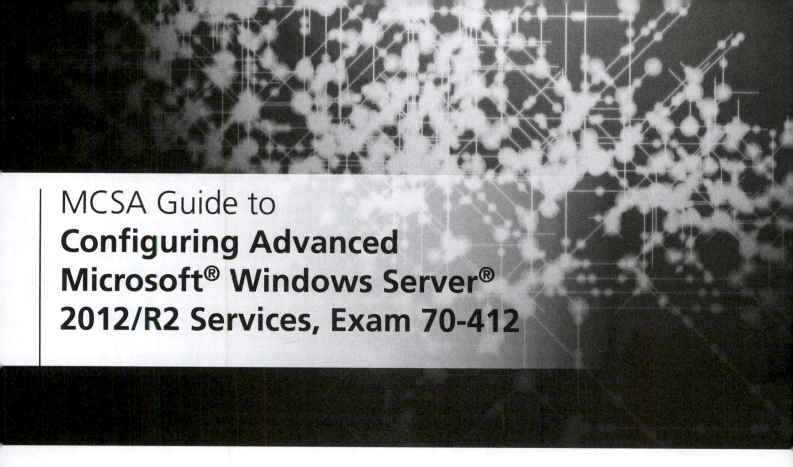

MCSA Guide to
Configuring Advanced Microsoft® Windows Server® 2012/R2 Services, Exam 70-412

Greg Tomsho

D0139112

CENGAGE
Learning·

Australia • Brazil • Mexico • Singapore • United Kingdom • United States

CENGAGE
Learning

MCSA Guide to Configuring Advanced Microsoft® Windows Server® 2012/R2 Services, Exam 70-412
Greg Tomsho

Vice President, General Manager: Dawn Gerrain

Product Director: Kathleen McMahon

Product Team Manager: Kristin McNary

Director, Development: Marah Bellegarde

Product Development Manager: Leigh Hefferon

Senior Content Developer:
  Michelle Ruelos Cannistraci

Developmental Editor: Lisa M. Lord

Product Assistant: Scott Finger

Marketing Manager: Eric La Scola

Senior Production Director: Wendy Troeger

Production Manager: Patty Stephan

Senior Content Project Manager:
  Brooke Greenhouse

Art Director: GEX Publishing Services

Cover image: ©Kheng Guan Toh/
Shutterstock.com

For product information and technology assistance, contact us at
Cengage Learning Customer & Sales Support, 1-800-354-9706.

For permission to use material from this text or product,
submit all requests online at **www.cengage.com/permissions.**
Further permissions questions can be e-mailed to
permissionrequest@cengage.com.

Library of Congress Control Number: 2015930282

ISBN-13: 978-1-285-86356-6

Course Technology
20 Channel Center St.
Boston, MA 02210
USA

Cengage Learning is a leading provider of customized learning solutions with office locations around the globe, including Singapore, the United Kingdom, Australia, Mexico, Brazil, and Japan. Locate your local office at **www.cengage.com/global.**

Cengage Learning products are represented in Canada by Nelson Education, Ltd.

To learn more about Cengage Learning, visit **www.cengage.com**

Purchase any of our products at your local college store or at our preferred online store **www.cengagebrain.com.**

Notice to the Reader
Publisher does not warrant or guarantee any of the products described herein or perform any independent analysis in connection with any of the product information contained herein. Publisher does not assume, and expressly disclaims, any obligation to obtain and include information other than that provided to it by the manufacturer. The reader is expressly warned to consider and adopt all safety precautions that might be indicated by the activities described herein and to avoid all potential hazards. By following the instructions contained herein, the reader willingly assumes all risks in connection with such instructions. The publisher makes no representations or warranties of any kind, including but not limited to, the warranties of fitness for particular purpose or merchantability, nor are any such representations implied with respect to the material set forth herein, and the publisher takes no responsibility with respect to such material. The publisher shall not be liable for any special, consequential, or exemplary damages resulting, in whole or part, from the readers' use of, or reliance upon, this material.

Printed in the United States of America
Print Number: 01   Print Year: 2015

Brief Contents

Contents

Introduction

*MCSA Guide to Configuring Advanced Microsoft® Windows Server®
2012/R2 Services, Exam 70-412*, gives you in-depth coverage of the 70-412 certification exam objectives and focuses on the skills you need to configure advanced services and features in Windows Server 2012/R2. With almost 90 hands-on activities and a number of skill-reinforcing case projects, you'll be well prepared for the certification exam and learn valuable skills to perform on the job.

After you finish this book, you'll have an in-depth knowledge of Windows Server 2012/R2, including advanced Active Directory configuration, advanced network services configuration, Dynamic Access Control (DAC) and IP Address Management (IPAM), server high availability and disaster recovery, and identity and access solutions, among other topics. Both the original release of Windows Server 2012 and the R2 release are covered.

Intended Audience

MCSA Guide to Configuring Advanced Microsoft® Windows Server® 2012/R2 Services, Exam 70-412, is intended for people who want to learn how to configure and manage an enterprise Windows Server 2012/R2 network and earn the Microsoft Certified Solutions Associate (MCSA) certification. This book covers in full the objectives of the third exam (70-412) needed to be MCSA: Windows Server 2012 certified. This book serves as an excellent tool for classroom teaching, but self-paced learners will also find that the clear explanations and challenging activities and case projects serve them equally well. Users of this book should have knowledge gained from studying the objectives of the 70-410 and 70-411 certification exams.

What This Book Includes

- A Windows Server 2012 R2 Datacenter Edition evaluation DVD is bundled with the book. It can be installed on a physical computer or in a virtual machine, using Microsoft Hyper-V, VMware Workstation, VMware Player, Oracle VirtualBox, or another compatible virtualization program.
- A lab setup guide is included in the "Before You Begin" section of this introduction to help you configure a physical or virtual (recommended) lab environment for doing the hands-on activities.

- Step-by-step hands-on activities walk you through tasks from configuring Active Directory trusts to advanced DNS and DHCP configurations and Windows Server clusters, among many other activities. All activities have been tested by a technical editor, reviewers, and validation experts.
- Extensive review and end-of-chapter materials reinforce your learning.
- Challenging case projects require you to apply the concepts and technologies learned throughout the book.
- Abundant screen captures and diagrams visually reinforce the text and hands-on activities.
- Appendix A contains a list of 70-412 exam objectives that's cross-referenced with chapters and sections covering each objective.

About Microsoft Certification: MCSA/MCSE

This book prepares you to take the third exam in the Microsoft Certified Solutions Associate (MCSA) Windows Server 2012 certification. The MCSA Windows Server 2012 certification is made up of three exams, which should be taken in order as follows:

- Exam 70-410: Installing and Configuring Windows Server 2012
- Exam 70-411: Administering Windows Server 2012
- Exam 70-412: Configuring Advanced Windows Server 2012 Services

Taking the exams in order is important because the objectives build on one another, with some topics introduced in an earlier exam and reinforced in subsequent exams.

Microsoft Certified Solutions Expert (MCSE): The Next Step   After achieving the MCSA Windows Server 2012 certification, you can move on to the MCSE certification. Microsoft offers three main options, and all require the three MCSA exams as a prerequisite:

- MCSE: Server Infrastructure
  - o Exam 70-413: Designing and Implementing a Server Infrastructure
  - o Exam 70-414: Implementing an Advanced Server Infrastructure
- MCSE: Desktop Infrastructure
  - o Exam 70-415: Implementing a Desktop Infrastructure
  - o Exam 70-416: Implementing Desktop Application Environments
- MCSE: Private Cloud
  - o Exam 70-246: Monitoring and Operating a Private Cloud with System Center 2012
  - o Exam 70-247: Configuring and Deploying a Private Cloud with System Center 2012

Chapter Descriptions

Each chapter in this book covers one or more important Microsoft Windows Server 2012 technologies. The 70-412 exam objectives are covered throughout the book, and you can find a mapping of objectives and the chapters in which they're covered on the inside front cover, with a more detailed mapping in Appendix A. The following list describes this book's chapters:

- **Chapter 1,** "Configuring Advanced Active Directory: Part I," describes an advanced Active Directory environment with multidomain and multiforest configurations. You learn to upgrade domains, configure users for multidomain environments, and configure trusts between domains and forests.
- **Chapter 2,** "Configuring Advanced Active Directory: Part II," discusses the details of configuring Active Directory sites, moving domain controllers between sites, and managing SRV record registration in a multisite environment. You also learn to configure domain controller replication on writeable and read only domain controllers.

- **Chapter 3**, "Advanced DHCP and DNS Configuration," explains how to set up advanced DHCP configurations, including superscopes, DHCPv6, DHCP high availability, and DHCP name protection. You also learn how to set up DNS security, including DNSSEC, DNS socket pools, cache locking, and DNS logging, and examine advanced DNS features, such as delegated administration, recursion, netmask ordering, and configuring the GlobalNames zone.

- **Chapter 4**, "Configuring Advanced File and Storage Solutions," describes advanced file and storage solutions, including Network File System, BranchCache, File Classification Infrastructure, and file auditing. You also learn how to set up an iSCSI SAN, which includes concepts such as Internet Storage Name Service (iSNS), thin provisioning, Features on Demand, and tiered storage.

- **Chapter 5**, "Configuring DAC and IPAM," discusses how to implement Dynamic Access Control (DAC), including configuring user and device claim types, policy changes and staging, access-denied remediation, and central access rules and policies. In addition, you learn about IP Address Management (IPAM), including group policy configuration, server discovery, managing IP blocks and ranges, and monitoring IP address space use.

- **Chapter 6**, "Configuring Server High Availability: Part I," describes Windows Server 2012 high-availability features, such as network load balancing (NLB) and failover clustering. You learn to install NLB nodes, configure affinity and port rules, and configure cluster operation modes. The material on failover clustering walks you through configuring cluster quorums, cluster networking configurations, configuring cluster storage, and Cluster-Aware Updating (CAU) as well as cluster shared volumes.

- **Chapter 7**, "Configuring Server High Availability: Part II," gives you an in-depth look at managing failover cluster roles, such as role-specific settings and continuously available shares. You also learn about using clusters with virtual machines, including guest clustering, live migration, storage migration, and other virtual machine movement operations.

- **Chapter 8**, "Server and Site Disaster Recovery," describes methods for surviving a server or site failure, such as the Windows Server Backup feature, working with Windows online backups, and using a variety of recovery methods. You also explore site-level fault tolerance features, such as using Hyper-V Replica, and multisite clustering techniques, including configuring quorum and failover settings.

- **Chapter 9**, "Implementing Active Directory Certificate Services," describes the purpose of digital certificates and explains the terminology that goes with them. You learn how to install an enterprise certification authority (CA), configure CRL distribution points, and use an online responder to automate CRL distribution, along with CA backup and recovery. You also learn how to manage certificates, certificate templates, and certificate deployment, validation, revocation, and renewal.

- **Chapter 10**, "Implementing AD FS and AD RMS," gives you an overview of Active Directory Federation Service (AD FS). You learn how to install AD FS, configure authentication policies, use the Workplace Join feature, and set up multi-factor authentication. Finally, you learn how to implement Active Directory Rights Management Services (AD RMS), including installing AD RMS, managing an AD RMS service connection point, working with RMS templates and exclusion policies, and backing up and restoring an AD RMS configuration.

- **Appendix A**, "MCSA 70-412 Exam Objectives," maps each 70-412 exam objective to the chapter and section where you can find information on it.

Features

This book includes the following features to help you master the topics in this book and the 70-412 exam objectives:

- *Chapter objectives*—Each chapter begins with a detailed list of the concepts to be mastered. This list is a quick reference to the chapter's contents and a useful study aid.

- *Hands-on activities*—Almost 90 hands-on activities are incorporated in this book, giving you practice in configuring advanced Windows Server 2012 services. Much of learning about Windows Server 2012 comes from doing the hands-on activities, and a lot of effort has been devoted to making them relevant and challenging.

- *A requirements table for hands-on activities*—A table at the beginning of each chapter lists the hands-on activities and what you need for each activity.

- *Screen captures, illustrations, and tables*—Numerous screen captures and illustrations of concepts help you visualize theories and concepts and see how to use tools and desktop features. In addition, tables are used often to give you details and comparisons of practical and theoretical information and can be used for a quick review.

- *Chapter summary*—Each chapter ends with a summary of the concepts introduced in the chapter. These summaries are a helpful way to review the material covered in the chapter.

- *Key terms*—All terms in the chapter introduced with bold text are gathered together in the Key Terms list at the end of the chapter. This list gives you a way to check your understanding of all important terms.

- *Review questions*—The end-of-chapter assessment begins with review questions that reinforce the concepts and techniques covered in each chapter. Answering these questions helps ensure that you have mastered important topics.

- *Case projects*—Each chapter closes with one or more case projects. Many of the case projects build on one another, as you take a small startup company to a flourishing enterprise.

- *On the DVD*—The DVD includes a free 120-day evaluation copy of Windows Server 2012 R2, Datacenter Edition.

Text and Graphics Conventions

Additional information and exercises have been added to this book to help you better understand what's being discussed in the chapter. Icons throughout the book alert you to these additional materials:

Tips offer extra information on resources, how to solve problems, and time-saving shortcuts.

Notes present additional helpful material related to the subject being discussed.

The Caution icon identifies important information about potential mistakes or hazards.

Each hands-on activity in this book is preceded by the Activity icon.

Case Projects icons mark the end-of-chapter case projects, which are scenario-based assignments that have you apply what you have learned in the chapter.

CertBlaster Test Preparation Questions

MCSA Guide to Configuring Advanced Microsoft® Windows Server® 2012/R2 Services, Exam 70-412, includes CertBlaster test preparation questions for the 70-412 MCSA exam. CertBlaster is a powerful online certification preparation tool from dti Publishing that helps prepare you for the certification exam.

To log in and access the CertBlaster test preparation questions for this book, go to *www.certblaster.com/login/*. The CertBlaster user's online manual describes features and gives navigation instructions. Activate your CertBlaster license by entering your name, e-mail address, and access code (found on the card bound in this book) in their fields, and then clicking Submit. CertBlaster offers three practice modes and all the types of questions required to simulate the exams:

- *Assessment mode*—Used to determine the student's baseline level. In this mode, the timer is on, answers aren't available, and the student gets a list of questions answered incorrectly, along with a Personal Training Plan.

- *Study mode*—Helps the student understand questions and the logic behind answers by giving immediate feedback both during and after the test. Answers and explanations are available. The timer is optional, and the student gets a list of questions answered incorrectly, along with a Personal Training Plan.

- *Certification mode*—A simulation of the actual exam environment. The timer as well as the number and format of questions from the exam objectives are set according to the exam's format.

For more information about dti test prep products, visit the Web site at *www.dtipublishing.com*.

Instructor Companion Site

Everything you need for your course in one place! This collection of book-specific lecture and class tools is available online via *www.cengage.com/login*. Access and download PowerPoint presentations, images, the Instructor's Manual, and more.

- *Electronic Instructor's Manual*—The Instructor's Manual that accompanies this book includes additional instructional material to assist in class preparation, including suggestions for classroom activities, discussion topics, and additional quiz questions.

- *Solutions Manual*—The instructor's resources include solutions to all end-of-chapter material, including review questions and case projects.

- *Cengage Learning Testing Powered by Cognero*—This flexible, online system allows you to do the following:

  o Author, edit, and manage test bank content from multiple Cengage Learning solutions.

  o Create multiple test versions in an instant.

  o Deliver tests from your LMS, your classroom, or wherever you want.

- *PowerPoint presentations*—This book comes with Microsoft PowerPoint slides for each chapter. They're included as a teaching aid for classroom presentation, to make available to students on the network for chapter review, or to be printed for classroom distribution. Instructors, please feel free to add your own slides for additional topics you introduce to the class.

- *Figure files*—All the figures and tables in the book are reproduced in bitmap format. Similar to the PowerPoint presentations, they're included as a teaching aid for classroom presentation, to make available to students for review, or to be printed for classroom distribution.

Acknowledgments

I would like to thank Cengage Learning Product Manager Nick Lombardi for his confidence in asking me to undertake this challenging book project. In addition, thanks go to Michelle Ruelos Cannistraci, the Senior Content Developer, who assembled an outstanding team to support this project. A special word of gratitude goes to Lisa Lord, the Development Editor, who has a knack for taking an unrefined product and turning it into a polished manuscript. Lisa's good humor and understanding as well as her commendable skills as an editor made my life considerably easier during the 8 months it took to complete this book. Serge Palladino, from the Manuscript Quality Assurance staff at Cengage Learning, tested chapter activities diligently to ensure that labs work as they were intended, and for that, I am grateful. I also want to include a shout-out to a student, Stephanie Garcia, who provided an extra layer of QA for hands-on activities.

Finally, my family: My beautiful and patient wife, Julie, daughters Camille and Sophia, and son, Michael, deserve special thanks and praise for going husbandless and fatherless for the duration of this project. Without their patience and understanding and happy greetings when I did make an appearance, I could not have accomplished this.

About the Author

Greg Tomsho has more than 30 years of computer and networking experience and has earned the CCNA, MCTS, MCSA, A+, Security+, and Linux+ certifications. Greg is the director of the Computer Networking Technology Department and Cisco Academy at Yavapai College in Prescott, AZ. His other books include *MCSA Guide to Installing and Configuring Microsoft Windows Server 2012/R2, Exam 70-410*; *MCSA Guide to Administering Windows Server 2012/R2, Exam 70-411*; *MCTS Guide to Microsoft Windows Server 2008 Active Directory Configuration*; *MCTS Guide to Microsoft Windows Server 2008 Applications Infrastructure Configuration*; *Guide to Networking Essentials*; *Guide to Network Support and Troubleshooting*; and *A+ CoursePrep ExamGuide*.

Contact the Author

I would like to hear from you. Please e-mail me at *books@tomsho.com* with any problems, questions, suggestions, or corrections. I even accept compliments! Your comments and suggestions are invaluable for shaping the content of future books. You can also submit errata, lab suggestions, and comments via e-mail. I have set up a Web site to support my books at *http://books.tomsho.com*, where you'll find lab notes, errata, Web links, and helpful hints for using my books. If you're an instructor, you can register on the site to contribute articles and comment on articles.

Before You Begin

Windows Server has become more complex as Microsoft strives to satisfy the needs of enterprise networks. In years past, you could learn what you needed to manage a Windows Server-based network and pass the Microsoft certification exams with a single server, some good lab instructions, and a network connection. Today, as you work with advanced technologies—such as DAC and IPAM, server clustering, Hyper-V, iSCSI server, just to name a few—your lab environment must be more complex, requiring two or even three servers and at least one client computer. Setting up this lab environment can be challenging, and this section was written to help you meet this challenge. Using virtual machines in VMware Workstation or VMware Player is highly recommended; other virtual environments work, too, but VMware allows you to install Hyper-V on a virtual machine. Hyper-V is used in Chapters 7 and 8.

If you can't set up a lab environment exactly as described in this section, you still have some options to help you gain the skills learned through hands-on activities:

- *Configure a partial lab*—If you have just one Windows Server 2012 R2 server available, you can still do many of the hands-on activities. Having one server and one client is even better, and having two servers and one client enables you to do the majority of the book's activities. If you can't do an activity, make sure you read the activity steps to learn important information about Windows Server 2012/R2.

- *Purchase the Web-Based Labs*—Cengage Learning offers Web-Based Labs for this book. This product gives you access to a real lab environment over the Internet by using a Web browser. Step-by-step lab instructions are taken directly from the hands-on activities in the book. See your sales representative or the Cengage Learning Web site for more information.

Lab Setup Guide

The lab equipment for hands-on activities consists of four computers (three of which are servers) and one client OS. Two servers with Windows Server 2012 R2 should be configured before doing the hands-on activities in Chapter 1. A client computer with Windows 8.1 Enterprise Edition should be available starting with Chapter 3. You need a third server to perform the high-availability and disaster recovery labs starting in Chapter 6. Figure 1 shows a diagram of the network.

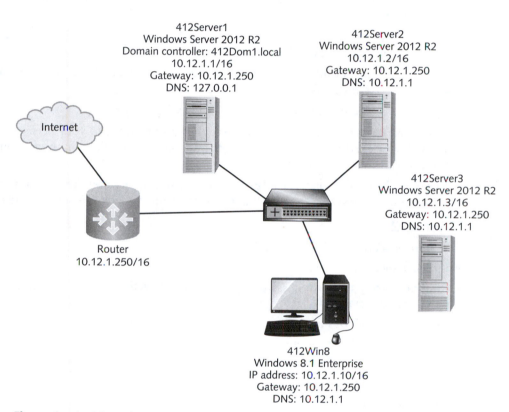

Figure 1   The lab configuration

©2016 Cengage Learning®

A few words about this diagram:

- No activities require access to the Internet; however, you might want to give servers Internet access to activate the evaluation copy of Windows Server 2012 R2. If this software isn't activated, the trial period is reduced to 10 days, and the server begins shutting down once an hour if the license isn't rearmed. Figure 1 shows a router with the address 10.12.1.250 for the purpose of activating the license, but you can use any address, and the router doesn't need to be part of the lab configuration for activities.
- Specific installation requirements for each server are explained in the following sections.

412Server1   This server should be configured as follows before beginning the activities in Chapter 1:

- Windows Server 2012 R2 Standard or Datacenter
- Server name: 412Server1
- Administrator password: Password01
- Memory: 1.5 GB or more
- Hard disk 1: 60 GB or more
- Hard disk 2: 60 GB or more
- Workgroup: 412Server2012
- Network interface card
  - o IP address: 10.12.1.1/16
  - o Default gateway: None required, but if you're using a router, 10.12.1.250 is recommended.
  - o DNS: 127.0.0.1
- Windows Update: Not configured
- If you're using an evaluation version of Windows Server 2012 R2, you can rearm the evaluation up to five times. To do so, follow these steps:

1. Open an elevated command prompt window as Administrator.
2. Type **slmgr -xpr** and press **Enter** to see the current status of your license. It shows how many days are left in the evaluation. If it says you're in notification mode, you need to rearm the evaluation immediately.
3. To rearm the evaluation, type **slmgr -rearm** and press **Enter**. You see a message telling you to restart the system for the changes to take effect. Click **OK** and restart the system.

412Server2

- Windows Server 2012 R2 Standard or Datacenter
- Server name: 412Server2
- Administrator password: Password02 (must be different from the 412Server1 administrator password to test trusts)
- Memory: 1.5 GB or more
- Hard disk 1: 60 GB or more
- Hard disk 2: 60 GB or more
- Workgroup: 412Server2012
- Network interface card
  - o IP address: 10.12.1.2/16
  - o Default gateway: None required, but if you're using a router, 10.12.1.250 is recommended.
  - o DNS: 10.12.1.1 (the address of 412Server1)
- Windows Update: Not configured

412Server3

- Windows Server 2012 R2 Standard or Datacenter
- Server name: 412Server3
- Administrator password: Password01
- Memory: 1.5 GB or more

- Hard disk 1: 60 GB or more
- Workgroup: 412Server2012
- Network interface card
  - o IP address: 10.12.1.3/16
  - o Default gateway: None required, but if you're using a router, 10.12.1.250 is recommended.
  - o DNS: 10.12.1.1 (the address of 412Server1)
- Windows Update: Not configured

412Win8 This computer should be configured as follows before beginning Chapter 5:

- Windows 8.1 Enterprise Edition
- Machine name: 412Win8
- Local administrator account with the username Win8User and the password Password01
- Memory: 1 GB or more
- Hard disk 1: 60 GB or more
- Network interface card
  - o IP address: 10.12.1.10/16
  - o Default gateway: None required, but if you're using a router, 10.12.1.250 is recommended.
  - o DNS: 10.12.1.1 (the address of 412Server1)
- Workgroup: 412Server2012
- Settings: Express settings
- Sign in without a Microsoft account
- Windows Update: Not configured

Deployment Recommendations

Using virtualization to configure your lab environment is recommended. If you're using physical computers, the requirements are much the same, but you need many more physical computers. If you're using physical computers, you can set up the network as shown previously in Figure 1 and configure the computers as described earlier.

Avoiding IP Address Conflicts Whether you're using physical computers or virtual computers, you must have a method for avoiding IP address conflicts. There are two setups for working in a classroom environment:

- *All students computers are on the same physical subnet*—In this setup, IP addresses and computer names must be changed to avoid conflict. One strategy for avoiding IP address conflicts is using the third octet of the address. Each student is assigned a number, such as from 1 to 50. When assigning IP addresses, simply change the third octet to the student-assigned number. For example, for student 15, address 10.12.1.1 becomes 10.12.15.1. Use the same number as a suffix for the computer and domain names. For example, 412Server1 becomes 412Server1-15, 412Server1-16, and so forth. The domain name also changes accordingly, such as 412Dom1-15.local, 412Dom1-16.local, and so on.
- *Each student works in a "sandbox" environment*—This setup, using virtualization, is preferred, if it's possible. Each student's VMs are configured on a private virtual network that doesn't connect to the physical LAN. In VMware, you can use a host-only or custom network configuration, and in Hyper-V, you can use an internal or a private virtual switch configuration.

Using Virtualization   Using virtualization is highly recommended, and you have the following options for virtualization software:

- *VMware Workstation*—This sophisticated virtualization environment is a free download if your school or organization is a member of the VMware Academic Program (*http://vmapss. onthehub.com*). The advantage of VMware Workstation is that you can take periodic snapshots of VMs and revert to one if something goes wrong with a virtual machine. In addition, you can install Hyper-V on a virtual machine with VMware Workstation 10 and later by setting the guest OS to Hyper-V Server.
- *VMware Player*—This product is a free download from the VMware Web site. You can't take snapshots, but otherwise, it's an excellent virtual environment.
- *Hyper-V*—If you install Windows Server 2012 R2 or Windows 8.1 on your host computers, you can run Hyper-V as your virtual environment. The advantage of using Hyper-V is that you can do the activities requiring Hyper-V without any additional configuration. The disadvantage is that you need Administrator access to your host computers to use Hyper-V Manager. Hyper-V doesn't support nested virtualization, so you can't install Hyper-V on a virtual machine if it's the host virtualization software.
- *VirtualBox*—This excellent open-source virtualization product from Oracle has many advanced features, as VMware Workstation does, but it's free. However, it doesn't support running Hyper-V on a virtual machine.

Host Computer Requirements When Using Virtualization   The following are recommendations for the host computer when you're using virtualization:

- Dual-core or quad-core CPU with Intel-VT-x/EPT or AMD-V/RVI support. You can see a list of supported Intel processors at *http://ark.intel.com/products/virtualizationtechnology*.

 Most activities can be done without a CPU that supports EPT, but you can't install Hyper-V on a VM if the host doesn't support EPT for Intel CPUs or VRI on AMD CPUs.

- 8 GB RAM.

 Most activities can be done with 4 GB RAM installed on the host. Only those requiring three VMs running at the same time need more than 4 GB.

- 150 GB free disk space.
- Windows 7 or Windows 8/8.1 if you're using VMware Workstation, VMware Player, or VirtualBox.
- Windows Server 2012 R2 or Windows 8.1 Pro or Enterprise 64-bit if you're using Hyper-V.

Where to Go for Help

Configuring a lab and keeping everything running correctly can be challenging. Even small configuration changes can prevent activities from running correctly. If you're using virtualization, use snapshots if possible so that you can revert virtual machines to an earlier working state in case something goes wrong. The author maintains a Web site that includes lab notes, suggestions, errata, and help articles that might be useful if you're having trouble, and you can contact the author at these addresses:

- Web site: *http://books.tomsho.com*
- E-mail: *books@tomsho.com*

chapter 1

Configuring Advanced Active Directory: Part I

After reading this chapter and completing the exercises, you will be able to:

- Describe the major features and components of Active Directory
- Configure a multidomain environment
- Configure a multiforest environment
- Describe Active Directory trusts
- Configure Active Directory trusts
- Upgrade domains and forests

The majority of day-to-day work in an Active Directory environment involves managing objects in a domain. With a single-domain, single-forest environment, administrators rarely need to use other tools besides Active Directory Users and Computers and Active Directory Administrative Center. However, multidomain and multiforest environments require configuring the Active Directory infrastructure in addition to user, group, and computer objects. For example, multiple forests or forests with several domains and trees might require trust configuration. In addition, a Windows network often has a mix of server OSs that must be integrated into the forest. If your network has older Windows versions, you might need to upgrade a domain or forest. Understanding domain and forest functional levels is critical to maintain this environment.

In this chapter, you review the major components and operation of Active Directory and then learn when you might need to configure a multidomain or multiforest network. You also learn how to configure trust relationships between domains and forests for efficient operation of Active Directory and to make using these complex environments easier for users. Finally, you learn about domain functional levels, what features are supported in the different functional levels, and how to upgrade domains and forests to the latest functional level.

This book covers Windows Server 2012 and its successor, Windows Server 2012 R2. When a topic or feature is relevant to both the original release of Windows Server 2012 and R2, the name "Windows Server 2012/R2" is used. If a feature is particular to the R2 version, "Windows Server 2012 R2" is used (without the "/" character). Microsoft has added a number of enhancements in Windows Server 2012 R2, and the new and modified features are included in the Windows Server 2012 certification exams.

Reviewing Active Directory

Before you begin this chapter, make sure you have completed *MCSA Guide to Installing and Configuring Windows Server 2012/R2, Exam 70-410*, and *MCSA Guide to Administering Windows Server 2012/R2, Exam 70-411*, or have equivalent knowledge. The topics covered in this book assume prerequisite knowledge of the topics the 70-410 and 70-411 certification exams cover. In addition, to do the hands-on activities, you must configure your lab environment according to the lab setup instructions in the "Before You Begin" section of this book's introduction. Table 1-1 lists what you need for the hands-on activities in this chapter.

Table 1-1   Activity requirements

Activity	Requirements	Notes
Activity 1-1: Installing Active Directory Domain Services	412Server1	See the "Before You Begin" section in this book's Introduction for the correct configuration of 412Server1 before you start activities.
Activity 1-2: Verifying an Active Directory Configuration	412Server1	
Activity 1-3: Installing a Subdomain	412Server1, 412Server2	
Activity 1-4: Removing a Subdomain	412Server1, 412Server2	
Activity 1-5: Adding a Tree to a Forest	412Server1, 412Server2	
Activity 1-6: Creating a New Forest	412Server1, 412Server2	
Activity 1-7: Creating Conditional Forwarders	412Server1, 412Server2	
Activity 1-8: Testing Cross-Forest Access Without a Trust	412Server1, 412Server2	
Activity 1-9: Creating a Forest Trust	412Server1, 412Server2	
Activity 1-10: Confirming Cross-Forest Access	412Server1, 412Server2	
Activity 1-11: Configuring Selective Authentication	412Server1, 412Server2	

Recall that Active Directory is a server role that, when installed, makes a Windows server a domain controller (DC). With a DC in your network, client computers and other servers can be joined to the domain, providing the benefits of centralized authentication, authorization, and network policy management. The Active Directory structure can be divided into physical components and logical components, discussed in the following sections.

Active Directory Physical Components

The physical components of Active Directory consist of servers configured as domain controllers and sites. A DC is a computer running Windows Server 2012/R2 with the Active Directory Domain Services role installed. Although an Active Directory domain can consist of many DCs, each can service only one domain. Each DC contains a full replica of the objects that make up the domain and is responsible for the following functions:

- Storing a copy of the domain data and replicating changes to that data to all other DCs throughout the domain

- Providing data search and retrieval functions for users attempting to locate objects in the directory

- Providing authentication and authorization services for users who log on to the domain and attempt to access network resources

An Active Directory **site** is a physical location in which DCs communicate and replicate information frequently. Microsoft defines a site as one or more Internet Protocol (IP) subnets connected by high-speed local area network (LAN) technology. A small business with no branch offices or other locations, for example, consists of a single site. A business with a branch office connected to the main office through a slow wide area network (WAN) link usually has two sites: the main office and the branch office. The main reasons for defining multiple sites are to control the frequency of Active Directory replication and to assign policies based on physical location.

Active Directory Logical Components

The logical components of Active Directory make it possible to pattern a directory service's look and feel after the organization in which it runs. There are four logical components of Active Directory:

- *Organizational units*—An **organizational unit** (OU) is an Active Directory container used to organize a network's users and resources into logical administrative units. An OU contains Active Directory objects, such as user accounts, groups, computer accounts, printers, shared folders, applications, servers, and DCs.

- *Domains*—A **domain** is Active Directory's core structural unit. It contains OUs and represents policy boundaries. To a lesser extent, a domain represents administrative and security boundaries, and each domain has a default domain administrator account. However, the forest root domain administrator has full access to all domains in the same forest.

- *Trees*—An Active Directory **tree** is a grouping of domains sharing a common naming structure. A tree consists of a parent domain and possibly one or more **child domains** (also called "subdomains") that have the same second-level and top-level domain names as the parent domain. Unlike domains and OUs, a tree isn't a container object in Active Directory; it's just a naming structure.

- *Forests*—An Active Directory **forest** is a collection of one or more trees. A forest can consist of a single tree with a single domain, or it can contain several trees, each with a hierarchy of parent and child domains. A forest's main purpose is to provide a common Active Directory environment in which all domains in all trees can communicate with one another and share information yet allow independent operation and differing policies in each domain. A single forest-wide administrator account is located in the forest root domain.

Before you go any further in reviewing Active Directory, now's a good time to install Active Directory so you can start working with it.

Activity 1-1: Installing Active Directory Domain Services

Time Required: 25 minutes or longer
Objective: Install Active Directory Domain Services.

Required Tools and Equipment: 412Server1 configured according to the "Before You Begin" section in this book's Introduction

Description: In this activity, you install the Active Directory Domain Services role and promote 412Server1 to a domain controller to create a new forest and a domain named 412Dom1.local.

1. Start 412Server1, and log on as **Administrator** with the password **Password01**. Server Manager opens automatically.

2. In Server Manager, click **Manage, Add Roles and Features** from the menu to start the Add Roles and Features Wizard. In the Before You Begin window, click **Next**.

3. In the Installation Type window, accept the default **Role-based or feature-based installation**, and click **Next**. In the Server Selection window, click **Next**.

4. In the Server Roles window, click to select **Active Directory Domain Services**. In the Add Roles and Features Wizard dialog box, click **Add Features**. Click **Next**.

5. In the Features window, click **Next**. The AD DS window describes Active Directory Domain Services and lists the prerequisites for installing it. Read this information, and then click **Next**.

6. In the Confirmation window, click **Install**. The Installation progress window shows a progress bar. The installation will probably take several minutes. Wait for the installation to finish, and then click **Close**.

7. On the Server Manager menu, click the notifications flag, and then click **Promote this server to a domain controller**. The Active Directory Domain Services Configuration Wizard starts.

8. In the Deployment Configuration window, click the **Add a new forest** option button, type **412Dom1.local** in the "Root domain name" text box (see Figure 1-1), and then click **Next**.

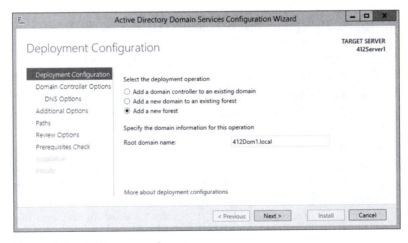

Figure 1-1   Adding a new forest

9. In the Domain Controller Options window (see Figure 1-2), verify that the forest and domain functional levels are set to **Windows Server 2012 R2**. In the "Specify domain controller capabilities" section, click to select the **Domain Name System (DNS) server** check box, if necessary. The Global Catalog (GC) check box is always selected by default for the first DC in a forest. Notice that the "Read only domain controller (RODC)" option isn't available because the first DC in a new forest or domain can't be an RODC.

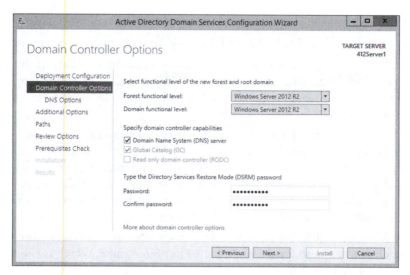

Figure 1-2   Setting domain controller options

10. In the Directory Services Restore Mode (DSRM) password section, type **Password01** in the Password and Confirm password text boxes. You can use a password that's different from the Administrator password, if you like, but for this activity, use the same password so that it's easier to remember. Click **Next**.

11. In the DNS Options window, you see a message about DNS delegation. Because you're creating a new domain, no action is necessary. Click **Next**.

12. In the Additional Options window, leave the default NetBIOS domain name, and click **Next**.

13. In the Paths window, you can choose locations for the database folder, log files, and SYSVOL folder. Specifying different disks for the database and log files is ideal, but leave the default settings for this activity, and click **Next**.

14. Review your choices in the Review Options window, and go back and make changes if necessary. When you're finished, click **Next**.

15. In the Prerequisites Check window, Windows verifies that all conditions for installing Active Directory successfully have been met. If all prerequisites have been met, a green circle with a check is displayed. If they haven't been met, Windows displays a list of problems you must correct before installing Active Directory. You might see some warnings about default security settings and DNS delegation, but you can ignore them. Click **Install**.

16. Watch the progress message at the top of the window to see the tasks being performed to install Active Directory. After the installation is finished, your computer restarts automatically. After the server restarts, log on as **Administrator**. (*Note*: You're now logging on to the 412Dom1.local domain.) In Server Manager, click **Local Server** and verify the domain information shown under Computer name.

17. Stay logged on if you're continuing to the next activity.

Activity 1-2: Verifying an Active Directory Configuration

Time Required: 10 minutes
Objective: Verify your Active Directory configuration.

Required Tools and Equipment: 412Server1
Description: In this activity, you verify the Active Directory configuration and review the features of Active Directory Administrative Center, Active Directory Users and Computers, Active Directory Sites and Services, and DNS Manager.

1. Start 412Server1, and log on as **Administrator** with the password **Password01**.

2. In Server Manager, click **Tools, Active Directory Administrative Center** from the menu.

3. In Active Directory Administrative Center, click **412Dom1 (local)** in the left pane. In the middle pane listing default folders and OUs, double-click **Domain Controllers**. You see 412Server1, which shows as a global catalog server in the Domain Controller Type column. Close Active Directory Administrative Center.

4. In Server Manager, click **Tools, Active Directory Users and Computers** from the menu. In the left pane, click to expand **412Dom1.local**, and then click **Users**. In the right pane, scroll through the list of users and groups. Note the groups named Enterprise Admins and Schema Admins. Only the forest root domain has these groups because they have forest-wide privileges. Double-click these groups to verify that the Administrator account is a member of them. Close Active Directory Users and Computers.

5. In Server Manager, click **Tools, Active Directory Sites and Services** from the menu. In the left pane, click to expand **Sites** and **Default-First-Site-Name**, which is the default site. Click **Servers** to see 412Server1 listed.

6. Click to expand **Servers** and then **412Server1**, and then right-click **NTDS Settings** and click **Properties**. In the General tab, you can configure whether this server is a global catalog server. Click **Cancel**, and close Active Directory Sites and Services.

7. In Server Manager, click **Tools, Active Directory Domains and Trusts** from the menu. In the left pane, right-click **412Dom1.local** and click **Properties**. The General tab shows the forest and domain functional levels. Click the **Trusts** tab. There are no trusts because there are no other domains. Close the Properties dialog box and Active Directory Domains and Trusts.

8. In Server Manager, click **Tools, DNS** to open DNS Manager. In the left pane, click to expand **412Server1** and **Forward Lookup Zones**. You see the 412Dom1.local and _msdcs.412Dom1.local zones. The _msdcs.412Dom1.local zone is a subdomain created in the forest root.

9. Click **412Dom1.local** in the left pane to see the default DNS records created for the zone, which include the SOA, NS, and A records. Close DNS Manager.

10. Stay logged on if you're continuing to the next activity.

Advanced Active Directory Functions

This chapter covers the configuration of advanced Active Directory functions. In addition to knowing the primary structural components, you need a solid understanding of some less visible components, including the following:

- *Forest root*—Every forest has a **forest root domain**, which is the first domain created in a new forest. It has a number of important responsibilities and serves as an anchor for other trees and domains added to the forest. Certain functions that affect all domains in the forest are conducted only through the forest root domain, and if this domain becomes inoperable, the entire Active Directory structure ceases functioning. The forest root domain provides functions that facilitate and manage communication between all domains in the forest as well as between forests, if necessary. Some functions it usually handles include DNS server, global catalog server, forest-wide administrative accounts, and operations masters. The DNS server and global catalog server functions can be installed on other servers in other domains for fault tolerance. However, the forest-wide operations masters and forest-wide administrative accounts can reside only on a DC in the forest root domain. For these reasons, it's a critical component of the Active Directory structure.

- *Flexible Single Master Operation roles*—**Flexible Single Master Operation (FSMO) roles** are functions operating on a single DC in the forest root domain. There are two forest-wide FSMO roles: domain naming master and schema master. There are three domain-wide FSMO roles: PDC emulator, RID master, and infrastructure master. The data maintained by FSMO roles uses single-master replication, meaning changes to the data can be made only on the server performing the FSMO role. The data is then replicated from this server to other DCs in the forest. The first DC installed in a forest holds all FSMO roles at first, but you transfer these roles to other DCs if needed.

- *Global catalog*—There's only one **global catalog** per forest, but unlike operations masters, multiple DCs can be designated as global catalog servers. **Global catalog (GC) servers** perform the following vital functions: facilitate forest-wide Active Directory searches, facilitate logon across domains in the forest, and hold universal group membership information.

- *Active Directory trusts*—In a multidomain environment, a trust allows users from one domain to access resources in another domain. Trusts are discussed in detail later in this chapter in "Active Directory Trusts."

- *Active Directory replication*—Replication is the process of maintaining a consistent database of information when the database is distributed among several locations. Active Directory contains several databases called "partitions" that are replicated between DCs by using intrasite replication or intersite replication. **Intrasite replication** takes place between DCs in the same site; **intersite replication** occurs between two or more sites. The replication process differs in these two types, but the goal is the same—to maintain consistent domain directory partitions. Whereas the data maintained by FSMO roles uses single-master replication, Active Directory uses **multimaster replication** for replicating Active Directory objects, such as user and computer accounts. Changes to these objects can occur on any DC and are propagated (replicated) to all other DCs. A process called the **Knowledge Consistency Checker (KCC)** runs on every DC to determine the replication topology, which defines the DC path that Active Directory changes flow through.

Active Directory and DNS

Windows domains and Active Directory rely exclusively on DNS for resolving names and locating services. When a workgroup computer attempts to join a domain, it contacts a DNS server to find records that identify a DC for the domain. When a member computer or server starts, it contacts a DNS server to find a DC that can authenticate it to the domain. When DCs replicate with one another and when trusts are created between domains in different forests, DNS is required to resolve names and services to IP addresses. Because of the importance of DNS for Active Directory operation, the first DC installed in a forest is usually also a DNS server. In fact, during Active Directory installation, Windows attempts to find a DNS server, and if it's unsuccessful, it asks whether you want to install DNS. If DNS is installed during Active Directory installation, the zone holding the records for the Active Directory domain is created automatically and populated with resource records.

Configuring Multidomain Environments

In the day-to-day administration of an Active Directory domain, most administrators focus on OUs and their child objects. In a small organization, a solid understanding of OUs and leaf objects might be all that's needed to manage a Windows domain successfully. However, in large organizations, building an Active Directory structure composed of several domains, multiple trees, and even a few forests might be necessary.

Reasons for a Single-Domain Environment

A domain is the primary identifying and administrative unit in Active Directory. A unique name is associated with each domain and used to access network resources. A domain administrator account has full control over objects in the domain, and certain security policies apply to all accounts in a domain. Additionally, most replication traffic occurs between DCs in a domain. Any of these factors can influence your decision to use a single-domain or multidomain design. Most small and medium businesses choose a single domain for reasons that include the following:

- *Simplicity*—The more complex something is, the easier it is for things to go wrong. Unless your organization needs multiple identities, separate administration, or differing account policies, keeping the structure simple with a single domain is the best choice.

- *Lower costs*—Every domain must have at least one DC and preferably two or more for fault tolerance. Each DC requires additional hardware and software resources, which increase costs.

- *Easier management*—Many management tasks are easier in a single-domain environment:

  o Having a single set of administrators and policies prevents conflicts caused by differing viewpoints on operational procedures and policies.

  o Object management is easier when personnel reorganizations or transfers occur. Moving user and computer accounts between different OUs is easier than moving them between different domains.

  o Managing access to resources is simplified when you don't need to consider security principals from other domains.

  o Placement of DCs and global catalog servers is simplified when your organization has multiple locations because you don't need to consider cross-domain replication.

- *Easier access to resources*—A single domain provides the easiest environment for users to find and access network resources. In a multidomain environment, mobile users who visit branch offices with different domains must authenticate to their home domain. If their home domain isn't available for some reason, they can't log on to the network.

Reasons for a Multidomain Environment

Although a single-domain structure is usually easier and less expensive than a multidomain structure, it's not always better. Using more than one domain makes sense or is even a necessity in the following circumstances:

- *Need for differing account policies*—Account policies that govern passwords and account lockouts apply to all users in a domain. If you need differing policies for different business units, using separate domains is the best way to meet this requirement. Although you can use a password settings object (PSO) to apply different password policies for users or groups in a domain, this feature can be difficult to manage when many users are involved.

- *Need for different name identities*—Each domain has its own name that can represent a separate company or business unit. If each business unit must maintain its own identity, child domains can be created in which part of the name is shared, or multiple trees with completely different namespaces can be created.

- *Replication control*—Replication in a large domain maintaining several thousand objects can generate substantial traffic. In addition, when multiple business locations are connected through a WAN, the amount of replication traffic could be unacceptable. Replication traffic can be reduced by creating separate domains for key locations because only global catalog replication is required between domains.

- *Need for internal versus external domains*—Companies that run public Web servers often create a domain used only for publicly accessible resources and another domain for internal resources.

- *Need for tight security*—With separate domains, stricter resource control and administrative permissions are easier, especially when dealing with hundreds or thousands of users in multiple business units. If a business unit prefers to have its own administrative staff, separate domains must be created.

The following sections discuss several aspects of multidomain environments, including adding subdomains, adding a tree to an existing forest, and configuring user accounts in multidomain environments.

Adding a Subdomain

Adding a subdomain is a common reason for expanding an Active Directory forest. A subdomain maintains a common naming structure with the forest root, so the top-level and second-level domain names remain the same. What makes a subdomain name different from the forest root's name is the third-level domain name. For example, if the forest root domain is csmtech. local, you might create subdomains named US.csmtech.local and Europe.csmtech.local to represent company branches organized by geography. A company might also create subdomains for different business units, such as widgets.csmtech.local and publishing.csmtech.local.

When you create a subdomain, you must consider a few questions before beginning:

- *What server will be the first DC for the new domain?* You can use an existing server or put a new computer into service. If you use an existing server that's currently a member of the forest root domain or a stand-alone server, you can just install the AD DS role and promote the server to a DC. If you use an existing DC, you must demote it and promote it again as the first DC in a new domain.

- *What are the names of the subdomain and the new DC?* You should have a naming convention established so that this question is easy to answer.

- *What Active Directory–related roles will the new DC fill?* Will the DC be a global catalog server, a DNS server, or another type?

- *In which site will the new DC be located?* Do you need to create a new site or add this DC to an existing site? Be sure the DC's IP addressing matches the site location.

- *Are you going to install a second DC for the subdomain immediately?* Remember that each domain should have a minimum of two DCs for fault tolerance and load balancing. In addition, you might want to offload FSMO roles to a second DC.

- *Who will administer the new domain?* Each domain or subdomain has a Domain Admins global group. Aside from the local administrator account, what other users should be a member of this group, if any?

These are some of the questions you should answer before you create a subdomain, and there might be others, depending on the circumstances. Activity 1-3 walks you through configuring a subdomain for the 412Dom1.local domain you created in Activity 1-1.

Activity 1-3: Installing a Subdomain

Time Required: 25 minutes or longer
Objective: Install a subdomain in an existing forest.

Required Tools and Equipment: 412Server1 and 412Server2 configured according to the instructions in "Before You Begin" in this book's introduction
Description: In this activity, you install the AD DS role on 412Server2, and promote 412Server2 to a domain controller, creating a subdomain named DomA.412Dom1.local in the 412Dom1.local forest.

It's important that 412Server2's IP address settings are correct. In particular, the Preferred DNS Server option must be set to 10.12.1.1 (the address of 412Server1).

1. Start 412Server1, if necessary. Start 412Server2, and log on as **Administrator** with the password **Password02**.

2. On 412Server2, install the Active Directory Domain Services role by following the same procedure as in Activity 1-1, Steps 2 through 6.

3. After the role is installed, click the notifications flag, and click **Promote this server to a domain controller**. The Active Directory Domain Services Configuration Wizard starts.

4. In the Deployment Configuration window, click the **Add a new domain to an existing forest** option button. In the "Select domain type" list box, make sure **Child Domain** is selected. Type **412Dom1.local** in the Parent domain name text box and **DomA** in the New domain name text box. Click **Change** to enter credentials. In the Windows Security dialog box, type **412Dom1\Administrator** for the username and **Password01** for the password, and then click **OK**. The Deployment Configuration window should look like Figure 1-3. Click **Next**.

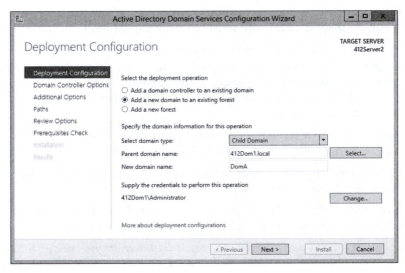

Figure 1-3   Adding a domain to an existing forest

5. In the Domain Controller Options window, verify that the domain functional level is set to **Windows Server 2012 R2**. In the "Specify domain controller capabilities and site information" section, click to clear the **Domain Name System (DNS) server** and **Global Catalog (GC)** check boxes (see Figure 1-4). You can specify the site to place the domain controller, but for this activity, leave the default **Default-First-Site-Name**.

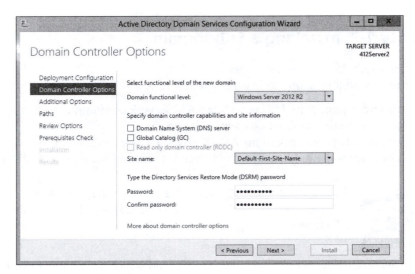

Figure 1-4   The Domain Controller Options window

6. In the Directory Services Restore Mode (DSRM) password section, type **Password02** in the Password and Confirm password text boxes, and then click **Next**.

7. In the Additional Options window, leave the default NetBIOS domain name, and click **Next**.

8. In the Paths window, leave the default settings, and click **Next**.

9. Review your choices in the Review Options window, and go back and make changes if necessary. When you're finished, click **Next**.

10. In the Prerequisites Check window, verify that all prerequisites have been met, and click **Install**.

11. Watch the progress message at the top of the window to see the tasks being performed to install Active Directory. After the installation is finished, your computer restarts automatically. After the server restarts, log on as **Administrator** with the password **Password02**. (*Note*: You're now logging on to the DomA.412Dom1.local domain.) In Server Manager, click **Local Server** and verify the domain information shown under Computer name.

12. Click **Tools, Active Directory Domains and Trusts** from the menu. In the left pane, click to expand **412Dom1.local**. You see the new subdomain. Right-click **412Dom1.local** and click **Properties**. Click the **Trusts** tab. You see an outgoing and incoming trust with DomA.412Dom1.local. Trusts are discussed later in "Configuring Active Directory Trusts." Click **Cancel**, and close Active Directory Domains and Trusts.

13. On 412Server1, log on as **Administrator**, if necessary. In Server Manager, click **Tools, DNS** from the menu.

14. In DNS Manager, click to expand **412Server1, Forward Lookup Zones**, and **412Dom1.local**. You see the DomA subdomain folder. Click **DomA** to see the records that were created automatically, which include an A record for 412Server2 and the folders holding Active Directory–related records. Close DNS Manager.

15. Stay logged on to both servers if you're continuing to the next activity.

Adding a Tree to an Existing Forest

As mentioned, an Active Directory tree is a grouping of domains sharing a common naming structure. A tree can consist of a single domain or a parent domain and child domains, which can have child domains of their own. An Active Directory tree is said to have a contiguous namespace because all domains in the tree share at least the second-level and top-level domain names. For example, csmtech.local has a second-level domain name of csmtech and a top-level domain name of local.

Organizations operating under a single name internally and to the public are probably best served by an Active Directory forest with only one tree. However, when two companies merge or a large company splits into separate business units that would benefit from having their own identities, a multiple tree structure makes sense. There's no functional difference between domains and subdomains in the same tree or domains in different trees, as long as they're part of the same forest. The only operational difference is the necessity of maintaining multiple DNS zones. Figure 1-5 shows a forest with two trees, each with two subdomains.

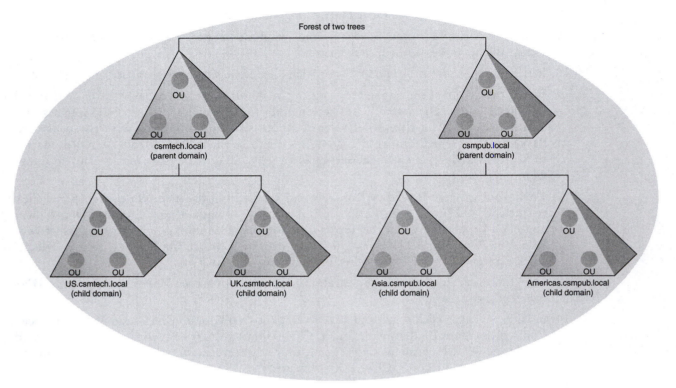

Figure 1-5   A forest with two trees

© Cengage Learning®

Adding a tree to an existing Active Directory forest isn't much different from adding a subdomain to an existing tree. Most of the same questions you should answer for adding a sub-domain apply to adding a new tree, except you need a name for the new tree that includes the top-level and second-level domain names. In Activity 1-4, you remove the DomA subdomain, and in Activity 1-5, you add a tree to the 412Dom1.local forest.

Activity 1-4: Removing a Subdomain

Time Required: 10 minutes
Objective: Remove a subdomain.

Required Tools and Equipment: 412Server1 and 412Server2
Description: In this activity, you demote 412Server2, which removes the DomA subdomain. Note that you aren't uninstalling the Active Directory Domain Services role because you need it later when you create a new tree.

1. Start 412Server1 and 412Server2, if necessary. On 412Server2, log on as **Administrator** with the password **Password02**.

2. On 412Server2, open a PowerShell prompt. Type **Uninstall-ADDSDomainController -LastDomainControllerInDomain -Credential (get-credential)** and press **Enter**. (*Hint*: Remember that you can use the Tab key to have commands completed. For example, you can enter uninstall-adds<TAB> -Last<TAB> to have PowerShell fill in the missing parts of the command for you.)

3. In the Enter your credentials dialog box, type **412dom1\administrator** in the User name text box and **Password01** in the Password text box, and then click **OK**. Because you're removing a domain from the forest, you must enter the forest root administrator's credentials.

4. When prompted for the local administrator password, type **Password02** and press **Enter**, and then type it again and press **Enter** to confirm it. This sets the local administrator account password because this server will no longer be a domain controller.

5. When you're prompted to continue the operation, press **Enter**. The server restarts. At this point, the Active Directory Domain Services role files aren't actually uninstalled, so you need to promote this server only if you want it to be a domain controller again.

6. Log on to 412Server2 as **Administrator**.

7. When Server Manager starts, click the notifications flag. (*Note*: Because you didn't uninstall the AD DS role, you can promote this server to a DC without having to reinstall the role.)

8. Stay logged on to 412Server2 and leave 412Server1 running if you're continuing to the next activity.

Activity 1-5: Adding a Tree to a Forest

Time Required: 25 minutes or longer
Objective: Add a tree to an existing forest.

Required Tools and Equipment: 412Server1 and 412Server2
Description: In this activity, you add a tree named 412Dom2.local to the 412Dom1.local forest.

1. Start 412Server1 and 412Server2, if necessary. On 412Server2, log on as **Administrator**, if necessary.

2. On 412Server2 in Server Manager, click the notifications flag, and then click **Promote this server to a domain controller**. The Active Directory Domain Services Configuration Wizard starts.

3. In the Deployment Configuration window, click the **Add a new domain to an existing forest** option button. In the "Select domain type" list box, click **Tree Domain**. Type **412Dom1.local** in the Forest name text box and **412Dom2.local** in the New domain name text box (see Figure 1-6). Click **Change** to enter credentials. In the Windows Security dialog box, type **412Dom1\Administrator** for the username and **Password01** for the password, and then click **OK**. Click **Next**.

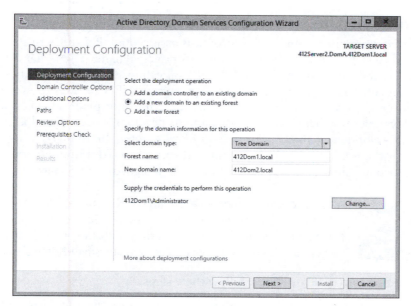

Figure 1-6 Adding a tree to an existing forest

4. In the Domain Controller Options window, verify that the domain functional level is set to **Windows Server 2012 R2**. In the "Specify domain controller capabilities and site information" section, leave the **Domain Name System (DNS) server** and **Global Catalog (GC)** check boxes selected. You should have a DNS server in each domain tree in the forest. Configuring this DC as a global catalog server is optional.

5. In the Directory Services Restore Mode (DSRM) password section, type **Password02** in the Password and Confirm password text boxes, and then click **Next**.

6. In the DNS Options window, you see a message about DNS delegation. Click **Next**.

7. In the Additional Options window, leave the default NetBIOS domain name, and then click **Next**.

8. In the Paths window, leave the default settings, and then click **Next**.

9. Review your choices in the Review Options window, and go back and make changes if necessary. When you're finished, click **Next**.

10. In the Prerequisites Check window, verify that all prerequisites have been met, and then click **Install**.

11. Watch the progress message at the top of the window to see the tasks being performed to install Active Directory. After the installation is finished, your computer restarts automatically. After the server restarts, log on as **Administrator**. (*Note*: You're now logging on to the 412Dom2.local domain.)

12. In Server Manager, click **Tools, Active Directory Domains and Trusts** from the menu. In the left pane, you see both 412Dom1.local and 412Dom2.local. Right-click **412Dom1.local** and click **Properties**. Click the **Trusts** tab. You see an outgoing and incoming trust with 412Dom2.local. Click **Cancel**. Right-click **412Dom2.local** and click **Properties**. Click the **Trusts** tab. You see an outgoing and incoming trust with 412Dom1.local. Click **Cancel**. Close Active Directory Domains and Trusts.

13. In Server Manager, click **Tools, DNS** to open DNS Manager.

14. In DNS Manager, click to expand **Forward Lookup Zones**, and click **412Dom2.local**. You see the records that were created automatically, which include an A record for 412Server2 and the folders containing Active Directory–related records. Close DNS Manager.

15. Stay logged on to 412Server2 and leave 412Server1 running if you're continuing to the next activity.

Configuring an Alternative UPN Suffix

When a user is created in a domain, the account is assigned a **UPN suffix** that's the same as the domain name. The UPN suffix is the part of the user principal name (UPN) that comes after the @. For example, in the UPN jsmith@csmtech.local, csmtech.local is the UPN suffix. In a multidomain environment, you might want to configure multiple UPN suffixes to make logons easier. For example, suppose you have a domain structure with multiple levels of subdomains, such as csmtech.local, development.csmtech.local, and us.development.csmtech.local. A user named jsmith in us.development.csmtech.local would have to enter jsmith@us.development.csmtech.local whenever the full UPN was required for authentication. To simplify logons, an alternative UPN suffix, such as csmtech.local, can be created and assigned to the jsmith account.

A user account assigned an alternative UPN suffix can still use the original domain name when entering credentials. So even though jsmith is assigned the csmtech.local UPN suffix, jsmith can enter credentials by using jsmith@us.development.csmtech.local or jsmith@csmtech.local.

To create alternative UPN suffixes, follow these steps:

1. Log on to the domain controller where you want to create the alternative suffix with enterprise administrator credentials. The account you log on with must be a member of Enterprise Admins.

2. In Server Manager, open Active Directory Domains and Trusts.

3. Right-click Active Directory Domains and Trusts [*server name*] and click Properties to open the dialog box shown in Figure 1-7.

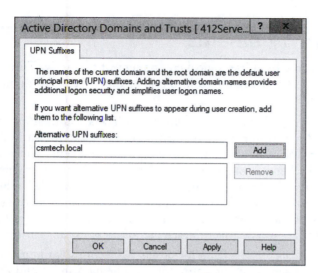

Figure 1-7   Creating an alternative UPN suffix

4. Type the suffix in the Alternative UPN suffixes text box, click Add, and then click OK. Close Active Directory Domains and Trusts.

5. In Active Directory Users and Computers, open the Properties dialog box for the user you want to assign the UPN suffix to and click the Account tab. Click the "User logon name" list arrow, and click the UPN suffix you want this user to use (see Figure 1-8). You can also assign a UPN suffix when you create a user.

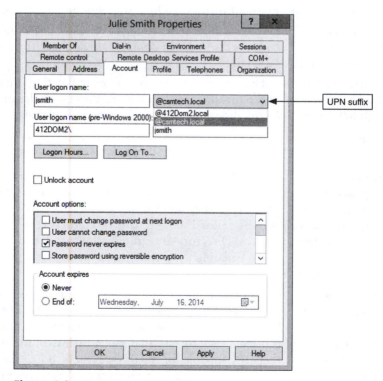

Figure 1-8   Assigning a UPN suffix to a user account

The UPN suffix doesn't need to have the same domain-naming structure as the account's actual domain. Although you should follow DNS naming rules when creating an alternative UPN suffix, the suffix name isn't required to be an actual DNS domain name. For example, you could create a single-level suffix named csm so that users assigned this suffix enter their usernames as *username*@csm.

Configuring Multiforest Environments

An Active Directory forest is the broadest logical component of the Active Directory structure. Forests contain domains that can be organized into one or more trees. All domains in a forest share some common characteristics:

- *A single schema*—The schema defines Active Directory objects and their attributes and can be changed by an administrator or an application to suit an organization's needs. All domains in a forest share the same schema, so a change to the schema affects objects in all domains. This shared schema is one reason that large organizations or conglomerates with diverse business units might want to operate as separate forests. With this structure, domains in different forests can still share information through trust relationships, but changes to the schema—perhaps from installing an Active Directory–integrated application, such as Microsoft Exchange—don't affect the schema of domains in a different forest.

- *Forest-wide administrative accounts*—Each forest has two groups with unique rights to perform operations that can affect the entire forest: Schema Admins and Enterprise Admins. Members of Schema Admins are the only users who can make changes to the schema. Members of Enterprise Admins can add or remove domains from the forest and have administrative access to every domain in the forest. By default, only the Administrator account for the first domain created in the forest is a member of these two groups.

- *Operations masters*—As discussed, certain forest-wide operations can be performed only by a DC designated as the operations master. Both the schema master and the domain naming master are forest-wide operations masters, meaning only one DC in the forest can perform these roles.

- *Global catalog*—There's only one global catalog per forest, but unlike operations masters, multiple DCs can be designated as global catalog servers. Because the global catalog contains information about all objects in the forest, it's used to speed searching for objects across domains in the forest and to allow users to log on to any domain in the forest.

- *Trusts between domains*—These trusts allow users to log on to their home domains (where their accounts are created) and access resources in domains throughout the forest without having to authenticate to each domain.

- *Replication between domains*—The forest structure facilitates replicating important information among DCs throughout the forest. Forest-wide replication includes information stored in the global catalog, schema directory, and configuration partitions.

With the preceding concepts in mind, you might need an additional forest for the following reasons:

- *Schema changes*—Business units in a large organization might require different schemas because of language or cultural differences or application differences. The schema controls the objects you can create in Active Directory and the attributes of these objects. If a new object or object attribute needs to be defined for language or cultural reasons, the schema must be changed. Likewise, an Active Directory–integrated application can make schema changes to accommodate its needs. Creating a separate forest isolates schema changes to the business unit requiring them.

- *Security*—Many industries and government entities have strict security requirements for access to resources. Domains in the same forest have a built-in trust, and members of the Enterprise Admins group have access to all domains, so the only way to have a true security boundary is with separate forests. Administrators in each forest can develop their own forest-wide security policies to ensure the degree of security suitable for the forest's assets. If necessary, a trust can be created between the forests to allow users in one forest to access resources in the other.

- *Corporate mergers*—Two businesses that merge might have their own established Active Directory forests and forest administrators. When the forests have different schemas or different security policies, merging them could be difficult or undesirable. Maintaining separate forests, with trusts for cross-forest access, is sometimes the best approach.

To create a forest, you simply choose the option to create a domain in a new forest when promoting a server to a domain controller. After the forest is created, you can choose whether to allow accounts in one forest to access resources in the other forest. You do that by creating a trust relationship, discussed next.

Activity 1-6: Creating a New Forest

Time Required: 25 minutes or longer
Objective: Create a new forest.

Required Tools and Equipment: 412Server1 and 412Server2
Description: You want to create a new forest, using 412Server2 as the DC for the new forest root. First, you demote 412Server2, and then you promote it, choosing the option to add a new forest. You name the new forest 412Forest2.local.

1. Start 412Server1 and 412Server2, if necessary. On 412Server2, log on as **Administrator**, if necessary.

2. On 412Server2 in Server Manager, click **Manage, Remove Roles and Features** from the menu to start the Remove Roles and Features Wizard.

3. In the Before You Begin window, click **Next**. In the Server Selection window, click **Next**.

4. In the Server Roles window, click to clear **Active Directory Domain Services**, and then click **Remove Features**. The Validation Results message box states that you must first demote the domain controller. Click **Demote this domain controller**.

5. In the Credentials window, you must enter enterprise administrator credentials. Click **Change**. In the Windows Security dialog box, type **412Dom1\Administrator** in the User name text box and **Password01** in the Password text box. Click **OK**.

6. Click the **Last domain controller in the domain** check box, and then click **Next**. In the Warnings window, click the **Proceed with removal** check box, and then click **Next**.

7. In the Removal Options window, click the Remove this DNS zone (this is the last DNS server that hosts the zone) check box, and then click Next.

8. Type **Password02** in the Password and Confirm password text boxes. (It's the password for the local Administrator account when the server is no longer a DC.) Click **Next**.

9. In the Review Options window, click **Demote**. When the demotion is finished, the server restarts. If the demotion isn't successful, start from the beginning and click the **Force removal of this domain controller** check box in the Credentials window.

10. After 412Server2 restarts, log on as **Administrator**. In Server Manager, click the notifications flag, and then click **Promote this server to a domain controller**. The Active Directory Domain Services Configuration Wizard starts.

11. In the Deployment Configuration window, click the **Add a new forest** option button. Type **412Forest2.local** in the Root domain name text box, and then click **Next**. Follow the remaining steps in the wizard, using the same options you did starting in Step 9 of Activity 1-1 but using **Password02** for the DSRM password.

12. After the server restarts, log on and verify the installation.

13. Stay logged on to 412Server2 and leave 412Server1 running if you're continuing to the next activity.

If you had to force the demotion of the domain controller, you might need to do some Active Directory cleanup on 412Server1 with `ntdsutil`. For details, read the article at *http://support.microsoft.com/kb/230306.*

Active Directory Trusts

In Active Directory, a **trust relationship** (or simply "trust") defines whether and how security principals from one domain can access network resources in another domain. Active Directory trust relationships are established automatically between all domains in the forest. Therefore, when a user authenticates to one domain, the other domains in the forest accept, or trust, the authentication. Because all domains in a forest have trust relationships with one another automatically, trusts must be configured only when an Active Directory environment includes two or more forests or when you want to integrate with other OSs.

Don't confuse trusts with permissions. Permissions are still required to access resources, even if a trust relationship exists.

Active Directory trusts can exist between domains and between forests. With a trust relationship between domains in the same forest or in different forests, users can access resources across domains without having to log on more than once. Moreover, a user account needs to exist in only one domain, which simplifies user management.

To say that Domain A trusts Domain B means that users in Domain B can be given permission to access resources in Domain A. Domain A is referred to as the "trusting domain," and Domain B is referred to as the "trusted domain." In Active Directory design documentation, a trust relationship is drawn with an arrow pointing from the trusting domain to the trusted domain, as shown in Figure 1-9. Trust relationship types are explained in the following sections.

Although configuring trusts in a single-forest environment might not be necessary, it can be a benefit in some configurations, as you see later in "Shortcut Trusts."

One-Way and Two-Way Trusts

A **one-way trust** exists when one domain trusts another, but the reverse is not true, as shown in Figure 1-9. Domain A trusts Domain B, but Domain B doesn't trust Domain A. This means Domain B's users can be given access to Domain A's resources, but Domain A's users can't be given access to Domain B's resources. More common is the **two-way trust**, in which users from both domains can be given access to resources in the other domain. The automatic trusts configured between domains in an Active Directory forest are two-way trusts. Both one-way and two-way trusts can be transitive or nontransitive, depending on the type of trust being created. Transitive trusts are discussed next.

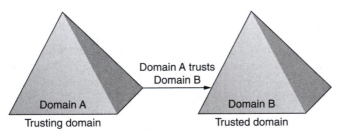

Domain A trusts
Domain B

Domain A
Trusting domain

Domain B
Trusted domain

Figure 1-9   A trust relationship
© *Cengage Learning*®

Transitive Trusts

A **transitive trust** is named after the transitive rule of equality in mathematics: If A = B and B = C, then A = C. When applied to domains, if Domain A trusts Domain B and Domain B trusts Domain C, then Domain A trusts Domain C. The automatic trust relationships created between domains in a forest are transitive two-way trusts. These trusts follow the domain parent-child relationship in a tree and flow from the forest root domain to form the trust relationship between trees. Figure 1-10 shows two-way transitive trusts between all domains in a forest. The trust relationship between branches of the tree (US.csmtech.local and UK.csmtech.local) and between trees flows through the forest root domain.

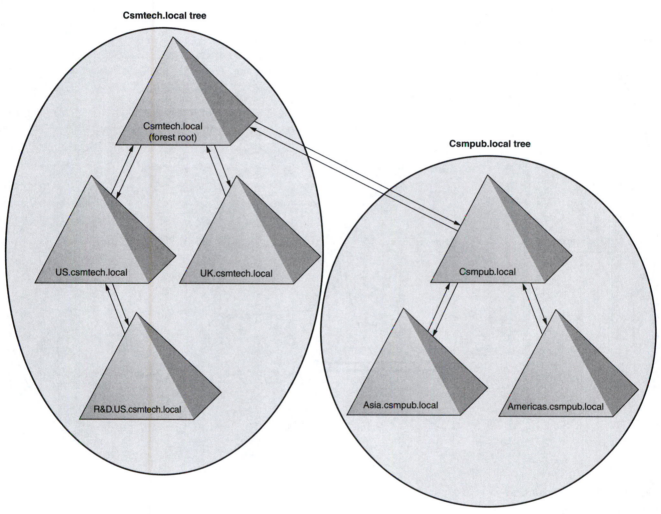

Figure 1-10   Two-way transitive trusts

© 2016 Cengage Learning®

The transitive nature of these trust relationships means that R&D.us.csmtech.local trusts Asia.csmpub.local because R&D.us.csmtech.local trusts US.csmtech.local, which trusts csmtech.local, which trusts csmpub.local, which trusts Asia.csmpub.local. Because the trusts are two-way, the reverse is also true.

Unfortunately, for Asia.csmpub.local to authenticate a user account in the R&D.us.csmtech.local domain, the authentication must be referred to a DC in each domain in the path from R&D.us.csmtech.local to Asia.csmpub.local. A **referral** is the process of a DC in one domain informing a DC in another domain that it doesn't have information about a requested object. The DC requesting the information is then referred to a DC in another domain and on through the chain of domains until it reaches the domain holding the object. This referral process can cause substantial delays when a user wants to access resources in a domain that's several referrals away. Fortunately, there's a solution to this problem in the form of shortcut trusts.

Shortcut Trusts

A **shortcut trust** is configured manually between domains in the same forest to bypass the normal referral process. Figure 1-11 shows the same forest as Figure 1-10 but with a manually configured two-way shortcut trust between R&D.us.csmtech.local and Asia.csmpub.local.

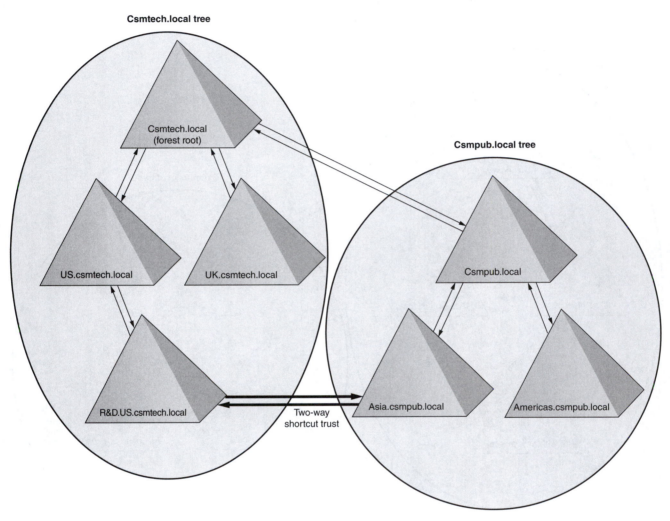

Figure 1-11   A shortcut trust

© 2016 Cengage Learning®

Shortcut trusts are transitive and can be configured as one-way or two-way trusts. Generally, they're configured when user accounts often need to access resources in domains that are several referrals away. Shortcut trusts can be used only between domains in the same forest. If users need access to resources in a different forest, you use a forest trust or an external trust.

Forest Trusts

A **forest trust** provides a one-way or two-way trust between forests that allows security principals in one forest to access resources in any domain in another forest. It's created between the forest root domains of Active Directory forests running Windows Server 2003 or later. Forest trusts aren't possible in Windows 2000 forests. A forest trust is transitive to the extent that all domains in one forest trust all domains in the other forest. However, the trust isn't transitive from one forest to another. For example, if a forest trust is created between Forest A and Forest B, all domains in Forest A trust all domains in Forest B. If there's a third forest, Forest C, and Forest B trusts Forest C, a trust relationship isn't established automatically between Forest A and Forest C. A separate trust must be configured manually between these two forests. In Figure 1-12, a two-way trust exists between Forest A and Forest B and between Forest B and Forest C, but there's no trust between Forest A and Forest C.

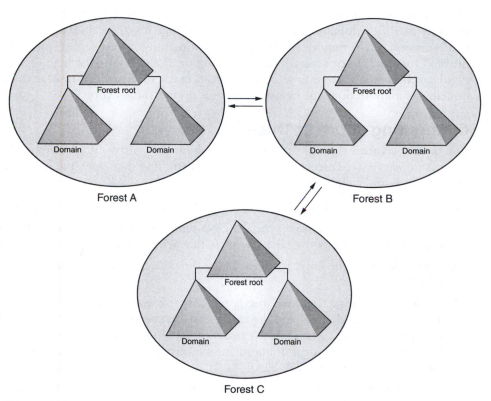

Figure 1-12   A forest trust

© 2016 Cengage Learning®

External Trusts and Realm Trusts

A forest trust is a powerful tool when having a trust relationship between all domains in two separate forests is an advantage. If the need for a trust relationship is limited to just a few domains in different forests, however, an external trust is a better option. An **external trust** is a one-way or two-way nontransitive trust between two domains that aren't in the same forest. External trusts are generally used in these circumstances:

- *To create a trust between two domains in different forests*—If no forest trust exists, an external trust can be created to allow users in one domain to access resources in another domain in a different forest. If a forest trust does exist, an external trust can still be used to create a direct trust relationship between two domains. This option can be more efficient than a forest trust when access between domains is frequent, much like a shortcut trust is used within a forest.

- *To create a trust with a Windows 2000 or Windows NT domain*—You probably won't run across many Windows 2000 or Windows NT domains, but if you do, an external trust is needed to create the trust relationship between a Windows Server 2003 and later forest and these older domains.

Networks are often composed of systems running different OSs, such as Windows, Linux, UNIX, and Mac OS. A **realm trust** can be used to integrate users of other OSs into a Windows domain or forest. It requires the OS to be running the Kerberos v5 or later authentication system that Active Directory uses.

Configuring Active Directory Trusts

One important requirement before creating any trust is that DNS must be configured so that the fully qualified domain names (FQDNs) of all participating domains can be resolved. DNS configuration might require Active Directory–integrated forest-wide replication of zones, conditional forwarders, or stub zones, depending on the type of trust being created and the OSs involved. Before you attempt to create a trust, make sure you can resolve the FQDNs of both domains from both domains by using `nslookup` or a similar tool.

Configuring Shortcut Trusts

You usually create a shortcut trust between subdomains of two domain trees. To create a shortcut trust, open Active Directory Domains and Trusts, and then open the Properties dialog box of the domain node. Follow these steps:

1. In the Trusts tab, click the New Trust button to start the New Trust Wizard, and then click Next.

2. In the Trust Name window, type the DNS name of the target domain, and then click Next. In the Trust Type window, click "Trust with a Windows domain," and then click Next.

3. In the Direction of Trust window, leave the default setting, Two-way, selected, and then click Next.

4. In the Sides of Trust window, specify whether to create the trust only in the local domain or in both the local domain and the target domain specified in Step 2. If you choose the latter, you must have the credentials to create a trust in the target domain. If you choose to create the trust only in the local domain, an administrator in the target domain must create the other side of the trust. Click Next.

5. In the User Name and Password window, if you choose to create the trust in both domains, you're prompted for credentials for an account in the target domain that can create the trust. You must be an administrator in the target domain and enter your credentials with the *username@domain* or *domain\username* syntax. If you're creating only the local side of the trust, you're prompted to enter a trust password. This password must also be used when creating the other side of the trust, so it must be communicated to the administrator who creates the trust in the other domain.

6. In the Trust Selections Complete window, you can review your choices. This window is the only place in the wizard where you actually see the word "shortcut" describing the trust type. After reviewing your choices, click Next to create the trust.

7. The next window shows the status of the created trust and summarizes the trust settings again. After reviewing the information, click Next.

8. Next, you can confirm the trust, which you should do if you created both sides of the trust.

After the wizard is finished, the Trusts tab shows the trust relationship and trust type. In Figure 1-13, the Trusts tab for the Sub1.ForestRoot.local domain shows an automatic parent trust with ForestRoot.local and a shortcut trust with Tree2.local, a domain in another tree in the forest.

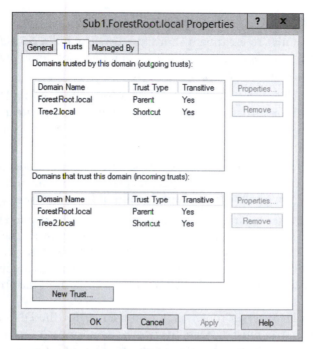

Figure 1-13   Reviewing a trust relationship

Figure 1-14 shows the entire forest and its trust relationships. The forest in Figure 1-14 is a small forest of only two trees and three domains. The path between Sub1.ForestRoot.local and Tree2.local is only two referrals away, and normally you don't need to create a shortcut trust for such a small forest. However, if four or five other domains were along the path between these two domains, a shortcut trust makes sense if users from these domains access each other's resources frequently.

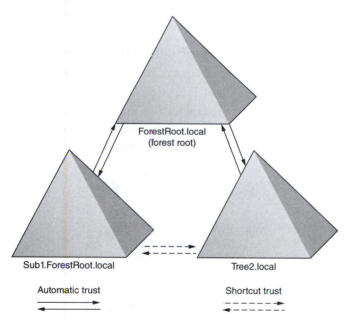

Figure 1-14   A forest with automatic trusts and a shortcut trust

© 2016 Cengage Learning®

In the preceding example, because all the domains are in the same forest, the DNS domains could be configured as Active Directory–integrated zones, and zone replication could be configured so that zones are replicated to all DNS servers in the forest. No further DNS configuration is necessary because the DNS servers in ForestRoot.local store the zone for Tree2.local, and vice versa. Trusts between forests and external trusts require additional DNS configuration.

Configuring Forest Trusts

Configuring a forest trust is similar to creating a shortcut trust. The main consideration before you begin is making sure DNS is configured correctly in both forest root domains. The following are the three most common ways to configure DNS for a forest trust:

- *Conditional forwarders*—They forward all DNS requests for a domain to a DNS server specified in the conditional forwarder record. With this method, you create a conditional forwarder in the forest root domain pointing to a DNS server in the other forest root domain. Do this in both forests involved in the trust.

- *Stub zones*—They're much like conditional forwarders, except they're updated dynamically if DNS servers' addresses change. To use this method, create a stub zone in the forest root domain of both forests pointing to the forest root domain of the other forest.

- *Secondary zones*—Creating a secondary zone for the purpose of configuring forest trusts is probably overkill. With secondary zones, you need to configure zone transfers, which causes more network traffic than stub zones do, especially if the primary zone's forest root domain contains a lot of records. However, you might want to use secondary zones as fault tolerance for the primary zone and to facilitate local hosts' name resolution for hosts in the primary domain.

You can also configure a DNS server to act as the root server for the DNS namespaces of both forests. On the root server, you must delegate the namespaces for each forest, and then configure root hints on DNS servers in the two forests to point to the root server.

After DNS is configured and you can resolve the forest root domain of both forests from both forests, you're ready to create the forest trust. This procedure is essentially the same as creating a shortcut trust, but there are a few important differences. You must initiate the forest trust in Active Directory Domains and Trusts from the forest root domain by following these steps:

1. In Active Directory Domains and Trusts, right-click the forest root domain and click Properties. In the root domain's Properties dialog box, click the Trusts tab. In this example, a two-way forest trust is created between one forest root domain named Forest1.local and another named Forest2.local.

2. Click the New Trust button to start the New Trust Wizard, and then click Next.

3. In the Trust Name window, specify the forest root domain of the target forest, which is Forest2.local.

4. In the Trust Type window, Windows recognizes that the specified domain is a forest root domain and gives you the option of creating an external trust or a forest trust, as shown in Figure 1-15. (*Note*: The forest trust option is available only from the forest root domain.) Click the Forest trust option button, and then click Next.

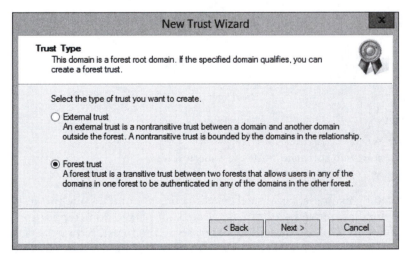

Figure 1-15   Selecting the trust type

5. In the Direction of Trust window, select Two-way, One-way: incoming, or One-way: outgoing, based on whether you need a two-way trust or just a one-way trust.

6. In the Sides of Trust window, specify whether you're creating the trust for the local domain only or for both domains. You need enterprise administrator credentials in both forests if you want to create both sides of the trust. If you create the trust for both domains, you're prompted for credentials for the other forest in the next window. Click Next.

7. In the Outgoing Trust Authentication Level—Local Forest window, the choices are forest-wide authentication or selective authentication (see Figure 1-16). **Forest-wide authentication** means Windows should authenticate all users in the specified forest for all resources in the local forest. With **selective authentication**, you can choose which local forest resources that users in the specified forest can be authenticated to. Authenticating a user for a resource doesn't grant the user access; permissions must also be set. Microsoft recommends forest-wide authentication when both forests belong to the same company and selective authentication when the forests belong to different organizations. Select the authentication level, and then click Next. If you're creating both sides of the trust, you're prompted to specify the trust authentication level for the other forest.

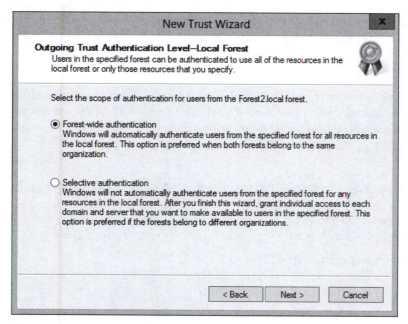

Figure 1-16   Selecting the trust authentication level

8. If multiple trees exist in one of the forests, you see the Routed Name Suffixes—Specified forest window. You're asked whether you want to prevent authentication requests from any of the name suffixes. Name suffix routing is discussed later in the "Configuring Trust Properties" section.

9. Last, you can confirm the trust if you created both sides of it, and you can confirm both the incoming and outgoing trusts if you created a two-way trust.

Activity 1-7: Creating Conditional Forwarders

Time Required: 15 minutes
Objective: Create a conditional forwarder.

Required Tools and Equipment: 412Server1 and 412Server2
Description: You want to create a forest trust between 412Dom1.local and 412Forest2.local, but first you must configure DNS. You decide to create a conditional forwarder on both DNS servers pointing to the other forest root domain.

1. Log on to 412Server1 as **Administrator**, if necessary, and open DNS Manager.

2. Click to expand the server node, and then click **Conditional Forwarders**. Right-click **Conditional Forwarders** and click **New Conditional Forwarder**.

3. In the New Conditional Forwarder dialog box, type **412Forest2.local** in the DNS Domain text box. Then click **<Click here to add an IP Address or DNS Name>**, type **10.12.1.2**, and press **Enter**. Click **OK**.

If you see an error message stating that the IP address isn't authoritative for the zone, wait a few minutes, and then come back to this dialog box. Usually, the error message is cleared after a short time.

4. To test the forwarder, open a command prompt window, and then type **nslookup 412forest2.local** and press **Enter**. The IP addresses of all DNS servers for 412forest2.local are displayed.

5. Log on to 412Server2 as **Administrator**, if necessary.

6. Open DNS Manager. Click to expand the server node, and then click **Conditional Forwarders**. Right-click **Conditional Forwarders** and click **New Conditional Forwarder**.

7. In the New Conditional Forwarder dialog box, type **412Dom1.local** in the DNS Domain text box. Then click **<Click here to add an IP Address or DNS Name>**, type **10.12.1.1**, and press **Enter**. Click **OK**.

8. To test the forwarder, open a command prompt window, and then type **nslookup 412Dom1.local** and press **Enter**. The IP addresses of all DNS servers for 412Dom1.local are displayed. Close the command prompt window.

9. Stay logged on to both servers for the next activity.

Activity 1-8: Testing Cross-Forest Access Without a Trust

Time Required: 10 minutes
Objective: Test access across forests before you create a forest trust.

Required Tools and Equipment: 412Server1 and 412Server2
Description: You plan to create a forest trust between 412Dom1.local and 412Forest2.local, but first you want to see what happens when you try to access resources across forests.

1. Log on to 412Server1 as **Administrator**, if necessary. Make sure 412Server2 is running.

2. On 412Server1, right-click **Start** and click **Run**. Type **\\412Server2.412forest2.local** in the Open text box, and press **Enter**.

3. You should see a Windows Security dialog box asking for your username and password. Type **Administrator** and **Password01**, and then click **OK**. The logon should be unsuccessful. Without a trust between the two forests, you can't log on to a domain in the other forest. Click **Cancel**.

4. Try to access the server again by repeating Step 2.

5. In the Windows Security dialog box, type **forest2\Administrator** and **Password02**, and then click **OK**. You're trying to log on with credentials from the other domain. This logon should be successful, and the NETLOGON and SYSVOL shares are displayed.

6. When no forest trust exists, you can still access a domain in another forest, but you need the logon credentials of a user in the other domain. The trust precludes the need for credentials in multiple domains, as you see later in Activity 1-10. Close File Explorer and any open windows.

7. Log off both servers to clear the existing connection between the two domains.

ACTIVITY

Activity 1-9: Creating a Forest Trust

Time Required: 15 minutes
Objective: Create a forest trust.

Required Tools and Equipment: 412Server1 and 412Server2
Description: Now that you have DNS set up between the two forests, you can create the forest trust.

1. Log on to 412Server1 as **Administrator**, and open Active Directory Domains and Trusts.

2. Right-click **412Dom1.local** and click **Properties**.

3. Click the **Trusts** tab, and click the **New Trust** button to start the New Trust Wizard. Click **Next** in the wizard's welcome window.

4. Type **412Forest2.local** in the Name text box, and then click **Next**.

5. In the Trust Type window, click the **Forest trust** option button. (*Note*: You can create an external trust in this window, but an external trust creates a trust only between two domains, whereas all domains in the forest are included in a forest trust.) Click **Next**.

6. In the Direction of Trust window, verify that the default **Two-way** option is selected, and then click **Next**.

7. In the Sides of Trust window, click **Both this domain and the specified domain**. If you're creating only one side of the trust, you're asked to enter a trust password, which must be used to create the second side of the trust. Click **Next**.

8. You need to specify credentials for the 412Forest2.local domain to create the other side of the trust. Type **Administrator** in the User name text box and **Password02** in the Password text box, and then click **Next**.

9. In the Outgoing Trust Authentication Level—Local Forest window, verify that **Forest-wide authentication** is selected for the authentication level, and then click **Next**.

10. In the Outgoing Trust Authentication Level—Specified Forest window, verify that **Forest-wide authentication** is selected, and then click **Next**.

11. Review your settings in the Trust Selections Complete window, and then click **Next**.

12. In the Trust Creation Complete window, the status of the trust creation and a summary of your choices are displayed. Click **Next**.

13. In the Confirm Outgoing Trust window, click **Yes, confirm the outgoing trust**, and then click **Next**.

14. In the Confirm Incoming Trust window, click **Yes, confirm the incoming trust**, and then click **Next**.

15. Click **Finish**. The Trusts tab should list 412Forest2.local in both the outgoing trusts and incoming trusts lists. Click **OK**, and close Active Directory Domains and Trusts.

16. Log on to 412Server2 as **Administrator**, and open Active Directory Domains and Trusts. Verify that the trust relationship with 412Dom1.local was created successfully, and then close Active Directory Domains and Trusts.

17. Stay logged on to both servers if you're continuing to the next activity.

Activity 1-10: Confirming Cross-Forest Access

Time Required: 10 minutes
Objective: Access resources from one forest to another.

Required Tools and Equipment: 412Server1 and 412Server2
Description: In this activity, you try to access resources in the 412Forest2.local domain from the 412Dom1.local domain, using credentials for the 412Dom1.local domain.

1. Log on to 412Server1 and 412Server2 as **Administrator,** if necessary.

2. On 412Server2, open File Explorer. On the root of the C drive, create a folder named **Share1.** Right-click the **Share1** folder, click **Share with,** and click **Specific people.** Add **Everyone** with **Read/Write** permission. Click **Share,** and then click **Done.**

3. Repeat Step 2, this time creating a share named **Share2** and leaving the default sharing permissions as they are. (Don't add the Everyone group to the list of users who can access the share.) Close File Explorer.

4. On 412Server1, right-click **Start,** click **Run,** type **\\412Server2.412forest2.local** in the Open text box, and press **Enter.** A File Explorer window opens and lists all shares on 412Server2. Notice that you didn't have to enter credentials because there's a trust between 412Dom1. local and 412Forest2.local.

5. Double-click **Share1,** and create a text file named `doc1.txt` to show that you can write files to the share across the forest. Share1 has Read/Write permission assigned to the Everyone group, which includes authenticated users from other forests.

6. In File Explorer, click the **back arrow** to see the list of shared folders on 412Server2. Double-click **Share2.** You see a "Windows cannot access" message. You can't access this share because you weren't given permission to do so. Click **Close.** Close File Explorer.

7. Stay logged on to both servers if you're continuing to the next activity.

Configuring External and Realm Trusts

External trusts and realm trusts are configured in Active Directory Domains and Trusts. An external trust involves Windows domains on both sides of the trust, but a realm trust is created between a Windows domain and a non-Windows OS running Kerberos v5 or later. Unlike a forest trust, an external trust isn't transitive and need not be created between the forest root domains of two forests. In addition, SID filtering (discussed later in "SID Filtering") is enabled by default for external trusts. Aside from these differences, configuring an external trust is nearly identical to creating a forest trust.

The only real consideration when creating a realm trust is whether it should be transitive. If it's transitive, the trust extends to all child domains and child realms. Otherwise, the procedure is much the same as configuring other trust types.

Configuring Trust Properties

After creating a trust, you might need to view or change its settings. To do this, in Active Directory Domains and Trusts, open the domain's Properties dialog box and click the Trusts tab. Select the trust you want to configure and click the Properties button. The Properties dialog box of a forest trust contains three tabs—General, Name Suffix Routing, and Authentication—discussed in the following sections.

A trust's Properties dialog box varies depending on the type of trust you're configuring. For example, an automatic trust has only a General tab.

The General Tab   The General tab, shown in Figure 1-17, contains the following fields and information:

- *This Domain*—The domain you're currently configuring.
- *Other Domain*—The domain a trust has been created with.
- *Trust type*—The type of trust, such as shortcut, forest, external, and so forth.
- *The other domain supports Kerberos AES Encryption*—Kerberos AES encryption enhances authentication security and is supported by Windows Server 2008 and later. If the forest trust is between two Windows Server 2008 or later domains, you can select this option for better security.
- *Direction of trust*—This field is for informational purposes only. You can't change the trust direction without deleting and re-creating the trust.
- *Transitivity of trust*—This field is for informational purposes only. You can't change the transitivity without re-creating the trust. Some trusts, such as forest and shortcut trusts, are always transitive.
- *Validate*—Click this button to confirm the trust. It performs the same action as the confirmation process at the end of the New Trust Wizard. If you didn't create both sides of the trust with the wizard, you should validate the trust with this option after both sides have been created.
- *Save As*—Click this button to create a text file containing details of the trust.

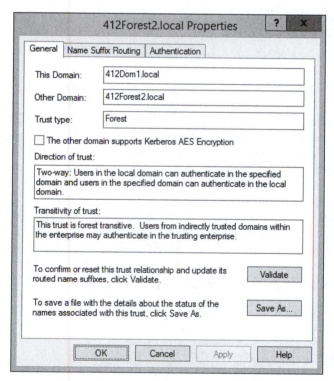

Figure 1-17   The General tab of a trust's Properties dialog box

The Name Suffix Routing Tab   In the Name Suffix Routing tab, you can control which name suffixes used by the trusted forest are routed for authentication. For example, the csmtech. local forest contains multiple trees—csmtech.local and csmpub.local—and csmtech.local is trusted by a second forest, csmAsia.local. Only users from the csmtech.local domain should have access to csmAsia.local resources, however. To do this, the csmAsia administrator can disable authentication requests containing the name suffix csmpub.local. The Name Suffix Routing tab displays all available name suffixes in the trusted forest, and you can disable or enable them. In Figure 1-18, only one name suffix is listed because there's only one domain tree in 412Forest2.local.

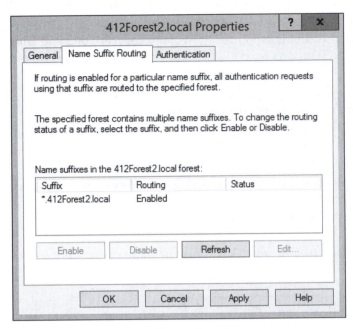

Figure 1-18   The Name Suffix Routing tab

The Authentication Tab   The Authentication tab has the same options as the Outgoing Trust Authentication Level window shown previously in Figure 1-16: forest-wide or selective authentication. As discussed, forest-wide authentication is recommended for forest trusts when both forests belong to the same organization. Selective authentication, recommended for forests in different organizations, enables you to specify users who can authenticate to selected resources in the trusting forest. After selecting this option, you add users and groups from the trusted forest to the DACL of computer accounts in the trusting forest and assign the "Allowed to authenticate" permission to these computer accounts. When selective authentication is enabled, by default, users from the trusted forest can't authenticate to the trusting forest. If users try to authenticate to a computer in the trusting domain and haven't been granted authentication permission, they see an error message indicating a logon failure.

Activity 1-11: Configuring Selective Authentication

Time Required: 10 minutes
Objective: Configure selective authentication.

Required Tools and Equipment: 412Server1 and 412Server2
Description: In this activity, you configure selective authentication and try to access resources in the 412Forest.local domain from the 412Dom1.local domain. You then add the Administrator account from 412Dom1.local to the DACL of 412Server2.412Forest2.local with the "Allowed to authenticate" permission.

1. Log on to 412Server1 as **Administrator**, and open Active Directory Domains and Trusts.

2. Right-click **412Dom1.local** and click **Properties**. Click the **Trusts** tab.

3. In the list box at the top, click **412Forest2.local**, and then click the **Properties** button. Review the options in the General tab, and then click the **Name Suffix Routing** tab to review the available options.

4. Click the **Authentication** tab, click the **Selective authentication** option button, and then click **OK** twice.

5. If necessary, log on to 412Server2 as **Administrator** with **Password02**.

6. Click **Start**, type **\\412Server1**, and press **Enter**. In the error message indicating that the machine you're logging on to is protected by an authentication firewall, click **OK**.

7. On *412Server1*, open Active Directory Users and Computers. Click **View, Advanced Features** from the menu so that you can view the Security tab in the next step. Click the **Domain Controllers** OU. Right-click **412Server1** and click **Properties**.

8. Click the **Security** tab. Click **Add** to open the Select Users, Computers, Service Accounts, or Groups dialog box, and then click **Locations**. Click the **412Forest2.local** forest, and then click **OK**.

9. Type **Domain Admins**, and click **Check Names**. All users who are members of the Domain Admins group in the 412Forest2.local domain are allowed to authenticate to 412Server1. Click **OK**.

10. Make sure **Domain Admins** is selected at the top of the Security tab, click the **Allowed to authenticate** check box in the Allow column, and then click **OK**.

11. On *412Server2*, try again to access **\\412Server1**. You should be successful.

12. In case you want other users to be able to access resources on 412Server1 from the 412Forest2. local domain, you should change the authentication type back to forest-wide authentication. On *412Server1*, open Active Directory Domains and Trusts. Right-click **412Dom1.local** and click **Properties**. Click the **Trusts** tab. In the list box at the top, click **412Forest2.local**, and then click the **Properties** button. Click the **Authentication** tab, click the **Forest-wide authentication** option button, and then click **OK** twice.

13. Close all open windows, and log off both servers.

SID Filtering

SID Filtering   Every account has an sIDHistory attribute that's used when migrating accounts from one domain to another to determine the account's rights and permissions in both the new and old domains. This attribute can also be used for nefarious purposes to gain administrative privileges in a trusting forest. Suppose ForestA is trusted by ForestB. An administrator in ForestA can edit the sIDHistory attribute of a user in ForestA to include the SID of a privileged account in ForestB. When this user logs on to a domain in ForestB, he or she has the same access as the privileged account.

To counter this security risk, Windows has a feature called **SID filtering** (also called "SID filter quarantining") that's enabled by default on external trusts but is disabled on forest trusts. It causes the trusting domain to ignore any SIDs that aren't from the trusted domain. Essentially, the trusting domain ignores the contents of the sIDHistory attribute. SID filtering should be enabled or disabled from the trusting side of the domain and should be used only between forests or with external domains. It shouldn't be used between domains in the same forest because it would break Active Directory replication and automatic transitive trusts.

For Active Directory migration purposes, SID filtering can be disabled but should be reenabled after the migration. To disable SID filtering, use the following command:

```
netdom trust TrustingDomainName /domain:TrustedDomainName /
  quarantine:No
```

To enable SID filtering, simply change the No to Yes. To check the status of SID filtering, omit the Yes or No at the end of the command.

You can view and clear the contents of sIDHistory in Attribute Editor and ADSI Edit, but you can't add or change existing values. If you attempt to do so, you get an access denied error.

Upgrading Domains and Forests

With each release of a Windows Server OS, features are added to make the Active Directory environment more capable and easier to manage. However, new features often aren't compatible with earlier releases. Instead of requiring administrators to upgrade servers before installing a new server OS, Windows enables administrators to configure functional levels on new domain controllers to maintain backward-compatibility.

When you install the first domain controller in a forest root domain with Windows Server 2012 R2, the forest and domain functional levels default to Windows Server 2012 R2. These levels ensure the highest level of Active Directory functioning, at least until the next version of Windows Server is released. Be aware that domain and forest functional levels are specific to domain controllers. Member servers and workstation computers don't have this setting and can be domain members of domains and forests running at any functional level. The following sections discuss the features and requirements of each forest and domain functional level.

 A functional level called "Windows 2000 mixed" provides backward-compatibility with Windows NT domain controllers. This functional level was deprecated in Windows Server 2008, and Windows NT domain controllers are no longer supported in the same network as Windows Server 2008 and later domain controllers.

Forest Functional Levels

The **forest functional level** determines the features of Active Directory that have forest-wide implications and which server OSs are supported on domain controllers in the forest. A Windows Server 2012 R2 domain controller supports the following forest functional levels:

- Windows Server 2003
- Windows Server 2008
- Windows Server 2008 R2
- Windows Server 2012
- Windows Server 2012 R2

The forest functional level can be raised from an earlier version to a newer version, but it can't be changed from a newer version to an earlier version. In addition, a domain in a forest can't operate at a lower functional level than the forest functional level, but it can operate at a higher level.

The following sections describe the available features and supported OSs for each functional level. Windows 2000 functional level is included for completeness but isn't supported as of Windows Server 2012.

Windows 2000 Native   The Windows 2000 Native forest functional level supports all the default features of an Active Directory forest. Because Windows 2000 was the first server OS supporting Active Directory, this functional level is considered the baseline for forest operation. Some notable features not supported at this functional level include creating forest trusts and renaming a domain. This level supports domain controllers running Windows 2000 Server through Windows Server 2008.

Windows Server 2003   The Windows Server 2003 forest functional level requires all domain controllers in all domains to be running at least Windows Server 2003. If there's a possibility of using a Windows 2000 Server computer as a DC in your network, don't raise the forest functional level to Windows Server 2003. This level supports all the forest-wide features of the Windows 2000 functional level and adds the following features:

- *Forest trusts*—Create a trust relationship between forests.

- *Knowledge Consistency Checker (KCC) improvements*—Large networks with more sites are supported by the Intersite Topology Generator (ISTG), a function the KCC performs on a DC in each site.

- *Linked-value replication*—Replicates only changes to group membership instead of replicating the entire group membership, which saves network and processor bandwidth.

- *Rename a domain*—Domains can be renamed by using the `rendom.exe` and `gpfixup.exe` command-line tools. This process is complex and should be attempted only after reviewing Microsoft documentation carefully.

- *Read only domain controller (RODC) deployment*—RODCs must be running Windows Server 2008 or later (because RODCs were introduced in Server 2008). In addition, a writeable Windows Server 2008 or later DC must be installed first to replicate with the RODC.

- *Additional features*—Other features, related mostly to the Active Directory schema, include creating the dynamic auxiliary class named `dynamicObject`, converting the `inetOrgPerson` object (used by some LDAP applications) to a user object and vice versa, creating new group types to support role-based authorization, and deactivating schema attributes and classes.

 A Windows Server 2012/R2 DC can be installed in an existing Windows Server 2003 domain or forest, but if you create a new forest in Windows Server 2012/R2, the lowest functional level you can choose is Windows Server 2008.

Windows Server 2008   No forest-wide features were added to this functional level. However, to operate at this forest functional level, all DCs must be running at the Windows Server 2008 domain functional level and, therefore, must be running Windows Server 2008 or later.

Windows Server 2008 R2   This forest functional level has all the features of the Windows Server 2003 forest functional level and adds the Active Directory Recycle Bin, which enables you to restore deleted Active Directory objects without taking Active Directory offline.

Windows Server 2012   No forest-wide features were added to this functional level. However, to operate at this forest functional level, all DCs must be running at the Windows Server 2012 domain functional level and, therefore, must be running Windows Server 2012 or later.

Windows Server 2012 R2   Again, no new forest-wide features were added at this functional level, but all DCs must be running at the Windows Server 2012 R2 domain functional level and, therefore, must be running Windows Server 2012 R2 or later.

Domain Functional Levels

Windows Server 2012 R2 supports five **domain functional levels** that have the same names as the forest functional levels. A domain controller can't be configured to run at a lower functional level than the functional level of the forest in which it's installed. Like forest functional levels, domain functional levels can be raised but not lowered. After a domain's functional level has been raised, no DCs running earlier versions of the OS can be installed in the domain. The following sections summarize the features available at each level.

Windows 2000 Native   The Windows 2000 native domain functional level includes all the original features given to domains by Active Directory. This functional level is supported only by Windows 2000 through Windows Server 2008 R2 but is described here for completeness. The following list of features can be thought of as upgrades to the Windows NT domain system:

- *Universal groups*—Allow administrators to assign rights and permissions to forest-wide resources to users from any domain.

- *Group nesting*—Allows most group types to be members of most other group types.

- *Group conversion*—Allows administrators to convert between security and distribution groups.

- *Security identifier (SID) history*—Facilitates migrating user accounts from one domain to another (which changes users' SIDs). A user's original SID is kept in the sIDHistory (meaning "SID history") attribute to determine the user's group memberships in the original domain and maintain the user's access to resources in the original domain.

Windows Server 2003   This level supports all the features in the Windows 2000 native domain functional level. All DCs must be running Windows Server 2003 or later. Added features for this functional level include the following:

- *Domain controller renaming*—The netdom.exe command-line tool makes renaming a domain controller possible without undue latency. Using the System Properties dialog box to rename a domain controller doesn't update DNS and Active Directory replication parameters completely, which could cause client authentication problems. Netdom does perform these updates.

- *Logon timestamp replication*—The lastLogonTimestamp user account attribute is updated with the time and date of a user's last logon. This attribute is replicated to all DCs in the domain.

- *Selective authentication*—With this feature, an administrator can specify users and groups from a trusted forest who can authenticate to servers in a trusting forest.

- *Users and Computers container redirection*—When creating users, groups, and computers with command-line tools that don't allow specifying a target OU (or if the location is omitted), these accounts are placed in the Users container or the Computers container. You can use the redirusr (for users and groups) and redircmp (for computers) commands to specify a different default location.

- *Additional features*—This level includes constrained delegation, Authorization Manager policy support, and the userPassword attribute set as the effective password on inetOrgPerson and user objects. These features are beyond the scope of this book, however.

 The Windows Server 2003 domain functional level is supported by Windows Server 2012/R2 when it's installed in an existing Windows Server 2003 domain. For new domains, Windows Server 2012/R2 supports only Windows Server 2008 and higher functional levels.

Windows Server 2008   This functional level supports all features in the Windows Server 2003 domain functional level with several additions, described in the following list. All DCs must be running Windows Server 2008 or later.

- *Distributed File System (DFS) replication*—DFS is used to replicate the contents of the SYSVOL share, which makes replication more reliable and efficient.

- *Fine-grained password policies*—This feature enables administrators to assign different password and account lockout policies for users and groups.

- *Interactive logon information*—Enabled through group policies, this option displays information about a user's most recent successful and unsuccessful logon attempts each time the user logs on. If you enable this policy in a domain with a functional level lower than Windows Server 2008, users who attempt to log on get a warning message explaining that the information couldn't be retrieved, and they can't log on.

- *Advanced Encryption Standard (AES) support*—AES 128 and AES 256 are supported encryption standards that can be used for Kerberos authentication to increase user logon security.

Windows Server 2008 R2   This functional level supports all features in the Windows Server 2008 domain functional level with the following additions. All DCs must be running Windows Server 2008 R2 or later.

- *Automatic Service Principal Name (SPN) management*—Includes automatic password management of service accounts and automatic DNS name changes if there's a name change on the computer where the service account is running.

- *Authentication mechanism assurance*—Simplifies authentication management when using a federated identity management structure. A federated identity is a person's electronic credentials that originate from a remote system, such as a nontrusted forest or a different operating system.

Windows Server 2012   This functional level supports all features in the Windows Server 2008 R2 domain functional level and adds Kerberos improvements in claims, compound authentication, and Key Distribution Center (KDC) armoring. All DCs must be running Windows Server 2012 or later.

Windows Server 2012 R2   This functional level supports all features in the Windows Server 2012 domain functional level with the following additions. All DCs must be running Windows Server 2012 or later.

- *Authentication improvements for Protected Users*—Older and less secure authentication methods can no longer be used by Protected Users, a security group introduced in Windows Server 2012 R2.

- *Authentication Policies*—Policies that define Kerberos properties for user, service, and computer accounts.

- *Authentication Policy silos*—New Active Directory containers to which authentication policies can be applied to restrict where high-privilege user accounts can be used in the domain.

Raising Domain and Forest Functional Levels

Functional levels can be set when a server is promoted to a DC, or they can be raised manually on the DC. Before you raise functional levels, make sure DCs meet the requirements for the functional level you want.

Functional levels apply only to DCs. Member servers can run any version of Windows Server, regardless of the domain or forest functional level.

Raising the Domain Functional Level   All DCs in the domain must be running the Windows version that supports the functional level you want. Raising the domain functional level affects all DCs in the domain. However, you need to raise the functional level on only one DC, and all other DCs reflect the change. To raise the domain functional level, right-click the domain node in Active Directory Domains and Trusts and click Raise Domain Functional Level. If the domain is already operating at the highest level, you can't change it.

Raising the Forest Functional Level   To raise the forest functional level, you must be a member of the Enterprise Admins group, and the Schema FSMO role must be available because the schema is changing. In addition, if you're raising both the forest and domain functional levels, you must raise the domain functional level first to at least the level you're raising the forest functional level. Remember that after a functional level is raised, it can't be changed back to a lower level, so be sure your DCs meet the functional level's requirements. To change the forest functional level in Active Directory Domains and Trusts, right-click the Active Directory Domains and Trusts node and click Raise Forest Functional Level. If the forest is already at the highest level, you can't change it.

To clear up any confusion about which configurations for forest and domain functional levels are valid, examine Figure 1-19. The first forest is set at the Windows Server 2012 R2 level with domains at the Windows Server 2008 and Windows Server 2003 levels. This configuration isn't valid because domain functional levels must be equal to or higher than forest functional levels. The second forest is set at the Windows Server 2008 level with domains at the Windows Server 2012 R2 and Windows Server 2008 levels, which is a valid configuration.

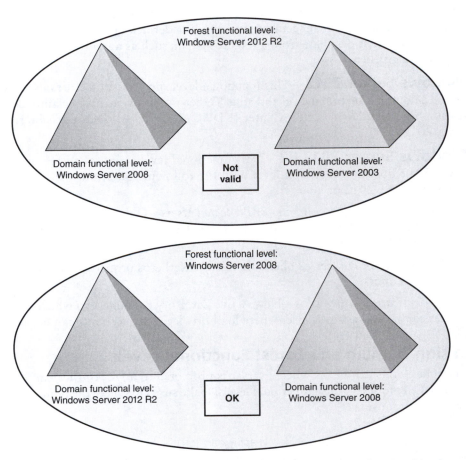

Figure 1-19   Valid and invalid configurations for forest and domain functional levels

© 2016 Cengage Learning®

Adding Domain Controllers to an Existing Domain

When you're installing Windows Server 2012 R2 DCs in a new forest, the process is straightforward, as you've seen. However, installing new Windows Server 2012 R2 DCs in existing Windows Server 2012 or Windows Server 2008 domains and forests is common, too. With each version of Windows Server, new features are added, and the schema changes, with new objects and object attributes. Before you can install a DC running a newer Windows Server version in an existing forest with a lower functional level, you must prepare existing DCs. Forest and domain preparation are done with the adprep.exe command-line program. It's built into the Windows

Server 2012/R2 Active Directory Domain Services role installation process, so there's no need to run it manually when adding a Windows Server 2012/R2 server to an existing domain or forest. However, you can run it manually if you want to prepare the environment before installation or extend the existing schema to support new features. `Adprep.exe` is in the \Support\Adprep folder on the Windows installation disc.

Versions of Windows Server before Windows Server 2012 require running `adprep.exe` manually before adding a DC to a domain or forest with an older functional level than the OS version you're installing.

Chapter Summary

- Active Directory is a server role that makes a Windows server a domain controller. Client computers and other servers can be joined to the domain for centralized authentication, authorization, and network policy management.

- Active Directory's physical components consist of servers configured as domain controllers and sites. A DC is a computer running Windows Server 2012/R2 with the Active Directory Domain Services role installed. A site is a physical location in which DCs communicate and replicate information.

- The logical components of Active Directory are OUs, domains, trees, and forests. They make it possible to pattern a directory service's look and feel after the organization in which it runs. Other important functions of Active Directory include the forest root, FSMOs, the global catalog, trusts, and replication.

- Windows domains and Active Directory rely on DNS for resolving names to IP addresses and locating services. The first DC installed in a forest is usually also a DNS server.

- Most small and medium businesses have a single domain, but using more than one domain makes sense when there's a need for differing account policies, different name identities, replication control, internal and external domains, and tighter security.

- Adding a subdomain is a common reason for expanding an Active Directory forest. A tree can consist of a single domain or a parent domain and child domains, which can have child domains of their own.

- When a user is created in a domain, the account is assigned a UPN suffix that's the same as the domain name. To simplify logons, an alternative UPN suffix can be created and assigned to user accounts.

- The Active Directory forest is the broadest logical component of the Active Directory structure. Forests contain domains that can be organized into one or more trees. All domains in a forest share some common characteristics: a single schema, forest-wide administrative accounts, operations masters, global catalogs, trusts between domains, and replication between all domains.

- A trust relationship defines whether and how security principals from one domain can access network resources in another domain. Trust relationship types include one-way and two-way trusts, transitive trusts, shortcut trusts, forest trusts, external trusts, and realm trusts. You configure trusts with Active Directory Domains and Trusts.

- The Properties dialog box for a forest trust has three tabs: General, Name Suffix Routing, and Authentication. In the Name Suffix Routing tab, you can control which name suffixes used by the trusted forest are routed for authentication. In the Authentication tab, you choose forest-wide or selective authentication. SID filtering, which is enabled by default on external trusts but disabled on forest trusts, causes the trusting domain to ignore any SIDs that aren't from the trusted domain.

- The forest functional level determines the features of Active Directory that have forest-wide implications and which server OSs are supported on domain controllers in the forest. The domain functional level determines the features Active Directory supports in a domain.

- Forest and domain preparation are done with the `adprep.exe` command-line program, which is included in the Active Directory Domain Services role installation.

Key Terms

child domains   Domains that have the same second-level and top-level domain names as the parent domain in the same tree and forest.

domain   The core structural unit of Active Directory; contains OUs and represents administrative, security, and policy boundaries.

domain functional levels   Properties of domains that determine which features of Active Directory have domain-wide implications and which server OSs are supported on domain controllers.

external trust   A one-way or two-way nontransitive trust between two domains that aren't in the same forest.

Flexible Single Master Operation (FSMO) roles   Specialized domain controller tasks that handle operations that can affect the entire domain or forest. Only one domain controller can be assigned a particular FSMO.

forest   A collection of one or more Active Directory trees. It can consist of a single tree with a single domain, or it can contain several trees, each with a hierarchy of parent and child domains.

forest functional level   A property of a forest that determines which features of Active Directory have forest-wide implications and which server OSs are supported on domain controllers.

forest root domain   The first domain created in a new forest.

forest trust   A trust that provides a one-way or two-way transitive trust between forests, which enables security principals in one forest to access resources in any domain in another forest.

forest-wide authentication   A property of a forest trust for granting users in a trusted forest access to the trusting forest.

global catalog   A partial replica of all objects in the forest. It contains the most commonly accessed object attributes and universal group membership information.

global catalog (GC) server   A server that holds the global catalog; it facilitates forest-wide Active Directory searches and logons across domains and stores universal group membership information. *See also* global catalog.

intersite replication   Active Directory replication that occurs between sites.

intrasite replication   Active Directory replication between domain controllers in the same site.

Knowledge Consistency Checker (KCC)   A process that runs on every domain controller to determine the replication topology.

multimaster replication   The process of replicating Active Directory objects; changes to the database can occur on any domain controller and are propagated to all other domain controllers.

one-way trust   A trust relationship in which one domain trusts another, but the reverse is not true.

organizational unit (OU)   An Active Directory container used to organize a network's users and resources into logical administrative units.

realm trust   A trust used to integrate users of other OSs into a Windows Server 2012/R2 domain or forest; requires the OS to be running Kerberos V5 authentication.

referral   The process of sending a request for information about an object to DCs in other domains until the information is found.

selective authentication A property of a forest trust that enables administrators to specify users who can be granted access to selected resources in the trusting forest.

shortcut trust A manually configured trust between domains in the same forest for the purpose of bypassing the normal referral process. *See also* referral.

SID filtering An option that causes a trusting domain to ignore any SIDs that aren't from the trusted domain.

site A physical location in which domain controllers communicate and replicate information.

transitive trust A trust relationship based on the transitive rule of mathematics; therefore, if Domain A trusts Domain B and Domain B trusts Domain C, then Domain A trusts Domain C.

tree A group of domains sharing a common naming structure.

trust relationship An arrangement that defines whether and how security principals from one domain can access network resources in another domain.

two-way trust A trust in which both domains in the relationship trust each other, so users from both domains can access resources in the other domain.

UPN suffix The part of the user principal name (UPN) that comes after the @.

Review Questions

1. What term is used for transferring Active Directory information among domain controllers?

   a. Zone transfer

   b. Replication

   c. Site topology

   d. Redundancy

2. Which of the following is a component of Active Directory's physical structure?

   a. Organizational units

   b. Domains

   c. Sites

   d. Folders

3. Which of the following is the responsibility of domain controllers? (Choose all that apply.)

   a. Storing a copy of domain data

   b. Providing data search and retrieval functions

   c. Servicing multiple domains

   d. Providing authentication services

4. Which of the following is *not* associated with an Active Directory tree?

   a. A group of domains

   b. A container object

   c. A common naming structure

   d. Parent and child domains

5. Which of the following is associated with an Active Directory forest? (Choose all that apply.)

   a. Can contain trees with different naming structures

   b. Allows differing domain policies

   c. Contains domains, each with a different schema

   d. Represents the broadest element in Active Directory

6. Which of the following best describes the first domain installed in a forest?

   a. Forest root

   b. Global catalog

   c. Master domain

   d. Primary tree

7. Which is responsible for facilitating forest-wide Active Directory searches?

   a. Knowledge Consistency Checker

   b. Infrastructure master

   c. Domain naming master

   d. Global catalog server

8. Which of the following is responsible for determining the replication topology?

   a. GPO

   b. PDC

   c. RID

   d. KCC

9. Your company has merged with another company that also uses Windows Server 2012 R2 and Active Directory. You want to give the other company's users access to your company's forest resources and vice versa without duplicating account information and with the least administrative effort. How can you achieve this goal?

   a. Transfer your global catalog to one of their servers

   b. Create a two-way forest trust

   c. Configure an external trust

   d. Configure selective authentication

10. All domains in a forest have which of the following in common? (Choose all that apply.)

    a. The same domain name

    b. The same schema

    c. The same user accounts

    d. The same global catalog

11. Which of the following is *not* a function of the global catalog?

    a. Facilitates forest-wide searches

    b. Keeps universal group memberships

    c. Facilitates intersite replication

    d. Facilitates forest-wide logons

12. You have an Active Directory forest of two trees and eight domains. You haven't changed any of the operations master domain controllers. On which domain controller is the schema master?

    a. All domain controllers

    b. The last domain controller installed

    c. The first domain controller in the forest root domain

    d. The first domain controller in each tree

1

13. Which of the following is a valid reason for using multiple forests?

    a. Centralized management

    b. Need for different schemas

    c. Easy access to all domain resources

    d. Need for a single global catalog

14. What can you do to reduce the delay caused by authentication referral?

    a. Create a forest trust

    b. Create an external trust

    c. Create a shortcut trust

    d. Create a transitive trust

15. What can you do to integrate user authentication between Linux and Active Directory?

    a. Create a realm trust

    b. Create an external trust

    c. Create a one-way trust

    d. Create a transitive trust

16. Which of the following is a reason to use multiple domains? (Choose all that apply.)

    a. Need for different name identities

    b. Replication control

    c. Need for differing account policies

    d. Easier access to resources

17. Bob is an administrator in a trusted forest, and you have some concerns about his trustworthiness. You want to be sure he can't gain privileged access to resources in your forest while masquerading as a user in his forest who doesn't normally have privileged access in your forest. What should you configure in the forest trust?

    a. SID filtering

    b. Trust transitivity

    c. Selective authentication

    d. One-way trust

18. Which of the following should you configure if you want users in a trusted forest to have access only to certain resources in your forest, regardless of permission settings on these resources?

    a. SID filtering

    b. Trust transitivity

    c. Selective authentication

    d. One-way trust

19. If you configure a trust between ForestA and ForestB, and a trust already exists between ForestB and ForestC, then ForestA trusts ForestC. True or False?

20. You're going to configure a forest trust between ForestA and ForestB and are logged on to a domain controller in the root of ForestA. You try to ping a domain controller in the root domain of ForestB and get the reply "Please check the name and try again." You have the IP address of the domain controller in the other forest, so you try pinging again with this IP address, and it's successful. You know you have the correct server and domain name. What should you do before you attempt to create the trust?

    a. Verify the IP address assignment of the remote domain controller.

    b. Configure a stub zone.

    c. Verify that Kerberos v5 is configured correctly in both forests.

    d. Configure a standard primary zone.

21. Which of the following is the default forest functional level for a Windows Server 2012 R2 domain controller installed in a new forest?

    a. Windows 2000 native

    b. Windows Server 2012 R2

    c. Windows Server 2008

    d. Windows Server 2012

22. Which of the following is true about forests running at the Windows Server 2012 R2 functional level? (Choose all that apply.)

    a. You can rename a domain.

    b. You can create a forest trust with a Windows 2000 forest.

    c. RODCs can be part of the forest.

    d. Windows 2000 domain controllers can be part of the forest.

23. The Windows Server 2008 R2 domain functional level supports Authentication Policy Silos. True or False?

24. Which of the following is a feature first introduced with the Windows Server 2012 R2 domain functional level?

    a. AES support

    b. Fine-grained password policies

    c. Domain controller renaming

    d. Protected Users group

25. You're going to introduce a Windows Server 2012 R2 domain controller into a Windows Server 2008 forest. Which of the following should you do first?

    a. Prepare the forest by running `adprep`.

    b. Install the AD DS role and promote the Windows Server 2012 R2 server.

    c. Create conditional forwarders on a Windows Server 2008 DNS server.

    d. Upgrade the Windows Server 2008 forest to a Windows Server 2012 R2 forest.

Case Projects

Case Project 1-1: Working with Trusts

Examine the network in Figure 1-20. You need to configure this network to meet the following requirements:

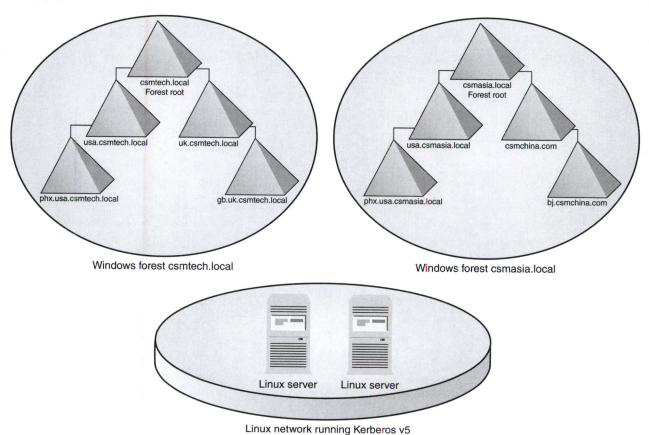

Figure 1-20 The network for Case Project 1-1

© 2016 Cengage Learning®

- Requirement 1: All users in the csmtech.local forest should be authenticated to all resources in the csmasia.local forest.

- Requirement 2: Selected users in the csmasia.local domains should be authenticated to selected resources in the csmtech.local forest.

- Requirement 3: No users in the csmchina.local domain tree should be authenticated to the csmtech.local forest.

- Requirement 4: Users in the bj.csmchina.local domain access resources in the phx.usa.csmtech.local domain frequently. Latency should be kept to a minimum.

- Requirement 5: Users in the phx.usa.csmtech.local domain access resources in the gb.uk.csmtech.local domain frequently. Latency should be kept to a minimum.

- Requirement 6: Users in the Linux network need to access resources in the csmasia.local forest frequently.

Given the preceding requirements, write a report describing how to configure trust relationships and listing configuration options, such as one-way or two-way, transitivity, authentication, and so forth.

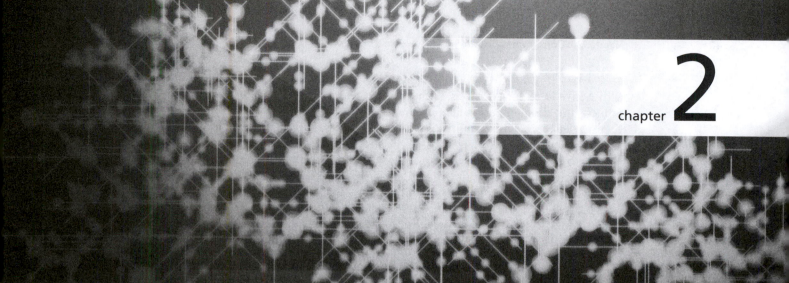

chapter 2

Configuring Advanced Active Directory: Part II

After reading this chapter and completing the exercises, you will be able to:

- Describe an Active Directory site and its components
- Configure Active Directory sites
- Manage Active Directory, RODC, and SYSVOL replication

The larger your network becomes, the more you need to be concerned with Active Directory features, such as replication and site configuration. A network with many subnets and domain controllers might require additional configuration to ensure efficient replication between DCs. A multisite network requires a solid understanding of site configuration and how domain controllers at different sites replicate with one another. This chapter discusses how to create new sites and configure them for optimal domain operation and replication. Replication between domain controllers is critical to a well-functioning domain. This chapter explains how to configure replication between DCs, including RODCs, within a site for both Active Directory and the SYSVOL share, which holds vital files related to group policies and user logon. You also learn how to optimize replication in a network with writeable domain controllers and RODCs operating in several site locations.

Understanding Sites

Table 2-1 summarizes what you need for the hands-on activities in this chapter.

Table 2-1   Activity requirements

Activity	Requirements	Notes
Activity 2-1: Creating a Subnet in Active Directory Sites and Services	412Server1	
Activity 2-2: Creating a Site	412Server1	
Activity 2-3: Adding a DC to the 412Dom1 Domain	412Server1, 412Server2	
Activity 2-4: Working with Connection Objects	412Server1, 412Server2	
Activity 2-5: Creating a Site Link	412Server1	
Activity 2-6: Managing Replication with Active Directory Sites and Services	412Server1, 412Server2	
Activity 2-7: Managing Replication at the Command Line	412Server1	

©2016 Cengage Learning®

As discussed in Chapter 1, Active Directory's physical components are sites and domain controllers. An Active Directory site represents a physical location where domain controllers are placed and group policies can be applied. When you're designing the logical components of Active Directory, such as domains and OUs, you don't need to consider the physical location of objects. In other words, an OU named Accounting could contain user accounts from both Chicago and New Orleans, and the domain controllers holding the Active Directory database could be located in San Francisco and New York. As long as there's a network connection between the location where a user logs on and the location of the DC, the system works.

Having said that, placing a DC physically near the accounts using it makes sense. Authentication and resource access work fine across a WAN link, but if a company location contains many users, placing domain controllers in that location is more efficient. Performance and reliability are less predictable on slower WAN links than on LAN links. So the extra cost of additional domain controllers can be outweighed by the productivity gained from faster, more reliable network access.

Overview of Sites

When the first DC of a forest is installed, a site named Default-First-Site-Name is created. Any additional domain controllers installed in the forest are assigned to this site until other sites are created. Figure 2-1 shows a single-site domain in two locations at the top and the same domain defined as two sites at the bottom.

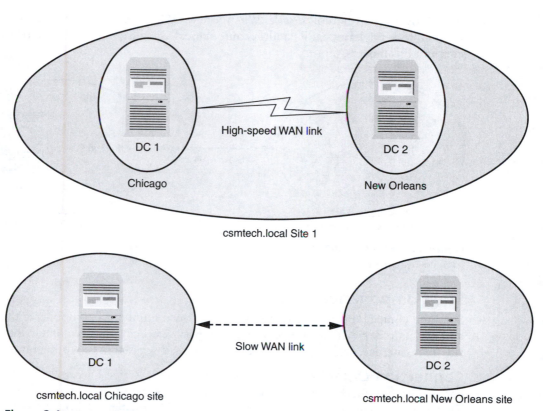

Figure 2-1 Active Directory sites
© 2016 Cengage Learning®

There are three main reasons for establishing multiple sites:

- *Authentication efficiency*—When a user logs on to a domain, the client computer always tries to authenticate to a DC in the same site to ensure that logon traffic is kept in the same site and off slower WAN links.

- *Replication efficiency*—A DC in every branch office facilitates faster and more reliable network access, but domain controllers must communicate with one another to replicate the Active Directory database. Using the default replication schedule, however, can create considerable replication traffic. Replication between domain controllers occurs within 15 seconds after a change is made and once per hour when no changes have occurred. In databases with several thousand objects, this schedule can take a toll on available resources needed for other network operations. With multiple sites, intersite replication can be scheduled to occur during off-peak hours and at a frequency that makes the most sense. For example, a small branch office site with a limited bandwidth connection to the main office can be configured to replicate less often than a larger branch office that requires more timely updates.

- *Application efficiency*—Some distributed applications, such as Exchange Server (an e-mail and collaboration application) and Distributed File System (DFS), use sites to improve efficiency. These applications ensure that client computers always try to access data in the same site before attempting to use the WAN link.

Sites are created by using Active Directory Sites and Services. A site is linked to an IP subnet that reflects the IP addressing scheme used at the physical location the site represents. A site can encompass one or more IP subnets, but each site must be linked to at least one IP subnet that doesn't overlap with another site. When a new DC is created and assigned an IP address, it's assigned to a site based on its address automatically. Figure 2-2 shows the relationship between sites and IP subnets.

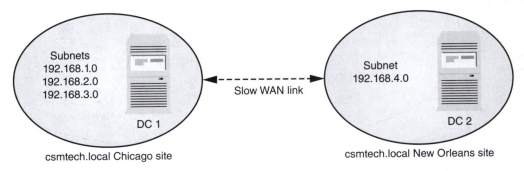

Figure 2-2   Sites and subnets
© 2016 Cengage Learning®

Site Components

Sites and connections between sites are defined by a number of components that can be created and configured in Active Directory Sites and Services. They include connection objects, subnets, site links, site link bridges, and bridgehead servers, discussed in the following sections.

Connection Objects   A **connection object** is an Active Directory object that defines the connection parameters between two replication partners (domain controllers) in the same site. They're generated automatically by the **Knowledge Consistency Checker (KCC)**, which is a process that runs on every DC to determine the replication topology, or they can be created manually if the situation warrants it. You can find connection objects under a server object's NTDS Settings node in Active Directory Sites and Services. Connection objects and the KCC are discussed in more detail later in "Active Directory Intrasite Replication."

Subnets   As mentioned, each site is associated with one or more IP subnets. In short, an IP subnet is a range of IP addresses shared by a group of computers. All computers assigned an address in a subnet can communicate with one another without requiring a router. By default, no subnets are created in Active Directory Sites and Services. However, when a new site is created, all subnets used by the default site should be created by an administrator and associated with the default site. Then the subnets for the new site should be created and associated with the new site. Figure 2-3 shows Active Directory Sites and Services with the Default-First-Site-Name Properties dialog box open.

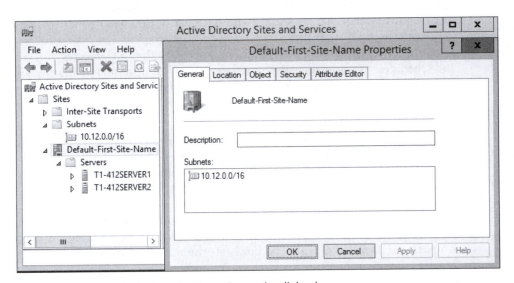

Figure 2-3   The Default-First-Site-Name Properties dialog box

ACTIVITY

Activity 2-1: Creating a Subnet in Active Directory Sites and Services

Time Required: 5 minutes
Objective: Create a subnet in Active Directory Sites and Services and associate it with a site.

Required Tools and Equipment: 412Server1
Description: You're creating multiple sites for your Active Directory structure. Before you create the second site, however, you must configure the existing site to use the subnets already on your network.

1. Log on to 412Server1 as **Administrator.**

2. Open Server Manager, and click **Tools, Active Directory Sites and Services** from the menu.

3. Click to expand **Sites**, if necessary. Right-click **Subnets** and click **New Subnet.**

4. In the Prefix text box, type **10.12.0.0/16** (assuming you're following the IP address scheme used in this book; otherwise, ask your instructor what to enter).

5. In the "Select a site object for this prefix" list box, click **Default-First-Site-Name** (see Figure 2-4), and then click **OK.**

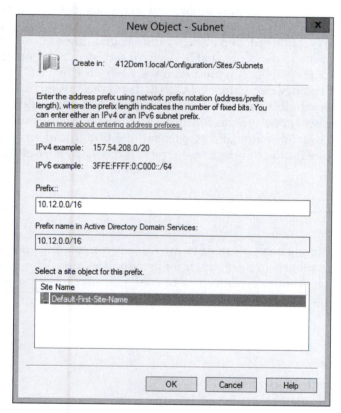

Figure 2-4   Creating a subnet

6. In the left pane, click **Subnets.** In the right pane, right-click **10.12.0.0/16** and click **Properties.** In the General tab, you can give the subnet a description and change the site the subnet is associated with, if necessary.

7. Click **Cancel.** Close Active Directory Sites and Services.

8. Stay logged on to 412Server1 if you're continuing to the next activity.

Site Links   A site link is an Active Directory object representing the path between sites for replication purposes. When Active Directory is installed, a default site link called DEFAULTIPSITELINK is created. Until new site links are created, all sites that are added use this site link. Site links connect sites and determine the replication schedule and frequency between two sites. If all locations in an organization are connected through the same WAN link or WAN links of equal bandwidth, a single site link might be suitable. If locations use different WAN connections at differing speeds, however, additional links can be created to configure different replication schedules. Site links are in the Inter-Site Transports node in Active Directory Sites and Services. Configuring site links is discussed later in "Configuring Site Links."

Site Link Bridges   A site link bridge is an Active Directory object representing one or more site links that use a common transport protocol. It provides transitivity in the connection between sites. This means when Site A is connected to Site B with a site link, and Site B is connected to Site C with a site link, Site A can still replicate with Site C even though no direct site link connection exists between Site A and Site C. A site link bridge allows data to flow from Site A through Site B to Site C. Site link bridges are discussed in more detail later in "Active Directory Intersite Replication."

Bridgehead Servers   A bridgehead server is a DC in a site that has been assigned to handle replication of directory partitions in that site. Bridgehead servers are assigned by the system automatically, although you can override the automatic assignment. A connection between bridgehead servers in each site is established, and all replication traffic flows through the designated bridgehead servers in each site to the designated bridgehead servers in every other site.

When the KCC detects that replication must occur between sites, one DC in each site is designated as the **Inter-Site Topology Generator (ISTG)**. The ISTG then assigns a bridgehead server to handle replication for each directory partition. Because bridgehead servers perform such a vital function in multisite networks, and this function can consume considerable server resources, the administrator can override automatic assignment of a bridgehead server and assign the role to a specific DC. Configuration of bridgehead servers is discussed later in "Active Directory Intersite Replication."

Configuring Sites

You've learned about basic site components and the reasons for creating additional sites, and you learned how to create subnets in preparation for creating new sites. This section covers the components of intersite replication, explains how to configure sites for optimal efficiency, and includes the following topics:

- Creating sites
- Configuring site links
- Registering SRV records
- Working with automatic site coverage
- Moving DCs between sites

Creating Sites

Sites are usually geographically dispersed and connected by WAN links, but they can also be different buildings on a campus or different floors of a building, for example. The only criteria for a site are that it's associated with one or more IP subnets and no two sites share the same subnet. When you create a site in Active Directory Sites and Services, you're asked to select a site link. DEFAULTIPSITELINK is the only choice unless you've created other site links.

The Significance of Subnets   After creating a site, you must associate one or more subnets with it, which essentially means you're assigning a range of IP addresses to the site. Active Directory uses this information in two important ways:

- *Placing new domain controllers in the right site*—Correct placement is necessary to determine optimum intrasite and intersite replication topology and to associate clients with the nearest domain controllers. When a new DC is installed, it's automatically placed in the site corresponding with its assigned IP address. If the DC existed before the site was created, you need to move it manually from Default-First-Site-Name to the new site.

- *Determining which site a client computer belongs to*—When a client requests a domain service, such as logging on to the domain or accessing a DFS resource, the request can be directed to a DC or member server in the same site. Use of a local resource is usually preferable, especially when remote sites are connected via slower WAN links.

Defining subnets is important when you have multiple sites. If a client's IP address doesn't match a subnet in any defined site, communication efficiency could degrade because the client might request services from servers in remote sites instead of local servers.

ACTIVITY

Activity 2-2: Creating a Site

Time Required: 10 minutes
Objective: Create a site.

Required Tools and Equipment: 412Server1

Description: To prepare Active Directory for a new location your company has opened, you're creating a new site. You want to rename the default site with a more descriptive name, so you use the third octet of the subnet's network address as part of the name. You configure the site in subsequent activities.

1. Log on to 412Server1 as **Administrator**, if necessary.

2. Open Active Directory Sites and Services, and click to expand the **Sites** folder, if necessary. You should see a Subnets folder, an Inter-Site Transports folder, and the Default-First-Site-Name site object.

3. Click to expand the **Subnets** folder. Right-click the **10.12.0.0/16** subnet you created in Activity 2-1 and click **Properties**. The General tab of the subnet's Properties dialog box shows that the subnet is assigned to Default-First-Site-Name. Click **Cancel**.

4. Right-click **Default-First-Site-Name** and click **Rename**. Type **Site12** and press **Enter**. Giving each site a descriptive name is a good idea; in this case, the 12 in the site name indicates the subnet the site is associated with.

5. Right-click the **Sites** folder and click **New Site**. In the New Object - Site dialog box, type **Site20** in the Name text box. Notice that you're prompted to select a site link object for the site. (Configuring site links is discussed in the next section.) Click **DEFAULTIPSITELINK**, and then click **OK**.

6. You should see a message from Active Directory Domain Services stating that more steps are needed to finish configuring the site: making sure site links are suitable, adding subnets for the site in the Subnets folder, and adding a domain controller to the site. Click **OK**.

7. Close Active Directory Sites and Services, but stay logged on if you're continuing to the next activity.

Activity 2-3: Adding a DC to the 412Dom1 Domain

Time Required: 20 minutes
Objective: Add a DC to the 412Dom1 domain.

Required Tools and Equipment: 412Server1 and 412Server2
Description: First, you delete the trust between 412Dom1.local and 412Forest2.local. Then you demote 412Server2 to have the 412forest2.local forest removed. Finally, you promote 412Server2 as an additional DC in the 412Dom1.local domain.

1. Turn on and log on to 412Server2 as **Administrator** with the password **Password02**. Log on to 412Server1 as **Administrator**, if necessary.

2. On 412Server1, open Server Manager, if necessary, and click **Tools, Active Directory Domains and Trusts** from the menu. Right-click **412Dom1.local** and click **Properties**. Click the **Trusts** tab.

3. Click **412Forest2.local** in the "Domains trusted by this domain" list box, and click **Remove**. In the Active Directory Domain Services dialog box, click **Yes, remove the trust from both the local domain and other domain**. In the User name text box, type **412forest2\administrator**, and in the Password text box, type **Password02**. Click **OK**, and click **Yes** to confirm.

4. Repeat Step 3 for the incoming trust. You don't need to reenter the credentials for Forest2. Click **OK**.

5. On 412Server2, open Server Manager, and click **Manage, Remove Roles and Features** from the menu to start the Remove Roles and Features Wizard.

6. In the Before You Begin window, click **Next**. In the Server Selection window, click **Next**.

7. In the Server Roles window, click to clear **Active Directory Domain Services**. Click **Remove Features**. The Validation Results message box states that you must demote the domain controller first. Click **Demote this domain controller**.

8. In the Credentials window, click the **Last domain controller in the domain** check box, and then click **Next**. In the Warnings window, click **Proceed with removal**, and then click **Next**.

9. In the Removal Options window, click **Remove this DNS zone** and **Remove application partitions**, and then click **Next**.

10. In the New Administrator Password window, type **Password01** in both the Password and Confirm password text boxes, and then click **Next**.

11. In the Review Options window, click **Demote**. After a while, the server restarts.

12. After 412Server2 restarts, log on as **Administrator** with the password **Password01**. Before you promote this server to a DC, change the Preferred DNS server address in the TCP/IPv4 Properties dialog box to **10.12.1.1**. Also, set the TCP/IPv6 DNS server to **Obtain DNS server address automatically**.

13. Open Server Manager, if necessary, and click the notifications flag. Next, click **Promote this server to a domain controller**. In the Deployment Configuration window, accept the default deployment operation, **Add a domain controller to an existing domain**, and type **412Dom1. local** in the Domain text box.

14. Click the **Change** button, and type **412dom1\administrator** for the username and **Password01** for the password. Click **OK**, and then click **Next**.

15. In the Domain Controller Options window, accept the default settings for domain controller capabilities and site information, and type **Password01** in the Password and Confirm password text boxes for the DSRM password. Click **Next**.

16. In the DNS Options window, click **Next**. In the Additional Options window, click **Next**.

17. In the Paths window, accept the default settings, and then click **Next**.

18. In the Review Options window, click **Next**. In the Prerequisites Check window, click **Install**.

19. Active Directory is installed, and the server restarts. After the server restarts, log on as **Administrator** with the password **Password01**. Note that you're now logging on to the 412Dom1.local domain.

20. Open Active Directory Users and Computers, and verify that 412Server1 and 412Server2 are in the Domain Controllers OU. Notice that the Site column shows that both servers are in Site12. Close Active Directory Users and Computers, and stay logged on to both servers if you're continuing to the next activity.

Configuring Site Links

Site links have two main configuration options: cost and replication frequency. The Cost field is an administrator-assigned value that represents the bandwidth of the connection between sites. The default value is 100. An administrator can alter this value to influence which path is chosen when more than one path exists between two sites. As shown in Figure 2-5, Site A replicates with Site B and Site C through the corresponding site links, but Site A has two options for replicating with Site D: the link with Site B or the link with Site C. The site link cost determines that Site A uses the link with Site B. Site link costs are additive, so the total cost for Site A to replicate with Site D through Site C is 400; the total cost to replicate with Site D via Site B is only 300. When you have more than one path between two sites, the lower cost path is always used unless links in the path become unavailable. In this case, the replication process reconfigures itself to use the next lower cost path, if available. Site links are transitive by default, which means Site A can replicate directly with Site D, and Site C can replicate directly with Site B, without creating an explicit link between the two sites.

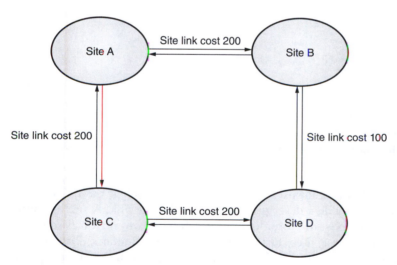

Figure 2-5 Site replication topology
© *Cengage Learning*®

Any new sites you create use the default site link, DEFAULTIPSITELINK, for their connection with other sites. If all company locations are connected via network links of similar speeds, you can use a single site link for all site connections. However, if connections between locations differ in speed or traffic volume, for example, you might want to create additional site links so that you can adjust the replication schedule according to the network links' characteristics.

Site links are in the Inter-Site Transports folder in Active Directory Sites and Services. This folder has two subfolders—IP and SMTP—and the DEFAULTIPSITELINK site link is in the IP folder. To configure a site link, right-click it and click Properties to open the dialog box shown in Figure 2-6.

In a site link's Properties dialog box, you can add or remove sites that use the link for replication. In Figure 2-6, Site100-Pittsburgh and Site150-Phoenix use DEFAULTIPSITELINK, but Site200-Dallas does not. You can change the replication cost and frequency in this dialog box, too. By default, intersite replication occurs every 180 minutes, seven days a week. If you click Change Schedule, you can specify days or times when replication shouldn't occur. For example, if your WAN link is busiest on Monday through Friday from 9 a.m. to noon, you could exclude these days and times from the replication schedule. Replication then occurs every three hours at all other times and days.

Figure 2-6   The Properties dialog box for a site link

To create a site link that uses the IP protocol, right-click the IP folder and click New Site Link. You should provide a descriptive name for the site link. A site link must contain at least two sites. A site can exist in more than one site link, however; for example, suppose your configuration includes three sites: Pittsburgh, Dallas, and Phoenix. Pittsburgh and Dallas could be contained in one site, and Dallas and Phoenix could be in the other site. Dallas, in this case, is contained in both sites. This arrangement makes sense if Dallas has WAN connections between both Pittsburgh and Phoenix. Domain controllers between Pittsburgh and Phoenix can still replicate with one another because of the transitive nature of site links. Because Pittsburgh can replicate with Dallas and Dallas can replicate with Phoenix, Pittsburgh can replicate with Phoenix.

Two other site link configuration options can be configured only in the Attribute Editor tab of a site link's Properties dialog box. By default, notification of changes doesn't occur between sites, and replication is based solely on the schedule. You can enable notifications by setting the options attribute to 1. In addition, data is compressed by default when it's replicated between sites. To turn compression off, set the options attribute to 4. To combine multiple options, simply add the values together. Therefore, to enable notification and disable compression, you set the options attribute to 5.

SRV Record Registration

Domain controllers advertise themselves by registering service (SRV) records with DNS servers so that clients can find DCs that offer services related to Active Directory. When a client needs the services of a DC (for example, to authenticate to the domain or join a domain), it queries a DNS server for SRV records for all DCs. It also queries for SRV records for DCs in its own site and uses these records first, if they exist, so that authentication and other procedures don't travel across a WAN.

The Netlogon service on the DC handles registration of SRV records for the Lightweight Directory Access Protocol (LDAP) and Kerberos services. These records are stored on the DNS server in folders in a subdomain named _msdcs located in the zone for the DC's domain. A folder for each site is maintained so that determining which sites offer these services is easier. For example, a DC in Site12 for domain 412Dom1.local registers SRV records under Forward Lookup Zones in _msdcs.412Dom1.local\dc_sites\Site12_tcp and _msdcs.412Dom1.local\dc_tcp (see Figure 2-7).

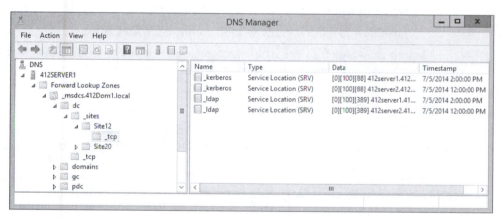

Figure 2-7   SRV records in DNS

If a DC fails to register its SRV records, you can force it to attempt to register the records by stopping and starting the Netlogon service in the Services MMC or with one of the following commands:

- At a command prompt: Type `net stop netlogon` and press Enter, and then type `net start netlogon` and press Enter.

- At a PowerShell prompt: Type `Restart-Service -Name netlogon` and press Enter.

Working with Automatic Site Coverage

Having a DC in each site is usually preferable so that authentication of clients occurs on the local LAN instead of having to traverse the WAN. However, having a DC at each site isn't always necessary or practical if you have a remote site with few users, an environment that isn't secure enough, or inadequate environmental controls for a DC.

When a site doesn't have a DC, other DCs in other sites in the domain can provide the services clients need. **Automatic site coverage** is a feature in which each DC advertises itself by registering SRV records in DNS in sites that don't have a DC if the advertising DC has the lowest cost connection to the site. When a client in the site attempts to contact a DC for authentication and other purposes, it performs a DNS lookup to request the closest DC. The SRV record for the advertising DC is returned. This process prevents clients from using DCs located across higher-cost links.

Generally, you want automatic site coverage enabled for efficient domain operation. However, if you have a Windows Server 2003 DC in your domain and RODCs in any sites, you might want to disable this feature on Windows Server 2003 servers. The reason is that a Windows Server 2003 DC doesn't recognize that an RODC is providing services for the site because Windows Server 2003 doesn't consider RODCs when evaluating site coverage. There are a few solutions to the problem:

- Install the RODC compatibility pack on Windows Server 2003 domain controllers. This solution is preferred.

- Make sure only Windows Server 2008 or later DCs are in the sites closest to any site with an RODC.

- Disable automatic site coverage on Windows Server 2003 DCs. To do so, you must edit the Registry by taking the following steps:

    1. Run `regedit` and navigate to the subkey HKEY_LOCAL_MACHINE\SYSTEM \CurrentControlSet\Services\Netlogon\Parameters.

    2. Create a new DWORD value with the name AutoSiteCoverage.

    3. Assign the value 0 to the new AutoSiteCoverage key to disable automatic site coverage. To reenable automatic site coverage, assign the value 1 to the key.

Moving DCs Between Sites

When a Windows server is first promoted to a DC, it's assigned to a site based on its IP address settings, or you can choose the site to install the DC during the promotion process. If there's only one site, the DC is placed in it. If you later change a DC's IP subnet address or change subnet assignments for sites, the affected DCs aren't moved to a different site automatically. You need to move DCs to new sites manually if changes in your site design or IP addressing warrant it. Here's the basic procedure for moving a DC to a new site:

1. Verify that the target site is created and has the right subnets assigned to it.

2. Change the DC's IP address, subnet mask, and default gateway as needed for the target site. If necessary, change the DC's DNS server addresses.

3. If the DC is used as a DNS forwarder, make the necessary changes in the forwarder configuration on other DNS servers.

4. If the DC hosts a delegated DNS zone, update the NS record in the parent domain's DNS zone to the new IP address of the DC.

5. If the DC being moved is a preferred bridgehead server, you must make the necessary adjustments in both the current site and the target site. In most cases, it's better to configure the DC so that it's not a preferred bridgehead server and ensure that no DCs in the current and target site are configured as bridgehead servers. By doing so, the ISTG assigns bridgehead servers automatically as needed when the DC is moved. After the move, you can then assign preferred bridgehead servers again, if necessary.

6. Move the server to the target site in Active Directory Sites and Services. To do so, right-click the server object in Active Directory Sites and Services and click Move, and then click the destination site name. If necessary, physically move the server to the new site location.

7. In DNS Manager, verify that SRV records are created for the DC in the target site folder. It could take up to an hour for these records to be created. The System event log contains any errors related to SRV record creation.

Active Directory Replication

Timely and reliable replication of data between domain controllers is paramount to a functioning Active Directory domain and forest. Active Directory replication includes the following types of information:

- Active Directory objects, such as OUs, user, group, and computer accounts
- Changes to data held in partitions maintained by FSMO role holders
- Trust relationships
- Global catalog data
- Group policy information
- Files located in SYSVOL, such as group policy templates and scripts

Most replication data is generated by changes to Active Directory objects and group policies. Active Directory replication occurs within sites (called **intrasite replication**) and between sites (called **intersite replication**). The following sections cover managing both types of replication along with RODC replication and SYSVOL replication as well as tools to help you monitor and troubleshoot replication.

Active Directory Intrasite Replication

Efficient and accurate replication of changes made to the Active Directory database is critical in a Windows domain. Intrasite and intersite replication use the same basic processes to replicate Active Directory data; the main goal is to balance replication timeliness and efficiency. To that end, the replication strategy between DCs within a site (intrasite) is optimized for high-speed, low-latency LAN links. Intersite replication involves two main components—the KCC and connection objects—and is optimized to take slower WAN links into account. It can be initiated in one of two ways:

- *Notification*—When a change is made to the Active Directory database, the DC on which the change was made notifies its replication partners. The partners then request replication from the notifying DC.

- *Periodic replication*—To account for missed updates, DCs request replication from their partners periodically. The interval can be configured in the connection object's Properties dialog box (explained later in "Connection Objects").

Knowledge Consistency Checker   For intrasite replication, the KCC builds a replication topology for DCs in a site and establishes replication partners. As shown in Figure 2-8, each DC in a site has one or more replication partners. For example, DC3 is partners with DC2, DC4, and DC5. The topology is designed to ensure that no more than two DCs lie in the replication path between two domain controllers. To put it another way, data in a replication transfer doesn't have to travel more than three hops to reach its destination DC. For example, if Active Directory data on DC1 changes, the changes have to hop through DC4 and DC6 to reach DC7. A domain controller waits 15 seconds after an Active Directory change before replicating with its partners, with a 3-second delay between partners. This arrangement guarantees that all DCs in a site receive changes in less than a minute.

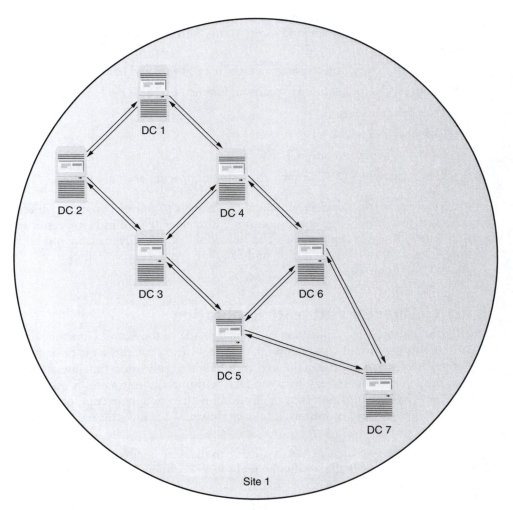

Figure 2-8   Intrasite replication partners
© Cengage Learning®

The KCC on each DC uses data stored in the forest-wide configuration directory partition to create the replication topology. The configuration directory partition is replicated to all DCs in the forest, so the KCCs don't need to communicate with one another. Because they all run the same algorithm on the same data, the KCCs on domain controllers create the same replication topology. The KCC recalculates the replication topology every 15 minutes by default to make sure the topology accurately reflects DCs that come online or go offline. If necessary, the replication topology can be recalculated manually in Active Directory Sites and Services. You might need to do this after you have added, changed, or removed connection objects, for example. To do so, right-click the NTDS Settings node under a domain controller, point to All Tasks, and click Check Replication Topology. The partnership between DCs is controlled by a connection object, which the KCC creates automatically for intrasite replication.

Connection Objects   A connection object defines the connection parameters between two replication partners. The KCC generates these parameters automatically between intrasite DCs. Generally, you don't need to make changes to intrasite connection objects, but if you do, you can change them in Active Directory Sites and Services. Figure 2-9 shows connection objects in Active Directory Sites and Services, and Figure 2-10 shows the Properties dialog box for one of the objects.

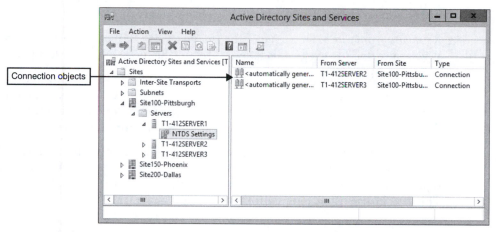

Figure 2-9   Connection objects in Active Directory Sites and Services

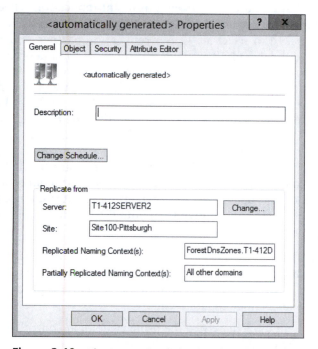

Figure 2-10   The Properties dialog box for a connection object

The General tab in the Properties dialog box is the only one of interest for connection objects; the other three tabs are the same for all Active Directory objects. The General tab contains the following options:

- *Change Schedule*—Click this button to view and change the KCC's default schedule (once per hour) for periodic replication. Periodic replication occurs in addition to triggered replication, which occurs after changes to Active Directory have been made. If you attempt to change the schedule on a KCC-generated connection object, Windows warns you that changes are overwritten by Active Directory, unless you mark the object as not automatically generated.

- *Replicate from Server*—Replication is a pull process, whereby a DC requests replication from its partners after being notified of changes and at the periodic replication interval. The name of the connection object's replication partner is specified in this field; to change it, click the Change button. For intrasite replication, in which the KCC creates the connection object, changing the server isn't recommended. As with the replication schedule, Windows warns you if you attempt to change the server name.

- *Replicate from Site*—The name of the site where the replication partner can be found. When only one site exists, this name is Default-First-Site-Name unless you rename it.

- *Replicated Naming Context(s)*—Specifies which partitions are replicated and from where. You might not see the full list because the text box isn't very wide. In Figure 2-10, several partitions are replicated, including the forest-wide and domain-wide DNS partitions, the domain partition, the schema partition, and the configuration partition.

- *Partially Replicated Naming Context(s)*—If the DC you're configuring is a global catalog server, you see a list of other domains from which partial Active Directory data is replicated, or you see "All other domains" if there are no additional domains in the forest. This text box is usually empty if the DC isn't a global catalog server.

Creating Connection Objects   You can create connection objects for intrasite replication if you want to alter the replication topology manually. You might want to alter the topology if a site includes WAN links that could benefit from a different replication schedule. To do so, right-click NTDS Settings under the applicable server and click New Active Directory Domain Services Connection. You're asked to select a DC as a replication partner, and the connection object is named after this server by default. By default, the schedule for a new connection object is set to every 15 minutes, but you can change this value.

Creating a connection object is usually unnecessary, but it can be useful for troubleshooting replication problems or for creating special replication schedules between DCs. The KCC uses a new connection object in its topology calculations and might alter the topology as a result. You must be sure of what you're doing before making manual changes to the intrasite replication topology, or you could break replication.

If you do make changes, right-click the NTDS Settings node, point to All Tasks, and click Check Replication Topology to run the KCC algorithm. If you created a connection manually to a server that already exists, the KCC deletes the automatically generated connection and leaves the manually created connection. If you remove the manually created connection, the KCC generally re-creates the original topology.

Special Replication Scenarios   Some changes to Active Directory objects require special handling, called **urgent replication**. This event triggers immediate notification that a change has occurred instead of waiting for the normal 15-second interval before replication partners are notified. Urgent replication events include the following:

- Account lockout changes sent immediately to the primary domain controller (PDC) emulator, which then replicates the event to other DCs

- Changes to the account lockout policy

- Changes to the password policy

- Changes to a local security authority secret, such as a trust relationship password

- Password changes to DC computer accounts

- Changes to the relative identifier (RID) master role holder

Password changes are handled slightly differently than other urgent replication events. When a password change occurs, the DC handling the change immediately transmits the new password to the PDC emulator, and the PDC emulator uses normal intrasite replication procedures. If a user attempts to log on to a DC with an incorrect password, the DC contacts the PDC emulator to see whether a password change has occurred before denying the authentication attempt. This process allows users to log on immediately after a password change, even if not all DCs have been updated with the change.

Checking Replication Status   You can use Active Directory Sites and Services to force the KCC to check the replication topology, but if you want to view detailed information about connections and replication status, use the command-line program `repadmin.exe`. Many arguments can be used with this command, but to view replication status, use `repadmin /showrepl`. Figure 2-11 shows the output of this command in a domain with three DCs. Each replication partner is listed.

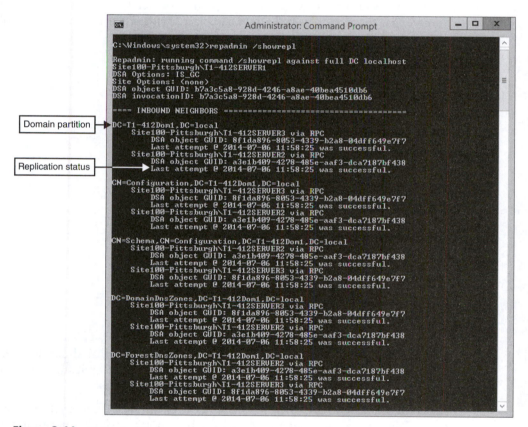

Figure 2-11   Output of the `repadmin /showrepl` command

Each section of the output lists a directory partition followed by the DCs from which the partition is replicated. For example, the first line under INBOUND NEIGHBORS specifies the domain partition, and the second line shows that the T1-412Server3 domain controller in Site100-Pittsburgh is a replication partner for this partition. The next two lines show the connection object's GUID and the status of the last replication attempt. Each replication partner is listed, along with the status of the last replication attempt. Other partitions are represented in the subsequent lines of output. You can also use `repadmin` to show the partitions being replicated by each connection object, force replication to occur, force the KCC to recalculate the topology, and other actions.

Entering `repadmin /?` doesn't show all the available parameters. To learn more about this command and see the full list of parameters, visit *http://technet.microsoft.com/en-us/library/cc736571.aspx.*

Activity 2-4: Working with Connection Objects

Time Required: 15 minutes
Objective: View and change properties of connection objects.

Required Tools and Equipment: 412Server1 and 412Server2
Description: You're trying to familiarize yourself with sites and site objects, so you explore the properties of NTDS Site Settings, server NTDS Settings, and connection objects.

1. Log on to 412Server1 as **Administrator**, if necessary, and open Active Directory Sites and Services.

2. Click to expand **Sites**, if necessary, and then click **Site12**. Two objects are displayed in the right pane: the Servers folder, which lists the DCs in the site, and NTDS Site Settings.

3. In the right pane, double-click to expand the **Servers** folder and then double-click **412Server1**. Right-click **NTDS Settings** and click **Properties** to open the dialog box shown in Figure 2-12. (Notice that there are NTDS Settings associated with server objects and site objects.)

Figure 2-12   The NTDS Settings Properties dialog box

4. In the General tab, you can configure the server as a global catalog server. Click the **Connections** tab. You should see 412Server2 in both the Replicate From and Replicate To text boxes. Click **Cancel**.

5. In the right pane, double-click to expand **NTDS Settings**. Right-click the connection object for 412Server2. Notice that Replicate Now is an option, which you can use to force replication to occur immediately. Click **Properties**.

6. Click the **Change Schedule** button. The regular schedule for intrasite replication is once per hour. Click **Cancel**, and then click **Cancel** again.

7. In the left pane, click **Site12**. Right-click **NTDS Site Settings** and click **Properties**.

8. In the Site Settings tab, click **Change Schedule**. In the Schedule for NTDS Site Settings dialog box, click **All**, and then click the **Four Times per Hour** option button. Changing the replication schedule here changes it for all automatically generated connections in the site. Click **OK** twice.

9. To verify that the schedule has changed, click **NTDS Settings** under 412Server1 again. Double-click the connection object to open its Properties dialog box, and click the **Change Schedule** button. (The schedule change might take a while to occur under each server.

Eventually, the change at the site level overwrites the server settings.) Click the **All** button at the upper left of the day/time table, click the **Once per Hour** option button, and then click **OK**.

10. Click **Apply**. You see a message indicating that changes to the connection will be overwritten because the connection object is generated automatically. When prompted to mark the connection as not automatically generated, click **Yes**, which changes the replication schedule for this connection only. Any other connections have their schedules set in NTDS Site Settings. Click **OK**. Notice that the connection object's name changes to a numeric GUID instead of "<automatically generated>."

11. Stay logged on and keep Active Directory Sites and Services open if you're continuing to the next activity.

Active Directory Intersite Replication

You've learned that intrasite replication occurs among several domain controllers after the KCC creates the topology. Intersite replication, however, occurs between bridgehead servers. When the KCC detects that replication must occur between sites, one DC in each site is designated as the ISTG, which assigns a bridgehead server to handle replication for each directory partition. Because bridgehead servers perform such a vital function in multisite networks, and this function can consume considerable server resources, the administrator can override automatic assignment of a bridgehead server and assign the role to a specific DC.

You might need to designate bridgehead servers manually. Perhaps you've identified a DC in a site that's less burdened by other server tasks and is better able to handle the task than the server the ISTG identified. You can use the `repadmin /bridgeheads` command to list which DCs in a site are acting as bridgehead servers to other sites.

After determining which DCs are currently acting as bridgehead servers, you can designate preferred bridgehead servers in Active Directory Sites and Services. Find the server in the Servers folder under the site, right-click the server object, and click Properties. Select the intersite transport protocol on the left (see Figure 2-13), and add it to the "This server is a preferred bridgehead

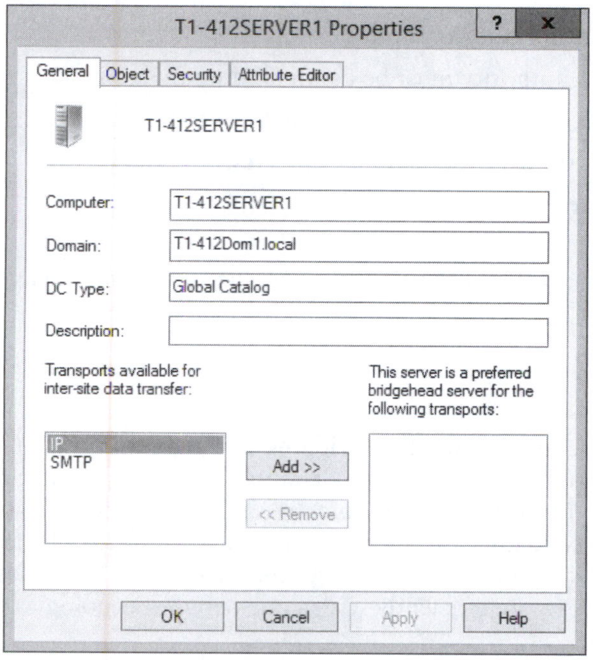

Figure 2-13 Configuring a bridgehead server

server for the following transports" list box. You need to make sure all directory partitions in the site are contained on the bridgehead servers you configure. If you don't, Windows warns you about which partitions the configured bridgehead servers won't replicate. Replication still takes place for these partitions because Windows configures the necessary bridgehead servers automatically, but relying on this automatic configuration defeats the purpose of assigning bridgehead servers manually.

If a manually configured bridgehead server fails, replication for the partitions it contains stops. The ISTG doesn't configure a new bridgehead server automatically for a failed manually configured one. However, if the ISTG assigns a bridgehead server and it fails, the ISTG attempts to assign a new one automatically.

Intersite Transport Protocols   Two protocols can be used to replicate between sites: IP and Simple Mail Transport Protocol (SMTP). By default, IP is used in the DEFAULTIPSITELINK site link and is recommended in most cases. To be precise, when you choose IP as the intersite transport protocol, you're choosing Remote Procedure Call (RPC) over IP. RPC over IP uses synchronous communication, which requires a reliable network connection with low latency. With synchronous communication, when a request is made, a reply is expected immediately, and the entire process of replication with one DC finishes before the process can begin with another DC.

If your network connections don't lend themselves to RPC over IP, you can use SMTP, which is used primarily for e-mail. It's an asynchronous protocol that works well for slower, less reliable, or intermittent connections. The advantage of SMTP is that a DC can send multiple replication requests simultaneously without waiting for a reply; the reply can occur sometime later. So if you think of SMTP as an e-mail conversation, you can liken RPC over IP to a chat session.

SMTP requires fairly complex configuration, and the administrative effort is rarely worth it, particularly with today's fast and reliable WAN connections. In addition, SMTP can't be used to replicate domain directory partitions, so it can't be used in domains spanning multiple sites. It can be used only to replicate the schema, global catalog, and configuration partitions. In a nutshell, here are the requirements for the bridgehead servers on both ends of an SMTP-configured site link:

- The SMTP feature must be installed on both servers.
- An enterprise certification authority must be configured on the network.
- The site link path must have a lower cost than an RPC over IP site link.
- You can't have DCs from the same domain in both sites.
- DCs must be configured to receive e-mail.

Remote Procedure Call over IP is the only replication protocol used in intrasite replication.

Site Link Bridges   As mentioned, **site link bridging** is a property of a site link that makes the link transitive. Site link bridging is enabled by default; however, in some circumstances, you don't want all site links to be transitive, as when some WAN links are slow or available only sporadically (with a dial-up connection, for example). To change the transitive behavior of site links, turn off site link bridging and create site link bridges manually, which enables you to manage replication traffic between sites more efficiently with some network topologies.

Figure 2-14 shows a network with a hub-and-spoke WAN topology. Because of the transitive nature of site links, Site1 replicates with bridgehead servers in Site2 and can also replicate with bridgehead servers in Site2A, Site2B, and Site2C. If WAN connections between all sites are fast and reliable, with plenty of bandwidth for replication traffic, this default behavior works well.

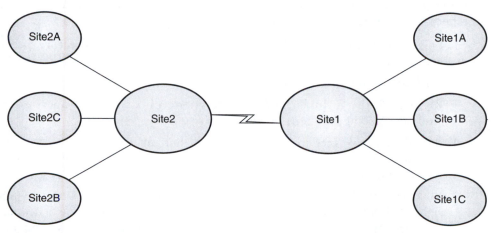

Figure 2-14   A hub-and-spoke topology

© Cengage Learning®

Keep in mind, however, that the same replication traffic is crossing WAN links four times, one for each site. On slower or heavily used WAN links between Site1 and Site2, this extra traffic could be excessive. To control the flow of replication traffic better, disable automatic site link bridging and create site link bridges between Site1 and Site2 and between Site2 and its satellites. Replication traffic still flows between Site1 and Site2, but Site2 distributes the traffic to satellite sites, so replication traffic crosses the Site1–Site2 WAN link only one time. You would probably want to create site link bridges in the opposite direction, too.

Other reasons to create site link bridges manually include the following:

- *Control traffic through firewalls*—You might want to limit which DCs can communicate with one another directly through firewalls. You can configure firewalls to allow traffic between DCs at specific sites and create site link bridges as needed.

- *Accommodate partially routed networks*—Normally, the KCC considers all possible connections when determining the replication topology. If sites are connected only intermittently, you can configure site link bridges between only the sites that map to full-time network connections, which bypasses intermittent links.

- *Reduce confusion of the KCC*—A complex network involving many alternative paths between sites can cause confusion when the KCC and ISTG create the replication topology. You can force what kind of topology is created by using custom site link bridges and disabling transitivity.

To disable transitivity of site links, right-click the IP or SMTP folder under Inter-Site Transports and click Properties, and then click to clear the "Bridge all site links" check box. To create a site link bridge, right-click the IP or SMTP folder and click New Site Link Bridge. Give a descriptive name to the site link bridge, and then add at least two site links to it.

Activity 2-5: Creating a Site Link

Time Required: 10 minutes
Objective: Create a site link.

Required Tools and Equipment: 412Server1
Description: You have created a site with a DC in it. Next, you create a site link to configure replication between Site12 and Site20.

1. Log on to 412Server1 as **Administrator**, and open Active Directory Sites and Services, if necessary.

2. Click to expand **Sites** and **Inter-Site Transports**, if necessary.

3. Right-click the **IP** folder and click **New Site Link**. In the Properties dialog box, type **SiteLink12-20** in the Name text box.

4. Because only two sites are defined, and a site link must contain at least two sites, both Site12 and Site20 are added to the "Sites in this site link" list box. If there were more than two sites, you would choose two or more sites to include in the site link. Click **OK**.

5. Make sure the **IP** folder is selected. In the right pane of Active Directory Sites and Services, right-click **SiteLink12-20** and click **Properties**. Click the **Change Schedule** button. Notice that replication takes place all day every day, which is the default setting for site links.

6. Drag to form a box around Monday through Friday from 8 a.m. to 3 p.m., and then click **Replication Not Available**. Now Site12 and Site20 won't attempt to replicate during these times. Click **OK**.

7. Click in the Cost text box and type **200**. Recall that the higher the cost of the link, the less attractive it is when the topology is generated. If there are multiple paths between destinations, the lower cost path is selected. In this case, DEFAULTIPSITELINK also contains Site12 and Site20 and has a cost of 100, so it's the preferred site link. Click **OK**.

8. Close Active Directory Sites and Services, and log off 412Server1.

Read Only Domain Controller Replication

There are special considerations for RODC replication, particularly when replicating credential information. Replication on an RODC is unidirectional, meaning the Active Directory database is replicated from a writeable DC to an RODC, but data is never replicated from an RODC to another DC. RODCs can replicate only with Windows Server 2008 and later writeable DCs. **Unidirectional replication** provides an extra level of security for networks with branch office locations. Even if a server is compromised and someone is able to make malicious changes to Active Directory on an RODC, the changes can't be propagated to DCs in the rest of the network.

One advantage of using RODCs is that you can limit which accounts' passwords are replicated to an RODC. To increase security of the Active Directory data stored on an RODC, administrators can configure a **filtered attribute set,** which specifies domain objects that aren't replicated to RODCs. The type of data to filter usually includes credential information that might be used by applications using Active Directory as a data store. Any data that might be considered security sensitive can be filtered, except objects required for system operation. Filtered attribute sets are configured on the schema master.

RODC placement in a site topology is important to ensure that replication occurs between an RODC and a writeable DC. A writeable DC is usually placed in the site nearest to the RODC's site. The nearest site is defined as the site with the lowest cost site link. If this placement isn't possible, you must create a site link bridge between the RODC site and a site with a writeable DC.

Password Replication Policy   By default, account passwords aren't stored on an RODC, which includes both user and computer account passwords. This arrangement makes the RODC more secure, in case an attacker tries to crack locally stored passwords. However, it also negates some advantages of having a DC on the local network. If the RODC stores no passwords, each user and computer authentication must be referred to a writeable DC, most likely located across a WAN link. To prevent this problem, you can specify accounts for which passwords are replicated. When an account password is replicated, its password is retrieved from a writeable DC the first time the account logs on, and thereafter, the password is retrieved from the RODC.

   Password replication is also known as "credential caching."

Password replication is controlled by the Password Replication Policy (PRP), accessed in the Properties dialog box of the RODC computer account (see Figure 2-15). A PRP lists users and groups along with a setting of Allow or Deny. Account Operators, Administrators, Backup Operators, and Server Operators are built-in domain local groups added to the PRP with the Deny setting by default. Passwords of these groups' members aren't stored on the RODC.

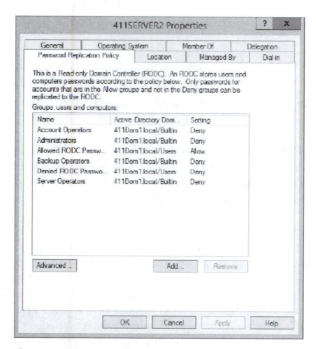

Figure 2-15   Viewing the Password Replication Policy

The PRP also contains the Allowed RODC Password Replication group and the Denied RODC Password Replication group. These two groups are added to the PRP of all RODCs. They have no members at first, but administrators can add users or groups to them to control password caching on all RODCs centrally. If a user is a member of a group with the Allow setting and a group with the Deny setting, the Deny setting takes precedence. Generally, groups or users with permission to sensitive information should be added to the Denied RODC Password Replication group. Users who often visit where RODCs are used might be candidates for membership in the Allowed RODC Password Replication group.

Besides the default groups added to the PRP for all RODCs, an administrator can customize each RODC's PRP. For example, a group can be created for all users at a branch office, and this group can be added to the PRP of the RODC at the branch office with an Allow setting. In addition, you can create a group for computer accounts in the branch office and add it to the PRP. Adding computer accounts to the PRP speeds up computer boot times and other actions that require the computer account to authenticate to the domain.

SYSVOL Replication

Not all Active Directory–related data is stored on Active Directory partitions. Some crucial information for domain operation is stored as files in the SYSVOL share on domain controllers, including group policy template files, the ADMX central store, and logon scripts. SYSVOL replication uses the same replication service as Distributed File System (DFS), called Distributed File System Replication (DFSR). Versions of Windows Server before Windows Server 2008 used File Replication Service (FRS).

Group Policy Replication   A Group Policy object (GPO) is composed of a group policy template (GPT) and a group policy container (GPC). A GPC is an Active Directory object stored in the Active Directory domain partition, and a GPT is a collection of files stored in the SYSVOL share. Because these two components are stored in different places on a DC, different methods are required to replicate GPOs to all domain controllers. GPCs are replicated during normal Active Directory replication, and GPTs are replicated with one of these methods:

- *File Replication Service*—FRS is used with DCs running Windows Server 2003 and Windows 2000 Server.
- *Distributed File System Replication*—DFSR is used when all DCs are running Windows Server 2008 and later.

Of these two methods, DFSR is more efficient and reliable. It's efficient because it uses the remote differential compression (RDC) algorithm, in which only data blocks that have changed are compressed and transferred across the network. It's reliable because of improvements in handling unexpected service shutdowns that could corrupt data and because it uses a multimaster replication scheme.

Because the GPC and GPT use different replication methods, they can become out of sync. As mentioned, GPCs are replicated when Active Directory replication occurs. Between DCs in the same site, this interval is about 15 seconds after a change occurs. Between DCs in different sites, the interval is usually much longer—minutes or even hours. Replication of the SYSVOL share (and, therefore, the GPT) occurs immediately after a change is made. Strange and unpredictable results could occur when a client computer attempts to apply a GPO when the GPC and GPT aren't synchronized. However, starting with Windows XP, the client computer checks the version number of both components before applying GPO settings.

As long as replication services are running correctly, the most likely problem with GPO replication is a delay in clients receiving changes in policy settings. This problem usually occurs when multiple sites are involved. Replication problems can be diagnosed with the Group Policy Management console (GPMC) by selecting the GPO in the left pane, clicking the Status tab in the right pane, and clicking the Detect Now button (see Figure 2-16).

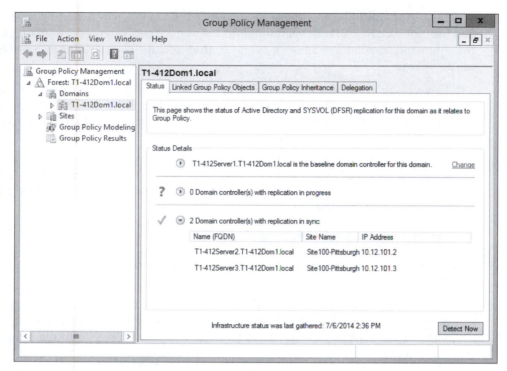

Figure 2-16   Checking the status of Group Policy replication

Upgrading to DFSR   If your domain includes Windows Server 2003 or older DCs, it's using FRS to replicate SYSVOL, and you should migrate to the more reliable DFSR as soon as possible. Even if you have upgraded all servers to Windows Server 2008 and later, FRS might still be running if your domain once contained older DCs and you haven't migrated to DFSR. Before migrating from FRS to DFSR, you need to understand the four phases of migration, referred to as "migration states":

- *State 0 - Start*—The C:\Windows\SYSVOL folder is present and mapped to the SYSVOL share and is being replicated with FRS.

- *State 1 - Prepared*—The SYSVOL share continues to be replicated with FRS. A new folder named SYSVOL_DFSR has been created; it contains a copy of the SYSVOL share and is being replicated with DFSR.

- *State 2 - Redirected*—The SYSVOL_DFSR folder is mapped to the SYSVOL share and is being replicated with DFSR. FRS continues to replicate the old C:\Windows\SYSVOL folder, which is no longer mapped to the SYSVOL share.

- *State 3 - Eliminated*—The SYSVOL_DFSR folder is mapped to the SYSVOL share and continues to be replicated with DFSR. The original C:\Windows\SYSVOL folder is deleted, and FRS replication no longer occurs.

You can use `dfsrmig /getmigrationstate` to see whether you need to perform DFSR migration. If you don't, you see the message "All domain controllers have migrated successfully to the Global state ('Eliminated'). Migration has reached a consistent state on all domain controllers."

Migrating from FRS to DFSR is done with the `dfsrmig` command-line tool on a writeable DC (not an RODC). Before beginning, do a system state backup on domain controllers with the command `wbadmin start systemstatebackup`. The steps for FRS-to-DFSR migration are as follows:

1. To verify that all DCs are operating in at least the Windows Server 2008 functional level, open Active Directory Domains and Trusts, and then right-click the domain and then click Raise Domain Functional Level. The current domain functional level is shown. Raise it to at least Windows Server 2008, if necessary.

2. To migrate the domain to the Prepared state, open a command prompt window, type `dfsrmig /setglobalstate 1`, and press Enter. To verify that all DCs have migrated to the Prepared state, type `dfsrmig /getmigrationstate` and press Enter. You see output similar to the following:

```
All domain controllers have migrated successfully to Global state
   ('Prepared').
Migration has reached a consistent state on all domain controllers.
Succeeded.
```

3. To migrate the domain to the Redirected state, type `dfsrmig /setglobalstate 2` and press Enter. To verify that all DCs have migrated to the Redirected state, type `dfsrmig /getmigrationstate` and press Enter. You see output similar to the following:

```
All domain controllers have migrated successfully to Global state
   ('Redirected').
Migration has reached a consistent state on all domain controllers.
Succeeded.
```

4. Before migrating the domain to the Eliminated state, verify that replication is working correctly by typing `repadmin /replsum` and pressing Enter. There should be no errors reported. After this final step, you can't revert to FRS replication. Type `dfsrmig /setglobalstate 3` and press Enter. To verify that all DCs have migrated to the Eliminated state, type `dfsrmig /getmigrationstate` and press Enter. You see output similar to the following:

```
All domain controllers have migrated successfully to Global state
   ('Eliminated').
Migration has reached a consistent state on all domain controllers.
Succeeded.
```

5. To verify the migration, type `net share` and press Enter on all DCs. The NETLOGON share should be mapped to the C:\Windows\SYSVOL_DFSR\sysvol*DomainName*\SCRIPTS folder, and the SYSVOL share should be mapped to the C:\Windows\SYSVOL_DFSR\sysvol folder.

6. Unless you're using FRS for some other purpose, stop and disable the service by typing `sc stop ntfrs` and pressing Enter on each DC, and then typing `sc config ntfrs start=disabled` and pressing Enter on each DC.

Managing Replication

Active Directory and SYSVOL replication usually work fine with the built-in scheduling and processes. However, you might want to force replication to occur for troubleshooting or testing purposes or just so that you don't have to wait for the normal replication schedule between sites. The main tool for controlling Active Directory replication is the `repadmin` command-line program. Some commonly used variations of the `repadmin` command are shown in the following list:

- `repadmin /replicate`—This command causes replication of a specified partition from one DC to another. For example, to replicate the domain directory partition from 412Server1 to 412Server2, use the following command. Note that the destination DC (the DC you're replicating to) is listed first followed by the source DC (the DC you're replicating from).

```
repadmin /replicate 412Server2 412Server1 dc=412Dom1,dc=local
```

If one of the servers is an RODC, add the `/readonly` switch to the end of the command.

- `repadmin /syncall`—This command forces replication to occur between the specified DC and all its replication partners. All partitions are synchronized unless you specify a partition. For example, the following command synchronizes all partitions on 412Server1 with all its replication partners:

```
repadmin /syncall 412Server1
```

You can include a number of options, called "flags," in this command. For more information on this command and other `repadmin` options, see *http://technet.microsoft.com/en-us/library/cc811569(v=ws.10).aspx*.

- `repadmin /kcc`—This command causes the KCC to check the replication topology and update it, if necessary. You should use it if you have recently made changes to the domain or forest, such as adding or removing domains or domain controllers, or if you have recently upgraded older DCs to Windows Server 2012/R2.

Managing Replication with Active Directory Sites and Services   With Active Directory Sites and Services, you can force replication to occur and force the KCC to check the replication topology. To cause replication to occur, expand the site node where the server on which you want to force replication is located. Expand the Servers node and click the target DC, and then click the NTDS Settings object. Right-click the connection object connecting the server on which you want to force replication and click Replicate Now (see Figure 2-17). In the figure, T1-412Server1 replicates immediately with T1-412Server2.

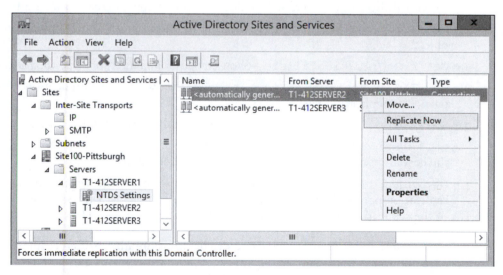

Figure 2-17   Forcing replication in Active Directory Sites and Services

To force the KCC to check the replication topology, right-click the NTDS Settings object under a DC, point to All Tasks, and click Check Replication Topology.

Surprisingly, there's only one PowerShell cmdlet to force replication. The `Sync-ADObject` cmdlet forces replication of a single specified Active Directory object between two specified DCs.

Monitoring Replication

There are several tools for monitoring Active Directory replication. You can use Performance Monitor to collect Active Directory replication statistics, using the predefined Active Directory Diagnostics data collector set, and you can monitor DFSR counters. In addition, you can use these command-line tools to get detailed replication status information:

- `repadmin`—Reports the replication status on each DC, allowing you to spot potential problems before they affect operations adversely. You can display replication partners for a DC with the `repadmin /showrepl` command, which informs you if a partner isn't available or communication problems are occurring. You can also display detailed information about connection objects with the `repadmin /showconn` command and view object replication information with the `repadmin /showobjmeta` command. For a less detailed summary of replication status, use the `repadmin /replsum` command. `Repadmin` can also be used to manage certain aspects of replication, as described earlier in "Managing Replication." For syntax help, type `repadmin /?`.

- `dcdiag`—Analyzes the status and overall health of Active Directory, performs replication security checks, and checks for correct DNS configuration and operation. Examples of some tests you can run include the following:

  - `dcdiag /test:Advertising`—Ensures that all DC roles are advertised so that client computers are aware of available services.

  - `dcdiag /test:Intersite`—Tests for failures in intersite replication.

  - `dcdiag /test:Replications`—Tests for timely and error-free replication.

  - `dcdiag /test:CheckSecurityError`—Verifies replication health, specifically its security.

There are also a few PowerShell cmdlets for monitoring and diagnosing replication problems:

- `Get-ADReplicationConnection`—Shows information about replication connection objects.

- `Get-ADReplicationFailure`—Shows replication failures for a specified DC, site, or domain.

- `Get-ADReplicationPartnerMetadata`—Shows detailed replication information for a particular replication partner.

- `Get-ADReplicationSite`—Shows replication information for a site.

- `Get-ADReplicationSiteLink`—Shows replication information for a site link, including the cost and replication frequency for the specified link.

- `Get-ADReplicationUpToDateNessVectorTable`—Shows how up to date a replication partner is. Displays the date and time of the last successful replication, the name of the replication partner, and the Update Sequence Number (USN).

Replication and general Active Directory health should be verified regularly when no problems are apparent. With a proactive approach, minor problems can be fixed before they turn into larger issues that affect domain functionality.

Activity 2-6: Managing Replication with Active Directory Sites and Services

Time Required: 10 minutes
Objective: Manage replication with Active Directory Sites and Services.

Required Tools and Equipment: 412Server1 and 412Server2
Description: You have two DCs and want to see how to force replication to occur and how to check the replication topology by using Active Directory Sites and Services.

1. Log on to 412Server1 as **Administrator**, and open Active Directory Sites and Services, if necessary. Make sure 412Server2 is running.

2. In Active Directory Sites and Services, navigate to 412Server1 under Site12. Click to expand **412Server1**, and click **NTDS Settings** in the left pane.

3. In the right pane, right-click the connection object connecting 412Server1 to 412Server2 and click **Replicate Now**. Click **OK** in the message box.

4. Open a command prompt window, and type **repadmin /showrepl** and press **Enter**. You see detailed information about partitions that were replicated and the date and time of the last attempt and whether it was successful. You should see that the last attempt just occurred and was successful.

5. Type **repadmin /replsum** and press **Enter**. You see a less detailed summary of the most recent replication (see Figure 2-18). There are two parts to the display: Source DSA and Destination DSA. The Source DSA indicates the server that data is being transferred from, and the Destination DSA indicates the server that data is being transferred to. The "largest delta" column shows the last time replication occurred. Notice that for 412Server2, under Source DSA, the time shows just a few seconds or minutes, and under Destination DSA, the times are reversed.

```
C:\Users\Administrator>repadmin /replsum
Replication Summary Start Time: 2014-07-08 17:40:36

Beginning data collection for replication summary, this may take awhile:
  .....


Source DSA          largest delta    fails/total %%   error
  412SERVER1              08m:04s       0 /   5     0
  412SERVER2                 :08s       0 /   5     0


Destination DSA     largest delta    fails/total %%   error
  412SERVER1                 :08s       0 /   5     0
  412SERVER2              08m:04s       0 /   5     0


C:\Users\Administrator>
```

Figure 2-18 Output of `repadmin /replsum`

6. In Active Directory Sites and Services, right-click the **NTDS Settings** object under 412Server1, point to **All Tasks,** and click **Check Replication Topology**. Click **OK** in the message box. Because no changes have been made to the domain, the topology won't change.

7. Stay logged on to 412Server1 if you're continuing to the next activity.

Activity 2-7: Managing Replication at the Command Line

Time Required: 10 minutes

Objective: Manage replication with the command-line programs `repadmin` and `dcdiag`.

Required Tools and Equipment: 412Server1 and 412Server2

Description: In this activity, you monitor replication and force replication to occur at the command line.

1. Log on to 412Server1 as **Administrator**, and open a command prompt window, if necessary. Make sure 412Server2 is running.

2. On 412Server1, type **`repadmin /replicate 412server1 412server2 dc=412dom1,dc=local`** and press **Enter**. You see a message stating that the sync was completed successfully. In this command, the source DC is 412Server2, and the destination DC is 412Server1. Recall that this command replicates only the domain partition unless additional partitions are specified.

3. Type **`repadmin /replsum`** and press **Enter**. You'll probably see that the replication doesn't seem to have happened because the timers weren't reset. However, `repadmin /replicate` replicates only changes; if no changes occurred since the last replication, no replication takes place.

4. Type **`repadmin /syncall`** and press **Enter**. This command replicates all partitions as needed.

5. Type **`repadmin /showrepl`** and press **Enter**. The most likely partition to have changed that requires replication is the Configuration partition.

6. Type **`dcdiag /test:replications`** and press **Enter**. The output indicates whether a connection can be made and the results of tests run on each Active Directory partition. Any replication errors are shown in the output.

7. Shut down 412Server2. On 412Server1, type **`dcdiag /test:replications`** and press **Enter**. The output indicates that replication failed.

8. Type **`repadmin /replicate 412server1 412server2 dc=412dom1,dc=local`** and press **Enter**. Because 412Server2 was shut down, the command takes a while to time out. After it does, type **`repadmin /showrepl`** and press **Enter**. You should see that there was an error replicating the domain partition because it's the partition you attempted to replicate.

9. Type **`repadmin /replsum`** and press **Enter**. The output indicates that errors occurred in replication. You see the message "The RPC server is unavailable."

10. Log off or shut down 412Server1.

Chapter Summary

- Active Directory's physical components are sites and domain controllers. An Active Directory site represents a physical location where domain controllers are placed and group policies can be applied.

- When the first domain controller of a forest is installed, a site named Default-First-Site-Name is created. Any additional domain controllers installed in the forest are assigned to this site until other sites are created.

- There are three main reasons for establishing multiple sites: authentication efficiency, replication efficiency, and application efficiency.

- Sites and connections between sites are defined by connection objects, subnets, site links, site link bridges, and bridgehead servers.

- Sites are usually geographically dispersed and connected by WAN links, but they can also be different buildings on a campus or different floors of a building, for example. When you create a site in Active Directory Sites and Services, you're asked to select a site link. DEFAULTIPSITELINK is the only choice unless you've created other site links.

- Site links have three configuration options: the cost field, the replication frequency, and the sites they connect. Any new sites you create use the default site link, DEFAULTIPSITELINK, for their connection with other sites.

- With automatic site coverage, each domain controller advertises itself by registering SRV records in DNS in sites that don't have a DC if the advertising DC has the lowest cost connection to the site.

- Timely and reliable replication of data between domain controllers is paramount to a functioning Active Directory domain and forest. Active Directory replication information includes Active Directory objects, such as OUs, user, group, and computer accounts; changes to data held in partitions maintained by FSMO role holders; trust relationships; global catalog data; group policy information; and files located in SYSVOL, such as group policy templates and scripts.

- The KCC is a process that runs on every DC and, for intrasite replication, builds a replication topology among DCs in a site and establishes replication partners.

- When the KCC detects that replication must occur between sites, one domain controller in each site is designated as the Inter-Site Topology Generator (ISTG). The ISTG then designates a bridgehead server to handle replication for each directory partition.

- Two protocols can be used to replicate between sites: IP and SMTP. By default, IP is used in the DEFAULTIPSITELINK site link and is recommended in most cases.

- There are special considerations for RODC replication. To increase security of the Active Directory data stored on an RODC, administrators can configure a filtered attribute set, which specifies domain objects that aren't replicated to RODCs.

- GPTs are replicated by using FRS or DFSR. Of these two methods, DFSR is the more efficient and reliable. If your domain includes Windows Server 2003 or older DCs, it uses the older FRS to replicate SYSVOL, and you should migrate to the more reliable DFSR as soon as possible.

- There are several tools for monitoring Active Directory replication. You can use Performance Monitor to collect Active Directory replication statistics, using the predefined Active Directory Diagnostics data collector set, and you can monitor DFSR counters. In addition, the command-line tools `repadmin` and `dcdiag` can give you detailed replication status information.

Key Terms

automatic site coverage   A feature in which each domain controller advertises itself by registering SRV records in DNS in sites that don't have a DC if the advertising DC has the lowest cost connection to the site.

bridgehead server   A domain controller in a site that has been assigned to handle replication of one or more directory partitions in that site.

connection object   An Active Directory object created in Active Directory Sites and Services that defines the connection parameters between two replication partners.

filtered attribute set   A feature of RODCs that specifies domain objects that aren't replicated to RODCs.

Inter-Site Topology Generator (ISTG)   A designated domain controller in each site that's responsible for assigning bridgehead servers to handle replication for each partition.

intersite replication   Active Directory replication that occurs between two or more sites.

intrasite replication   Active Directory replication between domain controllers in the same site.

Knowledge Consistency Checker (KCC) A process that runs on every domain controller to determine the replication topology.

site link An Active Directory object that represents the path between sites and determines the replication schedule and frequency between sites.

site link bridge An Active Directory object that represents site links using a common transport protocol.

site link bridging A default property of a site link that makes it transitive. To control the transitive nature of site links, you can create site link bridges manually.

unidirectional replication The type of replication used by RODCs, in which writeable DCs replicate to RODCs, but RODCs don't replicate to other DCs.

urgent replication An event triggering immediate notification that a change has occurred instead of waiting for the normal 15-second interval before replication partners are notified.

Review Questions

1. What term is used for transferring Active Directory information among domain controllers?

   a. Zone transfer

   b. Replication

   c. Site topology

   d. Redundancy

2. Which of the following is a component of Active Directory's physical structure?

   a. Organizational units

   b. Domains

   c. Sites

   d. Folders

3. You want to change the replication schedule between two domain controllers in the same site—and only these two domain controllers—to occur four times per hour. The KCC has generated all your intrasite connection objects. What's the best way to make this change?

   a. In the General tab of the connection object's Properties dialog box, click Change Schedule, and change the replication schedule to four times per hour. Make sure the object is marked as automatically generated.

   b. Create a new connection object for the two domain controllers, and set the schedule to four times per hour. Tell the KCC to check the replication topology.

   c. In the Site Settings tab of the NTDS Site Settings Properties dialog box, click Change Schedule, and set the schedule to four times per hour.

   d. In the Schedule tab of the server's Properties dialog box, click Change Schedule, and set the schedule to four times per hour.

4. A user calls the help desk to change her forgotten password. A minute later, she attempts to log on with the new password but gets a logon failed message. She verifies that she's entering the correct password. She tries logging on again about 30 minutes later and is successful. What's the most likely cause of the delay in her ability to log on?

   a. The domain controller where the password was changed was in a different site, and normal replication between sites caused the delay.

   b. The domain controller that authenticated the user must have gone down and didn't receive the password change until it was brought back online.

   c. The domain controller holding the PDC emulator role wasn't contacted by the domain controller that authenticated the user.

   d. The intrasite replication schedule is set for 30 minutes instead of 15 seconds.

2

5. Users of a new network subnet have been complaining that logons and other services are taking much longer than they did before being moved to the new subnet. You discover that many logon requests from workstations in the new subnet are being handled by domain controllers in a remote site instead of local domain controllers. What should you do to solve this problem?

    a.   Create a new subnet and add it to the site that maps to the physical location of workstations.

    b.   Enable automatic site coverage on the DCs in the site where users are having the problem.

    c.   Create a new connection object between the DCs in the site where users are having a problem and the main site.

    d.   Move the users' computer accounts to a new site and turn on automatic site coverage on the DCs in the old site.

6. You have three sites: Boston, Chicago, and LA. You have created site links between Boston and Chicago and between Chicago and LA with the default site link settings. What do you need to do to make sure replication occurs between Boston and LA?

    a.   Do nothing; replication will occur between Boston and LA with the current configuration.

    b.   Create a new connection object between Boston and LA.

    c.   Create a site link bridge between Boston and LA.

    d.   Configure a site link between Boston and LA with SMTP.

7. Which of the following is true about using SMTP in site links? (Choose all that apply.)

    a.   A certification authority must be configured.

    b.   Domains can span the sites included in the site link.

    c.   It's best used on slow or unreliable network links.

    d.   It's the preferred transport protocol for intersite links.

8. A partition stored on a domain controller in SiteA isn't being replicated to other sites, but all other partitions on domain controllers in SiteA are being replicated. The problem partition is stored on multiple domain controllers in SiteA. What should you investigate as the source of the problem?

    a.   An automatically configured bridgehead server

    b.   A manually configured bridgehead server

    c.   A failed site link bridge

    d.   A failed ISTG

9. Your network is configured in a hub-and-spoke topology. You want to control the flow of replication traffic between sites, specifically reducing the traffic across network links between hub sites to reach satellite sites. What should you configure?

    a.   Connection objects between domain controllers in each site

    b.   Intersite transports

    c.   Site link bridges

    d.   NTDS settings

10. Which is responsible for determining the replication topology?

    a.   GPO

    b.   PDC

    c.   RID

    d.   KCC

11. Which of the following is a reason for establishing multiple sites? (Choose all that apply.)

    a. Improving authentication efficiency

    b. Enabling more frequent replication

    c. Reducing traffic on the WAN

    d. Having only one IP subnet

12. Where is a GPT stored?

    a. In the SYSVOL share

    b. In Active Directory

    c. In GPMC

    d. In GPME

13. Several months ago, you installed a new forest with domain controllers running Windows Server 2012. You're noticing problems with GPT replication. What should you check?

    a. Verify that Active Directory replication is working correctly.

    b. Verify that FRS is operating correctly.

    c. Verify that DFSR is operating correctly.

    d. Check the GPOReplication flag for the GPT in the Attribute Editor.

14. Which of the following is created automatically by the KCC and is responsible for replication parameters between intrasite replication partners?

    a. Site link bridge

    b. Site link

    c. Bridgehead server

    d. Connection object

15. Which of the following is true about site links? (Choose all that apply.)

    a. Determine replication schedule between DCs

    b. Involved in intrasite replication

    c. Involved in intersite replication

    d. Can be configured with differing schedules

16. Which site-related object provides transitivity in the connection between sites?

    a. Site link bridge

    b. Bridgehead server

    c. Connection object

    d. Subnet

17. You have a network with three sites named Site1, Site2, and Site3 that are assigned the subnets 192.168.1.0/24, 192.168.2.0/24, and 192.168.3.0/24, respectively. You just changed the IP address of a DC in Site1 to 192.168.3.5/24. What should you do next?

    a. Move the computer object in Active Directory Users and Computers to a new OU.

    b. Nothing. Active Directory will make the necessary changes.

    c. Move the computer object in Active Directory Sites and Services to Site3.

    d. Right-click the computer object and click Check Replication Topology.

18. By default, how often does intersite replication occur?

    a. Every 180 seconds

    b. Every 15 seconds

    c. Every 15 minutes

    d. Every 180 minutes

19. What should you do if client computers can't find domain controller services?

    a. Manually add A records to the DNS server.

    b. Stop and start the Netlogon service.

    c. Configure entries in the hosts file.

    d. Restart the client computers.

20. When might you want to disable automatic site coverage?

    a. When you have Windows Server 2003 DCs and RODCs

    b. When your site has too many DCs

    c. When you don't have any DCs at a particular site

    d. When your DNS server has too many SRV records

21. How can intrasite replication be initiated? (Choose all that apply.)

    a. When the site link schedule timer expires

    b. Through partner notification

    c. Periodically, according to the connection object schedule

    d. Each time the KCC process runs

22. When does nonurgent intrasite replication occur?

    a. Immediately after any change occurs, with a 15-second delay between partners

    b. 15 seconds after any change occurs, with a 3-second delay between partners

    c. On a fixed schedule every 15 minutes, with a random delay between partners

    d. Only according to the schedule you set on each connection object

23. Which of the following requires urgent replication? (Choose all that apply.)

    a. Changes to the password policy

    b. User password changes

    c. Changes to the schema master role holder

    d. Changes to the account lockout policy

24. Which command shows you detailed information about replication status, including information on each partition?

    a. `Get-ADReplication /all`

    b. `dcdiag /replsum`

    c. `repadmin /showrepl`

    d. `showrepl /detailed`

25. When might you want to upgrade Active Directory replication from FRS to DFSR?

    a. You recently installed the DFS role service.

    b. You have at least one RODC in the site.

    c. You have one or more Linux computers running LDAP.

    d. You upgraded domain controllers from Windows Server 2003.

Case Projects

Case Project 2-1: Designing Sites

You're called in as a consultant to create a site design. The company has a network consisting of four hub sites and six satellite sites (see Figure 2-19). There are four domains, one for each city. Note the following facts about the company's site requirements:

- The satellite sites are in the same domain as the city to which they're connected.
- No sites contain domain controllers from outside their domain.
- Each hub site has 750 to 1000 users and 10 to 15 domain controllers.
- Each satellite site has 50 to 100 users and 2 to 4 domain controllers.

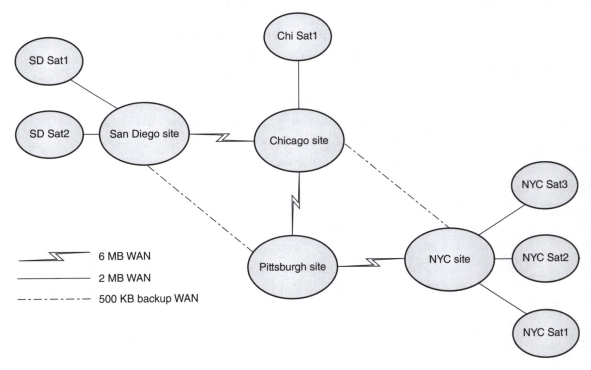

Figure 2-19   The site design for Case Project 2-1

© Cengage Learning®

Write a memo of one to two pages describing some factors to consider when designing this site, and take the following into account:

- Site links
- Intersite transport protocols
- Site link bridges
- Bridgehead servers
- FSMO role holders
- Global catalog servers

What additional information do you need to choose an efficient site design for this network?

chapter 3

Advanced DHCP and DNS Configuration

After reading this chapter and completing the exercises, you will be able to:

- Describe DHCP components and operation
- Configure superscopes and multicast scopes
- Use DHCPv6
- Configure DHCP for high availability
- Configure DHCP for DNS registration
- Describe the DNS structure and components
- Configure DNS security
- Configure advanced DNS options

All screenshots, unless otherwise noted, are used with permission from Microsoft Corporation.

Two of the most important network services are DHCP and DNS. You've learned about these network services in your earlier studies of Windows Server 2012/R2, and in this chapter you learn some of their advanced features. Starting with DHCP, you review its operation and components and then learn how to configure superscopes and multicast scopes. Next, you learn how to configure DHCPv6 for IPv6 environments and configure fault-tolerant and load-balancing DHCP solutions. To transition to DNS, you see how DHCP works with DNS for name registration.

DNS is a required service for Windows networks, and most networks would be almost unusable without it. The dependence on DNS makes it a ripe target for attackers trying to disrupt network operations or redirect users to fraudulent Web sites. Securing DNS is critical for a secure network, and you learn three techniques for securing DNS from attackers. Finally, you learn about advanced options to optimize DNS and simplify its management.

An Overview of DHCP

Table 3-1 lists what you need for the hands-on activities in this chapter.

Table 3-1   **Activity requirements**

Activity	Requirements	Notes
Activity 3-1: Installing and Authorizing a DHCP Server	412Server1	
Activity 3-2: Creating and Testing a DHCP Scope	412Server1, 412Win8	
Activity 3-3: Creating a Superscope	412Server1, 412Win8	
Activity 3-4: Creating a Multicast Scope	412Server1	
Activity 3-5: Creating and Testing a DHCPv6 Scope	412Server1, 412Win8	
Activity 3-6: Working with Split Scopes	412Server1, 412Server2, 412Win8	
Activity 3-7: Configuring DHCP Failover	412Server1, 412Server2, 412Win8	
Activity 3-8: Configuring DNSSEC	412Server1	
Activity 3-9: Configuring Netmask Ordering	412Server1, 412Win8	
Activity 3-10: Displaying DNS Zone Level Statistics	412Server1	

© 2016 Cengage Learning®

From your study of the 70-410 certification exam objectives, you should already be familiar with DHCP, so this first section of the chapter serves as a review. **Dynamic Host Configuration Protocol (DHCP)** is a component of the TCP/IP protocol suite, which is used to assign an IP address to a host automatically from a defined pool of addresses. The following sections cover these aspects of DHCP, and advanced DHCP configuration topics are covered next:

- DHCP operation
- DHCP server installation and authorization
- DHCP scopes
- Scope options
- DHCP relay agents

DHCP Operation

IP addresses assigned via DHCP are usually leased, not permanently assigned. When a client receives an IP address from a server, it can keep the address until the lease expires, at which point the client can request a new IP address. However, to prevent a disruption in communication, the client attempts to renew the lease when the lease interval is 50% expired, and then again when it's 87% expired if the first renewal attempt was unsuccessful. DHCP is based on broadcast packets, so there must be a DHCP server or DHCP relay agent (discussed later in "DHCP Relay Agents") in the same subnet as the client. Recall that broadcast packets are forwarded by switches but not by routers, so they're heard only by devices on the same LAN. DHCP is a fairly simple protocol, consisting of just eight message types. These message types and the DHCP address assignment and renewal processes are discussed in the following sections.

DHCP Address Assignment   Like most TCP/IP protocols, DHCP is a client/server protocol. A client makes a request for an IP address, and the server responds. The process of a DHCP client requesting an IP address and a DHCP server fulfilling the request is actually a four-packet sequence. All four packets are broadcast packets. DHCP was designed to use broadcast packets because a client that doesn't have an IP address can't be sent a unicast packet; it can, however, receive and respond to a broadcast packet. DHCP uses the UDP Transport-layer protocol on ports 67 and 68. Port 67 is for sending data from the client to the server, and port 68 is for sending data from the server to the client. The four-packet sequence is explained in the following list and illustrated in Figure 3-1:

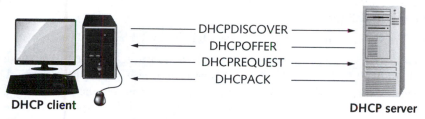

Figure 3-1   The packet sequence for DHCP address assignment
© 2016 Cengage Learning®

1. *DHCPDISCOVER*—The client transmits a broadcast packet via UDP source port 68 and UDP destination port 67 to the network, asking for an IP address from an available DHCP server. The client can request its last known IP address and other IP address parameters, such as the subnet mask, router (default gateway), domain name, and DNS server.

2. *DHCPOFFER*—A DHCP server receives the DHCPDISCOVER packet and responds with an offer of an IP address and subnet mask from the pool of addresses, along with the lease duration. The broadcast packet is transmitted via UDP source port 67 and UDP destination port 68.

3. *DHCPREQUEST*—The client responds by requesting the offered address. Because it's possible that multiple DHCP servers responded to the DHCPDISCOVER, the client might get multiple offers but accepts only one offer. The DHCPREQUEST packet includes a server identifier, which is the IP address of the server the offer is accepted from.

4. *DHCPACK*—The server the offer was accepted from acknowledges the transaction and sends any other requested IP parameters to the client. The client binds the IP address and other parameters to its network interface and is ready to communicate on the network by using TCP/IP.

DHCP Address Renewal   The DHCPDISCOVER broadcast packet is sent only when the client currently has no IP address configured on the interface the packet is transmitted from or after its current address has expired. As mentioned, a client attempts to renew the address lease when it's 50% expired. The lease renewal process is somewhat different, and because the client already has an IP address and the address of the DHCP server, the client uses unicast packets rather than broadcast packets. A successful renewal is a two-packet sequence:

1. *DHCPREQUEST*—When the lease is 50% expired, the client sends a unicast packet to the DHCP server, requesting a renewal lease for its current IP address. If the server doesn't respond, the client retries the renewal request up to three more times, occurring at 4, 8, and 16 seconds after the first renewal request.

2. *DHCPACK*—If the server responds and can honor the renewal request, the server sends a unicast packet to the client granting and acknowledging the renewal request.

The two-packet sequence for a lease renewal occurs when a server is available to service the request and the server can honor the renewal request. The renewal request might fail in these common situations:

- The server responds but can't honor the renewal. This situation can occur if the requested address has been deleted or deactivated from the scope or the address has been excluded from the scope since the time the client received it. The server sends a DHCPNAK to the client, and the client unbinds the address from its network interface and begins the process anew with a broadcast DHCPDISCOVER packet.

- The server doesn't respond. If the server has been taken offline, moved to another subnet, or can't communicate (perhaps because of a hardware failure), the DHCPREQUEST packet can't be serviced. In this case, the following steps occur:

1. The client keeps its current address until 87.5% of the lease interval has expired. At that time, the client sends a broadcast DHCPREQUEST requesting a lease renewal from any available DHCP server.

2. There are two possible results from the DHCPREQUEST broadcast:

   o A DHCP server responds to the request. If it can provide the requested address, it replies with a DHCPACK and the address is renewed; otherwise, it replies with a DHCPNAK (negative acknowledgement) indicating that it can't supply the requested address. In this case, the client immediately unbinds the address from the network interface and starts the DHCP sequence over, beginning with a DHCPDISCOVER broadcast packet.

   o No DHCP server responds. In this case, the client waits until the lease period is over, unbinds the IP address, and starts the sequence over with a DHCPDISCOVER broadcast packet. If no server responds, a Windows client (other client OSs might behave differently) binds an Automatic Private IP Addressing (APIPA) address to the network interface and sends a DHCPDISCOVER every 5 minutes in an attempt to get a DHCP-assigned address. If an alternate IP address configuration has been configured on the interface, it's used instead of an APIPA address, and no further attempts are made to get a DHCP-assigned address until the interface is reset or the computer restarts.

DHCP Messages   Table 3-2 describes all the message types exchanged between a DHCP server and client. The first column includes the message type number found in the DHCP packet. Message types that have been covered already are described briefly.

Table 3-2   DHCP message types

Message number	Message name	Description
1	DHCPDISCOVER	Sent by a client to discover an available DHCP server and request a new IP address.
2	DHCPOFFER	Sent by the server in response to a DHCPDISCOVER with an offer of an IP address.
3	DHCPREQUEST	Sent by a client to request a lease on an offered IP address in response to a DHCPOFFER or to renew an existing lease.
4	DHCPDECLINE	Sent by a client in response to a DHCPOFFER to decline an offered IP address. Usually occurs when the client has determined that the offered address is already in use on the network.
5	DHCPACK	Sent by the server to acknowledge a DHCPREQUEST or DHCPINFORM. This message also contains DHCP options requested by the client.
6	DHCPNAK	Sent by the server in response to a DHCPREQUEST. Indicates that the server can't fulfill the request. Usually occurs when a client is attempting a renewal, and the requested address is no longer available for lease.
7	DHCPRELEASE	Sent by a client to release a leased address. Usually occurs when a user issues the `ipconfig /release` command or a command of a similar function. However, it can also occur if a client is configured to release its address when the computer is shut down. (By default, Windows clients don't release an address when they are shut down.)
8	DHCPINFORM	Sent by a client to request additional configuration. The client must already have an IP address and a subnet mask. Can be used by a client that has a static IP address but has been configured to get a DNS address or router address via DHCP.

DHCP Installation and Authorization

The DHCP service is installed as a server role, aptly named DHCP Server. There are no role service components for this server role; the DHCP management tool is the only additional component installed. DHCP Server can be installed by using the Add Roles and Features Wizard via Server Manager or the following PowerShell cmdlet:

```
Install-WindowsFeature DHCP -IncludeManagementTools
```

After you install this role, the DHCP console is available on the Tools menu in Server Manager. You'll see a red down arrow on the IPv4 and IPv6 nodes indicating the server isn't currently providing services. In a Windows domain network, the DHCP server must be authorized, and a scope must be created before the server can begin providing DHCP services. In a workgroup network, authorization is automatic.

DHCP Server Authorization
A DHCP server must be authorized on a domain network before it can begin providing services. The reason is that DHCP clients have no way of determining whether a DHCP server is valid. When a client transmits a DHCPDISCOVER packet, any DHCP server receiving the broadcast can respond. The client accepts the first offer it gets that meets the requirements in the DHCPDISCOVER packet. If a rogue DHCP server is installed on a network, whether accidentally or on purpose, incorrect IP address settings could be configured on client computers. These settings likely include the DNS server and default gateway the client uses in addition to the IP address and subnet mask. At best, incorrect IP address settings cause the client to stop communicating correctly. At worst, servers set up by an attacker to masquerade as legitimate network resources can capture passwords and other sensitive information.

On a domain network, a DHCP server can be installed on a domain controller, a member server, or a stand-alone server. However, for authorization to work correctly, installing DHCP on a stand-alone server in a domain network isn't recommended. If you use this setup in a network that already has an authorized server, the stand-alone server can't lease addresses.

After a DHCP server is installed, you authorize it by right-clicking the server name in the DHCP console and clicking Authorize. DHCP server authorization requires Enterprise Administrator credentials, so if you aren't logged on as an Enterprise Administrator (the Administrator account in the forest root domain or a member of the Enterprise Administrators universal group), you're prompted for credentials. To authorize a DHCP server with PowerShell, use the `Add-DhcpServerInDC` cmdlet.

Activity 3-1: Installing and Authorizing a DHCP Server

Time Required: 10 minutes
Objective: Install and authorize a DHCP server.

Required Tools and Equipment: 412Server1
Description: You want to assign IP addresses dynamically to client computers, so you install the DHCP Server role on 412Server1 and authorize it.

1. Start 412Server1, and log on as **Administrator**, if necessary.

2. Open Server Manager, if necessary, and open a PowerShell prompt by clicking **Tools, Windows PowerShell** from the Server Manager menu. Type **Install-WindowsFeature DHCP -IncludeManagementTools** and press **Enter**.

3. When the DHCP Server installation finishes, close PowerShell and click **Tools, DHCP** from the Server Manager menu to open the DHCP console.

4. Click to expand the server node in the left pane. Notice that both the IPv4 and IPv6 nodes show red down arrows, indicating that the service is not currently operational. The server first needs to be authorized.

5. Right-click **412server1.412dom1.local** (the server node), and click **Authorize**. Nothing obvious occurs, but right-click **412server1.412dom1.local** again and you'll see the Unauthorize option, indicating that the server has been authorized. Because this server is on a DC in the root domain and you're already logged on as Administrator, you weren't asked to enter credentials.

6. Click the **IPv4** node. Read the information in the middle pane about adding a scope, which you do in the next activity. Notice that the red down arrow is replaced by a check mark in a green circle, indicating that IPv4 services are available. Click the **IPv6** node to see the same result. Close the DHCP console.

7. Stay logged on to 412Server1 if you're continuing to the next activity.

DHCP Scopes

A **scope** is a pool of IP addresses and other IP configuration parameters that a DHCP server uses to lease addresses to DHCP clients. A scope consists of the following required parameters:

- *Scope name*—A descriptive name for the scope.
- *Start and end IP addresses*—The start and end IP addresses define the address pool.
- *Prefix length or subnet mask*—Specify a prefix length or subnet mask that's assigned with each IP address. For example, you can specify 16 for the prefix length or 255.255.0.0 for the subnet mask.
- *Lease duration*—The lease duration specifies how long a DHCP client can keep an address. The lease duration is specified in days, hours, and minutes, with a minimum lease of 1 minute and a maximum lease of 999 days, 23 hours, and 59 minutes. The default lease duration is 8 days. The lease can also be set to unlimited, but this setting isn't recommended because if the client is removed from the network or its NIC is replaced, the address is never returned to the pool for lease to other clients. An unlimited duration can also cause DNS records to become stale when DHCP is configured to update DNS records on behalf of the client.

You can configure other options when you create a scope with the New Scope Wizard or PowerShell, or change the scope's properties after it's created. To create a scope for the 10.1.0.0 subnet with address range 10.1.0.100 through 10.1.0.255 and subnet mask 255.255.0.0 using PowerShell, use the following cmdlet from a PowerShell prompt:

```
Add-DhcpServerV4Scope -Name "NewScope" -StartRange 10.1.0.100
   -EndRange 10.1.0.255 SubnetMask 255.255.0.0
```

Exclusion Ranges   A DHCP scope contains a continuous range of IP addresses that are leased to DHCP clients. You might want to exclude certain addresses or a range of addresses from the scope for use in static address assignments. Static addresses are usually assigned to servers, routers, and other critical infrastructure devices to make sure they always have an address that never changes. So to avoid IP address conflicts, you need to exclude addresses that are assigned statically. Addresses can be excluded in two ways:

- *De facto exclusion*—You don't actually create an exclusion with this method; you simply set the start and end IP addresses in the scope so that several addresses in the subnet fall outside the scope's range. For example, if you set a scope's start address to 10.1.1.10 and end address to 10.1.1.240 with a 24-bit prefix, you have addresses 10.1.1.1 through 10.1.1.9 and addresses 10.1.1.241 through 10.1.1.254 to use for static address assignments. You might not need to create an exclusion range unless you use all these addresses.
- *Create an exclusion range*—Sometimes a scope is created after static address assignments have been made, and the static addresses occupy several ranges of addresses throughout the subnet (instead of at the beginning or end). For example, if your subnet is 10.1.1.0/24, and you have devices with static addresses in the range 10.1.1.100 through 10.1.1.110, you probably need to create one or more exclusion ranges because these addresses fall right in the middle of the subnet. An exclusion range consists of one or more addresses in the scope that the DHCP server doesn't lease to clients. They can be created when the scope is created with the New Scope Wizard or afterward by right-clicking the Address Pool node under the scope and clicking New Exclusion Range. In the Add Exclusion dialog box, type the start and end IP addresses. You can exclude a single IP address by specifying only the start address. You can create as many exclusion ranges as you need.

Reservations   A reservation is an IP address associated with the MAC address of a DHCP client to ensure that when the client requests an IP address, it always gets the same one, along with any configured options. The IP address in the reservation must fall within the same subnet as the scope and uses the same subnet mask that's configured for the scope. If options are configured for the reservation, they take precedence over options configured at the scope or server level (discussed later in "DHCP Options"). A reservation address can be any address in the subnet defined by the scope's address range and can even be within an exclusion range.

If the IP address you want to use in the reservation is already in use by another DHCP client, the client using the address continues to use it until it attempts to renew it. You can force the client to release the address and get a different address by entering `ipconfig /release` and `ipconfig /renew` at a command prompt. The client the reservation is made for can be forced to start using the reserved address by entering `ipconfig /renew` at the command prompt, or you can wait until it attempts to renew its current address.

DHCP Options

An IP address and subnet mask are the minimum settings needed for a computer to communicate on a network. However, almost every network requires a DNS server IP address for name resolution and a default gateway to communicate with other subnets and the Internet. The DHCP server can be configured to send both these addresses to DHCP clients along with the IP address and subnet mask. Many other options can be configured and might be necessary, depending on the network environment. DHCP options can be assigned at the following levels:

- *Server options*—Options configured at the server level affect all scopes but can be overridden by a scope, policy, or reservation option.

- *Scope options*—Scope options affect clients that get a lease from the scope in which the option is configured. Scope options can be overridden by reservation options or DHCP policies.

- *Policy options*—DHCP policies allow an administrator to assign IP address options to clients based on client properties, such as device type, MAC address, or OS. Options specified at the policy level can be overridden only by reservation options.

- *Reservation options*—Options set on a reservation take precedence over any conflicting options set at any other level.

Common DHCP Options   DHCP options are specified in the format *NNNOptionName*, with *NNN* representing a three-digit number that uniquely identifies the option in the DHCP packet, and *OptionName* being the option's user-friendly name. Some of the most common options include the following:

- *003 Router*—This option configures the client's default gateway setting. It's usually configured at the scope level because each scope has a different default gateway associated with it. If you have only one scope, you can configure it at the server level. If you use policies or reservations, you can configure the router option at these levels so that selected computers can use a different default gateway than the rest of the scope does, if needed.

- *006 DNS Servers*—The DNS Servers option consists of a list of IP addresses of DNS servers the client can use for name resolution. This option is often configured as a server option that applies to all scopes. However, if the option is configured on a scope, the scope option takes precedence.

- *015 DNS Domain Name*—This option provides a domain name, such as csmtech.local, to DHCP clients, which is needed when performing a DNS query with a single-label name. The client also uses the domain name when registering its computer name with the DNS server. Domain members configure their DNS domain names automatically with the name of the domain they're a member of, so this option is unnecessary if all computers receiving DHCP addresses are domain members.

Configuring Options   Server options are configured by clicking the IPv4 or IPv6 node in the DHCP console, right-clicking Server Options, and clicking Configure Options. The Server Options dialog box has two tabs. The General tab has a list of options in the upper pane. If you click the check box for an option, the lower pane is enabled so that you can enter information for the option. For example, in Figure 3-2, the 003 Router option is selected. For this option, you add one or more router addresses that clients use for their default gateway configuration.

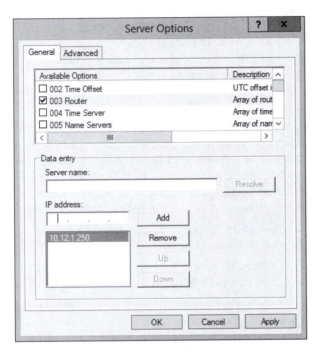

Figure 3-2   The Server Options dialog box

The Advanced tab of the Server Options dialog box has the same list of options as well as a list box to choose the Vendor class, a field in the DHCP packet that device manufacturers or OS vendors use to identify a device model or an OS version. You can use this field to set different DHCP options.

Scope and reservation options are set the same way as server options. To configure scope options, click the scope in the DHCP console, and then right-click Scope Options in the right pane and click Configure Options. To configure reservation options, right-click a reservation and click Configure Options. You can configure different options for each reservation.

Activity 3-2: Creating and Testing a DHCP Scope

Time Required: 15 minutes
Objective: Create a DHCP scope and test it.

Required Tools and Equipment: 412Server1 and 412Win8
Description: You have installed the DHCP Server service and authorized it. Before it can start leasing addresses, you need to define a scope and then test it by leasing an address with 412Win8.

1. Log on to 412Server1 as **Administrator**, and open the DHCP console, if necessary.

2. Click to expand the server node, if necessary, and then click to select **IPv4**. Right-click the **IPv4** node and click **New Scope** to start the New Scope Wizard. In the welcome window, click **Next**.

3. In the Scope Name window, type **10.12-Scope** in the Name text box, add a description, if you like, and then click **Next**.

4. In the IP Address Range window, type **10.12.1.100** in the Start IP address text box and **10.12.1.255** in the End IP address text box. In the Length text box, type **16** (see Figure 3-3), and then click **Next**.

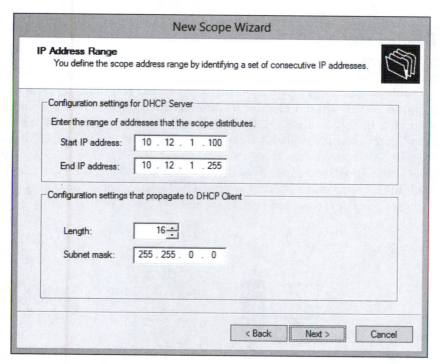

Figure 3-3   Specifying the IP address range

5. In the Add Exclusions and Delay window, click **Next**.

6. In the Lease Duration window, type **0** in the Days text box, **1** in the Hours text box, and **0** in the Minutes text box. One hour is a short lease time, but it's adequate for testing. Click **Next**.

7. In the Configure DHCP Options window, click **No, I will configure these options later**, and then click **Next**.

8. In the Completing the New Scope Wizard window, click **Finish**.

9. In the DHCP console, you see the new scope, but a red down arrow indicates it's not activated. Click the scope you just created. You see additional nodes under it, such as Address Pool, Address Leases, Reservations, and so forth. Right-click the scope and click **Activate**.

10. Start 412Win8 and log on as **Win8User** with the password **Password01**.

11. Open an elevated command prompt window on 412Win8 (right-click **Start**, click **Command Prompt (Admin)**, click **Yes** in the UAC message box, and then type **powershell** and press **Enter**). Type **Set-NetIPInterface -InterfaceAlias Ethernet -Dhcp Enabled** and press **Enter**. To set the DNS server address for DHCP, type **Set-DnsClientServerAddress -InterfaceAlias Ethernet -ResetServerAddresses** and press **Enter**.

12. Type **ipconfig /all** and press **Enter**. You see that the address 10.12.1.100 with subnet mask 255.255.0.0 was assigned. Look for the line starting with "DHCP Server"; the address is 10.12.1.1, the address of 412Server1. (You might have to enter **ipconfig /renew** for the new address to take effect). When you're finished, close the command prompt window.

13. On 412Server1, in the DHCP console, click **Address Leases**. You see the address leased to 412Win8.

14. Stay logged on to 412Server1 and 412Win8 if you're continuing to the next activity.

DHCP Relay Agents

A DHCP relay agent is a device that listens for broadcast DHCPDISCOVER and DHCPREQUEST messages and forwards them to a DHCP server on another subnet. You configure a DHCP relay agent on a subnet that doesn't have a DHCP server so that you can still manage DHCP addresses from a central server without having to configure the DHCP server with network interfaces in each subnet. In this setup, a DHCP server is configured on one subnet and has multiple scopes configured, one for each subnet in the internetwork that has DHCP clients, as shown in Figure 3-4. This figure shows three subnets. The DHCP server in the 10.1.1.0/24 subnet has three scopes configured, one for each of the three subnets. When a DHCP client in the 10.1.2.0 or 10.1.3.0 subnet requests an IP address, the DHCP relay agent in the same subnet forwards the request to the DHCP server on the 10.1.1.0 subnet.

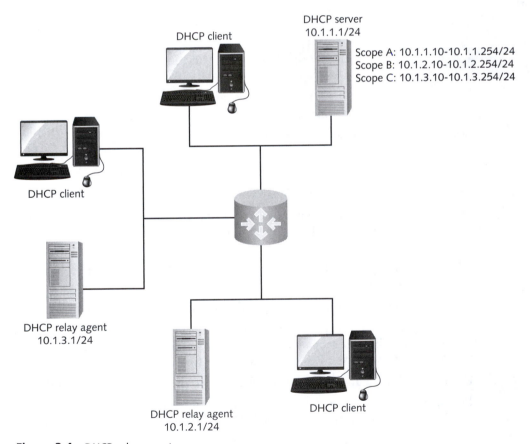

Figure 3-4   DHCP relay agents

© *Cengage Learning*®

Most commercial routers can be configured as DHCP relay agents, eliminating the need to configure a Windows server as a relay agent in each subnet.

3

The details of the DHCP relay process are as follows:

1. A client on the same subnet as the DHCP relay agent sends a DHCPDISCOVER broadcast requesting an IP address.

2. The relay agent forwards the message to the DHCP server's IP address as a unicast.

3. The DHCP server receives the unicast DHCPDISCOVER. The relay agent's address is contained in the message, so the DHCP server knows to draw an address from the scope matching the relay agent's IP address. For example, if the relay agent has the address 10.1.2.10, the DHCP server looks for a scope containing a range of addresses that includes 10.1.2.10.

4. The DHCP server sends a unicast DHCPOFFER message to the relay agent.

5. The relay agent forwards the DHCPOFFER as a broadcast to the subnet the DHCPDISCOVER was received from. Because the client doesn't yet have an IP address, the agent must forward the DHCPOFFER as a broadcast message.

6. The DHCP client broadcasts a DHCPREQUEST.

7. The relay agent receives the DHCPREQUEST and forwards it to the DHCP server.

8. The DHCP server replies with a DHCPACK to the relay agent.

9. The relay agent forwards the DHCPACK to the client, and the client binds the address to its interface.

10. Renewal requests are unicast packets, so the DHCP client can communicate directly with the DHCP server for renewals.

Configuring Superscopes and Multicast Scopes

A **superscope** is a special type of scope consisting of one or more member scopes that allows a DHCP server to service multiple IPv4 subnets on a single physical network. (Superscopes aren't supported in IPv6.) Although it isn't a common configuration for a network, it can and does occur. A superscope directs the DHCP server to draw addresses from both scopes, even though it has only a single interface configured for one of the IP subnets. This configuration can be useful if the number of computers on a physical network exceeds the original subnet's size or when a second subnet has been added to a physical network for testing purposes. To configure a superscope, first configure two or more scopes to include in the superscope; each scope that's part of a superscope is referred to as a "member scope." Then create the superscope and add the member scopes. Superscopes don't have any DHCP options of their own, and you can't create an IP address pool for a superscope. All IP address pools and options are configured in member scopes. However, you can deactivate a superscope, which deactivates all member scopes as well.

Figure 3-5 is an example of a network with a superscope. Two subnets are configured: 10.1.1.0/24 and 10.1.2.0/24. The router interface is configured with two IP addresses and can route between the two subnets. The DHCP server is configured with a superscope named Superscope1 that has two member scopes, one for each subnet.

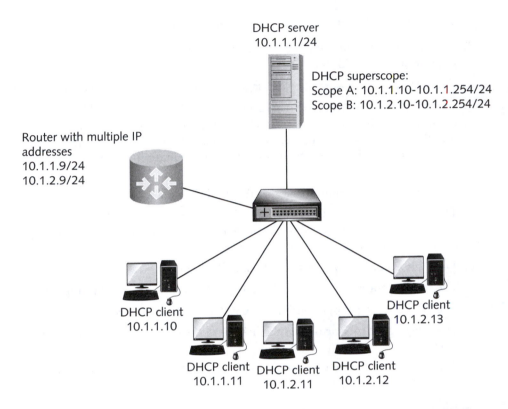

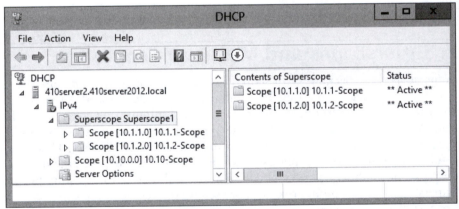

Figure 3-5   A network that uses a superscope

© Cengage Learning®

You create superscopes in the DHCP console by right-clicking the IPv4 node and clicking New Superscope, and then following the New Superscope Wizard. You can also create a superscope with PowerShell, as in the following example:

```
Add-DhcpServerv4SuperScope -SuperscopeName "NewSuperScope"
    -ScopeID 10.12.0.0,10.1.0.0
```

The IP addresses that follow the -ScopeID option are the subnet addresses of the two scopes you want to add to the superscope.

Activity 3-3: Creating a Superscope

Time Required: 15 minutes
Objective: Create a superscope and test it.

Required Tools and Equipment: 412Server1 and 412Win8

Description: You want to see how to use superscopes. You already have one scope, so you create a new scope, and then create a superscope and add both scopes to it.

1. Log on to 412Server1 as **Administrator**, and open a PowerShell window.

2. At the PowerShell prompt, type `Add-DhcpServerV4SuperScope -Name "10.1-Scope"` `-StartRange 10.1.0.100 -EndRange 10.1.0.255 -SubnetMask 255.255.0.0` and press **Enter**.

3. To create the new superscope, type `Add-DhcpServerv4Scope  -SuperscopeName` `"SuperScope-1" -ScopeID 10.12.0.0,10.1.0.0` and press **Enter**. Close the PowerShell prompt.

4. Open the DHCP console, if necessary. Click the **IPv4** node to see the new superscope. If you don't see it, click the **Refresh** icon on the DHCP console. Click **Superscope SuperScope-1** to see the two scopes that are members of the superscope.

5. Start 412Win8, and log on as **Win8User**, if necessary. Open a command prompt window. Type `ipconfig /release` and press **Enter**, and then type `ipconfig /renew` and press **Enter**. The 412Win8 computer will probably be assigned the same address it had before you created the superscope.

6. On 412Server1, click to expand **Scope [10.12.0.0] 10.12-Scope** and click **Address Leases**. You see the address leased by 412Win8.

7. Right-click **Scope [10.12.0.0] 10.12-Scope** and click **Deactivate**. Click **Yes** to confirm.

8. On 412Win8, at the command prompt, type `ipconfig /renew` and press **Enter**. You might see an error message, but an address from the 10.1.0.0 scope should be leased. Type `ipconfig` and press **Enter** to see the address the computer was leased, which should be 10.1.0.100.

9. On 412Server1, right-click **Scope [10.12.0.0] 10.12-Scope** and click **Activate**. You're finished with the 10.1.0.0 scope, so right-click **Scope [10.1.0.0] 10.1-Scope** and click **Delete**. Click **Yes** to confirm, and then click **Yes** again. Now right-click **Superscope SuperScope-1** and click **Delete**. Click **Yes** to confirm. Deleting the superscope doesn't delete the member scopes, so 10.12-Scope remains.

10. On 412Win8, type `ipconfig /release` and press **Enter**, and then type `ipconfig /renew` and press **Enter**. You might see an error message. Type `ipconfig` and press **Enter** to verify that you have an address from the 10.12.0.0 subnet again. Close the command prompt window.

11. Stay logged on to 412Server1 and 412Win8 if you're continuing to the next activity.

Configuring Multicast Scopes

Most network packets are addressed as unicast packets, meaning a single host is the intended recipient, or broadcast packets, meaning all hosts on the network should process them. An IPv4 multicast packet is a network packet addressed to a group of hosts listening on a particular multicast IP address. These hosts listening for multicast packets receive and process them while other hosts ignore them. A multicast address doesn't replace a host's regular IP address assignment. Recall that the first octet of IPv4 multicast addresses is in the range 224 to 239 and is classified as a class D IP address. Multicast addresses can't be assigned as a host's IP address; instead, a network service or application informs the IP protocol that it wants to "join" a multicast group. By doing so, the network software listens for the specified multicast address in the destination field of packets and processes them rather than ignore them.

Although IPv6 does support multicasting and uses it much more than IPv4 does, there's no support for IPv6 DHCP multicast scopes.

Most multicast applications use a reserved multicast address known by the server running the multicast service and by the clients that might join the multicast group, and there's no need for dynamic multicast address allocation. For example, several routing protocols use multicast addresses to exchange information. Routing Information Protocol version 2 (RIPv2) uses the reserved multicast address 224.0.0.9, and Open Shortest Path First (OSPF) uses addresses 224.0.0.5 and 224.0.0.6. All routers supporting these protocols have these addresses statically assigned, so there's no need to use DHCP for multicast address assignment in these cases. However, if you're using an application that doesn't use a reserved multicast address, you might want to use DHCP to assign multicast addresses temporarily on your network. If you want to reserve an address permanently, you must register it with the Internet Assigned Numbers Authority (IANA).

You can find a list of multicast addresses reserved by the IANA for designated purposes at *www.networksorcery.com/enp/protocol/ip/multicast.htm.*

A **multicast scope** allows assigning multicast addresses dynamically to multicast servers and clients with the Multicast Address Dynamic Client Allocation Protocol (MADCAP). Typically, a multicast server (MCS) is allocated a multicast address, and multicast clients register or join the multicast group, which allows them to receive multicast traffic from the MCS.

All devices using TCP/IP must be assigned a unicast IP address before they can be assigned and begin using multicast addresses.

There are two common ranges of multicast addresses you can use to create a multicast scope:

- *Administrative scopes*—An administrative scope is composed of multicast addresses intended to be used in a private network. This range of addresses is similar to the private unicast IP address ranges beginning with 10, 172.16-172.31, and 192.168. The range most recommended for this purpose is 239.192.0.0/14, which has plenty of addresses for a large enterprise. The range you specify when configuring the multicast scope must contain at least 256 addresses.

- *Global scopes*—In a global scope, the multicast application is used across the public Internet and has the recommended range of 233.0.0.0/24. There's no minimum number of addresses in a global scope.

The preceding ranges are recommended. You can use any range of multicast addresses for creating a scope, as long as it doesn't include any addresses reserved by the IANA.

You configure multicast scopes in the DHCP console or with PowerShell cmdlets. You don't configure options for a multicast scope, but you can configure exclusions, and you must specify a lease time. (The default value is 30 days.) The multicast scope consists of start and end IP addresses in the multicast address range, along with a time to live (TTL) value that specifies how many routers a multicast packet can pass through before being discarded. No subnet mask is specified in the scope because multicast addresses are considered secondary addresses, and a host already has a subnet mask assigned along with its unicast IP address. Activity 3-4 walks you through creating a multicast scope in the DHCP console.

Activity 3-4: Creating a Multicast Scope

Time Required: 10 minutes
Objective: Create a multicast scope.

Required Tools and Equipment: 412Server1
Description: You want to see how to create a multicast scope, so you create an administrative multicast scope with the minimum required 256 addresses.

1. Log on to 412Server1 as **Administrator**, and open the DHCP console.

2. Right-click the **IPv4** node and click **New Multicast Scope** to start the New Multicast Scope Wizard. In the welcome window, click **Next**.

3. Type **Admin1** in the Name text box (because you're creating an administrative scope), and then click **Next**.

4. In the Start IP address text box, type **239.192.0.0**, and in the End IP address text box, type **239.192.0.255**, which provides the minimum 256 addresses required for an administrative scope. Leave the TTL at the default value, **32**, and then click **Next**.

5. In the Add Exclusions window, click **Next**. In the Lease Duration window, note that the default lease time is 30 days, compared with 8 days for a unicast scope. Click **Next**.

6. In the Activate Multicast Scope window, accept the default value **Yes**, and click **Next**. Click **Finish**.

7. In the DHCP console, click to expand **Multicast Scope [Admin1]**. You see an Address Pool node and an Address Leases node (see Figure 3-6).

8. Stay logged on to 412Server1 if you're continuing to the next activity.

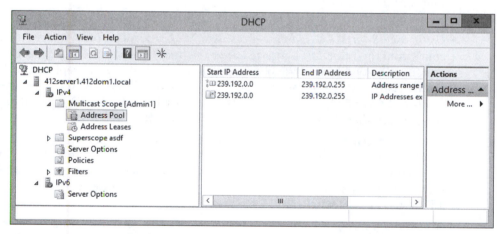

Figure 3-6   A multicast scope

For a good tutorial on IPv4 multicasting, see *http://technet.microsoft.com/en-us/library/cc759719(v=ws.10).aspx#w2k3tr_mcast_how_kgyu*.

Using DHCPv6

Up to now, you have learned how to use DHCP in an IPv4 environment. Although IPv6 provides automatic address assignment without using a DHCP server, you might still want to use DHCPv6 for IPv6 address assignment. DHCPv6 enables you to manage IPv6 address assignment better, see which addresses are being used on the network, and control IPv6 address options. Before you get into configuring DHCPv6, the following sections review some IPv6 concepts. You can find more detailed coverage in *MCSA Guide to Installing and Configuring Windows Server 2012/R2, Exam 70-410* (Cengage Learning, 2015).

IPv6 Address Structure

An IPv6 address is a 128-bit number written as eight 16-bit hexadecimal numbers separated by colons. There's no official name for each part of the address, so each 16-bit value is simply called a "field." A valid IPv6 address looks like this:

`fe80:0:0:0:18ff:0024:8e5a:60`

IPv6 addresses often have several 0 values. One or more consecutive 0 values can be written as a double colon (`::`), so the preceding address can be written as `fe80::18ff:0024:8e5a:60`. However, you can have only one double colon in an IPv6 address. Leading 0s are optional. The value `0024` in the previous example could just as easily have been written as `24`, and the value `60` could have been written as `0060`. The hexadecimal numbering system was chosen to represent IPv6 addresses largely because it's much easier to convert to binary than decimal is. Each hexadecimal digit represents 4 bits, so to convert an IPv6 address to binary, simply convert each hexadecimal digit (accounting for leading 0s) to its binary equivalent.

The IPv6 Interface ID
The prefix length (network ID) of an IPv6 host address is always 64 bits. Therefore, the interface ID of an IPv6 address is 64 bits, too. For this reason, you can identify the network ID of an IPv6 address easily by looking at the first 64 bits (16 hex digits or four fields) and the interface ID by looking at the last 64 bits. For example, in the address `fe80:0:0:0:18ff:0024:8e5a:60`, the network ID is `fe80:0:0:0` and the interface ID is `18ff:0024:8e5a:60`.

Because the prefix isn't a variable length, working with IPv6 addresses is somewhat easier because you don't have to do a binary calculation with a subnet mask to determine the network and interface IDs.

An IPv6 interface ID can be assigned to a host in these ways:

- *Using the 48-bit MAC address*—Because a MAC address is only 48 bits, the other 16 bits come from the value `fffe` inserted after the first 24 bits of the MAC address. In addition, the first two zeros that compose most MAC addresses are replaced with 02. For example, given the MAC address 00-0C-29-7C-F9-C4, the host ID of an IPv6 address is `020c:29ff:fe7c:f9c4`. This autoconfigured 64-bit host ID is called an Extended Unique Identifier (EUI)-64 interface ID, defined in RFC 4291.

- *A randomly generated permanent interface identifier*—The interface ID is generated randomly but is a permanent assignment maintained through system restarts. Windows Server 2008 and later use this method by default for permanent interfaces, such as Ethernet ports. However, you can specify that Windows use EUI-64 addresses with the `netsh` command or a PowerShell cmdlet.

- *A temporary interface identifier*—Some connections, such as dial-up Point-to-Point Protocol (PPP) connections, might use this method for interface IPv6 address assignment, defined in RFC 4941, whereby the interface ID is assigned randomly and changes each time IPv6 is initialized to maintain anonymity.

- *Via DHCPv6*—Addresses are assigned via a DHCPv6 server to IPv6 interfaces when they're initialized.

- *Manually*—Similar to IPv4 configuration, the IPv6 address is entered manually in the interface's Properties dialog box.

IPv6 Address Types

IPv4 defines unicast, multicast, and broadcast addresses, and IPv6 defines unicast, multicast, and anycast addresses. Unicast and multicast addresses in IPv6 perform much like their IPv4 counterparts, with a few exceptions. Anycast addresses are an altogether different animal.

- *IPv6 unicast addresses*—A unicast address specifies a single interface on a device. To participate in an IPv6 network, every device must have at least one network interface that has been assigned a unicast IPv6 address. In most cases, each interface on a device is assigned a separate unicast address, but for load-balancing purposes, multiple interfaces on a device can share the same IPv6 unicast address. There are three main types of IPv6 unicast addresses: link-local, unique local, and global.

- *Link-local addresses*—Addresses starting with `fe80` are called link-local IPv6 addresses and are self-configuring. They can't be routed and are somewhat equivalent to Automatic Private IP Addressing (APIPA) in IPv4. Link-local addresses can be used for computer-to-computer communication in small networks where no routers are needed.

- *Unique local addresses*—Unique local IPv6 addresses are analogous to the familiar private IPv4 addresses that most companies use behind a network firewall. Like private IPv4 addresses, unique local addresses can't be routed on the Internet (but can be routed inside the private network). These addresses begin with `fc` or `fd`.

- *Global addresses*—Global unicast IPv6 addresses are analogous to public IPv4 addresses. They're accessible on the public Internet and can be routed. These addresses begin with 2 or 3, and the rest of the address space is reserved and will be made available as needed.

IPv6 Autoconfiguration

IPv6 autoconfiguration occurs by two methods: stateless and stateful. With Windows Vista/ Windows Server 2008 and later computers, these methods can actually be used together.

- *Stateless autoconfiguration*—With **stateless autoconfiguration**, the node listens for router advertisement messages from a local router. If the Autonomous flag in the router advertisement message is set, the node uses the prefix information contained in the message. In this case, the node uses the advertised prefix and its 64-bit interface ID to generate the IPv6 address. If the Autonomous flag isn't set, the prefix information is ignored, and the node can attempt to use DHCPv6 for address configuration or an automatically generated link-local address.

- *Stateful autoconfiguration*—With **stateful autoconfiguration**, the node uses an autoconfiguration protocol, such as DHCPv6, to get its IPv6 address and other configuration information. A node attempts to use DHCPv6 to get IPv6 address configuration information if there are no routers on the network providing router advertisements or if the Autonomous flag in router advertisements isn't set.

How Autoconfiguration Works on Windows Hosts The Windows autoconfiguration process in Windows 8/8.1 and Windows Server 2012/R2 hosts involves the following steps:

1. At initialization, a link-local address is determined.

2. The link-local address is verified as unique by using duplicate address detection.

3. If the address is verified as unique, the address is assigned to the interface; otherwise, a new address is generated and Step 2 is repeated.

4. The host transmits a router solicitation message. This message is addressed to the `all-routers` multicast address.

5. If no router advertisement messages are received in response to the solicitation message, the host attempts to use DHCPv6 to get an address.

6. If a router advertisement message is received and has an Autonomous flag set, the prefix in the router advertisement is used along with the interface ID to configure the IPv6 address on the interface. The host can also use a DHCPv6 server to acquire other IPv6 configuration parameters if specified in the router advertisement. If the Autonomous flag isn't set, the host uses DHCPv6 to acquire the address.

Note that the IPv6 client maintains its link-local address even if it successfully gets an address via autoconfiguration or DHCPv6. Also, it's possible for the router advertisement to have the Autonomous flag set, causing the IPv6 client to autoconfigure an address *and* specify that the client should use DHCPv6 to get an address. In this case, the client does both and ends up with two addresses. It's also possible for more than one router to advertise an IPv6 prefix, causing the client to autoconfigure multiple addresses.

Configuring DHCPv6 Scopes

You configure a DHCPv6 scope in the DHCP console or with the `Add-DhcpServerv6Scope` PowerShell cmdlet. To configure a DHCPv6 scope, you need to provide the following information:

- *Scope name*—A name for your scope that identifies its purpose.
- *Prefix*—The 64-bit prefix value for the scope. The **prefix** is the part of the IPv6 address that's the network identifier. For example, a valid prefix is `2001:0db8:0412::`. You can use the standard abbreviated methods for entering each field, including omitting leading zeroes. You must terminate the prefix with a double colon. Unlike with an IPv4 scope, you don't specify start and end addresses for the range. The entire address range is used based on the prefix you enter. To exclude servers and other devices with static IPv6 addresses, use exclusions.
- *Preference*—The **preference** value is used to indicate priority when there are multiple DHCPv6 servers. It's an optional value in the DHCPv6 message. A higher preference value indicates a higher priority. The default value is 0, meaning no preference value should be included in the message. If the preference option is included and a DHCPv6 client receives replies from more than one server, it chooses the reply with the highest priority (highest preference value). If the preference values are the same, the client chooses the reply with the best configuration options.
- *Exclusions*—You add exclusions just as you do for an IPv4 scope. You can specify a range of addresses or a single address.
- *Scope lease*—The lease duration has two values: Preferred Life Time and Valid Life Time. The Preferred Life Time is the initial lease time, but when the time expires, the address remains valid until the Valid Life Time expires. The Valid Life Time must be equal to or greater than the Preferred Life Time. The default Preferred Life Time is 8 days, and the default Valid Life Time is 12 days.

As with IPv4 scopes, you can create reservations and include options for DNS servers and other service; however, you can't assign a default gateway (router) with DHCPv6. IPv6 relies on router advertisements to get the address of its default gateway, or it can be assigned manually in the network interface's Properties dialog box.

 Before Windows Server 2012/R2 can begin assigning IPv6 addresses via DHCPv6, you must assign a static IPv6 address to the server, using the same prefix you do for the DHCPv6 scope.

DHCPv6 Operation

Unlike DHCPv4, the client's MAC address isn't used to lease an address and create reservations. DHCPv6 uses a **DHCP Unique Identifier (DUID)**. In Windows, a DUID is a hexadecimal number, usually derived from the network interface's MAC address. It's created when Windows is installed and doesn't change even if the NIC changes. The DUID is stored in the HKLM\System\CurrentControlSet\Services\TCPIP6\Parameters Registry key. If you delete this key, the DUID is created when the system is restarted. You can see it by using the `ipconfig /all` command.

After a DHCPv6 scope is created and activated, the DHCPv6 server is ready to begin assigning IPv6 addresses. The dynamic assignment of IPv6 addresses is similar to the process for IPv4 addresses. It consists of a series of four packets between the client and the server, using UDP ports 546 and 547. The DHCPv6 client listens on port 546, and the DHCPv6 server listens on port 547. The four-message exchange is as follows:

1. The DHCPv6 client sends a Solicit message from its link-local address via UDP source port 546 to the IPv6 multicast address `ff02::1:2` on destination port 547.

2. The DHCPv6 server replies with an Advertise message to the link-local address of the client on destination port 546. This message contains the IPv6 address offered to the client.

3. The DHCPv6 client replies with a Request message from its link-local address, accepting the offered address. The message is still addressed to the IPv6 multicast address `ff02::1:2` at UDP port 547.

4. The DHCPv6 server responds with a Reply message confirming the address assignment. At this point, the client binds the assigned IPv6 address to its interface, the server adds the address to its list of leased addresses, and the process is completed.

To test a DHCPv6 scope, open a command prompt window on a Windows client computer, and enter the `ipconfig /renew6` command. You need to use the `/renew6` parameter because the `/renew` parameter is only for IPv4 addresses.

Activity 3-5: Creating and Testing a DHCPv6 Scope

Time Required: 10 minutes
Objective: Create and test a DHCPv6 scope.

Required Tools and Equipment: 412Server1 and 412Win8
Description: You want to begin using DHCPv6 for IPv6 address assignment, so you create a DHCPv6 scope and then test it with a Windows 8.1 client.

1. Log on to 412Win8 as **Win8User**, if necessary. Log on to 412Server1 as **Administrator**, if necessary, and open the DHCP console.

2. Click to expand the server node, if necessary, and then click to select **IPv6**. Right-click the **IPv6** node and click **New Scope** to start the New Scope Wizard. In the welcome window, click **Next**.

3. Type **Scope412** in the Name text box, and then click **Next**.

4. In the Prefix text box, type **2001:db8:412::**. Recall that addresses starting with **2001:db8** are reserved for testing and documentation purposes. Leave the Preference setting at the default value 0, and then click **Next**.

5. In the Add Exclusions window, type **1** in the Start IPv6 Address text box, and type **10** in the End IPv6 Address text box, to exclude the first 10 addresses. Click **Add** and then **Next**.

6. In the Scope Lease window, accept the defaults, and click **Next**.

7. In the final window, accept the default **Yes** to activate the scope now, and then click **Finish**.

8. On 412Win8, open a command prompt window, and then type `ipconfig /renew6 "Ethernet"` and press **Enter**. You might see an error message, and you won't be leased an IPv6 address on the Ethernet interface until you assign the server an address within the scope you created. If you don't specify the interface to renew, Windows takes longer to configure ISATAP and Teredo interfaces.

9. On 412Server1, right-click **Start** and click **Network Connections**. Right-click **Ethernet** and click **Properties**. Double-click **Internet Protocol Version 6 (TCP/IPv6)** and click the **Use the following IPv6 address** option button. In the IPv6 address text box, type **2001:db8:412::1**, and in the Subnet prefix length text box, type **64**, if necessary. Click **OK** twice, and close Network Connections.

10. On 412Win8, type `ipconfig /renew6 "Ethernet"` and press **Enter**. You should see that your Ethernet interface was assigned an address starting with `2001:db8:412`. Close the command prompt window.

11. On 412Server1, click **Address Leases** in the DHCP console under the scope you created. You should see the leased address and the name of the client, 412Win8.

12. Stay logged on to 412Server1 and 412Win8 if you're continuing to the next activity.

DHCPv6 Options

You configure DHCPv6 options just as you do for standard DHCPv4. However, there's no option in DHCPv6 to assign a default gateway (router) because this task is handled by router advertisements sent by routers on the network. You can configure domain names, DNS servers, and other options, however. As with DHCPv4, you can configure options at the server level, the scope level, and the reservation level, but there are no policies or filters for DHCPv6, unlike DHCPv4.

DHCP High Availability

DHCP is a crucial service in networks that use it. If the DHCP server fails to respond to client requests, clients can't communicate on the network. Microsoft offers the following ways to achieve high availability for DHCP:

- Split scopes
- DHCP failover
- DHCP server cluster
- Hot standby

Using a DHCP server cluster requires a complex network setup, including shared storage for the DHCP database that multiple DHCP servers have access to. This method works well, but setup and configuration can be difficult, and the shared storage can be a single point of failure. The hot standby method consists of two DHCP servers configured with identical scopes and options. If the primary DHCP server fails, an administrator must manually restore the DHCP database from backup to the standby server, which might not have the most recent lease data. The following sections cover the most recommended methods for providing DHCP high availability and fault tolerance: split scopes and DHCP failover.

DHCP Split Scopes

A **split scope** is a fault-tolerant DHCP configuration in which two DHCP servers share the same scope information, allowing both servers to offer DHCP services to clients. One server is configured as the primary DHCP server and the other as the secondary. In most cases, the secondary server leases addresses only if the primary server is unavailable. With Windows Server versions before Windows Server 2008 R2, you had to configure a split scope manually. Starting with Windows Server 2008 R2, however, the DHCP Server role has the Dhcp Split-Scope Configuration Wizard to automate the process. You create a split scope by using the wizard as follows:

1. Install the DHCP Server role on two servers designated DHCP1 and DHCP2 for this example. DHCP1 is the primary DHCP server, and DHCP2 is the secondary.

2. Create a scope on DHCP1, including any options, and activate it.

3. Run the DHCP Split-Scope Wizard on DHCP1. To do so, right-click the scope in the DHCP console, point to Advanced, and then click Split-Scope. The wizard prompts you for the following information:

   o The name or address of the secondary DHCP server.

   o The percentage of split. A typical split percentage is 80/20, meaning the primary server can lease 80% of the addresses and the secondary server has 20%, but you can configure the split as needed for your environment. If you're configuring the split scope for load balancing rather than fault tolerance, you can set the split to 50%.

   o Delay in DHCP offer. Specify the number of milliseconds each server should delay between receiving a DHCPDISCOVER and sending a DHCPOFFER. You usually set the primary server for a 0 delay. You want the secondary server to delay long enough that the primary server services most client requests. You might have to adjust this value until you get the intended results. A value of 1000 is a good place to start. If you're configuring a split scope for load balancing, leave the delay at 0 for both servers. Both servers will respond to all requests, but the client will accept only the first response. With the delay set at 0 for both servers and assuming similar load and network conditions, each server should be the first to respond about half the time, which is what you want in a load-balancing arrangement.

4. The wizard creates the scope on the secondary server and creates the necessary exclusion range, according to the split percentage on both servers, to ensure that IP addresses aren't duplicated.

5. Create reservations on both servers. If you're using reservations, you need to create them manually on both servers so that either server can offer reserved addresses; the split scope function doesn't replicate reservations.

Activity 3-6: Working with Split Scopes

Time Required: 10 minutes
Objective: Install a second DHCP server and configure a split scope.

Required Tools and Equipment: 412Server1, 412Server2, and 412Win8
Description: You want to work with split scopes, so you install the DHCP Server role on 412Server2, configure a split scope between 412Server1 and 412Server2, and then test it.

1. Start 412Server2, and log on as **Administrator**.

2. Open a PowerShell prompt by clicking the **PowerShell** taskbar icon. Type `Install-WindowsFeature DHCP -IncludeManagementTools` and press **Enter**.

3. When the DHCP Server installation finishes, close PowerShell, and click **Tools, DHCP** from the Server Manager menu to open the DHCP console. Right-click **412server2.412dom1.local** (the server node) and click **Authorize**.

4. On 412Server1, click to select **Scope [10.12.0.0] 10.12-Scope**. Then right-click it, point to **Advanced**, and click **Split-Scope** to start the Dhcp Split-Scope Configuration Wizard. Click **Next**.

5. In the Additional DHCP Server window, type **412Server2** in the Additional DHCP Server text box, and then click **Next**.

6. In the Percentage of Split window, move the slider so that both the Host DHCP Server and Added DHCP Server text boxes show **50** (see Figure 3-7). You use this kind of configuration for load-balancing DHCP. Click **Next**.

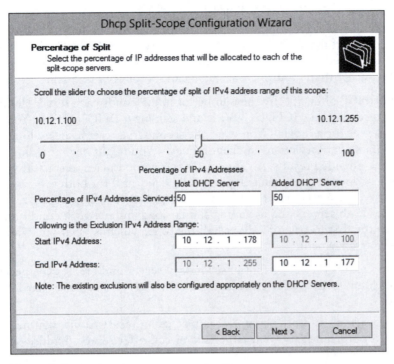

Figure 3-7   Setting the percentage of split

7. In the Delay in DHCP Offer window, leave both values at 0 for a load-balancing arrangement. (If you were more concerned with having a secondary DHCP server in case the primary server failed, you would set the delay for Added DHCP Server to about 1000.) Click **Next**, and then Click **Finish**. Click **Close**.

8. Click **Address Pool** to see that an exclusion range has been added that excludes addresses 10.12.1.178 to 10.12.1.255, which are the addresses 412Server2 will allocate. (*Note:* You might need to click **Refresh** to see the exclusion range.) Right-click the scope and click **Deactivate** so that 412Server1 can no longer allocate IP addresses. Click **Yes** to confirm.

9. On 412Server2, open the DHCP console, if necessary. Right-click **10.12-Scope** and click **Activate**. Click **Address Pool** to see the exclusion range of 10.12.1.100 through 10.12.1.177, the addresses 412Server1 will allocate.

10. Log on to **412Win8**, and open a command prompt window. Type `ipconfig /release` and press **Enter**, and then type `ipconfig /renew` and press **Enter**. You'll see that an address from 412Server2 was assigned. Close the command prompt window.

11. On 412Server2, right-click **10.12-Scope** and click **Delete**. Click **Yes** twice to confirm the deletion. On 412Server1, delete the exclusion in 10.12-Scope and reactivate the scope. Stay logged on to both servers if you're continuing to the next activity.

One problem with split scopes is that if one DHCP server fails, the lease information it stores is lost. In addition, because the second server has only a portion of the IP addresses available to lease, it could run out of IP addresses before the failed server is back up and running. Both these problems are solved by DHCP failover, discussed next.

Split scopes are an option only on IPv4 scopes, not on IPv6 scopes.

DHCP Failover

DHCP failover, a new feature in Windows Server 2012, allows two DHCP servers to share the pool of addresses in a scope, giving both servers access to all the addresses in the pool. Lease information is replicated between the servers, so if one server goes down, the other server maintains the lease information. Like split scopes, DHCP failover is available only in IPv4 scopes; if you need fault tolerance for IPv6 scopes, you have to use traditional server clustering or hot standby servers. There are two modes for DHCP failover:

- *Load-balancing mode*—With **load-balancing mode**, the default, both DHCP servers participate in address leasing at the same time. You can configure the load-balancing priority if you want one server to service the majority of DHCP clients. If one server fails, the other server takes over all leasing duties, and because the DHCP database is replicated between the servers, no lease information is lost.

- *Hot standby mode*—With **hot standby mode**, one server is assigned as the active server that provides DHCP services to clients while the other server is placed in standby mode. The standby server begins providing DHCP services if the primary server becomes unresponsive.

Because DHCP failover is configured per scope, not per server, you can configure load balancing for one scope and hot standby for another. In addition, with hot standby mode, you can configure one server as the primary server for one scope and the secondary server for another scope.

DHCP failover requires close time synchronization between servers. Server clocks should be synchronized within one minute of each other, so make certain all servers use the same reliable time source.

Configuring Load-Balancing Modes   You configure DHCP failover in the DHCP console by right-clicking the IPv4 node or the target scope and then clicking Configure Failover. The Configure Failover Wizard guides you through the process, including whether you want to use load sharing or hot standby mode. In the first window, you choose the scope or scopes on which you want to configure failover. If you configure failover from the IPv4 node, all scopes are listed and selected by default (see Figure 3-8).

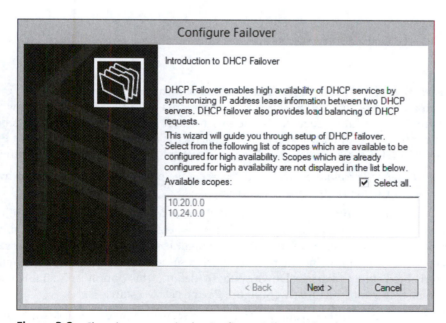

Figure 3-8   Choosing a scope in the Configure Failover Wizard

You can configure DHCP failover with the `Add-DhcpServerV4Failover` PowerShell cmdlet.

Next, you choose the partner server, which must be an authorized server that already has the DHCP Server service configured. If any servers have an existing failover configuration, you can select one from a list.

In the next window, you name the failover relationship and choose whether the failover configuration will be load balancing or hot standby. By default, the relationship name is composed of the names of the servers. Load balancing is the default configuration mode, and you configure the following additional parameters (see Figure 3-9):

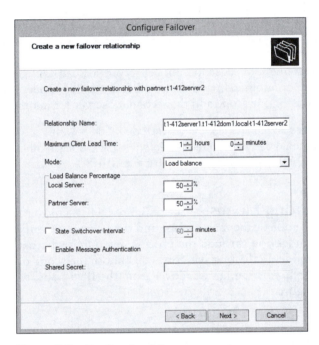

Figure 3-9   Configuring failover parameters

- *Maximum Client Lead Time*—The maximum client lead time (MCLT) defines the maximum amount of time a DHCP server can extend a lease for a DHCP client without the partner server's knowledge. It also defines the amount of time a server waits before assuming control over all DHCP services if its partner is in Partner Down state. In Partner Down state, the DHCP server assumes that its failover partner is no longer operational.

- *Load Balance Percentage*—Define the percentage of client requests serviced by each server. The default value is 50% for each server.

- *State Switchover Interval*—When a DHCP server loses communication with its partner, it enters the Communication Interrupted state, whereby each server operates independently but assumes the other server is still operational. If the State Switchover Interval option is enabled, you can define the time in which a server transitions from Communication Interrupted state to Partner Down state. By default, this option isn't enabled, and an administrator must manually configure Partner Down state.

- *Enable Message Authentication*—To increase security, you can enable authentication between failover partners. If you do, you must enter a shared secret on both DHCP servers.

Finally, review the selected options and click Finish to create the failover relationship. After the failover relationship is established, both inbound and outbound rules for TCP port 647 (DHCP Server Failover) are configured on the Windows firewall to allow communication between the two servers.

Configuring Hot Standby Mode   The process for configuring hot standby mode is almost identical to configuring load balancing mode, with the following exceptions:

- Select the "Hot standby" option for the failover mode.

- Instead of choosing a load balancing percentage, specify whether the failover partner is the active server or the standby server, and assign a percentage of addresses reserved for the standby server (see Figure 3-10).

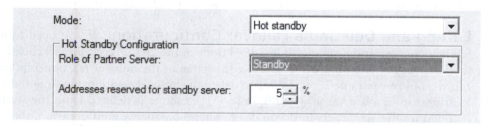

Figure 3-10   Configuring hot standby mode

In hot standby mode, the standby server doesn't normally lease IP addresses. However, if communication between the servers is interrupted, the standby server leases the addresses defined in the "Addresses reserved for standby server" option. If these addresses are exhausted before the MCLT timer has expired, the standby server no longer leases new addresses, but it can continue to renew existing address leases. If the MCLT timer expires, and the primary server is in Partner Down state, the standby server takes full control of the address pool.

Activity 3-7: Configuring DHCP Failover

Time Required: 10 minutes
Objective: Configure DHCP failover.

Required Tools and Equipment: 412Server1, 412Server2, and 412Win8
Description: In this activity, you configure DHCP failover in hot standby mode.

1. Log on to 412Server1 as **Administrator**, and open the DHCP console, if necessary. Make sure 412Server2 is running.

2. Right-click **10.12-Scope** and click **Configure Failover** to start the Configure Failover Wizard. In the welcome window, click **Next**.

3. In the Partner Server text box, type **412Server2**, and click **Next**. The partnership is validated.

4. In the "Create a new failover relationship" window, type **412Server1-412Server2-HotStandby** in the Relationship Name text box. Leave the Maximum Client Lead Time set at the default **1 hour**. In the Mode list box, click **Hot standby**.

5. In the Role of Partner Server list box, leave the default **Standby**, and leave the default **5%** for the "Addresses reserved for standby server" setting.

6. Click the **State Switchover Interval** check box, and leave the default value 60 in the minutes text box. Click to clear the **Enable Message Authentication** check box, and then click **Next**.

7. Confirm the configuration, and then click **Finish**. The failover configuration might take several seconds. After it's finished, click **Close**.

8. On 412Server2, open the DHCP console, if necessary. If you don't see 10.12-Scope, click the **Refresh** icon. Click **Address Leases** under 10.12-Scope. You should see the current address lease for 412Win8. (If you don't, click the **Refresh** icon.)

9. Log on to 412Win8, and open a command prompt window, if necessary. Type **ipconfig /release** and press **Enter**. Verify that the lease is no longer shown on 412Server1 and 412Server2. (You probably need to click the **Refresh** icon in the DHCP console on both servers.)

10. On 412Win8, type **ipconfig /renew** and press **Enter** to lease an address. Verify that the address lease can be seen on both servers, and then close the DHCP console on both servers. Log off 412Win8 and shut down 412Server2.

11. Stay logged on to 412Server1 if you're continuing to the next activity.

Editing and Deleting a Failover Configuration   If you need to edit or delete a failover configuration, right-click the IPv4 node in the DHCP console and click Properties. Click the Failover tab (see Figure 3-11). Select the name of the failover relationship, and click Edit to edit the failover parameters or Delete to delete the failover relationship. If you delete the failover relationship in a hot standby configuration, the scope is deleted from the standby server but retained on the active server. If you delete a load balancing configuration, the scope is deleted from the partner server, and all addresses are available to the local server.

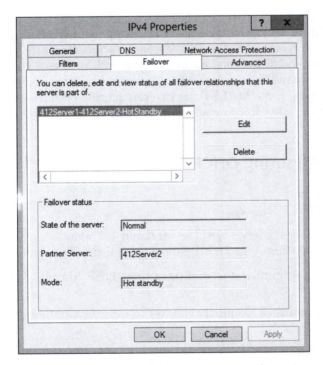

Figure 3-11   Editing or deleting a failover configuration

If you view the Failover tab in the Properties dialog box for a scope, you see information about the failover relationship (if any) of that scope, but you can't make changes. Changes must be made in the Failover tab of the IPv4 node's Properties dialog box.

Configuring DHCP for DNS Registration

A DHCP server can work with DNS to provide name resolution on behalf of DHCP clients. Configure DNS registration in the DNS tab (see Figure 3-12) of the Properties dialog box of the IPv4 or IPv6 server nodes or of the Properties dialog box of a scope. The DNS tab has the following options for configuring DNS registration:

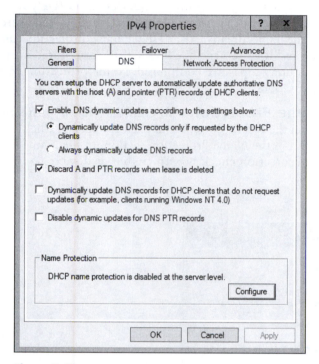

Figure 3-12 The DNS tab of the IPv4 Properties dialog box

- *Dynamically update DNS records only if requested by the DHCP clients*—This option is the default. When a client leases an IP address or renews a lease and sends option 81 in the DHCPREQUEST packet, the DHCP server attempts to register records dynamically with the DNS server on behalf of the client. Option 81 in the DHCPREQUEST packet contains the client's FQDN. By default, Windows clients configure option 81 so that the client updates its own A record and requests that the server update the PTR record.

- *Always dynamically update DNS records*—If this option is set, the DHCP server always attempts to register A and PTR records for the client as long as the client supports option 81.

- *Discard A and PTR records when lease is deleted*—If a lease is deleted and this option is selected (the default), the DHCP server attempts to contact the DNS server to delete the A and PTR records associated with the lease.

- *Dynamically update DNS records for DHCP clients that do not request updates*—If a client doesn't support option 81 (you have to go all the way back to Windows NT 4.0 for Windows clients that don't support it), and this option is set, the server attempts to register DNS records on the client's behalf.

- *Disable dynamic updates for DNS PTR records*—If set, the DHCP server doesn't attempt to register PTR records for DHCP clients.

DHCP Name Protection

On networks with both Windows and non-Windows computers, a problem known as **name squatting** can occur when a non-Windows computer registers its name with a DNS server, but the name has already been registered by a Windows computer. Name squatting isn't a problem on networks where all computers are members of a Windows domain because Active Directory ensures that all computer names are unique.

DHCP name protection prevents name squatting by non-Windows computers by using a DHCP resource record called Dynamic Host Configuration Identifier (DHCID). It's a resource record used by DHCP and DNS to verify that a name being registered in DNS is from the original computer that registered it if the name already exists. DHCP name protection can be configured at the scope level or the IPv4 and IPv6 server node levels. If it's configured at the IPv4 or IPv6 server level, all the corresponding scopes are configured. Name protection configured at the scope level doesn't affect other scopes.

Configuring DHCP Name Protection   To configure name protection, right-click the scope, IPv4, or IPv6 node in the DHCP console and click Properties. Click the DNS tab, and then click the Configure button in the Name Protection section. In the Name Protection dialog box, click the Enable Name Protection check box to enable or disable name protection (see Figure 3-13).

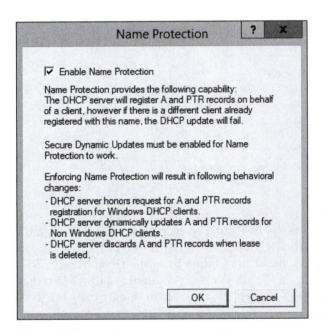

Figure 3-13   Configuring name protection

Overview of DNS

DNS is a critical network service in most networks because it provides name-to-address resolution, and a Windows domain network depends on DNS for name resolution and resolving client requests for Active Directory services. Without DNS, client computers couldn't locate domain controllers to download group policies or authenticate user logons. You learned about DNS in your study of the objectives for Exams 70-410 and 70-411. This section reviews the fundamentals of DNS, and later sections cover some advanced DNS topics.

DNS Fundamentals

Domain Name System (DNS) is a distributed hierarchical database composed mainly of computer name and IP address pairs. A distributed database means no single database contains all data; instead, data is spread out among many different servers. In the worldwide DNS system, data is distributed among thousands of servers throughout the world. A hierarchical database, in this case, means there's a structure to how information is stored and accessed in the database. In other words, unless you're resolving a local domain name for which you have a local server, DNS lookups often require a series of queries to a hierarchy of DNS servers before the name can be resolved.

The Structure of DNS   To better understand the DNS lookup process, reviewing the structure of a computer name on the Internet or in a Windows domain is helpful. Computer names are typically expressed as *host.domain.top-level-domain*; the *top-level-domain* can be com, net, org, us, edu, and so forth. This naming structure is called the fully qualified domain name (FQDN). The DNS naming hierarchy can be described as an inverted tree with the root at the top (named "."), top-level domains branching out from the root, and domains and subdomains branching off the top-level domains (see Figure 3-14).

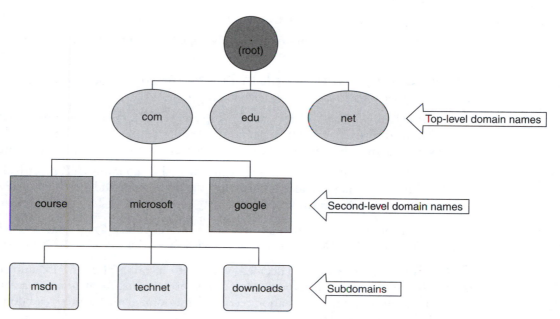

Figure 3-14   A partial view of the DNS naming hierarchy
© Cengage Learning®

The entire DNS tree is called the "DNS namespace." When a domain name is registered, the domain is added to the DNS hierarchy and becomes part of the DNS namespace. Every domain has one or more servers that are authoritative for the domain, meaning the servers contain a master copy of all DNS records for that domain. A single server can be authoritative for multiple domains.

Each shape in Figure 3-14 has one or more DNS servers managing the names associated with it. For example, the root of the tree has 13 DNS servers called "root servers" scattered about the world that keep a database of addresses of other DNS servers managing top-level domain names. These other servers, aptly named, are called "top-level domain (TLD) servers." Each top-level domain has servers that maintain addresses of other DNS servers. For example, the com TLD servers maintain a database containing addresses of DNS servers for each domain name ending with com, such as tomsho.com and microsoft.com. Each second-level DNS server can contain hostnames, such as www or server1. Hostnames are associated with an IP address, so when a client looks up the name www.microsoft.com, the DNS server returns an IP address. Second-level domains can also have subdomains, such as the technet in technet.microsoft.com.

DNS Zones

DNS servers maintain a database of information that contains zones. A zone is a grouping of DNS information that belongs to a contiguous portion of the DNS namespace, usually a domain and possibly one or more subdomains. Each zone contains a variety of record types called "resource records" containing information about network resources, such as hostnames, other DNS servers, domain controllers, and so forth; they're identified by letter codes. These records are discussed in more detail later in "DNS Resource Records."

DNS zones are created automatically during Active Directory installation, but you might need to create a zone manually in the following situations:

- When you don't install DNS at the time you install Active Directory
- When you install DNS on a server that's not a domain controller
- When you create a stub zone
- When you create a secondary zone for a primary zone
- When you create a primary or secondary zone for an Internet domain

Forward and Reverse Lookup Zones   Before you begin creating a zone, you must decide whether it's a forward or reverse lookup zone:

- *Forward lookup zone*—A forward lookup zone (FLZ), the type you work with most often, contains records that translate names to IP addresses, such as A, AAAA, and MX records. It's named after the domain whose resource records it contains, such as csmtech.local.
- *Reverse lookup zone*—A reverse lookup zone (RLZ) contains PTR records that map IP addresses to names and is named after the IP network address (IPv4 or IPv6) of the computers whose records it contains.

To create one of these zones, right-click the Forward Lookup Zones folder or the Reverse Lookup Zones folder in the DNS Manager console and click New Zone to start the New Zone Wizard.

Zone Type   After you have decided whether to install a FLZ or RLZ and started the New Zone Wizard, you select the type of zone you want to create. As mentioned, a zone is a database containing resource and information records for a domain and possibly subdomains. There are three different zone types:

- *Primary zone*—Contains a read/write master copy of all resource records for the zone. Updates to resource records can be made only on a server configured as a primary zone server, referred to as the "primary DNS server." A primary DNS server is considered authoritative for the zone it manages. A primary zone can be an Active Directory–integrated or a standard zone.
- *Secondary zone*—Contains a read-only copy of all resource records for the zone. Changes can't be made directly on a secondary DNS server, but because it contains an exact copy of the primary zone, it's considered authoritative for the zone. Although a secondary zone can be only a standard zone, not an Active Directory–integrated zone, a file-based secondary zone can be created on a server that's not a DC or on a DC in another Active Directory domain or forest. Secondary zones can be used in this way to resolve names for domain-based resources outside the domain.
- *Stub zone*—Contains a read-only copy of only the SOA and NS records for a zone and the necessary A records to resolve NS records. A stub zone forwards queries to a primary DNS server for the zone it holds SOA and NS records for and isn't authoritative for the zone. A stub zone can be an Active Directory–integrated or a standard zone.

Active Directory–Integrated Zones

When you're selecting the zone type in the New Zone Wizard, the "Store the zone in Active Directory" option means you want the zone to be stored in an Active Directory partition; and the zone is referred to as an "Active Directory–integrated zone." It's not a new zone type; it's just a primary or stub zone with the DNS database stored in an Active Directory partition. The server where you're creating the new zone must be a writeable domain controller (as opposed to a read only domain controller). When you're storing the zone in Active Directory, the only valid zone type options are primary and stub zones. If you select a secondary zone, the option to store the zone in Active Directory is disabled.

Standard Zones

A zone that isn't Active Directory integrated is referred to as a "standard zone," and the zone data is stored in a text file that can be opened and edited with a simple text editor (although using DNS Manager is preferable on a Windows system). This text file is named *zone-name*.dns (with *zone-name* typically the domain name) and is in the %*systemroot*%\System32\dns folder on the DNS server. A standard zone can be a primary, secondary, or stub zone. Standard zones are mostly installed on stand-alone servers that need to provide name resolution services for network resources outside the domain or in networks that don't use Active Directory at all, such as Linux or UNIX-based networks. In addition, standard zones are used for Internet name resolution.

DNS Resource Records

As mentioned, each zone contains resource records containing information about network resources. Table 3-3 lists resource record types and identifying codes and describes each record type.

Table 3-3   DNS resource record types

Record type (code)	Description
Start of Authority (SOA)	Less a resource than an informational record, the SOA identifies the name server that's authoritative for the domain and includes a variety of timers, dynamic update configuration, and zone transfer information.
Host (A)	The most common resource record; consists of a computer name and an IPv4 address.
IPv6 Host (AAAA)	Like an A record but uses an IPv6 address.
Name Server (NS)	The FQDN of a name server that has authority over the domain. NS records are used by DNS servers to refer queries to another server that's authoritative for the requested domain.
Canonical Name (CNAME)	A record containing an alias for another record that enables you to refer to the same resource with different names yet maintain only one host record. For example, you could create an A record for a computer named "web" and a CNAME record that points to the A record but allows users to access the host with the name "www."
Mail Exchanger (MX)	Contains the address of an e-mail server for the domain. Because e-mail addresses are typically specified as *user@domain.com*, the mail server's name is not part of the e-mail address. To deliver a message to the mail server, an MX record query supplies the address of a mail server in the specified domain.
Pointer (PTR)	Used for reverse DNS lookups. Although DNS is used mainly to resolve a name to an address, it can also resolve an address to a name by using a reverse lookup. PTR records can be created automatically on Windows DNS servers.
Service Records (SRV)	Allows DNS clients to request the address of a server that provides a specific service instead of querying the server by name. This type of record is useful when an application doesn't know the name of the server it needs but does know what service is required. For example, in Windows domains, DNS servers contain SRV records with the addresses of domain controllers so that clients can request the logon service to authenticate to the domain.

DNS records can be added to a zone and changed by using one of two methods:

- *Static updates*—With this method, an administrator must enter DNS record information manually. Using this method is reasonable with a small network of only a few resources accessed by name, but in a large network, static updates can be an administrative burden.

- *Dynamic updates*—Referred to as Dynamic DNS (DDNS), computers in the domain can register or update their own DNS records, or DHCP can update DNS on the clients' behalf when a computer leases a new IP address. Both the client computer and the DHCP server must be configured to use this feature.

The DNS Lookup Process

When a computer needs to acquire information from a DNS server, it sends a lookup or query to the server. A computer making a DNS query is called a "DNS client" or "DNS resolver." Two types of DNS queries can be made:

- *Iterative query*—When a DNS server gets an **iterative query**, it responds with the best information it currently has in its local database to satisfy the query, such as the IP address of an A record it retrieves from a local zone file or cache. If the DNS server doesn't have the specific information, it might respond with the IP address of a name server that *can* satisfy the query; this type of response is called a referral because the server is referring the DNS client to another server. If the server has no information, it sends a negative response that essentially says "I can't help you." DNS servers usually query each other by using iterative queries.

- *Recursive query*—A **recursive query** instructs the DNS server to process the query until it responds with an address that satisfies the query or with an "I don't know" message. A recursive query might require a DNS server to contact several other DNS servers before it finally sends a response to the client. Most queries made by DNS clients are recursive queries, and DNS servers also use recursive queries when using a forwarder.

A typical DNS lookup made by a DNS client can involve both recursive and iterative queries. A sample query demonstrating the hierarchical nature of DNS (see Figure 3-15) is outlined in the following steps:

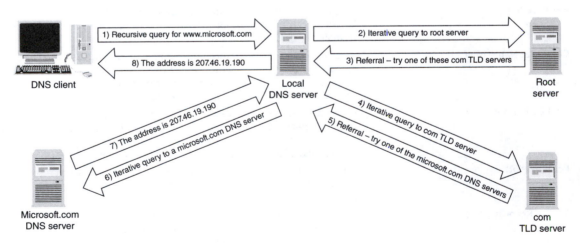

Figure 3-15   A DNS hierarchical lookup
© *Cengage Learning*®

1. A user types www.microsoft.com in the Web browser's address bar. The computer running the Web browser, called the DNS client or resolver, sends a recursive query to the DNS server's address in its IP configuration. Typically, this DNS server, called the "local DNS server," is maintained on the network or at the client's ISP.

2. The local DNS server checks its local zone data and cache. If the name isn't found locally, it sends an iterative query to a DNS root server.

3. The root server sends a referral to the local DNS server with a list of addresses for the TLD servers handling the com top-level domain.

4. The local DNS server sends another iterative query to a com TLD server.

5. The com TLD server responds with a referral to DNS servers responsible for the microsoft.com domain.

6. The local DNS server then sends another iterative query to a microsoft.com DNS server.

7. The microsoft.com DNS server replies with the host record IP address for www.microsoft.com.

8. The local DNS server responds to the client with the IP address for www.microsoft.com.

Configuring DNS Security

DNS is a common target for attacks because it figures so prominently in network transactions. The types of attacks on DNS include spoofing, DNS cache poisoning, denial of service, domain registration hijacking, and man-in-the-middle attacks, to name a few. The goal of most of these attacks is to compromise DNS so that users are unable to access network resources or are redirected to a different resource than was intended, often one with nefarious intentions. The techniques discussed in the following sections are steps that most DNS administrators should take to help prevent or at least mitigate the effectiveness of many DNS attacks.

Domain Name System Security Extension

Domain Name System Security Extension (DNSSEC) is a suite of features and protocols for validating DNS server responses. DNSSEC provides DNS clients with three critical methods to ensure that data they receive from DNS queries is accurate and secure:

- *Origin authentication of DNS data*—Verifies that the DNS server replying to a query is authentic

- *Authenticated denial of existence*—Allows verifying that a resource record couldn't be found

- *Data integrity*—Verifies that data hasn't been tampered with in transit

With DNSSEC in place, DNS is much less susceptible to spoofing and DNS cache poisoning. DNSSEC can secure zones by using a process called **zone signing** that uses digital signatures in DNSSEC-related resource records to verify DNS responses. By verifying the digital signature, a DNS client can be assured that the DNS response is identical to the information published by the authoritative zone server. Zones that are signed using DNSSEC have the following additional resource records:

- *DNSKEY*—The **DNSKEY** record is the public key for the zone that DNS resolvers use to verify the digital signature in Resource Record Signature records.

- *RRSIG*—A **Resource Record Signature (RRSIG)** key contains the signature for a single resource record, such as an A or MX record. RRSIG records are returned with the requested resource records so that each returned record can be validated.

- *NSEC*—Next Secure (NSEC) records are returned when the requested resource record doesn't exist. They're used to fulfill the authenticated denial of existence security feature of DNSSEC.

- *NSEC3*—Next Secure 3 (NSEC3) records are an alternative to NSEC records. They can prevent zone-walking, which is a technique of repeating NSEC queries to get all the names in a zone. Zones can use NSEC or NSEC3 records but not both.

- *NSEC3PARAM*—Next Secure 3 (NSEC3) **Parameter** records are used to determine which NSEC3 records should be included in responses to queries for nonexistent records.

- *DS*—**Delegation Signer (DS)** records hold the name of a delegated zone and are used to verify delegated child zones.

Zone signing uses public key cryptography. To secure a zone with a digital signature, a key master must be designated. It can be a Windows Server 2012/R2 server that's authoritative for the zone. Two keys must be generated:

- *Key-signing key*—A **key-signing key (KSK)** has a private and public key associated with it. The private key is used to sign all DNSKEY records, and the public key is used as a trust anchor for validating DNS responses. A **trust anchor** is usually the DNSKEY for the zone but can also be a DS key for a delegated zone.

- *Zone-signing key*—A **zone-signing key (ZSK)** is a public and private key combination stored in a certificate used to sign the zone. The KSK is used to sign the ZSK to validate it.

Trust anchors are distributed from authoritative DNS servers to nonauthoritative DNS servers that request DNSSEC validation. For example, when a client queries its local DNS server for a record in a zone not held by the local DNS server, the local DNS server must query the authoritative DNS server for that zone. When it does so, if the zone is protected by DNSSEC, the returned record contains the trust anchor (the DNSKEY or DS record) with the necessary public key to validate the record.

DNSSEC doesn't provide confidentiality of data; that is, data isn't encrypted, only authenticated.

Validating DNS Responses   When a client requests a resource record from a zone secured with DNSSEC, the following steps take place:

1. A DNS client sends a query to the local DNS server configured in its network interface settings. If the client is DNSSEC aware, that information is included in the query message.

2. The local DNS server sends a query to a root server and top-level domain (TLD) server, as necessary. The message contains information indicating that the DNS server is DNSSEC aware.

3. The local DNS server receives a response containing the IP address of a DNS server authoritative for the zone.

4. The local DNS server sends a query to the authoritative DNS server. The message indicates that the DNS server is DNSSEC aware and the server can validate signed resource records.

5. The authoritative DNS server returns the resource record information requested plus the RRSIG records needed to validate the response.

6. The local DNS server returns the response to the DNS client with an indication of whether the response was validated.

Configuring DNSSEC   To configure DNSSEC in Windows Server 2012/R2, use the following procedure:

1. In DNS Manager, right-click the zone you want to configure, point to DNSSEC, and click Sign the Zone to start the Zone Signing Wizard. Click Next to begin.

2. You have three options for signing a zone (see Figure 3-16):

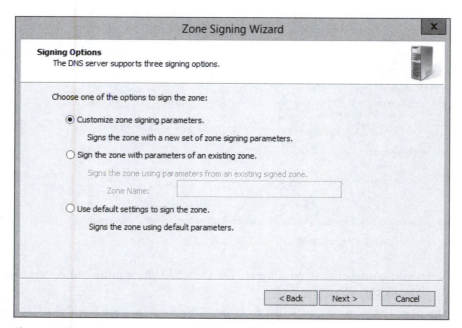

Figure 3-16   Choosing zone-signing options

- o *Customize zone signing parameters*—Allows you to choose the details for signing the zone, including the DNS server that will serve as the key master and the KSK and ZSK parameters.

- o *Sign the zone with parameters of an existing zone*—Use the zone-signing parameters from an existing signed zone. If you choose this option, click Next and then Finish, and zone signing is completed.

- o *Use default settings to sign the zone*—Default values are configured for zone signing, and you can review them before continuing. If you choose this option, click Next and then Finish.

3. If you selected "Customize zone signing parameters" in Step 2, continue with the wizard; otherwise DNSSEC configuration is complete for this zone. The next step is to choose the Key Master. By default, the current DNS server is chosen as the key master, but you can choose another primary server for the zone.

4. Next, you configure parameters for the KSK (see Figure 3-17). You can use the default values or select new values. A globally unique ID (GUID) is generated automatically. You can configure between one and three KSKs.

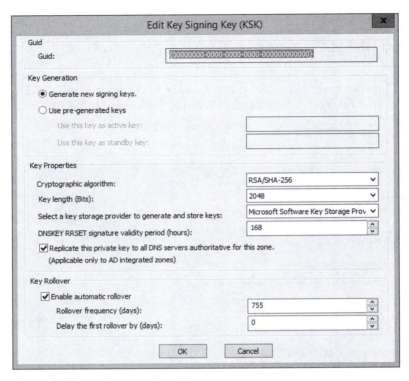

Figure 3-17   Configuring the KSK

5. Next, you configure the parameters for the ZSK; the window looks similar to the one for configuring the KSK.

6. The next step is to select NSEC or NSEC3 for authenticated denial of existence. NSEC3 is the default option (see Figure 3-18).

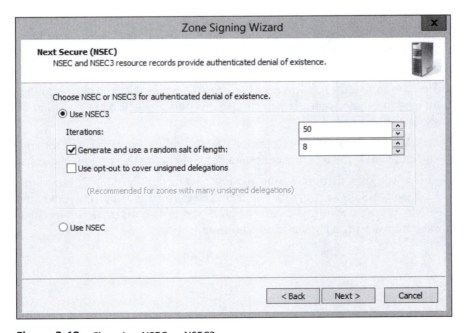

Figure 3-18   Choosing NSEC or NSEC3

7. Next, you specify how trust anchors are distributed. Trust anchors aren't required on authoritative DNS servers. You should distribute trust anchors only if other DCs provide nonauthoritative responses for the zone.

8. Last, you configure signing and polling parameters. You can accept the defaults for most situations. If you don't need to change any default values in the wizard, you could have selected the option to use the default settings in Step 2.

To test DNSSEC, do a DNS query with the PowerShell cmdlet `Resolve-DnsName`:

```
Resolve-DnsName 412Server2.412Dom1.local -dnssecok
```

This command must include the –dnssecok parameter to inform the DNS server that the DNS client is DNSSEC aware. The output looks similar to Figure 3-19.

```
PS C:\Users\Administrator> resolve-dnsname t1-412server2 -dnssecok

Name                                    Type   TTL   Section   IPAddress
----                                    ----   ---   -------   ---------
t1-412server2.T1-412Dom1.local          AAAA   3600  Answer    2001:db8:412:0:35c4:cda8:c285:9ead
t1-412server2.T1-412Dom1.local          A      3600  Answer    10.12.101.2

Name        : t1-412server2.T1-412Dom1.local
QueryType   : RRSIG
TTL         : 3600
Section     : Answer
TypeCovered : AAAA
Algorithm   : 8
LabelCount  : 3
OriginalTtl : 3600
Expiration  : 8/2/2014 6:32:41 PM
Signed      : 7/23/2014 5:32:41 PM
Signer      : t1-412dom1.local
Signature   : {48, 213, 147, 71...}
```

Figure 3-19   Output of the `Resolve-DnsName` cmdlet for testing DNSSEC

The `nslookup` command doesn't support DNSSEC.

Activity 3-8: Configuring DNSSEC

Time Required: 10 minutes
Objective: Configure DNSSEC.

Required Tools and Equipment: 412Server1
Description: In this activity, you configure DNSSEC and test it.

1. Log on to 412Server1 as **Administrator**, and open DNS Manager.

2. Click to expand **Forward Lookup Zones**, and click to select **412Dom1.local**. Then right-click **412Dom1.local**, point to **DNSSEC**, and click **Sign the Zone** to start the Zone Signing Wizard. In the welcome window, click **Next**.

3. In the Signing Options window, leave the default option **Customize zone signing parameters** selected. (Note that you aren't changing any default options, so you could select the "Use the default settings to sign the zone" option, but this way you can see the configurable options.) Click **Next**.

4. In the Key Master window, leave the default option that selects 412Server1 as the key master, and click **Next**.

5. In the Key Signing Key (KSK) window, read the information about the KSK, and then click **Next**. Click **Add**. In the New Key Signing Key (KSK) dialog box, accept the defaults, and click **OK**. Click **Next**.

6. In the Zone Signing Key (ZSK) window, read the information about the ZSK, and then click **Next**. Click **Add**. In the New Zone Signing Key (ZSK) dialog box, accept the defaults, and click **OK**. Click **Next**.

7. In the Next Secure (NSEC) window, accept the default option **Use NSEC3**, and then click **Next**.

8. In the Trust Anchors (TAs) window, accept the default **Enable automatic update of trust anchors on key rollover**, and then click **Next**.

9. In the Signing and Polling Parameters window, accept the default settings, and click **Next**. Review the selected options, and then click **Next** and **Finish**.

10. In DNS Manager, click the **Refresh** icon to see the RRSIG, DNSKEY, and NSEC3 resource records that were created.

11. Open a PowerShell prompt. Type `Resolve-DnsName 412server2` and press **Enter**. The output is what a client that's not DNSSEC aware sees. To get a secure reply, type `Resolve-DnsName 412server2 -dnssecok` and press **Enter**. You see the normal output followed by signature information. Close the PowerShell prompt.

12. Now you remove DNSSEC. In DNS Manager, right-click **412Dom1.local**, point to **DNSSEC**, and click **Unsign the Zone**. Click **Next** and then **Finish**. Click the **Refresh** icon in DNS Manager to see that the DNSSEC-related records are gone.

13. Stay logged on to 412Server1 if you're continuing to the next activity.

The DNS Socket Pool

The **DNS socket pool** is a pool of port numbers used by a DNS server for DNS queries. It protects against DNS cache poisoning by enabling a DNS server to randomize the source port when performing DNS queries. **DNS cache poisoning** is an attack on DNS servers in which false data is introduced into the DNS server cache, causing the server to return incorrect IP addresses. At best, this attack keeps clients from accessing requested network resources; at worst, clients are redirected to an attacker's server. By using a random source port chosen from the socket pool, an attacker must successfully guess the source port of a query issued by the server, along with a random transaction ID.

As you've learned, DNS uses recursive queries. A client issues a query for a network resource, such as the www.cengage.com host record. The DNS server first looks in its local zone database or cache. If the record can't be found, the DNS server queries other DNS servers until it finds a DNS server that's authoritative for the cengage.com zone. This is where DNS cache poisoning comes in. If an attacker knows that the DNS server has requested the record for www.cengage.com, it can issue its own response to the query first, providing false information. The DNS server caches the information for www.cengage.com, and the current client query and future queries are resolved to the IP address supplied by the attacker.

However, to issue a valid response, the attacker must know what port the DNS server used to issue the query. By default, DNS servers issue queries via UDP port 53. With that knowledge, an attacker can send the response, causing the DNS server to accept the response as though it came from the authoritative server. However, by randomizing the port, the attacker's job is much more difficult because he or she must guess which port number to use.

Configuring the DNS Socket Pool   By default, a socket pool is enabled on Windows Server 2008 R2 and higher servers, but you can configure the socket pool size and excluded port ranges with `dnscmd.exe`. By default, the socket pool size is 2500 port numbers, and you can increase this value up to 10,000. For example, to change the socket pool size to 5000, enter the following command:

```
dnscmd /config /socketpoolsize 5000
```

To exclude a range of ports from 100 to 500 from the socket pool, use the following command:

```
dnscmd /config /socketpoolexcludedportranges 100-500
```

DNS Cache Locking

DNS cache locking is a DNS security feature that allows you to control whether data in the DNS cache can be overwritten. When a DNS server receives a record as the result of a query to another DNS server, it caches the data. Each cached record has a time to live (TTL) value that tells the server when the record should be deleted from the cache, preventing cached data from becoming stale. Normally, if updated information about the cached record is received, the record can be overwritten. An attacker can falsify update information, causing cached data to be overwritten by the attacker's data, resulting in cache poisoning. Cache locking prevents any updates to a cached record until the TTL expires.

Configuring DNS Cache Locking   DNS cache locking is configured as a percentage of the TTL. For example, if the cache locking value is set to 50, the cached data can be overwritten when the TTL is 50% expired. If the cache locking value is 100, the data can never be overwritten. Starting with Windows Server 2008 R2, cache locking is enabled and set at 100% by default. To change the cache locking value, use `dnscmd.exe`. For example, to change the value so that records can be overwritten when the TTL is 75% expired, enter the following command:

```
dnscmd /config /cachelockingpercent 75
```

To see the current cache locking percent, replace `/config` with `/info` in the preceding command. This tip also applies to the DNS socket pool commands in the previous section.

Configuring Advanced DNS Options

As you have learned, DNS plays a vital role in almost all network transactions. This chapter wraps up the coverage of DNS by discussing some additional configuration options you might need in a DNS environment with multiple DNS servers at multiple locations, explaining how to configure DNS for single-label name resolution, and describing how to monitor your DNS server. Finally, you learn how to delegate some administrative tasks for maintaining a DNS environment.

Recursion

Recursive queries, used in DNS queries, were defined earlier in "The DNS Lookup Process." Typically, resolving DNS queries involves iterative queries to a root server first, then to a TLD server, and finally to an authoritative server for the domain name being resolved. However, a recursive query might involve a forwarder instead, in which the DNS server sends a recursive query to the forwarder. The forwarder resolves the query and responds to the DNS server or performs a recursive query starting with a root server.

Recursion is enabled on Windows DNS servers by default, but there are two ways to change this setting. The first involves configuring forwarders. When configuring a forwarder (see Figure 3-20), the "Use root hints if no forwarders are available" check box is selected by default. If this check box isn't selected, recursion is disabled, meaning that if no forwarders are available, the DNS server stops trying to resolve the query instead of trying to contact a root server.

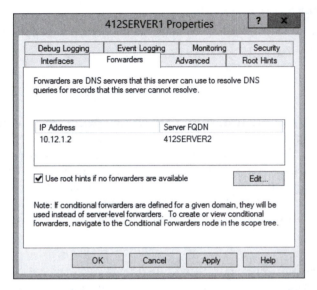

Figure 3-20 Enable or disable recursion when forwarders are used

The second is the "Disable recursion (also disables forwarders)" option in the Advanced tab of the DNS server's Properties dialog box (see Figure 3-21). If this check box is selected, the DNS server doesn't attempt to contact any other DNS servers, including forwarders, to resolve a query.

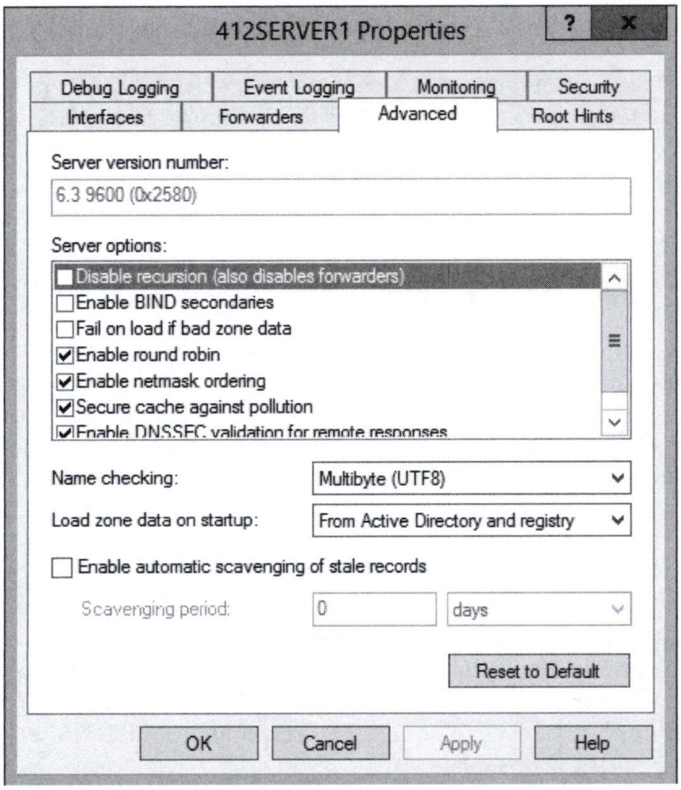

Figure 3-21 Configuring recursion on a DNS server

For example, you might want to disable recursion when you have a public DNS server containing resource records for your publicly available servers (Web, e-mail, and so forth). The public DNS server is necessary to resolve iterative requests from other DNS servers for your public domain, but you don't want unauthorized Internet users using your DNS server to field recursive client requests.

Netmask Ordering

When multiple DNS records exist for the same hostname but have different IP addresses, the DNS server returns an ordered list of the addresses in response to a DNS query for that hostname. In your studies of the objectives for Administering Windows Server 2012, Exam 70-411, you learned about round-robin DNS, where the list of IP addresses is returned in a different order for each query, which load-balances access to the target host.

Netmask ordering is a DNS feature that causes the DNS server to order the list of addresses so that addresses with a closer match to the client making the query are returned at the top of the list. For example, suppose you have a Web site being serviced by six servers. The A record entries in DNS for the servers are as follows:

```
www   172.31.1.200
www   172.31.2.200
www   172.31.3.200
www   172.31.3.201
www   172.16.10.200
www   172.16.11.200
```

If a client with address 172.31.3.10 queries the DNS server for the www host, the netmask ordering feature returns the list of addresses with 172.31.3.200 and 172.31.3.201 alternating between first and second in the list. Windows bases netmask ordering on the first three octets of the client by default. For example, if the client making the query has address 172.31.2.10, the host address 172.31.2.200 is always first in the list. However, if the client has address 172.31.5.10, all six addresses are returned in alternating order because the first three octets of 172.31.5.10 don't match the first three octets in any host addresses. In another example, if a client making the query has address 172.16.1.10, all six host addresses are again returned in alternating order.

This default behavior of netmask ordering might not be what you want. Because netmask ordering is based on the first three octets, it's assuming that the subnets in your network use a /24 or 255.255.255.0 subnet mask. If you're using a /16 or 255.255.0.0 subnet mask, the default behavior is not ideal. If your client with address 172.31.5.10 has a 255.255.0.0 subnet mask, you want the host addresses starting with 172.31 to be returned first in the order, with the 172.16 addresses always returned last. Fortunately, there's a way to change the default behavior by using the dnscmd.exe command. To see the current netmask DNS is using to prioritize the list of addresses, enter the following command:

```
dnscmd /info /localnetprioritynetmask
```

The output is similar to Figure 3-22. The value 255 (000000FF) is essentially the inverse of the subnet mask 255.255.255.0. This tells you that DNS is looking at the first three octets to determine whether there's a match.

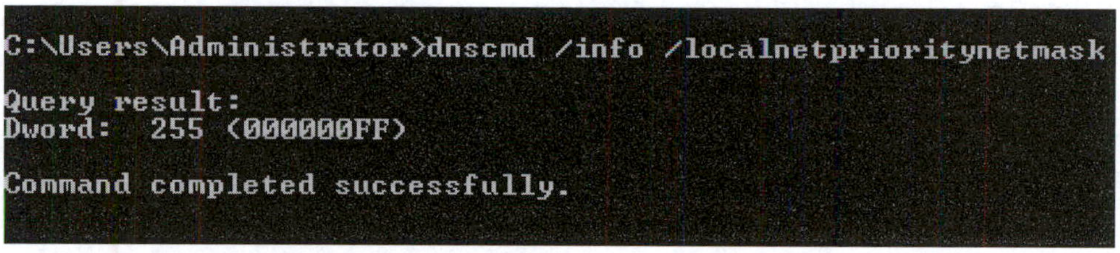

```
C:\Users\Administrator>dnscmd /info /localnetprioritynetmask

Query result:
Dword:   255 (000000FF)

Command completed successfully.
```

Figure 3-22   Viewing the current netmask setting

To change the netmask so that DNS looks only at the first two octets to determine a match, enter the following command:

```
dnscmd /config /localnetprioritynetmask 0x0000FFFF
```

Netmask ordering is enabled by default. You can disable it by clearing the check box in the DNS server's Properties dialog box (refer back to Figure 3-21) or at the command line with `dnscmd /config /localnetpriority 0`.

Netmask ordering doesn't appear to work with DNSSEC enabled on the zone. When DNSSEC is enabled, all records for the host are returned in round-robin fashion, regardless of the client's IP address or the `/localnetprioritynetmask` setting.

Activity 3-9: Configuring Netmask Ordering

Time Required: 10 minutes

Objective: Configure netmask ordering.

Required Tools and Equipment: 412Server1 and 412Win8

Description: In this activity, you create several A records in DNS with the same hostname and different IP addresses. Then you use `nslookup` to see how DNS returns the list of IP addresses, change the `localnetprioritynetmask` setting, and observe the difference in the ordering of the address list.

1. Log on to 412Server1 as **Administrator**, and open DNS Manager, if necessary. Start 412Win8 and log on, if necessary. On 412Win8, open a PowerShell prompt. Type **Set-DnsClientServerAddress -InterfaceAlias Ethernet -ServerAddresses ("10.12.1.1")** and press Enter to set the DNS server address for 412Win8.

2. Click to expand **Forward Lookup Zones**, if necessary. Click to select **412Dom1.local** and then right-click **412Dom1.local** and click **New Host (A or AAAA)**.

3. In the New Host dialog box, type **www** in the Name text box. Type **10.12.1.200** in the IP address text box. Click **Add Host**. Click **OK**. The New Host dialog stays open allowing you to add more hosts if desired.

4. Repeat Step 3 five more times, each time typing **www** in the Name text box and using the following IP addresses: **10.12.1.201, 10.12.20.1, 10.12.30.1, 172.16.2.200,** and **172.16.1.200**. When you're finished creating host records, click **Done** in the Add Host dialog box.

5. On 412Win8, open a command prompt window. Type **nslookup www.412dom1.local** and press **Enter**. You see the hostname and list of six IP addresses that `nslookup` displays. Addresses 10.12.1.200 and 10.12.1.201 are listed first and second (although not necessarily in that order, as 10.12.1.201 might be listed first).

6. Press the **up arrow** to repeat the command and press **Enter**. The list is displayed again with 10.12.1.200 and 10.12.1.201 listed first and second. Continue to press the **up arrow** and **Enter** several times to repeat the command. The addresses 10.12.1.200 and 10.12.1.201 should always be listed first and second.

7. On 412Server1 in DNS Manager, right-click **412Server1** (the server node) and click **Properties**. Click the **Advanced** tab. Click to clear **Enable netmask ordering**, and then click **Apply**. Leave this Properties dialog box open for Step 9.

8. On 412Win8, press the **up arrow** to repeat the `nslookup` command and press **Enter**. Repeat the command several times to see all six addresses rotated through the order, with each address eventually being listed first.

9. On 412Server1, in the Properties dialog box opened in Step 7, click **Enable netmask ordering**, and then click **OK**. Open a command prompt window. Type `dnscmd /config /localnetprioritynetmask 0x0000FFFF` and press **Enter** so that netmask ordering considers only the first two octets when ordering the list of IP addresses.

10. On 412Win8, press the **up arrow** to repeat the `nslookup` command and press **Enter**. Repeat the command several times. You should see that addresses 10.12.20.1 and 10.12.30.1 are sometimes listed first because they share the same first two octets with 412Win8. Close the command prompt window. Log off or shut down 412Win8.

11. On 412Server1, close the command prompt window and DNS Manager.

12. Stay logged on to 412Server1 if you're continuing to the next activity.

Using the GlobalNames Zone

The **GlobalNames zone (GNZ)** provides a way for IT administrators to add single-label names (computer names that don't use a domain suffix) to DNS, thereby allowing client computers to resolve these names without including a DNS suffix in the query. The GNZ feature is intended to help IT administrators migrate away from Windows Internet Name Service (WINS). The GNZ isn't a replacement for a dynamically created WINS database (which is also used to resolve single-label, or NetBIOS, names) because records in this zone must be added manually. For important servers with names currently being resolved by WINS, however, a GNZ is an option worth considering, especially if only a few hosts are the sole reason for maintaining WINS.

The GNZ feature isn't just a partial replacement for WINS, however. If your network supports mobile users whose laptops and other mobile devices are unlikely to have the correct DNS suffixes configured, GNZ can make access to servers these users need more convenient. Instead of mobile users having to remember resource FQDNs, they can simply access them by using a single-label name, such as Web1.

You must enable the GNZ feature on servers hosting this zone before you create a GNZ. Use the following command to enable GNZ at a PowerShell prompt:

`Set-DnsServerGlobalNameZone -Enable $true`

The GNZ can also be enabled with the following command:

`dnscmd /config /enableglobalnamessupport 1`

After GNZ support is enabled, you create a new zone that can be (but need not be) Active Directory integrated and named GlobalNames (not case sensitive). Dynamic updates should be disabled because GNZ doesn't support DDNS. For each host to be accessed with a single-label name, create a CNAME record in the GNZ that references the host's A record. You must enable GNZ support on each server the zone is replicated to.

DNS Monitoring

To maintain a healthy network, you need a healthy domain name system. A number of tools are available to monitor and debug DNS. The following sections cover DNS events and debug logging along with a new feature in Windows Server 2012 R2 called "zone level statistics."

Event and Debug Logging   When DNS is installed, a new event log is created to record informational, error, and warning events generated by the DNS server. You can configure which event types should be logged in the Event Logging tab of the server's Properties dialog box (shown in Figure 3-23). Events you're likely to find in the DNS Server log include zone serial number (referred to as "version number" in the DNS Server log) changes, zone transfer requests, and DNS server startup and shutdown events. The event log can help you diagnose problems, such as when an error causes the server to stop or keeps it from starting or when communication between servers for replication or zone transfers has failed. When DNS problems are evident and can't be traced easily to misconfiguration, the event log is the first place to look.

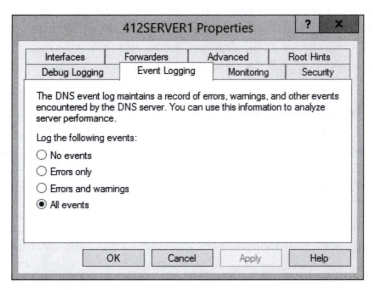

Figure 3-23 Configuring event logging

When serious DNS debugging is warranted, you can enable debug logging in the server's Properties dialog box. Debug logging records selected packets coming from and going to the DNS server in a text file. Figure 3-24 shows the packet-capturing options for debug logging.

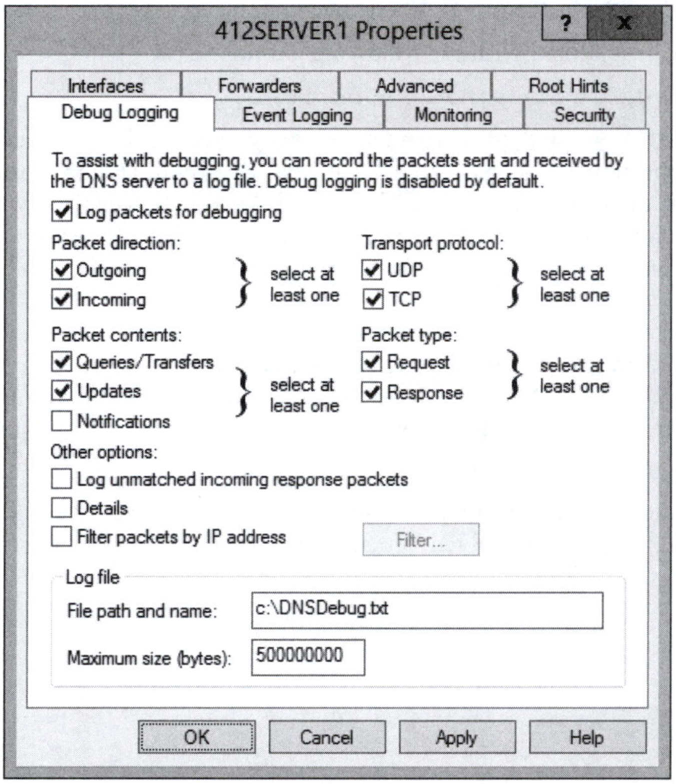

Figure 3-24 The Debug Logging tab

Figure 3-25 shows a sample of debug logging output. The first part of the file is a key to help you interpret the captured data. Each line of the file starting with date and time is a summary of a captured packet. If necessary, you can enable logging of detailed packet contents. The information from debug logging can help you solve problems related to "Web page not found" errors, zone transfer problems, redirect errors, and other DNS operational errors that aren't easy to find by examining the DNS configuration and event logs alone.

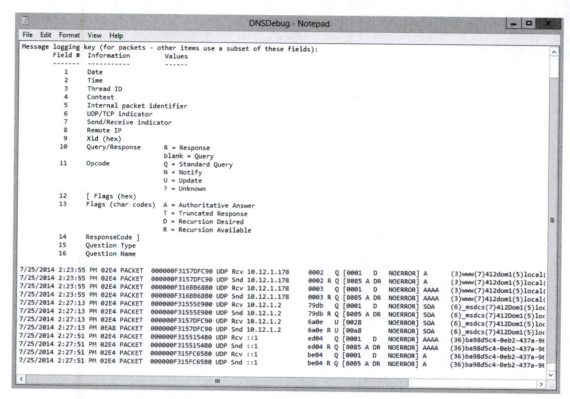

Figure 3-25 Debug logging output

Analyzing DNS Zone Level Statistics

Analyzing DNS Zone Level Statistics A new feature in Windows Server 2012 R2 called **zone level statistics** provides a detailed look at how a DNS server is used. The following types of statistics are available for each authoritative zone on a DNS server:

- *Zone queries*—Show queries received and responded to successfully as well as query failures.

- *Zone transfers*—Show zone transfers between primary and secondary zone servers. If a zone is Active Directory integrated, no information is shown.

- *Zone updates*—Show how many dynamic updates the server received and rejected.

You can view zone level statistics with the PowerShell cmdlet Get-DnsServerStatistics. Statistics are returned as a list that can be stored in a variable. The data can then be retrieved based on the category of statistic you want to examine. The following PowerShell commands show how to access zone level statistics. To store zone level statistics for the 412Dom1.local zone in a variable named $zonestatistics, enter the following command:

```
$zonestatistics = Get-DnsServerStatistics -ZoneName 412Dom1.local
```

To retrieve zone query statistics and display them onscreen, enter this command:

```
$zonestatistics.ZoneQueryStatistics
```

To retrieve zone transfer statistics and display them onscreen, use this command:

`$zonestatistics.ZoneTransferStatistics`

To retrieve zone update statistics and display them onscreen, enter this command:

`$zonestatistics.ZoneUpdateStatistics`

Activity 3-10: Displaying DNS Zone Level Statistics

Time Required: 10 minutes
Objective: Display DNS zone level statistics.

Required Tools and Equipment: 412Server1
Description: In this activity, you use the `Get-DnsServerStatistics` PowerShell cmdlet to display DNS statistics.

1. Log on to 412Server1 as **Administrator**, and open a PowerShell prompt.

2. Type **$zonestatistics = Get-DnsServerStatistics -ZoneName 412Dom1. local** and press **Enter**.

3. Type **$zonestatistics.ZoneQueryStatistics** and press **Enter**. You see a list of statistics for queries received and sent by the DNS server.

4. Type **$zonestatistics.ZoneTransferStatistics** and press **Enter**. Because this zone is Active Directory integrated and this statistic shows information only for zone transfers between primary and secondary zones, all the statistics are 0.

5. Type **$zonestatistics.ZoneUpdateStatistics** and press **Enter**. You see a list of statistics for dynamic updates the server has received and rejected.

6. Close the PowerShell prompt, and log off or shut down the server.

Delegated Administration

In a large network, there might be several zones, both Active Directory–integrated and standard zones, and dozens of DNS servers. As you have learned, there's a lot to keep up with to make sure DNS is running well on your network. Members of the Domain Admins or Enterprise Admins group have full access to manage the DNS service, but you might want to delegate DNS administration to an employee without allowing the broader domain administrative rights these groups afford. To that end, the DnsAdmins group in Active Directory enables its members to manage the DNS server without giving them broader administrative rights. The DnsAdmins group has Read, Write, Create all child objects, and Delete all child objects permissions on the DNS server and DNS zones, and it has Read and Write permission on DNS resource records. DnsAdmins is a domain local group and has no members by default. If you want users to have this group's rights and permissions, you should follow best practices by creating a global group, adding user accounts to it, and adding the global group to the DnsAdmins group.

Chapter Summary

- Dynamic Host Configuration Protocol (DHCP) is a component of the TCP/IP protocol suite, which is used to assign an IP address to a host automatically from a defined pool of addresses. IP addresses assigned via DHCP are usually leased, not permanently assigned.

- A DHCP scope is a pool of IP addresses and other IP configuration parameters that a DHCP server uses to lease addresses to DHCP clients. It contains a continuous range of IP addresses leased to DHCP clients. You might want to exclude certain addresses or a range of addresses from the scope for use in static address assignments.

- A superscope is a special type of scope consisting of one or more member scopes that allows a DHCP server to service multiple IPv4 subnets on a single physical network. It directs the DHCP server to draw addresses from both scopes, even though it has only a single interface configured for one of the IP subnets.

- An IPv4 multicast packet is a network packet addressed to a group of hosts listening on a particular multicast IP address. Multicast DHCP scopes allow assigning multicast addresses dynamically to multicast servers and clients by using Multicast Address Dynamic Client Allocation Protocol (MADCAP).

- DHCPv6 enables you to manage IPv6 address assignment, see which addresses are being used on the network, and control IPv6 address options. You configure a DHCPv6 scope in the DHCP console or with the `Add-DhcpServerV6Scope` PowerShell cmdlet.

- DHCPv6 uses a DHCP Unique Identifier (DUID) to lease an address and create reservations. A DUID in Windows is a hexadecimal number, usually derived from the network interface's MAC address.

- Microsoft has several ways to achieve high availability for DHCP: split scopes, DHCP failover, DHCP server cluster, and hot standby. A split scope is a fault-tolerant DHCP configuration in which two DHCP servers share the same scope information, allowing both servers to offer DHCP services to clients.

- DHCP failover, a new feature in Windows Server 2012, allows two DHCP servers to share the pool of addresses in a scope, giving both servers access to all addresses in the pool. There are two modes for DHCP failover: load balancing mode and hot standby mode.

- A DHCP server can work with DNS to provide name resolution on the behalf of DHCP clients. Configure DNS registration in the DNS tab of the Properties dialog box of the IPv4 or IPv6 server nodes or in the Properties dialog box of a scope.

- DNS is a critical network service in most networks because it provides name-to-address resolution, and a Windows domain network depends on DNS for name resolution and resolving client requests for Active Directory services.

- DNS is a common target of attacks because it figures so prominently in most network transactions. The types of attacks on DNS include spoofing, DNS cache poisoning, denial of service, domain registration hijacking, and man-in-the-middle attacks, to name a few.

- Domain Name System Security Extension (DNSSEC) is a suite of features and protocols for validating DNS server responses. It gives DNS clients several methods to ensure that data they receive from DNS queries is accurate and secure.

- A DNS socket pool is a pool of port numbers used by a DNS server for DNS queries. It protects against DNS cache poisoning by enabling a DNS server to randomize the source port when performing DNS queries.

- DNS cache locking is a DNS security feature that allows controlling whether data in the DNS cache can be overwritten. It's configured as a percentage of TTL. For example, if the cache locking value is set to 50, the cached data can be overwritten when the TTL is 50% expired.

- Recursion is enabled on Windows DNS servers by default, but it can be disabled. You might want to disable recursion when you have a public DNS server containing resource records for your publicly available servers

- Netmask ordering causes the DNS server to order the list of IP addresses so that the ones with a closer address match to the client making the query are returned at the top of the list.

- The GlobalNames zone (GNZ) gives IT administrators a way to add single-label names to DNS, thereby allowing client computers to resolve these names without including a DNS suffix in the query.

- A number of tools are available to monitor and debug DNS, including DNS events and debug logging. Debug logging records selected packets coming from and going to the DNS server in a text file.

- A new feature in Windows Server 2012 R2 called zone level statistics provides a detailed look at how a DNS server is used.

- You can delegate DNS administration to an employee without allowing broader domain administrative rights. The DnsAdmins group in Active Directory enables its members to manage the DNS server without giving them broader administrative rights.

Key Terms

Delegation Signer (DS)   A DNSSEC record that holds the name of a delegated zone and is used to verify delegated child zones. *See also* Domain Name System Security Extension (DNSSEC).

DHCP failover   A new feature in Windows Server 2012 that allows two DHCP servers to share the pool of addresses in a scope, giving both servers access to all addresses in the pool.

DHCP name protection   A feature in DHCP that prevents name squatting by non-Windows computers by using a DHCP resource record called Dynamic Host Configuration Identifier (DHCID). *See also* name squatting.

DHCP Unique Identifier (DUID)   A hexadecimal number, usually derived from the MAC address of the network interface used by DHCPv6 to identify clients for address leases and to create reservations.

DNS cache locking   A DNS security feature that allows you to control whether data in the DNS cache can be overwritten.

DNS cache poisoning   An attack on DNS servers in which false data is introduced into the DNS server cache, causing the server to return incorrect IP addresses.

DNS socket pool   A pool of port numbers used by a DNS server for DNS queries to protect against DNS cache poisoning. *See also* DNS cache poisoning.

DNSKEY   The public key for the zone that DNS resolvers use to verify the digital signature contained in Resource Record Signature (RRSIG) records.

Domain Name System Security Extension (DNSSEC)   A suite of features and protocols for validating DNS server responses.

Dynamic Host Configuration Protocol (DHCP)   A component of the TCP/IP protocol suite used to assign an IP address to a host automatically from a defined pool of addresses.

GlobalNames zone (GNZ)   A DNS feature that gives IT administrators a way to add single-label names to DNS, thereby allowing client computers to resolve these names without including a DNS suffix in the query.

hot standby mode   A DHCP failover mode in which one server is assigned as the active server to provide DHCP services to clients, and the other server is placed in standby mode. *See also* DHCP failover.

iterative query   A DNS query in which the server responds with the best information it currently has in its local database to satisfy the query.

key-signing key (KSK)   A DNSSEC key that has a private and public key associated with it. The private key is used to sign all DNSKEY records, and the public key is used as a trust anchor for validating DNS responses. *See also* Domain Name System Security Extension (DNSSEC).

load balancing mode   The default DHCP failover mode in which both DHCP servers participate in address leasing at the same time from a shared pool of addresses. *See also* DHCP failover.

multicast scope   A type of DHCP scope that allows assigning multicast addresses dynamically to multicast servers and clients by using Multicast Address Dynamic Client Allocation Protocol (MADCAP).

name squatting   A DNS problem that occurs when a non-Windows computer registers its name with a DNS server, but the name has already been registered by a Windows computer.

netmask ordering   A DNS feature that causes the DNS server to order the list of addresses so that the ones with a closer address match to the client making the query are returned at the top of the list.

Next Secure (NSEC)   A DNSSEC record that is returned when the requested resource record does not exist. *See also* Domain Name System Security Extension (DNSSEC).

Next Secure 3 (NSEC3)   An alternative to NSEC records. They can prevent zone-walking, which is a technique of repeating NSEC queries to get all the names in a zone. *See also* Next Secure (NSEC).

Next Secure 3 (NSEC3) Parameter   DNSSEC records used to determine which NSEC3 records should be included in responses to queries for nonexistent records. *See also* Next Secure 3 (NSEC3).

preference   A value used to indicate priority when there are multiple DHCPv6 servers.

prefix   The part of the IPv6 address that's the network identifier.

recursive query   A DNS query in which the server is instructed to process the query until it responds with an address that satisfies the query or with an "I don't know" message.

Resource Record Signature (RRSIG)   A key containing the signature for a single resource record, such as an A or MX record.

scope   A pool of IP addresses and other IP configuration parameters that a DHCP server uses to lease addresses to DHCP clients.

split scope   A fault-tolerant DHCP configuration in which two DHCP servers share the same scope information, allowing both servers to offer DHCP services to clients.

stateful autoconfiguration   A method of IPv6 autoconfiguration in which the node uses an autoconfiguration protocol, such as DHCPv6, to obtain its IPv6 address and other configuration information.

stateless autoconfiguration   A method of IPv6 autoconfiguration in which the node listens for router advertisement messages from a local router.

superscope   A special type of scope consisting of one or more member scopes that allows a DHCP server to service multiple IPv4 subnets on a single physical network.

trust anchor   In public key cryptography, it's usually the DNSKEY record for a zone.

zone level statistics   A new feature in Windows Server 2012 R2 that provides detailed statistics for each zone to show how a DNS server is used.

zone signing   A DNSSEC feature that uses digital signatures contained in DNSSEC-related resource records to verify DNS responses. *See also* Domain Name System Security Extension (DNSSEC).

zone-signing key (ZSK)   A public and private key combination stored in a certificate used to sign the zone.

Review Questions

1. Which of the following is true about the DHCP protocol? (Choose all that apply.)
   a. There are eight message types.
   b. DHCPDISCOVER messages sent by clients traverse routers.
   c. It uses the UDP Transport-layer protocol.
   d. An initial address lease involves three packets.

2. After you install the DHCP Server role on a member server, what must you do before the server can begin providing DHCP services?
   a. Configure options.
   b. Activate the server.
   c. Authorize the server.
   d. Create a filter.

3. Which of the following is a required element of a DHCP scope? (Choose all that apply.)

    a. Subnet mask

    b. Scope name

    c. Router address

    d. Lease duration

4. What's the default lease duration on a Windows DHCP server?

    a. 8 hours

    b. 16 minutes

    c. 8 days

    d. 16 hours

5. What should you define in a scope to prevent the DHCP server from leasing addresses that are already assigned to devices statically?

    a. Reservation scope

    b. Exclusion range

    c. Deny filters

    d. DHCP policy

6. You have four printers that are accessed via their IP addresses. You want to be able to use DHCP to assign addresses to the printers, but you want to make sure they always have the same address. What's the best option?

    a. Create reservations.

    b. Create exclusions.

    c. Configure filters.

    d. Configure policies.

7. You want high availability for DHCP services, a primary server to handle most DHCP requests, and a secondary server to respond to client requests only if the primary server fails to in about a second. The primary server has about 85% of the IP addresses to lease, leaving the secondary server with about 15%. You don't want the servers to replicate with each other. What should you configure?

    a. Multicast scope

    b. Failover

    c. Superscope

    d. Split scope

8. A subnet on your network uses DHCP for address assignment. The current scope has the start address 192.168.1.1 and the end address 192.168.1.200 with the subnet mask 255.255.255.0. Because of network expansion, you have added computers, bringing the total number that needs DHCP for address assignment to 300. You don't want to change the IP addressing scheme or the subnet mask for computers already on the network. What should you do?

    a. Create a new scope with the start address 192.168.2.1 and the end address 192.168.2.200 with the prefix length 24, and add the existing scope and new scope to a superscope.

    b. Add a scope with the start address 192.168.1.1 and the end address 192.168.2.200 with the subnet mask 255.255.255.0. Then delete the existing scope.

    c. Create a new scope with the start address 192.168.1.1, the end address 192.168.2.200, and the prefix length 16.

    d. Add another DHCP server. Using the split scope wizard, split the existing scope with the new server and assign each server 100% of the addresses.

9. Some of your non-Windows clients aren't registering their hostnames with the DNS server. You don't require secure updates on the DNS server. What option should you configure on the DHCP server so that non-Windows clients names are registered?

   a. Update DNS records dynamically only if requested by the DHCP clients.

   b. Always dynamically update DNS records.

   c. Update DNS records dynamically for DHCP clients that don't request updates.

   d. Configure name protection.

10. Which of the following listens for broadcast DHCPDISCOVER and DHCPREQUEST messages and forwards them to a DHCP server on another subnet?

    a. Superscope

    b. Multicast scope

    c. DHCPv6 server

    d. Relay agent

11. What should you create if you need to service multiple IPv4 subnets on a single physical network?

    a. Split scope

    b. Relay agent

    c. Superscope

    d. Multicast server

12. What do you configure if you need to assign addresses dynamically to applications or services that need a class D IP address?

    a. IPv6 relay

    b. Multicast scope

    c. Dynamic scope

    d. Autoconfiguration

13. What type of address begins with `fe80`?

    a. APIPA address

    b. Global address

    c. Link-local address

    d. EUID address

14. What type of IPv6 address configuration uses DHCPv6?

    a. Unicast allocation

    b. Stateless autoconfiguration

    c. Dynamic allocation

    d. Stateful autoconfiguration

15. Which of the following is *not* part of a DHCPv6 scope configuration?

    a. Default gateway

    b. Prefix

    c. Preference

    d. Scope lease

16. Which of the following is a DHCP high-availability option that includes hot standby mode?

    a. Load balancing

    b. Superscopes

    c. DHCP split scope

    d. DHCP failover

17. When a DNS server responds to a query with a list of name servers, what is the response called?

    a. Iterative

    b. Recursive

    c. Referral

    d. Resolver

18. Which type of DNS query instructs the DNS server to process the query until it responds with an address that satisfies the query or with an "I don't know" message?

    a. Iterative

    b. Recursive

    c. Referral

    d. Resolver

19. Which of the following uses digital signatures contained in DNSSEC-related resource records to verify DNS responses?

    a. Zone signing

    b. Data integrity

    c. Socket pool

    d. Cache locking

20. Which of the following protects against DNS cache poisoning by enabling a DNS server to randomize the source port when performing DNS queries?

    a. Zone signing

    b. Data integrity

    c. Socket pool

    d. Cache locking

21. Which security feature should you use if you want to prevent DNS records retrieved from other DNS servers from being overwritten until the TTL is at least 75% expired?

    a. Cache locking

    b. TTL expiration

    c. Record overwrite

    d. Socket prevention

22. If you disable the option to use root hints when no forwarders are available, what are you doing?

    a. Enabling the socket pool

    b. Locking the cache

    c. Disabling recursion

    d. Configuring the netmask

23. You have four Web servers, all with the same name for load balancing. Your client computers are using a Web server in a remote subnet, even though there's a Web server in their local subnet. What should you do to ensure that client computers use the Web server in their local subnet whenever possible?

    a. Configure netmask ordering.

    b. Create a GlobalNames zone.

    c. Disable recursion.

    d. Configure zone delegation.

24. You want client computers from all domains in your network to be able to access a server named CorpDocs without having to know which domain the server is in. What can you configure in DNS to make this happen?

    a. Netmask inclusion

    b. Recursive queries

    c. DNS suffix ordering

    d. GlobalNames zone

25. You want to give a junior administrator access to DNS servers so that he can configure zones and resource records, but you don't want to give him broader administrative rights in the domain. What should you do?

    a. Make his account a member of DnsAdmins.

    b. Add his account to the Administrators group on all DNS servers.

    c. Delegate control for the OU where the DNS computer accounts are.

    d. Add his account to the Administer DNS Servers policy.

Case Projects

Case Project 3-1: Using IPv6 Autoconfiguration

You're beginning to use IPv6 in your network and want your client computers to use stateful autoconfiguration for IPv6 address assignments. You have five servers, a router, and two printers that will have static IPv6 addresses with the prefix 2001:db8:100::. You might have as many as 20 devices with static addresses, and you also want to ensure fault tolerance. Explain how you will achieve goals. What features and options should you consider when setting up the necessary services?

Case Project 3-2: Setting Up DNS Security

Your DNS servers have been hacked, and you've been asked to set up DNS security measures. Your supervisor wants to know the options for preventing attackers from tampering with your DNS servers. Write a memo to your supervisor discussing DNSSEC, a DNS socket pool, and DNS cache locking and how they can help secure DNS.

chapter 4

Configuring Advanced File and Storage Solutions

After reading this chapter and completing the exercises, you will be able to:

- Configure advanced file service solutions
- Configure advanced file storage solutions

Convenient and secure access to files and storage for files are driving forces in developing innovations in server operating systems. Whether you're trying to make shared files more convenient for branch offices and users of Linux/UNIX, trying to organize and audit sensitive data, or better manage server storage, the quest for improvements in file and storage management continues. This chapter begins by describing four features in Windows Server 2012/R2 that can help you perform file service tasks: BranchCache, File Classification Infrastructure, file auditing, and Services for NFS. The second half of the chapter describes solutions for managing organizations' ever-increasing storage requirements: iSCSI SAN, thin provisioning, tiered storage, and Features on Demand.

Configuring Advanced File Services

Table 4-1 lists what you need for the hands-on activities in this chapter.

Table 4-1   **Activity requirements**

Activity	Requirements	Notes
Activity 4-1: Configuring BranchCache on a File Server	412Server1	
Activity 4-2: Configuring BranchCache on a Client	412Server1, 412Win8	
Activity 4-3: Installing the File Server Resource Manager Role Service	412Server1	
Activity 4-4: Classifying Files with FCI	412Server1	
Activity 4-5: Auditing Folder Access	412Server1	
Activity 4-6: Configuring Global Object Access Auditing	412Server1	
Activity 4-7: Installing the iSCSI Target Server Role Service	412Server1	
Activity 4-8: Creating an iSCSI Virtual Disk	412Server1, 412Server2	
Activity 4-9: Configuring an iSCSI Initiator	412Server1, 412Server2	

© 2016 Cengage Learning®

Being able to share files was one of the factors that compelled businesses to begin networking computers. You have learned about creating file shares with a single server and using Distributed File System (DFS) to provide fault tolerance and load balancing. This chapter focuses on some advanced file service topics that go beyond basic file sharing, including the following:

- *BranchCache*—Optimizing file sharing across WAN links
- *File Classification Infrastructure*—Organizing sensitive data
- *File auditing*—Configuring policies to audit access and track changes to files
- *Network File System*—Sharing files with Linux/UNIX-based systems

BranchCache

Sharing files across a WAN link can be slow and sometimes expensive. Organizations with branch offices can solve some problems of sharing files across WAN links by placing traditional file servers in branch offices and using file replication to synchronize files between branch offices and the main office. However, this solution requires servers and someone to maintain servers and file shares, which isn't always practical or economical. **BranchCache** is a file-sharing technology that allows computers at a branch office to cache files retrieved from a central server across a WAN link. When a computer in the branch office requests a file for the first time, it's retrieved from the a server in the main office and then cached locally. When a subsequent request for the file is made, only information about the file is transferred, not actual file contents. This **content information** indicates to the client where the file can be retrieved from the cache in the branch office. The content information that's transferred is very small compared with the original file contents and can also be used by clients to secure cached information so that it can be accessed only by authorized users.

BranchCache supports content stored on Windows Server 2008 R2 and later servers running the following roles and protocols:

- *File Server role*—A file server sharing files by using the Server Message Block (SMB) protocol
- *Web Server (IIS) role*—A Web server using the HTTP or HTTPS protocol
- *Background Intelligent Transfer Service (BITS) feature*—An application server running on a Windows server with BITS installed

BranchCache has two modes of operation, so you can configure it depending on the resources available at a branch office:

- *Distributed*—With **distributed cache mode,** cached data is distributed among client computers in the branch office. Client computers must be running Windows 7 or later.
- *Hosted*—With **hosted cache mode,** cached data is stored on one or more file servers in the branch office. Servers operating in this mode must be running Windows Server 2008 R2 or later, and clients must be running Windows 7 or later.

If you have more than one branch office, you can choose the mode for each office, but only one can be used at each branch office. Figure 4-1 shows a central office with a connection to two branch offices using different BranchCache modes. In the figure, Branch office1 uses hosted cache mode, in which client PCs access a central BranchCache server to retrieve cached

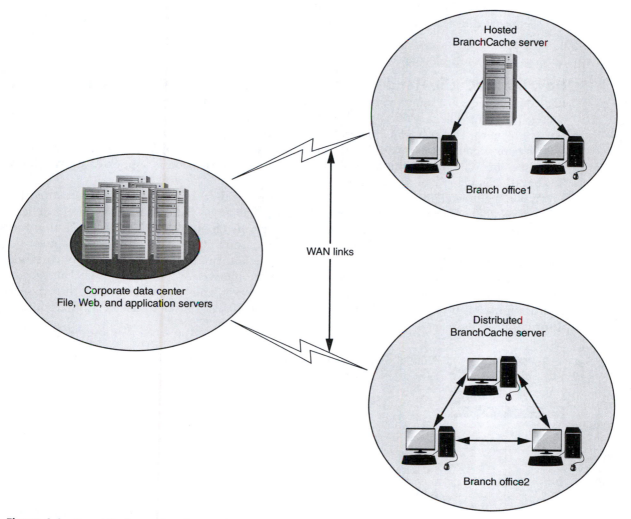

Figure 4-1   BranchCache modes of operation
© 2016 Cengage Learning®

files. Branch office2 uses distributed cache mode, in which cached files are distributed among all client computers, which retrieve the files from one another. In this case, the content information retrieved from servers in the main office specifies which computer hosts a requested file.

Benefits of Distributed Cache Mode   Distributed cache mode is the best solution for small branch offices when having a dedicated server is neither practical nor desirable. Servers require more expertise to maintain and secure and have a higher cost than client computers. No extra equipment and no additional resources or personnel for server maintenance are necessary when using BranchCache in distributed cache mode.

Benefits of Hosted Cache Mode   Hosted cache mode is best for branch offices that already have servers performing other functions, such as a domain controller or a DHCP server. Using hosted cache mode has the following advantages over distributed cache mode:

- *Increased availability of cached files*—In distributed cache mode, if the client that cached the file is turned off, the file is unavailable to other clients. With hosted cache mode, all cached files are stored on servers, which are rarely turned off.

- *Support for multiple subnets*—A larger branch office might have more than one IP subnet. Distributed cache mode works only in a single subnet, so files cached by computers on one subnet aren't available to computers on another subnet. Hosted cached mode works across subnets, so files cached by a server on one subnet are available to client computers on all subnets. You can also deploy multiple servers operating in hosted cache mode, and clients are directed to the server hosting the requested file, even if it's on a different subnet from the client.

How BranchCache Handles Changes to Cached Files   When a change is made to a cached file, clients accessing the file after the change has occurred must have a way to access the changed content. The fact that a file has changed is reflected in the content information clients retrieve from the server hosting the original file. There are two versions of the content information. Version 1 content information is the original version supported by Windows Server 2008 R2 and later and Windows 7 and later. Version 2 content information is supported by Windows Server 2012 and later and Windows 8 and later.

When a file is changed, some or all of it must be retrieved from the server hosting the original content. With version 1 content information, changes made to a file require the client to retrieve the entire file, starting with the part that changed. With version 2, only the changed part of the file must be retrieved, saving bandwidth because fewer bytes must be transferred across the WAN link. Version 2 content information can be used only when all devices involved in BranchCache support version 2; otherwise, version 1 is used. This means the client requesting the file, the local hosted cache server, and the server hosting the original content must all be Windows 8 or Windows Server 2012 or later to use version 2 content information.

With distributed cache mode, clients using different content information versions can't share cached files with each other.

Installing and Configuring BranchCache

The procedure to install and configure BranchCache depends on the type of content you want to cache and whether you're using hosted or distributed cache mode, as shown in Table 4-2.

Table 4-2 BranchCache installation

Content type	Installed on content server	Hosted cache mode	Distributed cache mode
File server using the SMB protocol	BranchCache for Network Files role service	BranchCache feature on hosting server	Enable BranchCache on client
Web server using HTTP or HTTPS	BranchCache feature	BranchCache feature on hosting server	Enable BranchCache on client
Application server using BITS	BranchCache feature	BranchCache feature on hosting server	Enable BranchCache on client

© 2016 Cengage Learning®

 **NOTE**   In all cases, BranchCache must be enabled on client computers, whether you're using hosted or distributed cache mode. After you enable BranchCache, you select the cache mode you want the client to use. If no mode is selected, the client uses only locally cached files. BranchCache is supported only in Windows 7 Ultimate and Enterprise editions and Windows 8/8.1 Enterprise editions.

Installing BranchCache on a File Server   To install BranchCache to cache files in shared folders, take the following steps:

1. Install the File Server role and the BranchCache for Network Files role service, as shown in Figure 4-2, on all servers that will host shared folders by using BranchCache.

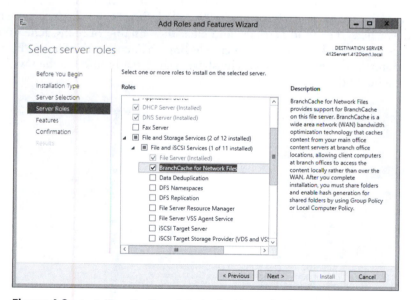

Figure 4-2   Installing the BranchCache for Network Files role service

2. Configure the Hash Publication for BranchCache group policy (see Figure 4-3), located under Computer Configuration, Policies, Administrative Templates, Network, Lanman Server. In most cases, you should place the computer accounts for servers using BranchCache for shared folders in a separate OU in Active Directory and link a GPO with this policy configured to this OU.

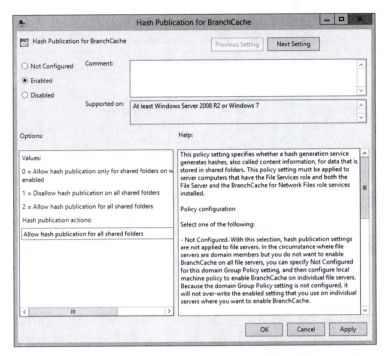

Figure 4-3   Configuring the Hash Publication for BranchCache policy

3. Set the BranchCache support tag on each shared folder that should be cached. Click File and Storage Services in Server Manager and click Shares. Right-click the share and click Properties. Click to expand Settings, and click the "Enable BranchCache on the file share" option (see Figure 4-4). You can also enable BranchCache in the Shared Folders snap-in in the Computer Management MMC. The share is now ready to be cached with hosted or distributed cache mode.

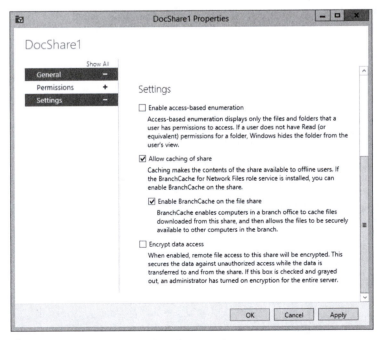

Figure 4-4   Enabling BranchCache on a share

Activity 4-1: Configuring BranchCache on a File Server

Time Required: 15 minutes
Objective: Install and authorize a DHCP server.

Required Tools and Equipment: 412Server1
Description: In this activity, you configure BranchCache on a file server and enable it on a share.

1. Start 412Server1, and log on as **Administrator,** if necessary.

2. In Server Manager, click **Manage, Add Roles and Features.** Click **Next** until you get to the Server Roles window. Click to expand **File and Storage Services** and **File and iSCSI Services.** The File Server role is already installed because the domain controller has the Netlogon and SYSVOL shares. Click to select **BranchCache for Network Files,** and then click **Next** twice.

3. Click **Install,** and then click **Close** after the installation is finished.

4. In Server Manager, click **Tools, Group Policy Management** from the menu. Right-click the **Domain Controllers** OU and click **Create a GPO in this domain, and Link it here.**

5. In the New GPO dialog box, type **BranchCache Server** in the Name text box, and click **OK.**

6. Click the **Domain Controllers** OU, if necessary, and in the right pane, right-click the **BranchCache Server** GPO and click **Edit.** In the Group Policy Management Editor, navigate to **Computer Configuration, Policies, Administrative Templates, Network, Lanman Server.**

7. In the right pane, double-click **Hash Publication for BranchCache.** Click the **Enabled** option button, and accept the default option **Allow hash publication for all shared folders.** Click **OK.** Close the Group Policy Management Editor and Group Policy Management console.

8. Create a share named **DocShare1** on the C drive of 412Server1. You can use the default settings.

9. In Server Manager, click **File and Storage Services** in the left pane, and then click **Shares.** (You might have to refresh the view.) Right-click **DocShare1** and click **Properties.** Click to expand **Settings.** Click the **Enable BranchCache on the file share** check box, and then click **OK.** Click the back arrow in Server Manager twice to return to the Dashboard. BranchCache is now enabled on the server.

10. Stay logged on to 412Server1 if you're continuing to the next activity.

Installing BranchCache on a Web Server or an Application Server To install BranchCache on a Web server or an application server, you just need to install the BranchCache feature in Add Roles and Features or use the PowerShell cmdlet `Install-WindowsFeature BranchCache`. The Web Server role or an application using BITS takes advantage of the BranchCache service automatically, so no additional configuration on the content server is needed.

Configuring a Server for Hosted Cache Mode If you're using BranchCache in hosted cache mode, you need to configure a server running Windows Server 2008 R2 or later. The hosted cache server must be trusted by BranchCache clients, so part of the process involves installing a certificate on the server that's trusted by the BranchCache client computers. This requires issuing a certificate from a Windows server configured as a certification authority (CA) or installing a certificate issued by a third-party CA. The details of working with a CA and issuing a certificate are beyond the scope of this chapter, but Chapter 10 discusses Active Directory Certificate Services in detail. The following steps outline the process for installing a hosted cache server:

1. Install the BranchCache feature by using Add Roles and Features or the PowerShell cmdlet `Install-WindowsFeature BranchCache`.

2. Import a certificate that's trusted by the branch office client computers.

3. Link the certificate to BranchCache with the `netsh HTTP ADD SSLCERT` command.

4. Configure BranchCache clients to use BranchCache in hosted cache mode.

Configuring Clients to Use BranchCache The BranchCache client feature is built into Windows client OSs that support BranchCache, so no installation is needed. Enabling client computers to use BranchCache is a simple three-step process:

1. To enable BranchCache with a group policy, open a GPO linked to the OU where the branch office computer accounts are located. Navigate to Computer Configuration, Policies, Administrative Templates, Network, BranchCache, and then double-click the Turn on BranchCache policy. Click the Enabled option button (see Figure 4-5).

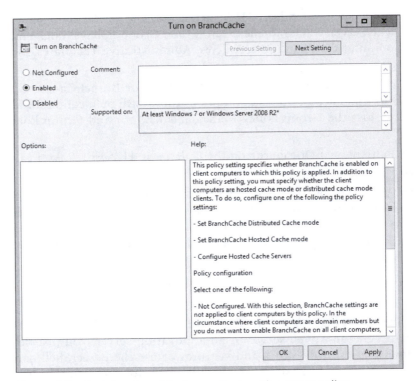

Figure 4-5   Enabling BranchCache on clients with a group policy

2. To configure BranchCache clients to use BranchCache in hosted cache mode, open the GPO you used in Step 1 and navigate to the same location. Double-click Set BranchCache Hosted Cache mode, and click the Enabled option button. Type the name of the hosted cache server under Options, as shown in Figure 4-6. The name must match the name on the certificate installed on the hosted cache server. If you're using distributed cache mode, enable the Set BranchCache Distributed Cache mode policy instead.

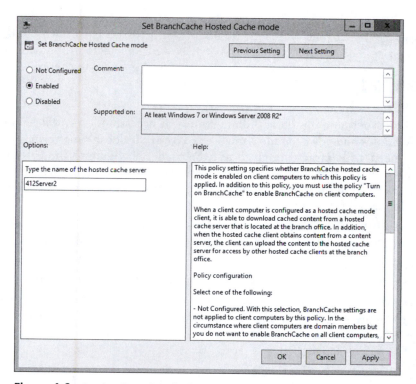

Figure 4-6   Setting BranchCache hosted cache mode on clients with a group policy

3. To configure Windows Firewall on client computers, use a group policy or the Windows Firewall with Advanced Security console to configure inbound rules that allow the following predefined rules:

   o BranchCache - Content Retrieval (uses HTTP)

   o BranchCache - Hosted Cache Server (uses HTTPS)

   o BranchCache - Peer Discovery (uses WSD): This rule is required only for distributed cache mode.

All three steps of the client configuration process can be done with a single `netsh` command: `netsh branchcache set service mode=hostedclient location=`*ServerName*. For distributed cache mode, use `netsh branchcache set service mode= distributed`. The `netsh` command configures the client firewall for the specified mode.

Activity 4-2: Configuring BranchCache on a Client

Time Required: 20 minutes

Objective: Configure BranchCache on a client computer with `netsh`.

Required Tools and Equipment: 412Server1 and 412Win8

Description: In this activity, you configure BranchCache on a client computer in distributed mode and test it.

> **NOTE**
>
> Configuring BranchCache in hosted cache mode requires a certificate, so this activity configures your 412Win8 computer to use distributed mode. There's only one computer, but you'll see how to check the status of BranchCache to know that it's working.

1. Start 412Server1, and log on as **Administrator**, if necessary. Open File Explorer. Navigate to **C:\Windows** and copy the file named **explorer**. It doesn't matter which file you copy; you just need a file large enough to test the cache. Navigate to the **C:\DocShare1** folder you shared in Activity 4-1, and paste the file you just copied. Create a text file named **mydoc.txt** in the folder, type your name in the text file, and save it. Now you have two files in the shared folder.

2. Log on to 412Win8 as **Win8User** with the password **Password01**. Right-click **Start** and click **Command Prompt (Admin)**. Click **Yes** in the User Account Control message box.

3. At the command prompt, type **netsh branchcache set service mode=distributed** and press **Enter**. You see a message that the command succeeded and the firewall rules were set.

4. Type **netsh branchcache show status all** and press **Enter**. You should see output similar to Figure 4-7. Type **netsh branchcache smb set latency 0** and press **Enter** to have BranchCache cache all files, even if there's no delay in retrieving them from the file server. The default latency value is set to 80 ms.

```
C:\Windows\system32>netsh branchcache show status all

BranchCache Service Status:
_____
Service Mode                 = Distributed Caching
Serve peers on battery power = Disabled
Current Status               = Running
Service Start Type           = Manual
This machine is not configured as a hosted cache client.

Local Cache Status:
_____
Maximum Cache Size         = 5% of hard disk
Active Current Cache Size  = 0 Bytes
Local Cache Location       = C:\Windows\ServiceProfiles\NetworkService\AppData\Lo
cal\PeerDistRepub (Default)

Publication Cache Status:
_____
Maximum Cache Size         = 1% of hard disk
Active Current Cache Size  = 0 Bytes
Publication Cache Location = C:\Windows\ServiceProfiles\NetworkService\AppData\L
ocal\PeerDistPub (Default)

Networking Status:
_____
Content Retrieval URL Reservation         = Configured      (Required)
Hosted Cache URL Reservation              = Configured      (Not Required)
Hosted Cache HTTP URL Reservation         = Configured      (Not Required)
SSL Certificate Bound To Hosted Cache Port = Not Configured (Not Required)
Content Retrieval Firewall Rules          = Enabled         (Required)
Peer Discovery Firewall Rules             = Enabled         (Required)
Hosted Cache Server Firewall Rules        = Disabled        (Not Required)
Hosted Cache Client Firewall Rules        = Enabled         (Not Required)
```

Figure 4-7 Checking the status of BranchCache on a client

5. Right-click **Start**, click **Run**, type **\\412Server1\docshare1**, and press **Enter**. When prompted for credentials, type **412dom1\administrator** for the username and **Password01** for the password.

6. When the share opens, double-click the text file to open it in Notepad. Type some text in the file, save it, and exit Notepad. Next, copy the **explorer** file and paste it to your desktop. In the command prompt window, type **netsh branchcache show status all** and press **Enter**. You should see that the line beginning with "Active Current Cache Size" shows a number of bytes in use by the cache. If the value is still 0, wait a while and try the command again. Sometimes it takes a while for the statistics to update. Review the command output to verify that the current status is running and the firewall rules are enabled.

7. Type **PowerShell** and press **Enter**. Type **Get-BCDataCache** and press **Enter**. You see information about the cache, such as the maximum percent of the volume used by the cache and the current use of the cache.

8. Close the command prompt window on 412Win8.

9. You're finished using BranchCache, so on 412Server1, unlink the **BranchCache Server** GPO from the **Domain Controllers** OU.

10. Stay logged on to 412Server1 if you're continuing to the next activity. You can log off or shut down 412Win8.

Configuring BranchCache with PowerShell   Table 4-3 lists some PowerShell cmdlets commonly used for configuring BranchCache.

Table 4-3   **BranchCache PowerShell cmdlets**

Cmdlet	Description
Clear-BCCache	Deletes all cached data
Disable-BC	Disables BranchCache
Enable-BCDistributed	Configures BranchCache in distributed cache mode
Enable-BCHostedClient	Configures a BranchCache client to operate in hosted cache mode
Enable-BCHostedServer	Configures a BranchCache server to operate in hosted cache mode
Get-BCDataCache	Shows information about the cache
Get-BCStatus	Shows detailed information about the BranchCache service and the cache
Reset-BC	Resets the configuration of BranchCache
Set-BCCache	Configures the cache parameters
Set-BCDataCacheEntryMaxAge	Configures the maximum time data remains in the cache
Set-BCMinSMBLatency	Sets the minimum latency between the client and server before caching can take place
Get-Command -Module BranchCache	Displays all cmdlets related to the BranchCache service

© 2016 Cengage Learning®

File Classification Infrastructure

File Classification Infrastructure (FCI) is a feature of File Server Resource Manager (FSRM) that allows you to classify files by assigning new properties to them. The properties can then be used to create rules for searching or perform tasks on files meeting the criteria of the assigned properties.

Because the number and size of files that organizations store on file servers keep increasing, users have more difficulty finding the files they want, even with advanced search algorithms to help with the task. In the past, the only way to classify a file was to organize files with descriptive filenames and folder names. With indexing, files can be searched based on file content, but finding certain words in a file doesn't always tell you whether it contains sensitive information or is related to a particular vendor or customer. File classification by filenaming or folder storage is often left up to users, which can result in inconsistencies and errors. FSRM's file classification feature helps you develop a consistent, reliable classification system for file management tasks. File classification management involves three basic steps:

1. Create file classification properties.

2. Create classification rules to apply classification properties to files and folders.

3. Carry out file management tasks based on the classified files.

File classification is also used by Dynamic Access Control (DAC), a new feature in Windows Server 2012/R2 for setting access permissions on files. DAC is covered in Chapter 5.

Classifying Files To begin classifying files, you need to install File Server Resource Manager, a role service under the File and Storage Services role. Next, you need to enable or create classification properties that are applied by using classification rules. A **classification property** is a file attribute containing a value that's used to categorize the data in a file or an aspect of the file, such as its location or creation time. For example, say you want to classify all files containing the word "confidential" so that they can be flagged for special handling. Activity 4-3 walks you through the process, and the following steps outline the procedure:

1. Enable or create a classification property. Windows has predefined classification properties called "resource properties," including one named Confidentiality. Before you can use resource properties, they must be enabled in Active Directory Administrative Center (ADAC) or by using the `Set-ADResourceProperty` PowerShell cmdlet.

2. Synchronize the resource properties in Active Directory with FSRM by using the PowerShell cmdlet `Update-FsrmClassificationPropertyDefinition`. This command causes FSRM to recognize resource properties you have enabled.

3. Create a classification rule to set the property in files containing the string `confidential`. The rule can be run manually, or you can create a schedule to run the rule periodically.

Activity 4-3: Installing the File Server Resource Manager Role Service

Time Required: 10 minutes
Objective: Install the File Server Resource Manager role service.

Required Tools and Equipment: 412Server1
Description: In this activity, you install the File Server Resource Manager role service.

1. Log on to 412Server1 as **Administrator**, if necessary.

2. Open Server Manager, and start the Add Roles and Features Wizard.

3. Click **Next** until you get to the Server Roles window. Click to expand **File and Storage Services** and **File and iSCSI Services**. Click to select **File Server Resource Manager**, and then click the **Add Features** button. Continue the installation with the default settings, and then click **Install**. When the role service is installed, click **Close**.

4. Stay logged on to 412Server1 for the next activity.

Activity 4-4: Classifying Files with FCI

Time Required: 20 minutes

Objective: Classify files with File Classification Infrastructure (FCI).

Required Tools and Equipment: 412Server1

Description: In this activity, you configure FCI on 412Server1 and test the results. First, create a couple of files in a folder and add some text to the files. Next, enable a resource property named Confidentiality. Then create a file classification rule to set the property on files based on their contents.

1. Start 412Server1, and log on as **Administrator**, if necessary. Open File Explorer, and navigate to C:\DocShare1. Open the **mydoc.txt** file you created in Activity 4-2. Type **confidential** anywhere in the file. Create a second text file named **mydoc2.txt** and type **public information** in the file. Save and close both files.

2. In Server Manager, click **Tools, Active Directory Administrative Center.** In the left pane, click to expand **Dynamic Access Control** and click **Resource Properties.** In the middle pane, right-click **Confidentiality** (see Figure 4-8) and click **Enable.**

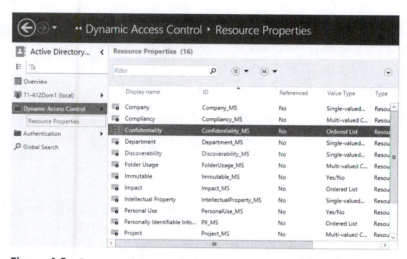

Figure 4-8   Resource properties in Active Directory Administrative Center

3. Double-click **Confidentiality** to open its properties. The Suggested Values list box has three possible values: Low, Moderate, and High. You can add values if you want. Close the Confidentiality dialog box, and then close Active Directory Administrative Center.

4. Open a PowerShell prompt. Type **Update-FsrmClassificationPropertyDefinition** and press **Enter.** This command updates FSRM with the Confidentiality property you just enabled. Close the PowerShell window.

5. In Server Manager, click **Tools, File Server Resource Manager.** In the left pane, click to expand **Classification Management,** and then click **Classification Properties.** In the middle pane, you see the Confidentiality property you just enabled. You can also create your own properties here.

6. In the left pane, click **Classification Rules.** In the Actions pane, click **Create Classification Rule.** In the Create Classification Rule dialog box, type **Confidential Files** in the Rule name text box and **Files that contain the word "confidential"** in the Description text box.

7. Click the **Scope** tab, where you choose which files to scan. You can choose file types and add folders that should be scanned. Click **Add.** In the Browse For Folder dialog box, click the **C:\DocShare1** folder, and then click **OK.**

8. Click the **Classification** tab. Under Classification method, leave the default setting **Content Classifier**. Under Property, the Confidentiality property is already selected with the value High (see Figure 4-9).

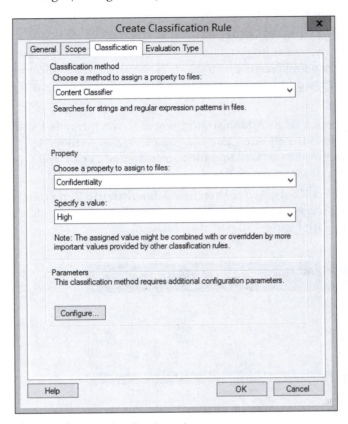

Figure 4-9   The Classification tab

9. Click the **Configure** button to open the Classification Parameters dialog box, where you specify what to look for in a file to make the classification. In the Expression Type column, click the list arrow and click **String**. In the Expression column, type **confidential** (see Figure 4-10), and then click **OK**. You can also combine strings and regular expressions.

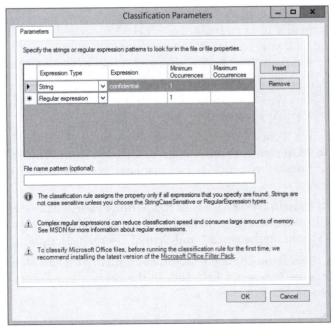

Figure 4-10   Configuring the search string

10. Click the **Evaluation Type** tab. Click **Re-evaluate existing property values,** and then click **OK.** Setting this option means that if the property already exists, it's overwritten if needed.

11. In File Server Resource Manager, right-click **Classification Rules** and click **Run Classification With All Rules Now.** Click the **Wait for classification to complete** option button, and then click **OK.** An Internet Explorer window opens to the page "Automatic Classification Report." Review this report to see its contents, and then close Internet Explorer.

12. Open File Explorer, and open **C:\DocShare1.** Right-click **mydoc.txt** and click **Properties.** Click the **Classification** tab. You see the Confidentiality property with the value High (see Figure 4-11). Click **Cancel.** Right-click **mydoc2.txt** and click **Properties,** and then click the **Classification** tab. You see the Confidentiality property with the value "(none)." Note that you can also set the property manually by clicking a value in the lower half of the dialog box. Click **Cancel,** and close File Explorer.

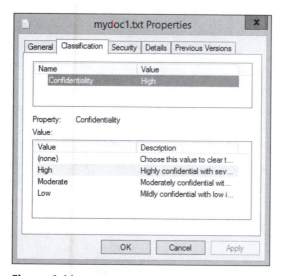

Figure 4-11   The Classification tab of a file's properties

13. Close File Server Resource Manager. Stay logged on to 412Server1 if you're continuing to the next activity.

Auditing File Access

You might think files on your servers are secure because you have set strong password policies and configured permissions correctly on files and folders. However, in a large network with many servers and shared folders, you need to verify that there are no gaps in file security, and you need to know whether someone is trying to bypass your security measures. This is where file access auditing comes in. With file access auditing enabled, events are created in the Security log to show that access to a file was attempted.

Auditing in Windows Server 2012/R2 includes the auditing features available in previous versions and adds the following improvements:

- Target specific files and users in audit policies to reduce the volume of auditing information logged.

- Combine global object access auditing with Dynamic Access Control (DAC) to zero in on specific activities. DAC is covered in Chapter 5.

- Data access events contain more information, so you can conduct more precise searches to find audit information.

- Audit removable storage devices to increase security.

The steps required to audit file access are as follows:

1. Enable the "Audit object access" policy in Group Policy. You can enable auditing for successful access attempts, failures, or both. You can link the GPO where you have enabled the policy to a particular OU containing the computer accounts on which you want to audit file access or link it to the domain to enable auditing on all computers.

2. Enable auditing on each file or folder you want to audit. Every file system object has a **system access control list (SACL)** that defines whether and how the file system object is to be audited. When you enable auditing on a folder, the files and subfolders inherit the auditing settings of the parent folder by default. You can create multiple auditing entries, each with different security principals and conditions for auditing. For each auditing entry (see Figure 4-12), set the following criteria:

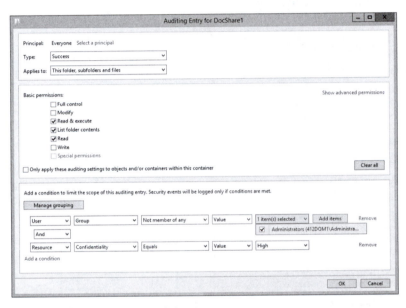

Figure 4-12   Creating an auditing entry

- o Choose a security principal. You can select a user or group account, including special identities such as Everyone or Authenticated Users. Only attempts to access the object by the specified accounts are audited.

- o Choose the type of access attempt: Success, Fail, or All.

- o Specify the inheritance property. On folders, auditing is applied to the folder, subfolders, and files by default.

- o Specify the type of access attempted based on permissions. You can select basic or advanced permissions.

- o Create additional conditions. You can narrow the scope of auditing by creating additional conditions for applying the audit policy. For example, you can choose the Everyone security principal but exclude members of the Administrators group. You can include file classifications, too. The bottom of Figure 4-12 shows that auditing occurs only if the account accessing the file isn't a member of the Administrators group and the file has a Confidentiality property value of High. Creating additional conditions is optional.

3. Verify the auditing policy by accessing an audited file. You should conduct tests to be sure auditing is performed only for the type of attempt (success or fail) and for the specified conditions.

Activity 4-5: Auditing Folder Access

Time Required: 15 minutes
Objective: Create an audit policy for a folder.

Required Tools and Equipment: 412Server1
Description: In this activity, you create an audit policy that records an event each time a designated folder is accessed successfully.

1. Log on to 412Server1 as **Administrator**, if necessary.

2. Open File Explorer, and then right-click **C:\DocShare1** and click **Properties**. Click the **Security** tab and click **Advanced**.

3. In the Advanced Security Settings for DocShare1 dialog box, click the **Auditing** tab. Currently there are no auditing entries. The list of auditing entries is the SACL. Click **Add**.

4. In the Auditing Entry for DocShare1, click **Select a principal**. Type **Everyone** in the "Enter the object name to select" text box, click **Check Names**, and click **OK**.

5. In the Type drop-down list, click **All**. Leave the default value in the "Applies to" drop-down list.

6. In the Basic permissions section, click to clear all check boxes except **Read** so that only read accesses are logged.

7. Click **Add a condition**. In the first drop-down list on the left, click **Resource**. Because you have only one resource property defined, Confidentiality is selected automatically. In the fifth drop-down list from the left (currently blank), click **High** so that this policy audits only files with the Confidentiality property set to High. Click **OK**. The Advanced Security Settings for DocShare1 dialog box should now look like Figure 4-13. Click **OK** twice.

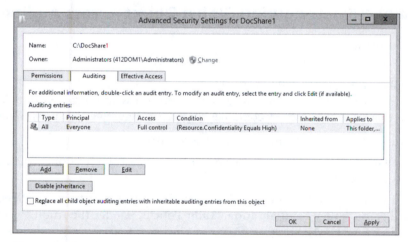

Figure 4-13   The Advanced Security Settings for DocShare1 dialog box

8. Now you need to enable auditing with Group Policy. In Server Manager, click **Tools, Group Policy Management** from the menu. Right-click the **Domain Controllers** OU and click **Create a GPO in this domain, and Link it here**. In the Name text box, type **EnableAuditing**, and then click **OK**.

9. Right-click the **EnableAuditing** GPO and click **Edit**. In the left pane, expand **Computer Configuration, Policies, Windows Settings, Security Settings, Local Policies**, and click **Audit Policy**. Double-click **Audit object access** in the right pane to open its Properties dialog box.

10. Click the **Define these policy settings** check box, click the **Success** and **Failure** check boxes, and then click **OK**. Close the Group Policy Management Editor and Group Policy Management console.

11. Open a command prompt window. Type **gpupdate** and press **Enter** to refresh the security policy. Close the command prompt window.

12. In File Explorer, open the **DocShare1** folder and double-click **mydoc**. Close the mydoc file. Right-click **Start** and click **Event Viewer**, expand **Windows Logs**, and click the **Security** log. Look for an event with Event ID 4663, which is an object access event. Several events were created for this simple file access, which is why you need to be careful with how many files you audit. Close Event Viewer and File Explorer.

13. Open the Group Policy Management console and click to expand the **Domain Controllers** OU. Right-click the **EnableAuditing** GPO and click **Delete** to disable auditing. Click **OK** to confirm.

14. Stay logged on if you're continuing to the next activity.

Global Object Access Auditing Using the steps outlined previously, you need to enable auditing on each file system object on each computer you want to audit. Obviously, this task can be tedious and difficult to track. Windows Server 2008 R2 introduced global object access auditing policy settings that allow administrators to manage auditing centrally by using group policies. A **global object access auditing policy** affects the entire file system or Registry on computers in the scope of the GPO where the policy is defined. Obviously, enabling auditing on so many files can take a toll on resources because many events are created. If you configure global object access auditing, it's best to narrow the criteria for triggering auditing events by using conditions with resource properties.

If a file system object has auditing defined from global object access auditing and from a SACL manually defined on the object, auditing is derived from a combination of both settings. If object access matches the global policy or the local SACL, an event is generated. To configure global object access auditing, follow the steps in Activity 4-6.

Activity 4-6: Configuring Global Object Access Auditing

Time Required: 15 minutes
Objective: Configure global object access auditing.

Required Tools and Equipment: 412Server1
Description: In this activity, you configure global object access auditing in Group Policy. You don't link the GPO to an Active Directory container to prevent triggering too many auditing events.

1. Log on to 412Server1 as **Administrator**, if necessary.

2. Open the Group Policy Management console, if necessary, and open the **EnableAuditing** GPO in the Group Policy Management Editor.

3. Navigate to **Computer Configuration, Policies, Windows Settings, Security Settings, Advanced Audit Policy Configuration, Audit Policies**. Under the Audit Policies node, click **Global Object Access Auditing**.

4. In the right pane, double-click **File system**. (You can also click Registry if you want to audit Registry access.) Click the **Define this policy setting** check box, and then click the **Configure** button.

5. The Advanced Security Settings for Global File SACL dialog opens. This dialog box looks similar to the Advanced Security Settings dialog box shown previously in Figure 4-13. Click **Add**.

6. The Auditing Entry for Global File SACL dialog box opens, which looks similar to Figure 4-12, except you don't define inheritance settings and you see the list of advanced permissions instead of the basic permissions. From this point, you would follow Steps 4 through 7 of Activity 4-5 to define the SACL if you were going to complete the configuration. You aren't going to do that now, however, so click **Cancel** three times to return to the Group Policy Management Editor.

7. After defining global object access auditing, you would link the GPO to a container that has the computer accounts you want to audit file object access for, but don't do that now. The purpose of this activity is to show you how to configure it if you want to use it. Close the Group Policy Management Editor and Group Policy Management console.

8. Stay logged on if you're continuing to the next activity.

Network File System

Not every network is composed solely of computers running Windows. Some networks include Linux and UNIX computers that use the native file-sharing system, Network File System. **Network File System (NFS)** is a file-sharing protocol that allows users to access files and folders on other computers across a network. From a user's standpoint, NFS makes network resources seem to be part of the local file system, much like mapping a drive does for Windows file shares. NFS has both a client and server component; both are installed by default on most Linux and UNIX systems.

Windows Server 2012/R2 supports an NFS server component as a role service under the File and Storage Services role and an NFS client component as a feature. You can install either component or both. The Enterprise Edition of Windows 8/8.1 supports an NFS client but not the NFS server component.

Installing and Configuring Server for NFS   You install Server for NFS like any other role service, by using the Add Roles and Features Wizard or the PowerShell cmdlet `Install-WindowsFeature`. After it's installed, a tab named NFS Sharing is added to the Properties dialog box of folders (see Figure 4-14).

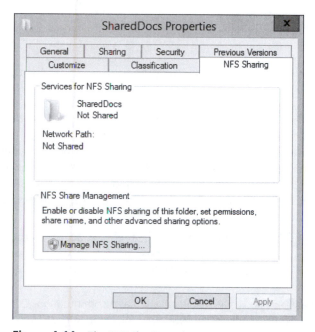

Figure 4-14   The NFS Sharing tab

The NFS Sharing tab shows the current status of NFS for the folder (whether or not the folder is shared by using NFS). Clicking the Manage NFS Sharing button opens the NFS Advanced Sharing dialog box shown in Figure 4-15. In the NFS Advanced Sharing dialog box, you can configure the following settings:

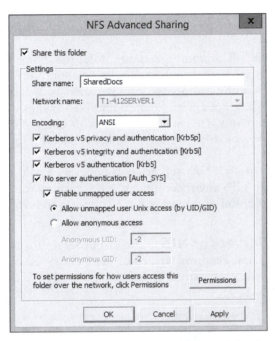

Figure 4-15 The NFS Advanced Sharing dialog box

- *Share this folder*—When this check box is selected, the folder is shared with NFS.

- *Share name*—Name the share; the default value is the name of the folder.

- *Encoding*—Choose the encoding method, which determines the characters that can be used in file and directory names.

- *Authentication*—Configure Kerberos authentication options and specify whether to allow unmapped user access and anonymous access. If you enable the "No server authentication" option, you can select "Enable unmapped user access." Doing so allows users of Linux and UNIX systems to access the NFS share without authenticating through Active Directory. You can also allow anonymous access.

- *Permissions*—By default, all NFS client computers that request access to the share are allowed Read-Only access. You can change the default access to Read-Write or No Access. You can add client groups and assign each group different access.

 This chapter covers basic NFS installation and configuration. Comprehensive configuration details are covered in the Designing and Implementing a Server Infrastructure, Exam 70-413, certification exam objectives.

Implementing an NFS Data Store Microsoft added the capability to provide fault tolerance and high availability to Server for NFS in Windows Server 2012 by allowing an NFS share to be configured on a Windows failover cluster. An NFS share on a Windows failover cluster is called an **NFS data store**, which provides a highly available storage solution for applications using NFS, such as VMware ESX Server and other Linux and UNIX applications. To implement an NFS data store, perform the following steps:

1. Install the File Services role, the Server for NFS role service, and the Failover Clustering feature.

2. Create a failover cluster (described in Chapter 6).

3. Configure the File Server role in Failover Cluster Manager, which is installed when the Failover Clustering feature is installed.

4. Add an NFS file share to the cluster in Failover Cluster Manager.

Configuring NFS with PowerShell Table 4-4 lists some PowerShell cmdlets for configuring NFS.

Table 4-4   NFS PowerShell cmdlets

Cmdlet	Description
Get-NfsServerConfiguration	Shows NFS server configuration settings
Get-NfsShare	Shows information about NFS shares on a server
New-NfsShare	Creates an NFS share
Remove-NfsShare	Stops sharing an NFS share
Set-NfsClientConfiguration	Configures settings on an NFS client
Set-NfsShare	Configures settings on an NFS share
Get-Command -Module NFS	Displays all cmdlets related to the NFS service

© 2016 Cengage Learning®

Configuring Advanced File Storage

One of the main reasons networks and servers were invented was to have a centralized repository for shared files. The need for faster, bigger, and more reliable storage is growing as fast as technology can keep up. Everything is stored on digital media now—documents, e-mail, music, photographs, videos—and this trend is continuing. You learned about managing local storage on a Windows Server 2012/R2 server when studying the objectives for Installing and Configuring Windows Server 2012, Exam 70-410. This chapter focuses on the following advanced storage topics:

- *iSCSI*—Set up a storage area network (SAN) with Internet Small Computer System Interface (iSCSI) and Internet Storage Name Service (iSNS).

- *Thin provisioning*—Implement thin provisioning by using dynamically expanding disks.

- *Tiered storage*—Configure tiered storage by using Storage Spaces and solid state disks.

- *Features on Demand*—Optimize server storage free space by using Features on Demand.

Implementing a SAN with iSCSI

A **storage area network (SAN)** is a storage system that uses high-speed networking technologies to give servers fast access to large amounts of shared disk storage. The storage on a SAN appears to the server OS as though it's physically attached to the server. You can set up a SAN with Windows servers by using the iSCSI protocol, which carries SCSI device commands over an IP network. There are two main components in a Windows Server 2012/R2 iSCSI SAN solution:

- *iSCSI target*—An **iSCSI target** is a logical storage space made available to iSCSI clients by a server running the iSCSI Target Server role service. The iSCSI target consists of one or more virtual disks on the iSCSI target server.

- *iSCSI initiator*—An **iSCSI initiator** is the iSCSI client that sends iSCSI commands to the iSCSI target. Each iSCSI initiator is assigned an **iSCSI qualified name (IQN)** that the iSCSI target uses to give it access to iSCSI storage. The IQN is an identifier that iSCSI targets and initiators use to identify the iSCSI device in an iSCSI connection. An IQN—for example, `iqn.1991-05.com.microsoft:412server1.412dom1.local`—follows this format:

o The literal string `iqn` followed by a period.

o The date the naming authority took ownership of the domain in the format **yyyy-mm** followed by a period. On Microsoft iSCSI devices, the date is always 1991-05.

o The reverse domain name of the authority followed by a colon. On Microsoft iSCSI devices, it's `com.microsoft:`.

o The name of the iSCSI target or initiator.

Windows Server 2012/R2 includes both the iSCSI initiator, which is preinstalled, and the iSCSI target, which is installed as a role service under File and Storage Services. Figure 4-16 shows a SAN and the relationship between an iSCSI target and iSCSI initiators. In the figure, the iSCSI target server makes storage available to iSCSI initiators as **block-level storage**, which the storage client sees as a local drive. The storage can be formatted, and volumes can be created like any other local storage device. Conversely, **file-level storage** is storage the client has access to only as files and folders. A Windows file share is file-level storage.

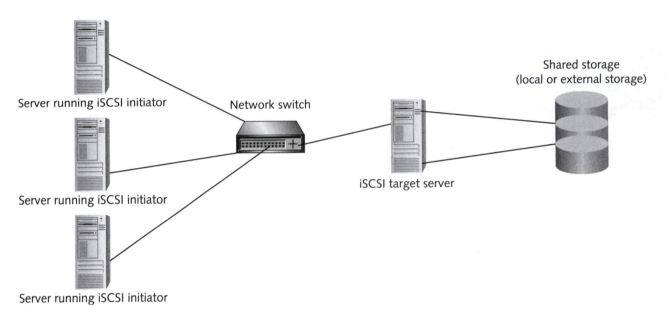

Figure 4-16   A SAN with iSCSI in Windows Server 2012/R2

© 2016 Cengage Learning®

The iSCSI target makes storage available to iSCSI initiators as an iSCSI virtual disk, also called an **iSCSI logical unit number (LUN)**. An iSCSI LUN is a reference ID to a logical drive the iSCSI initiator uses when accessing storage on the iSCSI target server. An iSCSI target can contain one or more iSCSI LUNs, depending on how many virtual disks are associated with the iSCSI target.

The iSCSI initiator is also available in Windows 8/8.1 from the Administrative Tools menu.

Configuring an iSCSI Target An iSCSI target is installed on the server hosting storage for the SAN. The storage can be internal hard drives or external storage devices connected through a high-speed bus, such as e-SATA or USB 3.0. An iSCSI target allows servers running the iSCSI initiator to access shared storage by using the iSCSI protocol over standard network technologies, such as Ethernet. From the viewpoint of an iSCSI initiator, the storage appears as a local volume.

Two components make up the iSCSI target software in Windows Server 2012/R2:

- *iSCSI target server*—This required component gives iSCSI initiators access to shared storage.

- *iSCSI target storage provider*—Although this component isn't required, it provides Virtual Disk Service (VDS) and Volume Shadow Copy Service (VSS) support to applications needing these services.

The steps for configuring an iSCSI target are as follows:

1. Install the iSCSI Target Server role service and optionally the iSCSI Target Storage Provider role service.

2. Create an iSCSI virtual disk.

3. Create an iSCSI target and assign one or more iSCSI virtual disks to the target.

Steps 2 and 3 are combined when you use the iSCSI Virtual Disk Wizard, described in the next section.

Creating an iSCSI Virtual Disk You create an iSCSI virtual disk with the iSCSI Virtual Disk Wizard accessed via File and Storage Services. This wizard walks you through the process as you provide the following information:

1. *Virtual disk location*—Select the server and volume for storing the virtual disk. By default, it's stored in a folder named iSCSIVirtualDisks the wizard creates in the root of the selected volume. You can also specify a custom path, such as E:\iSCSI\disks.

2. *Virtual disk name*—Assign a name and optional description to the virtual disk. The name, in VHDX virtual disk format, is the name of the virtual disk file. For example, if you accepted the default folder location on volume E and assigned the name vdisk1, the virtual disk is stored in E:\iSCSIVirtualDisks\vdisk1.vhdx.

3. *Virtual disk size*—Specify the size of the virtual disk. You can also specify whether the disk should be a fixed-size, dynamically expanding, or differencing disk. A fixed-size disk results in the best performance. A differencing disk requires a path to a parent virtual disk. You learned about virtual disk types when studying the objectives of Installing and Configuring Windows Server 2012, Exam 70-410.

4. *iSCSI target*—Specify an existing iSCSI target, if available, or create one. If you create one, you assign a name and optional description. iSCSI initiators use this descriptive name to access the storage. Every virtual disk is assigned to a target, and more than one virtual disk can be assigned to a single target. A sample target name might be Cluster1 if the target is to be used by a server cluster. If you specify an existing target, creating the virtual disk is complete, so you don't need to perform Steps 5 and 6.

5. *Identify iSCSI initiators*—Specify the iSCSI initiators that can access the virtual disk. iSCSI initiators that have been given access to the virtual disk can discover and connect to the target. They can be identified by IQN, DNS name, IP address, or MAC address. If an iSCSI initiator is running Windows Server 2012 or later, and you have already started the iSCSI initiator client software on it, you can query the initiator computer for its ID. You can identify more than one iSCSI initiator if the storage will be used in a server cluster.

6. *Select authentication*—Challenge-Handshake Authentication Protocol (CHAP) can be enabled for an iSCSI initiator to authenticate to the iSCSI target, and reverse CHAP can be enabled for the target to authenticate to the initiator. Authentication is optional and in most cases, you don't need to enable it. If you need a secure connection to the iSCSI target, you can configure IPsec after the virtual disk is created.

Activity 4-7: Installing the iSCSI Target Server Role Service

Time Required: 5 minutes
Objective: Install the iSCSI Target Server role service.

Required Tools and Equipment: 412Server1
Description: In this activity, you install the iSCSI Target Server role service.

1. Log on to 412Server1 as **Administrator**, if necessary.

2. Open Server Manager, and start the Add Roles and Features Wizard. Click **Next** until you see the Server Roles window.

3. Click to expand **File and Storage Services** and **File and iSCSI Services**. Click to select **iSCSI Target Server** and **iSCSI Target Storage Provider**. Click **Next** twice, and click **Install** in the Confirmation window.

4. After the role services are installed, click **Close**.

5. Stay logged on if you're continuing to the next activity.

Activity 4-8: Creating an iSCSI Virtual Disk

Time Required: 10 minutes
Objective: Create an iSCSI virtual disk.

Required Tools and Equipment: 412Server1 and 412Server2
Description: In this activity, you create a 10 GB iSCSI virtual disk and assign it to an iSCSI target. This activity assumes you have a second disk drive installed on 412Server1 and assigned to drive letter E. If you don't, you can use the C drive as long as you have at least 15 GB of free space. If you have a second disk on 412Server1 but no volumes have been created, create a 20 GB NTFS volume on it in Desk Management before continuing.

1. Log on to 412Server2 as **Administrator**, if necessary. Open Server Manager, if necessary, and click **Tools, iSCSI Initiator** from the menu. In the Microsoft iSCSI message box, click **Yes** to start the iSCSI service. (Starting the iSCSI initiator now makes configuration of the iSCSI target go more smoothly.) For now, close the iSCSI Initiator Properties dialog box.

2. On 412Server1, in the left pane of Server Manager, click **File and Storage Services**. Click **iSCSI**.

3. In the right pane, click the **To create an iSCSI virtual disk, start the New iSCSI Virtual Disk Wizard link**.

4. In the iSCSI Virtual Disk Location window, click the **Select by volume** option button, click the **E:** volume (or another volume specified by your instructor), as shown in Figure 4-17, and click **Next**.

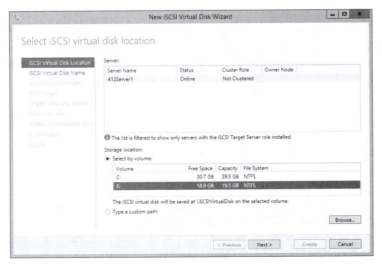

Figure 4-17   Specifying the iSCSI virtual disk location

5. In the iSCSI Virtual Disk Name window, type **vdisk1** in the Name text box, and click **Next**.

6. In the iSCSI Virtual Disk Size window, type **10** in the Size text box, click the **Dynamically expanding** option button (see Figure 4-18), and click **Next**.

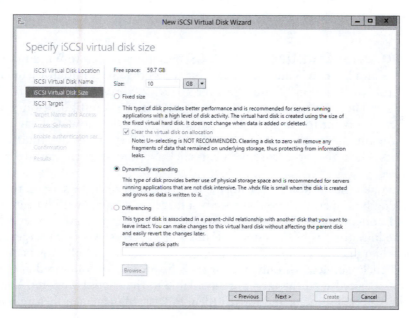

Figure 4-18   Specifying the size and type of virtual disk

7. In the iSCSI Target window, because there are no existing targets, accept the default option **New iSCSI target**, and click **Next**.

8. In the Target Name and Access window, type **target1**, and click **Next**.

9. In the Access Servers window, click **Add**. In the Add initiator ID dialog box, click the **Query initiator computer for ID** option button, if necessary, and type **412server2.412dom1.local** in the text box (see Figure 4-19). Click **OK**. The server queries 412Server2 to get its IQN, which is why you started the iSCSI service on 412Server2 first. If you were configuring shared storage for use by a server cluster, you could add more initiators. Click **Next**.

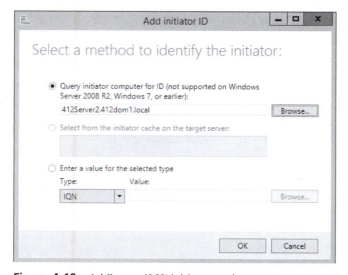

Figure 4-19   Adding an iSCSI initiator to the target

10. In the "Enable authentication service" window, click **Next**. In the Confirmation window, verify the settings, and click **Create**. After the iSCSI virtual disk is created, click **Close**.

11. In File and Storage Services, you see the new virtual disk and the iSCSI target. If you need to make changes to either, you can right-click it and click Properties. Stay logged on to both servers if you're continuing to the next activity.

Configuring an iSCSI Initiator   The iSCSI initiator is built into Windows Server 2012/R2 and Windows 8 and later. In Windows 8/8.1, you access the iSCSI initiator from Administrative Tools in Control Panel, and in Windows Server 2012/R2, you access it from the Tools menu in Server Manager. The first time you run the iSCSI initiator configuration software, you're asked whether you want to start the Microsoft iSCSI service now and each time Windows starts. If you want the computer to connect to the iSCSI target automatically each time Windows starts, click Yes; otherwise, you can click No and start the service manually in the Services console.

When you open the iSCSI initiator for the first time and start the service, the iSCSI Initiator Properties dialog box opens, where you specify a target to connect with by entering the server's fully qualified domain name. The initiator software queries the server to see whether it hosts any targets the initiator has been granted permission to access. An iSCSI target server might be hosting more than one target, so a dialog box opens with a list of all targets discovered. Select the target and click Connect. (If only one target is listed, you're connected automatically.) Any virtual disks associated with the target are available to the client computer. You have to bring the disks online, initialize them, and format them in Disk Management before the first time you connect to them.

The iSCSI initiator doesn't reconnect to a target automatically each time Windows starts unless you configure it to do so. In the Volumes and Devices tab of the iSCSI Initiator Properties dialog box, you can configure specific devices or all available devices to reconnect automatically at Windows startup. Activity 4-9 steps you through configuring the iSCSI initiator to connect to the target you configured in Activity 4-8.

Activity 4-9: Configuring an iSCSI Initiator

Time Required: 10 minutes
Objective: Configure an iSCSI initiator.

Required Tools and Equipment: 412Server1 and 412Server2
Description: In this activity, you start the Microsoft iSCSI service and configure the iSCSI initiator to connect to the iSCSI target you configured in Activity 4-8.

1. Log on to 412Server2 as **Administrator**, if necessary. Make sure 412Server1 is running.

2. Open Server Manager, if necessary, and click **Tools**, **iSCSI Initiator** from the menu.

3. In the iSCSI Initiator Properties dialog box, type **412server1.412dom1.local** in the Target text box, and click **Quick Connect**. The target you created on 412Server1 is listed in the Quick Connect dialog box (see Figure 4-20). Click **Done**.

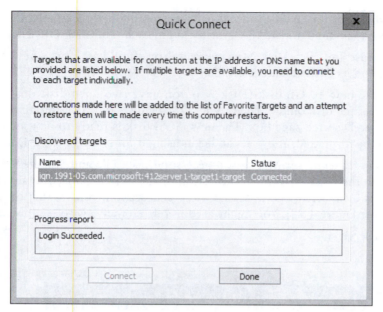

Figure 4-20   The Quick Connect dialog box showing discovered targets

4. The Targets tab lists the target and its status as Connected (see Figure 4-21). To configure the iSCSI initiator to reconnect to the iSCSI target when the system restarts, click the **Volumes and Devices** tab. Click **Auto Configure** so that the virtual disk on the target is connected automatically when the system restarts.

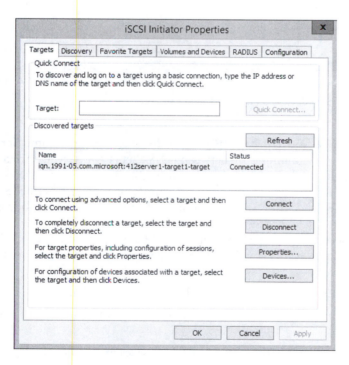

Figure 4-21   The Targets tab

5. Click the other tabs in the iSCSI Initiator Properties dialog box to see other configuration options. Take some time to read the information in each tab. Click **OK** when you're done.

6. Right-click **Start** and click **Disk Management.** You should see that a new 10 GB disk has been added, and its current state is offline.

7. Right-click the new 10 GB disk (Disk 2, if you have two hard disks installed) and click **Online** to bring the disk online. Then right-click the disk and click **Initialize Disk.** Click **OK** in the Initialize Disk message box. The new iSCSI disk is ready to be used by 412Server2. The disk can be formatted, and you can begin using it for storage. Close Disk Management.

8. On 412Server1, open Server Manager, if necessary. Click **File and Storage Services,** and then click **iSCSI.** In the iSCSI Virtual Disks section of the middle pane, you see that the virtual disk's status is Connected, and in the iSCSI Targets section, you see that the target status is Connected (see Figure 4-22). You might need to refresh the view to see this status.

9. Log off both servers.

Figure 4-22   The status of iSCSI devices on the iSCSI target server

The Internet Storage Name Service   The **Internet Storage Name Service (iSNS)** is an IP-based protocol used to communicate between iSNS clients and servers. An iSNS client is an iSCSI initiator running the iSNS protocol that discovers iSCSI targets. An iSNS server provides a management platform for iSCSI devices similar to those in a Fibre Channel SAN. The iSNS protocol can actually be used in networks running Fibre Channel SANs, but the Microsoft iSNS server supports only iSCSI devices.

iSNS is essentially a central storage location for iSCSI devices, so iSCSI can be managed centrally when you have many servers providing iSCSI targets. iSNS offers the following benefits for iSCSI SANs on large networks:

- *Scalability*—Setting up iSCSI SANs on larger IP networks is easier.

- *Manageability*—Management of iSCSI targets, initiators, and management nodes can be centralized.

- *Monitoring*—You can monitor the status of iSCSI devices and receive change notifications.

iSCSI initiators use iSNS by sending queries to the iSNS server to discover iSCSI targets and receive notifications about new iSCSI targets or targets that are no longer available. iSCSI targets use iSNS by registering with the iSNS server so that their status is available to iSCSI initiators.

Implementing iSNS   To implement iSNS in Windows Server 2012/R2, install the iSNS Server feature with the Add Roles and Features Wizard or PowerShell. After the feature is installed, configure it by opening iSNS Server from the Tools menu in Server Manager (see Figure 4-23). The General tab of the Properties dialog box shows the currently registered iSCSI devices.

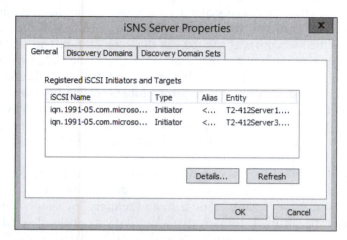

Figure 4-23   The iSNS Server Properties dialog box

You must configure an iSCSI initiator to register with the iSNS server. To register an iSCSI initiator, add an iSNS server in the Discovery tab of the iSNS Initiator Properties dialog box. The Discovery Domains tab of the iSNS Server Properties dialog box is where you create groups of iSCSI devices to partition iSCSI resources. Creating discovery domains lets you limit which targets iSCSI initiators can discover and connect to. A discovery domain named Default DD is created automatically, and all registered iSCSI devices are added to it. You can create additional domains and move devices to them as needed to group devices together. An iSCSI target can be discovered by an initiator only if they're in the same discovery domain.

You can further partition devices by creating discovery domain sets, which consist of one or more discovery domains. A discovery domain set named Default DDS is created automatically and contains Default DD. Discovery domain sets can be enabled or disabled. iSCSI targets in disabled discovery domain sets can't be discovered by an iSCSI initiator.

Configuring iSCSI with PowerShell   Table 4-5 lists some commands for configuring iSCSI.

Table 4-5   iSCSI PowerShell cmdlets

Cmdlet	Description
Get-IscsiServerTarget	Shows information about an iSCSI target
Get-IscsiVirtualDisk	Shows information about an iSCSI virtual disk
New-IscsiServerTarget	Creates an iSCSI target
New-IscsiVirtualDisk	Creates an iSCSI virtual disk
Set-IscsiServerTarget	Configures settings of an iSCSI target
Set-IscsiVirtualDisk	Configures settings of an iSCSI virtual disk
Get-Command -Module IscsiTarget	Displays all cmdlets related to iSCSI targets
iSCSI initiator cmdlets	**Description**
Connect-IscsiTarget	Connects an initiator to a target
Disconnect-IscsiTarget	Disconnects an initiator from a target
Get-IscsiTarget	Shows information about all currently connected targets
Get-Command -Module iSCSI	Displays all cmdlets related to iSCSI initiators

Storage Thin Provisioning

An advantage of using virtual disks is the capability of **thin provisioning**, which is using dynamically expanding virtual disks so that they occupy only the amount of space on the physical disk that's currently used on the virtual disk. For example, if you create a dynamically expanding virtual disk, as you did in Activity 4-8, and make it 10 GB, the virtual disk occupies only about 70 MB on the physical disk until you start saving files to it. The virtual disk can grow to a maximum of the size specified when it was created—in this case, 10 GB. This feature allows you to store virtual disks with a maximum size that's actually larger than the physical disk they're stored on. If the limits of the physical disk are almost reached, you can add storage whenever needed or move some virtual disks to another storage location. The bottom line is that thin provisioning allows you to use just-in-time storage allocation by allocating only the space you currently need instead of allocating all the space you might need in the future. You can use thin provisioning with dynamically expanding virtual disks on Hyper-V virtual machines, with Storage Spaces virtual disks, and when creating iSCSI virtual disks.

Although dynamically expanding disks expand automatically as files are written to them, they don't necessarily shrink automatically when files are deleted. However, Windows Server 2012 R2 introduced a feature called "automatic trim and unmap," or simply **trim**, that allows a thinly provisioned disk to shrink automatically when data has been deleted from it. This feature is available for Hyper-V virtual machines with VHDX virtual disks. When Hyper-V recognizes that space on a virtual machine's disk is no longer needed, it informs the storage system where the virtual disk is located, and the storage system can reclaim the space by shrinking the VHDX file.

Tiered Storage

Tiered storage, a new feature in Windows Server 2012 R2 Storage Spaces, combines the speed of solid state drives (SSDs) with the low cost and high capacity of hard disk drives (HDDs). You can add SSDs to a storage pool with HDDs, and Windows keeps the most frequently accessed data on the faster SSD disks and moves less frequently accessed data to HDDs. This scheme improves performance substantially without the expense of moving all storage to costly SSDs.

To configure tiered storage, you must have at least one SSD and one HDD as part of a Storage Spaces storage spool. You specify tiered storage when you create a virtual disk with the New Virtual Disk Wizard in Storage Spaces. In the Virtual Disk Name window, click the "Create storage tiers on this virtual disk" check box, as shown in Figure 4-24. If Storage Spaces doesn't recognize a disk as an SSD, you can configure it as one with the following PowerShell cmdlet after the disk has been added to a storage pool:

```
Set-PhysicalDisk diskname -MediaType SSD
```

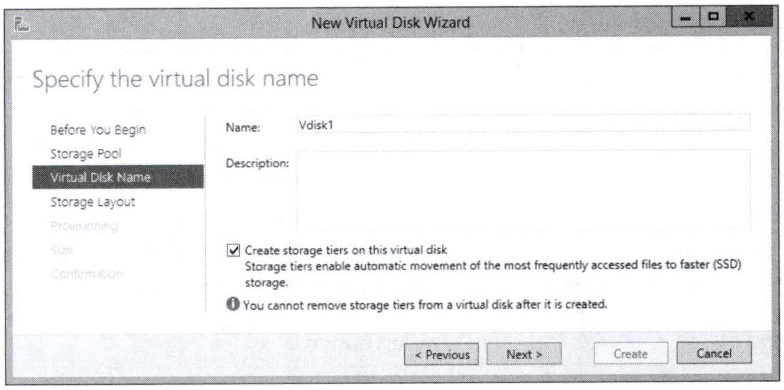

Figure 4-24 Creating a storage tier

After you select the storage layout and provisioning type, you configure the size of the virtual disk and how you want to use the SSDs and HDDs in the tier (see Figure 4-25). Normally, the amount of space you allocate from SSDs is considerably smaller than from HDDs. A typical ratio of HDD space to SSD space might be 4 to 1, 5 to 1, or higher. If you need to create more than one virtual disk, you can distribute space from a single SSD among several virtual disks.

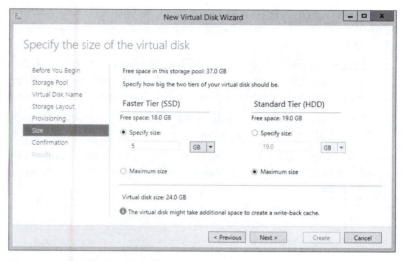

Figure 4-25   Configuring the size of storage tiers

Configuring Tiered Storage with PowerShell   Table 4-6 list some common commands for configuring tiered storage.

Table 4-6   Tiered storage PowerShell cmdlets

Cmdlet	Description
`Set-PhysicalDisk diskname -MediaType SSD`	Sets the media type of a physical disk in the pool to SSD
`New-StorageTier SSDTier -MediaType SSD`	Creates a storage tier named `SSDTier` and sets the media type to SSD
`New-StorageTier HDDTier -MediaType HDD`	Creates a storage tier named `HDDTier` and sets the media type to HDD
`$SSD=Get-StorageTier SSDTier` `  $HDD=Get-StorageTier HDDTier`	Stores information about storage tiers `SSDTier` and `HDDTier` in variables named `$SSD` and `$HDD`
`New-VirtualDisk diskname -StorageTiers` `  $SSD, $HDD -StorageTierSizes 40GB, 200GB`	Creates a virtual disk named `diskname` and assigns 40 GB to `SSDTier` and 200 GB to `HDDTier`
`Get-Command -Module Storage`	Displays all cmdlets related to storage

© 2016 Cengage Learning®

Features on Demand

When you install Windows Server 2012/R2, all the files you need to install server roles and features are copied to the C:\Windows\WinSxS folder, so you don't need any installation medium to install new roles and features. However, these files use a lot of disk space. Although disk space is fairly cheap and abundant, it's neither free nor infinite. When you're talking about a server hosting several virtual machines, the disk space used for server roles and features can have an impact, and it can be used for better purposes.

To address this problem, Windows Server 2012/R2 has added **Features on Demand**, which enables you to remove these files and free up the disk space they normally consume. If the files are needed later, such as for adding a server role, Windows can be directed to a network share, an installation medium, or Windows Update to get them. Another advantage of removing features you don't need is that Windows Update runs faster because it doesn't have to update files that have been removed.

Keep in mind that you can't remove these files from a feature you want to remain installed; it's used only to remove features you aren't currently using. Say you have Windows Server 2012/R2 installed with a GUI, along with Active Directory and DHCP. You have configured the server the way you need it and now find that you can manage it remotely and no longer need the GUI components. To convert the server to a Server Core installation, use this command in PowerShell:

```
Uninstall-WindowsFeature Server-Gui-Shell, Server-Gui-Mgmt-Infra
  -Restart
```

This command removes the GUI features of Windows Server 2012/R2 and restarts the server, but it leaves the installation files in the C:\Windows\WinSxS folder. To uninstall the feature and remove these files, you add the -Remove option to the command:

```
Uninstall-WindowsFeature Server-Gui-Shell,
  Server-Gui-Mgmt-Infra -Remove -Restart
```

You can use this command on any role, role service, or feature you want. To see a list of available roles and features, use the Get-WindowsFeature command, which yields the output shown in Figure 4-26.

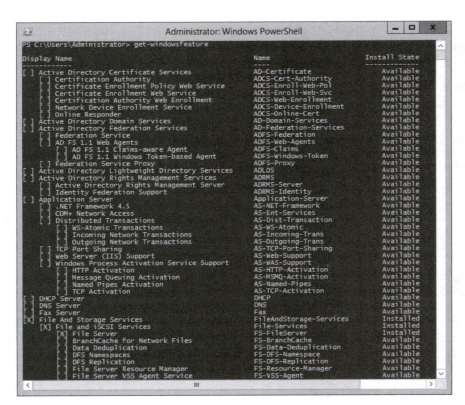

Figure 4-26   A list of all Windows features and their status

If you want to narrow the display down to only those features that are installed, use the following command to yield the output in Figure 4-27.

```
Get-WindowsFeature | where InstallState -eq Installed
```

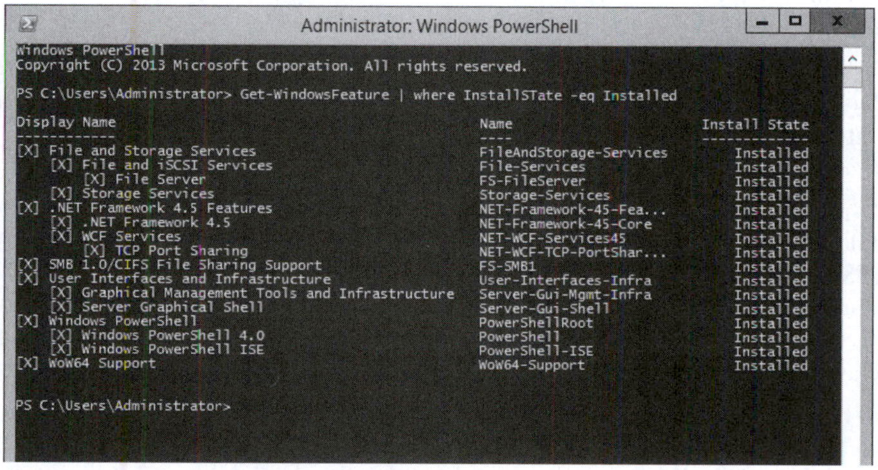

Figure 4-27   Viewing only installed features

You can replace the string `Installed` with `Removed` or `Available`, depending on the list you want to see. The `Removed` option displays features that no longer have installation files in the C:\Windows\WinSxS folder. The `Available` option shows features that are in the folder but not currently installed. For example, to remove all available features (leaving the installed features as they are) and restart the server, use the following command:

```
Get-WindowsFeature | where InstallState -eq Available|
  Uninstall-WindowsFeature -Remove
```

This command removes all files from the C:\Windows\WinSxS folder for features that aren't currently installed, and you need to specify another source if you want to install any removed features. It also creates a list of all features that have an install state of `Available` and pipes this list to the `Uninstall-WindowsFeature` cmdlet, which uninstalls the features (if necessary) and then removes the files. You can verify the results by using this command:

```
Get-WindowsFeature | where InstallState -eq Removed
```

Using this command also reduces the C:\Windows\WinSxS folder by about 2 GB, which, of course, is the objective.

If you have removed installation files and need to install a role or feature later, you can do so by specifying another location where Windows can find the installation files. The most common way to do this is to create a feature file store (also called a "side-by-side store"). A **feature file store** is a network share containing the files required to install roles, role services, and features on Windows Server 2012/R2 servers. To create a feature file store, create a network share and assign Read permissions for the Everyone group (or a group containing the computer accounts that will access the store). Then copy the Sources\SxS folder from the Windows Server 2012/R2 installation medium to the shared folder. You can then install a role or feature from the feature file store by using the following command.

```
Install-WindowsFeature FeatureName -Source \\Server\Share
```

In this command, you replace *FeatureName* with the name of the role or feature you want to install and *Server**Share* with the UNC path of the share you created for the feature file store.

Chapter Summary

- BranchCache is a file-sharing technology that allows computers at a branch office to cache files retrieved from a central server across a WAN link. It supports content stored on Windows Server 2008 R2 and later servers running the File Server Role for SMB shares, the Web Server role, and the BITS feature.

- BranchCache has two modes of operation: distributed cache mode and hosted cache mode. Distributed cache mode is the best solution for small branch offices where having a dedicated server is neither practical nor desirable. Hosted cache mode is best for branch offices that already have servers performing other functions, such as a domain controller or a DHCP server.

- File Classification Infrastructure (FCI) is a feature of File Server Resource Manager (FSRM) that allows classifying files by assigning new properties to them. To use it, you must install File Server Resource Manager, a role service under the File and Storage Services role, and then enable or create classification properties that are applied by using classification rules.

- With file access auditing enabled, events are created in the Security log to show that access to a file was attempted. Auditing in Windows Server 2012/R2 includes the auditing features available in previous versions and adds the following improvements: targeting specific files and users, combining global object access auditing with Dynamic Access Control (DAC), including data access events that contain more information, and auditing removable storage devices.

- A global object access auditing policy affects the entire file system or Registry on computers in the scope of the GPO where the policy is defined. If a file system object has auditing defined from global object access auditing and from a SACL manually defined on the object, auditing is derived from a combination of both settings.

- Network File System (NFS) is a file-sharing protocol that allows users to access files and folders on other computers across a network. Windows Server 2012/R2 supports an NFS server component as a role service under the File and Storage Services role and an NFS client component as a feature.

- Microsoft added the capability to provide fault tolerance and high availability to Server for NFS in Windows Server 2012 by allowing an NFS share (called an "NFS data store") to be configured on a Windows failover cluster.

- A storage area network (SAN) uses high-speed networking technologies to give servers fast access to large amounts of shared disk storage. You can set up a SAN with Windows servers by using the iSCSI protocol. The iSCSI protocol carries SCSI device commands over an IP network.

- An iSCSI target is a logical storage space made available to iSCSI clients by a server running the iSCSI Target Server role service. An iSCSI initiator is the iSCSI client that sends iSCSI commands to the iSCSI target.

- The Internet Storage Name Service (iSNS) is an IP-based protocol used to communicate between iSNS clients and servers. iSNS offers these benefits for iSCSI SANs on large networks: scalability, manageability, and monitoring.

- Thin provisioning is using dynamically expanding virtual disks so that they occupy only the amount of space on the physical disk that's currently in use on the virtual disk. Trim allows a thinly provisioned disk to shrink automatically when data has been deleted from it.

- Tiered storage is a new feature in Windows Server 2012 R2 Storage Spaces that combines the speed of SSDs with the low cost and high capacity of HDDs. To configure tiered storage, you must have at least one SSD and one HDD as part of a Storage Spaces storage spool.

■ Features on Demand enables you to remove unneeded installation files and free up the disk space they normally consume. If you have removed installation files and need to install a role or feature later, you can do so by specifying another location where Windows can find the installation files.

■ A feature file store is a network share containing the files required to install roles, role services, and features on Windows Server 2012/R2 servers.

Key Terms

block-level storage   Storage seen by the storage client as a local drive.

BranchCache   A file-sharing technology that allows computers at a branch office to cache files retrieved from a central server across a WAN link.

classification property   A file attribute containing a value that's used to categorize the data in a file or an aspect of the file, such as its location or creation time.

content information   A message transferred from a BranchCache server to a client that indicates to the client where the file can be retrieved from the cache in the branch office. *See also* BranchCache.

distributed cache mode   A BranchCache mode of operation in which cached data is distributed among client computers in the branch office. *See also* BranchCache.

feature file store   A network share containing the files required to install roles, role services, and features on Windows Server 2012/R2 servers.

Features on Demand   A feature in Windows Server 2012/R2 that enables you to remove unneeded installation files and free up the disk space they normally consume.

File Classification Infrastructure (FCI)   A feature of File Server Resource Manager that allows classifying files by assigning new properties to them. The properties can then be used to create rules for searching or perform tasks on files meeting the criteria of the assigned properties.

file-level storage   Storage that the client has access to only as files and folders.

global object access auditing policy   A group policy setting that affects the auditing status of an entire file system or Registry on computers in the scope of the GPO where the policy is defined.

hosted cache mode   A BranchCache mode of operation in which cached data is stored on one or more file servers in the branch office. *See also* BranchCache.

Internet Storage Name Service (iSNS)   An IP-based protocol used to communicate between iSNS clients and servers for the purpose of allowing iSCSI devices to discover and monitor one another.

iSCSI initiator   An iSCSI client that sends iSCSI commands to an iSCSI target. *See also* iSCSI target.

iSCSI logical unit number (LUN)   A reference ID to a logical drive the iSCSI initiator uses when accessing storage on the iSCSI target server.

iSCSI qualified name (IQN)   An identifier for iSCSI targets and initiators used to identify the iSCSI device in an iSCSI connection.

iSCSI target   A logical storage space made available to iSCSI clients by a server running the iSCSI Target Server role service.

Network File System (NFS)   A file-sharing protocol that allows users to access files and folders on other computers across a network; it's the native file-sharing protocol of Linux and UNIX systems.

NFS data store   An NFS share on a Windows failover cluster that provides a highly available storage solution for applications using NFS. *See also* Network File System (NFS).

storage area network (SAN) A storage system that uses high-speed networking technologies to give servers fast access to large amounts of shared disk storage.

system access control list (SACL) An attribute of a file system object that defines whether and how a file system object is to be audited.

thin provisioning The use of dynamically expanding virtual disks so that they occupy only the amount of space on the physical disk that's currently in use on the virtual disk.

tiered storage A feature of Storage Spaces that combines the speed of solid state drives with the low cost and high capacity of hard disk drives.

trim A feature that allows a thinly provisioned disk to shrink automatically when data has been deleted from the disk. *See also* thin provisioning.

Review Questions

1. Which of the following features or services should you install on Windows Server 2012 if you want to improve file-sharing performance in a remote office connected to the main office by a WAN link?

   a. File Classification Infrastructure

   b. Network File System

   c. BranchCache

   d. iSCSI Target Server

2. Which of the following can benefit from using the BranchCache role service? (Choose all that apply.)

   a. File Server

   b. Web Server

   c. Network File System

   d. BITS

3. Which mode should you configure if you want to support multiple subnets?

   a. Hosted cache mode

   b. Distributed cache mode

   c. File classification mode

   d. Tiered storage mode

4. Which of the following is a requirement for configuring a server in hosted cache mode?

   a. Windows Server 2012 or later

   b. Windows Server 2008 R2 or later

   c. Windows Server 2003 or later

   d. Windows Server 2008 or later

5. Which FSRM feature should you use if you want to set certain attributes of a file automatically based on its contents?

   a. File Screening Management

   b. Quota Management

   c. Classification Management

   d. Storage Reports Management

6. Which of the following is a file attribute containing a value that's used to categorize the data in a file or an aspect of the file, such as its location or creation time?

   a. File extension

   b. Catalog property

   c. Classification property

   d. File policy

7. You want to use a predefined classification property named Confidentiality. What should you do before you use this property the first time?

   a. Enable it in ADAC and synchronize resource properties.

   b. Create it in ADAC and move it to FSRM.

   c. Run the `Update-FsrmClassificationPropertyDefinition` cmdlet.

   d. Create the property by using the `Set-ADResourceProperty` cmdlet.

8. You want a security event to be created whenever a user who's a member of the accounting group accesses a file named payroll on any server on the network. What should you do?

   a. Create a new resource property named Payroll and add it to the global DACL.

   b. Create a file classification for the payroll file that searches for the string `accounting`.

   c. Add the accounting group to the DACL of each file on each server.

   d. Create a global object access auditing policy and add the accounting group to the SACL.

9. A group of consultants has been hired to do some work for your company. The consultants need access to some shared files on your Windows Server 2012 R2 systems. They will be bringing their laptops that run Linux. You have learned that they're required to use the native file-sharing system on their laptops. What should you do to facilitate sharing the files on your servers?

   a. Install the SMB protocol on your servers.

   b. Configure a Linux to Windows gateway server.

   c. Install the iSCSI shared storage feature.

   d. Install the Server for NFS role service on your servers.

10. You need a highly available file-sharing system that accommodates the native Linux and UNIX file-sharing protocol. What do you need to configure?

    a. A Network File System data store

    b. A round-robin SMB file share

    c. A SAN using the iSNS protocol

    d. A server cluster using SMB

11. Which of the following is a logical storage space consisting of one or more virtual disks in an iSCSI system?

    a. iSCSI qualified name

    b. iSCSI target

    c. iSCSI initiator

    d. iSNS server

12. What does iSCSI use to reference a logical drive provided by the iSCSI target?

    a. iSCSI LUN

    b. IQN value

    c. iSNS ID

    d. Target ID

13. If you enable authentication on an iSCSI target, what authentication protocol is used?

    a. PAP

    b. CHAP

    c. EAP

    d. PEAP

14. When looking over an iSCSI configuration, you see the string `iqn.1991-05.com.microsoft:SAN.domain1.local`. What are you looking at?

    a. iSCSI initiator handle

    b. iSCSI target name

    c. Internet Storage Name

    d. iSCSI qualified name

15. You want to be able to group iSCSI devices and manage them from a central server. What should you install?

    a. iSCSI LUN

    b. iSCSI Management Service

    c. iSNS Server

    d. iSCSI Target Server

16. You have a Hyper-V server with about 1 TB of free disk space. You want to configure four virtual machines, with each having a 300 GB disk drive. The VMs' virtual disks will reside on the Hyper-V server. How should you configure these VMs?

    a. Using Features on Demand

    b. Using tiered storage

    c. Using thin provisioning

    d. Using differencing disks

17. You're configuring some virtual disks with Storage Spaces. The disks should balance high performance with reasonable cost. What new feature in Windows Server 2012 R2 should you consider using to achieve this goal?

    a. Tiered storage

    b. NFS data store

    c. Features on Demand

    d. Thin provisioning

18. You want to optimize the space used by your Hyper-V virtual machine's virtual disks. You're running Hyper-V on Windows Server 2012 R2 servers. What feature can you use to ensure that your VMs are taking no more space than necessary on your storage system?

    a. On-demand tiering

    b. Automatic trim and unmap

    c. Automatic provisioning

    d. On-demand storage

19. When you install Windows Server 2012 R2, where are the files you need to install roles and features copied to by default?

    a. C:\Windows\WinSxS

    b. NFS data store

    c. Feature file store

    d. C:\Program Files\Install

20. Which of the following is a network share containing the files required to install roles, role services, and features on Windows Server 2012/R2 servers?

    a. Network install cache

    b. Shared installation folder

    c. Feature file store

    d. On-demand file share

Case Projects

Case Project 4-1: Using Advanced File and Storage Features

You're the IT administrator for CSM Tech Publishing. You've just had a meeting with the general manager about some data storage problems the company has been having. You've been asked to find solutions for the following problems:

- Two satellite offices have been complaining about slow access to shared files on the servers at the company's headquarters. One office has about 25 client computers running Windows 8.1, and there's one server running Windows Server 2012 R2 that provides DHCP and DNS services but isn't heavily loaded. The other office has only four client machines running Windows 8.1. There's no budget for additional hardware at either location.

- You have a database application that has been exhibiting poor performance caused by latency from the drives it uses for storage. The storage system uses Storage Spaces and consists of four 200 GB HDDs. You have been asked to see what you can do to improve the performance of the storage used by the database application. You have a limited budget for the project—certainly not enough for a new server but probably enough for some new components.

What solutions do you propose for these two file and storage problems? Include implementation details.

Case Project 4-2: Solving a File Management Problem

Your boss has asked you to find a way to track files on the servers containing confidential employee information: in particular, Social Security numbers. She wants to be able to locate and audit files containing this information easily. What steps should you take to accommodate this request?

chapter 5

Configuring DAC and IPAM

**After reading this chapter and completing
the exercises, you will be able to:**

- Configure Dynamic Access Control
- Configure Internet Protocol Address Management

This chapter expands on the File Classification Infrastructure feature you learned about in Chapter 4 by explaining how to use file classification to control access to files. This powerful new method for controlling file access is called Dynamic Access Control (DAC). You learn how to build the DAC infrastructure, configure user claims, and set permission conditions on files and folders.

In Chapter 3, you learned about advanced DHCP configurations. In this chapter, you learn how to use a new management tool called Internet Protocol Address Management (IPAM) to centrally manage DHCP servers and IP address spaces. You learn how to install and provision an IPAM server, select servers to manage, collect server data, and delegate IPAM administration.

Configuring Dynamic Access Control

Table 5-1 lists what you need for the hands-on activities in this chapter.

Table 5-1   **Activity requirements**

Activity	Requirements	Notes
Activity 5-1: Configuring Resource Properties	412Server1	
Activity 5-2: Creating and Classifying Folders and Files	412Server1	
Activity 5-3: Creating Claim Types	412Server1	
Activity 5-4: Configuring Group Policy for Claims Support	412Server1	
Activity 5-5: Setting Permission Conditions On a Folder	412Server1	
Activity 5-6: Creating Users to Test DAC	412Server1	
Activity 5-7: Checking Effective Access	412Server2	
Activity 5-8: Testing Access to a Folder	412Server1, 412Win8	
Activity 5-9: Creating Central Access Policies	412Server1	
Activity 5-10: Configuring Group Policies to Deploy a Central Access Policy	412Server1	
Activity 5-11: Testing Central Access Policy Deployment	412Server1	
Activity 5-12: Removing DAC Group Policies	412Server1	
Activity 5-13: Demoting a Server Before Installing IPAM	412Server1, 412Server2	
Activity 5-14: Installing and Provisioning the IPAM Server	412Server1, 412Server2	
Activity 5-15: Discovering and Selecting Servers	412Server1, 412Server2	
Activity 5-16: Using IPAM	412Server1, 412Server2	
Activity 5-17: Removing IPAM	412Server1, 412Server2	

© 2016 Cengage Learning®

Dynamic Access Control (DAC) gives administrators another method for securing access to files that's more powerful than file and folder permissions based simply on group memberships. With DAC, administrators can control file access by using complex criteria that can include file classification and user attributes. For example, suppose you have a file share named Marketing. Inside the file share is a variety of files with differing levels of confidentiality. You want everyone in the Marketing Department to have Read access to all the files with low confidentiality and the Marketing Department executives to have Modify access to all files in the share, including those with a higher level of confidentiality.

You could set up this access by using a few groups, careful placement of users in these groups, and careful assessment of which files have what level of confidentiality. However, using DAC along with File Classification Infrastructure (FCI, introduced in Chapter 4) makes the job easier and more accurate in the long run and helps reduce the complexity of security group management. DAC and FCI require somewhat substantial time and effort to learn, but after you understand how to use them, you'll see they're very powerful tools for organizing and securing data.

DAC works *with* sharing and NTFS permissions; it's not a replacement for them. Perhaps the best way to illustrate DAC is with screenshots of a folder with a file classification and DAC conditions applied, as in Figures 5-1 and 5-2. Figure 5-1 shows the Classification tab in the Properties dialog box for the Marketing folder, which is classified as low confidentiality and belonging to the Marketing Department. Figure 5-2 shows the Advanced Security Settings dialog

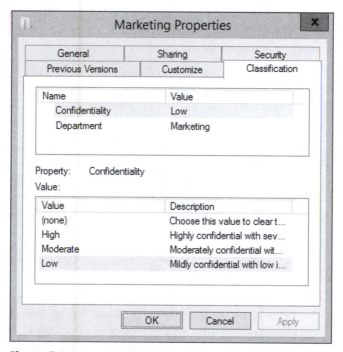

Figure 5-1   The Classification tab

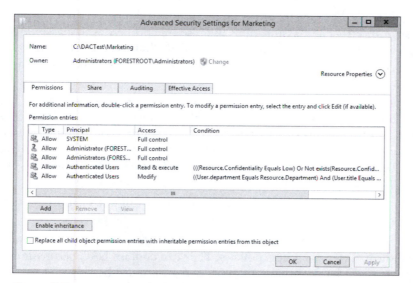

Figure 5-2   DAC settings in a folder's Advanced Security Settings dialog box

box for the Marketing folder. There are two Authenticated Users entries with a value in the Condition column, which is where you find DAC information. The first Authenticated Users entry states that "Authenticated Users have Read & execute access if the confidentiality of the file is low and the user's department is the same as the file's department." The second Authenticated

Users entry states that "Authenticated Users have Modify access if the user's department is the same as the file's department and the user is an executive."

What these permissions mean is that users with the Department attribute set to Marketing have Read access to all files belonging to the Marketing Department that have low confidentiality. Users with the Department attribute set to Marketing and the Title attribute set to Executive have Modify access to all files in the Marketing Department, regardless of confidentiality. So executives have Modify access to files classified as low, moderate, or high confidentiality. Users who aren't in the Marketing Department have no access to any files in the folder. You can use compound conditions joined by And and Or to create permissions based on user attributes, file classifications, and traditional group memberships.

 The Department and Title attributes are set in the Organization tab of the user account's Properties dialog box.

Now that you have an overview of DAC, the following sections explore some details of using it. You must take several steps before using DAC, and there are two ways to set conditions for file access: manually and with group policies. First, you see how to set up the DAC infrastructure and set permission conditions manually, and then you see how to use central access policies to set permissions with the Group Policy tool.

Building a DAC Infrastructure

The DAC infrastructure consists of several parts:

- *Resource properties*—Resource properties were discussed in Chapter 4 when you learned about FCI. A **resource property** is an attribute that can be applied to a resource, such as a file or folder, and is used to classify resources. For example, a file can be assigned the resource property Department with the value Marketing so that it's known the file belongs to the Marketing Department. Resource properties are managed in Active Directory Administrative Center (ADAC). Those defined by Microsoft have an "_MS" suffix after the resource property ID.

- *File classifications*—File classifications use resource properties to classify data in files and folders. They aren't a required component of DAC, but using them is what makes DAC so powerful. The File Server Resource Manager (FSRM) role service must be installed to use file classifications.

- *Claim types*—A claim type is a property of a user or computer used in a claim. A **claim** is an assertion an entity (user or computer) makes about what it is or what it does for the purpose of authenticating or gaining access to a resource. For example, a user account can use the value of its Job Title field in a claim to access an object that has an access condition set, such as "Users with Title=Executive have read access." For use in DAC and Kerberos authentication, claims must be enabled on DCs by using group policies.

- *Central access policies*—**Central access policies** consist of one or more central access rules and are used to configure resource permissions with group policies.

- *Central access rules*—**Central access rules** set permissions on targeted resources and are deployed through central access policies. They can contain DAC permissions and regular NTFS permissions based on user accounts and group memberships.

An example of file access requirements is used to illustrate configuring the DAC infrastructure, and you walk through the steps needed to satisfy these requirements. To simplify it, files are classified manually rather than automatically. After you review the process, you work through hands-on activities to set up and test DAC. Here are the requirements:

- There's a file share named Marketing.

- The Marketing file share contains files of varying levels of confidentiality.

- User accounts with the Department attribute set to Marketing have read access to all files classified as Department=Marketing and Confidentiality=Low.

- User accounts with the Department attribute set to Marketing and the Job Title attribute set to Executive have modify access to all files classified as Marketing, regardless of the confidentiality.

- Administrators have full control access to all files.

For this example, access rules are created manually at first, and then you set up central access rules and central access policies.

Configuring Resource Properties

You need to define the resource properties for classifying files. To find them, click Dynamic Access Control in ADAC and double-click Resource Properties. Several predefined resource properties (see Figure 5-3), which are disabled by default, are available.

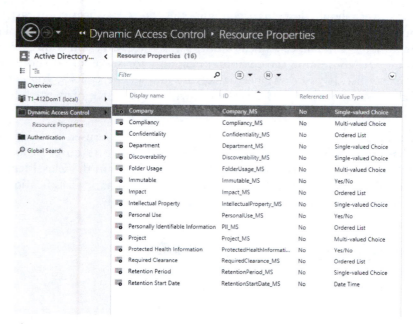

Figure 5-3   Predefined resource properties in ADAC

You can enable existing resource properties defined by Microsoft or create your own if none fit your needs. When you create a resource property, enter the following pieces of information:

- *Display name*—The name of the resource property.

- *Value type*—The type of value the resource property contains. Choices are Date Time, Multi-valued Choice, Multi-valued Text, Number, Ordered List, Single-valued Choice, Text, and Yes/No.

- *Description*—An optional description of how the resource property should be used.

- *Is used for authorization*—If enabled, the resource property can be used to determine access to a resource. If this option isn't enabled, the resource property can't be used for authorization.

- *Suggested values*—You can populate the resource property with a list of suggested values. If the resource property is named Business Unit, for instance, you can add suggested values such as Office Products, Software, Publishing, and so forth. Not all value types can have suggested values.

For example, if you want to classify a resource based on whether it contains budget information, you can create a resource property named BudgetInfo and give it the value type Yes/No. If a file or folder contains budget information, you can set the BudgetInfo property to Yes in the Classification tab of the file's Properties dialog box.

Getting back to the example, you need to classify files based on the department the file belongs to and the file's level of confidentiality. You can use the predefined resource properties named Department and Confidentiality. The Department resource property is already populated with some department names, including Marketing, so all you need to do is enable the property by right-clicking it and clicking Enable. You can add suggested values, if you like. The Confidentiality resource property is populated with the values Low, Moderate, and High, which suits the needs of this example, so you just need to enable this resource property, too.

Resource properties must be a member of a **resource property list** for file servers to download and use them. To access resource property lists in ADAC, click Dynamic Access Control and then double-click Resource Property Lists. The Global Resource Property List is defined by default and contains all resource properties. You can create new resource property lists if you want to categorize resource properties for easier management. To specify which resource property lists your servers should download, configure the "File Classification Infrastructure: Specify classification properties list" policy, which is under Computer Configuration, Policies, Administrative Templates, System, File Classification Infrastructure. After you configure the policy, link the GPO to the OU containing the computer accounts for servers that should download the resource property list. If you don't need to create new property lists, you can skip this step because all file servers with FSRM installed download resource properties from the Global Resource Property List.

Classifying Files   After a resource property is enabled, it can be used to classify files. Figure 5-4 shows the Classification tab of the Marketing folder after two resource properties have been enabled. Each resource property you enable or create is listed in the Classification tab of files and folders. At this point, you might use FSRM to set up automatic classification of files, as you did in Chapter 4, but for now, you just classify the files manually.

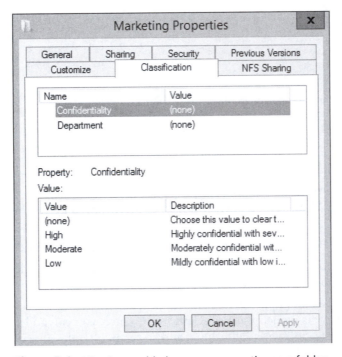

Figure 5-4   Viewing enabled resource properties on a folder

After a resource property is enabled, it might not show up in the Classification tab immediately. To see it immediately, run the PowerShell cmdlet `Update-FsrmClassificationPropertyDefinition` on each server containing files you want to classify; otherwise, the server downloads resource properties automatically, usually within several minutes.

To classify a file, open the file's Properties dialog box and click the Classification tab. As Figure 5-4 shows, the resource properties you enabled are listed with the value "(none)." Click a property in the top pane, and click a value in the bottom pane. If you want to clear an existing value, click (none) in the bottom pane. For this example, set Confidentiality to Low and Department to Marketing. Because the property is set on the folder, all files (and subfolders) in the Marketing folder inherit the values you set.

Next, two files are created in the Marketing folder: LowConfidential and HighConfidential. These files inherit the settings from the folder, so the Confidentiality property on the HighConfidential file is just changed to High (see Figure 5-5).

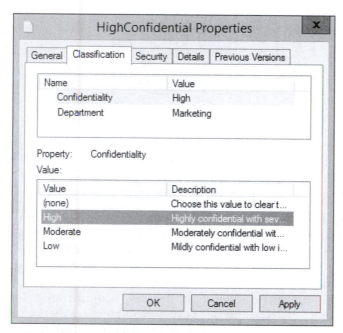

Figure 5-5   Setting a file classification

Files and folders can be classified only on computers running Windows Server 2008 R2 and later. The Classification tab isn't available on computers running a Windows client OS, such as Windows 7 or 8.1.

Configuring Claims   In the example, you want to restrict access to marketing files based on a user account's Department and Job Title attributes. Before you can set permissions on files with these attributes, you need to create claims so that you can use account attributes in permission conditions. To create a claim, click Dynamic Access Control in ADAC, and then double-click Claim Types. Create a claim type by clicking New in the Tasks pane and clicking Claim Type. In the Create Claim Type window, you see a list of Active Directory attributes. Click the attribute named Department, and click OK, and then repeat for the attribute named Title, which corresponds to a user's job title. When you click an attribute, you can change the display name; for example, in Figure 5-6, the display name for the title attribute is changed to Job Title.

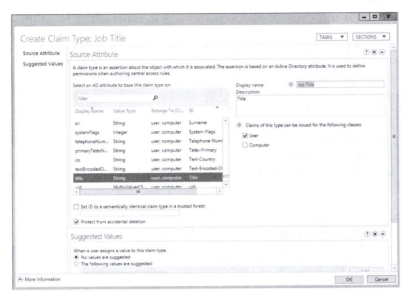

Figure 5-6   Creating a claim type

In the Suggested Values section, you can add values to suggest for attributes. For example, for the Department attribute, you can add Marketing, Accounting, and so forth. For the Title attribute, you can add Executive, Manager, and so on. When you use the claim in a permission condition, you can choose from the suggested values or enter a new value.

Configuring Group Policy for Claims Support   Before a domain controller can support claims and resource properties for controlling authorization to resources, a group policy setting must be configured on a GPO linked to the Domain Controllers OU. You can create a GPO or edit the Default Domain Controllers GPO, but best practices suggest creating a GPO and linking it to the Domain Controllers OU. Open the GPO in the Group Policy Management Editor and navigate to Computer Configuration, Policies, Administrative Templates, System, KDC. Open the policy named "KDC support for claims, compound authentication and Kerberos armoring" and enable it. To make sure the policy takes effect immediately, run `gpupdate` at a command prompt.

At this point, domain controllers running Windows Server 2012/R2 support claims and resource properties in file and folder permission conditions, which you set next. However, client computers must also have claims support enabled so that they pass the necessary information to Kerberos during authentication and authorization. Client support for DAC is configured in Group Policy by enabling the "Kerberos client support for claims, compound authentication and Kerberos armoring" policy under Computer Configuration, Policies, Administrative Templates, System, Kerberos. The GPO the policy is enabled on must be linked to the domain or an OU containing the computer accounts from which users access resources secured by DAC. After the policy is updated on client computers, users' access to resources across the network is governed by sharing and NTFS permissions along with DAC conditions, when configured.

The domain functional level must be set to Windows Server 2012 or later to support DAC, and client computers must be running Windows 8 or later.

Setting Permission Conditions   For the purposes of this example, you set permission conditions on the Marketing folder manually. Later, you create central access policies that automatically set permission conditions on targeted resources. First, you create a folder named Marketing and share it with the default permissions. These permissions give Everyone and the local Administrators group Full Control sharing permissions and give the Administrator account and the local Administrators group Full Control NTFS permissions.

Next, set permission conditions. First, add Authenticated Users to the permissions list of the Marketing folder and give Authenticated Users Read access with the following conditions: "If the resource named Confidentiality has a value of Low and the Department attribute of the user equals the Department resource property." Figure 5-7 shows what the condition looks like in the permissions entry for the Marketing folder.

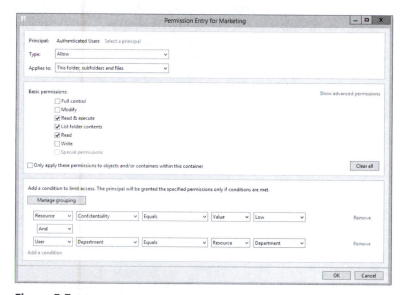

Figure 5-7   A permissions entry with a condition added

In the second condition, you could have specified that the user's Department attribute equals Marketing, but by specifying that the user's Department attribute equals the Department resource property, the same condition works for other departments.

Now you can add a second permission entry that gives Marketing users who have the title Executive Modify access to all files belonging to Marketing. This condition looks like Figure 5-8.

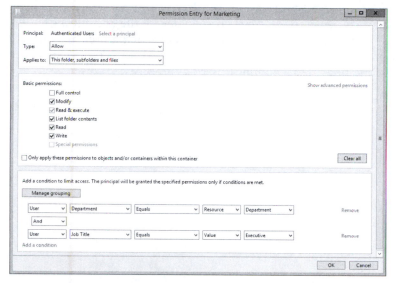

Figure 5-8   A permission entry to give Modify access to executives

It's important to understand that the Confidentiality and Department resource properties aren't available in the Permission Entry dialog box until they're enabled in ADAC, and the User Department and Title attributes aren't available in the Permission Entry dialog box until claim types have been created for them.

You don't need to include resource properties or claim types in permission conditions. You can create a condition based solely on a user's group memberships. For example, you can create a condition that says, in effect, "Allow read access if the user is a member of the Accounting group and is also a member of the Accounts Payable group."

Testing Dynamic Access Control   Now that DAC is configured on some shares, it's time to test everything. First, some user accounts are created, and then you look at the effective access for these users for the Marketing folder and files. Next, you verify that permissions are enforced on a user logging on from a client computer.

An OU named TestDAC is created, and three users are added to this OU: accounting1, marketing1, and executive1. Table 5-2 shows their attribute settings.

Table 5-2   Attribute settings for the TestDAC OU

User account	Department	Job title
accounting1	Accounting	None set
marketing1	Marketing	Manager
executive1	Marketing	Executive

© 2016 Cengage Learning®

The Department and Job Title attributes are set in the Organization tab of the user account's Properties dialog box. From a client computer, you can verify policy setting and claims of the currently logged-on user account by entering `whoami /claims` at a command prompt. The output shows the claims the currently logged-on user presents to Kerberos when attempting to access resources.

To test the access conditions set on the Marketing folder, open the Advanced Security Settings dialog box for the folder. In the Effective Access tab, select the accounting1 user. Next, you include a user claim and set the Department attribute to Accounting. The effective access function requires specifying claims for the user; it doesn't access user attributes automatically. By specifying claims in the Effective Access tab, you can perform what-if functions on users. To view the effective access to the Marketing folder by the accounting1 user, click the "View effective access" button. Because the condition specifies that a user must have the same Department attribute as the resource property, and the user's department is Accounting and the folder's department is Marketing, the accounting1 user has no access.

Then you do the same thing for the marketing1 and executive1 users. According to the condition, the marketing1 user should have Read permission to the folder, and executive1 should have Modify permission. Figure 5-9 shows the settings in the Effective Access tab and results for the executive1 user.

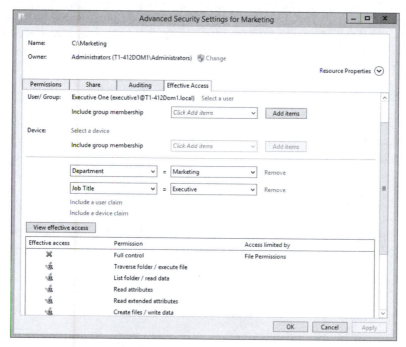

Figure 5-9 The Effective Access tab for the executive1 user

Based on the conditions set on the Marketing folder and its files, the accounting1 user should have no access to the folder or its files, and the marketing1 user should have Read access to the folder and any files in the folder classified as Confidentiality=Low. The executive1 user should have Modify access to all files.

Now that you have an understanding of the process for setting up and using DAC, the next several activities step you through setting it up and testing it on a server and client.

Activity 5-1: Configuring Resource Properties

Time Required: 5 minutes
Objective: Configure resource properties for DAC deployment and testing.

Required Tools and Equipment: 412Server1
Description: In this activity, you enable and configure resource properties for deploying and testing DAC. The File Server Resource Manager must already be installed, which you did in Activity 4-3.

1. Start 412Server1 and log on as **Administrator**, if necessary.

2. In Server Manager, click **Tools, Active Directory Administrative Center** from the menu. In the Active Directory Administrative Center, click **Dynamic Access Control** in the left pane.

3. In the right pane, double-click **Resource Properties**. Verify that the Confidentiality resource is enabled (which you did in Activity 4-4). An enabled resource property has a dark gray icon next to it; a disabled resource property is light gray with a dark circle and a white down arrow.

4. Right-click the **Department** resource property and click **Enable**. Double-click the **Department** resource property. In the Suggested Values list box, scroll through the prepopulated values and verify that Marketing is among them. Click **Cancel**.

5. In the left pane, click **Dynamic Access Control**, and in the right pane, double-click **Resource Property Lists**. Double-click the default resource property list named **Global Resource Property List**.

6. If you needed to organize properties for use by specific servers, you could create new property lists, add resource properties to them, and deploy the lists via Group Policy. The Global Resource Property List window (see Figure 5-10) contains all resource properties and is available to all servers. You don't need to create new resource property lists because the global list is enough, so click **Cancel**.

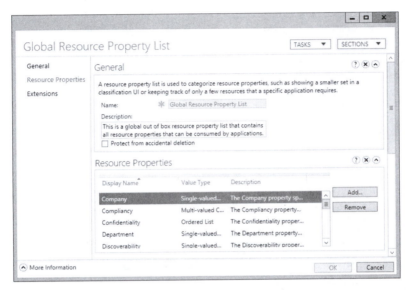

Figure 5-10   The Global Resource Property List window

7. You need to update the availability of the resource properties (although the server eventually updates it automatically). Open a PowerShell prompt, and then type **Update-FsrmClassificationPropertyDefinition** and press **Enter**. Close the PowerShell prompt.

8. Stay logged on to 412Server1 if you're continuing to the next activity.

Activity 5-2: Creating and Classifying Folders and Files

Time Required: 10 minutes
Objective: Create a folder and some files to classify.

Required Tools and Equipment: 412Server1
Description: In this activity, you create a folder named Marketing and create two files in the folder so that you can set classifications on them.

1. Start 412Server1, and log on as **Administrator**, if necessary.

2. Open File Explorer. Create a folder named **Marketing** in the root of the C drive. Right-click the **Marketing** folder, point to **Share with**, and click **Specific people**. The Administrator user already has Read/Write access, and the Administrators group is the owner. Click the list arrow, click **Everyone**, and click **Add**. In the Permission Level column next to Everyone, click **Read/Write**, and then click **Share**. Click **Done**. Sharing permissions are set so that Everyone and Administrators have Full Control sharing permissions.

3. To change the NTFS permissions accordingly, right-click the **Marketing** folder and click **Properties**. Click **Security**, and then click **Edit**. Click **Everyone** in the top pane and click **Remove**. Now only System, the Administrator user, and the Administrators group have NTFS permissions. You add new permissions later. Click **OK**.

4. Click the **Classification** tab. You see the Confidentiality and Department resource properties. The Confidentiality property is selected by default, so click **Low** in the bottom pane. Click the **Department** property in the top pane, and click **Marketing** in the bottom pane. Click **Apply**. The Classification tab should look similar to Figure 5-11. Click **OK**.

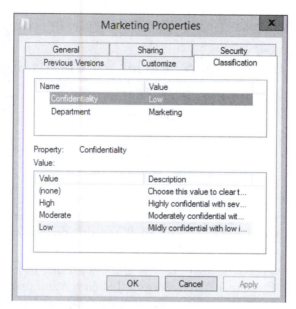

Figure 5-11   Classifying the Marketing folder

5. Open the Marketing folder, and create two text files named **HighConfidential** and **LowConfidential**. Right-click the **HighConfidential** file and click **Properties**. Click the **Classification** tab. Like permissions, classifications are inherited from the parent folder. With the Confidentiality property selected, click **High** in the lower pane, and then click **OK**. You now have two files, both with the Department property set to Marketing and one with the Confidentiality property set to Low and one with it set to High. Close File Explorer.

6. Stay logged on to 412Server1 if you're continuing to the next activity.

Activity 5-3: Creating Claim Types

Time Required: 15 minutes
Objective: Create claim types for use in DAC.

Required Tools and Equipment: 412Server1
Description: In this activity, you use the Active Directory Administrative Center to create claim types for the Department and Job Title attributes of user accounts.

1. Start 412Server1, and log on as **Administrator**, if necessary.

2. Open the Active Directory Administrative Center, if necessary. In the left pane, click **Dynamic Access Control**, and in the right pane, double-click **Claim Types**.

3. In the Tasks pane, under Claim Types, click **New**, and then click **Claim Type**. In the Create Claim Type window, you see a list of attributes you can create claims from. To find the Department attribute quickly, type **department** in the Filter text box. Click **department**, if necessary, and in the Display name text box, type **Department**. By default, the object class for the claim type is set to User. You can also set claim types for computer accounts.

4. Scroll down to the Suggested Values section. Click the **The following values are suggested** option button, and click **Add**. In the Value and Display name text boxes, type **Marketing**, and then click **OK**. Repeat this step, and add **Accounting** as a suggested value. Click **OK**.

5. In the Tasks pane, under Claim Types, click **New**, and then click **Claim Type**. To find the title attribute quickly, type **title** in the Filter text box. Click **title**, and in the Display name text box, type **Job Title**.

6. Add the following suggested values: **Executive** and **Manager**. Click **OK**. Close the Active Directory Administrative Center.

7. Stay logged on to 412Server1 if you're continuing to the next activity.

Activity 5-4: Configuring Group Policies for Claims Support

Time Required: 15 minutes
Objective: Configure group policies for claims support.

Required Tools and Equipment: 412Server1
Description: In this activity, you configure group policies so that DCs can use claims in resource authorization and client computers use claims when presenting credentials for resource access.

1. Start 412Server1, and log on as **Administrator**, if necessary.

2. In Server Manager, click **Tools, Group Policy Management** from the menu. In the left pane, right-click **Domain Controllers** and click **Create a GPO in this domain, and Link it here**. Type **DACforDCs** in the Name text box and then click **OK**.

3. Right-click the **DACforDCs** GPO you just created and click **Edit**. In the Group Policy Management Editor, expand **Computer Configuration, Policies, Administrative Templates, System**, and **KDC**. Double-click **KDC support for claims, compound authentication and Kerberos armoring**.

4. Click the **Enabled** option button, and leave the default value, **Supported**, selected under Options. Click **OK**. Close the Group Policy Management Editor.

5. Open a command prompt window. Type **gpupdate** and press **Enter** so that the policy is effective immediately. Close the command prompt window.

6. Next, you configure client support for claims by setting the client policy for the entire domain. In the Group Policy Management console, right-click the **412Dom1.local** node and click **Create a GPO in this domain, and Link it here**. Type **DACforClients** in the Name text box, and then click **OK**. If you wanted to limit which computers supported DAC, you could have created an OU for the computer accounts and linked the GPO to the OU.

7. Right-click the **DACforClients** GPO you just created and click **Edit**. In the Group Policy Management Editor, expand **Computer Configuration, Policies, Administrative Templates, System**, and **Kerberos**. Double-click **Kerberos client support for claims, compound authentication and Kerberos armoring**. Click the **Enabled** option button, and then click **OK**. Close the Group Policy Management Editor and the Group Policy Management console.

8. Stay logged on to 412Server1 if you're continuing to the next activity.

Activity 5-5: Setting Permission Conditions On a Folder

Time Required: 10 minutes
Objective: Set permission conditions on a folder.

Required Tools and Equipment: 412Server1
Description: Your DAC infrastructure is set up. Now you can set permission conditions by using resource properties and claims. You create two conditions on the Marketing folder: one that lets all Marketing Department users have Read access to low-confidentiality files owned by the

Marketing Department and one that gives Marketing users who are executives Modify access to all files owned by the Marketing Department.

1. Start 412Server1, and log on as **Administrator**, if necessary.

2. Open File Explorer, open the Properties dialog box for the Marketing folder, and click the **Security** tab. Click **Advanced**.

3. In the Advanced Security Settings for Marketing dialog box, click the **Add** button. In the Permissions Entry for Marketing dialog box, click the **Select a principal** link.

4. In the Select User, Computer, Service Account, or Group dialog box, type **Authenticated Users**, click **Check Names**, and click **OK**.

5. Leave these default basic permissions selected: **Read & execute, List folder contents**, and **Read**. Click the **Add a condition** link at the bottom.

6. In the list boxes for condition information, click these options: **Resource, Confidentiality, Equals, Value**, and **Low**.

7. Click **Add a condition**. Leave the joiner as **And**. (*Note*: You can also create Or conditions.) Click these options in the condition list boxes: **User, Department, Equals, Resource**, and **Department**.

8. The first condition states that the Confidentiality classification of the resource (the Marketing folder) must be Low. The second condition specifies that the Department attribute of the user account must be the same as the Department classification of the resource. Click **OK**.

9. Click the **Add** button, and then click the **Select a principal** link. Type **Authenticated Users** as the principal again. In the Basic permissions section, click the **Modify** check box, and then click **Add a condition**. In the list boxes for condition information, click these options: **User, Department, Equals, Resource**, and **Department**.

10. Click **Add a condition**. Leave the joiner as **And**. Click these options in the condition list boxes: **User, Job Title, Equals, Value**, and **Executive**. Click **OK**.

11. The final Advanced Security Settings for Marketing dialog box should look like Figure 5-12. Click **OK** twice to close the Advanced Security Settings for Marketing and the Marketing Properties dialog boxes.

12. Stay logged on to 412Server1 if you're continuing to the next activity.

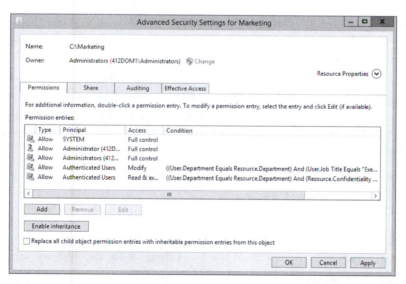

Figure 5-12   The Advanced Security Settings for Marketing dialog box

Activity 5-6: Creating Users to Test DAC

Time Required: 10 minutes
Objective: Create three users to test DAC.

Required Tools and Equipment: 412Server1
Description: Now that you have a folder set up with conditions by using DAC, you can create some users to test your access conditions.

1. Start 412Server1, and log on as **Administrator**, if necessary.

2. In Server Manager, click **Tools, Active Directory Users and Computers** from the menu.

3. Create an OU at the root of the domain named **TestDAC**.

4. Create a user in the TestDAC OU with the following properties:

   First name: **Accounting**

   Last name: **One**

   User logon name: **accounting1**

   Password: **Password01**

   Set the password to never expire

5. Create a second user with the following properties:

   First name: **Marketing**

   Last name: **One**

   User logon name: **marketing1**

   Password: **Password01**

   Set the password to never expire

6. Create a third user with the following properties:

   First name: **Executive**

   Last name: **One**

   User logon name: **executive1**

   Password: **Password01**

   Set the password to never expire

7. Open the properties of **Accounting One**, click the **Organization** tab, and type **Accounting** in the Department text box.

8. Open the properties of **Marketing One**, click the **Organization** tab, and type **Marketing** in the Department text box. Type **Manager** in the Job Title text box.

9. Open the properties of **Executive One**, click the **Organization** tab, and type **Marketing** in the Department text box and **Executive** in the Job Title text box. Close Active Directory Users and Computers.

10. Stay logged on to 412Server1 if you're continuing to the next activity.

Activity 5-7: Checking Effective Access

Time Required: 10 minutes
Objective: Check effective access to the Marketing folder and files for users.

Required Tools and Equipment: 412Server1
Description: You're ready to check effective access to the Marketing folder.

1. Start 412Server1, and log on as **Administrator**, if necessary.

2. Open File Explorer, open the Properties dialog box for the Marketing folder, and click the Security tab. Click **Advanced**.

3. Click the **Effective Access** tab. Click **Select a user**. Type **accounting1**, click **Check Names**, and then click **OK**.

4. The Accounting One user presents the claim Department=Accounting, so click **Include a user claim**. Click the list arrow, and click **Department**. Click the other list arrow, and click **Accounting**. The Accounting and Marketing values listed are the suggested values you added when you created the Department claim type in Activity 5-3.

5. Click the **View effective access** button. You should see that the user has no permissions to the folder.

6. Click **Select a user** again. Type **marketing1**, click **Check Names**, and then click **OK**. In the Accounting text box from Step 4, click the list arrow, and click **Marketing**.

7. This user has the Job Title attribute set to Manager. Click **Include a user claim**. Click the list arrow, and click **Job Title**. Click the other list arrow, and click **Manager**.

8. Click the **View effective access** button. You should see that the user has Read permissions.

9. At this point, you could check effective access for the Executive One user, but because the user differs from Marketing One only in the job title, you can just change the Job Title attribute to see what access a user with the Department attribute set to Marketing and the Job Title attribute set to Executive would have. Click the **Manager** list arrow, and click **Executive**.

10. Click the **View effective access** button. You should see that the user has all the permissions that Modify grants. Keep in mind that this view feature doesn't actually have access to an account's claims, so when you add claims, the "View effective access" button shows you what-if results rather than actual permissions for that user. Click **Cancel** twice to close the Advanced Security Settings for Marketing and the Marketing Properties dialog boxes.

11. Stay logged on to 412Server1 if you're continuing to the next activity.

Activity 5-8: Testing Access to a Folder

Time Required: 15 minutes

Objective: Test access to the Marketing folder with different users.

Required Tools and Equipment: 412Server1 and 412Win8

Description: You're ready to test access to the Marketing folder. First, you need to join the 412Win8 computer to the domain. Then you log on to the domain from the 412Win8 computer with the accounts you created in Activity 5-6 and try to access files in the Marketing folder.

1. Start 412Server1, if necessary. Start 412Win8, and log on as **win8user** with the password **Password01**. Change the preferred DNS server on the Ethernet interface to 412Server1's IP address (10.12.1.1).

2. Next, right-click **Start** and click **System**. Next to Computer name, click **Change settings**.

3. In the System Properties dialog box, click the **Change** button. Click the **Domain** option button, type **412dom1.local**, and click **OK**.

4. In the Windows Security dialog box, type **administrator** for the username and **Password01** for the password. Click **OK** twice. In the Computer Name/Domain Changes message box, click **OK**, and then click **Close**. When prompted to restart the computer, click **Restart Now**.

5. When the computer restarts, click the **back arrow**, click **Other user**, and log on as **accounting1** with the password **Password01**. Preparing your profile might take a while.

6. When you're logged on, go to the desktop and open a command prompt window. Type **whoami /claims** and press Enter. This command displays any claims the user presents to Kerberos for authorization. If the Kerberos client group policy you configured in Activity 5-4 wasn't set, you wouldn't see any claims information. You should see an indication that the Department attribute is Accounting. Because you didn't set the Job Title attribute for accounting1, no claim is configured for this attribute.

7. Right-click **Start** and click **Run**. Type **\\412server1** in the Open text box, and click **OK**. Double-click the **Marketing** share. You should see a message indicating that you don't have permission to access to the share, which is correct because your Department attribute isn't Marketing. Click **Close**.

8. Log off, and log back on as **marketing1**. Open a command prompt window, type **whoami /claims**, and press **Enter**. You should see that marketing1 has Department = Marketing and Job Title=Manager claims.

9. Right-click **Start** and click **Run**. Type **\\412server1** in the Open text box, and click **OK**. Double-click the **Marketing** share. You see the LowConfidential file. You don't see the HighConfidential file because only Marketing executives can access files with high confidentiality. Open the LowConfidential file, type some characters in it, and then try to save it. A Save As dialog box opens because you don't have permission to write to the file. You can't create a new file, either, because you have only Read permission to the Marketing folder. Click **Cancel**.

10. Close all open windows, and log off. Log on as **executive1**. Verify that this user can open, change, and save both the LowConfidential and HighConfidential files in the Marketing folder. Close all open windows.

11. Shut down 412Win8. Stay logged on to 412Server1 if you're continuing to the next activity.

Configuring DAC with Central Access Policies

As you're starting to see, DAC is a powerful tool for setting complex conditions on access permissions to folders and files. However, you can also see that it might get cumbersome if you have to set conditions on each folder on every server that requires them. This is where central access policies (CAPs) come in. Central access policies enable you to target resources on servers and set DAC permissions with the Group Policy tool. As mentioned, central access policies consist of one or more central access rules containing both DAC and regular permissions. They can be targeted to specific servers by linking the GPO in which they're defined to an OU containing computer accounts of the target servers. The central access rules in central access policies can be targeted at resources meeting specific criteria. For example, a central access rule that applies the conditions you configured in Activity 5-5 can be targeted at files classified as belonging to the Marketing Department and having a value for the Confidentiality resource property.

There's one important difference between setting permission conditions on folders and files manually, as you did in Activity 5-5, and setting permissions by using a central access policy. When you set conditions manually, they act just like NTFS permissions with the added conditions. However, when you use central access policies, NTFS permissions are evaluated first, and then permissions set with a CAP are evaluated. Of the two, the most restrictive is the effective permission. For example, if the NTFS permissions on a folder include Administrators only in the discretionary access control list (DACL), permissions applied by a CAP can't *add* users or groups to the effective permissions. A CAP can only further restrict access to the resource. Therefore, when using CAPs to deploy permissions, you need to be sure existing NTFS permissions are less restrictive than those you set with the CAP. One way to do this is to set a baseline of Authenticated Users with Modify permission, and then you can further restrict access as needed with a CAP.

Deploying Central Access Policies   The process for deploying central access policies is as follows:

1. Create one or more central access rules in the ADAC.

2. Create a central access policy, and add one or more central access rules to the policy.

3. Deploy the central access policy with the Group Policy tool.

Start by creating one or more central access rules. In the ADAC, double-click Dynamic Access Control, and then double-click Central Access Rules. Central access rules have the following properties (shown in Figure 5-13).

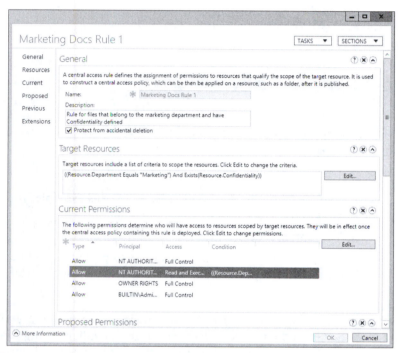

Figure 5-13   Creating a central access rule

- *Name*—Specify the name of the central access rule. For this example, you might give the rule a name such as Marketing Docs Confidentiality because the rule applies only to files with the Confidentiality property defined.

- *Description*—Add an optional description.

- *Target Resources*—Specify the criteria to limit the rule's scope so that it affects only files with certain properties. For example, you can specify that the rule applies to files belonging to the Marketing Department with the Confidentiality property defined. Criteria are defined much like permission conditions.

- *CurrentPermissions*—Specify the permissions that should be applied to the targeted resources, just as you do in the Advanced Security Settings dialog box for a folder or file. You have the option to "Use following permissions as proposed permissions," which doesn't actually apply permissions to the targeted resources but allows you to audit access to the resource as though the permissions were applied. This option enables you to test what-if settings with your permissions strategy without causing access problems. After you know that the permissions do what you expect, they can be applied by choosing this option.

Create additional rules as needed, and then create a central access policy. In the ADAC, click Dynamic Access Control, and then double-click Central Access Policies. Central access policies have the following properties (shown in Figure 5-14):

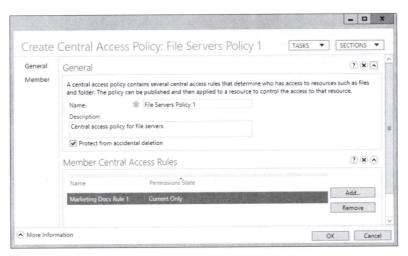

Figure 5-14   Creating a central access policy

- *Name*—Specify the name of the central access policy. For this example, you might give the policy a name such as File Servers Policy 1.
- *Description*—Add an optional description.
- *Member Central Access Rules*—Add the central access rules that should be deployed with this policy. A central access rule can be a member of more than one central access policy, if needed.

When you have created all the rules and added them to the policies, you deploy central access policies with the Group Policy tool. The Central Access Policy setting is under Computer Configuration, Policies, Windows Settings, Security Settings, File System. Right-click the Central Access Policy setting and click Manage Central Access Policies to open a dialog box where you add the policies you want to add to the GPO. You can deploy different central access policies to different servers by adding them to a GPO and linking the GPO to different OUs. You can also deploy multiple policies in a single GPO.

That's it! After your servers update their policies, the permissions you set in the central access rules are deployed to the targeted resources on the servers in the scope of the GPO. The next three activities walk you through deploying central access policies.

Activity 5-9: Creating Central Access Policies

Time Required: 10 minutes
Objective: Create a central access policy.

Required Tools and Equipment: 412Server1
Description: In this activity, you create central access rules and add them to a central access policy.

1. Start 412Server1, and log on as **Administrator**, if necessary.
2. Open the Active Directory Administrative Center. In the left pane, click **Dynamic Access Control**, and in the right pane, double-click **Central Access Rules**.

3. In the Tasks pane, under Central Access Rules, click **New**, and then click **Central Access Rule**. In the Create Central Access Rule window, type **Marketing Docs Confidentiality**.

4. In the Description text box, type **Rule for Marketing files with Confidentiality set**.

5. In the Target Resources section, click the **Edit** button, and then click **Add a condition**. Set the conditions according to Figure 5-15, and then click **OK**.

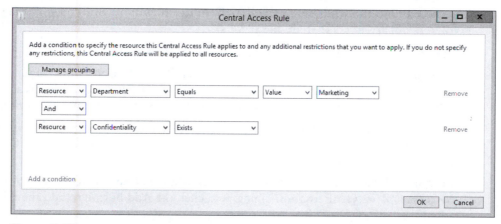

Figure 5-15   Setting conditions to target resources

6. Click the **Use following permissions as current permissions** option button, and then click **Edit**.

7. At this point, you add conditions. Click **Add**, and then click the **Select a principal** link. Type **Authenticated Users**, click **Check Names**, and click **OK**.

8. Leave the default basic permissions selected, and click **Add a condition**. Click these options in the condition list boxes: **Resource, Confidentiality, Equals, Value**, and **Low**.

9. Click **Add a condition**. Leave the joiner as **And**. Click these options in the condition list boxes: **User, Department, Equals, Resource**, and **Department**.

10. Click **OK**. Click the **Add** button, click the **Select a principal** link, and type **Authenticated Users** as the principal again. In the Basic permissions section, click the **Modify** check box. Click these options in the condition list boxes: **User, Department, Equals, Resource**, and **Department**.

11. Click **Add a condition**. Leave the joiner as **And**. Click these options in the condition list boxes: **User, Job Title, Equals, Value**, and **Executive**.

12. Click **OK** until you're back to the Active Directory Administrative Center. In the left pane, click **Dynamic Access Control**, and in the right pane, double-click **Central Access Policies**.

13. In the Tasks pane, under Central Access Policies, click **New**, and then click **Central Access Policy**. In the Create Central Access Policy window, type **File Servers Policy 1** in the Name text box. In the Description text box, type **CAP for file servers**.

14. Click the **Add** button. In the Add Central Access Rules dialog box, because there's only one rule, click the right arrow to add the **Marketing Docs Confidentiality** rule, and then click **OK**. Click **OK** to close the Create Central Access Policy window, and then close the Active Directory Administrative Center.

15. Stay logged on to 412Server1 if you're continuing to the next activity.

Activity 5-10: Configuring Group Policies to Deploy a Central Access Policy

Time Required: 10 minutes
Objective: Configure group policies to deploy a central access policy.

Required Tools and Equipment: 412Server1
Description: In this activity, you configure the central access policy setting in Group Policy and link the GPO to the Domain Controllers OU (although typically, you link the GPO to an OU holding member servers that are file servers).

1. Start 412Server1, and log on as **Administrator**, if necessary.

2. Open Server Manager, if necessary, and click **Tools, Group Policy Management** from the menu. In the left pane, right-click **Domain Controllers** and click **Create a GPO in this domain, and Link it here.** Type **DeployCAP** in the Name text box, and click **OK**.

3. Right-click the **DeployCAP** GPO you just created and click **Edit**. In the Group Policy Management Editor, expand **Computer Configuration, Policies, Windows Settings, Security Settings,** and **File System.**

4. Right-click **Central Access Policy** and click **Manage Central Access Policies.** In the Central Access Policies Configuration dialog box, click the **Add** button to add the File Servers Policy 1 to the GPO. Click **OK**.

5. Open a command prompt window, and then type **gpupdate** and press **Enter** so that the policy is effective immediately. Close the command prompt window and the Group Policy Management console.

6. Stay logged on to 412Server1 if you're continuing to the next activity.

Activity 5-11: Testing Central Access Policy Deployment

Time Required: 20 minutes
Objective: Test the central access policy.

Required Tools and Equipment: 412Server1
Description: In this activity, you create some folders and enable the central access policy on the folders. Then view effective permissions to see how the CAP affects permissions.

1. Start 412Server1, and log on as **Administrator**, if necessary.

2. First, you remove the conditional permissions from the Marketing folder. Open File Explorer, and open the Advanced Security Settings dialog box for the Marketing folder. Click each **Authenticated Users** entry, and click **Remove**.

3. Click **Add**. Click the **Select a principal** link, and type **Authenticated Users**. Click **Check Names**, and then click **OK**. In the Basic permissions section, click the **Modify** check box, and then click **OK**. Click **OK** twice.

4. Create another folder on the C drive named **Marketing2**. Right-click **Marketing2** and click **Properties**, and then click the **Classification** tab. Set the Confidentiality property to **High** and the Department property to **Marketing**.

5. Click the **Security** tab, and click **Edit**. Click **Add**. Type **Authenticated Users**, click **Check Names**, and then click **OK**. Click the **Authenticated Users** entry and click **Allow** for the Modify permission. Click **OK** twice.

6. Create another folder named **Marketing3**. Open Marketing3's Properties dialog box, and click the **Classification** tab. Set the Department property to **Marketing**, but leave the Confidentiality property set to **(none)**. Set the permissions by following Step 5. Now all three folders have the baseline of Authenticated Users with the Modify permission.

7. Next, you need to enable the policy on each folder. Perform the following steps for all three folders: Open the Advanced Security Settings dialog box for the folder. Click the new **Central Policy** tab. Click **Change**, and then click **File Servers Policy 1** in the list box (see Figure 5-16). Click **OK** twice.

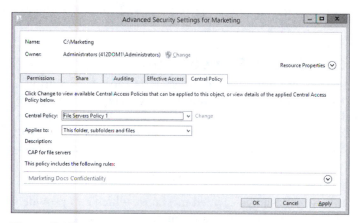

Figure 5-16   Enabling a central access policy on a folder

8. Next, you check the effective access for each folder. Open the Advanced Security Settings dialog box for the Marketing folder, and click **Effective Access**. Click **Select a user**. Type **marketing1**, click **Check Names**, and click **OK**.

9. Click **Include a user claim** and include claims for Department="Marketing" and Job Title= "Manager." Click **View effective access**. You should see that Read permissions are allowed and most of the Write permissions are limited by the Marketing Docs Confidentiality rule (see Figure 5-17). View effective access for the other two users in the TestDAC OU, and verify that the permissions are what you expect. Close the Marketing folder's Properties dialog box when you're done.

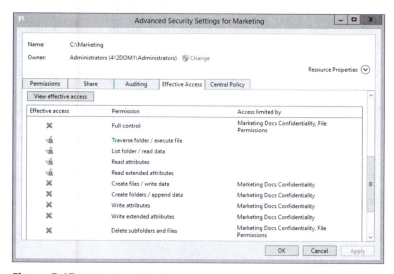

Figure 5-17   Viewing effective access

10. View the effective access for the Marketing2 folder. Try different combinations of users and claims. You should see that a user who has the Department="Marketing" and the Job Title="Executive" claims has Modify access, but other users (except Administrators) are denied access. This is because the Marketing2 folder has the Confidentiality property set to High.

11. View the effective access for the Marketing3 folder. Try different combinations of users and claims. You should see that none of the users are limited by a central access rule because the

rule you created was targeted to folders with the Department resource set to Marketing and the Confidentiality resource set to a value other than "none." Because the Marketing3 folder doesn't have a value set for Confidentiality (which is set to "none"), the folder isn't affected by the central access rule.

12. Close all File Explorer windows. Stay logged on to 412Server1 if you're continuing to the next activity.

Configuring Access-Denied Remediation

NTFS permissions and DAC are powerful administrative tools for securing access to files and folders. What about the user side of the equation, however? Users who are denied access to files they need to perform their jobs can become frustrated. Windows Server 2012 introduced **access-denied assistance** to help solve problems with file and folder access. This feature gives file users, file owners, and administrators ways to remediate access-denied messages when the user requesting the shared file should be allowed access.

Access-denied assistance has the following options:

- Administrators can customize access-denied messages, which can provide more details about why the user was denied access to a resource.

- Users can send an e-mail message to the responsible file owner or an administrator to request access to a resource.

- Administrators can create a distribution list for shared folders so that the folder owner is notified via e-mail when someone requests access to a folder.

Configuring Access-Denied Assistance with FSRM   You can configure access-denied assistance on file servers by using the File Server Resource Manager (FSRM) or remotely with the Group Policy tool. To configure it with FSRM, follow these steps:

1. Open the FSRM on the file server where you want to enable access-denied assistance.

2. In the left pane, right-click File Server Resource Manager (Local) and click Configure Options.

3. Click the Access-Denied Assistance tab. Click the "Enable access-denied assistance" check box. In the message box, you can customize the message users see if they're denied access to a file or folder. You can include troubleshooting instructions and links to more information (see Figure 5-18). You can also include the following macros in the message:

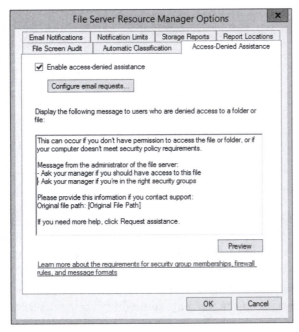

Figure 5-18   Configuring access-denied assistance with FSRM

o [Original File Path]: The path to the file on the server

o [Original File Path Folder]: The parent folder of the file, if applicable

o [Admin Email]: The administrator e-mail address, configured in the Email Notifications tab

o [Data Owner Email]: The e-mail address of the person who owns the file

4. To allow users to request assistance or access to a folder, click the "Configure email requests" button, and then click the "Enable users to request assistance" check box. You can choose to include user information, including claims, and device state information in the e-mail. You can also choose to include the file owner and the administrator as e-mail recipients and specify whether an event should be generated (see Figure 5-19).

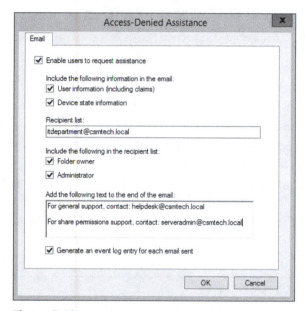

Figure 5-19   Configuring e-mail requests

5. After access-denied assistance is configured, users see a message similar to Figure 5-20 if access is denied to a resource on the configured server. If the user clicks Request Assistance, a message box opens where the user can write a message explaining why access to the resource is required. For this feature to work, an SMTP server must be configured in the Email Notifications tab of the File Server Resource Manager Options dialog box.

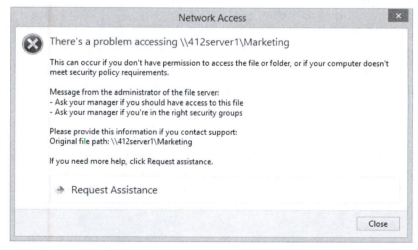

Figure 5-20   A customized access-denied message

Configuring Access-Denied Assistance with Group Policies   If you want to deploy access-denied assistance to several or all of your file servers, you can do so with group policies. Open a GPO in the Group Policy Management Editor, and browse to Computer Configuration, Policies, Administrative Templates, System, Access-Denied Assistance. Double-click the "Customize message for Access Denied errors" policy, and click the Enabled option button. The options in this policy are the same as those in the Access-Denied Assistance tab of the File Server Resource Manager Options dialog box. Link the GPO to an OU containing file servers that should provide the access-denied assistance message. You can organize file servers in different OUs and apply GPOs with different access-denied assistance settings, such as different e-mail recipients.

Activity 5-12: Removing DAC Group Policies

Time Required: 5 minutes
Objective: Remove DAC group policies.

Required Tools and Equipment: 412Server1
Description: In this activity, you unlink the GPOs you used to deploy DAC.

1. Start 412Server1, and log on as **Administrator**, if necessary.

2. Open the Group Policy Management console. Expand the domain node, if necessary. Right-click **DACforClients** and click **Delete**. Click **OK**.

3. Expand the **Domain Controllers** OU. Right-click **DACforDCs** and click **Delete**. Click **OK**. Right-click **DeployCAP** and click **Delete**. Click **OK**.

4. If you're continuing to the next activity, restart 412Server1; otherwise, shut down 412Server1.

Configuring IP Address Management

A large enterprise network has thousands of IP addresses in use, usually configured by several DHCP servers, and thousands of hostnames maintained by DNS servers. With so many addresses, hostnames, and servers to manage, IP address management can become unwieldy. **IP Address Management (IPAM)** is a new feature in Windows Server 2012 that enables an administrator to manage the IP address space. IPAM has monitoring, auditing, and reporting functions to help you manage key server components in an IP network. IPAM handles forest-wide discovery and management of all Microsoft DHCP, DNS, NPS, and DC servers and monitors DHCP scopes and DNS zones throughout the network. The following problems are some you might be able to solve with IPAM:

- Manual address management with spreadsheets or another custom solution
- Inefficiency in keeping track of and managing multiple DNS and DHCP servers
- Difficulties keeping track of address use across multiple domains and sites
- Global changes to all DHCP scopes across several servers, such as changing a DNS server address
- Problems identifying available IP addresses quickly

This chapter describes the IPAM infrastructure and shows you how to set up an IPAM solution, including IPAM requirements and installation, server provisioning, server discovery and selection, IP address block management and monitoring, migrating to IPAM, and configuring IPAM storage.

The IPAM Infrastructure

The IPAM infrastructure consists of IPAM servers and managed servers. You can also install the IPAM management console on another server, called an **IPAM client**, so that you can manage the IPAM server remotely. The IPAM client can also be on a computer running Windows 8/8.1 with remote server administration tools installed.

The **IPAM server** discovers servers you want to manage and collects and stores data from IPAM-managed servers in the IPAM database. A **managed server** is a Windows server running one or more of these Microsoft services: DHCP, DNS, Active Directory, and NPS. You can install more than one IPAM server on your network, particularly when it includes multiple sites, domains, or forests, and select which servers each IPAM server manages. An IPAM deployment has three topology options:

- *Centralized*—In a **centralized topology**, a single IPAM server is deployed for the entire enterprise (see Figure 5-21). The central server collects information from all managed servers. With this type of topology, the IPAM server should be centrally located with a reliable and high-performance connection to the network. A variation on this topology is to have multiple IPAM servers centrally located, with each IPAM server dedicated to managing a particular type of server. For example, one IPAM server can manage DHCP servers, another can manage DNS servers, and a third can manage DCs and NPS servers.

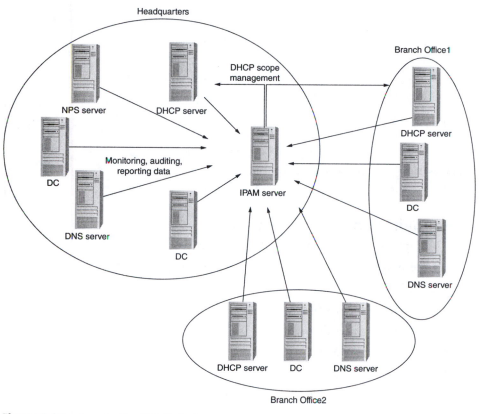

Figure 5-21   A centralized IPAM deployment

© *2016 Cengage Learning*®

- *Distributed*—In a **distributed topology**, an IPAM server is deployed at every site in the network. Each server is assigned a group of managed servers in the same site. There's no communication between IPAM servers.

- *Hybrid*—Like the centralized topology, in a **hybrid topology**, a single IPAM server collects information from all managed servers in the enterprise; however, an IPAM server is also deployed at key branch locations. You might use this method when you have some large branch locations with IT staff so that they can easily manage servers in their locations. Figure 5-22 shows a hybrid IPAM deployment, with an IPAM server in the headquarters and the larger branch office locations and an IPAM client running the IPAM management console at the headquarters location. In this topology, the IPAM server in the headquarters collects data from servers in all three locations. The IPAM server in the branch office collects data only from servers in that location.

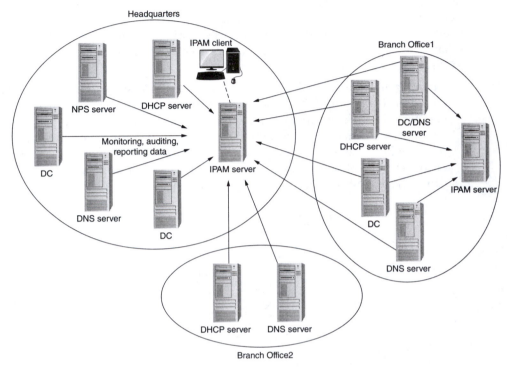

Figure 5-22   A hybrid IPAM deployment
© 2016 Cengage Learning®

Deploying an IPAM Solution

IPAM deployment involves the following steps:

- Determining the requirements for an IPAM deployment
- Installing the IPAM Server feature
- IPAM server provisioning
- Performing server discovery
- Provisioning IPAM GPOs
- Selecting servers and services to manage
- Collecting data from managed servers

IPAM Requirements   Before you deploy IPAM, you should have a good understanding of its requirements and limitations. The following list describes the requirements for the IPAM server, client, and managed servers:

- *IPAM server*—The IPAM server must be running the Standard or Datacenter Edition of Windows Server 2012 or later and must be a domain member. It can manage only domain member servers in the same Active Directory forest, and it can't be a domain controller. IPAM should be the sole server role installed on the server, although IPAM can coexist with other server roles. However, if IPAM is installed on a DHCP server, DHCP server discovery is disabled, which defeats one of the primary purposes of using IPAM.

- *IPAM client*—An IPAM client isn't a necessary component in an IPAM deployment, as you can manage IPAM from the IPAM server. However, if you want to manage IPAM from a different computer, you can install the IPAM management console on a computer running Windows Server 2012 or later or a Windows 8/8.1 computer with the Remote Server Administration Tools (RSAT) installed.

- *IPAM managed server*—All servers managed by IPAM must be joined to a domain in the same forest as the IPAM server and must be running Windows Server 2008 or later. As mentioned, IPAM can collect monitoring, reporting, and auditing data from the following services: Active Directory, DHCP, DNS, and NPS. IPAM can manage DHCP scopes.

Installing the IPAM Server Feature IPAM Server is a feature you install with the Add Roles and Features Wizard or the `Install-WindowsFeature` PowerShell cmdlet. To install it, run the Add Roles and Features Wizard from Server Manager, and in the Select Features window, select IP Address Management (IPAM) Server. Group Policy Management and the Windows Internal Database are also required, and you're prompted to include these features in the installation. By default, the IPAM management console is also installed. To use PowerShell, enter the following command at a PowerShell prompt:

```
Install-WindowsFeature IPAM -IncludeManagementTools
```

If you just want to install the IPAM client feature on a server to manage an IPAM server remotely, in the Select Features window, expand Remote Server Administration Tools and then expand Feature Administration Tools and select IP Address Management (IPAM) Client. Enter the following command at a PowerShell prompt:

```
Install-WindowsFeature IPAM-Client-Feature
```

To install the IPAM feature in Windows 8/8.1, download the Remote Server Administration Tools for Windows 8.1 from the Microsoft Download Center and follow the installation instructions. Then add the IPAM server to Server Manager, and the IPAM console is installed on your Windows 8/8.1 computer.

After IPAM Server is installed, IPAM is added to the left pane in Server Manager. To get started, click IPAM in the left pane of Server Manager, and you see a list of IPAM server tasks you can perform (see Figure 5-23). If you're running the management console on the server, the first task, Connect to IPAM server, takes place automatically. Now you're ready to provision the IPAM server.

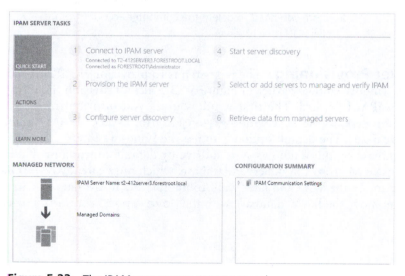

Figure 5-23   The IPAM server management console

Activity 5-13: Demoting a Server Before Installing IPAM

Time Required: 20 minutes or longer
Objective: Demote 412Server2 and uninstall DHCP and DNS.

Required Tools and Equipment: 412Server1 and 412Server2
Description: Before you can install the IPAM Server feature on 412Server2, you must demote 412Server2 to a member server and uninstall DHCP Server because IPAM Server can't run on a DC or a DHCP server. You also uninstall DNS.

1. Start 412Server1, if necessary. Start 412Server2, and log on as **Administrator**.

2. On 412Server2, open Server Manager, and click **Manage, Remove Roles and Features** from the menu. Click **Next** twice, and in the Server Roles window, click to clear the **Active Directory Domain Services** check box. Click the **Remove Features** button.

3. You see an error in the Validation Results window indicating that the server must be demoted before the role can be uninstalled. Click the **Demote this domain controller** link.

4. In the Credentials window, click **Next**. In the Warnings window, click the **Proceed with removal** check box and click **Next**.

5. In the New Administrator Password window, type **Password01** in the Password and Confirm password check boxes. Click **Next**.

6. In the Review Options window, click **Demote**. After the demotion is complete, the server will restart.

7. Log on the 412Server2 as Administrator when it restarts. In Server Manager, click **Manage, Remove Roles and Features**. Click **Next** twice. Click to clear the **Active Directory Domain Services** check box, and click **Remove Features**. Repeat for DHCP Server and DNS Server. Click **Next** twice, and click **Remove**. Click **Close** when the feature removal is finished.

8. Restart 412Server2. Log on to the 412Dom1 domain as **Administrator**, and leave 412Server1 running if you're continuing to the next activity.

When you demote a domain controller, the computer normally becomes a member server. If the demotion of the domain controller doesn't work correctly, you might need to use the Force Removal option. In this case, the computer isn't a domain member after the demotion, and you need to join it to the domain before installing IPAM. In addition, if you use this option, you need to delete the computer account from the Domain Controllers OU on 412Server1.

IPAM Server Provisioning   The next step is to provision the IPAM server. In the IPAM Server Tasks window (shown earlier in Figure 5-23), click "Provision the IPAM server" to start the Provision IPAM Wizard. The first window gives you information about IPAM and the provisioning process. In the next window, you select the type of IPAM database you want to use (see Figure 5-24). The default option is to use the Windows Internal Database (WID), which stores the database on the Windows system drive by default. Starting in Windows Server 2012 R2, you can use a Microsoft SQL Server database, which must already be installed and running. If you choose to use the WID and later want to migrate the IPAM database to a Microsoft SQL server, you can move the IPAM database with the Move-IpamDatabase PowerShell cmdlet.

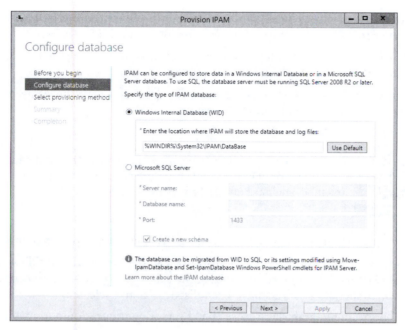

Figure 5-24   Configuring the IPAM database

In the next window, you select the method to provision managed servers. The default and recommended method is to use Group Policy provisioning. **Group Policy provisioning** uses group policies to perform tasks such as creating security groups, setting firewall rules, and creating shares for each IPAM-managed server. **Manual provisioning** requires configuring each IPAM server task and managed server manually. If you choose Group Policy provisioning, you must enter a GPO name prefix, which is used to name the GPOs that are created. For example, if you enter the name prefix IPAMdom1 (see Figure 5-25), the following GPOs are created and linked to the domain object:

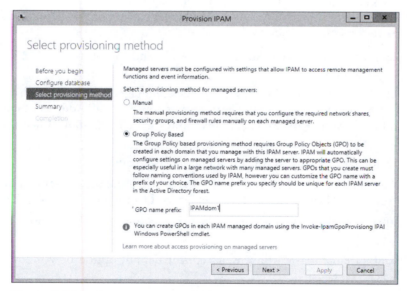

Figure 5-25   Selecting the IPAM provisioning method

- *IPAMdom1_DC_NPS*—This GPO sets the firewall rules and other policies needed for the IPAM server to collect data from domain controllers and NPS servers.

- *IPAMdom1_DHCP*—This GPO sets the firewall rules and other policies needed to collect data from and manage DHCP servers.

- *IPAMdom1_DNS*—This GPO sets the firewall rules and other policies needed for the IPAM server to collect data from DNS servers.

You can't change the IPAM provisioning method after you have finished the Provision IPAM Wizard. If you need to change the provisioning method, you must uninstall and reinstall IPAM.

The next window shows a summary of tasks performed by the provisioning process:

- Prepares GPO settings so that an administrator can deploy the IPAM GPOs discussed earlier. GPOs must be deployed by running the `Invoke-IpamGPOProvisioning` PowerShell cmdlet after servers have been discovered and selected.

- Creates the specified database to store IPAM server configuration parameters and collected data.

- Creates scheduled tasks on the IPAM server to discover servers and collect data from managed servers.

- Creates local security groups used to assign IPAM administrator permission.

- Enables the IPAM server to track IP addressing.

Activity 5-14: Installing and Provisioning the IPAM Server

Time Required: 10 minutes
Objective: Install the IPAM Server feature and provision the IPAM server.

Required Tools and Equipment: 412Server1 and 412Server2
Description: In this activity, you install the IPAM Server feature on 412Server2 and provision the IPAM server with the Group Policy tool.

1. Start 412Server1, if necessary. Start 412Server2, and log on to the 412Dom1 domain as **Administrator**, if necessary.

2. On 412Server2, open Server Manager, and click **Manage, Add Roles and Features** from the menu. Click **Next** until you get to the Features window. Click **IP Address Management (IPAM) Server**, and click **Add Features**. Click **Next**, and then click **Install**. When the installation is finished, click **Close**.

3. In Server Manager, click the **IPAM** node that has been added.

4. In the IPAM Server Tasks window, verify that you see the server name under "Connect to IPAM server." Click **Provision the IPAM server** to start the Provision IPAM Wizard.

5. In the "Before you begin" window, read the information about IPAM provisioning, and then click **Next**.

6. In the "Configure database" window, accept the default option of **Windows Internal Database** and click **Next**.

7. In the "Select provisioning method" window, accept the default option, **Group Policy Based**, and type **IPAMdom1** in the GPO name prefix text box. Click **Next**.

8. In the Summary window, verify the settings. Read the information describing what tasks are performed with Group Policy provisioning. Click **Apply**. When provisioning is finished, read the information under "Next steps." You're performing these steps in the next activity. Click **Close**.

9. In the IPAM Server Tasks window, click to expand **Access Provisioning Method** to see a summary of how IPAM is provisioned, including the names of GPOs to be created. Click the other configuration categories to see IPAM scheduled tasks, IPAM security groups, and IPAM communication settings.

10. Stay logged on to 412Server2 and leave 412Server1 running if you're continuing to the next activity.

Configuring Server Discovery

After the IPAM server has been provisioned, you configure server discovery. In the Configure Server Discovery dialog box, you select the domains where the IPAM server should search for servers to manage. If you're using a distributed IPAM topology, you might want to limit the search to a single domain, but with a central or hybrid topology, you might want to select all domains in the forest. You can also choose the server roles the IPAM server should discover. By default, all services are selected (see Figure 5-26).

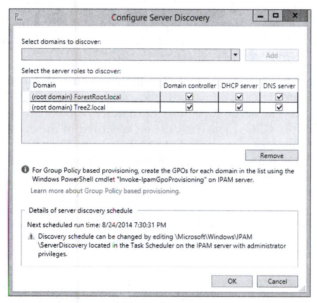

Figure 5-26   Configuring server discovery

After server discovery is configured, click "Start server discovery" in the IPAM Server Tasks window. IPAM probes the network in the specified domains to find servers that run the specified services. Server discovery might take several minutes or longer, depending on the number of domains and servers in the network. A message is displayed in the IPAM Server Tasks window indicating the status of server discovery. When discovery is finished, servers that have been discovered are listed in the Server Inventory window (see Figure 5-27).

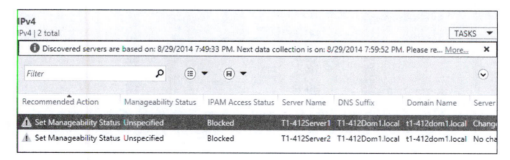

Figure 5-27   The Server Inventory window

Verifying IPAM Server Group Membership Before the IPAM server can manage DHCP, the server account must be added to the DHCP Administrators group in Active Directory. This should be done automatically during the IPAM server provisioning process, but it's a good idea to verify it. On any DC in the domain, open Active Directory Users and Computers and open the Users folder. Open the IPAMUG group, and verify that the IPAM server account is a member of this group. Next, open the DHCP Administrators group, and verify that the IPAMUG group is a member of this group.

 The DHCP server service on all DHCP servers managed by IPAM should be restarted after you have verified the IPAM server group membership.

Provisioning GPOs The IPAM server provisioning process doesn't actually create and link the IPAM GPOs to the domain. After the managed servers have been identified, run the following PowerShell cmdlet to provision the GPOs:

```
Invoke-IpamGpoProvisioning –domain yourdomain –GpoPrefixName
  GPOprefix –DelegatedGpoUser IPAMUser
```

In this command, replace *yourdomain* with your domain name. If you're managing multiple domains, run the command for each domain. Replace *GPOprefix* with the prefix specified in the Provision IPAM Wizard. The account running the cmdlet requires domain administrator privileges to create and link the GPOs. The `IPAMUser` specified in the command is a list of users who are delegated permissions to edit the IPAM GPOs later. The `DelegatedGpoUser` parameter isn't required. After running the cmdlet, the three GPOs are created and linked to the domain node of the specified domain.

After provisioning the GPOs, you can open the Group Policy Management console on a DC in the domain to see the IPAM GPOs that have been linked to the domain. You'll see that the security filtering on each GPO is blank, which means the GPOs aren't applied to any servers. The next step in the process, selecting servers to manage, adds the managed server to the security filtering on the GPOs.

Selecting Servers to Manage As you can see in Figure 5-27, the manageability status of discovered servers is Unspecified, and the IPAM access status is Blocked. To select a server to manage, right-click the server in the Server Inventory window and click Edit Server. In the Add or Edit Server dialog box, you can change the manageability status to Managed if you want this IPAM server to manage the server; otherwise, it should be Unmanaged. You can also choose the services you want to manage on the selected server (see Figure 5-28).

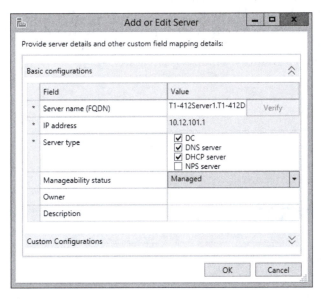

Figure 5-28 Changing the manageability status to Managed

When you set a server's manageability status to Managed, the server account is added to the security filter of the corresponding GPOs (depending on which services the server is running). However, you'll see that the IPAM access status remains in the Blocked state because the GPOs must be applied to each server. You can wait until the servers refresh their computer policies or run `gpupdate /force` at a command prompt on each managed server. After the policies are updated, right-click a server in the Server Inventory window and click Refresh Server Access Status, and then click the Server Manager refresh icon. The IPAM access status should then be Unblocked (see Figure 5-29). Alternatively, you can wait until the IPAM scheduled task automatically refreshes the access status, which is every 15 minutes. IPAM can then collect data from servers and manage DHCP addressing.

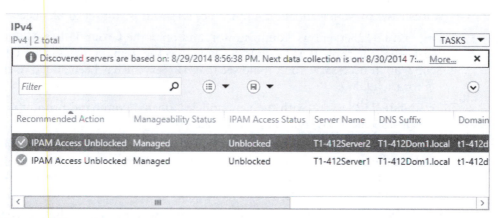

Figure 5-29   Unblocking servers

 After running gpupdate on servers, you might need to refresh the access status and the Server Manager window more than one time to see servers' Unblocked status.

Activity 5-15: Discovering and Selecting Servers

Time Required: 15 minutes
Objective: Discover and select servers to manage.

Required Tools and Equipment: 412Server1 and 412Server2
Description: With IPAM installed and provisioned, you can start server discovery and then select servers to manage. Because you have only one other server, IPAM discovers it, and you select 412Server1 to manage.

1. Start 412Server1, if necessary. Start 412Server2, and log on to the 412Dom1 domain as **Administrator**, if necessary.

2. On 412Server2, open Server Manager, and click **IPAM**, if necessary. In the IPAM Server Tasks window, click **Configure server discovery**. In the Configure Server Discovery dialog box, your domain (412Dom1.local) is listed. Click **Add**. By default, the selected server roles are domain controller, DHCP server, and DNS server. Click **OK**.

3. In the IPAM Server Tasks window, click **Start server discovery**. You see a message near the top of the window indicating that an IPAM task is running. After a while, you see the message "Discovered servers are based on: *date and time*" (with *date and time* representing the current date and time). When you see this message, click **Select or add servers to manage and verify IPAM access**.

4. You see 412Server1 in the list of servers to select. The manageability status is Unspecified, and the IPAM access status is Blocked. Before you change the manageability status, you need to provision the GPOs. Open a PowerShell prompt. Type **Invoke-IpamGpoProvisioning -domain 412dom1.local -GpoPrefixName IPAMdom1** and press **Enter**. You see a message stating that you didn't specify the DelegatedGpoUser parameter, but it's needed only if you want non-administrator users to be able to edit the IPAM GPOs. Press **Enter** to confirm. After the command finished running, close the PowerShell window.

5. Right-click **412Server1** and click **Edit Server**. In the Add or Edit Server dialog box, in the Server type section, the DC, DNS server, and DHCP server check boxes are selected. Click the **Manageability status** list arrow and click **Managed**. Click **OK**. You see the manageability status is set to Managed, but the IPAM access status is still set to Blocked.

6. Log on to 412Server1 as **Administrator**, and open the Group Policy Management console. Verify that the three IPAM GPOs are linked to the domain. Click each GPO and click the **Scope** tab, if necessary. You should see that 412Server1 has been added to the security filtering for each GPO.

7. To update 412Server1 with the new policies, open a command prompt window, and then type gpupdate /force and press **Enter**.

8. Next, restart the DHCP Server service. You need to do this on each DHCP server that's managed. At the command prompt, type **net stop dhcpserver** and press **Enter**. Then type **net start dhcpserver** and press **Enter**. After the command finishes running, close the command prompt window.

9. On 412Server2, in the IPAM Server Inventory window, right-click **412Server1** and click **Refresh Server Access Status**. You see a message that IPAM tasks are running. After you see the "Discovered servers" message you saw in Step 3, click the **Refresh** icon in Server Manager to refresh the view. If all went well, you should see that the IPAM access status is set to Unblocked, and you'll see a white check mark in a green circle next to the 412Server1 entry.

10. With 412Server1 selected, in the IPAM Server Inventory window, scroll down to the Details View. You see detailed status information for the server. If access to the IPAM server is blocked, you can see which service is causing IPAM access to be blocked. For example, if Event Log Access is blocked, the IPAM server needs to be added to the Event Log Readers group on the managed server.

11. Stay logged on to 412Server2 and leave 412Server1 running if you're continuing to the next activity.

Retrieving Server Data   The next step is to retrieve data from the managed servers. In the IPAM Server Tasks window, click "Retrieve data from managed servers" to begin the process, or in the Server Inventory window, right-click a server and click Retrieve All Server Data. When data retrieval is finished, you see a message at the top indicating the date and time of the last data collection and the schedule for the next data collection. You're now ready to start using the IPAM server and administering the IP address space.

Understanding the IP Address Space

Before you start using IPAM, it's helpful to understand how IPAM views the IP address space, which is divided into the following units:

- *IP address block*—An **IP address block** is the largest unit used to refer to the IP address space. It consists of a contiguous range of IP addresses with a corresponding subnet mask. Each IP address block is categorized as a public or private block, as defined by the Internet Assigned Numbers Authority (IANA). For example, 172.16.0.0/16 is a private address block. IP address blocks are divided into IP address ranges. By default, no IP address blocks are defined until you create them. One of the first things you do with IPAM is create one or more IP address blocks to be the parent block to IP address ranges.

- *IP address range*—An **IP address range** is a pool of continuous addresses in an IP address block and usually corresponds to a DHCP scope. Every IP address range is a member of a parent IP address block. There can be one or more IP address ranges in an IP address block. For example, you might have IP address ranges of 172.16.1.0/24 and 172.16.2.0/24 in the 172.16.0.0/16 IP address block. IP address ranges contain IP addresses that are used to assign to host IP devices.

- *IP address range group*—An **IP address range group** consists of one or more IP address ranges that are logically grouped by some criteria. A default group called Managed by Service contains all address ranges. You can create new IP address range groups based on criteria you assign to IP address ranges, such as the Active Directory site, country or region, or device type in which the IP address range is used. For example, you can assign two IP address ranges to the Active Directory site named Site100. You can then create a custom group named SiteGroup that groups IP address ranges by Active Directory site. Then you can view information and statistics about both ranges as a group instead of individually.

- *Unmapped address space*—**Unmapped address space** is any IP address or IP address range that hasn't been assigned to an IP address block. By default, all IP address ranges are unmapped until you create IP address blocks.

Administering IPAM

After the IPAM server has collected data from selected servers and services, you can start working with IPAM. The IPAM console's navigation pane (see Figure 5-30) contains links to several monitoring and management views of your IP address space and DNS zone data:

Figure 5-30   The IPAM console's navigation pane

- *OVERVIEW*—Shows the IPAM Server Tasks window (shown earlier in Figure 5-23).
- *SERVER INVENTORY*—Lists the servers the IPAM server has discovered (shown earlier in Figure 5-27).
- *IP ADDRESS SPACE*—Allows you to choose three different views:
  - IP Address Blocks: You can view and manage current IP address blocks. As mentioned, no IP address blocks are defined until you create them.
  - IP Address Inventory: Displays the IP address range group that's organized by device type.

o IP Address Range Groups: Displays the IP address ranges organized by IP address range groups. By default, IP address ranges are organized by the Managed by Service field, which is MS DHCP if the address range is from a Microsoft DHCP server.

- *VIRTUALIZED IP ADDRESS SPACE*—This IPAM enhancement in Windows Server 2012 R2 enables you to manage virtual IP address spaces created with Microsoft System Center Virtual Machine Manager.

- *MONITOR AND MANAGE*—Enables you to monitor and manage DNS and DHCP server status, DHCP scopes, DNS zones, and server groups with the following views:

o DNS and DHCP Servers: Lists managed servers by service type along with their current status. You can right-click a DHCP server to edit its properties and options and create a scope. New in Windows Server 2012 R2 is the capability to define MAC address filters and manage DHCP policies. You can also open the DHCP management console (MMC) for the selected server. If you right-click a DNS server, you can open the DNS MMC for that server.

o DHCP Scopes: Lists available scopes on all managed servers and allows you to edit, delete, duplicate, and activate or deactivate the scope. New in Windows Server 2012 R2 is the capability to create a reservation or superscope, configure DHCP failover, configure DHCP policies, and set the access scope. You use the access scope to customize which objects on a managed server a user can access. The default access scope is Global, and all IPAM objects are a member of it.

o DNS Zone Monitoring: Displays the status of all DNS server zones and enables you to set the access scope, but you can't manage zones.

o Server Groups: Servers can be grouped by using custom criteria, much as you do with IP address ranges. For example, you might want to group servers by region or country.

- *EVENT CATALOG*—Displays information about IPAM and DHCP configuration events and allows you to track IP addresses by address, client ID, hostname, and username.

- *ACCESS CONTROL*—Shows the defined roles for IPAM administration, allowing you to configure role-based access control (RBAC). There are a number of built-in roles, such as IPAM Administrator, DNS Record Administrator, IPAM DHCP Administrator, and so forth. Each built-in role has permissions assigned to it. For example, the IP Address Record Administrator role can create, edit, and delete IP addresses. You can't change the permissions of built-in roles, but you can create custom roles and define custom permissions for them.

Creating IP Address Blocks and Ranges   Each IP address range should be a member of an IP address block. To create an IP address block, click IP Address Blocks in the IPAM console's navigation pane, and in the right pane, click Tasks and then Add IP Address Block. The address block requires a network ID and prefix length. The Start and End IP address is filled in automatically, but you can change these values as long as they fall within the range specified by the network ID and prefix length. If you're creating a public IP address range, you need to select the Regional Internet Registry (RIR) that issued IP addresses to your organization. After you have created one or more IP address blocks, your existing IP address ranges are listed when you click IP Address Blocks in the navigation pane. From the IP Address Blocks view, click Tasks to see other tasks you can perform, which include adding and importing IP address ranges, IP address subnets, and IP addresses.

Activity 5-16: Using IPAM

Time Required: 10 minutes
Objective: Retrieve server data and create an IP address block.

Required Tools and Equipment: 412Server1 and 412Server2
Description: In this activity, you start using IPAM by retrieving server data and creating an IP address block.

1. Start 412Server1, if necessary. Start 412Server2, and log on to the 412Dom1 domain as **Administrator**, if necessary.

2. On 412Server2, open Server Manager, and click **IPAM**, if necessary. Click **OVERVIEW** in the IPAM console's navigation pane. In the IPAM Server Tasks window, click **Retrieve data from managed servers**.

3. After a while, you see the message "Server data is based on *date and time*." In the navigation pane, click **IP ADDRESS SPACE**. Read the information displayed. Click to expand the following items and read more about each: **IP Address Blocks, IP Address Inventory,** and **IP Address Range Groups**.

4. In the navigation pane, click **IP Address Blocks**. There are no IP address blocks at first. Click the **TASKS** list arrow, and click **Add IP Address Block**.

5. In the Add or Edit IPv4 Address Block dialog box, type **10.0.0.0** in the Network ID text box, and in the Prefix length list box, click 8. The Start IP address and End IP address text boxes are filled in automatically (see Figure 5-31). Click **OK**. You should see the IP address range 10.12.0.0/16 from the scope defined on 412Server1. If you don't see the address range, click the **Refresh** icon in Server Manager.

5

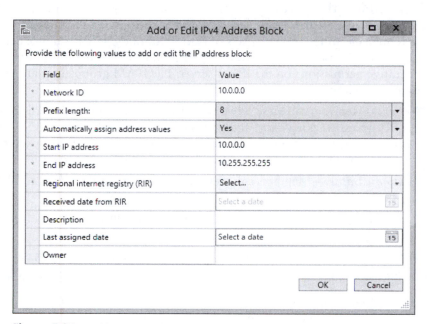

Figure 5-31   Adding an IP address block

6. Click **DNS and DHCP Servers** under MONITOR AND MANAGE in the IPAM console's navigation pane. You see one entry for each DNS and DHCP server you're managing. Right-click the DHCP server entry and click **Edit DHCP Server Properties**. Browse through the settings in the Edit DHCP Server Properties dialog box. You can manage all your DHCP servers in this console. Click **Cancel** when finished.

7. Click **DHCP Scopes** in the navigation pane. You see the scope defined on 412Server1. Scroll down to the Details view, and look at the Scope Properties tab. You can view details about the scope and see the current scope utilization. Scroll up and right-click the scope to see the management tasks you can perform.

8. Click **DNS Zone Monitoring** in the navigation pane to see the DNS zones defined on 412Server1.

9. Stay logged on to 412Server2 and leave 412Server1 running if you're continuing to the next activity.

Activity 5-17: Removing IPAM

Time Required: 10 minutes
Objective: Uninstall the IPAM feature.

Required Tools and Equipment: 412Server1 and 412Server2
Description: In this activity, you remove the IPAM feature.

1. Start 412Server1, if necessary. Start 412Server2, and log on to the 412Dom1 domain as **Administrator**, if necessary.

2. On 412Server2, start the Remove Roles and Features Wizard. Click **Next** until you reach the Features window. Click to clear the **IP Address Management (IPAM) Server** check box, and then click **Remove Features**. Click **Next**, and then click **Remove**.

3. On 412Server1, log on as **Administrator**, if necessary. Open the Group Policy Management console, and delete the **ipamdom1_DC_NPS**, **ipamdom1_DHCP**, and **ipamdom1_DNS** GPOs from the Domain node.

4. Shut down 412Server1 and 412Server2.

IPAM Administration Delegation   As you have seen, a number of IPAM-related groups are created to allow delegation of IPAM administration. You add users to these groups to allow them to manage and monitor aspects of IPAM without giving them broader administrative authority. There are no users in these groups by default; however, the Administrator account has full administrative permissions on the IPAM server. The IPAM groups that are created and their capabilities are as follows:

- *IPAM Users*—Members can view server inventory information and IP address space data (but not IP address tracking data) and access the MONITOR AND MANAGE view in the IPAM console. They can also view the event catalog. All the other groups in this list have the same access as this group plus the additional capabilities described.

- *IPAM Administrators*—Members can view all IPAM data and perform all IPAM administrative tasks.

- *IPAM ASM Administrators*—Members can perform IP address space management (ASM) tasks.

- *IPAM IP Audit Administrators*—Members can view IP address tracking data.

- IPAM MSM Administrators—Members can monitor and manage IPAM tasks.

As described, you can also create custom IPAM administrator roles by using the ACCESS CONTROL option in the IPAM console's navigation pane.

For a user to manage a remote IPAM server in Server Manager, the user must also be a member of the winRMRemoteWMIUsers group on the target IPAM server as well as a member of one of the groups in the preceding list.

Managing IPAM Data Collection Tasks   A number of IPAM scheduled tasks are created when you provision an IPAM server. Open the Task Scheduler on the IPAM server to see the list of scheduled tasks and, if necessary, change their frequency (see Figure 5-32). Table 5-3 lists the tasks along with their purpose and default frequency.

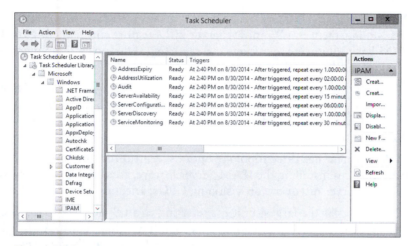

Figure 5-32 IPAM scheduled tasks

Table 5-3   IPAM scheduled tasks

Task name	Purpose	Default frequency
AddressExpiry	Tracks IP address lease expiration states and logs notifications	1 day
AddressUtilization	Collects IP address space use from DHCP servers	2 hours
Audit	Collects DHCP and IPAM operational events and events from DCs and NPS servers plus IP address tracking events from DHCP servers	1 day
ServerAvailability	Gets status information from managed DNS and DHCP servers	15 minutes
ServerConfiguration	Get DHCP and DNS server configuration information	6 hours
ServerDiscovery	Discovers DCs and DHCP and DNS servers in the selected domains	1 day
ServiceMonitoring	Gets DNS zone status event information	30 minutes

© 2016 Cengage Learning®

Chapter Summary

- Dynamic Access Control gives administrators another method for securing access to files that's more powerful than file and folder permissions based simply on group memberships. DAC enables administrators to control file access by using complex criteria that can include file classification and user attributes.

- The DAC infrastructure consists of resource properties, file classifications, claim types, central access policies, and central access rules. Resource properties must be a member of a resource property list for file servers to use them. A resource property list contains a list of resource properties that are downloaded by servers.

- Before a domain controller can support claims and resource properties for controlling authorization to resources, a group policy setting must be configured on a GPO linked to the Domain Controllers OU.

- Central access policies allow targeting resources on servers and setting DAC permissions with group policies. They consist of one or more central access rules containing both DAC and regular permissions and can be targeted to specific servers.

- Access-denied assistance helps resolve issues in file and folder access. This feature gives file users, file owners, and administrators methods to remediate access-denied messages when users requesting shared files should be allowed access.

- IP Address Management is a Windows Server 2012 feature for managing the IP address space. IPAM has monitoring, auditing, and reporting functions to help manage key server components in an IP network.

- The IPAM infrastructure consists of IPAM servers and managed devices. The IPAM server discovers servers you want to manage and collects and stores data from IPAM-managed devices in the IPAM database. Managed devices are Windows servers running DHCP, DNS, Active Directory, or NPS.

- An IPAM deployment has three topology options: centralized, distributed, and hybrid. IPAM deployment includes installing the IPAM Server feature, conducting IPAM server provisioning, performing server discovery, provisioning GPOs, selecting servers, and collecting data.

- An IP address block is the largest unit for referring to an IP address space. It consists of a contiguous range of IP addresses with a corresponding subnet mask. An IP address range is a pool of continuous addresses in an IP address block and usually corresponds to a DHCP scope. An IP address range group consists of one or more IP address ranges that are logically grouped by some criteria.

- The IPAM console's navigation pane contains links to several monitoring and management views of the IP address space and DNS zone data. Each IP address range should be a member of an IP address block.

- IPAM-related groups are created to allow delegation of IPAM administration, and IPAM scheduled tasks are created when you provision an IPAM server.

Key Terms

access-denied assistance   A feature in Windows Server 2012/R2 that gives file users, file owners, and administrators methods to remediate access-denied messages when users requesting shared files should be allowed access.

central access policies   A component of DAC consisting of one or more central access rules; used to target resources on servers and set DAC permissions with group policies. *See also* Dynamic Access Control (DAC).

central access rules   A DAC component for setting permissions on targeted resources; deployed through central access policies. *See also* Dynamic Access Control (DAC).

centralized topology   An IPAM deployment option that has a single IPAM server for the entire enterprise. *See also* IP Address Management (IPAM).

claim   An assertion an entity (user or computer) makes about what it is or what it does for the purpose of authenticating or gaining access to a resource.

distributed topology   An IPAM deployment option that places an IPAM server at every site in a network. *See also* IP Address Management (IPAM).

Dynamic Access Control (DAC)   A feature in Windows Server 2012/R2 that gives administrators another method for securing access to files that's more powerful than file and folder permissions based on group memberships.

Group Policy provisioning   A method of provisioning IPAM that uses the Group Policy tool to perform tasks such as creating security groups, setting firewall rules, and creating shares for each IPAM-managed server. *See also* IP Address Management (IPAM).

hybrid topology An IPAM deployment option that has a single IPAM server collecting information from all managed servers in the enterprise and IPAM servers at key branch locations. *See also* IP Address Management (IPAM).

IP address block The largest unit for referring to an IP address space; consists of a contiguous range of IP addresses with a corresponding subnet mask.

IP Address Management (IPAM) A new feature in Windows Server 2012 that enables an administrator to manage the IP address space with monitoring, auditing, and reporting functions to help manage DHCP and DNS.

IP address range A pool of continuous addresses in an IP address block; usually corresponds to a DHCP scope.

IP address range group One or more IP address ranges that are logically grouped by some criteria.

IPAM client A Windows computer with the IPAM management console installed; typically used for remote management. *See also* IP Address Management (IPAM).

IPAM server A Windows Server 2012/R2 member server with the IPAM Server feature installed. *See also* IP Address Management (IPAM).

managed server An IPAM component that's a Windows server running one or more of these Microsoft services: DHCP, DNS, Active Directory, and NPS. *See also* IP Address Management (IPAM).

manual provisioning A method of provisioning IPAM that requires configuring each IPAM server task and managed server manually. *See also* IP Address Management (IPAM).

resource property An attribute that can be applied to a resource, such as a file or folder, and is used to classify resources.

resource property list A DAC component of containing a list of resource properties that are downloaded by servers.

unmapped address space An IP address or address range that hasn't been assigned to an IP address block.

Review Questions

1. Which of the following features or services should you install if you want to control file access with file classifications?

   a. BranchCache

   b. Dynamic Access Control

   c. NTFS permissions

   d. IPAM

2. You want to set DAC permissions on folders on several servers in the domain by using group policies. Which of the following should you do first?

   a. Configure the Central Policy tab for a folder.

   b. Create a central access policy.

   c. Configure central access policy settings in a GPO.

   d. Create a central access rule.

3. Which of the following is an attribute that can be applied to a file or folder and is used to classify resources?

   a. Resource property

   b. Central access policy

   c. Claim type

   d. Conditional access rule

4. You want to restrict access to a folder based on a user's job title. What do you need to create to use this criteria in a permission condition?

   a. Resource property

   b. Central access policy

   c. Claim type

   d. Conditional access rule

5. Which of the following is true about Dynamic Access Control? (Choose all that apply.)

   a. File classifications are a necessary component of DAC.

   b. DAC can use user claims for access control.

   c. You can set permissions based on compound conditions.

   d. Central access rules can contain NTFS permissions.

6. Which of the following is true about resource properties? (Choose all that apply.)

   a. They're disabled by default.

   b. You have to create any resource property you might want to use.

   c. You always have to add a resource property to a resource property list.

   d. They're used to classify resources.

7. What do you use to set up automatic classification of files with resource properties?

   a. FSRM

   b. ADAC

   c. ADUC

   d. GPME

8. A user named Mike has some files on his computer that contain sensitive information. His computer is running Windows 8.1 Enterprise Edition and is a member of a Windows Server 2012 R2 domain. You want to be able to classify Mike's files so that access to them can be restricted based on their classification. What should you do first?

   a. Create a group policy that classifies the files on Mike's computer.

   b. Move the files from Mike's computer to a server running Windows Server 2012 R2.

   c. Open the Properties dialog box for the folder containing the files and click the File Classification tab.

   d. Create a central access rule to classify the files on Mike's computer.

9. You want to classify some files on a Windows Server 2012 R2 server, using the Confidentiality and Department resource properties. What should you do to use these resource properties in a permission entry?

   a. Open FSRM and create the resource properties.

   b. Configure a GPO to allow resource properties on the server.

   c. Install the File Classification role service.

   d. Open ADAC and enable the resource properties.

10. You've configured permissions on a folder by using user claims and resource properties and want to test permissions for several different users. What should you do so that you don't have to log on as each user to verify that these permissions are doing what you want?

   a. Run the Resultant Set of Policy Wizard from the Group Policy Management console.

   b. Enter the `whoami` *UserName* `/claims` command for each user.

   c. Open the Advanced Security Settings dialog box and click the Effective Access tab.

   d. Run the `Get-Permissions` *UserName* `-Whatif` PowerShell cmdlet for each user.

11. A user account named msmith with the job title Manager is a member of the Accounting global security group. The Accounting group has Modify permission to the acctdocs folder. Msmith is also a member of the Finance group, which has Read permission to the acctdocs folder. You create a central access policy granting Full Control access to users with the job title Manager. What is msmith's permission to the acctdocs folder?

    a. Read

    b. Modify

    c. Full Control

    d. Denied

12. You want to create a central access rule that affects only folders classified as highly confidential. You don't want the rule to affect other folders on any servers. What should you do?

    a. Configure the Target Resources property on the central access rule.

    b. Configure the Scope property on the central access policy.

    c. Link the central access policy to a specific OU.

    d. Create a Folder Exception in the central access policy.

13. You have just configured file servers in a new facility to share documents among all users. Users have been complaining that they're getting obscure messages when they try to access some shared folders, and they can't access the files. What should you do so that users get more helpful messages when they can't access shared folders?

    a. Create a central access policy after configuring the Access-Denied property.

    b. Use FSRM to create new file classifications.

    c. Create custom messages in ADAC.

    d. Configure access-denied assistance with a group policy.

14. You want to deploy IPAM in your network. You have four servers running and need to decide on which server you should install the IPAM Server feature. Which of the following server configurations is the best solution?

    a. Windows Server 2012 R2 domain controller

    b. Windows Server 2012 standalone server running DHCP

    c. Windows Server 2012 R2 member server running Web Server

    d. Windows Server 2012 member server running DHCP

15. Your company has a main office with four branch offices; each has about 30 computers and a single server running file and print services, DNS, and DHCP. There are no IT personnel at branch offices. You want to set up IPAM in your network. Which IPAM topology makes the most sense?

    a. Centralized

    b. Distributed

    c. Unified

    d. Hybrid

16. You recently configured IPAM in your Windows Server 2012 R2 domain. When you view the Server Inventory window, you notice that one DHCP server isn't displayed. This missing server runs Windows Server 2008 in a workgroup configuration and is located in the Engineering Department. Which of the following actions is most likely to display the missing server in the Server Inventory window?

    a. Upgrade the server to Windows Server 2012 R2.

    b. Join the server to the domain.

    c. Configure the server's firewall.

    d. Uninstall DHCP from the server.

17. You have recently installed IPAM on a server running Windows Server 2012 R2. Your network has four DHCP servers, six DNS servers, and three DCs. All the DHCP and DNS servers are domain members. When you look at the Server Inventory window, you don't see any of the DHCP servers, but you do see the DNS servers and DCs. What should you do to solve this problem?

    a. Reinstall IPAM on a server that isn't a DC.

    b. Configure the DHCP servers as workgroup servers.

    c. Demote the IPAM server.

    d. On the IPAM server, uninstall DHCP.

18. You have recently installed the IPAM Server feature on a server running Windows Server 2012 R2. You chose manual provisioning during installation. You have 15 servers to be managed by IPAM and have decided the manual provisioning tasks are too much work. You want to use Group Policy provisioning instead. What should you do?

    a. Delete any GPOs you have created. In the Overview window of the IPAM console, enable Group Policy provisioning.

    b. Uninstall IPAM and reinstall it, making sure to select Group Policy provisioning in the "Provision the IPAM server" step.

    c. Run the `Invoke-IpamGpoProvisioning -GroupPolicy` PowerShell cmdlet.

    d. Create a GPO, configure the IPAM-Provisioning setting, and link the GPO to an OU containing the IPAM server account.

19. You have just installed a Microsoft SQL server and want to use it to store IPAM data, which is currently using the WID. What should you do?

    a. Copy the files from C:\Windows\System32\ipam\database folder to the SQL server and import the files.

    b. Uninstall IPAM and reinstall it, making sure to choose Microsoft SQL Server during server provisioning.

    c. In the IPAM Overview window, run the Change Database Storage Method Wizard.

    d. Run the `Move-IpamDatabase` PowerShell cmdlet from the IPAM server.

20. You have just finished the Add Roles and Features Wizard and clicked the IPAM node in Server Manager. The IPAM Server Tasks window indicates that you're connected to the IPAM server. What should you do next?

    a. Provision the IPAM server.

    b. Configure server discovery.

    c. Start server discovery.

    d. Select servers to manage.

Case Projects

Case Project 5-1: Using Dynamic Access Control

You're the IT administrator for CSM Tech Publishing and have been given a new project to classify files on three file servers and set access permission conditions on these files based on certain criteria. The project's goals are as follows:

- Classify files based on customer accounts. There are three customer accounts: Spalding, Wilson, and Champion. All files containing these account names should be classified accordingly.

- Classify files based on type of customer project: Baseball, Basketball, Football, and Soccer. If a project name is found in a file, the file should be classified accordingly.

- Your company uses the Department attribute on user accounts to specify which type of product the user is involved with. Access to files you classify should be based on the user's Department attribute; for example, if the Department attribute=Baseball, the user should have access to the files classified as Baseball. Access should be as follows:

  o If the user's Department doesn't equal the product type, the user shouldn't have any access.

  o If the user's Department is equal to the product type, the user should have Read access.

  o If the user's Department is equal to the product type and the user job title is Manager, the user should have Modify access to the files.

  o If the user is a member of the Administrators group, the user should have Full Control access to all files.

- Only files that have been classified with both the customer account and the project should be subject to DAC permissions.

Outline the steps you should take to achieve this project's goals. Supply enough detail so that someone who has a good understanding of DAC and FCI could perform these tasks.

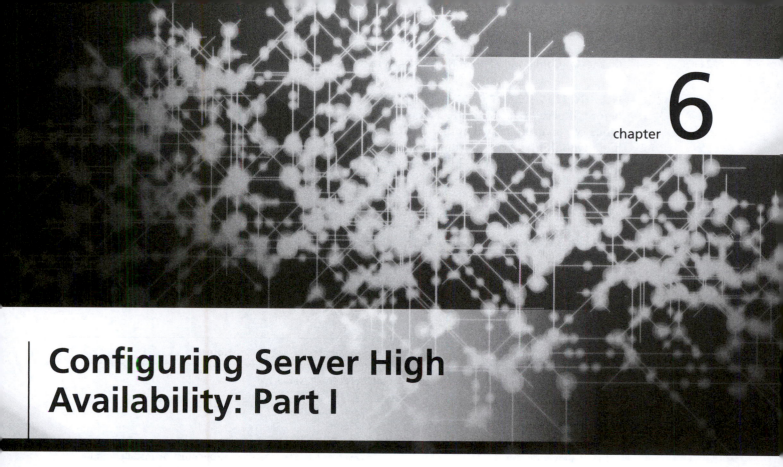

chapter 6

Configuring Server High Availability: Part I

After reading this chapter and completing the exercises, you will be able to:

- Configure network load balancing
- Configure a failover cluster

Businesses depend on their networks and network data more than ever before. If network servers aren't available, productivity can come to a grinding halt. The importance of server high availability can't be overstated, so Windows Server 2012/R2 has several high-availability server options to ensure that productivity continues even if one server fails. This chapter discusses two high-availability options in Windows Server 2012/R2: network load balancing and failover clustering.

Configuring Network Load Balancing

Table 6-1 lists what you need for hands-on activities in this chapter.

Table 6-1   Activity requirements

Activity	Requirements	Notes
Activity 6-1: Installing the Network Load Balancing Feature	412Server1, 412Server2, 412Server3	
Activity 6-2: Creating an NLB Cluster	412Server1, 412Server2, 412Server3	
Activity 6-3: Configuring the iSCSI SAN for a Failover Cluster	412Server1, 412Server2, 412Server3	The iSCSI Target Server role must be installed and configured from Activities 4-7 through 4-9 on 412Server1.
Activity 6-4: Installing the Failover Clustering Feature	412Server1, 412Server2, 412Server3	
Activity 6-5: Validating a Cluster Configuration	412Server1, 412Server2, 412Server3	
Activity 6-6: Creating a Failover Cluster	412Server1, 412Server2, 412Server3	
Activity 6-7: Creating a File Server Failover Cluster	412Server1, 412Server2, 412Server3	

© 2016 Cengage Learning®

The Windows Server 2012/R2 **network load balancing (NLB)** feature uses server clusters to provide both scalability and fault tolerance. A **server cluster** is a group of servers configured to respond to a single virtual IP address. Based on an internal algorithm, the servers decide which server should respond to each incoming client request. To provide scalability, the servers in an NLB cluster share the load of incoming requests based on rules you can define. To provide fault tolerance, a failed server can be removed from the cluster, and another server can take its place and begin servicing client requests that were handled by the failed server. Although NLB does provide some fault tolerance, its main function is to handle a large volume of client traffic efficiently.

From a client computer's perspective, a server cluster appears on the network as a single device with a single name and IP address. A cluster is assigned a name, much as a server is assigned a hostname, and an IP address. Client computers connect to the cluster instead of to the servers that make up the cluster. Figure 6-1 shows an NLB cluster with three servers participating. The clients use a single virtual IP address—in this example, 10.12.1.100—to access the cluster. The NLB software running on the servers responds to the virtual IP address and decides which of the three servers should respond to each client request.

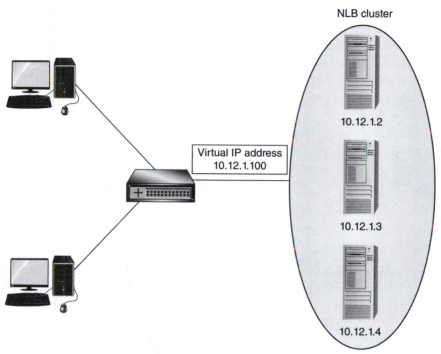

Figure 6-1   A logical depiction of network load balancing
© 2016 Cengage Learning®

NLB is well suited to TCP/IP-based applications, such as Web servers and streaming media servers where the data can be replicated easily between participating servers and isn't changed by users. NLB clusters are also effective in distributing the load among VPN servers and terminal server farms.

NLB isn't advisable if the data being accessed on the servers requires exclusive access, as with database, file and print, and e-mail applications. Failover clusters, discussed later in this chapter, are a better fit for these types of applications.

Installing Network Load Balancing

NLB is available in Windows Server 2012/R2 Datacenter and Standard editions but not in Essentials or Foundation editions. NLB clusters don't have any special hardware requirements, but it's important that each server in the cluster is configured with the same OS version and updates are consistent on all servers. Typically, servers participating in an NLB cluster shouldn't provide services other than the ones the cluster is providing. For example, using a domain controller as a cluster server isn't recommended.

NLB must be installed on each server in the cluster, and the networking services to be load balanced must be installed and configured identically. NLB doesn't provide data replication, so the cluster administrator must make sure the data provided by cluster servers is consistent among all servers.

Ideally, the servers in an NLB cluster should be configured with two NICs. One NIC is used for communication with network clients that request cluster services, and the other NIC is dedicated for communication among cluster members. Figure 6-2 shows this arrangement. The second NIC can be configured to operate on a separate logical IP network, as this figure shows, or it can be configured for the same IP network as NLB clients.

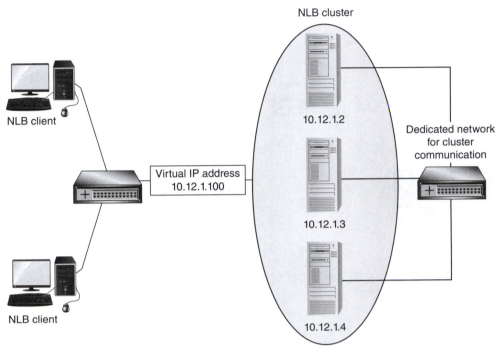

Figure 6-2   An NLB cluster with a separate cluster network

© 2016 Cengage Learning®

NLB is installed as a feature in Server Manager, as you see in Activity 6-1. After it's installed, NLB is configured for all participating servers in the Network Load Balancing Manager. An NLB cluster can be configured on any server running the NLB Manager.

Activity 6-1: Installing the Network Load Balancing Feature

Time Required: 5 minutes

Objective: Install the network load balancing feature.

Required Tools and Equipment: 412Server1, 412Server2, and 412Server3

Description: In this activity, you install the NLB feature on 412Server2 and 412Server3. 412Server1 is the DC for the network and should be running during this activity.

1. Start 412Server1. Start 412Server2, and log on to the domain as **Administrator**.

2. On 412Server2, install **Network Load Balancing** by using the Add Roles and Features Wizard in Server Manager or the PowerShell cmdlet `Install-WindowsFeature NLB -IncludeManagementTools`.

3. Start 412Server3, and log on to the domain as **Administrator**. Install the **Network Load Balancing** feature.

4. Stay logged on to both servers for the next activity and leave 412Server1 running.

Creating a Network Load Balancing Cluster

After NLB is installed on each server, you can create a load-balancing cluster and configure load-balancing options. Creating an NLB cluster involves the following tasks:

- Create a new cluster.
- Select a host and network interface to participate in the cluster.
- Configure the host priority and host ID.
- Set the cluster IP address.
- Set the cluster name and operation mode.
- Configure port rules.
- Add servers to the cluster.

Additional configuration of the cluster can be done later if you want to change how traffic is distributed between servers. You take a closer look at each task before you configure an NLB cluster in Activity 6-2.

Creating a New Cluster   To create an NLB cluster, open the Network Load Balancing Manager from the Tools menu in Server Manager on one of the servers with the NLB feature installed. You have the option of creating a new cluster or connecting to an existing cluster (see Figure 6-3).

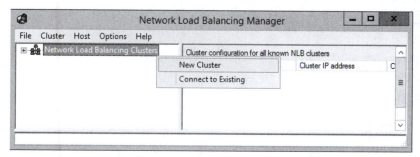

Figure 6-3   The Network Load Balancing Manager

Selecting a Host and Network Interface to Participate in the Cluster   When you create a new cluster, you must specify a host to participate in the new cluster. You can enter the name of the server where you're running the Network Load Balancing Manager or a different server. After the NLB Manager is connected to the server you specify, you're asked to select the network interface the server will use in the new cluster. If you have more than one network interface, you should choose the interface to be used to communicate with client computers accessing the cluster. If you have only one NIC, it's used for both cluster communication and client communication. In addition, if you're using two NICs, you should remove the dedicated IP address.

Configuring the Host Priority and Host ID   Each host participating in an NLB cluster is assigned a unique host ID, which is also the host's priority in the cluster. You can have up to 32 servers in an NLB cluster, so you can choose a priority value from 1 to 32. The cluster member with the lowest priority (ID) handles all cluster traffic that isn't associated with a port rule. This behavior can be overridden by defining specific port rules (discussed later in "Configuring Port Rules"). Every server in a cluster must have a unique priority value.

Setting the Cluster IP Address   The cluster IP address, or **virtual IP address**, is the address network clients use to access the networking services provided by the cluster. A DNS host record should exist for the cluster name mapped to this address. If you're using a single NIC configuration for NLB servers, the cluster IP address is added to the NIC's TCP/IP properties, although, depending on your NIC, you might have to add this address manually. If you're using two NICs, the cluster address replaces the current address assigned to the NLB NIC, assuming you removed the dedicated IP address on the NLB NIC. You can use IPv4 or IPv6 addresses.

Setting the Cluster Name and Operation Mode   The cluster name and operation mode are set in the Cluster Parameters dialog box shown in Figure 6-4. The cluster name is the fully qualified domain name (FQDN) that clients use to access the cluster and is specified in the "Full Internet name" text box in the figure. The name should have a corresponding DNS host record entry associated with the cluster IP address. So in this figure, you need a DNS zone named 412Dom1.local with an A record for host nlb with the IP address 10.12.1.100.

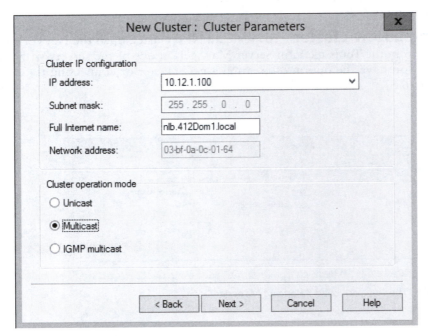

Figure 6-4   Setting cluster parameters

You must have DNS set up correctly for NLB to work. You need to configure a zone for the FQDN specified for the cluster name and A records for each server. In addition, you must create an A record for the cluster name and cluster virtual IP address (NLB and 10.12.1.100 in Figure 6-4).

The **cluster operation mode** specifies the type of network addressing used to access the cluster: Unicast, Multicast, or IGMP multicast. The default option is Unicast. The multicast options can make network communication more efficient, but multicast support must be available and configured on your routers. If you're using only one NIC on cluster servers, multicast mode is the best option. Using unicast mode with a single NIC has some limitations: Regular (non-NLB) network traffic among cluster hosts isn't supported; regular network traffic directed to one of the cluster hosts causes additional network overhead for all cluster hosts; and you can't manage other NLB hosts by using the Network Load Balancing Manager from another NLB host.

If you must use unicast mode, it's preferable to install two NICs so that one can be assigned to the NLB cluster and the other dedicated to regular traffic.

If NLB hosts are Hyper-V virtual machines and you configure unicast mode with a single NIC, you must enable MAC address spoofing in the NIC properties of the virtual machine.

Configuring Port Rules   The last step in the initial configuration of an NLB cluster is defining port rules. A **port rule** specifies which type of TCP or UDP traffic the cluster should respond to and how the traffic is distributed between cluster members. The default port rule, shown in Figure 6-5, specifies that all TCP and UDP traffic on all ports are balanced across cluster members according to each member's load weight. Each cluster member can be assigned a load weight, with the traffic distributed proportionally based on the load weight of other members. The higher the load weight, the more traffic that member handles. Port rules can be modified at any time if you want to change the cluster's default behavior. Cluster configuration is discussed later in "Configuring an NLB Cluster."

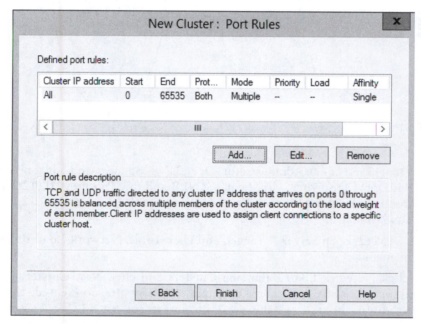

Figure 6-5   The default port rule

Adding Servers to the Cluster   After the cluster is created, you can add servers to it in the Network Load Balancing Manager by right-clicking the cluster and clicking Add Host to Cluster. However, the Network Load Balancing feature must be installed on the server you want to add to the cluster. Again, you must select the network interface the server will use for communication with clients, and you must assign a priority. Because the value 1 is already used for the first server in the cluster, the priority value defaults to 2. You have the opportunity to assign port rules for the new server and, if necessary, change the load weight. The load weight value defaults to Equal, and valid values are 0 to 100. After you have at least two servers in the cluster, you can further configure the cluster.

Activity 6-2: Creating an NLB Cluster

Time Required: 15 minutes
Objective: Create an NLB cluster.

Required Tools and Equipment: 412Server1, 412Server2, and 412Server3
Description: In this activity, you configure DNS for the NLB cluster and then configure the NLB cluster. You configure the NLB cluster hosts with a single NIC using multicast mode. The topology looks like Figure 6-6, except you don't have NLB clients in your network.

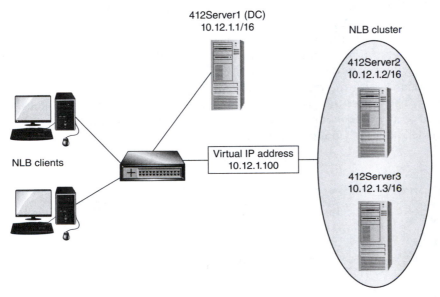

Figure 6-6   The NLB topology

© 2016 Cengage Learning®

1. Log on to 412Server1 as **Administrator**. Open DNS Manager and add a new host (A) record in the 412Dom1.local zone with the name **NLB** and the IP address **10.12.1.100**. Verify that there are A records for 412Server2 and 412Server3 (10.12.1.2 and 10.12.1.3, respectively). Close DNS Manager.

2. On 412Server2, open Server Manager, and click **Tools, Network Load Balancing Manager** from the menu.

3. Right-click **Network Load Balancing Clusters** and click **New Cluster**. Type **412Server2** in the Host text box, and click **Connect**. After you're connected, the New Cluster: Connect dialog box shows the available interfaces for 412Server2 (see Figure 6-7).

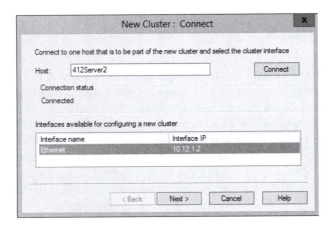

Figure 6-7   The New Cluster: Connect dialog box

If you were using a setup with two adapters, you would choose the adapter you want to use for NLB traffic. Because you're using a single adapter, click **Next**.

4. In the New Cluster: Host Parameters dialog box (see Figure 6-8), accept the default value **1** in the "Priority (unique host identifier)" text box. The "Dedicated IP addresses" section lists the IP address used when an external device communicates directly with the server. This address is used only if you're using a single-adapter configuration. If you were using multiple adapters, you would remove the listed IP address. The "Default state" option specifies how this host should behave when it boots. The default state is Started, which means this host participates in the cluster when the system boots. Click **Next**.

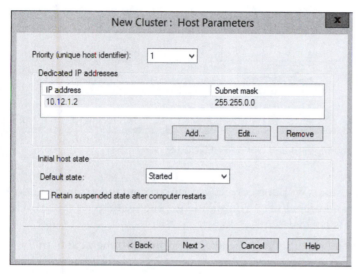

Figure 6-8   The New Cluster: Host Parameters dialog box

5. In the New Cluster: Cluster IP Addresses dialog box, click **Add**. Type **10.12.1.100** in the IPv4 address text box and **255.255.0.0** in the Subnet mask text box. This is the virtual IP address client computers will use to access the cluster. Click **OK**, and then click **Next**.

6. In the New Cluster: Cluster Parameters dialog box, type **nlb.412dom1.local** in the "Full Internet name" text box. This is the name client computers use to access the cluster and corresponds to the DNS record you created in Step 1. In the "Cluster operation mode" section, click the **Multicast** option button (see Figure 6-4, shown earlier). Click **Next**.

7. In the New Cluster: Port Rules dialog box (shown previously in Figure 6-5), read the port rule description for the default port rule, and then click **Finish**.

8. If you don't see any error messages in the Network Load Balancing Manager, go on to Step 9. If you see an error stating "The bind operation was successful but NLB is not responding to queries," you have to set the cluster IP address manually on the network interface. To do so, open the Properties dialog box for the Ethernet connection, double-click **Internet Protocol Version 4 (TCP/IPv4)**, and click **Advanced**. Click **Add** in the "IP addresses" section. Type **10.12.1.100** for the IP address and **255.255.0.0** for the subnet mask, and then click **Add**. Click **OK** until you see the Network Connections window. Shut down and restart 412Server2, and then open the Network Load Balancing Manager.

9. To add 412Server3 as a second cluster host, right-click **nlb.412Dom1.local** and click **Add Host To Cluster**.

10. Type **412Server3** in the Host text box, and click **Connect**. After the Ethernet interface is listed in the "Interfaces available for configuring the cluster" list box, click **Next**.

11. In the Add Host to Cluster: Host Parameters dialog box, leave the Priority setting at the default value of **2**, and click **Next**.

12. In the Add Host to Cluster: Port Rules dialog box, click **Finish**. You might have to add the cluster IP address (10.12.1.100) as a second IP address to the Ethernet adapter on 412Server3 if you get the error message mentioned in Step 8. A correctly configured and working NLB cluster shows the status of both servers as Converged, and both servers are outlined in green, as shown in Figure 6-9.

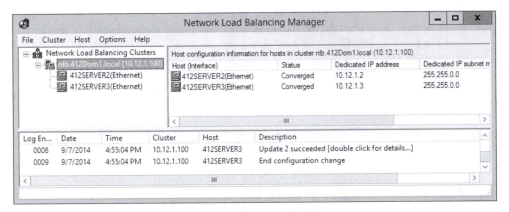

Figure 6-9   A correctly configured and working NLB cluster

13. To test that the cluster is working correctly, open a command prompt window on 412Server1. Type **ping nlb** and press **Enter**. You should get successful ping replies. The first ping might time out, but this is normal.

14. Stay logged on to all three servers if you're continuing to the next activity.

Configuring an NLB cluster can be complex, and much can go wrong. DNS must be set up correctly, NICs must be capable of dynamic MAC address changes, and the IP configuration must be correct. If you believe you have everything set correctly but the NLB Manager still reports errors, shut down both servers and restart them. Open the NLB Manager after both servers have restarted to see whether the problem has been solved.

Configuring an NLB Cluster

After you have a running NLB cluster, you can configure the cluster and host settings. Configuration of an NLB cluster is divided into three categories, discussed in the following sections:

- Cluster properties
- Port rules
- Host properties

Configuring Cluster Properties   To configure cluster properties, right-click the cluster name in the Network Load Balancing Manager and click Cluster Properties. A cluster's properties include the cluster's IP address and several cluster parameters. These settings affect the cluster as a whole, not any particular cluster server. The cluster IP address is set when you create the cluster and can be changed in the Cluster IP Addresses tab of the cluster's Properties dialog box (see Figure 6-10). You can also add or remove IP addresses in this tab. You might want to assign more than one IP address to a cluster when you're running multiple instances of the same service on the cluster, such as two Web servers, each responding to a different IP address.

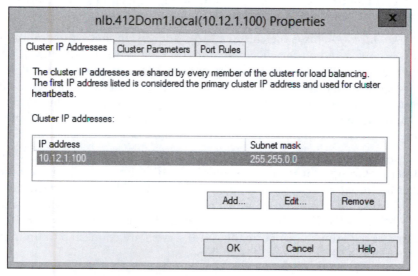

Figure 6-10   The Cluster IP Addresses tab

The cluster address is a virtual IP address, but it's still configured in the TCP/IP Properties dialog box of an adapter on each server that's a cluster member. When you add a host to the cluster and select an adapter, the Add Host to Cluster Wizard might configure the adapter for you, but if it's not successful in doing so, you might have to configure the adapter with the cluster address manually.

Cluster parameters are configured in the Cluster Parameters tab of the cluster's Properties dialog (see Figure 6-11) and consist of the following:

- *IP address*—Select the cluster's primary IP address. If more than one IP address is configured for the cluster, you can choose the primary address in the list box.

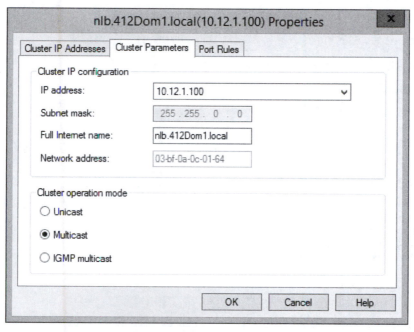

Figure 6-11   The Cluster Parameters tab

- *Subnet mask*—The subnet mask for the specified IP address. If you need to change this setting, you must do so in the Cluster IP Addresses tab.

- *Full Internet name*—This is the fully qualified domain name (FQDN) assigned to the cluster. This name must have an entry in DNS that resolves to the cluster's primary IP address.

- *Network address*—This is the cluster's MAC address. In unicast operation mode, this address is configured on the cluster adapter on each server in the cluster. The NICs on your servers must support changing the built-in MAC address. The NLB service automatically makes this change to the selected cluster adapter on each host server. In multicast mode, the MAC address is a multicast MAC address assigned to the cluster. A multicast MAC address can be identified by the least significant bit of the first octet being set to binary 1.

- *Cluster operation mode*—The choices for cluster operation mode are unicast, multicast, and Internet Group Management Protocol (IGMP) multicast. The default mode is unicast. If either multicast mode is selected, the cluster MAC address is changed to a multicast MAC address. In addition, in multicast mode, the server adapter can also use its built-in MAC address. If IGMP multicast mode is selected, switches that support IGMP forward NLB frames only out switch ports that NLB servers are connected to. In multicast mode, switches flood NLB traffic out all switch ports.

Configuring Port Rules   If you created the cluster leaving the default port rules in place, the cluster responds to all IP communication directed to the cluster's virtual IP address. (In this chapter's example, the virtual IP address is 10.12.1.100.) In most cases, you should change the port rules to accept communication on the cluster address only for services specifically offered by all cluster members. For example, if the cluster's purpose is to provide scalable access to a Web site, create port rules that allow TCP port 80 and possibly port 443 (for secure HTTP) yet disallow all other ports. Port rules apply to all hosts in a cluster and are configured in the Port Rules tab of the cluster's Properties dialog box. In Figure 6-12, three port rules were created. The first rule instructs the cluster to discard all traffic directed to the cluster in which the TCP or UDP ports are in the range 0 to 22. The second rule instructs the cluster to accept traffic that arrives on TCP port 23. The third rule instructs the cluster to discard all traffic for all ports higher than 23.

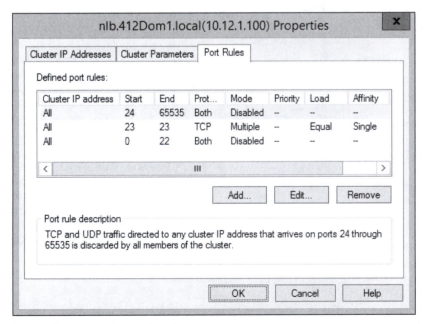

Figure 6-12   The Port Rules tab

To create or edit a rule, click Edit or Add in the Port Rules tab of the cluster's Properties dialog box to open the Add/Edit Port Rule dialog box shown in Figure 6-13. The port rule properties are as follows:

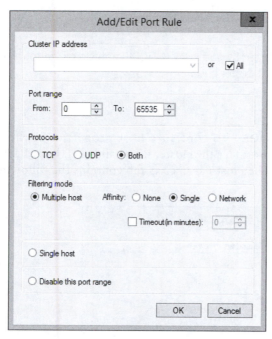

Figure 6-13   The Add/Edit Port Rule dialog box

- *Cluster IP address*—The port rule can apply to all cluster IP addresses (the default), or you can select an address if more than one IP address is assigned to the cluster.

- *Port range*—You specify the port range from 0 to 65535. To select a single port, make the From and To values the same.

- *Protocols*—You can specify TCP or UDP or both.

- *Filtering mode*—The options for **filtering mode** are Multiple host or Single host. Multiple host is the default and provides scalability so that network traffic on the specified hosts is load-balanced between all cluster hosts, according to each cluster host's assigned weight value. If Single host is selected, the host with the highest priority handles all traffic on the specified ports. If the host with the highest priority doesn't respond, the host with the next highest priority responds. The Single host option provides a level of fault tolerance but not scalability. In Multiple host mode, you select a **client affinity value** of one of the following:

  o *None*: With this option, any cluster member can respond to any client request, even multiple requests from the same client. For example, if the cluster is serving a Web site, a client can request multiple Web pages or multiple elements of a single Web page. In addition, one cluster member might handle one of the page requests, and another cluster member handles another request. This option works well with the TCP protocol only and only when the content being served is fairly static and stateless.

  o *Single*: This default affinity setting for port rules specifies that multiple requests from the same client are directed to the same cluster host. It must be used if the application has some level of dynamic data or if the client state must be maintained—for example, if the client must authenticate or establish an encrypted session.

  o *Network*: This affinity setting ensures that a single cluster host responds to client connections coming from a specific IP network, assuming a /24 prefix. This setting is used when clients access the cluster from behind multiple proxy servers, which might cause the client's source address to appear different on subsequent requests. This setting assumes that all proxy servers are in the same /24 subnet.

- *Timeout (in minutes)*—Set the amount of time to extend single or network affinity, which preserves the affinity configuration if the NLB cluster is changed while a client is connected.
- *Disable this port range*—Select this option when you want the cluster to discard packets matching the specified protocol and ports.

ICMP isn't affected by port rules. All ICMP traffic directed to the cluster is forwarded to all cluster hosts.

Configuring Host Properties   To configure host properties in the Network Load Balancing Manager, right-click a host under the cluster name and click Host Properties to open a dialog box similar to Figure 6-14. The Host Parameters tab contains the following settings:

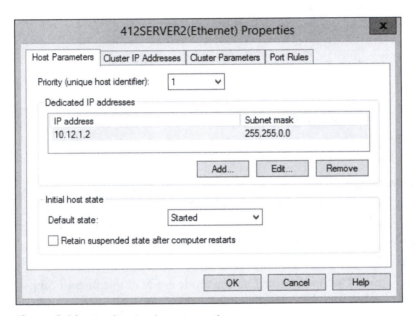

Figure 6-14   Configuring host properties

- *Priority (unique host identifier)*—This property, as discussed earlier, serves two purposes: an identifier for each host so that no two hosts can be assigned the same value and a priority value specifying that the host with the lowest value handles all traffic not covered by a port rule directed toward the cluster.
- *Dedicated IP addresses*—This setting is one or more IP addresses configured on the host's cluster adapter used for noncluster (dedicated) communication. If a second NIC is used for noncluster communication, this list can be empty because the second adapter's IP address is used automatically as the dedicated IP address.
- *Initial host state*—This property controls how the NLB service behaves when the OS boots. It has three options: Started, Stopped, and Suspended. The default option is Started, specifying that the host should join the cluster when the OS starts. If Stopped is selected, the host doesn't join the NLB cluster until it's started manually. If Suspended is selected, the host doesn't join the cluster when the OS starts and doesn't respond to remote NLB commands until it's resumed.

- *Retain suspended state after computer restarts*—If this check box is selected, the cluster host remains suspended if the host restarts while in a suspended state, regardless of the default state option that's selected.

The Cluster IP Addresses tab shows the cluster's IP addresses. The Cluster Parameters tab shows you the cluster parameters shown earlier in Figure 6-4, but you can't change these parameters in this tab; you need to open the cluster's Properties dialog box to change values in this tab. You use the Port Rules tab to edit port rules that aren't set to the Disabled mode. Port rules for each host can be configured as follows (see Figure 6-15):

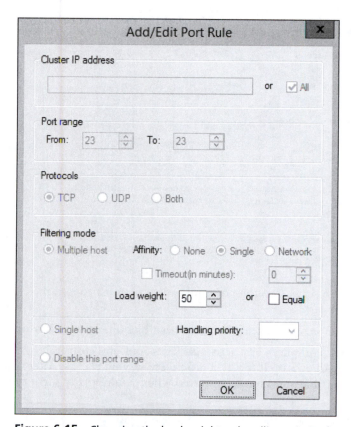

Figure 6-15   Changing the load weight or handling priority for a host

- *Multiple host filtering mode*—If the port rule filtering mode is set to Multiple host, a **load weight** can be assigned to the host for that port rule. By default, all hosts have equal weight, but if you want certain hosts to handle more traffic than others, you can set the load weight on each host. The load weight should be looked at as a percentage and can be set from 0 to 100. The total weight of all hosts should equal 100.

- *Single host filtering mode*—If the port rule filtering mode is set to Single host, the Handling priority value can be set. The host with the highest **handling priority** handles all traffic meeting the port rules' criteria. This value overrides the host priority value and allows you to assign different hosts to handle different types of traffic.

Managing an NLB Cluster

You might need to perform maintenance tasks on cluster servers as you would on any network server. To that end, you can change the state of hosts or the cluster as a whole. Figure 6-16 shows the options for controlling hosts that are cluster members. To control all hosts, right-click the cluster node and click Control Hosts. To control a single host, right-click the host and click Control Host. Then select one of these options:

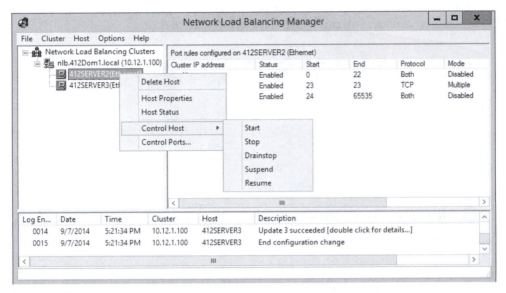

Figure 6-16   Controlling hosts

- *Start*—Starts the NLB service on the host and causes the host to join the cluster and begin handling NLB traffic.

- *Stop*—Stops the NLB service so that the host doesn't handle any NLB traffic.

- *Drainstop*—The host completes any active NLB sessions and stops taking new sessions. Use this option instead of Stop if the host is actively serving clients. After using this option, the host is in the Stop state and must be started when you're ready for it to begin handling NLB traffic again.

- *Suspend*—This option places the host in the Suspend state, which prevents it from handling new NLB traffic as well as NLB control commands, except for Resume.

- *Resume*—Resumes a suspended host but places it in the Stop state. The host can take NLB commands and must be started before it can resume handling NLB traffic.

Upgrading an NLB Cluster   You can upgrade an NLB cluster to a new version of Windows Server by taking all the cluster hosts offline, upgrading each host, and then bringing the cluster back online. You can also use a **rolling upgrade**, which involves taking each cluster node offline, upgrading the host, and then bringing it back online. A rolling upgrade maintains uninterrupted access to cluster services, but not all NLB applications support it. Before you perform an NLB cluster upgrade, you should keep the following in mind:

- Verify that all cluster services are supported on the new version of the OS you're upgrading to.

- Use the Drainstop option on each host before you begin the upgrade, and set the initial host state to Stop.

- After finishing the upgrade, verify that all services using NLB work correctly before bringing the host back into the cluster.

Using PowerShell to Configure NLB Clusters
Table 6-2 shows some PowerShell cmdlets you can use to configure NLB clusters. To see the full list of NLB-related PowerShell cmdlets, enter `Get-Command *nlb*`.

Table 6-2 PowerShell cmdlets for configuring NLB clusters

Cmdlet	Description
`Add-NlbClusterNode`	Adds a host to an existing NLB cluster
`Add-NlbClusterNodeDip`	Adds a dedicated IP address to an NLB cluster
`Add-NlbClusterPortRule`	Adds a port rule to an NLB cluster
`Add-NlbClusterVip`	Adds a virtual IP address to an NLB cluster
`Disable-NlbClusterPortRule`	Disables a port rule on an NLB cluster or host
`Enable-NlbClusterPortRule`	Enables a port rule on an NLB cluster or host
`New-NlbCluster`	Creates an NLB cluster
`Remove-NlbCluster`	Deletes an NLB cluster
`Remove-NlbClusterNode`	Removes a host from an NLB cluster
`Remove-NlbClusterNodeDip`	Removes a dedicate IP address from an NLB cluster
`Remove-NlbClusterPortRule`	Removes a port rule from an NLB cluster
`Remove-NlbClusterVip`	Removes a virtual IP address from an NLB cluster
`Resume-NlbCluster`	Resumes all hosts in an NLB cluster
`Resume-NlbClusterNode`	Resumes a suspended host in an NLB cluster
`Set-NlbCluster`	Edits the configuration of an NLB cluster
`Set-NlbClusterNode`	Changes settings of an NLB host
`Set-NlbClusterPortRule`	Edits the port rules for an NLB cluster
`Set-NlbClusterPortRuleNodeHandlingPriority`	Sets the host priority of a port rule for an NLB host
`Set-NlbClusterPortRuleNodeWeight`	Sets the load weight of a port rule for an NLB host
`Set-NlbClusterVip`	Edits the virtual IP address of an NLB cluster
`Start-NlbCluster`	Starts all hosts in an NLB cluster
`Start-NlbClusterNode`	Starts an NLB cluster host
`Stop-NlbCluster`	Stops all hosts in an NLB cluster
`Stop-NlbClusterNode`	Stops a host in an NLB cluster
`Suspend-NlbCluster`	Suspends all hosts in an NLB cluster
`Remove-NlbClusterNode`	Removes a host from an NLB cluster

© 2016 Cengage Learning®

Failover Clusters

A failover cluster has different objectives than an NLB cluster does. An NLB cluster is targeted toward scalability, but a failover cluster is deployed for **high availability**. An NLB cluster works best with fairly static, read-only data access, and a failover cluster is well suited to back-end database applications, file-sharing servers, messaging servers, and other mission-critical applications dealing with dynamic read/write data.

Before getting into failover clusters in more detail, take a few moments to review some terms used in describing failover clusters:

- A **clustered application** is an application or a service that's installed on two or more servers participating in a failover cluster. It's also called a "clustered service."
- A **cluster server** is a Windows Server 2012/R2 server participating in a failover cluster. It's also called a "cluster node" or "cluster member."
- An **active node** is a cluster member responding to client requests for a network application or service. It's also referred to as an "active server."
- A **passive node**, also called a "passive server," is a cluster member that's not responding to client requests for a clustered application but is in standby to do so if the active node fails.

- The term **standby mode** describes a cluster node that isn't active.

- A **quorum** is a database containing cluster configuration information about the status of each node (active or passive) for clustered applications. It's also used to determine, in a server or communication failure, whether the cluster is to remain online and which servers should continue participating in the cluster.

- The **cluster heartbeat** is communication between cluster nodes that provides the status of each node to the cluster quorum. The cluster heartbeat, or lack of it, informs the cluster when a server is no longer communicating.

- A **witness disk** is shared storage used to store cluster configuration data and help determine the cluster quorum.

A **failover cluster** consists of two or more servers, usually of identical configuration, that access common storage media. Typically, storage is in the form of a storage area network (SAN), which is external storage that can be shared among several servers that see SAN volumes as locally attached storage. The servers are connected to the SAN device through a secondary high-speed network connection, such as iSCSI (discussed in Chapter 4). One server in a failover cluster is considered the active server, and the other servers are considered passive. The active server handles all client requests for the clustered application, and passive servers wait in a type of standby mode. If the active server fails and stops responding, one of the passive servers becomes active and begins handling client requests, as shown in Figure 6-17. In this diagram, Server1 is initially the active server, and Server2 is passive.

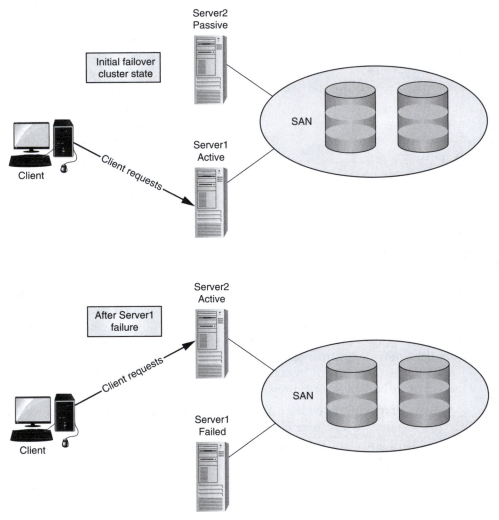

Figure 6-17   A logical depiction of a failover cluster

© 2016 Cengage Learning®

You might think that setting up a failover cluster wastes a lot of resources and money, if only one server in a cluster is actually doing anything. Keep in mind, however, that you're providing high availability for an application or a service. If you need high availability for several services or applications, you can design clusters so that each server is active for a particular application or service and in standby mode for the services or applications the other servers are handling. That way, each server is active, just not for the same application or service.

How a Failover Cluster Works

Failover clusters work by using two or more servers and shared storage to provide fault tolerance and high availability. Like an NLB cluster, client computers see the failover cluster as a single entity that can be accessed by a single name or IP address. All servers have access to the application data so that if the active server fails, another server can take over the clustered application. So how do passive servers know when the active server is no longer able to serve client requests? They do so by using a process called a "quorum," which is a consensus among cluster elements about the cluster's status. Because hardware and software can't actually have opinions, the quorum is really just a database containing cluster configuration information. This database defines the role of each cluster member and specifies which server should be active and which are passive. Each cluster member must have the same configuration information for the cluster to operate correctly. If a cluster server can't access the quorum data, it can't participate in the cluster.

A failover cluster can operate correctly only if all cluster members can communicate with one another so that they have access to the same quorum data. A cluster network is **partitioned** if communication fails between cluster servers, resulting in two or more subclusters, each with the objective of providing the clustered service. Because only one server can be active, this situation poses a problem. To solve this problem, the quorum process is designed so that only one partition, or subcluster, can continue participating in the cluster.

Quorum Models   Because failover clusters can be designed in a variety of configurations, there are a variety of models for maintaining quorums. The best model is usually selected automatically during cluster installation. There are four quorum models:

- *Node Majority quorum*—This model is used for failover clusters that have an odd number of members. Quite simply, the majority rules. If fewer than half the nodes fail, the cluster continues to run. If the cluster becomes partitioned, the partition with the majority of nodes (more than half the total) owns the quorum, and the other nodes are removed from the cluster. For example, in a five-node cluster, if two servers fail or become partitioned, they're removed from the cluster, and the cluster continues to run with the remaining three servers.

- *Node and Disk Majority quorum*—This model is used by default on clusters with an even number of cluster nodes and uses the witness disk. The cluster quorum data is stored on the witness disk, which is shared among all nodes. With this configuration, the cluster is operational as long as at least half the cluster members are online and can communicate with the witness disk. However, if the witness disk fails, the cluster can continue running only if a majority (at least half plus one) of servers are communicating.

- *Node and File Share Majority quorum*—This model uses a file share rather than shared storage to store the quorum data but is otherwise similar to Node and Disk Majority.

- *No Majority: Disk Only quorum*—This model allows the cluster to remain operational as long as the witness disk is available to at least one server. This model can endure the failure of all but one server, but if the witness disk fails, the entire cluster is unavailable.

Requirements for a Failover Cluster

The first requirement for a failover cluster is that all cluster servers must have Windows Server 2012/R2 Standard or Datacenter Edition installed. Either edition supports up to 64 cluster members. Also, be aware that the application you want to cluster might limit the total number of cluster members.

Aside from the Windows Server edition, a few other hardware and software requirements must be met before you can build a failover cluster:

- Identical or nearly identical server components.
- Identical CPU architecture.
- Components should meet the "Certified for Windows Server 2012" logo requirements.
- Separate adapters for shared storage communication and network client communication.
- A supported cluster-compatible storage technology that meets these requirements:
    o Serial Attached SCSI (SAS), Fibre Channel, or iSCSI storage technology should be used. SATA is acceptable, but not recommended. Parallel SCSI for cluster storage is not supported.
    o For iSCSI, you must use a separate network adapter that's dedicated to cluster storage.
    o A minimum of two volumes, one of which serves as the witness disk for the cluster.
- Cluster servers must run the same edition of Windows Server 2012/R2.
- Cluster servers must be members of a Windows domain. A cluster server can be a domain controller, but this configuration isn't recommended.
- All clustered applications or services must be the same version, and all cluster servers should have the same updates and service packs installed.

Cluster Storage Requirements   The storage requirements for a failover cluster are unique in that, in most configurations, the clustered application's data must be available to all cluster members, even though only one cluster member at a time accesses it. If the currently active cluster server fails, another cluster member must have access to the same data so that it can begin serving client requests. Shared storage is required on clusters using the Disk Majority and No Majority: Disk Only quorum models. Most clustered applications use these models. In addition, all components of the storage system should be Windows Server 2012/R2 certified and use digitally signed device drivers.

Failover Cluster Installation

The failover cluster function on Windows Server 2012/R2 is installed as a feature in Server Manager. The procedure for installing and creating a failover cluster is generally as follows:

1. Install the Failover Clustering feature on all servers.
2. Verify the cluster server network and shared storage access.
3. Run the cluster validation wizard.
4. Create the cluster.

The first step simply involves using the Add Roles and Features Wizard in Server Manager or the `Install-WindowsFeature` PowerShell cmdlet. Note that you shouldn't configure failover clustering and network load balancing on the same server. The remaining steps are explained in the following sections.

Verifying the Cluster Server Network and Shared Storage Access   You can actually perform this step before installing the Failover Clustering feature, but just make sure this step is complete before moving on to the next step. The procedure you use to do this depends on the type of shared storage you're using for the cluster and the configuration of your network. In short, verify that all the servers can communicate with computers on the client network, and shared storage is visible in Disk Management.

Running the Cluster Validation Wizard   Before you create a new cluster, you should run the Validate a Configuration Wizard in the Failover Cluster Manager, shown in Figure 6-18. The Failover Cluster Manager is added to Administrative Tools after you install the Failover Clustering feature. If your server isn't in a domain or you aren't logged on with a domain account, you get a warning message declaring that some management functions aren't available. In fact, your server must be in a domain and the account you're logged on with must be able to create a cluster object in Active Directory before any useful cluster management tools are available.

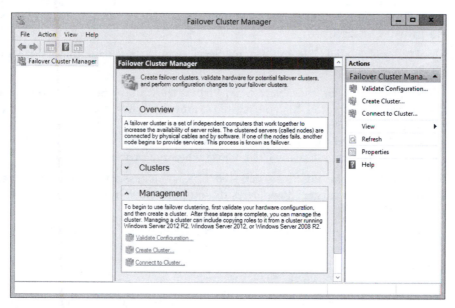

Figure 6-18   The Failover Cluster Manager

You can run the Validate a Configuration Wizard as many times as you need until the cluster configuration is validated correctly. You should even run this wizard periodically on an active cluster to make sure the configuration is still in good working order. In the second window of the wizard, you're prompted to enter the names of servers to participate in the cluster. If you're running the wizard on an existing cluster, you can enter the cluster name instead.

Next, you choose the testing options you want. The choices are to run all tests or only selected tests. When you're validating a cluster configuration for the first time, you should run all tests. If you're validating an existing cluster, you can limit the tests to suspected problem areas. The selected tests run, and a summary report is displayed on the window. Any errors are listed in the report and should have enough information for you to solve the problems. If there are no errors, the report indicates that the configuration is suitable for clustering.

Setting up a failover cluster is a complex task requiring at least two Windows Server 2012/R2 Standard or Datacenter servers and a shared storage server, such as an iSCSI target server. If your lab doesn't have enough hardware for all students to do the following activities, your instructor could do them as a demonstration.

Activity 6-3: Configuring the iSCSI SAN for a Failover Cluster

Time Required: 15 minutes
Objective: Configure the iSCSI SAN for a failover cluster.

Required Tools and Equipment: 412Server1, 412Server2, 412Server3, and the iSCSI Target Server role installed on 412Server1 and configured in Activities 4-7 through Activity 4-9
Description: First, you add another virtual disk to the iSCSI target on 412Server1, which serves as a cluster witness disk. Then you give 412Server3 access to the target. Last, you bring the disks online and create a volume on each disk so that they can be used in the cluster.

1. Log on to 412Server3 as **Administrator,** if necessary. Open Server Manager, if necessary, and click **Tools, iSCSI Initiator** from the menu. In the Microsoft iSCSI message box, click **Yes** to start the iSCSI service.

2. On 412Server1, click **File and Storage Services** in the left pane of Server Manager, and click **iSCSI.**

3. Click **Tasks,** and then click **New iSCSI Virtual Disk.** In the Select by volume list box, click **E:** (or the right drive letter for your system), and then click **Next.** In the Name text box, type **vdisk2,** and then click **Next.** Type **10** in the Size text box, click the **Dynamically expanding** option button, and then click **Next.** In the iSCSI Target window, click **Next.** In the Confirmation window, click **Create.** Click **Close** when the process is finished.

4. Scroll down to the iSCSI Targets list box, if necessary. Right-click **target1** and click **Properties.** In the target1 Properties dialog box, click **Initiators** in the left pane, and then click **Add.**

5. In the "Select a method to identify initiator" dialog box, click the **Query initiator computer for ID** option button, if necessary, and type **412server3.412dom1.local** in the text box. Click **OK.** The server queries 412Server3 to get its iSCSI qualified name (IQN). The configuration might take a while to finish. Click **OK.**

6. On 412Server3, open Server Manager, and click **Tools, iSCSI Initiator** from the menu.

7. In the iSCSI Initiator Properties dialog box, type **412server1.412dom1.local** in the Target text box, and click **Quick Connect.** The target you created on 412Server1 is listed in the Quick Connect dialog box. Click **Done.**

8. The Targets tab lists the target and its status as Connected. To configure the iSCSI initiator to reconnect to the iSCSI target when the system restarts, click the **Volumes and Devices** tab. Click **Auto Configure** so that the virtual disks on the target are connected automatically when the system restarts. Click **OK.**

9. Right-click **Start** and click **Disk Management.** You should see that two new 10 GB disks have been added, and their current state is offline. Right-click each disk and click **Online** to bring the disks online. Close Disk Management.

10. On 412Server2, open Disk Management. Look for the new disk with the offline status. Right-click the disk and click **Online.** Right-click the disk again and click **Initialize Disk.** Click **OK.**

11. Create a simple volume on both 10 GB disks. Assign drive letter **G** to the first volume and name it **Cluster1.** Assign drive letter **H** to the second volume and name it **Cluster2.** Use the defaults for the remaining settings. Close Disk Management.

12. Leave all three servers running if you're continuing to the next activity.

Activity 6-4: Installing the Failover Clustering Feature

Time Required: 15 minutes
Objective: Install the Failover Clustering feature on two servers.

Required Tools and Equipment: 412Server1, 412Server2, and 412Server3
Description: The topology for this cluster configuration is shown in Figure 6-19. In this topology, 412Server1 is the iSCSI target, which has iSCSI shared storage for 412Server2 and 412Server3, the cluster servers. Because you can't have both Network Load Balancing and Failover Clustering installed, first you uninstall the Network Load Balancing feature from 412Server2 and 412Server3.

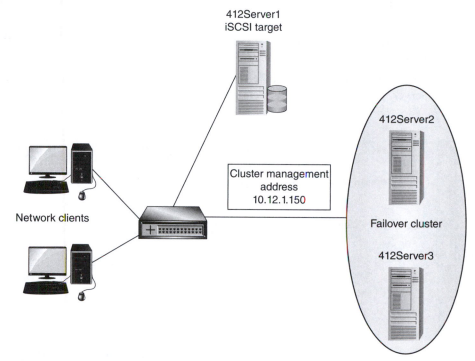

Figure 6-19 A failover cluster topology
© 2016 Cengage Learning®

1. Log on to 412Server2 as the domain **Administrator**.
2. Open Server Manager, if necessary and uninstall the **Network Load Balancing** feature.
3. Open the Advanced TCP/IP Settings dialog box for the Ethernet network connection, and remove the **10.12.1.100** IP address.
4. Log on to 412Server3 as the domain **Administrator**.
5. Open Server Manager, if necessary and uninstall the **Network Load Balancing** feature.
6. Open the Advanced TCP/IP Settings dialog box for the Ethernet network connection, and remove the **10.12.1.100** IP address.
7. On 412Server2, install the **Failover Clustering** feature, and then restart the server.
8. Log on to 412Server3 as the domain **Administrator**, and install the **Failover Clustering** feature.
9. On 412Server1, open DNS Manager and delete the NLB A record from the 412Dom1.local zone. Close DNS Manager.
10. Stay logged on to all three servers for the next activity.

Activity 6-5: Validating a Cluster Configuration

Time Required: 10 minutes
Objective: Run the Validate a Configuration Wizard.

Required Tools and Equipment: 412Server1, 412Server2, 412Server3
Description: You have two servers ready to be deployed in a failover cluster configuration. You have installed the Failover Clustering feature and need to validate the configuration before creating the cluster.

1. Make sure 412Server1 is running. Log on to 412Server2 as the domain **Administrator**, if necessary.

2. On 412Server2, open Server Manager, and click **Tools, Failover Cluster Manager** from the menu.

3. Click **Validate Configuration** in the Actions pane to start the wizard. Read the information in the Before You Begin window, and then click **Next**.

4. In the Select Servers or a Cluster window, type **412Server2**, and click **Add**. Then type **412Server3**, and click **Add** again (see Figure 6-20). Click **Next**.

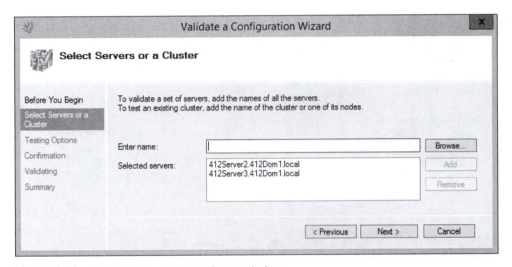

Figure 6-20 The Select Servers or a Cluster window

5. In the Testing Options window, leave the default option **Run all tests (recommended)** selected, and click **Next**.

6. In the Confirmation window, review your validation settings, and then click **Next**.

7. The validation test runs, and each test reports results as it runs. The Summary window has a button you can click to review the validation report when the tests are finished. If errors or warnings are reported in this window, click **View Report** to get additional information. Because you're using only one NIC in this configuration, you see a warning about a single point of network failure, and you'll probably see a warning about disk latency. In a production environment, you would have two NICs and a faster storage system. If you see a

message that testing has completed successfully (see Figure 6-21), click to clear the **Create the cluster now using the validated nodes** check box because you don't want to create the cluster just yet, and then click **Finish**. If there are errors, try to solve any problems and run the validation wizard again.

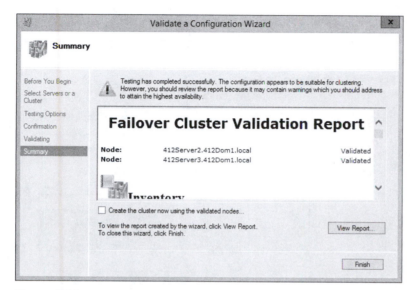

Figure 6-21   The Summary Window

8. Leave the Failover Cluster Manager open if you're continuing to the next activity.

Creating the Cluster   After your network and servers are validated, you can create a new failover cluster. The process is similar to the processes for validating the configuration and for creating an NLB cluster and is explained in the following activity. During the process of creating the cluster, you're asked to enter a name for the cluster in the Access Point for Administering the Cluster window. You're also asked to provide an IP address. This name and address is used for accessing the cluster to administer it. The name and IP address are added to DNS as a host record. In addition, a new computer object is created in Active Directory with the name of the cluster. The IP address is assigned to the network adapter selected for handling cluster clients on one of the servers (usually the one where you're running the Failover Cluster Manager). If this server becomes unavailable, the address is assigned to the other cluster server.

Activity 6-6: Creating a Failover Cluster

Time Required: 15 minutes
Objective: Create a failover cluster.

Required Tools and Equipment: 412Server1,412Server2, and 412Server3
Description: Your cluster servers and network environment have been validated, so it's time to create the failover cluster.

1. Log on to 412Server2 as the domain **Administrator**, if necessary.

2. Open the Failover Cluster Manager, if necessary.

3. Click **Create Cluster** in the Actions pane to start the wizard. Read the information in the Before You Begin window, and then click **Next**.

4. In the Select Servers window, type **412Server2**, and click **Add**. Then type **412Server3**, and click **Add**. Click **Next**.

5. In the Access Point for Administering the Cluster window, type **Failover1** in the Cluster Name text box. Click **Click here to type an address**, and type **10.12.1.150** (see Figure 6-22). A host record with the name and address is added to DNS, and an Active Directory computer object is created. Click **Next**.

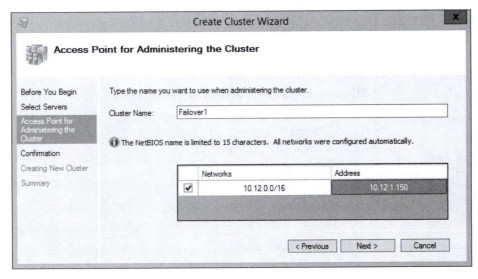

Figure 6-22 Entering the cluster name and address

6. The Confirmation window shows the settings for creating the cluster, which include the cluster name, IP address, and the nodes (servers) in the cluster. Click **Next**.

7. If errors or warnings are reported in the Summary window, click **View Report** to get additional information. If the cluster was created successfully, you see that the quorum mode of Node and Disk Majority was selected automatically (see Figure 6-23). Click **Finish**.

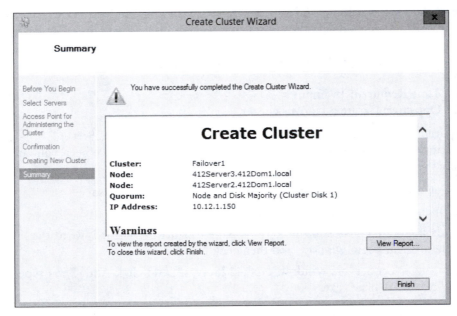

Figure 6-23 The Summary window showing the quorum mode

8. The next step is to review the cluster configuration in the Failover Cluster Manager. In the middle pane, review the cluster summary. In the left pane, click to expand the cluster name, and then click **Nodes** to view the servers and their status in the middle pane. Click **412Server2** in the middle pane to see more details about this node (see Figure 6-24).

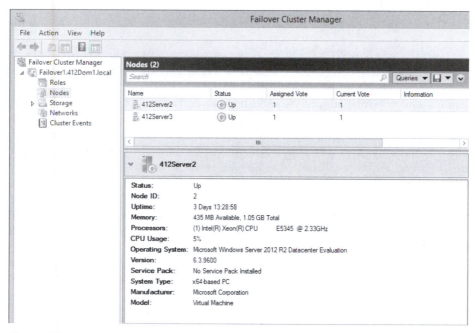

Figure 6-24   Reviewing the cluster nodes

9. In the left pane, click to expand **Storage** and then click **Disks** to see the disks available for the cluster. Two of the disks are shared storage from the iSCSI SAN. The third disk is on 412Server2. Notice that Cluster Disk 1 has been assigned as "Disk Witness in Quorum."

10. In the left pane, click **Networks** to review the cluster networks. Because you have only one NIC, there's only one network assigned Cluster Network 1, and its cluster use is listed as Cluster and Client. If you had a two-NIC configuration, one network would be listed as Internal. Close the Failover Cluster Manager.

11. Log on to 412Server1 as **Administrator,** and open Active Directory Users and Computers. Click the **Computers** folder. You should see the new computer account created for the cluster named FAILOVER1. Close Active Directory Users and Computers.

12. Open DNS Manager and look in the 412Dom1.local zone. You should see that the Failover1 A record has been created. Close DNS Manager.

13. Stay logged on to all servers if you're continuing to the next activity.

Configuring Failover Clustering

After a cluster is created, a number of configuration tasks should be performed, including the following:

- Configuring the cluster networks
- Configuring the quorum model
- Configuring cluster storage
- Configuring a cluster role

Configuring the Cluster Networks   The networks in a cluster are the critical link between clients and clustered applications and between cluster nodes and their shared storage. Cluster networks are used for the following types of communication:

- *Client access*—The network clients use to access clustered services

- *Cluster communication*—Heartbeat and quorum vote communication and other cluster management communication

- *Storage network*—Access shared storage, such as an iSCSI or a Fibre Channel SAN

Ideally, you should have at least two separate networks: one for client access to the cluster nodes and another for the storage network. Having three networks is even better, one for each type of cluster communication. Each network adapter should be connected to a different subnet, and network adapters should be renamed to reflect the network function. For example, you could name one adapter FOCAdapter (for Failover Cluster Adapter) and another Storage-Adapter. In the Failover Cluster Manager, the networks are simply named Cluster Network 1, Cluster Network 2, and so forth. You should rename them to reflect the network's purpose. To do so, in the Failover Cluster Manager, expand the Networks node in the left pane and click a cluster network. In the Actions pane, click Properties, and enter a new name for the network. If you have two networks (one for cluster client access and one for storage), you should select the option to not allow cluster network communication on the network used for storage (see Figure 6-25). On a cluster with only one network, you can leave the default settings.

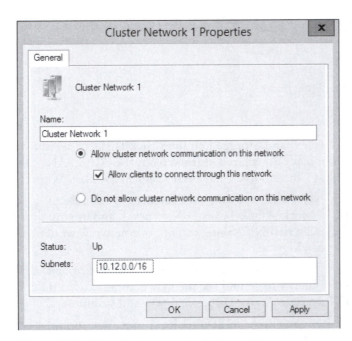

Figure 6-25   Viewing cluster network properties

Configuring the Quorum Model   If the quorum model selected by the Create Cluster process isn't suitable for your environment, you can change it. In the Failover Cluster Manager, click the name of the cluster in the left pane, and in the Actions pane, click More Actions and then Configure Cluster Quorum Settings. The Configure Cluster Quorum Wizard walks you through changing the model (discussed earlier in "How a Failover Cluster Works"). In this wizard, you have the following options:

- *Use the default quorum configuration*—With this option, the cluster determines the quorum model to use and selects the witness disk. If you're unsure how to configure the quorum, use this option.

- *Select the quorum witness*—You select the quorum witness disk, but the cluster determines other quorum options.

- *Advanced quorum configuration*—You select all quorum options. If you choose this option, you must select which servers vote in the quorum and select the witness disk or choose a file share witness.

Configuring Cluster Storage   During the cluster creation process, Windows detects shared storage that's available for use in the cluster and assigns one of the cluster nodes as the owner. If more than one shared disk is available, one is usually assigned as the witness disk for the quorum. If there are other shared disks that aren't recognized by the cluster, you can add them for use by the entire cluster by clicking Add Disk in the Actions pane. You can also add storage to a particular clustered service or application after one has been configured.

 Dynamic disks can't be used in a failover cluster; only basic disks can be added to a failover cluster.

By default, each cluster disk is owned by one cluster node, and all other cluster nodes see the disk as offline. Starting in Windows Server 2008 R2, you can configure a **cluster shared volume** in which all cluster nodes have access to the shared storage for read and write access. In Windows Server 2012, cluster shared volumes are enabled by default; in Windows Server 2008 R2, you have to enable them. To create a cluster shared volume (CSV), click Disks (under the Storage folder) in the left pane of the Failover Cluster Manager, and then right-click a disk assigned to Available Storage and click Add to Cluster Shared Volumes. After a disk has been added to a cluster shared volume, it appears in Disk Management as a CSVFS (cluster shared volume file system) disk. The underlying format is still NTFS or ReFS but with additional attributes indicating to cluster nodes that the volume is a CSV. When you configure a CSV, a folder named ClusterStorage is created at the root of the Windows OS drive, and the CSV is mounted in that folder.

The original purpose of CSVs was for use in Hyper-V clusters to store the files that compose VMs, but CSVs in Windows Server 2012/R2 have expanded uses, including file sharing with Server Message Block (SMB) 3.0. The following list includes some features and advantages of using CSVs in Windows Server 2012/R2 clusters:

- Better backup and restore functions for CSV volumes

- Support for BitLocker volume encryption on CSV volumes

- Improved CSV performance

- SMB 3.0 file share support

- Support for multiple subnets

- Support for ReFS-formatted volumes (starting with Windows Server 2012 R2)

- Data deduplication (starting with Windows Server 2012 R2)

- Support for tiered and parity storage spaces (starting with Windows Server 2012 R2)

Configuring a Cluster Role   To configure a server role to use failover clustering, right-click Roles in the left pane of the Failover Cluster Manager and click Configure Role to start the High Availability Wizard. A number of Windows Server 2012/R2 roles and features can be configured for failover clustering, as shown in Figure 6-26.

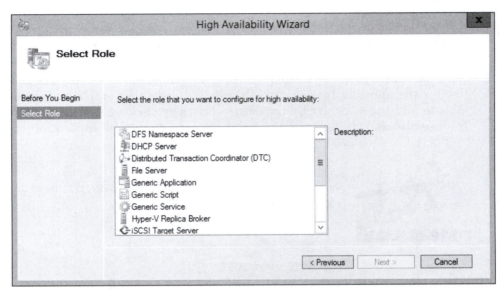

Figure 6-26   Selecting a role

Before you run the High Availability Wizard, in most cases you must install the role or feature on each server in the cluster. This procedure is shown in the next activity with the File Server role. During the configuration of a service, you're prompted to enter a name that clients use when accessing it, called the **client access point**. For example, if you configure the File Server role on the Failover1 cluster, you might name the client access point Failover1FS. You're also prompted for the IP address that clients use to access this cluster service. As with the access point for administering the cluster, a host record is created in DNS, and a new computer object is created in Active Directory.

Activity 6-7: Creating a File Server Failover Cluster

Time Required: 15 minutes
Objective: Configure the File Server role on the failover cluster.

Required Tools and Equipment: 412Server1, 412Server2, and 412Server3
Description: Your cluster is up and running, so now it's time to configure the File Server role for high availability.

1. Log on to 412Server3 as the domain **Administrator**, if necessary. You need to install the File Server role on 412Server3 so that it can participate in the cluster role. Open a PowerShell window, and then type **Install-WindowsFeature FS-FileServer** and press **Enter**. After the role is installed, close the PowerShell window.

2. Log on to 412Server2 as the domain **Administrator**, if necessary, and open the Failover Cluster Manager.

3. Click to expand **Failover1.412Dom1.local** in the left pane. Right-click **Roles** and click **Configure Role** to start the High Availability Wizard.

4. Read the information in the Before You Begin window, and then click **Next**.

5. In the Select Role window, click **File Server**, and then click **Next**. In the File Server Type window, leave the default option **File Server for general use** selected, and click **Next**.

6. In the Client Access Point window, type **Failover1FS** in the Name text box, and then click **Click here to type an address**. Type **10.12.1.151** for the address of this cluster service, and then click **Next**.

7. In the Select Storage window, you select the storage volume you want to use. These servers were set up to share two iSCSI volumes, and one of them is used as the witness disk. Click the check box next to the cluster disk, and then click **Next**.

8. Review the information in the Confirmation window, and then click **Next**.

9. If any errors or warning were generated, click **View Report** in the Summary window and try to correct the problems; otherwise, click **Finish**.

10. In the Failover Cluster Manager, click **Roles** and then **Failover1FS** to review the summary information for the clustered service. Notice that one of the servers is designated as the current owner. The other server is in passive or standby mode.

11. Click the **Shares** tab at the bottom of the Roles window. Notice that a default administrative share is created. You can create new shared folders on the shared volume by using Share and Storage Management or the Add File Share link in the Actions pane.

12. To test the failover configuration, right-click **Failover1FS** under Roles, point to **Move**, and click **Select Node**. In the Move Clustered Role dialog box, click **412Server3** or **412Server2** (whichever is listed), and then click **OK**. The summary window shows the new owner of the service.

13. Close the Failover Cluster Manager.

After the service is configured, you can configure other high-availability options, including the following:

- *Preferred owner*—The **preferred owner** is the server selected as the active server for the service or application. To configure the preferred owner, right-click the role and click Properties. The available servers are listed, and you can click the check box next to servers to specify the preferred owner. By default, there's no preferred owner. If you select more than one preferred server, the most preferred server is at the top (see Figure 6-27).

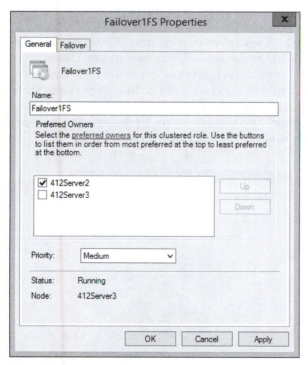

Figure 6-27   Selecting a preferred owner

- *Failover options*—Set **failover options** in the Failover tab of the clustered service's Properties dialog box. The "Maximum failures in the specified period" value specifies how many times the service attempts to restart or fail over to another server in the specified period. In Figure 6-28, the service attempts to fail over two times within 6 hours. If the service fails a third time within the 6 hours, the service is left in the failed state.

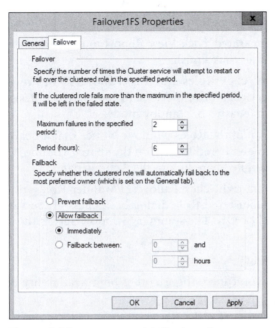

Figure 6-28   Failover and failback options

- *Failback options*—**Failback options** are also set in the Failover tab of the clustered service's Properties dialog box. If a preferred owner is specified, you have the option to revert to the most preferred owner when that server is available again. The failback can occur immediately or between certain hours of the day. The default option is to prevent failback.

Cluster-Aware Updating   Cluster-Aware Updating (CAU) is a new failover cluster feature in Windows Server 2012. CAU automates software updates on cluster servers and maintains cluster service availability. With this feature, you can control how the nodes in a cluster handle updates from Windows Update so that the cluster can continue providing services while updates take place. To enable CAU, right-click a cluster in Failover Cluster Manager, click More Actions, and click Cluster-Aware Updating. The Cluster-Aware Updating window (see Figure 6-29) lists cluster nodes, and you can choose from the following actions:

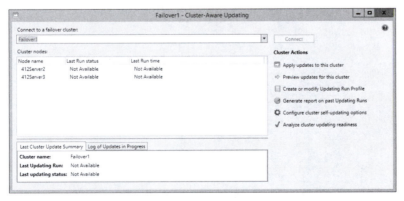

Figure 6-29   The Cluster-Aware Updating window

- *Apply updates to this cluster*—Configure and start a software update on the cluster.

- *Preview updates for this cluster*—See which updates each node in the cluster receives. You should choose this action before applying an update.

- *Create or modify Updating Run Profile*—Create an update profile to control updates.

- *Generate report on past Updating Runs*—Create a report showing update runs that have already occurred along with their status.

- *Configure cluster self-updating options*—Schedule updates, including the frequency and time of day that updates occur. You can also specify the order in which nodes are updated, run a script before or after updates occur, and specify retry and failure options (see Figure 6-30).

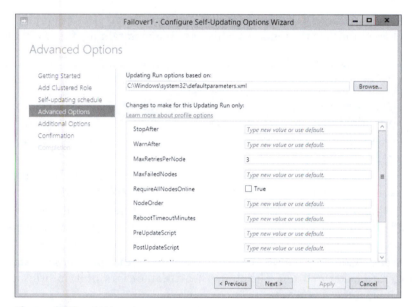

Figure 6-30   CAU options

- *Analyze cluster updating readiness*—Generate a report on whether the cluster is prepared for using CAU. The analyzer checks for cluster availability, whether remote management is enabled on cluster nodes, firewall settings, and other CAU requirements.

Chapter Summary

- Network load balancing uses server clusters to provide scalability and fault tolerance. A server cluster is a group of servers configured to respond to a single virtual IP address. To provide scalability, the servers in an NLB cluster share the load of incoming requests based on rules you can define. To provide fault tolerance, a failed server can be removed from the cluster, and another server can take its place and begin servicing client requests that were handled by the failed server.

- NLB is a feature available in Windows Server 2012/R2 Datacenter and Standard editions. Creating an NLB cluster involves creating the cluster, selecting host and network interfaces, configuring the host ID, setting the cluster IP address, setting the cluster name and operation mode, configuring port rules, and adding servers to the cluster.

- Cluster configuration involves setting cluster properties, port rules, and host properties.

- You can control NLB cluster hosts with the following commands: Start, Stop, Drainstop, Suspend, and Resume.
- A failover cluster is deployed for high availability. It's well suited to back-end database applications, file-sharing servers, messaging servers, and other applications that are both mission critical and deal with dynamic read/write data.
- Failover clusters consist of two or more servers, usually of identical configuration, that access common storage media. Typically, storage is in the form of a SAN. One server in a failover cluster is considered the active server while one or more other servers are passive.
- All failover cluster servers have access to the application data so that if the active server fails, another server can take over the clustered application. The passive servers know when the active server is no longer able to serve client requests using a process called a quorum. A quorum is a consensus among the cluster elements of the status of the cluster.
- Cluster-Aware Updating is a new feature in Windows Server 2012 that allows updating failover cluster nodes with Windows updates while maintaining high availability.

Key Terms

active node   A cluster member that's responding to client requests for a network application or service; also referred to as an "active server."

client access point   A name and IP address by which clients can access a clustered service in a failover cluster. *See also* failover cluster.

client affinity value   An option specified in multiple host filtering modes that determines whether the same or a different host handles successive requests from the same client.

Cluster-Aware Updating (CAU)   A new failover cluster feature in Windows Server 2012 that automates software updates on cluster servers while maintaining cluster service availability. *See also* failover cluster.

cluster heartbeat   Communication between cluster nodes that provides the status of each cluster member to the cluster quorum. The cluster heartbeat, or lack of it, informs the cluster when a server is no longer communicating.

cluster operation mode   A cluster parameter that specifies the type of network addressing used to access the cluster: unicast, multicast, or IGMP multicast.

cluster shared volume   A storage option in a failover cluster in which all cluster nodes have access to the shared storage for read and write access. *See also* failover cluster.

cluster server   A Windows Server 2012/R2 server that participates in a failover cluster; also referred to as a "cluster node" or "cluster member." *See also* failover cluster.

clustered application   An application or service installed on two or more servers participating in a failover cluster; Also called a "clustered service." *See also* failover cluster.

failback options   Settings that specify a cluster should revert to the most preferred owner when the server is available again. The failback can occur immediately or between certain hours of the day.

failover cluster   Two or more servers appearing as a single server to clients. One server is considered the active server, and other servers are passive. The active server handles all client requests for the clustered application, and the passive servers wait in standby mode until the active server fails.

failover options   Settings that specify how many times a service attempts to restart or fail over to another server in the specified period.

filtering mode   An option in a port rule that specifies whether multiple hosts or a single host respond to traffic identified by the port rule. Multiple host is the default mode and allows scalability. Single host mode specifies that the server with the highest priority value handles traffic.

handling priority   An NLB parameter used in single host mode that determines which host handles all traffic meeting the port rules' criteria. *See also* filtering mode and network load balancing (NLB).

high availability   A network or computer configuration in which data and applications are almost always available, even after a system failure.

load weight   An NLB parameter that allows configuring how much network traffic, as a percentage, each node should handle. *See also* network load balancing (NLB).

network load balancing (NLB)   A Windows Server feature that uses server clusters to provide scalability and fault tolerance. *See also* server cluster.

partitioned   A cluster status that can occur if communication fails between cluster servers, resulting in two or more subclusters, each with the objective of handling the clustered service. *See also* cluster server.

passive node   A cluster member that's not currently responding to client requests for a clustered application but is in standby in case the active node fails; also called a "passive server."

port rule   A setting that specifies which type of TCP or UDP traffic an NLB cluster should respond to and how the traffic is distributed among cluster members. *See also* network load balancing (NLB).

preferred owner   The server selected as the active server for a service or an application.

quorum   A database containing cluster configuration information about the status of each node (active or passive) for clustered applications. It's also used to determine, in a server or communication failure, whether the cluster is to remain online and which servers should continue to participate in the cluster.

rolling upgrade   An NLB cluster upgrade method that involves taking each cluster node offline, upgrading the host, and then bringing it back online. *See also* network load balancing (NLB).

server cluster   A group of two or more servers configured to respond to a single virtual IP address.

standby mode   A cluster node that isn't active.

virtual IP address   The IP address by which networking services provided by an NLB cluster are accessed by network clients. A DNS host record should exist for the cluster name mapped to this address. *See also* network load balancing (NLB).

witness disk   Shared storage used to store cluster configuration data and help determine the cluster quorum.

Review Questions

1. Which of the following describes high availability? (Choose all that apply.)

   a. Applications that are available even in the event of a system failure

   b. A server that requires no more than one restart per week

   c. Fast response time from a service or application when two or more servers spread the workload

   d. An OS that detects when a memory error has occurred

2. How does an NLB cluster provide fault tolerance?

   a. Based on an internal algorithm, the servers decide which server should respond to each incoming client request.

   b. A failed server can be removed from the cluster and another server can take its place.

   c. DNS records are changed to point clients to a different server if one fails.

   d. RAID and multiple NICs are used.

3. You have a Web site serving mostly static content, and the current server is unable to handle the traffic load. You think you need three servers to handle the traffic load adequately, but you want to be able to prioritize how much traffic each server handles. Which high-availability solution makes the most sense?

    a. Create a round-robin load balancing configuration by using DNS.

    b. Use the failover cluster feature in Windows Server 2012.

    c. Use the distributed Web server feature in Windows Server 2012.

    d. Use the network load balancing feature in Windows Server 2012.

4. Which of the following is *not* a step in creating and configuring an NLB cluster?

    a. Configuring the host priority

    b. Setting the cluster IP address

    c. Configuring port rules

    d. Configuring a preferred owner

5. Which of the following is a valid NLB cluster operation mode?

    a. Single host

    b. Network

    c. Multicast

    d. Suspended

6. Which filtering mode should you use when you want to provide scalability for several servers in an NLB cluster?

    a. Multiple host

    b. Failback immediate

    c. IGMP multicast

    d. Node majority

7. Under which circumstances should you use the None option when setting the client affinity value?

    a. When you want multiple requests from the same client to be directed to the same cluster host

    b. When clients access the cluster from behind multiple proxy servers

    c. When the content being served is fairly static and stateless

    d. When you want the cluster to discard packets matching the specified protocol and ports

8. Which of the following serves as an NLB cluster server identifier and determines which server will handle traffic not covered by a port rule?

    a. Dedicated IP address

    b. Port range

    c. Priority

    d. Affinity value

9. You manage an NLB cluster composed of three servers: Server1, Server2, and Server3. Your maintenance schedule indicates that Server1 is due for cleaning maintenance, which involves vacuuming dust and reseating all components. The NLB cluster is in constant use, so you don't want to interrupt any clients currently being served by Server1. Which option should you use to take Server1 temporarily offline yet allow it to complete active client requests?

    a. Stop

    b. Suspend

    c. Resume

    d. Drainstop

10. Which of the following is a failover cluster server that doesn't respond to client requests but is available to do so if the active server fails?

    a. Passive node

    b. Quorum node

    c. Active node

    d. Suspended node

11. Which of the following describes a cluster that has been divided into two or more subclusters because of lack of communication?

    a. Quorum

    b. Partitioned

    c. No majority

    d. Sanctioned

12. Which of the following is a valid quorum model? (Choose all that apply.)

    a. Node Majority

    b. No Majority: Disk Only

    c. Node and Disk Majority

    d. File Share and Disk Majority

13. Which of the following is a requirement for creating a failover cluster? (Choose all that apply.)

    a. Two or more stand-alone servers

    b. Two or more quad-core CPUs

    c. Windows Server 2012 Standard or Datacenter edition

    d. Servers that are Active Directory domain members or domain controllers

14. You're configuring a failover cluster and want a quorum configuration that can endure the failure of all but one server and remain operational. Which quorum configuration should you choose?

    a. Node Majority

    b. No Majority: Disk Only

    c. Node and File Share Majority

    d. Node and Disk Majority

15. What's created in Active Directory during the failover cluster creation process?

    a. A computer object with the name of the cluster

    b. A SAN object with the name of the witness disk

    c. An A record with the name and IP address of the cluster

    d. A cluster object containing the names of all the cluster servers

16. Which of the following is true about the network configuration of failover clusters?

    a. The shared storage should be on the same subnet as cluster clients.

    b. Cluster servers require a minimum of three NICs.

    c. The iSCSI storage server should be on a separate subnet from cluster clients.

    d. All NICs on each server must be configured on the same subnet.

17. Which of the following failover cluster options specifies how many times a clustered service can restart or fail to another server in a certain period before the service is left in the failed state?

    a. Preferred owner

    b. Failover options

    c. Affinity value

    d. Failback options

18. Which cluster storage option grants all cluster nodes read and write access to shared storage?

    a. Cluster shared volume

    b. Volume pool

    c. Affinity storage system

    d. Mirrored storage volume

19. Which of the following is the name assigned to a clustered service?

    a. Network cluster name

    b. Cluster DNS name

    c. Cluster service name

    d. Client access point

20. Which failover cluster feature do you use to configure cluster self-updating options?

    a. NLB

    b. CAU

    c. CSV

    d. SAS

Case Projects

CASE PROJECTS

Case Project 6-1: Choosing a High-Availability Solution

You have been hired to set up the network and servers for a new company, using Windows Server 2012 R2. The company is investing in an application critical to the company's business that all employees will use daily. This application uses a back-end database and is highly transaction oriented, so data is read and written frequently. To simplify maintenance of the front-end application, users will run it on remote desktop servers. The owner has explained that the back-end database must be highly available, and the remote desktop servers must be highly scalable to handle hundreds of simultaneous sessions. What high-availability technologies do you recommend for the back-end database server and the remote desktop servers? Explain your answer.

Case Project 6-2: Server Requirements for a Failover Cluster

You're setting up the application discussed in Case Project 6-1. Because the company is new, there are no servers—you're setting everything up from scratch. Describe the minimum requirements for this solution, including the number of servers and what they will be used for, the editions of Windows Server 2012 R2, the basic network configuration, and any other devices you might need. Make a drawing of the network.

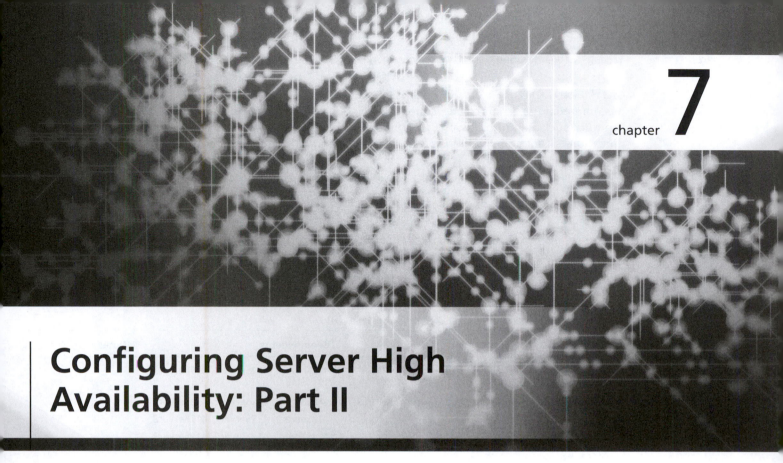

chapter 7

Configuring Server High Availability: Part II

After reading this chapter and completing the exercises, you will be able to:

- Configure advanced failover clusters
- Configure highly available virtual machines
- Configure virtual machine movement

Failover clusters have some advanced configuration options to accommodate different cluster configurations. In this chapter, you learn about several of these options, such as quorum configuration and Active Directory–detached clusters. Because virtualization is common technology used in data centers, it's only natural to want to make virtual machines highly available. You can configure high availability at the Hyper-V host level, referred to as "highly available" or "clustered" virtual machines, at the guest OS level, called "guest clustering," or both. One advantage of using VMs is their portability, and in this chapter, you learn several methods for moving VMs and their storage.

Advanced Failover Clusters

Table 7-1 lists what you need for the hands-on activities in this chapter.

Table 7-1   Activity requirements

Activity	Requirements	Notes
Activity 7-1: Exploring Failover Cluster Management Options	412Server1, 412Server2, 412Server3	
Activity 7-2: Configuring Advanced Quorum Settings	412Server1, 412Server2, 412Server3	
Activity 7-3: Destroying a Failover Cluster	412Server1, 412Server2, 412Server3	
Activity 7-4: Remove the iSCSI Configuration	412Server1, 412Server2, 412Server3	

© 2016 Cengage Learning®

In Chapter 6, you learned how to create a failover cluster and configure basic failover cluster settings. This chapter explores additional failover cluster settings and shows you how to configure roles for high availability. In addition, you learn how to back up and restore a failover cluster configuration. In this section, you look at the following advanced failover cluster configuration:

- Managing a failover cluster
- Configuring advanced quorum settings
- Configuring roles for high availability
- Upgrading a failover cluster
- Creating Active Directory–detached clusters
- Using storage spaces with clusters
- Backing up and restoring cluster configurations

Managing a Failover Cluster

After a cluster has been created, you might need to perform some management tasks, including validating the cluster, adding nodes to it, or shutting down or destroying a cluster. You might also need to move cluster roles or resources from one cluster to another. In this section, you look at the following failover cluster management tasks:

- Validating a configuration
- Adding and removing a cluster node
- Shutting down and restarting a cluster
- Removing a cluster role and destroying a cluster
- Copying cluster roles
- Moving core cluster resources

Validating a Configuration Before you create a cluster or add servers to an existing cluster, you can validate the cluster's configuration or the servers to be added to it. To validate a configuration, right-click the Failover Cluster Manager node in the Failover Cluster Manager console and click Validate Configuration. The Validate a Configuration Wizard starts, and you're prompted to select the servers or clusters you want to validate. If you select a server that's already a member of a cluster, all the cluster members are validated. If you select a server that isn't currently a member of a cluster, the server is validated for its suitability to be added to a cluster.

You can run all tests or selected tests. If you're validating a single server, the tests check for a suitable storage and network configuration as well as a valid system configuration. System configuration tests check for signed drivers, a valid OS edition, processor architecture, Active Directory configuration, and so forth (see Figure 7-1).

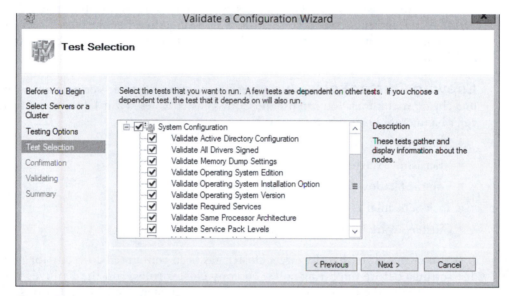

Figure 7-1 Validating a configuration

The Validate a Configuration Wizard creates a report and warns of any configuration parameters that might be a problem. The Summary window reports whether the cluster is valid or the server is suitable for clustering.

Adding and Removing a Cluster Node To add a node to a cluster, right-click a cluster and click Add Node to start the Add Node Wizard. Then enter the server name in the Select Servers window. The selected server must have the Failover Clustering feature already installed. The Add Node Wizard validates the server for use in the cluster if hasn't already been validated; however, running the Validate a Configuration Wizard on the server and the cluster is recommended before adding a node to the cluster. The server is added to the cluster, and the quorum settings are updated, if necessary.

To remove a node from a cluster, right-click the node, point to More Actions, and click Evict. You can add the cluster node back to the cluster by using the Add Node Wizard.

Shutting Down and Restarting a Cluster If you need to take a cluster offline, you can shut down the entire cluster, which stops all clustered roles and the cluster service on all nodes in the cluster. This approach is preferable to stopping the cluster service separately on each node. To shut down a cluster, right-click the cluster name in the Failover Cluster Manager, point to More Actions, and click Shut Down Cluster. This action doesn't shut down Windows on the cluster nodes, but all cluster activities are stopped. To restart a cluster that has been shut down, right-click the cluster and click Start Cluster.

You can also stop and start the cluster service on a single cluster node. To do so, click Nodes in the Failover Cluster Manager, right-click the node, point to More Actions, and click Stop Cluster Service or Start Cluster Service.

Removing a Cluster Role and Destroying a Cluster   To remove a clustered role, click the Roles node, right-click the role, and click Remove in the Actions pane. When you remove cluster roles, the corresponding computer accounts in Active Directory are disabled, and the DNS entries for the cluster roles are deleted. To destroy a cluster, right-click it, click More Actions, and click Destroy Cluster. If any clustered roles are configured, you need to delete the roles from the cluster before you can destroy it. The Destroy Cluster option deletes the cluster permanently, and the servers in the cluster can be used in other clusters, if needed. Also, the corresponding computer account in Active Directory is disabled, and the DNS entry for the cluster is deleted.

Copying Cluster Roles   If you need to migrate clustered services and applications from one cluster to another, you can use the Copy Cluster Roles Wizard. However, the following roles can't be migrated by using this wizard:

- Microsoft SQL Server
- Microsoft Exchange Server
- Volume Shadow Copy Service tasks
- Task Scheduler tasks
- Cluster-Aware Updating settings

You must ensure that the target cluster has been configured correctly for network and storage settings before migrating roles. To copy cluster roles, run the Failover Cluster Manager from a node in the target cluster. Right-click the cluster, click More Actions, and click Copy Cluster Roles. In the Copy Cluster Roles Wizard, specify the source cluster and roles you want to copy. (The source cluster can't be the cluster from which you're running the Copy Cluster Roles Wizard.) The Copy Cluster Roles Wizard copies the clustered role configuration and IP address setting if the target cluster is in the same subnet as the source. However, you still need to install the clustered role or feature on each node in the target cluster. In addition, if you're using existing storage for the clustered role data, you need to take the storage offline on the old cluster and make it available to the new cluster. If you're using new storage, you must copy any folders and data the clustered role uses to the new storage.

Moving Core Cluster Resources   If you need to perform maintenance operations on a cluster node, you should move any cluster resources from that node to another node in the cluster. **Core cluster resources** include the quorum resource, which is usually the witness disk or witness share; the IP address resource that provides the cluster IP address; and the network name resource that provides the cluster name. This command can also be used to simulate a failover if the server providing core resources fails. To move core cluster resources, right-click the cluster, point to More Actions, point to Move Core Cluster Resources, and click Best Possible Node or Select Node. If you choose Select Node, you can specify which server to transfer the core cluster resources to. To see which server currently owns the cluster core resources, click the cluster name in the left pane to see its summary in the middle pane, including the current host server of the cluster resources. In the bottom of the middle pane is a list of cluster core resources (see Figure 7-2).

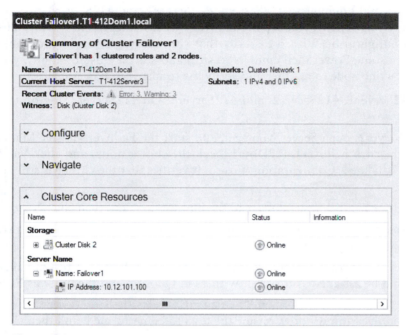

Figure 7-2   Cluster core resources

Managing a Cluster with PowerShell   Table 7-2 lists PowerShell cmdlets you can use to manage failover clusters. To see a list of all commands related to failover clusters, enter `Get-Command -Module FailoverClusters` at a PowerShell prompt.

Table 7-2   **PowerShell cmdlets for managing failover clusters**

Cmdlet	Description
Test-Cluster	Runs validation tests on a cluster, nodes in a cluster, or a server that's not yet a member of a cluster
Get-Cluster	Displays information about a cluster
Get-ClusterGroup	Displays the owner and status of a cluster group
Add-ClusterNode	Adds a server to a failover cluster
Stop-Cluster	Shuts down a cluster
Start-Cluster	Starts the cluster service on all nodes in a cluster
Stop-ClusterNode	Shuts down the cluster service on a node in a cluster
Start-ClusterNode	Starts the cluster service on a node in a cluster
Remove-ClusterGroup	Removes a clustered role from a cluster
Remove-Cluster	Destroys a cluster
Remove-ClusterNode	Removes (evicts) a cluster node from the cluster
Move-ClusterGroup	Moves (copies) a cluster role from one cluster to another cluster or moves core cluster resources from one node to another

© 2016 Cengage Learning®

Activity 7-1: Exploring Failover Cluster Management Options

Time Required: 15 minutes
Objective: Explore failover cluster management options.

Required Tools and Equipment: 412Server1, 412Server2, and 412Server3
Description: In this activity, you explore failover cluster management options. First, you run the Validate a Configuration Wizard to verify that your cluster is still in good operational order. Next, you use some PowerShell cmdlets to stop and start a cluster. Finally, you move cluster resources from one node to another and verify the results with PowerShell.

1. Start 412Server1, 412Server2, and 412Server3. On 412Server2, log on to the domain as **Administrator**.

2. On 412Server2, open Server Manager, and start the Failover Cluster Manager. In the left pane, right-click **Failover1.412Dom1.local** (the cluster node) and click **Validate Cluster** to start the Validate a Configuration Wizard. It verifies that the cluster is still in good working order.

3. In the Before You Begin window, read the information, and then click **Next**.

4. In the Testing Options window, leave the default option **Run all tests (recommended)** selected, and then click **Next**.

5. In the Review Storage Status window, click the check box next to both cluster disks. One disk should be assigned as the Disk Witness in Quorum and the other as Failover1FS. Click **Next**.

6. In the Confirmation window, review the tests to be performed, and then click **Next** to start the validation tests.

7. Watch the progress of the tests. You might get warnings, particularly about the network tests because you have only one network connection. When the tests are finished, click **View Report**. An Internet Explorer window opens and displays the tests by category.

8. Click the **Network** category because you have a warning in this category. Then click **Validate Network Communication** to see details about the warning. You see a message indicating that you should have more than one network interface to prevent a single point of failure in the cluster. Click any other test categories with warnings or errors. There shouldn't be any errors, but if there are, review the suggested steps to fix the error. When you're finished, close Internet Explorer and click **Finish** in the Summary window.

9. Next, you shut down and restart a cluster. In the Failover Cluster Manager, right-click **Failover1.412Dom1.local**, point to **More Actions**, and click **Shut Down Cluster**. In the Shut-down Cluster dialog box, click **Yes**.

10. To start the cluster, open a PowerShell window. Type **Start-Cluster** and press **Enter**.

11. To see all information about the cluster, type **Get-Cluster | Format-List -Property *** and press **Enter**.

12. In the Failover Cluster Manager, verify that the cluster is started. To see which server owns cluster core resources, click **Failover1.412Dom1.local**. The Summary section in the middle pane shows that the server listed after Current Host Server owns the core resources.

13. To view the core resources, scroll down until you see Cluster Core Resources. Click to expand the **Server Name** resource and then the **Storage** resource. The disk listed under Cluster Disk 1 is the witness disk.

14. To change the owner of the cluster core resources, right-click **Failover1.412Dom1.local**, point to **More Actions**, point to **Move Core Cluster Resources**, and click **Select Node**. Click the node shown (which is 412Server2 or 412Server3, depending on which node currently doesn't own the cluster core resources). Click **OK**. In the Summary section of the Failover Cluster Manager, you should see that the Current Host Server has changed, indicating the new owner of the cluster core resources.

15. In the PowerShell window, type **Get-ClusterGroup "Cluster Group"** and press **Enter** to display the current owner of the core cluster resources. Type **Move-ClusterGroup "Cluster Group"** and press **Enter** to move the core cluster resources to the best possible node, which is the node that doesn't currently own the resources. Type **Get-ClusterGroup "Cluster Group"** and press **Enter** to see that the cluster resources have been moved. Close the PowerShell window.

16. Leave all servers running for the next activity.

Configuring Advanced Quorum Settings

Although the cluster creation process configures suitable cluster quorum settings for the cluster, you might want to change the quorum configuration if you add or remove cluster nodes or a witness disk. To configure quorum settings, right-click the cluster in the Failover Cluster Manager, point to More Actions, and click Configure Cluster Quorum Settings to start the Configure Cluster Quorum Wizard. In the Select Quorum Configuration Option window, you have three options, as you can see in see Figure 7-3. If you choose "Use default quorum configuration," the cluster configures the quorum settings and configures a witness disk, if applicable. The next two options are explained in the following sections.

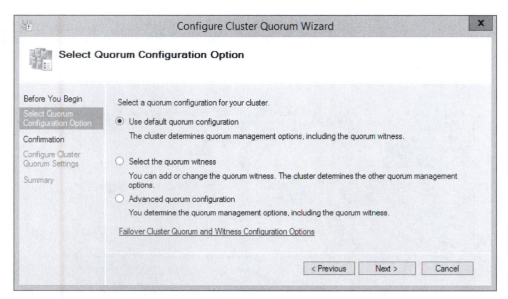

Figure 7-3   Selecting quorum configuration options

Selecting the Quorum Witness   If you choose the "Select the quorum witness" option, you can specify how you want the quorum witness to be configured, and the cluster determines the other quorum options. There are three options for configuring the quorum witness:

- *Configure a disk witness*—If you choose this option, you're prompted to select a volume to act as the disk witness. The volume must be available to all cluster nodes through the cluster shared storage network.

- *Configure a file share witness*—With this option, you provide the path to a file share hosted on a server that's not in the cluster. The administrator configuring the file share witness must have Full Control permission to the file share. A file share witness should be used only if there's no shared storage between cluster nodes to create a disk witness, as might be the case in a multisite cluster. In addition, the server hosting the file share should be in a site separate from any of the cluster nodes using the file share witness.

- *Do not configure a quorum witness*—This option is not recommended as of Windows Server 2012 R2, which has added the **dynamic witness** feature, in which the cluster determines whether to give the witness a quorum vote. If there are an odd number of cluster nodes, the witness doesn't have a quorum vote, but with an even number of cluster nodes, the witness does. This feature attempts to prevent a **split vote**, in which no quorum can be reached. The cluster must be configured to use dynamic quorum (discussed in "Using New Quorum Features") to use the dynamic witness feature.

Setting Advanced Quorum Configuration Options   The advanced quorum configuration option allows you to choose which nodes have a quorum vote in the cluster. By default, all nodes have a quorum vote, but you can remove nodes from the voting process (see Figure 7-4). If you remove voting from all nodes, you must have a disk witness. This configuration isn't recommended because if the disk witness fails, the cluster fails. After you select which nodes can vote, you select the quorum witness, as described in the preceding section.

You can remove a vote from a node with the PowerShell cmdlet (Get-ClusterNode *ServerName*).NodeWeight=0 (replacing *ServerName* with the name of the server where you want to set the NodeWeight value).

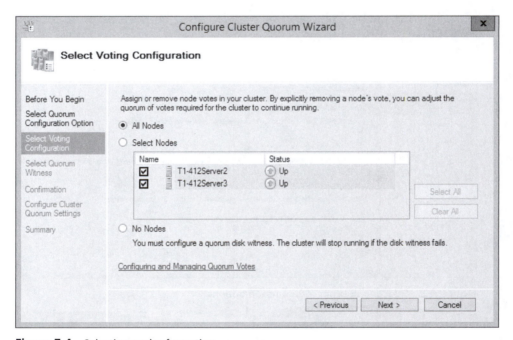

Figure 7-4   Selecting nodes for voting

Using New Quorum Features   Starting in Windows Server 2012, failover clusters have a feature called **dynamic quorum**, which is enabled by default. This feature assigns a cluster node vote dynamically depending on whether the node is an active member of the cluster. If a node is no longer active in the cluster, its vote is removed. In earlier versions of Windows Server, the number of node votes was static, based on the initial cluster configuration. So if a cluster lost more than half its members, it stopped operating. With dynamic quorum, a cluster can continue running with only one active node because the number of votes needed to reach a quorum is adjusted dynamically. Therefore, it's not advisable to remove a node's vote manually because the cluster manager can't assign a node vote dynamically if it's manually overridden.

Another new quorum feature in Windows Server 2012 R2 is the capability to change node votes dynamically to create a **tie breaker for 50% node split**. For example, say you have a cluster consisting of four nodes and a file share witness. Two nodes are in Site1, and the other two nodes are in Site2. The file share witness is on a server in Site3. The quorum consists of a total of five votes. The link to Site3 goes down, and you're left with a total of four votes. The goal in a cluster quorum is always having an odd number of votes to prevent a tie. In this case, the cluster picks one of the four nodes and removes its vote, leaving a total of three votes. With three votes, two votes are required to reach a quorum. If one node in Site1 is selected to have its vote removed, Site1 has one vote, and Site2 has two votes. If the link between Site1 and Site2 goes down, the Site1 cluster partition goes offline, leaving the cluster partition in Site2 operational. You can also determine which cluster site will continue running in the event of a 50% node split. In Windows Server 2012 R2, Microsoft introduced the cluster property LowerQuorumPriorityNodeID. You set it to the ID of a node in the site that should go down if there's a 50% node split by using `(Get-Cluster).LowerQuorumPriorityNodeID=X` (replacing *X* with the node ID). To get a node's ID, use the PowerShell cmdlet `Get-ClusterNode` *ServerName* `| Format-List -Property Id`, replacing *ServerName* with the name of the node you want to get an ID for.

Dynamic quorum can be disabled by using the PowerShell cmdlet `(Get-Cluster).DynamicQuorum=0`.

Activity 7-2: Configuring Advanced Quorum Settings

Time Required: 15 minutes
Objective: Configure advanced quorum settings.

Required Tools and Equipment: 412Server1, 412Server2, and 412Server3
Description: In this activity, you configure advanced quorum settings with the Configure Cluster Quorum Wizard and PowerShell cmdlets.

1. Start 412Server1, 412Server2, and 412Server3, if necessary. On 412Server2, log on to the domain as **Administrator**.

2. On 412Server2, open Server Manager, and start the Failover Cluster Manager, if necessary. In the left pane, right-click **Failover1.412Dom1.local**, point to **More Actions**, and click **Configure Cluster Quorum Settings** to start the Configure Cluster Quorum Wizard.

3. In the Before You Begin window, read the information, and then click **Next**.

4. In the Select Quorum Configuration Option window, click the **Advanced quorum configuration** option button, and then click **Next**.

5. In the Select Voting Configuration window, All Nodes is selected by default. You can deselect nodes by clicking Select Nodes or No Nodes, as shown previously in Figure 7-4. Recall that removing all votes from nodes requires a disk witness, which represents a single point of failure. Click **Next**.

6. In the Select Quorum Witness window, you can configure a disk witness, a file share witness, or no witness. Configuring a witness is always recommended, so leave the default option **Configure a disk witness**, and then click **Next**.

7. In the Configure Storage Witness window, you can choose the storage device that should be the witness. Accept the default, and then click **Next**.

8. In the Confirmation window, review the selected options. You aren't making any changes, so click **Cancel**.

9. Open a PowerShell window. Type **Get-ClusterNode 412Server2 | Format-List -Property NodeWeight** and press Enter. The value of `NodeWeight` is 1, which means 412Server2 has a quorum vote.

10. Type `(Get-ClusterNode 412Server2).NodeWeight=0` and press **Enter**. Type `Get-ClusterNode 412Server2 | Format-List -Property NodeWeight` and press **Enter**. The value of `NodeWeight` is now 0, meaning 412Server2 no longer has a quorum vote.

11. In the Failover Cluster Manager, click **Nodes** in the left pane. Look in the Assigned Vote and Current Vote columns to see that 412Server2 doesn't have a vote.

12. In the PowerShell window, type `Get-Cluster | Format-List -Property DynamicQuorum` and press **Enter**. The value is 1, indicating that the dynamic quorum feature is enabled.

13. Type `Get-Cluster | Format-List -Property LowerQuorumPriorityNodeID` and press **Enter**. The default value is 0, indicating that no nodes have a lower quorum priority.

14. To get the ID of a node, type `Get-ClusterNode 412Server2 | Format-List -Property Id` and press **Enter**. You can use the ID value if you want to set the `LowerQuorumPriorityNodeID` property discussed previously in "Using New Quorum Features."

15. Close the PowerShell window. Leave all servers running for the next activity.

Configuring Roles for High Availability

In Chapter 6, you configured the File Server role to use failover clustering. In this section, you take a closer look at the roles you can configure to use failover clustering and examine the File Server role in more detail.

When you configure an application or service for high availability, there are two broad categories: cluster-aware and generic. A cluster-aware service or application is designed to work with the failover clustering feature. A generic cluster application or service might be able to work in a clustered environment, but additional configuration tasks might be necessary for it to work correctly in a cluster. The cluster-aware roles in Windows Server 2012/R2 include the following, most of which you're already familiar with:

- DFS Namespace Server
- DHCP Server
- Distributed Transaction Coordinator (DTC)
- File Server
- Hyper-V Replica Broker
- iSCSI Target Server
- iSNS Server
- Message Queuing
- Virtual Machine
- WINS Server

One other role called Other Server provides a client access point and storage for an application you install later that can use the access point and storage.

Three categories of generic applications or services can be deployed in a failover cluster: Generic Application, Generic Script, and Generic Service. Applications, scripts, and services deployed with the "generic" failover cluster option are not cluster aware and, therefore, might not respond to a failover situation as quickly or in the same way that a cluster-aware role does. With generic applications and services, the cluster software starts the application or service and then periodically queries Windows to check whether the application or service is still running. Generic applications and services have fewer ways to let the cluster software know its operational state. So the application or service might still appear to be running but can't perform its normal function. In this case, the cluster software doesn't know that action should be taken.

Using the generic script option, you can create a script that starts and monitors an application or service. The script can communicate to the cluster service the precise state of the application or service, thereby ensuring a more accurate and timely response to application or service problems.

Configuring Highly Available Shares   There are two main options for configuring highly available shares by using the File Server role (see Figure 7-5). The default option is "File Server for general use," which supports standard Windows SMB shares and NFS shares and role services such as data deduplication, Distributed File System (DFS) replication, and File Service Resource Manager (FSRM). The ideal application for this option is a centralized share containing files that are opened and closed frequently.

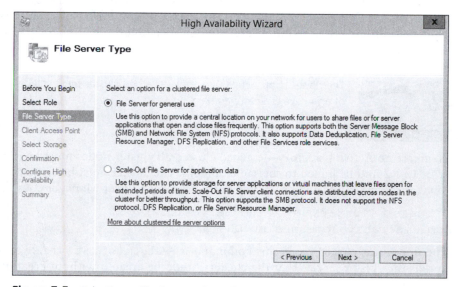

Figure 7-5   Selecting a File Server role option

The "Scale-Out File Server for application data" option is used for applications that leave files open for extended periods. A common use of this option is for a Hyper-V server where virtual machine files are stored on a file share. When using this option for virtual machine storage, performance and reliability are on par with typical SAN storage. With a **scale-out file server**, you have the reliability of failover clusters and the load distribution of an NLB because client connections are distributed among all nodes in the cluster. This option is recommended for Hyper-V deployments that use SMB shares for VM storage and for SQL deployments that use SMB. It doesn't support Network File System (NFS), FSRM, or DFS replication.

Upgrading a Failover Cluster

If you're running a Windows Server 2008/R2 failover cluster and want to migrate to a Windows Server 2012/R2 cluster, you have a few options. One option is to add two nodes running Windows Server 2012/R2 to the existing cluster and then transfer the roles and resources to the new nodes. After the resources and roles have been transferred, you can evict (remove) the older Windows Server 2008/R2 nodes from the cluster. To evict a node from a cluster, right-click the node in Failover Cluster Manager, point to More Actions, and click Evict.

This option might not be feasible if you don't have extra servers available, however. Another option is to perform an in-place upgrade, in which you evict one of the nodes running Windows Server 2008/R2 from the cluster, upgrade the server to Windows Server 2012/R2, and then add the node back to the cluster. After the node is rejoined to the cluster, transfer resources and roles to the new Windows Server 2012/R2 node and evict another node running Windows Server 2008/R2. Upgrade this node, and then rejoin it to the cluster. Perform this process until all nodes have been upgraded to Windows Server 2012/R2. You should then validate the configuration to make sure the upgraded cluster is in good working order.

A third option is to build a new cluster with nodes running Windows Server 2012/R2 and run the Copy Cluster Roles Wizard from one of the nodes in the new cluster. Then you can destroy the old Windows Server 2008/R2 cluster. The Copy Cluster Roles Wizard was described earlier in "Copying Cluster Roles."

Creating Active Directory–Detached Clusters

A new feature in Windows Server 2012 R2 is the capability to deploy a failover cluster without needing Active Directory for network name management. As you know, when you create a failover cluster, a computer account is created in Active Directory for the cluster and any clustered roles you configure, and DNS entries are created for the cluster and cluster roles. An **Active Directory–detached cluster** still creates the DNS entries for name resolution, but computer accounts aren't created in Active Directory. This option for creating clusters allows someone who doesn't have permission to create computer objects in Active Directory to create a failover cluster.

The nodes in an Active Directory–detached cluster must still be members of an Active Directory domain.

To create an Active Directory–detached cluster, all cluster nodes must be running Windows Server 2012 R2 and be joined to the same domain. The cluster must be created with the following PowerShell cmdlet; it can't be created in the Failover Cluster Manager console:

```
New-Cluster ClusterName -Node Server1,Server2
  -AdministrativeAccessPoint DNS
```

The important parameter in this command is `-AdministrativeAccessPoint DNS`, which tells the cluster service that the cluster should be created without creating Active Directory computer accounts.

Deploying Clustered Storage Spaces

You learned about Storage Spaces when you studied the objectives for the Installing and Configuring Windows Server 2012, 70-410 exam. This section briefly describes the steps for deploying a clustered storage space. This topic is covered more thoroughly in the Implementing an Advanced Server Infrastructure, 70-414 exam. Before you can create a clustered storage space, your cluster and storage configuration must meet the following prerequisites:

- All servers must be running at least Windows Server 2012.

- You must have at least three disks that haven't had any volumes allocated on them.

- Disk controllers must be serially attached SCSI (SAS) and must not have RAID functionality enabled.

- Windows Server 2012 supports simple and mirror spaces, and Windows Server 2012 R2 also supports parity spaces for a failover cluster.

- Use a Windows Server 2012–certified just a bunch of disks (JBOD) storage enclosure that has an SAS connection for each cluster node. The Windows Server Catalog lists available certified enclosures.

- The disks used for the clustered storage pool must be dedicated to that pool.

There are two main methods for deploying a clustered storage space:

- Create a storage space before you create the failover cluster, and then add the storage to the failover cluster when running the Create Cluster Wizard.

- Create the failover cluster, and then create a clustered storage space in the Failover Cluster Manager.

After the prerequisites are met, perform the following steps. Steps 1 through 4 are used for the first method, and Steps 1, 2, 4, and 5 are used for the second method:

1. Install the Multipath I/O (MPIO) feature on all cluster nodes.

2. Verify that the shared disks are available in Disk Management or File and Storage Services.

3. Create the storage spaces by using File and Storage Services. (Skip this step for Method 2.)

4. Create a failover cluster.

5. *Don't do this step for the first method.* Create storage spaces in the Failover Cluster Manager instead of using File and Storage Services. To do so, expand the Storage node in the Failover Cluster Manager, click Pools, and click New Storage Pool in the Actions pane.

You can then add a clustered storage space volume, if you want, to a cluster shared volume (CSV) if you're using CSVs.

Cluster Configuration Backup and Restore

You can see by now that configuring a failover cluster can be complex. After you have created and configured a failover cluster, you don't want to lose all your hard work if disaster strikes. You can get some peace of mind by using Windows Server Backup to back up a failover cluster configuration. First, you need to install the Windows Server Backup feature on at least one node in the cluster by using the Add Roles and Features Wizard or PowerShell. Before backing up the cluster configuration, verify that the cluster node where you're doing the backup is active in the cluster, the cluster is running, and it has a quorum.

Any Windows Server Backup that allows a system recovery includes the cluster configuration data, such as a full server backup or a custom backup incorporating the system state. Because the witness disk also includes cluster configuration data, it's a good idea to include it in the backup. You should also back up the data on clustered disks. Only disks that are online and owned by the node where you're performing the backup can be backed up, so you might need to do a backup on more than one server to make sure all the cluster data is backed up.

Restoring a Failover Cluster Configuration
Cluster configuration data is replicated automatically to all cluster nodes and the witness disk, if present. If you need to restore the cluster configuration on a single cluster node, you have two options:

- *Authoritative restore*—In this case, the configuration contained in the backup is replicated to all cluster nodes after the backup is finished. You use this type of restore when you need to roll back the cluster configuration to an earlier point, perhaps because of an administrative error made when changing the cluster configuration.

- *Nonauthoritative restore*—In this case, you restore a node from the system state backup, and it rejoins the cluster. Then the current cluster configuration stored on the other cluster nodes is replicated to it.

Activity 7-3: Destroying a Failover Cluster

Time Required: 15 minutes
Objective: Destroy a failover cluster.

Required Tools and Equipment: 412Server1, 412Server2, and 412Server3
Description: You're finished working with failover clusters, so in this activity, you remove the Failover1FS role, evict 412Server3 from the cluster, and then destroy the cluster. Although evicting nodes from the cluster first isn't necessary, you do it for practice.

1. Start 412Server1, 412Server2, and 412Server3, if necessary. On 412Server2, log on to the domain as **Administrator**.

2. On 412Server2, open Server Manager, and start the Failover Cluster Manager, if necessary. In the left pane, click to expand **Failover1.412Dom1.local**, and then click **Roles**.

3. In the middle pane, right-click **Failover1FS** and click **Remove**. In the Remove File Server message box, click **Yes**.

4. Next, you evict 412Server3; however, you can't evict a node that causes the cluster to lose a quorum. So first you need to give 412Server2 its quorum vote back that you removed in Activity 7-2. Open a PowerShell window, and then type **(Get-ClusterNode 412Server2).NodeWeight=1** and press **Enter**. Close the PowerShell window.

5. In the left pane of the Failover Cluster Manager, click **Nodes**. 412Server2 has its vote restored. In the middle pane, right-click **412Server3**, point to **More Actions**, and click **Evict**. In the Evict node 412Server3 message box, click **Yes**.

6. In the left pane of the Failover Cluster Manager, right-click **Failover1.412Dom1.local**, point to **More Actions**, and click **Destroy Cluster**. In the Destroy Cluster message box, click **Yes**. Close the Failover Cluster Manager.

7. Leave all servers running for the next activity.

Activity 7-4: Removing the iSCSI Configuration

Time Required: 15 minutes
Objective: Remove the iSCSI configuration.

Required Tools and Equipment: 412Server1, 412Server2, and 412Server3
Description: You're finished working with iSCSI, so in this activity, you disconnect the iSCSI volumes, delete the iSCSI targets, and then delete the volume on the second disk on 412Server1.

1. Start 412Server1, 412Server2, and 412Server3, if necessary. On 412Server2, log on to the domain as **Administrator**.

2. On 412Server2, open Server Manager, if necessary, and click **Tools, iSCSI Initiator** from the menu. Click the **Targets** tab, if necessary. Click the target in the Discovered targets list box, and click **Disconnect**. In the Disconnect From All Sessions message box, click **Yes**. Click **OK**.

3. On 412Server3, log on to the domain as **Administrator**. Open Server Manager, if necessary, and click **Tools, iSCSI Initiator** from the menu. Click the **Targets** tab, if necessary. Click the target in the Discovered targets list box, and click **Disconnect**. In the Disconnect From All Sessions message box, click **Yes**. Click **OK**.

4. On 412Server1, log on as **Administrator**. Open Server Manager, if necessary. Click **File and Storage Services**, and then click **iSCSI**.

5. In the middle pane, scroll down until you see the iSCSI Targets section. Right-click the target and click **Remove Target**. In the Remove Target message box, click **Yes**.

6. Scroll up to the iSCSI Virtual Disks section, and then right-click **vdisk1** and click **Remove iSCSI Virtual Disk**. In the Remove iSCSI Virtual Disk message box, click the **Delete the iSCSI virtual disk file from the disk** check box, and click **OK**. Repeat this step for **vdisk2**.

7. Right-click **Start** and click **Disk Management**. Right-click the **Data** volume and click **Delete Volume**. In the "Delete simple volume" message box, click **Yes**. In the Disk Management dialog box, click **Yes** to force deletion of the volume.

8. Shut down all servers.

Configuring Highly Available Virtual Machines

The use of virtual machines has become standard practice in both small and large organizations. Because so many organizations depend on virtual servers for enterprise applications, being able to provide high availability to virtual servers is as important as being able to provide high availability to the physical hosts that run them. This section describes the steps for configuring a

highly available virtual machine (also known as a "clustered virtual machine") and configuring virtual machine monitoring. Later in "Configuring Guest Clustering," you look at configuring a guest cluster and virtual machine movement, when you learn how to move VMs easily from one Hyper-V server to another.

Configuring Highly Available Virtual Machines

A highly available virtual machine allows you to make applications and services highly available simply by installing them on a virtual machine (VM) configured for high availability. In other words, configuring each application or service for high availability isn't necessary because the VM it's running on already is. To configure a highly available (clustered) VM, you need to create a failover cluster on two or more host computers running the Hyper-V role. In addition, it's best to use CSVs to store the highly available VMs because multiple VMs hosted by different Hyper-V servers can be put on the same CSV. If you use traditional shared storage, each node in the cluster requires a separate volume for its hosted VMs. Before creating a highly available VM, you should perform the following tasks:

- Verify that you have two host computers that meet requirements for the Hyper-V role and the Failover Clustering feature.

- Be sure all host computers are members of the same domain.

- Install the Hyper-V role and Failover Clustering feature on all servers participating in the failover cluster.

- Configure the shared storage the failover cluster will use.

- In Hyper-V Manager, configure the virtual networks the VMs will use.

- Validate the failover cluster configuration by running the Validate a Configuration Wizard in the Failover Cluster Manager.

- Create the failover cluster.

- Add storage to a cluster shared volume if you're using CSVs (recommended).

Creating a Highly Available VM   You can create a highly available VM directly in the Failover Cluster Manager, which configures a VM for high availability automatically. In the Failover Cluster Manager, click the Roles node, and in the Actions pane, click Virtual Machines and then New Virtual Machine to start the New Virtual Machine Wizard. In the first window, choose the target cluster node to host the VM (see Figure 7-6). From that point, the New Virtual Machine Wizard runs normally as though you had started it in Hyper-V Manager.

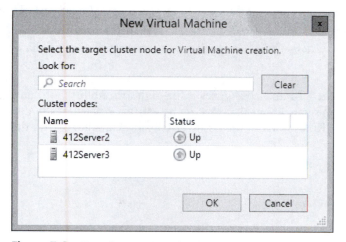

Figure 7-6   Choosing a target cluster node

In the Specify Name and Location window, select the option "Store the virtual machine in a different location." If you're using a CSV, select a volume in the C:\ClusterStorage folder (see Figure 7-7). If you're using traditional shared storage, specify the shared storage currently owned by the target cluster node you selected.

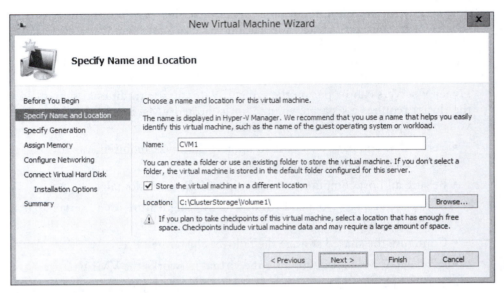

Figure 7-7   Choosing shared storage for the VM

After you specify the location, continue with the New Virtual Machine Wizard as usual. You need to select the following options for the new VM:

- *Specify the generation*—You can choose generation 1 or 2. Generation 2 VMs offer some advanced features and are recommended.

- *Assign memory*—Choose the right amount of memory for applications the VM will run.

- *Configure networking*—You should have created the virtual switches earlier; select one from the available choices.

- *Configure the virtual hard disk*—Be sure the path to the virtual hard disk points to the shared storage location—for example, C:\ClusterStorage\Volume1 if you're using CSVs. You can also attach a hard disk later or use an existing virtual hard disk. In any case, the virtual disk must be on shared storage.

- *Install an operating system*—You can specify a path to installation media or install an OS later.

The wizard creates the VM and configures it for high availability automatically. A report is generated so that you can see whether there were any errors or warnings in configuring the VM for high availability. The Roles node in the Failover Cluster Manager shows the highly available

VM and its current status (see Figure 7-8). If you click the VM, you can manage it in the Failover Cluster Manager. You can test failover by using the Move option in the Actions pane, which enables you to choose Live Migration, Quick Migration, or Virtual Machine Storage. To test failover of a running VM, choose Live Migration. You can specify which node to fail over to, or you can select Best Possible Node to have the cluster service choose for you. The status of the live migration process is shown in the middle pane of the Failover Cluster Manager. Live migration and other virtual machine movement options are discussed later in "Configuring Virtual Machine Movement." If the live migration is successful, you have a highly available VM.

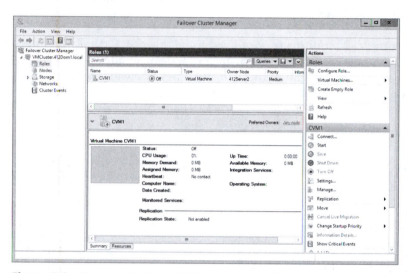

Figure 7-8 The new highly available VM in the Failover Cluster Manager

Configuring an Existing VM for High Availability
If the VM you want to configure for high availability already exists, you can move it to shared storage (with the Move option in Hyper-V Manager) and configure it for high availability in the Failover Cluster Manager. Click Configure Role in the Actions pane to start the High Availability Wizard. In the Select Role window, click Virtual Machine. You see a list of VMs you can configure for high availability. Select one or more of the VMs and continue with the High Availability Wizard.

Using Drain on Shutdown
What happens if you shut down a Hyper-V host that's configured in a cluster hosting one or more VMs? The best way to shut down a node in a Hyper-V cluster is to place it in maintenance mode by pausing it and selecting Drain Roles. Doing so signals the cluster that the host is going to be unavailable and the VMs are live-migrated automatically to another node in the cluster. To pause a node, right-click it in the Failover Cluster Manager, point to Pause, and click Drain Roles. Then you can take the node offline for maintenance and so forth. When you resume the node, you can choose Fail Roles Back if you want the VMs (and any other clustered roles that were running on the server when it was paused) to be migrated back to that node.

Suppose, however, you simply shut down a clustered Hyper-V server without pausing it first. In Windows Server 2012, the state of running VMs is saved, the VMs are moved, and then the VMs are resumed on another cluster node. This process results in downtime for VMs that are moved. Windows Server 2012 R2 introduces the **drain on shutdown** feature, which drains roles automatically and live-migrates the VMs to another cluster node before the Hyper-V server shuts down. Drain on shutdown is enabled by default.

Configuring Virtual Machine Monitoring

A new feature in Windows Server 2012, **virtual machine monitoring**, enables you to monitor resources, applications, and services running on highly available VMs. If a resource fails, the cluster node can take actions to recover, such as attempting to restart a service or moving the resource to another cluster node. VM monitoring has the following prerequisites:

- The guest OS and Hyper-V host must be running at least Windows Server 2012.
- The guest OS must be a member of the same domain as the Hyper-V host.
- The user running the Failover Cluster Manager must be a member of the local Administrators group in the VM's guest OS.

To configure VM monitoring, you need to enable the Virtual Machine Monitoring firewall rule on each guest to be monitored. To do so, open Windows Firewall from Control Panel and click "Allow an app or feature through Windows Firewall." Then click to select the Virtual Machine Monitoring rule, making sure the Domain check box is selected (see Figure 7-9).

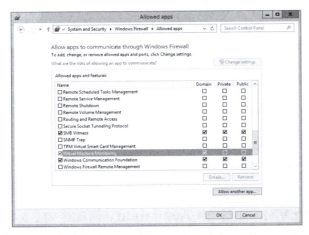

Figure 7-9   Enabling the Virtual Machine Monitoring firewall rule

In the Failover Cluster Manager on a VM's host machine, click Roles, right-click the VM you want to monitor, point to More Actions, and click Configure Monitoring. In the list of services that's displayed, click to select each one you want to monitor. For example, in Figure 7-10, the Print Spooler and File Server Resource Manager services are selected for monitoring.

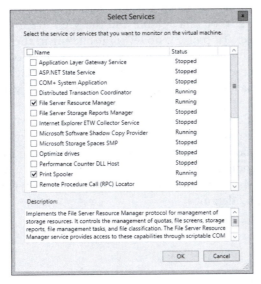

Figure 7-10   Selecting VM services to monitor

If a service being monitored is determined to have failed, a service restart is attempted up to two times by default. If the service fails to start after the second restart attempt, an event with ID 1250 is generated in the System log, and the VM is restarted. If another failure occurs, the VM is moved to another cluster node and started. This behavior is the default action for a failed service. You can change the failure response policy by selecting the VM in the Failover Cluster Manager and clicking the Resource tab at the bottom of the Roles pane. Then right-click the VM and click Properties to open the VM's Properties dialog box. In the Policies tab (see Figure 7-11), you can choose whether to perform a restart and specify the time between restart attempts. In the Advanced Policies tab, you can select which cluster hosts can be owners of the resource and the resource health check intervals. Use the Settings tab to determine the actions to take if the virtual machine stops and whether automatic recovery is enabled for the virtual machine.

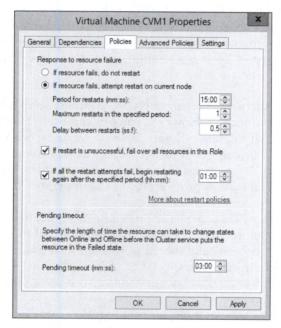

Figure 7-11   Configuring VM failure response policies

Using Virtual Machine Network Health Detection   An additional feature in Windows Server 2012 R2 is **virtual machine network health detection**. If a network disconnect is detected on a virtual machine's virtual NIC, the cluster moves the virtual machine to another cluster node. Virtual machine network health detection is configured on the network interface on each VM and is enabled by default. To enable or disable the feature, open the settings for a VM in Hyper-V Manager or the Failover Cluster Manager, click to expand the network adapter you want to change, and click Advanced Features. Click to enable or disable the "Protected network" check box (see Figure 7-12).

Figure 7-12   Configuring network health detection

Configuring Guest Clustering

Guest clustering is different from a highly available or clustered VM in that it requires two or more VMs with a guest OS installed and configured for failover clustering. A highly available VM requires configuring the Hyper-V host server with the Failover Clustering feature, but in a guest cluster, the failover clustering occurs in the VM's guest OS. Each application requiring high availability must be configured in the guest OS by using the Failover Cluster Manager. The benefits of using guest clustering versus a clustered VM are as follows:

- *Monitoring clustered resources in the guest OS*—A clustered VM can fail over only to another Hyper-V server if the entire VM fails, but a guest cluster monitors each clustered resource, such as applications and services, network, and storage, and can initiate recovery or failover if a failure is detected.

- *Hyper-V host optimization*—VMs participating in a guest cluster can be moved easily between Hyper-V hosts to optimize Hyper-V host resource use.

- *Host failure protection*—VMs participating in a guest cluster can reside on multiple Hyper-V hosts so that clustered applications and services are protected from VM failure as well as host failure. In addition, the Hyper-V hosts can be configured in a failover cluster, adding resiliency for highly available applications.

Ideally, the VMs in a guest cluster are on separate Hyper-V servers so that if the Hyper-V host fails, the cluster can continue to function. However, you can run a guest cluster on a single Hyper-V cluster to provide some fault tolerance. If you choose a single Hyper-V server to host the cluster, each cluster node should be connected to a separate virtual network assigned to its own physical NIC. In addition, each VM participating in the cluster should be stored on a separate physical disk on the host. These measures provide cluster fault tolerance in case of component failure on the Hyper-V host.

To create a guest cluster, you follow the same basic procedure as for creating a failover cluster with physical hosts, and the same prerequisites apply. For example, all the guest OSs must belong to the same Active Directory domain, and shared storage must be available to all cluster nodes. Shared storage can be provided by a SAN using iSCSI or Fibre Channel as with a physical host cluster. Starting in Windows Server 2012 R2, a guest cluster can use a **shared virtual hard disk** instead of traditional SAN storage.

The steps for configuring a two-node guest cluster running Windows Server 2012 R2 and using a two-node Hyper-V failover cluster are as follows:

1. Configure the Hyper-V failover cluster as described earlier in "Configuring Clustered Virtual Machines." The Hyper-V failover cluster can use a CSV or a scale-out file server for shared storage.

2. Create two highly available virtual machines.

3. Install Windows Server 2012 R2 on both virtual machines.

4. Join each VM to an Active Directory domain.

5. Install the Failover Clustering feature on both VMs.

6. Make sure both VMs have access to the shared storage, which can be an iSCSI SAN or a shared virtual hard disk (discussed next in "Configuring a Shared Virtual Hard Disk").

7. Create the guest cluster and add both VMs to the cluster.

You can avoid having to configure traditional SAN storage for the guest cluster by using a shared virtual hard disk, which is a virtual disk created on one of the cluster nodes and made available to all cluster nodes. Using a shared virtual hard disk is a good solution for applications running on the guest cluster, such as file sharing and database applications. In these applications, the shared folders or database files are stored on the shared virtual hard disk.

Configuring a Shared Virtual Hard Disk To use a shared virtual hard disk for a guest cluster, you need to make sure the following requirements are met:

- You have configured a Hyper-V failover cluster as described earlier in "Configuring Clustered Virtual Machines." The Hyper-V hosts must be running Windows Server 2012 R2.

- You're using cluster shared volumes or a share on a scale-out file server to store the virtual hard disk.

- The guest OS on all cluster nodes must be running Windows Server 2012/R2. If Windows Server 2012 is used, the guest must be updated with Windows Server 2012 R2 Integration Services.

- The shared virtual hard disk must be connected to a virtual SCSI controller and be in the VHDX format. The shared virtual hard disk can be a fixed-size or dynamically expanding disk but not a differencing disk.

Configuring Virtual Machine Movement

A big advantage of using a virtual machine is making efficient use of computer and network resources. You can put multiple VMs to work on a single host server to concentrate workloads or distribute VMs among multiple hosts to spread out the workload. As you've seen, you have more resiliency with highly available VMs by using Hyper-V failover clusters, creating guest clusters, or combining both functions to have multilevel fault tolerance.

To get the most out of VMs using multiple Hyper-V hosts, you need to be able to move VMs and VM storage quickly and easily from one host to another with limited service disruption. There are a number of methods for moving a virtual machine, depending on why you want to move it and how your VMs and Hyper-V hosts are configured:

- Live migration
- Quick migration
- Storage migration
- VM import and export

Live Migration

Live migration is a Hyper-V feature that enables an administrator to move a VM from one Hyper-V server to another while maintaining the VM's availability. Live migration of a single VM was introduced in Windows Server 2008 R2, and Windows Server 2012 adds the capability to live-migrate multiple VMs simultaneously. Before you can use live migration, the environment must meet these prerequisites:

- Two or more servers running the Hyper-V role or Hyper-V server that are in the same Active Directory domain or are in trusting domains.

- Same processor manufacturer. For example, both servers must be running Intel processors or AMD processors. You can't live-migrate between Hyper-V servers with processors from different manufacturers.

- The VM to be migrated must be using virtual hard disks.

Live migration is enabled by default on clustered Hyper-V servers but not on nonclustered servers. In addition, the initial live migration setting allows you to perform two simultaneous live migrations. You can enable or disable live migrations or change the limit in Hyper-V Manager by opening the Hyper-V Settings window and clicking Live Migrations in the left pane (see Figure 7-13). The Live Migrations dialog box is also where you can specify which IP addresses can be used to perform migrations. If you have multiple NICs, for example, you can specify a network to use.

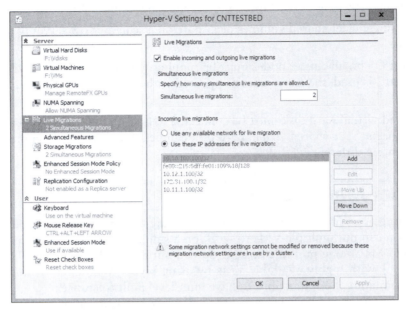

Figure 7-13 Changing live migration settings

Virtual machines can be live-migrated in different ways, depending on the virtual environment configuration. The preceding prerequisites apply to all live migration methods. Specific live migration settings might have additional requirements. The following types of live migrations are discussed in this section:

- Cluster live migration
- Live migration with SMB shares
- Shared-nothing live migration
- Cross-version live migration

Cluster Live Migrations VM live migrations between two Hyper-V servers configured in a cluster are usually very fast. Because the VM files are stored on shared storage, ownership of the VM transfers between the cluster nodes quickly, and then the memory state of the running VM must be transferred. A typical clustered live migration generally occurs in seconds rather than minutes. Additional requirements for clustered live migrations include the following:

- Two or more Hyper-V servers configured in a cluster by using the Failover Clustering feature.
- Shared storage is set up with CSVs.

To perform a cluster live migration, select a virtual machine in the Failover Cluster Manager, click Move in the Actions pane, point to Live Migration, and then click Best Possible Node if you want the Failover Cluster Manager to select the node to migrate to, or click Select Node if you want to choose the node. The live migration starts, and its status is shown in the Information column for the VM in the middle pane.

Live Migrations with SMB Shares You can perform live migration between two Hyper-V servers that aren't clustered if the VMs are stored on an SMB share. In this case, the VM's configuration files and virtual hard disks are in a file share accessible by both Hyper-V servers.

The permissions on the share must grant access to both Hyper-V server computer accounts. When you create the VMs, you must use the share's UNC path to specify the VM's location and its virtual disk location.

In addition, you must log on to the source Hyper-V server (the one currently running the VM) to perform the migration or configure constrained delegation. By default, live migration uses the Credential Security Support Provider (CredSSP) authentication protocol, which is suitable if you perform the migration from the source Hyper-V server. If you want to use remote management with PowerShell or Remote Desktop to perform the migration, you must use the Kerberos protocol and configure constrained delegation. You learned about constrained delegation when you studied the objectives of the 70-411 exam. You can configure the authentication protocol in Hyper-V Manager by clicking Advanced Features under the Live Migrations setting shown previously in Figure 7-13.

Shared-Nothing Live Migrations   Another option for performing live migrations between nonclustered Hyper-V servers is **shared-nothing live migration**. As the name implies, the live migration is done between Hyper-V servers that have no common storage. The VM's files are stored in local storage on the Hyper-V server. This type of live migration takes the longest because all the VM's files must be copied across the network to the destination Hyper-V server. The virtual machine storage is copied from the source Hyper-V server while it continues to run, and then the configuration files and the running VM's memory contents are copied. The VM remains available to clients throughout the operation. To perform shared-nothing live migration, follow these steps:

1. Verify that all prerequisites for live migration, discussed earlier, have been met.

2. Enable live migrations on all Hyper-V servers.

3. Log on to the source Hyper-V server, and open Hyper-V Manager.

4. Select the VM to be migrated and click Move in the Actions pane.

5. In the Choose Move Type window, click Move the virtual machine. (You also have the option to move just the VM's storage, but for a live migration, you must move the entire VM.)

6. Specify the name of the destination Hyper-V server.

7. Choose whether to move the VM's data and configuration file to a single location or specify the location of each item. Moving the VM's data and configuration file to a single location is easiest, but you can specify different locations for the configuration file, virtual disks, snapshot files, and paging file, if necessary.

8. Select the locations on the destination server.

You can also use shared-nothing live migration to move VMs between servers that are members of different clusters. To do so, first remove the VM from the cluster in the Failover Cluster Manager. Next, use Hyper-V to move the VM to the destination Hyper-V server that's a member of a different cluster, using the shared-nothing live migration procedure described previously. Finally, add the VM to the cluster in the Failover Cluster Manager. You don't need to shut down a VM to remove it from or add it to a cluster.

Cross-Version Live Migrations   You can move a VM running on a Windows Server 2012 server to a Windows Server 2012 R2 server, but the reverse isn't possible. This option allows you to upgrade Hyper-V servers to Windows Server 2012 R2 without any VM downtime. All the live migration methods discussed in this section are available.

Quick Migration

Quick migration is a migration option available only between Hyper-V servers in a failover cluster. The advantage is that it's available in Windows Server 2008 Hyper-V servers and later. Unlike live migration, in which there's no downtime for the migrated VM, a quick migration usually results in a minute or more of downtime, depending on how much memory the VM uses. It involves copying the VM data to the destination Hyper-V node, saving the VM's state on the source node, and then copying the machine state to the destination Hyper-V node and resuming the servers. To perform a quick migration, select the VM you want to use in the Failover Cluster Manager, click Move in the Actions pane, and click Quick Migration. Like a live migration, you can choose the node you want to move the VM to, or you can let the Failover Cluster Manager select the best possible node. You can use quick migration in the following situations:

- Your Hyper-V servers are running Windows Server 2008. (Live migration wasn't available until Window Server 2008 R2.)

- You want to distribute VMs to different cluster nodes during off hours and don't require live migrations.

- You need to perform maintenance on the current host server.

Storage Migration

A **storage migration** is usually used when you simply need to move a VM's storage from one volume to another without actually moving the VM to another Hyper-V server. You can perform a storage migration while the VM is still running or when it's shut down. You might want to do a storage migration for the following reasons:

- The current storage location is running low on free space, and you have added new storage.

- You want to move the VM's virtual disks from local storage to shared storage in preparation for making the VM highly available.

- You want to move VM storage to a temporary location while the server's storage system is upgraded.

- You want to move the VM's virtual disks to higher performing storage, such as an SSD.

You can perform a storage migration on a Hyper-V cluster or a stand-alone Hyper-V server. In the Failover Cluster Manager, select the VM, click Move in the Actions pane, and then click Virtual Machine Storage. You can choose some or all of the VM's data files, including the virtual hard disks, checkpoints, paging file, and configuration files. You see a list of available shared storage as the destination, or you can add an SMB share to the list of destinations.

On a stand-alone Hyper-V server, select the VM, and click Move in the Actions pane. In the Move Wizard, you can choose between moving the entire VM or just the VM storage. You can move all storage items to the same location, choose different locations for each item, or just move the machine's virtual hard disks (see Figure 7-14).

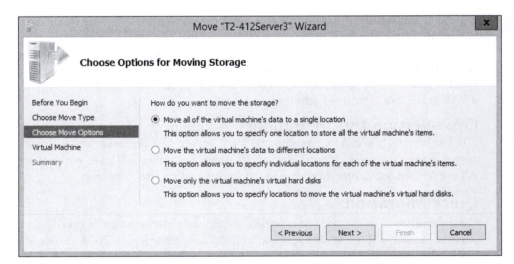

Figure 7-14 Moving VM storage

VM Export and Import

The virtual machine movement options discussed earlier simply move a VM, its data, or both to a different location on the same server, within a cluster, or on different servers. Virtual machine export creates a copy of an existing VM, and virtual machine import creates a new VM. You can export or import a VM by using the Actions pane in Hyper-V Manager or using the PowerShell cmdlets `Export-VM` and `Import-VM`. The following list describes a situation in which you might want to use VM exporting and importing:

- Export a virtual machine to create a backup. The VM can later be imported on the same Hyper-V host to replace an existing VM that became corrupted or on another Hyper-V host if the original host fails or is being replaced.

- Export a virtual machine to create a copy. After you export the VM, you can import it into a new VM, thereby saving the time needed to install the OS.

- Export a VM to be moved to another host. The virtual machine move or live migration options discussed earlier are generally preferable to performing an export and then an import, but circumstances might prevent you from using the other options, such as a failure on the original host or the target Hyper-V server not being on the same network as the original.

Exporting VMs   Virtual machines can be exported and then imported to create virtual machines. Starting in Windows Server 2012 R2, you can even export a running VM. In previous versions of Hyper-V, the VM had to be shut down. Because you can export a VM while it's running, this feature allows you to back up a VM without shutting it down first. You can use an exported VM as a backup or to make a copy of an existing VM. When you select the Export option for a VM, you're prompted to enter a path for storing the exported VM. Starting in Windows Server 2012, you can enter a path to a network share; previous versions required a path to local storage. After a VM is exported, it can be moved to archival storage as a backup, imported on another server running Hyper-V, or imported on the same server.

Importing VMs   In previous versions of Windows Server, you had to export a VM before you could import it. Starting in Windows Server 2012 R2, you can import a VM that hasn't been exported first. This new feature can come in handy if, for example, the Hyper-V host suffers a hardware or software failure; you can simply move the hard disk containing VMs to another host and import them in place. When you import a virtual machine, you have three options for the type of import:

- *Register the virtual machine in-place (use the existing unique ID)*—This option registers the exported VM in Hyper-V from its current location. No copy of the exported VM is made. Use this option only if you're restoring a failed or corrupt VM or rebuilding a Hyper-V host, and the files are already where you want them. The advantage of this option is that the import process is fast.

- *Restore the virtual machine (use the existing unique ID)*—This option is usually best for restoring VMs. It copies the VM files to their original location on the host, leaving the exported files unchanged and available for future restoration if needed. You can't use this option if the original exported VM is already running on the Hyper-V host.

- *Copy the virtual machine (create a new unique ID)*—Use this option to make a copy or clone of a virtual machine and register it in Hyper-V. For example, use this option if you want to use a VM as a template for additional VMs that you can run on the same Hyper-V host or another Hyper-V host. Because a new unique ID is created, the VMs can run on the same Hyper-V host as the exported VM.

Exporting a VM doesn't change the original VM in any way. You can continue to use the original VM as before.

P2V and V2V Migration

A **physical to virtual (P2V) migration** converts a physical computer to a virtual machine. A **virtual to virtual (V2V) migration** converts a virtual machine from one vendor's format to another vendor's format. The next sections discuss these two processes.

P2V Migration   Hyper-V has no built-in tools to create a virtual machine from a physical computer (P2V migration), but other tools are available for this task. One comes with the Microsoft System Center Virtual Machine Manager (SCVMM), which is a tool for managing multiple Hyper-V hosts. It has the Convert Physical Server Wizard that walks you through the conversion process.

SCVMM is a component of System Center, an add-on product that can be purchased from Microsoft and installed on Windows Server 2012/R2 computers.

A less expensive and complex option is downloading the free `disk2vhd` utility from *http://technet.microsoft.com/sysinternals/*. It runs on the physical server and creates a virtual hard disk file from the disk on the physical server. You can then create a VM in Hyper-V and choose the option to use an existing virtual hard disk to convert your physical computer to a virtual machine. Be aware that the OS on the physical disk was originally meant for a particular hardware configuration, so you might have to change other settings. The original physical disk is unaltered and can be used as always.

You can create a virtual disk by copying the contents of one of the host machine's physical disks. In Hyper-V Manager, just click New, Hard Disk. If you remove a computer's OS disc and install it in the Hyper-V host machine, you can essentially create a VM from a physical disk. The `disk2vhd` utility is usually an easier solution, however.

P2V migrations with SCVMM can be done as online conversions or offline conversions. With an online conversion, the physical computer being converted remains fully functional throughout the process. All local NTFS volumes are copied to create a virtual hard disk. An online conversion is usually the default method. An offline conversion is usually required only if the source computer is running Windows 2000 Server, if FAT volumes are involved, or if the source computer is a domain controller.

V2V Migration   Like P2V migrations, you need to step up to SCVMM if you want to perform V2V migrations. SCVMM can convert virtual machines running on VMware ESX/ESXi Update 5 and later. Versions of SCVMM before the version that comes with System Center 2012 R2 could convert XenServer virtual machines, but XenServer conversions are no longer supported.

Chapter Summary

- After a cluster has been created, you might need to perform some management tasks, including validating the cluster, adding nodes to it, or shutting down or destroying a cluster. You might also need to move cluster roles or resources from one cluster to another.

- Although the cluster creation process configures suitable cluster quorum settings, you might want to change the quorum configuration if you add or remove cluster nodes or a witness disk.

- Windows Server 2012 R2 adds a feature called dynamic witness in which the cluster determines whether to give the witness a quorum vote. If there are an odd number of cluster nodes, the witness doesn't have a vote, but if there are an even number of cluster nodes, the witness does have a quorum vote.

■ Starting in Windows Server 2012, failover clusters have a feature called dynamic quorum, which is enabled by default. With dynamic quorum, a cluster node vote is assigned dynamically, depending on whether the node is an active member of the cluster.

■ When you configure an application or service for high availability, there are two broad categories: cluster-aware and generic. A cluster-aware service or application is designed to work with the Failover Clustering feature.

■ A new feature in Windows Server 2012 R2 is the capability to deploy a failover cluster without needing Active Directory for network name management. An Active Directory–detached cluster still creates the DNS entries for name resolution, but computer accounts aren't created in Active Directory.

■ You can use Windows Server Backup to back up the failover cluster configuration. First, verify that the cluster node you're performing the backup from is active in the cluster, the cluster is running, and it has a quorum.

■ The ability to provide high availability to virtual servers is as important as the ability to provide high availability to the physical hosts that run them. A highly available virtual machine allows you to make applications and services highly available simply by installing them on a VM configured for high availability.

■ A new feature in Windows Server 2012, virtual machine monitoring, allows you to monitor resources, applications, and services running in highly available VMs. If a resource fails, the cluster node can take actions to recover.

■ A new feature in Windows Server 2012 R2 is virtual machine network health detection. If a network disconnect is detected on a virtual machine's virtual NIC, the cluster moves the virtual machine to another cluster node. Virtual machine network health detection is configured on the network interface on each VM and is enabled by default.

■ Guest clustering is different from a highly available or clustered VM in that a guest cluster requires two or more VMs with a guest OS installed and configured for failover clustering.

■ A big advantage of using virtual machines is the ability to make efficient use of computer and network resources. You can put multiple VMs to work on a single host server to concentrate workloads, or you can distribute VMs among multiple hosts to spread out the workload.

■ Live migration is a Hyper-V feature that allows an administrator to move a virtual machine from one Hyper-V server to another while maintaining the availability of the VM.

■ Quick migration is a migration option available only between Hyper-V servers in a failover cluster. The advantage of quick migration is that it's available in Windows Server 2008 Hyper-V servers and later.

■ A storage migration is usually used when you simply need to move a VM's storage from one volume to another without actually moving the VM to another Hyper-V server. You can perform a storage migration while the VM is still running or when it's shut down.

■ Virtual machines can be exported and then imported to create one or more virtual machines. Starting in Windows Server 2012 R2, you can export a running VM.

■ A physical to virtual (P2V) migration converts a physical computer to a virtual machine. A virtual to virtual (V2V) migration converts a virtual machine from one vendor's format to another vendor's format.

Key Terms

Active Directory–detached cluster   A new cluster configuration option that allows deploying a failover cluster without needing Active Directory for network name management.

core cluster resources   Resources in a failover cluster that include the quorum resource, which is usually the witness disk or witness share; the IP address resource that provides the cluster IP address; and the network name resource that provides the cluster name.

drain on shutdown   A new feature in Windows Server 2012 R2 that drains roles automatically and live-migrates VMs to another cluster node before the Hyper-V server shuts down.

dynamic quorum   A feature that assigns a cluster node vote dynamically depending on whether the node is an active member of the cluster. If a node is no longer active in the cluster, its vote is removed.

dynamic witness   A quorum feature in Windows Server 2012 R2 in which the cluster determines whether to give the witness a quorum vote, based on whether there's an odd or even number of cluster nodes.

guest clustering   A clustering feature that requires two or more VMs with a guest OS installed and configured for failover clustering; the failover clustering occurs in the VM's guest OS.

highly available virtual machine   A failover cluster configuration in which two or more servers with the Hyper-V role are configured in a failover cluster, and the VMs are stored on shared storage. Also called a "clustered virtual machine."

live migration   An application or service installed on two or more servers participating in a failover cluster; also called a "clustered service."

physical to virtual (P2V) migration   A migration that converts a physical computer to a virtual machine.

quick migration   A migration option available only between Hyper-V servers in a failover cluster; usually results in a minute or more of downtime, depending on how much memory the VM uses.

scale-out file server   A highly available share option that provides the reliability of failover clusters and the load distribution of an NLB because client connections are distributed among all nodes in the cluster.

shared virtual hard disk   A virtual hard disk configured on a VM in a guest cluster that's used for shared storage among VMs in the guest cluster instead of traditional SAN storage.

shared-nothing live migration   A live migration done between Hyper-V servers that have no common storage.

split vote   A quorum situation in which no quorum can be reached.

storage migration   A VM migration process used to move a VM's storage from one volume to another without moving the VM to another Hyper-V server.

tie breaker for 50% node split   A situation in which a cluster is partitioned into equal numbers of nodes, and the dynamic quorum feature is used to change node votes to break the tie. *See also* dynamic quorum.

virtual machine monitoring   A new feature in Windows Server 2012 that allows monitoring resources, applications, and services running on highly available VMs. *See also* highly available virtual machine.

virtual machine network health detection   A failover cluster feature that automatically live migrates a virtual machine to another node if its network connection fails.

virtual to virtual (V2V) migration   A migration that converts a virtual machine from one vendor's format to another vendor's format.

Review Questions

1. Before you create a cluster, what task should you perform in the Failover Cluster Manager?

   a. Connect to the cluster.

   b. Live migrate one or more servers.

   c. Validate a configuration.

   d. Configure cluster quorum settings.

2. When you add a node to an existing cluster, which of the following can take place?

   a. Quorum settings are updated.

   b. A new iSCSI target is created.

   c. A new DNS record is created.

   d. An existing cluster node is disabled.

3. You need to perform maintenance on a cluster and must take the entire cluster offline. Which of the following is the best approach?

   a. For each node, right-click the node, point to More Actions, and click Stop Cluster Service.

   b. Right-click the cluster name, point to More Actions, and click Shut Down Cluster.

   c. Use the Windows shutdown procedure on each cluster node.

   d. Click the cluster name, and then click Close Connection in the Actions pane.

4. Which of the following is true about copying cluster roles?

   a. You should run the Copy Cluster Wizard from the source cluster.

   b. You need to install the clustered role on the nodes in the target cluster.

   c. Storage used by the current clustered role must remain online during the copy.

   d. Data is copied automatically to new cluster storage.

5. Which of the following is considered a core cluster resource?

   a. Cluster node

   b. Central processor

   c. CSV data disk

   d. Witness disk

6. Which cmdlet displays a list of all PowerShell cmdlets related to failover clusters?

   a. `Show-All -Commands FailoverCl*`

   b. `Get-Module -Name Failover`

   c. `Get-Command -Module FailoverClusters`

   d. `Show-Module -Display Cluster*`

7. Which of the following is *not* a quorum witness configuration option?

   a. Configure a local disk witness.

   b. Configure a file share witness.

   c. Do not configure a quorum witness.

   d. Configure a disk witness.

8. What new feature in Windows Server 2012 R2 attempts to prevent a split vote from occurring?

    a. Cluster shared volume

    b. Node majority quorum

    c. Witness share

    d. Dynamic witness

9. In Windows Server 2012 R2 failover clusters, why isn't it advisable to remove a node's vote manually?

    a. Dynamic quorum won't work.

    b. The node will go offline.

    c. Quorum can never be reached.

    d. The witness disk will be disabled.

10. You have six cluster nodes split evenly between SiteA and SiteB and no witness. The link between the sites goes down, leaving two separate cluster partitions. The SiteA cluster continues to function, and the SiteB cluster goes offline. All nodes are running Windows Server 2012 R2. Why did this problem occur?

    a. A node in SiteA was given an extra vote.

    b. A witness share was created in SiteB.

    c. Dynamic quorum removed a vote from SiteB.

    d. SiteA was assigned a disk witness automatically.

11. Why is it better to use cluster-aware roles instead of generic applications or services for high-availability applications?

    a. The cluster might not know whether the generic application failed.

    b. Generic services can't access witness disks.

    c. A client access point can't be configured for a generic application.

    d. Dynamic quorum is disabled on generic services.

12. Which configuration results in the best performance and reliability for a Hyper-V failover cluster with VMs stored on a file share?

    a. SMB share

    b. Scale-out file server

    c. NFS share

    d. DFS replication

13. You need to upgrade a two-node cluster that has Windows Server 2008 R2 servers. You have added two Windows Server 2012 R2 servers to the cluster and transferred the roles and resources to the new servers. What should you do next?

    a. Live-migrate the new servers.

    b. Restart the cluster service on the new servers.

    c. Put the cluster in maintenance mode.

    d. Evict the Windows Server 2008 R2 nodes.

14. You're configuring a new failover cluster but don't want to create new accounts in Active Directory. What should you do?

    a. In the New Cluster Wizard, choose the Active Directory–Detached option.

    b. Run the `New-Cluster` cmdlet with the `-AdministrativeAccessPoint` parameter.

    c. Don't join the cluster nodes to an Active Directory domain.

    d. Use the NETBios option for resolving cluster and role names.

15. Which of the following is a prerequisite for deploying a clustered storage space?

    a. All servers must be running Windows Server 2008 R2 or later.

    b. RAID must be enabled on the SAS disk controller.

    c. You need at least three unallocated disks.

    d. A mirror space requires Windows Server 2012 R2.

16. There are two methods for deploying a clustered storage space. Which of the following steps is used in both methods?

    a. Install the MPIO feature.

    b. Create storage spaces with File and Storage Services.

    c. Create a storage space in the Failover Cluster Manager.

    d. Verify that none of the disks are shown in Disk Management.

17. Which of the following is true about a clustered virtual machine? (Choose all that apply.)

    a. You need to have shared storage available to the VM's guest OS.

    b. You need two or more host computers running Hyper-V.

    c. All host computers should be members of the same domain.

    d. CSVs aren't recommended for shared storage.

18. If you're using cluster shared volumes for highly available VMs, which of the following is a likely path for storing the VM files?

    a. \\Server\SharedVM

    b. D:\

    c. C:\ClusterStorage

    d. FTP:\\Server

19. What new feature in Windows Server 2012 R2 causes a highly available VM to be live-migrated automatically if the host it's running on is shut down?

    a. Cluster shared volume

    b. Authoritative restore

    c. Dynamic witness

    d. Drain on shutdown

20. Which option on a VM should you select if you want to enable virtual machine network health detection?

    a. Protected network

    b. Hardware acceleration

    c. Virtual machine queue

    d. NIC teaming

7

Case Projects

Case Project 7-1: Choosing a Quorum Configuration

You're going to set up a high-availability share configuration with failover clusters. You have four sites, and three will have cluster nodes. Site1 has three cluster nodes, Site2 has four cluster nodes, Site3 has two cluster nodes, and Site4 has no cluster nodes. What quorum configuration should you choose for this configuration? Describe some new quorum features in Windows Server 2012 R2 that will make configuration easier and improve cluster availability.

Case Project 7-2: Setting Up a Guest Cluster

You have three Hyper-V servers, and you're currently running four VMs on each server for a total of 12 VMs. You want to be sure that if a Hyper-V server fails or you need to take one down for maintenance, the VMs will continue to run. Describe the configuration you plan to use, including options for shared storage.

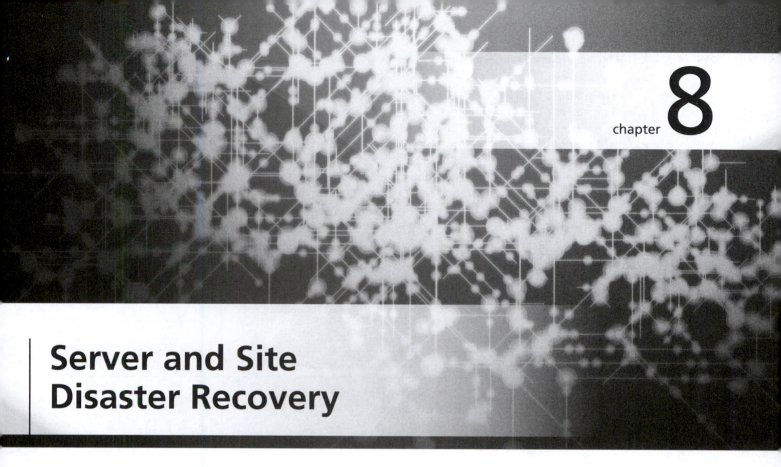

chapter 8

Server and Site Disaster Recovery

After reading this chapter and completing the exercises, you will be able to:

- Back up Windows servers
- Recover Windows servers
- Configure online backups
- Perform site-level disaster recovery
- Configure multisite clustering

The idea of a server going down or a hard disk crashing on a mission-critical server keeps IT administrators up at night, especially if they don't have procedures in place to recover from these events quickly. Even if procedures are in place, have they been tested, and will they work if they need to be carried out? Most IT administrators do have a plan for server or hardware component failures, but what about the failure of an entire data center caused by a natural or manmade disaster? This chapter covers some features in Windows Server 2012/R2 that can help IT administrators sleep better knowing their data centers can recover from almost any disaster. You learn about Windows Server Backup, techniques to recover Windows servers, Hyper-V Replica, and configuring a multisite failover cluster.

Backing Up Windows Servers

Table 8-1 lists what you need for the hands-on activities in this chapter.

Table 8-1   **Activity requirements**

Activity	Requirements	Notes
Activity 8-1: Installing Windows Server Backup	412Server1	
Activity 8-2: Performing a Scheduled Full Server Backup	412Server1	
Activity 8-3: Performing a One-Time Backup of Selected Files	412Server1	
Activity 8-4: Recovering a File	412Server1	
Activity 8-5: Using Windows Recovery Environment	412Server1	

© 2016 Cengage Learning®

In Chapters 6 and 7, you learned about failover clusters, which provide fault tolerance for network services. If a cluster node fails, the network services running on that node fail over to other servers in the cluster. So who needs backups, right? Well, sooner or later, you have to get the failed node back into service so that the cluster is fully operational. Of course, you're not likely to have all network services configured on cluster nodes, so server backups and restores are critical components of every network's disaster recovery toolkit. This section covers server backup procedures, including role-specific backups and online backups. It does no good to back up, however, if you don't know how to recover a server. This section describes server recovery procedures, including several methods to restore a server from backup, using system restore snapshots, and configuring the boot loader store.

Server Backup

A server backup is the cornerstone of any disaster recovery procedure. Backups are necessary for the following reasons, among others:

- *Server hardware failure*—The server can't start or no longer functions normally because of a hardware failure. In this case, you might need to perform a full restore on another server.

- *Disk failure*—Disk drives have failed and must be replaced, and their volumes must be restored from backup.

- *Volume corruption*—Volumes have become corrupted and can't be fixed. The physical disk might still be okay, but the affected volume must be restored from backup.

- *Deletion of files*—If a user deletes files that can't be recovered through other methods, such as the Previous Versions feature, files can be restored from backup.

- *Software failure*—A critical application or service no longer functions. This problem could be caused by an unsuccessful update or misconfiguration, among other reasons. The remedy can include restoring the OS volume plus the volume where the software is stored, doing a system restore, and restoring just the software configuration.

- *Theft or disaster*—Servers were stolen or damaged by an environmental disaster (such as fire or flood) and must be restored to new hardware.

Third-party backup programs with loads of features are available for backing up servers in an enterprise, but this book focuses on the Windows Server Backup feature. The following sections explain configuring Windows Server Backup to perform full and partial backups as well as restores. You also look at using online or cloud-based backups with Microsoft Azure.

Configuring Windows Server Backup

The Tools menu in Server Manager includes a link for Windows Server Backup, but when you click it, you get a message stating that Windows Server Backup isn't installed. You need to install it with the Add Roles and Features Wizard or the PowerShell cmdlet `Install-WindowsFeature Windows-Server-Backup`. After installing it, you can configure backups with the Windows Server Backup console, the `wbadmin` command-line program, or PowerShell cmdlets (listed later in Table 8-2).

Configuring Backup Permissions

Backups are a critical function in any network, and it's important to assign the task of backing up servers to a reliable and responsible person. However, not just any user can perform backups. By default, members of the local Administrators group, Backup Operators group, and Server Operators group can back up and restore files. Administrators have full rights to the server, and Backup Operators and Server Operators are given the following rights:

- Back up files and directories.
- Restore files and directories.
- Shut down the system.

If this list of rights doesn't suit your situation, you can assign each right separately. For example, you might want a user to be able to back up files but not restore them. You can assign the user only the "Back up files and directories" right without making the user a member of Backup Operators. You can assign rights to users or groups by editing the Local Security Policy or using group policies (in Computer Configuration, Policies, Windows Settings, Security Settings, Local Policies, User Rights Assignment).

Activity 8-1: Installing Windows Server Backup

Time Required: 10 minutes
Objective: Install Windows Server Backup.

Required Tools and Equipment: 412Server1
Description: In this activity, you install Windows Server Backup with PowerShell on 412Server1 and explore the Windows Server Backup console. You also explore the commands in PowerShell for performing Windows backup and restore procedures.

1. Start 412Server1, and log on as **Administrator**.

2. Open a PowerShell prompt. Type **Install-WindowsFeature Windows-Server-Backup** and press **Enter**. After the installation is finished, close the PowerShell window.

3. In Server Manager, click **Tools, Windows Server Backup.** In the left pane, click **Local Backup.** There's not much to see because you haven't performed a backup before (see Figure 8-1). Look in the Actions pane to see what tasks you can perform.

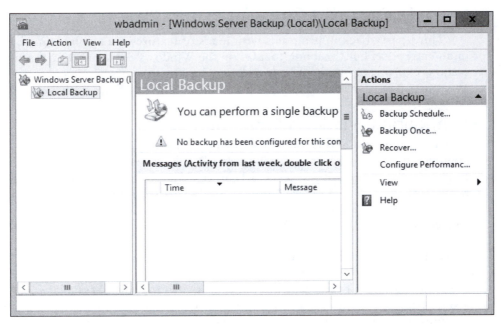

Figure 8-1   The Windows Server Backup console

4. Open a command prompt window. Type **wbadmin /?** and press **Enter** to see a list of options for performing backup and restore tasks with the wbadmin command. Close the command prompt window.

5. Open a PowerShell prompt. Type **Get-Command *-WB*** and press **Enter** to see the list of PowerShell cmdlets for performing backup and restore tasks. Close the PowerShell window.

6. Stay logged on to 412Server1 if you're continuing to the next activity.

After installing the Windows Server Backup feature, you can perform the following tasks in the Windows Server Backup console:

- Create a scheduled backup job.
- Perform a one-time backup.
- Perform a recovery operation.
- Configure backup performance.

Configuring Backups   Whether you're scheduling a backup to occur regularly or are performing a one-time backup, you can configure the backup with the following options:

- *Full backup*—Backs up all local volumes, including the system state. A full backup allows you to perform all types of server recoveries, discussed later in "Windows Server Recovery."

- *Custom backup*—Select which data you want to back up from the following options (see Figure 8-2):

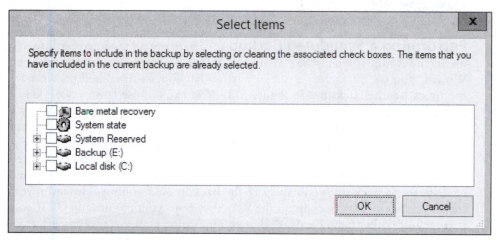

Figure 8-2   Selecting items to back up

- o Bare metal recovery: A **bare metal recovery** backs up the critical volumes needed to recover a server's OS; data volumes aren't included. It includes the system state, the system reserved volume, and the volume where Windows is stored.

- o System state: A **system state backup** backs up boot files, Windows system files, and the Registry. On a domain controller (DC), the system state includes the Active Directory database and the SYSVOL folder. On a cluster server, it includes the cluster configuration, and on a certificate server, the certificate store is included.

- o System Reserved: Backs up files on the system partition, which includes the boot loader files, the boot manager, system volume information, and Windows Recovery Environment (RE).

- o Individual volumes: Backs up only the volumes you select. If you choose this option, you can back up the entire volume or select specific files and folders. You can also exclude particular file types by file extension.

- *Specify the destination*—Specify a dedicated hard disk (scheduled backup only), volume, or shared folder. The destination drive or share should have at least one and a half times the free space required to store the backup and can be one of the following:

- o Shared folder: Both one-time backups and scheduled backups can be stored on a shared folder. A single backup can be stored on a remote folder; any existing backups in the same location are overwritten. If you want to keep multiple backups, you must use an internal or external hard drive.

- o DVD or other removable media: Only one-time backups can be stored on optical or removable media.

- o Internal hard drive: Both one-time backups and scheduled backups can be stored on an internal drive. For scheduled backups, you can dedicate the disk to backups, and it's no longer available for other purposes. (You see the disk in Disk Management but not File Explorer.) Dedicating a disk to backups is recommended but not required. You can use a volume on an internal disk to store backups along with other data. However, you can't store a bare metal recovery or full server backup on a critical volume (which is required to perform a bare metal recovery). If you use a volume to store the backup, it must be formatted as NTFS.

- o External hard drive: Similar to an internal hard drive, but an external drive has the advantage of being easily rotated with other drives, and backups can be stored off-site for disaster recovery.

Other backup destination considerations: First, you can use a virtual hard disk as a backup destination, but it shouldn't be stored on a critical volume. Second, you can't do a bare metal recovery from a backup stored on a dynamic disk. Third, tape drives aren't supported as a backup destination.

Performing a Scheduled Backup   To perform a **scheduled backup,** click Backup Schedule in the Actions pane of the Windows Server Backup console to start the Backup Schedule Wizard. You need to select a full or custom backup, as discussed previously, and then specify the times for the backup (see Figure 8-3). You can choose from once a day or multiple times throughout the day. In either case, you select the time the backup runs. By default, it runs at 9:00 p.m. once per day. Next, you specify the destination for the backup, as described previously. You can specify a hard disk that's dedicated for backups. External drives are preferable because you can remove them easily and store backups off-site. If you choose to dedicate a drive, it's formatted, and any existing volumes and data on the drive are deleted. If you don't have a drive to dedicate to backups, you can store the backup on a volume. However, you can't store a full server or system state backup on the Windows boot volume (usually C). If you choose a volume that includes other data, be aware that volume performance is severely affected when the backup is in progress. You can also store the backup on a network share, but only a single backup can be stored on a share, and any subsequent backups overwrite existing backups. Finally, you confirm the scheduled backup, and the backup begins at the scheduled time each day.

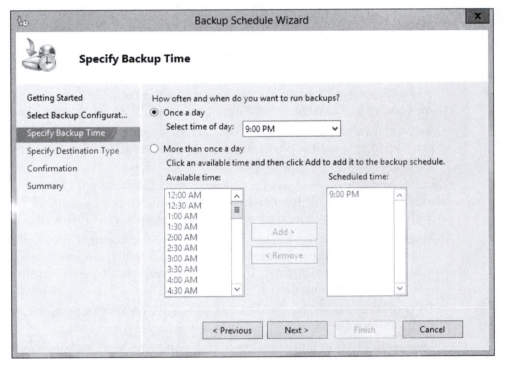

Figure 8-3   Scheduling a backup

You can have only one scheduled backup. If you click Backup Schedule after a scheduled backup has already been created, you're prompted to modify the existing scheduled backup or stop it. If you stop it and you're using a dedicated disk, the disk is released for normal use, and a drive letter is assigned to it.

Performing a One-Time Backup   A **one-time backup** creates a backup to a local volume or a share. The backup begins immediately, and the progress is shown in the Windows Server Backup console. You can close the console, and the backup continues to run. To configure a one-time backup, click Backup Once in the Actions pane to start the Backup Once Wizard. If you have any existing scheduled backups, you have the option to do the one-time backup using the options from one of the scheduled backups; otherwise, you select options as you do when creating a scheduled backup.

One-time backups shouldn't be used as the sole method of backing up your server. You should always have at least one regularly scheduled backup, and then use a one-time backup for particular situations, such as the following:

- Immediately before a software or hardware upgrade.

- Periodically, to store a full backup off-site, such as a once per month archival backup.

- To back up a volume not included in the scheduled backup.

- To test the backup and restore process. You might want to verify that backups are working by backing up a volume and restoring it.

Configuring Backup Performance   Backup performance can be optimized for backups of entire volumes. Windows uses the Volume Shadow Copy Service (VSS) to perform full volume backups. VSS doesn't copy individual files; it copies the volume block by block, essentially making a mirror image of the volume. Windows Server Backup uses this image to create the backup. You can choose from the following options (shown in Figure 8-4):

Figure 8-4   Optimizing backup performance

- *Normal backup performance*—This default setting is used with all backup types. The time needed to do the backup is proportional to the amount of data being backed up. The full contents of the source volume are transferred, but if a backup already exists on the destination, only the space required by the changed blocks is used.

- *Faster backup performance*—This option results in a **differential backup**, in which only the blocks that have changed are transferred to the destination if there's an existing backup. Volumes used by disk-intensive applications shouldn't use this option because write performance on the source volume is decreased.

- *Custom*—You can choose a full backup or differential backup for each volume.

Even if you choose a differential backup option, Windows Server Backup performs a full backup after 14 incremental backups have occurred or if more than 14 days have passed since the last full backup.

Configuring the Volume Shadow Copy Service   To configure the Volume Shadow Copy Service used for full volume backups, you can use the vssadmin command-line program. You can create and delete shadow copies and list existing shadow copies. In addition, you can revert a volume to an existing shadow, which overwrites the volume on a previously created shadow copy. The revert operation requires that no files be open on the volume to be reverted. To see the full list of vssadmin commands (see Figure 8-5), enter vssadmin /? at an elevated command prompt.

```
C:\Users\Administrator>vssadmin /?
vssadmin 1.1 - Volume Shadow Copy Service administrative command-line tool
(C) Copyright 2001-2013 Microsoft Corp.

---- Commands Supported ----

Add ShadowStorage      - Add a new volume shadow copy storage association
Create Shadow          - Create a new volume shadow copy
Delete Shadows         - Delete volume shadow copies
Delete ShadowStorage   - Delete volume shadow copy storage associations
List Providers         - List registered volume shadow copy providers
List Shadows           - List existing volume shadow copies
List ShadowStorage     - List volume shadow copy storage associations
List Volumes           - List volumes eligible for shadow copies
List Writers           - List subscribed volume shadow copy writers
Resize ShadowStorage   - Resize a volume shadow copy storage association
Revert Shadow          - Revert a volume to a shadow copy
Query Reverts          - Query the progress of in-progress revert operations.
```

Figure 8-5   The list of vssadmin commands

Activity 8-2: Performing a Scheduled Full Server Backup

Time Required: 20 minutes
Objective: Perform a scheduled full server backup.

Required Tools and Equipment: 412Server1
Description: In this activity, you perform a scheduled full server backup of 412Server1 to a dedicated backup disk. This activity requires the second disk in 412Server1 to be unallocated.

1. Start 412Server1, and log on as **Administrator**, if necessary. In Server Manager, click **Tools**, **Windows Server Backup**, if necessary.

2. In the Actions pane, click **Backup Schedule**. In the Getting Started window, click **Next**.

3. In the Select Backup Configuration window, accept the default option **Full server (recommended)**, and then click **Next**.

4. In the Specify Backup Time window, review the options for scheduling the backup. You can perform the backup once per day or more than once per day, but you don't have any options for specific days of the week. Accept the default option **Once a day**, and select a time close to the current time on your computer so that the backup runs as soon as possible. Click **Next**.

5. In the Specify Destination Type window, accept the default option **Back up to a hard disk that is dedicated for backups (recommended)**, and click then **Next**.

6. In the Select Destination Disk window, only external disks are shown by default. Click **Show All Available Disks**. In the Show All Available Disks dialog box, click the **Disk 1** check box, and then click **OK**.

7. In the Select Destination Disk window, click the check box next to **Disk 1**, and then click **Next**. You see a Windows Server Backup message stating that the disk will be formatted and all volumes and data will be erased. Click **Yes**.

8. In the Confirmation window, review the options you have selected, and click **Finish**. You see a message stating that the disk is being formatted and then a message stating when the backup will occur. Click **Close**.

9. While you're waiting for the backup to begin, click **Configure Performance Settings** in the Actions pane.

10. In the Optimize Backup Performance dialog box, review the options. If you want Windows Server Backup to perform differential backups on subsequent backup runs, you click the "Faster backup performance" option button. You can also click the Custom option button and choose the performance method (full or differential backup) for each volume. For now, click **Cancel**.

11. If you want to begin the full backup, wait until the backup starts, and you see its status in the middle pane of the Windows Server Backup console. Continue to the next activity immediately, where you stop the scheduled backup.

Activity 8-3: Performing a One-Time Backup of Selected Files

Time Required: 10 minutes
Objective: Perform a one-time backup of selected files.

Required Tools and Equipment: 412Server1
Description: In this activity, you stop the scheduled backup, and then perform a one-time backup of selected files on 412Server1.

1. On 412Server1, log on as **Administrator**, if necessary. In Server Manager, click **Tools**, **Windows Server Backup**, if necessary.

2. Click **Backup Schedule** in the Actions pane. In the Modify Scheduled Backup Settings window, click the **Stop backup** option button, and then click **Next**.

3. The Confirmation window has a message stating that the disk will be released for normal use. Click **Finish**. Click **Yes** when prompted, if you're sure you want to stop the scheduled backup. Click **Close**.

4. In the Actions pane, click **Backup Once**. In the Backup Options window, you see that you can base the one-time backup on the existing scheduled backup, if one exists. Accept the default option **Different options**, and then click **Next**.

5. In the Select Backup Configuration window, click the **Custom** option button, and then click **Next**.

6. In the Select Items for Backup window, click **Add Items**. Click to expand **Local disk (C:)**, and click the **DocShare1** check box, a folder you created in Chapter 4. You're backing up just a single folder so that the restore is easy to do. Click **OK** and then **Next**.

7. In the Specify Destination Type window, accept the default option **Local drives** (with a one-time backup, there's no option for using a dedicated disk), and then click **Next**.

8. In the Select Backup Destination window, click the **Backup destination** list arrow, and click the drive with **E:** assigned to it. (The drive letter might be different on your system, but the volume name includes the date and time of the scheduled backup you just stopped.) Click **Next**.

9. In the Confirmation window, click **Backup** to start the backup. You see its status in the Windows Server Backup Progress window. When the backup is finished, click **Close**.

10. Open File Explorer, and click the **E:** drive (or the drive letter of the backup destination). Double-click the **WindowsImageBackup** folder, and then double-click the **412Server1** folder. You see a number of folders including the folder Backup *date and time* (with *date and time* representing the date and time of the backup you created). Double-click the folder to see a virtual disk and several XML documents. The virtual disk contains the files in the backup. Close File Explorer.

11. Stay logged on to 412Server1 if you're continuing to the next activity.

Backing Up Server Roles   Most server role data is stored in locations that are backed up when you perform a backup containing the system state, such as a system state or full server backup. If you restore the system state, data associated with the roles installed on the server is restored, too. A system state backup contains the following data, depending on which roles and features are installed:

- The Registry
- Boot files and Windows system files
- Component Services Class registration database
- Performance counter data
- Local users and groups
- Active Directory and SYSVOL
- Cluster configuration database
- Certificate Services database
- DFS namespace configuration
- Web Server role settings

In addition, some roles, features, applications, and services register themselves with Windows Server Backup so that you can recover application-specific data without having to do a more extensive recovery. When you perform a server recovery (discussed later in "Windows Server Recovery"), applications that have registered with Windows Server Backup are listed in the Select Application window (see Figure 8-6), and you have the option to restore only that application's data.

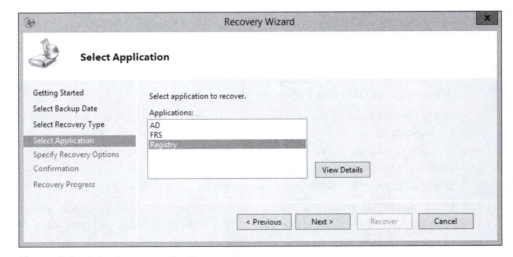

Figure 8-6   Selecting an application to restore

Many server roles and features, such as DNS and DHCP, maintain a separate data store. Backing up and restoring the data associated with these roles was discussed in the *MCSA Guide to Installing and Configuring Microsoft Windows Server 2012/R2, Exam 70-410*, and *MCSA Guide to Administering Microsoft Windows Server 2012/R2, Exam 70-411*, books (Cengage Learning, 2015). The data for these roles is also backed up in a full server backup or a backup that includes the C:\Windows folder.

Performing Backups from the Command Line Table 8-2 lists many PowerShell cmdlets you can use for Windows Server Backup operations. For detailed help and examples of using each cmdlet, type Get-Help *cmdletname* -detailed at a PowerShell prompt.

Table 8-2 **PowerShell cmdlets for Windows Server Backup**

Cmdlet	Description
Add-WBBackupTarget	Adds a backup storage location to the backup policy
Add-WBBareMetalRecovery	Adds to the backup policy items needed to perform a bare metal recovery
Add-WBSystemState	Adds to the backup policy items needed to perform a system state recovery
Add-WBVolume	Adds a volume to the list of items to be backed up
Get-WBBackupSet	Lists backups created for a server
Get-WBJob	Shows the backup job currently in operation
Get-WBPolicy	Gets the current backup policy
New-WBPolicy	Creates a new backup policy
Set-WBPolicy	Sets the backup policy used for scheduled backups
Set-WBSchedule	Sets the schedule for the backup policy
Start-WBBackup	Starts a one-time backup
Get-Command *-WB*	Lists all the Windows Backup Server PowerShell cmdlets

© 2016 Cengage Learning®

Table 8-3 lists many of the wbadmin commands you can use for Windows Server Backup operations. For a complete list of commands and examples of using them, see *http://technet.microsoft.com/en-us/library/cc742130.aspx*.

Table 8-3 **Wbadmin commands for Windows Server Backup**

Command	Description
wbadmin enable backup	Enables and configures a scheduled backup
wbadmin disable backup	Disables a scheduled backup
wbadmin start backup	Starts a one-time backup
wbadmin get items	Lists the items in a backup
wbadmin start recovery	Runs a recovery operation
wbadmin start systemstaterecovery	Runs a system state recovery operation
wbadmin start systemstatebackup	Runs a system state backup
wbadmin start sysrecovery	Starts a full server backup recovery
wbadmin /?	Lists all wbadmin commands

© 2016 Cengage Learning®

Windows Server Recovery

The reason you back up a server is so that you can recover lost data. Server recovery is a task you hope you never have to perform, but if you maintain a server for any length of time, a recovery of some sort is inevitable. Server recovery can mean different things, from recovery of a single file or folder to a full server restore. This section covers the following server recovery procedures:

- Recovering files, folders, and volumes
- System state recovery
- Bare metal recovery
- Windows Recovery Environment
- Configuring boot configuration data

Recovering Files, Folders, and Volumes

Windows Server Backup can recover single files, selected files and folders, or entire volumes. If you find you have to restore single files often because of accidental deletion or to recover a previous version of a file, you should enable the Shadow Copies feature on the volumes storing these documents. This feature enables users to restore files themselves in the Previous Versions tab of a shared or local folder's Properties dialog box. (You learned about this feature when you studied the objectives of the Installing and Configuring Windows Server 2012, 70-410, exam.)

Of course, Shadow Copies isn't always enabled on the volumes containing files that might need to be recovered; in that case, you have to turn to a backup of the volume. In addition, sometimes you need to restore an entire volume because of file system corruption or a failed drive. To recover a file or folder with Windows Server Backup, follow the procedure in Activity 8-4. To recover a file or folder at the command line, you can use the wbadmin start recovery command or the Start-WBFileRecovery PowerShell cmdlet. In both cases, you need to know the backup set's version identifier and the path of the file to recover. The following is an example of using wbadmin to recover the D:\Docs\Myfile.txt file from a backup with the version identifier 10/09/2014-21:00:

```
wbadmin start recovery –version:10/09/2014-2100 –itemType:File
  –items:D:\Docs\Myfile.txt
```

Using PowerShell, the same file recovery looks similar. In this example, the $Backup variable contains the backup set information:

```
Start-WBFileRecovery –Backupset $Backup
  –FilePathToRecover D:\Docs\Myfile.txt
```

Activity 8-4: Recovering a File

Time Required: 10 minutes
Objective: Recover a file from backup.

Required Tools and Equipment: 412Server1
Description: In this activity, you delete one of the files you backed up earlier and then recover it.

1. On 412Server1, log on as **Administrator**, if necessary. Open File Explorer, and delete **C:\DocShare1\mydoc.txt**. Leave File Explorer open.

2. In Server Manager, click **Tools, Windows Server Backup,** if necessary. Click **Recover** in the Actions pane. In the Getting Started window, click **Next**.

3. In the Select Backup Date window, accept the default backup because you have only one backup, and then click **Next**.

4. In the Select Recovery Type window, accept the default option **Files and folders.** Review the other recovery types, most of which are grayed out because you don't have a suitable backup to perform them (see Figure 8-7). Click **Next.**

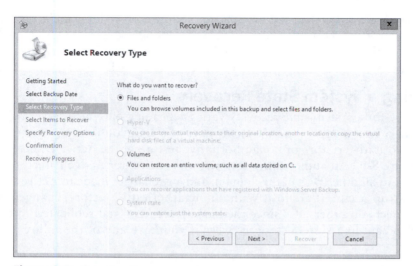

Figure 8-7   Selecting the recovery type

5. In the Select Items to Recover window, click to expand **412Server1** and **Local disk (C:)**, and click **DocShare1.** In the right pane, click `mydoc.txt`, and then click **Next.**

6. In the Specify Recovery Options window, you can recover the file to the original location or a new location. You also have the option to create a copy of the file if the original file exists, and you can choose to restore permissions to the file being recovered (see Figure 8-8). Accept the default options, and then click **Next.**

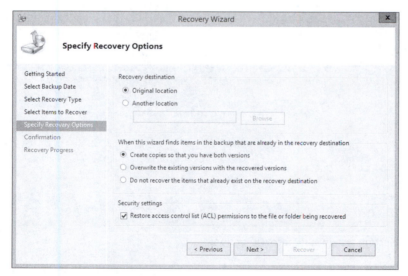

Figure 8-8   Specifying recovery options

7. In the Confirmation window, click **Recover**. In the Recovery Progress window, you see the progress of the recovery. After the recovery is finished, click **Close**.

8. In File Explorer, verify that the file has been recovered, and then close this window. Stay logged on to 412Server1 if you're continuing to the next activity.

If you need to restore an entire volume, you follow a procedure similar to restoring a single file or folder. You can't, however, do a volume recovery on a volume containing OS components. To perform a volume recovery involving OS components, you should perform a system state recovery or use Windows Recovery Environment (Windows RE) to do a bare metal recovery.

Performing a System State Recovery

The procedure for a system state recovery varies depending on which server roles are installed. In particular, if you're restoring the system state of a DC, you need to decide whether to perform an authoritative restore or nonauthoritative restore of the Active Directory database and files (see Figure 8-9). An **authoritative restore** means that after Active Directory is restored, the DC replicates to all other DCs in the domain, and any changes made to Active Directory objects since the backup occurred are lost. With a **nonauthoritative restore**, changes made to Active Directory objects on other DCs since the backup are kept and replicated to the server being restored. You can do a system state recovery if you have any of the following backup types available:

- System state
- Bare metal recovery
- Full server

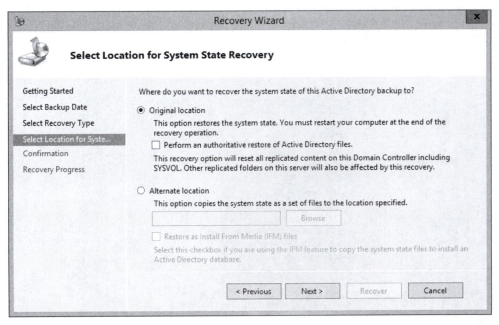

Figure 8-9   Selecting system state recovery options

You can also restore the system state as a set of files to another location without affecting the current OS installation. If you restore the system state to the original location, the server restarts after the system state recovery is completed.

Performing a Bare Metal Recovery

A bare metal recovery (BMR) restores a server from a full server backup. You perform this task when your server has suffered catastrophic failure and can't boot to Windows. To do it, you need to be able to boot to the Windows installation medium. If you're restoring a physical server, you need an installation medium, such as a DVD, and if you're restoring a virtual machine, you can use an ISO file of the installation medium. To do a BMR, follow these steps:

1. Insert the installation medium into the system's DVD drive, or configure a VM's DVD drive to point to an ISO file.

2. Boot the system you want to restore to from the installation medium. The Windows Setup process starts.

3. Confirm the language options, and click "Repair your computer" to start Windows Recovery Environment.

4. You see a menu with the following options: Continue (exits Windows RE and attempts to reboot the system), Troubleshoot (displays a menu where you can specify a system image recovery or open a command prompt window), and Turn off your PC (shuts down the computer). Select the Troubleshoot option, and then select System Image Recovery.

5. When prompted to select an OS to recover, choose Windows Server 2012 R2 (or another suitable OS).

6. Windows RE scans your system for a suitable backup. You're prompted to choose from the latest available system image (see Figure 8-10) or select a different system image, such as one on a share.

8

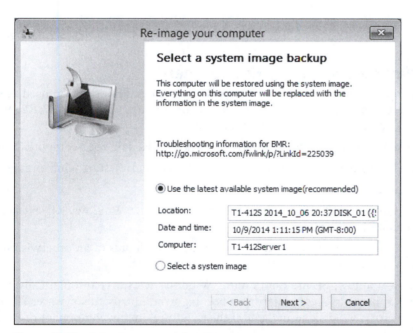

Figure 8-10   Selecting a system image to restore

7. Next, you choose restore options. You can format and repartition disks, and you can exclude disks from the restore operation. For example, you might want to exclude data disks if you want only the Windows system disk to be restored (see Figure 8-11). If necessary, you can load drivers for the disk controller if the disk isn't recognized. If you click the Advanced button, you see options to restart the computer and check for disk errors. (Both options are enabled by default.)

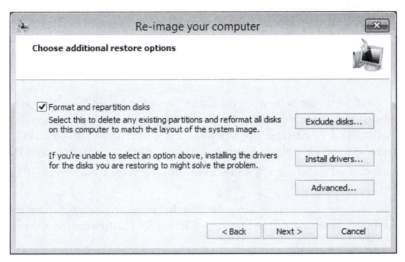

Figure 8-11   Selecting restore options

8. Finally, you have the option to review your choices and begin the restore procedure.

Using Windows Recovery Environment

Windows Recovery Environment (Windows RE) is a special boot option used to solve common Windows startup problems. It's a standard part of Windows Server 2012/R2, Windows 8/8.1, and later OSs and can be started in the following ways:

- Boot to Windows installation media, and click the "Repair your computer" option.
- On the Charms bar, click Settings, Power, and then click Restart while pressing the Shift key.
- Type shutdown /r /o at a command prompt.
- If Windows Server 2012/R2 fails to start twice in a row, Windows RE starts automatically on the second failed attempt.
- If there are two unexpected shutdowns within two minutes of an otherwise successful boot, Windows RE starts automatically on the second restart.
- If there's a Windows Secure Boot failure, Windows RE starts automatically. **Secure Boot** is a feature that prevents a computer from booting from untrusted software. The boot software is checked for a valid signature, and if the signature on any component of the boot software is invalid, the computer boots to Windows RE.

Windows RE includes the following tools:

- *Push-button reset*—Available in Windows 8 and later (but not in Windows Server), this option allows repairing a Windows system without a backup. Options include "Refresh your PC," which performs a factory image install while keeping accounts, data, apps, and customizations, and "Reset your PC," which resets the computer to its original state.
- *System Image Recovery*—Available in Windows Server 2012/R2, this option restores the entire server or just the OS disk from a full server backup.

- *Command prompt*—Provides access to advanced troubleshooting tools for recovering from boot failures, including the following:

  o `bcdedit`: Allows displaying and editing the boot configuration data (BCD) store. For example, you can use it to ensure that Windows boots to Safe Mode on the next restart. In Windows Server 2003 and earlier, you use the `bootcfg` command to modify the `boot.ini` file.

  o `bcdboot`: Configures or repairs the system partition; can also configure Windows to boot to a virtual hard disk or repair the system partition on a virtual disk.

  o `bootrec`: Allows you to repair the master boot record (MBR), the boot sector, and the BCD store; also used to solve "Bootmgr is Missing" errors.

  o `diskpart`: Enables you to perform advanced disk partitioning and management tasks.

  o `bootsect`: Updates the MBR code on hard disk partitions to switch between BOOTMGR and NTLDR and allows restoring the boot sector.

  o `sfc`: Verifies the versions of protected system files. If a protected file has been overwritten, this tool (which stands for "system file checker") retrieves the original version from \Windows\System32\dllcache. To check system files, use `sfc /scannow`.

- *Startup Settings*—You can change how Windows attempts to start. If you click Restart, you see a list of startup options and then the Advanced Boot Options menu (see Figure 8-12). They're the same boot options displayed when you press F8 while booting Windows.

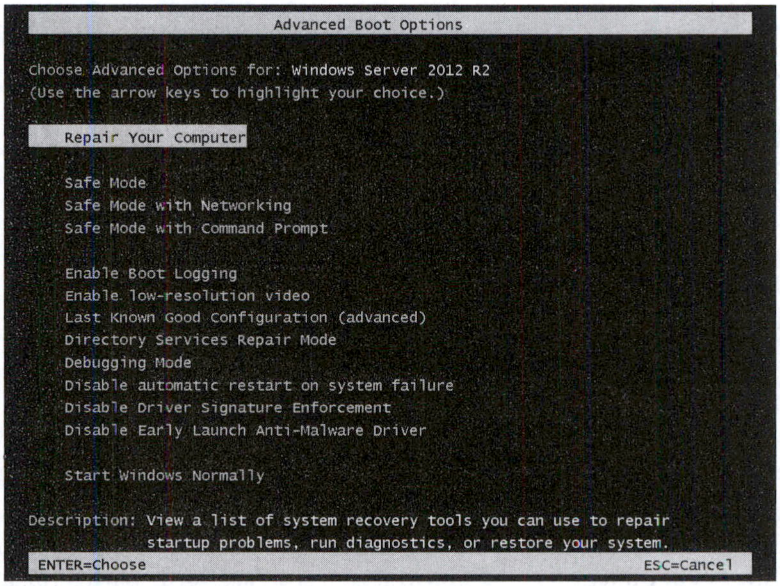

Figure 8-12   The Advanced Boot Options menu

Using Advanced Boot Options

You can access the Advanced Boot Options menu from Startup Settings in Windows RE or by pressing F8 when Windows begins to boot. The following list describes the options in this menu:

- *Safe Mode*—Starts Windows with the minimal number of drivers to boot the OS; only basic video resolution is available. Use this option if Windows won't start normally, and you need to stop a service or uninstall a driver to get Windows to boot correctly.

- *Safe Mode with Networking*—Adds network drives to the regular Safe Mode boot option. Use this option if you need to access a network share or the Internet to install a driver or gain access to other troubleshooting tools.

- *Safe Mode with Command Prompt*—Allows access only to the command prompt and Windows PowerShell. There's no GUI environment, and only minimal drivers and services are started.

- *Enable Boot Logging*—Creates a log file name `ntbtlog.txt` containing a list of drivers that started during the boot process.

- *Enable low-resolution video*—Boots normally except for low video resolution and refresh rate settings; allows troubleshooting video problems.

- *Last Known Good Configuration*—Loads the last set of Registry entries and drivers that allowed a successful boot and user logon. Use this option if you just installed a new driver or made changes to the Registry, and the computer fails to boot the next time it's restarted.

- *Directory Services Repair Mode*—Used to boot the computer to allow restoring Active Directory. You need the Directory Services Repair Mode (DSRM) password to use this option.

- *Debugging Mode*—Enables an advanced debug mode intended for Windows developers.

- *Disable automatic restart on system failure*—By default, Windows attempts to restart after a system crash or a boot failure. Use this option if Windows is stuck in a continuous loop of attempting to restart.

- *Disable Driver Signature Enforcement*—Disables the requirement that Windows drivers must be signed.

- *Disable Early Launch Anti-Malware Driver*—Select this option if a startup problem might be related to a recent installation of or change to antimalware software.

- *Start Windows Normally*—Performs a normal boot.

Activity 8-5: Using Windows Recovery Environment

Time Required: 10 minutes
Objective: Start Windows in Windows RE.

Required Tools and Equipment: 412Server1
Description: In this activity, you restart 412Server1 so that it enters Windows RE and explore some Windows RE options.

1. On 412Server1, log on as **Administrator**, if necessary. Open a command prompt window, and then type **shutdown /r /o** and press **Enter**.

2. 412Server1 shuts down within a minute and restarts in Windows RE. You see a menu with the options to continue and boot to Windows Server 2012 R2, use a device, turn off the computer, or troubleshoot. Click **Troubleshoot** to open the Advanced options window.

3. In the Advanced options window, you see three choices: System Image Recovery, Command Prompt, and Startup Settings. Click **Command Prompt**. You must choose an account to log on with to continue. Click **Administrator**. Type **Password01** when prompted, and click **Continue**.

4. There's no help command to see the available commands, but type **dir *.exe** and press **Enter** to see a list of executable programs in the C:\Windows\System32 folder. There are quite a few commands, including those discussed in the preceding section: `bcdboot.exe`, `bcdedit.exe`, `bootrec.exe`, `diskpart.exe`, and `sfc.exe`.

5. Type **sfc /scannow** and press **Enter** to run the system file checker. You see a message indicating that a system repair is pending because you started the system in Windows RE. Type **exit** and press **Enter** to return to the main Windows RE window.

6. Click **Troubleshoot** and then **Startup Settings**. You see the startup options (the same ones displayed if you press F8 during the Windows boot). Click **Restart** to see the Advanced Boot Options menu shown earlier in Figure 8-12.

7. Using the arrow keys, select **Enable Boot Logging** and press **Enter**. After Windows boots, log on as **Administrator**.

8. Open File Explorer, navigate to **C:\Windows**, and double-click the **ntbtlog** file to see its contents in Notepad. You see a list of files that Windows loads at boot time and a list of files that aren't loaded. To troubleshoot a Windows boot that hangs, you can start Windows by using Enable Boot Logging, and then start Windows in Safe Mode and examine the ntbtlog file to see that the last file that was loaded successfully. Close ntbtlog and any open windows.

9. Shut down 412Server1.

Configuring the Boot Configuration Data Store

The **boot configuration data (BCD) store** contains settings that determine how a Windows system boots. It's usually on the reserved partition created when you install Windows. In versions of Windows before Windows Server 2008 and Vista, the boot configuration was stored as plain text in the boot.ini file and could be changed easily with a text editor, such as Notepad. Now it's a binary file that requires a program such as bcdedit.exe or bcdboot.exe to view and modify it.

The BCD store contains entries describing each installed OS that can be started by the Windows boot loader. Each entry is identified with a globally unique identifier (GUID) that must be referenced if you want to change an entry. The main tool for working with the BCD store is bcdedit.exe, which you can run from a command prompt with administrator privileges. Most bcdedit commands follow the format bcdedit /*optionname*. You can get more information on using these commands by adding /? at the end. For example, bcdedit /enum /? shows you detailed help for the /enum option. The following list describes some options you can specify and tasks you can perform with bcdedit.exe; for a complete list of options, enter bcdedit /? at a command prompt.

- /enum—Lists the boot entries. It's the default option, so simply typing bcdedit at a command prompt produces the same result as bcdedit /enum. Adding /v to the command shows the output in verbose mode. Figure 8-13 shows the output of the bcdedit /enum command, which is in two sections. The first section is the Windows Boot Manager, the program loaded by the computer's BIOS that reads the BCD store to see which OSs are installed and available to boot. The second section is the Windows Boot Loader, which describes the installed OS and where it's located. There's a boot loader section for each installed OS.

```
C:\Users\Administrator>bcdedit /enum

Windows Boot Manager
--------------------
identifier              {bootmgr}
device                  partition=\Device\HarddiskVolume4
description             Windows Boot Manager
locale                  en-US
inherit                 {globalsettings}
bootshutdowndisabled    Yes
default                 {current}
resumeobject            {8f80e408-1dcb-11e3-a6f5-e7eb3ff17813}
displayorder            {current}
toolsdisplayorder       {memdiag}
timeout                 30

Windows Boot Loader
-------------------
identifier              {current}
device                  partition=C:
path                    \Windows\system32\winload.exe
description             Windows Server 2012 R2
locale                  en-US
inherit                 {bootloadersettings}
recoverysequence        {8f80e40a-1dcb-11e3-a6f5-e7eb3ff17813}
recoveryenabled         Yes
allowedinmemorysettings 0x15000075
osdevice                partition=C:
systemroot              \Windows
resumeobject            {8f80e408-1dcb-11e3-a6f5-e7eb3ff17813}
nx                      OptOut

C:\Users\Administrator>
```

Figure 8-13 Output of the bcdedit /enum command

- /copy—Creates a copy of a boot entry. Use bcdedit /enum to list the boot entries, and then use bcdedit /copy to copy one with the GUID.

- /create—Creates a new boot entry.

- /delete—Deletes a boot entry.

- /export—Exports the BCD store to a file that can be used as a backup.

- /import—Imports the BCD store from a file created by using the /export option.

- /set—Sets a value for a BCD store entry. For example, you can set the OS device from a physical volume to a virtual disk with bcdedit /set {GUID} osdevice vhd= D:\virtual\vdisk.vhd. Replace GUID with the actual GUID of the entry, and specify the actual path to the virtual disk. You can also use /set to force Windows to start in a particular mode. For example, bcdedit /set {default} /safeboot minimal configures the default boot entry to start in Safe Mode with Command Prompt.

- /default—Sets the default boot entry after the timeout expires. If there are multiple boot entries and you want to change the default OS that boots, do so with bcdedit /default {GUID}.

- /timeout—Sets the default timeout. If there are multiple boot entries, the boot manager displays the OSs you can start. If none is chosen within the timeout period, the boot manager starts the default entry.

With the bcdboot command, you can manage files related to the boot process that are stored on the system partition, including the BCD store. For example, if an entry is missing from the boot menu, you can use bcdboot to restore it. In addition, if files on the system partition have been damaged, you can use bcdboot to repair them. Another common use of bcdboot is to configure Windows to boot to a virtual disk. Following are some examples of using bcdboot:

- bcdboot E:\Windows—Initializes the system partition with BCD files from the E:\Windows folder and creates a boot entry in the BCD store for the OS in E:\Windows.

- bcdboot C:\Windows /s V:—Copies BCD files from the C:\Windows folder to the system partition on the V drive. The V drive can be a physical drive containing a Windows OS from another computer or a mounted virtual disk containing a Windows OS. You can use this command to repair the system partition on a disk from another computer or on a virtual disk from a VM.

- bcdboot C:\Windows /l ja-jp—Sets the locale in the BCD store to Japanese.

Configuring Online Backups

Managing backups and backup media can be a chore, but **Microsoft Azure Backup** can help ease the task of performing regular backups. With Microsoft Azure Backup, backups are stored in the cloud and can be accessed from anywhere you have an Internet connection. Backups made with Azure are compressed and encrypted, making them both efficient and safe. To use Microsoft Azure Backup, you need to be aware of the following:

- You need at least Windows Server 2012.

- You can't do system state, bare metal, or OS volume recoveries. Only file and folder recoveries are possible. You can back up and restore an entire data volume but not the OS volume.

- You can't back up BitLocker-encrypted volumes. If you want to back up an encrypted volume, you must unlock it first.

- The volume you want to back up must be online and formatted with NTFS.

- The volume you want to back up must be a fixed disk; removable storage, such as USB flash drives, can't be backed up with Microsoft Azure Backup, but you can back them up with Windows Server Backup.

- You must download and install the Microsoft Azure Backup agent on each server you want to back up.

- Windows Server Backup should be installed. The Microsoft Azure Backup agent integrates with the Windows Server Backup console, but it also has a stand-alone console.

- You must set up a Microsoft Azure Backup account.

- Microsoft Azure Backup is a fee-based subscription service, but you can sign up for a one-month free trial.

- You need a reliable Internet connection.

Here are the basic steps for using Microsoft Azure Backup:

1. Verify that Windows Server Backup is installed.

2. Set up a Microsoft Azure Backup account. If you already have a Microsoft Live Login account, you can use it instead.

3. Download and install the Microsoft Azure Backup agent.

4. Register the server with the Azure service.

5. Configure a backup schedule.

6. Run the backup.

 Because Microsoft Azure is an online service, the steps and look of the interface might change. The steps in this section are accurate as of this writing.

Installing Microsoft Azure Backup

To install Microsoft Azure Backup, go to the Azure Web page at *http://azure.microsoft.com*. You have the option of signing up for a free trial account, which gives you 30 days of use and some credit toward Azure services, including the online backup service. As of this writing, the credit is $200. During the sign-up process, you're required to enter your cell phone number to get a verification code. After you enter the code, you're prompted to enter credit card information, which is used only if you exceed the trial amount of credit.

After you're signed up with Azure, you need to create a backup vault. To do so, log on to your Azure account, click Storage, Data Services, Recovery Services, Backup Vault, and then Quick Create. Enter a name for the backup vault and a region that's close to your location (see Figure 8-14), and then click Create Vault. Azure creates your backup vault account.

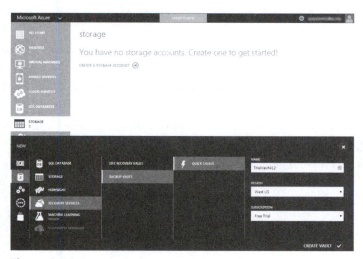

Figure 8-14   Creating a backup vault

Microsoft changed the name of Windows Azure to Microsoft Azure in 2014 and the name of the backup service from Windows Azure Online Backup to Microsoft Azure Backup. However, you might still see the name Windows Azure Online Backup on certification test questions.

After the vault is created, click All Items in the left pane, and then click the new backup vault. From there, you can download and install the Microsoft Azure Backup agent, but first, you need to download vault credentials that are used when installing the agent by clicking the "Download vault credentials" link. After the credentials are downloaded, click the link under Download Azure Backup Agent (see Figure 8-15). After the agent is downloaded, double-click the downloaded file to begin the installation. Here are the steps for installing the agent:

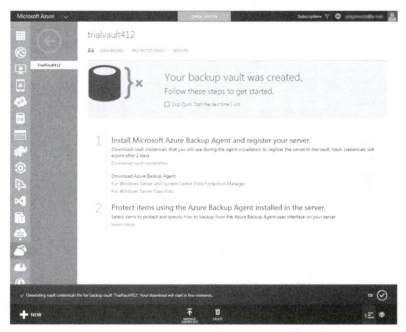

Figure 8-15   Installing the Microsoft Azure Backup Agent

1. In the Installation Settings window, enter the agent installation path and the cache location or accept the default locations.

2. In the Proxy Configuration window, enter the proxy settings if you're using a proxy to access the Internet.

3. In the Microsoft Update Opt-In window, you can choose to use Windows Update to keep the agent up to date.

4. In the Installation window, click Proceed to Registration to start the Register Server Wizard.

5. In the Vault Identification window, click Browse to select the credentials file you downloaded from the Azure Web site.

6. In the Encryption Setting window, enter a passphrase for encrypting stored data or click Generate Passphrase. The passphrase must be at least 16 characters. Enter a location to save it in a text file in case it's lost or forgotten (see Figure 8-16). You should specify a network location or external storage. Click Register to register the server.

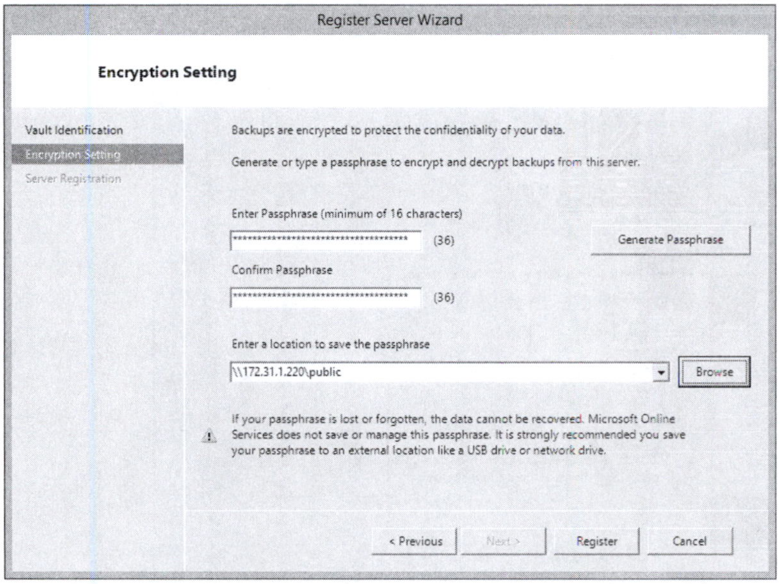

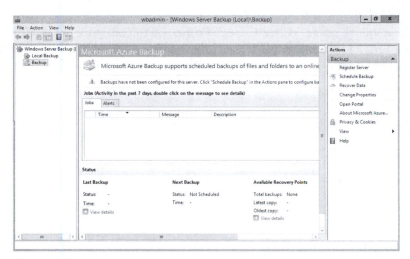

Figure 8-16   Setting a passphrase

7. In the Server Registration window, review the summary, and then click Close. When the server is registered, you can begin using Microsoft Azure Backup.

A link is created on your desktop to run the Microsoft Azure Backup agent software, or you can start it in the Windows Server Backup console by clicking the Backup icon in the left pane. The Local Backup icon opens the standard Windows Server Backup program (see Figure 8-17).

Figure 8-17   The Microsoft Azure Backup agent

To use Microsoft Azure Backup, you must schedule a backup first, which is similar to scheduling a backup with Windows Server Backup. First, you select the items you want to back up, which can include any or all files and folders from any or all of the volumes on your server. You can exclude particular file types, if you want. Microsoft Azure Backup doesn't create a volume image backup, however, so you can't do a system state, volume, or bare metal restore.

Next, you specify the times you want to back up. The scheduling options are more flexible than in Windows Server Backup (see Figure 8-18):

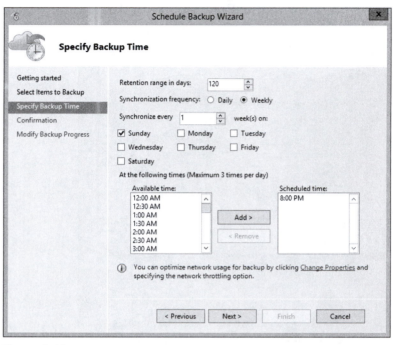

Figure 8-18   Scheduling an Azure backup

- *Retention range in days*—The **retention range** specifies how long the backup should be kept. The default is 120 days, and the maximum is 3360 days.

- *Synchronization frequency*—Specify whether files should be synchronized daily or weekly. If you select Weekly (the default), specify which days of the week and what time of day, up to a maximum of three times per day. If you select Daily, specify which times of the day, up to a maximum of three times per day.

- *Optimize network usage*—Click Change Properties to configure encryption, proxy configuration, and throttling (used to set the maximum bandwidth the backup uses during work hours and nonwork hours). You can also set work hours and days of the week (see Figure 8-19).

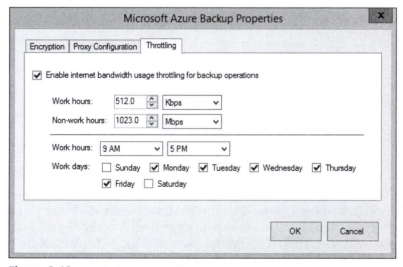

Figure 8-19   Optimizing network usage

As with Windows Server Backup, you can create only one scheduled backup. If you click Backup Now in the Microsoft Azure Backup console, the scheduled backup runs immediately.

Configuring Microsoft Azure Backup with PowerShell

You can use several PowerShell cmdlets to configure Microsoft Azure Backup. Table 8-4 lists some commonly used ones.

Table 8-4   **PowerShell cmdlets for Microsoft Azure Backup**

Cmdlet	Description
`Get-OBPolicy`	Displays the current backup policy, which includes the backup schedule, selected files to back up, and retention range
`New-OBPolicy`	Creates a backup policy
`Set-OBMachineSetting`	Configures an `OBMachineSetting` object that includes Microsoft Azure Backup settings, such as proxy server, throttling settings, and the encryption passphrase
`Set-OBPolicy`	Sets the backup policy to be used for scheduled backups
`Set-OBRetentionPolicy`	Sets the retention policy
`Set-OBSchedule`	Sets the backup schedule
`Start-OBBackup`	Starts a backup operation based on a specified policy
`Start-OBRecovery`	Starts a recovery operation
`Start-OBRegistration`	Registers the current computer with Microsoft Azure Backup
`Get-Command *-OB*`	Lists all Microsoft Azure Backup cmdlets

© 2016 Cengage Learning®

Site-Level Disaster Recovery

Site-level disaster recovery includes procedures and technologies that an organization uses to get its network and servers running quickly after a disaster that affects some or all of its IT infrastructure. You have learned how to recover servers from a disaster involving loss of data, and this section covers some features in Hyper-V for recovering from a disaster involving Hyper-V host servers and associated VMs. In Chapter 7, you learned how to configure failover clusters, and in this chapter, you see how to configure clustering for a multisite network and recover a multisite failover cluster.

Configuring Hyper-V Site-Level Fault Tolerance

Chapter 7 covered how to manage VM movement by using live migration as well as VM import, export, and copy and how to configure VM network health detection. The following sections explain Hyper-V Replica, a new feature in Windows Server 2012, along with the related technologies Hyper-V Replica Broker and Hyper-V Extended Replication (new in Windows Server 2012 R2).

Configuring Hyper-V Replica   Hyper-V Replica periodically replicates changes in a VM to a mirror VM hosted on another Hyper-V server. It works over a regular IP network and can be enabled on stand-alone servers or servers in a failover cluster. There are no domain requirements, so the Hyper-V servers might or might not be members of a domain or can even be members of different domains. In addition, the Hyper-V servers can be at the same site or at different sites, so you can continue VM operation easily if a single server goes down or an entire site suffers a catastrophic failure. There are no shared storage requirements, so there's no need to configure a SAN or cluster.

Replication occurs asynchronously, so although the replica VM is always in operational condition, its state might lag behind the original VM by a few seconds to a few minutes, depending on the settings and connection speed between hosts. You can configure encryption so that the data transfer between hosts is secure, and you can configure compression to reduce bandwidth requirements.

Hyper-V Replica can also be used for site-level disaster recovery if your organization maintains a **hot backup site,** a location that duplicates much of the main site's IT infrastructure and can be switched to if a disaster occurs at the main site. With Hyper-V Replica operating between these sites, your VMs can be running at the hot backup site immediately. Minimal data loss occurs because the replica VMs lag behind the primary VMs by only a few seconds or minutes.

The source and destination Hyper-V servers involved in replication must be running the same version of Windows Server. For example, you can't replicate from a Windows Server 2012 R2 server to a Windows Server 2012 server.

To configure Hyper-V Replica, follow these steps:

1. Enable replication on the Hyper-V server to receive replicated VMs. In the Settings window of Hyper-V Manager, click Replication Configuration in the left pane, and click "Enable this computer as a Replica server" (see Figure 8-20). The Hyper-V server you enable replication on is called the **replica server.** Note that if the Hyper-V server is a member of a failover cluster, the option to enable replication in Hyper-V Manager is grayed out; you need to configure replication settings in the Failover Cluster Manager console.

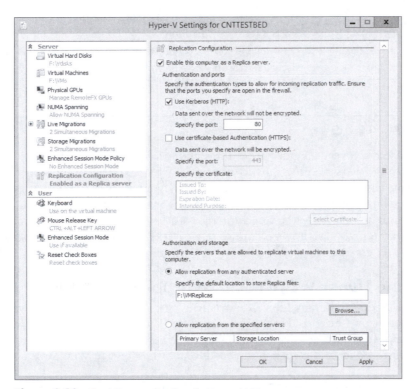

Figure 8-20   Enabling replication in Hyper-V Manager

2. Select the authentication method. You can select Kerberos authentication (using port 80 by default, but you can change the port), but data transfers aren't encrypted with this authentication method. Certificate-based authentication encrypts data transfers over HTTPS. You should choose certificate-based authentication if the two Hyper-V servers aren't members of the same forest.

3. Specify servers that can replicate to this server and the storage location. You can allow any server that authenticates to replicate to this server or select specific servers. If you select specific servers, you can specify a different storage location for each one. After you finish configuring replication, you're prompted to configure the firewall.

4. Configure firewall rules to allow replication. Create a new inbound firewall rule on the replication server that enables the predefined Hyper-V Replica HTTP Listener (TCP-In) rule (see Figure 8-21).

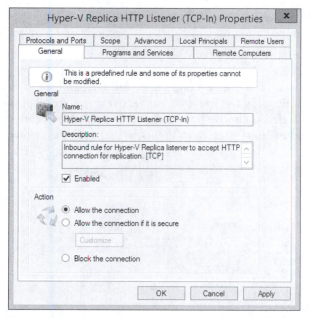

Figure 8-21   Enabling the Hyper-V Replica HTTP Listener (TCP-In) rule

5. Configure each VM you want to replicate on one or more source servers that you want to replicate to the replica server. These steps are explained in the next section.

Enabling Replication on a Virtual Machine   Before a VM can be replicated to the replica server, replication must be configured in the VM's settings. To do so, follow these steps:

1. In Hyper-V Manager, click the VM you want to enable replication for, and in the Actions pane, click Enable Replication. The Enable Replication Wizard begins.

2. In the Specify Replica Server window, type the name of the replica server or click Browse to select one.

3. In the Specify Connection Parameters window, you choose the authentication method and whether to compress network data (see Figure 8-22). The authentication method must match the authentication method on the replica server.

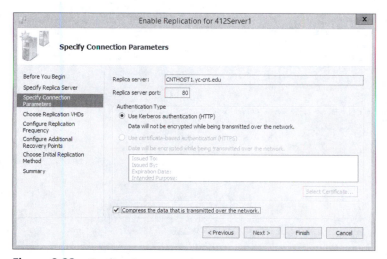

Figure 8-22   Configuring connection parameters

4. In the Choose Replication VHDs window, exclude the virtual disks that shouldn't be replicated. By default, all virtual disks are replicated, but you can deselect any that shouldn't be.

5. In the Configure Replication Frequency window, you specify how often changes to the VM should be checked and replicated. (This feature is new in Windows Server 2012 R2.) The default frequency is 5 minutes, and you can choose 30 seconds or 15 minutes.

6. In the Configure Additional Recovery Points window, you configure options for recovery points. A **recovery point** is a checkpoint that can be generated automatically so that you can revert to an earlier server state if there's an unplanned failover, and the VM is in an unworkable state. You can maintain only the most recent recovery point, or you can have hourly recovery points generated. If you choose hourly recovery points, you can specify how many hours of coverage (how many hourly recovery points to maintain), as shown in Figure 8-23.

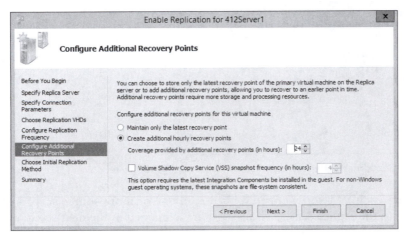

Figure 8-23   Configuring recovery points

7. In the Choose Initial Replication Method window, you can send the initial replica over the network or export a copy of the VM to external media. If the VM is very large or the replica server is located across a low bandwidth link, using external media might be the best option. The initial replica copy requires the most bandwidth; from then on, only changes are replicated. You can also start the replication immediately or at a scheduled date and time (see Figure 8-24).

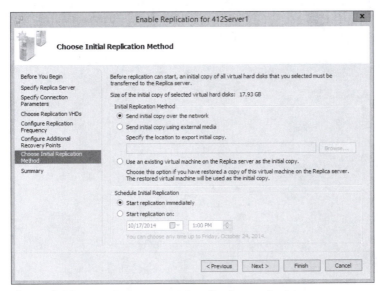

Figure 8-24   Specifying the initial replication method

8. When you have finished configuration and replication begins, you're prompted to configure the network connection settings on the replicated VM if the virtual networks on the source and destination Hyper-V server don't match. When replication begins, check the status by clicking the VM, and in the Actions pane, click Replication, View Replication Health. The following are other options on the Replication menu in the Actions pane from the replica VM side (not the original VM):

- o Failover: This option should be used when the primary VM fails. If the primary VM is still running, this option won't work.

- o Test Failover: Verify the replica's health so that you know it will work in an actual failover. The original VM continues to work normally.

- o Pause Replication: Pause the replication process.

- o Extend Replication: This option is discussed later in "Configuring Hyper-V Extended Replication."

- o Import Initial Replica: This option is available only if you specified using external media for initial replication.

- o Remove Replication: This option stops replication but doesn't delete the replica VM.

From the source Hyper-V server, the replication actions you can perform on a replicated VM include the Pause Replication, Remove Replication, and View Replication Health options already discussed. In addition, you have the Planned Failover option. A planned failover is initiated only on the source Hyper-V server. It should be used when you need to take the source server down for maintenance or when you know a service outage is imminent, such as a planned power outage or a coming storm.

Configuring Hyper-V Replica Broker   Hyper-V Replica Broker is used to configure Hyper-V Replica between failover cluster nodes. You configure it by adding the Hyper-V Replica Broker role in the Failover Cluster Manager console (see Figure 8-25). Then right-click the role in the Failover Cluster Manager console and click Replication Settings to enable and configure Hyper-V Replica. The process is similar to using Hyper-V Manager as described earlier.

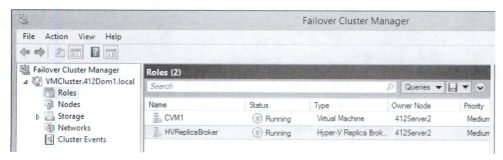

Figure 8-25   Configuring Hyper-V Replica Broker

Configuring Hyper-V Extended Replication   Extended replication, a new option in Windows Server 2012 R2, is used to replicate a replica. This feature, which you can think of as a "backup of a backup," gives you a third location from which to run a VM. If there's a catastrophic failure at your primary site, your backup site can begin running replicated VMs, and your extended replica site is already configured to act as a backup if your backup site goes offline.

After the initial replication between the original VM and the first replica server is finished, you can configure extended replication. On the replica server in Hyper-V Manager, click the replica VM on the replica server, click Replication in the Actions pane, and click Extend Replication. The process is nearly identical to configuring replication on the original VM, except the replication frequency is limited to 5 minutes or 15 minutes, with no 30-second option. Of course, you need to enable replication on another Hyper-V server and specify that server as the replica server.

Configuring Multisite Clustering

As you have seen, Hyper-V Replica is a powerful feature for disaster recovery and can work with or without a Hyper-V failover cluster configuration and both within a site and across multiple sites. The one drawback of using Hyper-V Replica for multisite fault tolerance is that some loss of data between the source VMs being replicated and the replica VMs is inevitable because there's a lag between changes occurring on the source VM and the time replication occurs. The lag can be from about 30 seconds to 15 minutes, depending on the replication schedule you configured. In addition, Hyper-V Replica provides fault tolerance only for VMs, not for physical computers. For real-time failover for both VMs and physical computers, a multisite failover cluster is the best solution.

Chapter 7 mentioned how to configure a failover cluster when the cluster nodes are in different physical sites. This section expands on multisite cluster configuration and explains the requirements for a multisite failover cluster, quorum configurations, the network configuration, data replication settings, and heartbeat settings to best support a multisite failover cluster:

- *Multisite failover cluster requirements*—The computer and software requirements for a multisite failover cluster are the same as for any failover cluster. The main consideration is the investment in physical servers and the infrastructure to support the servers and network. You should use similar server hardware for the cluster nodes in all sites, and you need to be sure the network infrastructure in all sites supports the shared storage scheme you're using. In addition, if you decide to use a file share witness, you need a third physical site for the share.

- *Multisite cluster node and quorum configuration*—Multisite clusters work best if there's an even number of cluster nodes with a node and file share majority quorum configuration. The file share used in the quorum should be in a neutral site, if possible. That way, if one site goes down, the file share is still available for the quorum, as shown in Figure 8-26. Site 1 is the primary site, with active cluster nodes providing services. Site 2 is the failover, or hot backup, site with cluster nodes in standby. The cluster storage at Site 1 is configured as read-write and is replicated to Site 2's storage, which is configured as read-only. Site 3 contains the file share witness, accessible to both sites. If Site 1 becomes inaccessible, Site 2 becomes active, and the storage becomes read-write.

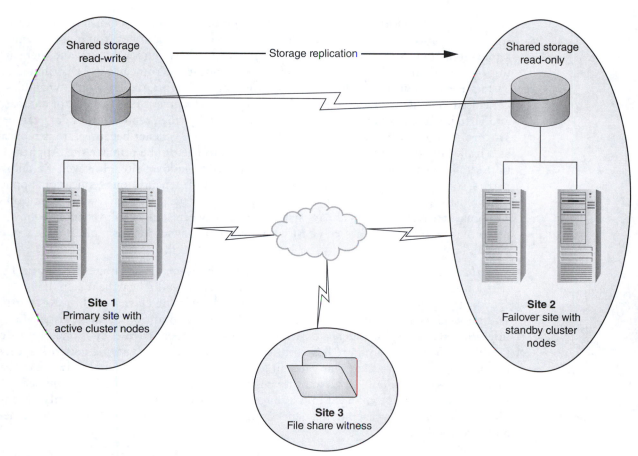

Figure 8-26   Multisite failover cluster configuration

© 2016 Cengage Learning®

If you can't configure the cluster with a file share witness at a neutral site, configure the quorum as node majority, being sure to have an odd number of nodes. The primary site has an odd number of servers, and the failover site has an even number of nodes. As discussed in Chapter 7, Windows Server 2012 and later supports dynamic quorum, which is enabled by default. This feature recalculates quorum votes automatically if a cluster node leaves or returns to the cluster. In addition, Windows Server 2012 R2 supports dynamic witness, which guarantees an odd number of votes by allowing the witness vote to be ignored if the total number of votes, including the witness, is an even number.

- *Multisite cluster network configuration*—When configuring a multisite cluster, your network design probably includes multiple IP subnets; at least one per physical site. Support for multisubnet clusters has been included in Windows failover clusters since Windows Server 2008. However, client computers must be able to discover network services on another subnet when a site failover occurs. The problem lies mainly with DNS because the cluster name's IP address changes. So the effectiveness of a multisite, multisubnet cluster partially depends on how fast DNS entries are replicated between DNS servers and how quickly these entries are reported to the client. You should also consider multisite/multisubnet Hyper-V clusters. If the VMs use static IP addresses, when failover occurs, their addresses need to be configured manually for the new subnet. Using DHCP addresses for VMs solves this problem, however. Another option to consider is configuring the network with VLANs so that the cluster nodes on each site are in the same IP subnet.

- *Data replication options*—Windows doesn't have an automatic mechanism to replicate storage data from the shared storage location on one site to another. You must provide the replication. Some SANs perform automatic replication between SAN units, and there are third-party solutions for file-level or block-level replication. You can't use Distributed File System Replication (DFSR) for file replication because it replicates data only when files are closed. So unless your cluster service is limited to document files (instead of databases and virtual machines), DFSR isn't a suitable solution. Further, replication of data can be synchronous or asynchronous. Asynchronous replication is faster because data is replicated as a background process after it's been written to storage on the primary site. Applications don't have to wait for data to be replicated to the failover site. However, if a failover occurs, some recent write operations might be lost. With synchronous replication, applications must wait for replication to occur to the secondary site after each write operation. This guarantees that data is always synchronized between sites but slows application performance. If site links are very fast with low latency, synchronous replication is a good choice; otherwise, asynchronous replication should be used.

- *Heartbeat settings*—The **heartbeat** is a signal sent between cluster nodes to inform them that a node is up and running. If a cluster node fails to send a heartbeat signal in a specific time, the node is considered unavailable. A multisite cluster might miss heartbeats sent between cluster nodes because of varying network conditions, and a cluster node might be mistakenly considered down. By default, heartbeat frequency is once per second (1000 ms). You can configure heartbeat settings to account for varying network speeds by increasing or decreasing that value in the range 250 ms to 4000 ms. If five heartbeats in a row are missed, failover to another cluster node occurs. The number of missed heartbeats can also be changed in the range of 3 to 10. Further, you can specify heartbeat settings differently for each node, depending on whether cluster nodes are in the same or a different subnet.

To configure the heartbeat frequency for cluster nodes in the same subnet, use the following PowerShell cmdlet (replacing *clustername* with the name of the cluster and *timeInms* with the number of milliseconds):

```
cluster /cluster:clustername /prop SameSubnetDelay=timeInms
```

To configure the heartbeat frequency for cluster nodes in a different subnet, change the `SameSubnetDelay` parameter to `CrossSubnetDelay`. To change the number of times the heartbeat can be missed (the threshold) before a failover occurs, use the following PowerShell cmdlet, setting *ThresholdValue* to a number between 3 and 10:

```
cluster /cluster:clustername /prop SameSubnetThreshold=ThresholdValue
```

To configure the threshold value for cluster nodes in a different subnet, change the `SameSubnetThreshold` parameter to `CrossSubnetThreshold`.

Chapter Summary

- A server backup is the cornerstone of any disaster recovery procedure. Backups are necessary for the following reasons: server hardware failure, disk failure, volume corruption, deletion of files, software failure, and theft or disaster.

- Administrators, Backup Operators, and Server Operators have permission to back up and restore files.

- Using Windows Server Backup, you can configure a one-time backup with the following options: full backup, bare metal recovery, system state backup, and backup of separate volumes or files. The destination can be a local or external disk, a DVD, or other removable media.

- A scheduled backup can dedicate a disk to the backup operation. You can have only one backup schedule.

- You can back up a server role if the role or service registers itself with the Windows Server Backup program.

- With the Windows Server Backup recovery options, you can recover files, folders and volumes and the system state or perform a bare metal restore. The data to perform a system state recovery is included in the system state, bare metal recovery, and full server backup options.

- Windows Recovery Environment (Windows RE) is a special boot option for solving common Windows startup problems. Windows RE is a standard part of Windows Server 2012/R2 and Windows 8/8.1 and later OSs.

- The boot configuration data (BCD) store contains settings that determine how a Windows system boots. The BCD store is usually on the reserved partition created when you install Windows.

- Windows offers Microsoft Azure Backup to help ease performing regular backups. Backups are stored in the cloud and can be accessed from anywhere you have an Internet connection. You can sign up for a free trial account of Microsoft Azure Backup, which gives you 30 days of use and some credit toward Azure services.

- Site-level disaster recovery includes procedures and technologies that allow an organization to get its network and servers up and running quickly after a disaster affecting some or all of its IT infrastructure.

- Hyper-V Replica is a feature that periodically replicates changes in a VM to a mirror VM hosted on another Hyper-V server. It works over a regular IP network and can be enabled on stand-alone servers or servers in a failover cluster.

- For real-time failover for both VMs and physical computers, a multisite failover cluster is the best solution. The computer and software requirements for a multisite failover cluster are the same as for any failover cluster. The main consideration is the investment in physical servers and the infrastructure to support the servers and network.

- Multisite clusters work best if there's an even number of cluster nodes with a node and file share majority quorum configuration. When configuring a multisite cluster, your network design probably includes multiple IP subnets; at least one per physical site. An option to consider is configuring the network with VLANs so that the cluster nodes on each site are in the same IP subnet.

- Windows doesn't have an automatic mechanism to replicate storage data from the shared storage location on one site to another. You must provide the replication. Replication of data can be synchronous or asynchronous. If site links are very fast with low latency, synchronous replication is a good choice; otherwise, asynchronous replication should be used.

- The heartbeat is a signal sent between cluster nodes that tell each other that a node is up and running. If a cluster node fails to send a heartbeat signal in a specific time, the node is considered unavailable.

Key Terms

authoritative restore   A type of Active Directory restore operation in which the restored DC replicates to all other DCs in the domain, and any changes made to Active Directory objects since the backup occurred are lost.

bare metal recovery   A backup option that includes the system state, the system reserved volume, and the volume where Windows is stored.

boot configuration data (BCD) store   A binary file containing settings that determine how a Windows system boots.

differential backup   A backup method in which only the blocks that have changed are transferred to the destination if there is an existing backup.

heartbeat   A signal sent between cluster nodes informing them that a node is up and running.

hot backup site   A location that duplicates much of the main site's IT infrastructure and can be switched to if a disaster occurs at the main site.

Hyper-V Replica   A new feature in Windows Server 2012 that periodically replicates changes in a VM to a mirror VM hosted on another Hyper-V server.

Microsoft Azure Backup   An online backup solution that stores backups in the cloud; they can be accessed from anywhere you have an Internet connection.

nonauthoritative restore   A type of Active Directory restore operation in which changes made to Active Directory objects on other DCs since the backup are kept and replicated to the server being restored.

one-time backup   A backup type that creates a backup to a local volume or a share; the backup begins immediately.

recovery point   A checkpoint that can be generated automatically so that you can revert to an earlier server state in case there's an unplanned failover and a VM is in an unworkable state.

replica server   In the Hyper-V Replica feature, the Hyper-V server where replication is enabled.

retention range   A setting in Microsoft Azure Backup that specifies how long a backup should be kept.

scheduled backup   A backup type that allows specifying how often a backup occurs and dedicating a disk to backups.

Secure Boot   A feature that prevents a computer from booting from untrusted software.

site-level disaster recovery   A process with procedures and technologies an organization uses to get its network and servers running quickly after a disaster.

system state backup   A backup option that backs up boot files, Windows system files, and the Registry. On a DC, the system state includes the Active Directory database and the SYSVOL folder.

Review Questions

1. Which of the following situations typically requires the availability of a backup created by Windows Server Backup? (Choose all that apply.)

    a. You need continuous availability of a network service.

    b. There's been accidental deletion of folders or files.

    c. Your need to fail over to a replica VM.

    d. A server's registry appears to be corrupted.

2. You have just installed Windows Server 2012 R2 and want to run a full server backup. What do you need to do first?

    a. Run `Install-WindowsFeature Windows-Server-Backup` from a PowerShell prompt.

    b. Run `Start-Backup` from a PowerShell Prompt.

    c. In Server Manager, click Tools, Windows Server Backup.

    d. At the command prompt, run `wbadmin start backup`.

3. You need to allow a junior administrator named jradmin to perform backup operations on a server named DataServ1. You don't want to give jradmin broader rights or permissions on the server, and this user shouldn't be able to restore files. What should you do?

    a. Add jradmin to the Backup Operators group.

    b. Add jradmin to the Server Operators group.

    c. Assign jradmin the "Back up files and directories" right.

    d. Add jradmin to the Allow list in the Software Restrictions policy.

4. Which command should you use if you want a Windows Server 2012 R2 server to start in Safe Mode the next time it restarts?

   a. `bootcfg`

   b. `diskpart`

   c. `bcdboot`

   d. `bcdedit`

5. You have started a Windows Server 2012 R2 server in Windows RE mode. What command should you use to restore the boot sector?

   a. `diskpart`

   b. `bootsect`

   c. `bcdboot`

   d. `bootcfg`

6. Which command enables you to replace corrupt boot files on a virtual disk you have mounted on the server's V drive? The server is running Windows Server 2012 R2, which is also loaded on the virtual disk.

   a. `bcdboot C:\windows /s V:`

   b. `bcdedit V:`

   c. `bootrec /repair V:`

   d. `bootcfg /scan V:`

7. A Windows Server 2012 R2 system has undergone system crashes, and you suspect a Windows system file is missing or corrupted. What command should you use to try to solve the problem?

   a. `bcdboot`

   b. `diskpart`

   c. `sfc`

   d. `scan`

8. What command should you use to revert a volume to an existing shadow copy?

   a. `diskpart`

   b. `Start-Backup`

   c. `wbadmin`

   d. `vssadmin`

9. Which of the following is a disadvantage of using differential backups?

   a. Disk performance can degrade.

   b. More space is required for backups.

   c. Backup operations can take longer.

   d. Restore operations can take longer.

10. Which of the following is true about a scheduled backup?

   a. You can create a separate schedule for each type of backup you want to perform.

   b. You can specify a destination disk that's dedicated to backup jobs.

   c. Only one backup set is stored on the destination.

   d. You can't use a network share as the destination for a scheduled backup.

11. Which item is *not* included in a system state backup of a member server?

    a. Local users and groups

    b. The Registry

    c. SYSVOL

    d. Windows system files

12. What feature can you enable in Windows Server 2012 R2 to reduce the need to perform restore operations from a backup for files?

    a. Shadow copies

    b. FSRM

    c. Disk quotas

    d. Windows RE

13. You have a domain controller that suffered a system crash, and you have to perform a full server recovery. You have two other DCs on the network, and they have been working fine during the two days the DC was offline. What type of Active Directory restore should you perform?

    a. Authoritative restore

    b. Shadow copy restore

    c. Nonauthoritative restore

    d. Bare metal recovery

14. Which of the following actions starts Windows RE? (Choose all that apply.)

    a. Enter `shutdown /s /t 0` at a command prompt.

    b. Enter `shutdown /r /o` at a command prompt.

    c. While pressing the Shift key, click Restart from the Power menu.

    d. While pressing the Ctrl key, click Shutdown from the Start menu.

15. You installed a new driver and tried to restart the computer, and now the computer won't boot. Which startup mode should you try first?

    a. Safe Mode

    b. Last Known Good Configuration

    c. Directory Services Restore Mode

    d. Debugging Mode

16. Which of the following contains settings that determine how Windows Server 2012 R2 boots?

    a. BMR

    b. SYSVOL

    c. `boot.ini`

    d. BCD store

17. Which command do you use to configure Windows Server 2012 R2 to boot to a virtual hard disk?

    a. `bcdboot C:\Windows`

    b. `bcdedit /set`

    c. `bootcfg vdisk.vhd`

    d. `diskpart /virtual`

18. Which of the following backup operations isn't possible with Microsoft Azure Backup? (Choose all that apply.)

    a. Data volume backup

    b. OS volume backup

    c. C:\Windows folder backup

    d. System State backup

19. You have two sites running Hyper-V servers. All servers in both sites are members of the same domain. You want to ensure high availability of the VMs running on Hyper-V servers and can't afford data loss as a result of a failover. What should you use?

    a. Multisite Hyper-V cluster

    b. Hyper-V Replica

    c. Microsoft Azure Backup

    d. Live migration

20. You're configuring Hyper-V Replica. You need to make sure that if an unplanned failover occurs and the replica VM is damaged, you can revert it to an earlier state when the VM was working. You want to be able to go back at least 24 hours on an hourly basis. What's the best option for doing this?

    a. Use Task Scheduler to create periodic checkpoints on the source VM.

    b. Configure Volume Shadow Copy Service by using `vssadmin`.

    c. Configure recovery points, and select the "Create additional hourly recovery points" option.

    d. Schedule backups of the VM to occur every hour by using `wbadmin`.

21. You have configured highly available virtual machines in the Failover Cluster Manager, and all cluster nodes are in the primary site. You want to make sure the VMs are available at a secondary site in case of a disaster. The secondary site is also running Hyper-V in a failover cluster. Some data loss is acceptable if there's a failover to the secondary site. What should you configure?

    a. Enable Hyper-V Replica in Hyper-V Manager on the secondary site nodes.

    b. Configure the Hyper-V Replica Broker role in the Failover Cluster Manager on the secondary site cluster.

    c. Configure Hyper-V Replica in Hyper-V Manager on the primary site nodes.

    d. Configure the Hyper-V Replica Broker role in the Failover Cluster Manager on the primary site cluster.

22. You want to configure a multisite cluster between two sites named SiteA and SiteB. You have a third site named SiteC. The cluster will have a total of six nodes. Which quorum configuration should you choose?

    a. Node majority

    b. Node and disk majority

    c. Disk only

    d. Node and file share majority

23. You have a multisite cluster named MultiCluster with a high latency link between sites and are using default failover settings. Periodically, a failover occurs when the primary server is still online. What command should you use to prevent these errant failovers?

    a. `cluster /cluster:MultiCluster /prop SameSubnetDelay=500`

    b. `cluster /cluster:MultiCluster /prop CrossSubnetDelay=2500`

    c. `cluster /cluster:MultiCluster /prop SameSubnetThreshold=2500`

    d. `cluster /cluster:MultiCluster /prop CrossSubnetThreshold=500`

Case Projects

Case Project 8-1: Choosing a Fault-Tolerant Solution

You have a network consisting of three sites and 15 member servers. Both SiteA and SiteB have six of the member servers, and SiteC has three member servers. SiteA and SiteB are across town from each other, and SiteC is in another state. Your environment is heavily virtualized, with Hyper-V running on 4 servers each in SiteA and SiteB and a total of 24 VMs spread evenly among the servers. Each server is capable of running double the number of VMs it's currently running. Hyper-V is running on two servers in SiteC. SiteC isn't currently running any VMs, but Hyper-V is installed on the servers for contingency purposes. The SiteC servers are capable of running all 24 VMs, if necessary.

Given this setup, describe a server and site disaster recovery plan. Include features of Windows Server 2012 R2 you have learned about in this chapter and other chapters that should be used in your plan. Be sure to include the following elements:

- Clustering, if any, including the quorum configuration
- Virtual machine fault-tolerance strategies, such as live migration and Hyper-V replicas
- Windows Server Backup and Microsoft Azure Backup, if necessary

chapter 9

Implementing Active Directory Certificate Services

After reading this chapter and completing the exercises, you will be able to:

- Describe the components of a PKI system
- Deploy the Active Directory Certificate Services role
- Configure a certification authority
- Maintain and manage a PKI

It's a matter of trust. Whether you're shopping on a Web site, engaging in online banking, or even reading an e-mail, you must have a certain level of trust that the entity you're exchanging information with is actually who it says it is. Unfortunately, digital fraud and scams have become all too common. Fortunately, there are ways to protect yourself and your organization in the form of digital certificates.

Microsoft Active Directory Certificate Services provides the infrastructure for issuing and validating digital certificates in a corporate environment. With digital certificates, users can provide proof of their identities to corporate resources and confirm the identity of resources they access. Active Directory Certificate Services is Microsoft's implementation of a public key infrastructure (PKI), which secures information transfer and identity management and verification. This chapter describes how a PKI works and defines the terms used to discuss a PKI and Active Directory Certificate Services. You learn how to install and configure the Active Directory Certificate Services role and how to configure and manage key elements of this role, such as certification authorities and certificate enrollments and revocations.

Introducing Active Directory Certificate Services

Table 9-1 lists what you need for the hands-on activities in this chapter.

Table 9-1 **Activity requirements**

Activity	Requirements	Notes
Activity 9-1: Installing the AD CS Role	412Server1, 412Server2	
Activity 9-2: Creating an EFS Certificate Template	412Server1, 412Server2	
Activity 9-3: Configuring Certificate Autoenrollment	412Server1, 412Server2	
Activity 9-4: Testing EFS Certificate Autoenrollment	412Server1, 412Server2, 412Win8	
Activity 9-5: Installing the Web Enrollment Role Service	412Server1, 412Server2, 412Win8	
Activity 9-6: Configuring an OCSP Response Signing Certificate Template	412Server1, 412Server2	
Activity 9-7: Requesting the OCSP Response Signing Certificate	412Server1, 412Server2	
Activity 9-8: Creating a Revocation Configuration for the OR	412Server1, 412Server2	
Activity 9-9: Backing Up the CA Server	412Server1, 412Server2	
Activity 9-10: Archiving a Key Manually	412Win8	
Activity 9-11: Recovering a Lost Key	412Win8	

© 2016 Cengage Learning®

Active Directory Certificate Services (AD CS) is a server role in Windows Server 2012/R2 that provides services for creating a public key infrastructure that administrators can use to issue and manage public key certificates. With AD CS, you can add security for a variety of applications, including e-mail, wireless networks, virtual private networks (VPNs), Encrypting File System (EFS), smart cards for user logons, Secure Sockets Layer/Transport Layer Security (SSL/TLS), and others. This section describes the basic components of a PKI and defines several terms used in implementing PKIs and AD CS.

Public Key Infrastructure Overview

A **public key infrastructure (PKI)** is a security system that binds a user's or device's identity to a cryptographic key that secures data transfer with encryption and ensures data authenticity with digital certificates. PKI provides the following services to a network:

- *Confidentiality*—Data and communications are protected by encryption algorithms, allowing only the authorized parties to access information.
- *Integrity*—Ensures that data received is the same as data sent.

- *Nonrepudiation*—Ensures that a party in a communication can't dispute the validity of the transaction, much like a signature on a letter or contract is used to verify that the signatory wrote the letter.

- *Authentication*—Verifies the identity of a person or system involved in a transaction.

Before going into the details of a PKI, first you need to understand why this service is necessary. Suppose you want to do some online banking, a transaction you want to be confidential. You open your Web browser and go to *www.mybank.com*. You enter your logon information and proceed with your transaction. Without some type of security system in place, a number of things can go wrong with this procedure, as in the following examples:

- DNS servers could be compromised, replacing the IP address of *www.mybank.com* with the IP address of a fraudulent site. All your logon information, including, perhaps, your account number, is actually being sent to the fraudulent Web site and could be used to access your real account. Without some type of security system in place, you can't be sure of the authenticity of the server you're communicating with.

- Someone could be electronically eavesdropping on your conversation. You might actually be communicating with *www.mybank.com*, but someone could be "listening" to the conversation with a packet-capturing program, which means your transaction is not confidential. The packets can be examined to find your logon information and account information for later use.

A public key security system, such as your Web browser using HTTPS instead of HTTP in a URL, can thwart both the preceding situations. In the first example, using digital certificates can authenticate the Web site's identity. If your browser is directed to a fraudulent site, the digital certificate doesn't match the site's URL. In the second example, encryption can ensure confidentiality and prevent an eavesdropper from interpreting information in captured packets.

Of course, for the security system to work, users have the responsibility of checking that the Web browser is using secure communication (usually indicated by a padlock icon in the browser). In addition, users must be vigilant in heeding warning messages about Web sites' certificate validity. PKI is commonly used in many other situations, but whenever a secure transaction is necessary between two parties that don't know each other, PKI is likely to be part of the transaction.

PKI Terminology

Before you delve into PKI transactions, review the following list of components that compose a PKI:

- *Plaintext*—Data that has been unaltered; as used in cryptography, this term defines the state of information before it's encrypted or after it has been decrypted.

- *Ciphertext*—Data that has been encrypted; it's the result you get when plaintext is transformed by an encryption algorithm.

- *Key*—In encryption, a key is a numeric value used by a cryptographic algorithm to change plaintext into ciphertext (encrypt) and ciphertext back to plaintext (decrypt).

- *Secret key*—A key used to both encrypt and decrypt data in a secure transaction. The secret key must be known by both parties because it's used in both ends of the cryptography process. The terms "symmetric key" and "shared secret key" are also used. Secret keys are used in symmetric cryptography, defined later in this list, and provide a lower-overhead secure transaction than using a public/private key pair.

- *Private key*—A key that's held by a person or system and is unknown to anyone else. A private key is part of a key pair used in asymmetric cryptography (defined later in this list) and is most often used by the owner to decrypt data that has been encrypted with the corresponding public key.

- *Public key*—A key owned by a person or system that's distributed to whoever wants to have a secure communication session with the key owner. The public key, part of the key pair used in asymmetric cryptography, is used to encrypt data, which can then be decrypted only by using the owner's private key. A public key is also used to verify a digital signature.

- *Symmetric cryptography*—An encryption/decryption process that uses a single secret key to encrypt and decrypt a message (also called "private key cryptography" or "secret key cryptography"). The key is often referred to as a shared secret because both parties involved in the communication must have the same key. Symmetric cryptography is vulnerable to attack because the shared secret must be transmitted to both parties, and the key used in the encryption algorithm tends to be easier to crack than those used in asymmetric cryptography.

 **NOTE**   Although symmetric cryptography is sometimes referred to as "private key cryptography" or "private key encryption," these terms are somewhat imprecise. A private key is used as part of a pair in asymmetric cryptography and should never be shared with another party.

- *Asymmetric cryptography*—An encryption/decryption process, used in a PKI system, that uses both a public key and a private key. Asymmetric cryptography is more complex and requires more computing resources than symmetric cryptography, but it's also more secure. Because of its higher resource requirements, asymmetric cryptography is often used with symmetric cryptography. It's used to exchange secret keys, which are then used symmetrically for the bulk of data encryption and decryption.

- *Digital certificate*—A digital document containing identifying information about a person or system; it's a central component of a PKI. Information in the certificate typically includes a person's or organization's name or a system's URL and IP address as well as the holder's public key, an expiration date, and the digital signature of the certification authority that issued the certificate. The certificate also defines the purpose it's used for.

- *Digital signature*—A numeric string created by a cryptographic algorithm, called a "hash" (discussed later in "Installing the AD CS Role"), that's used to validate a message or document's authenticity. The signature is verified by an algorithm that uses the stated owner of the signature's public key to accept or reject the signature as authentic. In a PKI, a certification authority's digital signature is used to verify the authenticity of digital certificates and other documents.

- *Certification authority (CA)*—An entity that issues and manages digital certificates and associated public keys and is an integral part of a PKI. Windows Server 2012/R2, with the Active Directory Certificate Services role installed, can be a CA for an enterprise network. Well-known companies, such as VeriSign, Comodo, and GlobalSign, are examples of universally trusted public CAs that issue certificates to people and systems needing to engage in secure communication with the public.

Now that you have a few terms down, take another look at an online banking session. The following steps are general because an actual secure Web session involves many variables, but these steps are the basic framework for most secure Web transactions (see Figure 9-1):

SSL client ················ Request secure transaction ·············▶ SSL Web server
◀············· Here's my certificate ·············
············· Certificate verified; here is the encrypted session key ·············▶
◀············· Data can be transferred securely by using the session key ·············

Figure 9-1   Steps of a secure Web transaction

© 2016 Cengage Learning®

1. The Web browser requests a secure transaction with *www.mybank.com* using HTTPS. HTTPS is a secure form of HTTP that uses SSL or TLS, both of which use a PKI.

2. The Web server sends information about the encryption protocols it will use and its certificate containing its public key.

3. The Web client verifies the certificate and extracts the CA's public key to verify the digital signature of the issuing CA. If the CA is trusted and the signature is verified, the Web client sends additional parameters to the server that are encrypted with the server's public key. One parameter is a session key, which is a shared secret key used to encrypt and decrypt data transferred during the rest of the communication session.

4. The Web server decrypts the session key with its private key. The session key is then used to encrypt and decrypt information communicated between the parties.

Notice in the preceding steps that both asymmetric and symmetric encryption are used. Asymmetric encryption is used in the beginning of the conversation to transmit several parameters, including the session key. After that point, symmetric encryption is used. So why not use asymmetric encryption throughout the conversation? Doing so require both client and the server to have a public/private key pair, and assuming every client has one might be unreasonable. Also, the additional processing asymmetric encryption requires slows communication. Because the shared secret key (session key) is exchanged by using more secure asymmetric encryption, the transaction remains highly secure.

The online banking transaction example is used because of its familiarity to most people. A Windows network with Active Directory Certificate Services installed is typically used to add an extra layer of security to enterprise network communication. AD CS not only ensures confidential communication, but can also protect users and resources by providing data integrity and authenticity.

 Don't confuse a PKI in which publicly trusted CAs are used to secure public transactions with a PKI used in a private organization. The fact that you set up a CA in your company doesn't mean certificates issued by your CA are trusted by the outside world.

AD CS Terminology

Now that you have a general understanding of a PKI, review some terms used with AD CS to give you an overview of this server role:

- *Certificate revocation list*—A **certificate revocation list (CRL)** is a list of certificates that the CA administrator has invalidated before their expiration dates. Reasons for certificate revocation include a private key that has been compromised or is suspected of having been compromised or a certificate deemed no longer necessary, as when an employee leaves the company that issued the certificate.

- *Certificate template*—A shell or model of a certificate used to create new certificates. **Certificate templates** define characteristics of the certificate, such as the intended use and expiration date. In Windows Server 2012/R2, AD CS includes more than 30 predefined certificate templates named for their intended purposes, such as Web Server for authenticating the identity of Web servers and Smart Card Logon, which enables users to authenticate by using smart cards. You can also create custom certificate templates.

- *CRL distribution point*—A **CRL distribution point (CDP)** is an attribute of a certificate that identifies where the CRL for a CA can be retrieved; can include URLs for HTTP, FILE, FTP, and LDAP locations.

- *Delta CRL*—A list of certificates revoked since the last base, or complete, CRL was published. Using Delta CRLs reduces the traffic created when downloading CRLs.

- *Enterprise CA*—A CA installation on a Windows Server 2012/R2 server that's integrated with Active Directory.

- *Stand-alone CA*—A CA installation that isn't integrated with Active Directory.

- *Enrollment agent*—A user authorized to enroll for smart cards on behalf of other users. A **restricted enrollment agent** limits the agent to enrolling only specific users or security groups; it's available only with an enterprise CA.

- *CA hierarchy*—The first CA installed in a Windows network is called the "root CA." The root CA's certificate is self-signed and distributed to Windows clients that automatically trust the root CA. Additional CAs, called "subordinate CAs," can be installed. Their certificates are signed by the root CA, and because Windows clients trust the root CA, by extension they trust subordinate CAs.

- *Online responder*—A server that supports Online Certificate Status Protocol (OCSP). This protocol is an alternative to clients downloading CRLs periodically to check certificate status. Clients can instead query an online responder for a certificate's status.

- *Certificate enrollment*—The process of issuing a certificate to a client. AD CS supports a number of enrollment methods, including autoenrollment, Web enrollment, smart card enrollment, and manual enrollment. In addition, AD CS supports Network Device Enrollment Service (NDES), which allows network devices to get certificates.

- *Key management*—Users' private keys are stored in their profiles. If a private key gets lost or corrupted, it might need to be restored. Key archival provides a method for storing a backup of a private key, and key recovery is the process of restoring a private key.

- *Authority Information Access (AIA)*—The AIA is a path configured on a CA server that specifies where to find the certificate for a CA.

Deploying the Active Directory Certificate Services Role

Before you decide to deploy AD CS on your network, you should have a clear understanding of how it will be used in your network and the options for implementing it. For example, if your reason for issuing certificates to employees is to give them secure access to external resources, such as Web servers and Internet e-mail, you should probably use a well-known external third-party CA. After all, a certificate your internal CA issues is unlikely to be trusted by outside entities. However, if your goal is to enhance the security of internal communication, that's the primary purpose of AD CS. All your internal clients and resources can be configured to trust the internal CA.

 It's possible to have a third-party CA as part of your PKI. In this case, the third-party CA acts as a root CA and issues certificates to your internal subordinate CAs. With this setup, your client computers can access external resources securely because the third-party CA is a point of common trust between internal computers and external entities.

Some AD CS options you should be aware of before deploying this server role include the following:

- Stand-alone and enterprise CAs
- Online and offline CAs
- CA hierarchy
- Certificate practice statements

Stand-alone and Enterprise CAs

An **enterprise CA** is a server running Windows Server 2012/R2 with the AD CS role installed. Enterprise CAs integrate with Active Directory and offer several advantages for a PKI running in a domain environment. A **stand-alone CA** is a server running Windows Server 2012/R2 with the

AD CS role installed, but it has little Active Directory integration. If you're issuing certificates only to domain member users and computers, you can install all enterprise CAs. If your network consists of non-Windows devices, you need at least one stand-alone CA. Although stand-alone CAs can be integrated with Active Directory somewhat for storing configuration information, the CA certificate, and CRL data, the integration must be done manually. Table 9-2 compares stand-alone and enterprise CAs.

Table 9-2   Stand-alone and enterprise CAs

Stand-alone CA server	Enterprise CA server
Active Directory not required	Active Directory required; server must be a member server (preferred) or domain controller
Can operate offline	Must operate online
Certificate requests must be approved manually	Certificate requests approved manually or automatically by using Active Directory information
No certificate templates available	Certificate templates available
Certificates not published in Active Directory	Certificates published in Active Directory
Requester must enter identifying information in certificate request manually	Identifying information taken from Active Directory
CA's certificate distributed to clients manually	CA's certificate distributed to clients automatically
CRL optionally published to Active Directory	CRL published automatically to Active Directory

© 2016 Cengage Learning®

Online and Offline CAs

A CA server is a critical component in a network's security. If a CA is compromised, all certificates the CA has issued are also compromised and must be revoked immediately. Given the critical nature of servers acting as CAs, running one or more servers in the CA hierarchy in offline mode is a common practice.

An offline CA isn't connected to the network, which makes it less vulnerable to attacks. However, all certificates and CRLs must be distributed with removable media. In a small network, using removable media to process certificate transactions works fine, but in a large network, depending on an offline CA for all certificate needs isn't practical. Typically, when a hierarchy of CAs is necessary, a mix of offline and online CAs is used.

The root CA is the most critical and is the server typically configured for offline operation. An offline CA must also be a stand-alone CA. The root CA issues certificates only to CAs in the next level of the hierarchy that can be accommodated by using removable media. The next section discusses this concept in more detail.

CA Hierarchy

A small organization might require only a root CA if certificate requirements are modest. Large organizations, however, might want to create a hierarchy of CAs, consisting of a root CA, intermediate CAs, and issuing CAs. A CA hierarchy distributes the load placed on CA servers and augments security.

The **root CA** is the first CA installed in a network. If it's an enterprise CA, its certificate is distributed to clients automatically via group policies. If it's a stand-alone CA, manual configuration of group policies is required to distribute its certificate. In either case, after clients are configured to trust the root CA's certificate, they also trust the certificate of any CA that's subordinate to the root. Administrators can use this fact to create a hierarchy that insulates the root CA from network exposure. This hierarchical arrangement is how you can operate a root CA in offline mode. The root CA needs to grant issuing certificates only to subordinate CAs, which are trusted by the clients they issue access certificates to.

Depending on an organization's needs, a CA hierarchy can be single-level, consisting of only the root CA; two-level, consisting of the root CA and one or more issuing CAs; or three-level, consisting of the root CA, one or more intermediate CAs, and one or more issuing CAs. Figure 9-2 shows two-level and three-level hierarchies.

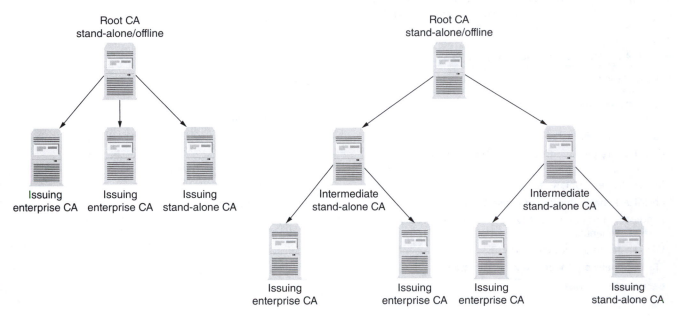

Figure 9-2 Two-level and three-level CA hierarchies
© 2016 Cengage Learning®

In the two-level hierarchy, the root CA issues certificates to subordinate CAs and then is usually taken offline for security. The subordinate CAs are called **issuing CAs** because they interact with clients to field certificate requests and maintain the CRL. Because the root CA issues certificates to issuing CAs and the clients trust the root CA, they also trust the issuing CAs. Issuing CAs are generally enterprise CAs or can be a combination of enterprise and stand-alone if the network includes non-Windows clients.

The three-level hierarchy is a common configuration and offers the most security because the issuing CAs, where user certificate requests are made, is farther removed from the root CA. In this arrangement, the root CA issues certificates to **intermediate CAs** (sometimes called "policy CAs"), authorizing them to issue certificates to other CAs. Intermediate CAs issue certificates to issuing CAs, which respond to user and device certificate requests. The root CA and intermediate CAs can be stand-alone and operate in offline mode. Issuing CAs can be a mix of enterprise and stand-alone CAs and operate in online mode.

Multilevel CA hierarchies are often used to distribute the certificate-issuing load in organizations with multiple locations. Each intermediate CA is responsible for one or more issuing CA in each location. In Figure 9-2, for example, one intermediate CA and its subordinate issuing CAs might handle certificate management for the U.S. location, and the other intermediate and issuing CAs handle certificates for the Europe location.

Certificate Practice Statements

A **certificate practice statement (CPS)** is a document describing how a CA issues certificates. A CPS isn't a required component of a PKI, but it should be developed as part of the planning process when an organization is designing its PKI. The document is usually published on the Internet, and every certificate the CA issues has a URL pointing to the CPS so that people examining the certificate can read the statement. Because the CPS describes the process used to issue certificates, it can be used as a guide when deploying your CA design. A CPS usually contains the following elements:

- Identification of the CA
- Security practices for maintaining CA integrity
- Types of certificates issued
- Policies and procedures for issuing, revoking, recovering, and renewing certificates
- Cryptographic algorithms used
- Certificate lifetimes
- CRL-related policies, including the location of CRL distribution points
- Renewal policy of the CA's certificate

The CPS is installed by creating a `CAPolicy.inf` file and placing the file in the CA server's *%systemroot%* directory before the AD CS role is installed. For more on creating this file, see *http://technet.microsoft.com/en-us/library/jj125373.aspx*.

Installing the AD CS Role

Best practices dictate that the AD CS role shouldn't be installed on a domain controller. In fact, for optimum security, AD CS should probably be the only role installed on the server. If you're installing a stand-alone CA, the server can be a member server if you want to take advantage of the limited Active Directory integration possible with stand-alone CAs. An enterprise CA must be installed on a member server running Windows Server 2012/R2 Standard or Datacenter Edition.

AD CS is installed in Server Manager by adding the AD CS role. During installation, you have the option to install several role services, including the following:

- *Certification Authority (selected by default)*—The CA component that issues, validates, and revokes certificates.

- *Certificate Enrollment Policy Web Service*—Enables users to get certificate enrollment policies via a Web browser.

- *Certificate Enrollment Web Service*—Allows users and computers to perform certificate enrollment via HTTPS. Works with Certificate Enrollment Policy Web Service to allow policy-based automated certificate enrollment for non-domain members. Supports Windows 7/Windows Server 2008 R2 and later.

- *Certification Authority Web Enrollment*—Allows users to request certificates, submit certificate requests by using a file, and retrieve the CRL via a Web browser. Supports a wide variety of OSs.

- *Network Device Enrollment Service*—Used to issue certificates to network devices, such as routers and switches.

- *Online Responder*—Allows clients to check a certificate's revocation status without having to download the CRL periodically.

Your selections of role services depend on how the CA will be used in your network. Will users enroll in certificates by using a Web browser? Will the CA issue certificates to only users and computers, or will you need to issue certificates to network devices, such as access points and routers? Will you use an online responder to automate CRL distribution?

Activity 9-1: Installing the AD CS Role

Time Required: 20 minutes
Objective: Install the AD CS role.

Required Tools and Equipment: 412Server1 and 412Server2
Description: You want to set up a PKI on your network to augment security, so in this activity, you install AD CS on 412Server2, a member server, and configure it as an enterprise CA.

9

1. Start 412Server1, if necessary. Start 412Server2, and log on to the domain as **Administrator**. (Be sure to log on with **412Dom1\Administrator** so that you log on to the domain instead of the local computer.)

2. In Server Manager, click **Manage, Add Roles and Features** to start the Add Roles and Features Wizard. Click **Next** until you get to the Server Roles window.

3. In the Server Roles window, click the **Active Directory Certificate Services** check box. Click **Add Features,** and then click **Next**. In the Features window, click **Next** again.

4. In the AD CS window, read the description and the paragraph under "Things to note." In particular, notice that you can't change the computer name, join a different domain, or promote the server to a domain controller after the role is installed. Click **Next**.

5. In the Role Services window, the Certification Authority option is selected by default. Click **Certification Authority Web Enrollment,** and then click **Add Features**. Click **Online Responder,** click **Add Features,** and then click **Next**. In the Web Server Role (IIS) window, click **Next**. In the Role Services window, click **Next**. In the Confirmation window, click **Install**. Click **Close** when the installation is finished.

6. In Server Manager, click the notifications flag, and then click the **Configure Active Directory Certificate Services on the destination server** link to start the AD CS Configuration Wizard. In the Credentials window, accept the default credentials **412Dom1\Administrator,** and click **Next**.

7. In the Role Services window, click **Certification Authority**. (You configure the other role services later.) Click **Next**.

8. In the Setup Type window, accept the default **Enterprise CA,** and then click **Next**.

9. In the CA Type window, accept the default **Root CA,** and then click **Next**.

10. In the Private Key window, accept the default option **Create a new private key** (see Figure 9-3). If this CA were replacing a failed CA or if you had an existing certificate you wanted to use, you would click "Use existing private key." Click **Next**.

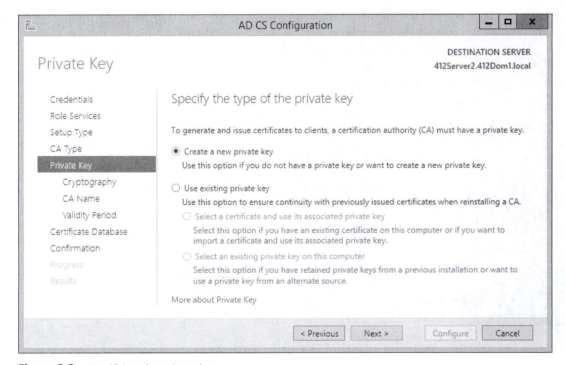

Figure 9-3   Specifying the private key

11. In the Cryptography window, accept the default selections (described after this activity), and then click **Next**.

12. The CA Name window requests a name for the CA (see Figure 9-4). By default, the name is generated automatically to include the domain name and server name followed by "CA." You can also enter the distinguished name suffix, but for most situations, the default is okay. Click **Next**.

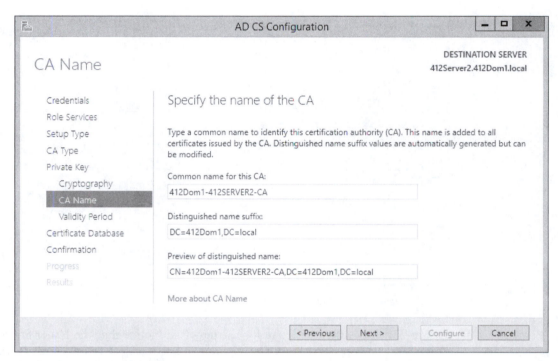

Figure 9-4   Specifying the CA name

13. In the Validity Period window, you can set the validity period of the certificate issued to this CA. The validity period should be specified in the certificate practice statement. The period you choose depends on how this CA is used and the types of certificates it will issue. If the certificate expires, the CA and any certificates it has issued are no longer valid. The validity period of the CA's certificate should be longer than that of the certificates it will issue. Certificates can be renewed as needed. Accept the default **5 years**, and then click **Next**.

14. In the Certificate Database window, you can choose where certificates and the certificate log should be stored. If the CA will be used heavily, these two databases should be stored on separate drives and shouldn't be placed on the same drive as the Windows folder. For testing purposes, you can use the default location C:\Windows\system32\CertLog for both databases. Click **Next**.

15. Click **Configure** in the Confirmation window. When the configuration is finished, click **Close**. If prompted to configure additional role services, click **No**.

16. Open a command prompt window. Type **certutil -viewstore** and press **Enter**. The View Certificate Store dialog box opens (see Figure 9-5), which lists all certificates currently published in Active Directory. Click the **412Dom1-412SERVER2-CA** certificate, and then click the **Click here to view certificate properties** link.

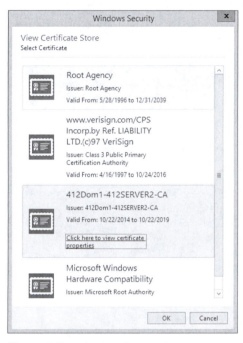

Figure 9-5 Viewing the certificate store

17. Figure 9-6 shows the certificate for the new CA. Notice that the Issuer Statement button is grayed out. If you publish a CPS, this button becomes active and links to your CPS. Click the **Details** tab to view more information about the certificate. Click the **Certification Path** tab, which shows the path through the CA hierarchy to the root CA where the certificate originates. In this case, only the current server is listed because you don't have a multilevel CA hierarchy. Click **OK**.

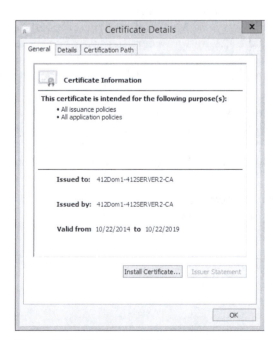

Figure 9-6 The General tab for the CA certificate

18. Click **OK** in the View Certificate Store dialog box to close it. Close the command prompt window.

19. Keep both servers running and stay logged on if you're continuing to the next activity.

A few figures shown in the preceding activity need some additional explanation. The Cryptography window in Step 11 of the AD CS installation includes several options (see Figure 9-7), described in the following list:

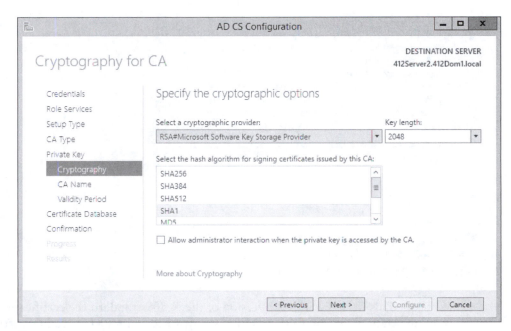

Figure 9-7   Options in the Cryptography window

- *Select a cryptographic provider*—This list box displays the cryptographic service providers (CSPs) already configured in Windows Server 2012/R2. A CSP is a library of algorithms for performing cryptographic functions, such as creating hashes and encrypting and decrypting data.

- *Key length*—This text box defines the number of bits that make up keys used in cryptography algorithms. Generally, the longer the key, the more difficult it is to crack. However, longer keys also take more CPU resources to perform cryptographic functions.

- *Select the hash algorithm for signing certificates issued by this CA*—A **hash algorithm** is a mathematical function that takes a string of data as input and produces a fixed-size value as output. Hash values are used to verify that the original data hasn't been changed and to sign the CA certificate and certificates issued by the CA.

- *Allow administrator interaction when the private key is accessed by the CA*—If this check box is selected, cryptographic operations require the administrator to enter a password, which helps prevent unauthorized use of the CA and its private key.

The Details tab you viewed in Step 17 of Activity 9-1 contains considerable information (see Figure 9-8). The following list describes some items in this tab:

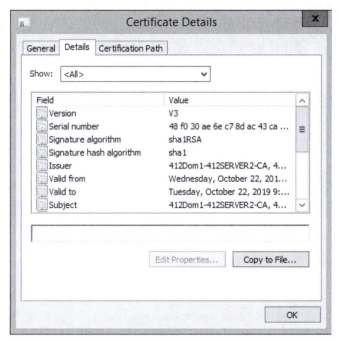

Figure 9-8 The Details tab for a certificate

- *Version*—This field specifies the version of the X.509 standard the certificate uses. X.509 is an international standard that defines many aspects of a PKI, including certificate formats.
- *Signature algorithm*—The hash algorithm used to sign the certificate.
- *Issuer*—The CA that issued the certificate. In this case, the certificate is self-signed, as all root CA certificates are.
- *Subject*—The device, computer, user, or other entity that has been issued the certificate. In this case, it's the CA itself.
- *Public key (not shown in the figure)*—Defines the algorithm and bit length for the public key.
- *Key usage (not shown in the figure)*—Specifies the purposes for which the certificate can be used. Examples are digital signatures and certificate signing.

Configuring a Certification Authority

After installing AD CS on a server, you must perform several configuration tasks, including the following, before using a new CA:

- Configure certificate templates.
- Configure enrollment options.
- Configure the online responder.
- Create a revocation configuration.

Configuring Certificate Templates

If you install an enterprise CA, some predefined certificate templates can be configured to generate certificates. Windows Server 2012/R2 supports four versions of certificate templates:

- *Version 1 templates*—Provided for backward-compatibility; Windows Server 2003 Standard Edition and Windows 2000 Server support only version 1 templates. These templates can't be modified or removed, and autoenrollment is not an option. Windows Server 2012/R2 includes several version 1 templates. You can duplicate these templates, and then they're converted to version 2 or 3 templates, which can be modified.

- *Version 2 templates*—Allow customization of most certificate settings and permit autoenrollment. They're supported by Windows Server 2003 Enterprise Edition and later.

- *Version 3 templates*—Provide advanced cryptographic functions; they can be issued only from Windows Server 2008 and later enterprise CAs and can be used only on Windows Server 2008/Windows Vista and later clients.

- *Version 4 templates*—Can only be used only on Windows Server 2012/R2 and Vista and later clients. Support cryptographic service providers and key service providers and enforcement of renewal with the same key. On Windows Server 2012 R2 and Windows 8.1 and later clients, they support Trusted Platform Module (TPM) key attestation, which lets the CA verify that the private key is protected by a hardware TPM.

Certificate templates are created and modified in the Certificate Templates snap-in (see Figure 9-9), which you can add to an MMC or open in the Certification Authority console via the Tools menu in Server Manager. Templates shown with Schema Version 1 must be duplicated before they can be modified. Each template type has different properties and a different number of tabs in the template Properties dialog boxes.

9

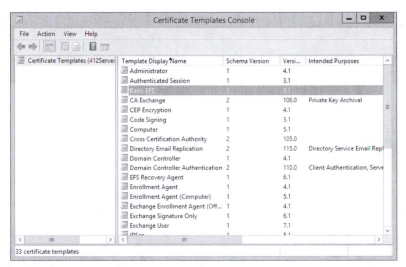

Figure 9-9   The Certificate Templates snap-in

A common certificate type is one used for EFS, which allows users to encrypt and decrypt files on a hard drive. The Basic EFS template is used to issue certificates to users so that they can protect files with EFS. The EFS Recovery Agent template is used to issue certificates to users who are designated as recovery agents so that EFS-encrypted files can be recovered if a user's EFS certificate becomes unusable for some reason.

Activity 9-2: Creating an EFS Certificate Template

Time Required: 10 minutes
Objective: Create an EFS certificate template.

Required Tools and Equipment: 412Server1 and 412Server2
Description: You want to issue certificates to employees so that they can use EFS throughout the domain. In this activity, you duplicate the version 1 Basic EFS template and create a version 3 EFS template for use on Windows 8.1 clients.

1. Log on to 412Server2 as **Administrator**, and open Server Manager, if necessary.

2. Click **Tools, Certification Authority** from the menu. Click to expand the server node. Right-click **Certificate Templates** and click **Manage** to open the Certificate Templates console.

3. Right-click **Basic EFS** in the right pane and click **Properties**. Notice that all options are grayed out because you must duplicate the version 1 template to make changes. Click **Cancel**.

4. Right-click **Basic EFS** and click **Duplicate Template**. In the Properties of New Template dialog box, you can select the minimum version of Windows Server that you want the certificate to be compatible with. In the Certification Authority list box, click **Windows Server 2012**. Click **OK** in the Resulting changes dialog box. In the Certificate recipient list box, click **Windows 8/Windows Server 2012**. Click **OK** in the Resulting changes dialog box.

5. Click the **General** tab, and type **EFS-2012** in the "Template display name" text box (see Figure 9-10). Notice that the certificate is set to publish in Active Directory automatically.

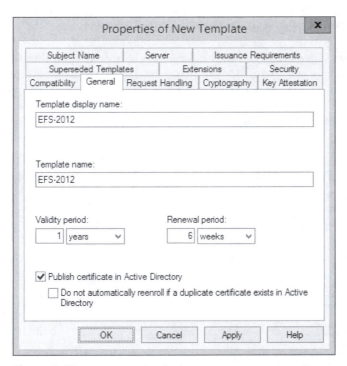

Figure 9-10   Changing the display name on a new template

6. Click the **Request Handling** tab. Click the **Purpose** list arrow to view the options for certificates created with this template. Leave **Encryption** as the selected purpose. Review the other options in this tab.

7. Click the **Superseded Templates** tab. Click **Add**, click **Basic EFS** in the Certificate templates list box, and then click **OK**. Now when a request for an EFS certificate is made, only the new EFS-2012 certificate is used.

8. Browse through the options in other tabs to see the configuration settings available for this template, and click **OK** when you're finished. Close the Certificate Templates console.

9. Stay logged on to 412Server2 and leave 412Server1 running if you're continuing to the next activity.

The following list describes some options in the General tab for certificate templates:

- *Template display name and Template name*—By default, these two fields have the same value, but they can be different. However, after the template has been created, you can't change either name.

- *Validity period*—The length of time the certificate is valid if it's not renewed. If the period elapses, the certificate expires; it's invalid and can no longer be renewed. You can specify the validity period in units of years, months, weeks, or days.

- *Renewal period*—The time window before a certificate's validity period expires in which the certificate can be renewed. For example, if a certificate is issued January 1, 2015, and has a validity period of 1 year and a renewal period of 1 month, the certificate can be renewed any time between December 1, 2015 and January 1, 2016. After a certificate is renewed, it's valid for another length of time specified by the validity period.

- *Publish certificate in Active Directory*—When this check box is selected, information about the template is available throughout the network.

- *Do not automatically reenroll if a duplicate certificate exists in Active Directory*—When this check box is selected, if a computer makes an enrollment request, a new enrollment request isn't made if a duplicate certificate already exists in Active Directory. Certificates can be renewed, but duplicate certificates aren't issued.

Configuring Certificate Enrollment Options

Certificate enrollment occurs when a user or device requests a certificate, and the certificate is granted. Enrollment can occur with several methods:

- Autoenrollment
- Certificates MMC
- Web enrollment
- Network Device Enrollment Service
- Smart card enrollment

Configuring Certificate Autoenrollment
When autoenrollment is configured, users and devices don't have to make explicit certificate requests to be issued certificates. Autoenrollment options are configured through group policies and the certificate template. In addition, the CA must be configured to allow autoenrollment, which is an option only on enterprise CAs.

Certificate autoenrollment is commonly used for EFS. A user must have a certificate to encrypt and decrypt a file with EFS. If no certificate server is operating on the network, Windows creates the certificate automatically but only on the computer where the encrypted file is created. Without a central store of certificates, certificates created this way could be deleted or lost too easily, resulting in loss of access to the encrypted file. In addition, the user would have to be logged on to the computer where the encrypted file is stored to access it; network access of the encrypted file wouldn't be possible.

By setting up autoenrollment for EFS certificates, a user's EFS certificate is created the first time he or she logs on to the domain after autoenrollment is configured. Furthermore, the certificate is available anywhere in the domain and is centrally stored, which makes backup and restore of the certificate easier. Because autoenrollment is configured through group policies, a user must be authenticated by a domain controller before a certificate is issued to make the process secure.

Autoenrollment is enabled in the Computer Configuration or User Configuration node of the Group Policy Management console. The Certificate Services Client - Auto-Enrollment policy, under Policies, Windows Settings, Security Settings, Public Key Policies and with the options shown in Figure 9-11, controls autoenrollment settings. The following list describes these options:

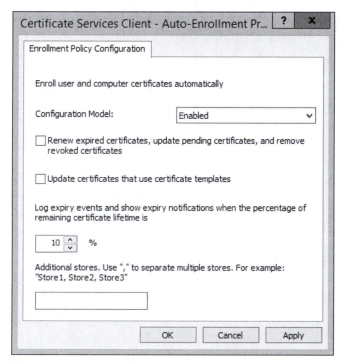

Figure 9-11   Options for the Auto-Enrollment policy

- *Configuration Model*—Options are Enabled, Disabled, and Not configured. If Enabled is selected, the Active Directory objects affected by the policy can autoenroll for certificates.
- *Renew expired certificates, update pending certificates, and remove revoked certificates*—When this check box is selected, autoenrollment is extended so that certificates are renewed, updated, and removed (for revoked certificates) automatically.
- *Update certificates that use certificate templates*—When this check box is selected, certificates created with a certificate template can be updated through autoenrollment if the template changes.
- *Log expiry events and show expiry notifications when the percentage of remaining certificate lifetime is*—Determines how much time can be left on a certificate's lifetime before a notification is issued and an event is logged.
- *Additional stores*—Specify additional certificate stores that should be monitored for certificate expiration. By default, the CurrentUser\My and LocalMachine\My stores are monitored.

Autoenrollment is configured for certificate templates in the Request Handling, Issuance Requirements, and Security tabs of a template's Properties dialog box. In the Request Handling tab, you can configure the amount of user interaction required during autoenrollment with the following options:

- *Enroll subject without requiring any user input*—This option is required for autoenrollment of computers and services. You can also select it if you want user autoenrollment to occur in the background without user interaction.

- *Prompt the user during enrollment*—Users must respond to prompts during autoenrollment.

- *Prompt the user during enrollment and require user input when the private key is used*—Users must enter a password during auto enrollment and each time their private keys are used. This option is the most secure but least user friendly.

The Issuance Requirements tab has options for specifying enrollment requirements for certificates issued from the template:

- *CA certificate manager approval*—If enabled, a CA manager must approve the certificate request before it's issued.

- *This number of authorized signatures*—If enabled and the number of signatures is more than zero, certificate enrollment requests must be signed with a digital signature. If more than one signature is required, autoenrollment is disabled.

- *Require the following for reenrollment*—Two options are available. If "Same criteria as for enrollment" is selected, users must use the same process for renewal that's required for initial enrollment. If "Valid existing certificate" is selected, renewal is automatic as long as the current certificate is valid.

The Security tab of a certificate template is similar to the Security tab of most Active Directory objects. By default, Domain Users group members have the Enroll permission. The Autoenroll permission must be set for users in the domain to autoenroll in the certificate.

The CA must be set to allow autoenrollment by configuring request-handling options (see Figure 9-12). To open this dialog box, click Properties in the Policy Module tab of a CA's Properties dialog box. The default option is "Follow the settings in the certificate template, if applicable. Otherwise, automatically issue the certificate." This option enables the CA to autoenroll applicable templates, so normally there's no need to change it unless you want to disallow autoenrollment. The "Set the certificate request status to pending" option accepts certificate requests but requires an administrator to issue the certificate manually in the Certificates MMC. Activity 9-3 explains this procedure.

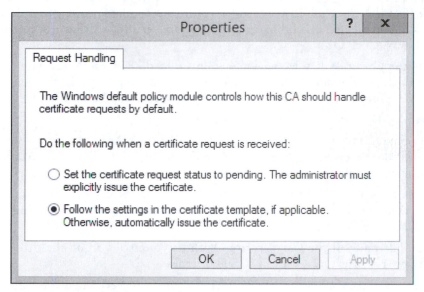

Figure 9-12   Request-handling options

The following list summarizes the steps for configuring autoenrollment after you have installed an issuing CA:

1. Create a certificate template.

2. Set options as needed in the Issuance Requirements and Request Handling tabs of the Properties dialog box.

3. Configure the template to allow autoenrollment by setting the Autoenroll permission for the users or groups who should autoenroll for the certificate.

4. Configure the Certificate Services Client - Auto-Enrollment policy.

5. Make sure the CA's request-handling options are configured to allow autoenrollment.

6. Add the template to the Certificate Templates folder under the CA server node.

Activity 9-3: Configuring Certificate Autoenrollment

Time Required: 20 minutes
Objective: Configure autoenrollment for users to use EFS.

Required Tools and Equipment: 412Server1 and 412Server2
Description: In this activity, you configure autoenrollment by configuring group policies and certificate template properties.

1. Log on to 412Server1 as **Administrator**, and open the Group Policy Management console.

2. Right-click the **Group Policy Objects** folder and click **New**. Type **CertAutoEnroll** in the Name text box, and then click **OK**.

3. Right-click **CertAutoEnroll** and click **Edit**. In the Group Policy Management Editor, click to expand **User Configuration, Policies, Windows Settings, Security Settings**, and **Public Key Policies**. In the right pane, double-click **Certificate Services Client - Auto-Enrollment**. (*Note:* Make sure you configure the policy in the User Configuration section of the GPO, not the Computer Configuration section.)

4. In the Enrollment Policy Configuration tab, click the **Configuration Model** list arrow and click **Enabled**. Click the **Renew expired certificates, update pending certificates, and remove revoked certificates** check box and the **Update certificates that use certificate templates** check box. Click **OK**.

5. Close the Group Policy Management Editor. In the Group Policy Management console, right-click the domain node and click **Link an Existing GPO**. In the Select GPO list box, click **CertAutoEnroll**, and then click **OK**. Close the Group Policy Management console.

6. Log on to 412Server2 as **Administrator**, if necessary.

7. Open Server Manager, and click **Tools, Certification Authority** from the menu. Click to expand the server node. Right-click **Certificate Templates** and click **Manage** to open the Certificate Templates console.

8. Double-click **EFS-2012** to open its Properties dialog box, and then click the **Security** tab. Click **Domain Users**, click the **Autoenroll** permission in the Allow column, and then click **OK**. Close the Certificate Templates console.

9. In the left pane of the Certification Authority console, right-click the CA server node (**412Dom1-412Server2-CA**) and click **Properties**.

10. Click the **Policy Module** tab, and then click **Properties**. Verify that the **Follow the settings in the certificate template, if applicable. Otherwise, automatically issue the certificate.** option button is selected, and then click **Cancel** twice.

11. In the Certification Authority console, click the **Certificate Templates** folder. The listed templates represent the certificates this CA can issue. Right-click the **Certificate Templates** folder, point to **New**, and click **Certificate Template to Issue**.

12. In the Enable Certificate Templates dialog box, click **EFS-2012**, and then click **OK**. Your CA is now ready to issue EFS certificates through autoenrollment. (*Note*: If you don't see the EFS-2012 template right away, close the Certification Authority console, wait a few minutes, and try Steps 9 to 12 again.)

13. Stay logged on to both servers if you're continuing to the next activity.

Activity 9-4: Testing EFS Certificate Autoenrollment

Time Required: 20 minutes
Objective: Test EFS certificate autoenrollment.

Required Tools and Equipment: 412Server1, 412Server2, and 412Win8
Description: You have configured a certificate template to autoenroll members of the Domain Users group with an EFS certificate. You test the configuration by logging on to the domain from 412Win8 and verifying that a new certificate has been issued. First, you create a user to test the certificate. (*Note*: If you're using virtual machines and can't accommodate three running simultaneously, you can log on to the domain controller instead of 412Win8. If you use the domain controller, you need to add Domain Users to the "Allow log on locally" policy in the Default Domain Controllers GPO.)

1. Log on to 412Server1 as **Administrator**, if necessary, and open Active Directory Users and Computers. In the Users folder, create a user with the first name **Test**, last name **Cert**, and logon name **TestCert**. Assign **Password01** and set the password to never expire. Start 412Win8, and log on to the domain as **TestCert**.

2. When you log on, autoenrollment of user certificates takes place. To verify that the EFS-2012 certificate has been issued, you can view your certificates. Right-click **Start**, click **Run**, type **MMC** in the Open text box, and press **Enter**.

3. Click **File**, **Add/Remove Snap-in** from the MMC menu. In the Available snap-ins list box, click **Certificates**, and then click **Add**. Click **OK**.

4. In the left pane, click to expand **Certificates - Current User** and **Personal**, and then click **Certificates**. The issued EFS-2012 certificate is displayed in the right pane (see Figure 9-13). (*Note*: If you don't see the certificate, you might need to run gpupdate from a command prompt on 412Win8, log off, log on again as TestCert, and then repeat this step.)

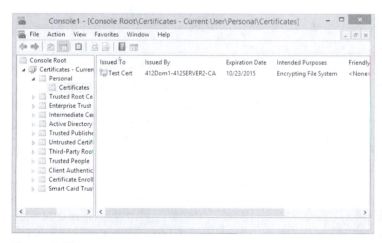

Figure 9-13   Viewing issued certificates

5. In the left pane, click to expand **Trusted Root Certification Authorities**, and click the **Certificates** folder to view certificates of CAs your computer trusts. 412Dom1-412Server2-CA should be listed near or at the top. (*Note*: Again, if you don't see it, try running the gpupdate command as described in Step 4.) Close the MMC. When prompted to save the console, click **No**.

6. On 412Server2 in the Certification Authority console, click the **Issued Certificates** folder. The TestCert certificate should be listed at the bottom. You might also see one or more certificates issued to 412Server1.

7. Close the Certification Authority console. Stay logged on to all computers if you're continuing to the next activity.

Requesting a Certificate with the Certificates Snap-in   Users can request certificates that aren't configured for autoenrollment by using the Certificates snap-in. To do so, make sure you're logged on to the domain. Then right-click the Certificates folder under the Personal folder, point to All Tasks, and click Request New Certificate to start the Certificate Enrollment Wizard.

The Request Certificates window (shown in Figure 9-14) lists the certificates available for this method. If you click the "Show all templates" check box, other templates are listed but have the status Unavailable. Select the certificates you want to enroll in, and click Details to see the certificate's validity period and how the certificate key can be used. This method for requesting certificates can be used only with enterprise CAs.

In most cases, autoenrollment is preferred over manual requests. If you want users to know their certificate information or you have specialized templates that only a few users require, you might want to use manual requests.

Figure 9-14   Using the Certificate Enrollment Wizard

Configuring Web Enrollment   After autoenrollment, the most common certificate request method is Web enrollment, which requires installing the Certification Authority Web Enrollment role service in Server Manager. This role service enables users to request and renew certificates, retrieve CRLs, and enroll for smart card certificates via their Web browsers. Web enrollment is the main method for accessing CA services on a stand-alone CA because, as mentioned, autoenrollment and the Certificates snap-in can be used only with enterprise CAs.

To access the Certification Authority Web Enrollment role service, users simply open a browser and go to *http://CAServer.domain/certsrv; CAServer* is the name of the CA server, and *domain* is the domain name. The server with the Web Enrollment role service installed can be, but need not be, the CA server. A server configured for Web enrollment is called a **registration authority** or a "CA Web proxy."

Starting with Windows Server 2012 R2, Windows XP clients aren't supported for Web enrollment.

Activity 9-5: Installing the Web Enrollment Role Service

Time Required: 20 minutes
Objective: Install the Web Enrollment role service.

Required Tools and Equipment: 412Server1, 412Server2, and 412Win8
Description: You have several certificates that you don't want to use autoenrollment for and have found that using the Certificates snap-in is cumbersome for users. You install the Certification Authority Web Enrollment role service with PowerShell and test it by requesting a certificate from 412Win8. (If you want to test the configuration from your CA server or domain controller, you must enable IE to run ActiveX controls.)

1. Log on to 412Server2 as **Administrator**, if necessary.

2. In Server Manager, click the notifications flag, and then click the **Configure Active Directory Certificate Services on the destination server** link. The AD CS Configuration Wizard starts. In the Credentials window, click **Next**.

3. In the Role Services window, click **Certification Authority Web Enrollment**, and then click **Next**. In the Confirmation window, click **Configure**. Click **Close**. If you're prompted to configure additional role services, click **No**.

4. IIS must have a Web Server Certificate. To request one, click **Tools, Internet Information Services (IIS) Manager** from the Server Manager menu.

5. In the left pane of IIS Manager, click the **412Server2** node. If you're prompted to get started with the Microsoft Web Platform, click **No**. In the middle pane, double-click **Server Certificates**.

6. In the Actions pane, click **Create Domain Certificate** to start the Create Certificate Wizard. In the Distinguished Name Properties window shown in Figure 9-15, fill in the following information:

- Common name: **412Server2.412Dom1.local**
- Organization: **Server 2012 412 Class**
- Organizational unit: *Your name*
- City/locality: *Your city*
- State/province: *Your state or province*
- Country/region: *Your country*

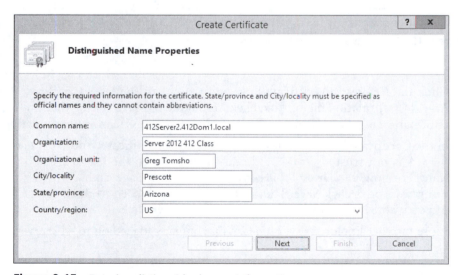

Figure 9-15   Entering distinguished name information

7. Click **Next**. In the Online Certification Authority window, click **Select**, click **412Dom1-412Server2-CA**, and then click **OK**. In the Friendly name text box, type **412Server2.412Dom1.local**, and then click **Finish**.

8. In the left pane of IIS Manager, click the **Sites** node. Right-click **Default Web Site** and click **Edit Bindings**.

9. In the Site Bindings dialog box, click **Add**. In the Add Site Binding dialog box, click the **Type** list arrow and click **https**. Click the **SSL certificate** list arrow, click **412Server2.412Dom1. local**, and then click **OK**. Click **Close**.

10. In the left pane of IIS Manager, click to expand **Sites**, click to expand **Default Web Site**, and then click **CertSrv**. In the middle pane, double-click **SSL Settings**. In the SSL Settings dialog box, click **Require SSL**, if necessary. Notice the options under "Client certificates." You can have the Web server ignore, accept, or require client certificates. If you want client computers to connect to the Web server to verify their identity, you would select Require. For now, leave the default **Ignore** selected. Click **Apply** in the Actions pane, and then close IIS Manager.

11. To test your configuration, log on to the domain from 412Win8 as **TestCert**. Open Internet Explorer, type **https://412Server2.412Dom1.local/certsrv** in the Address text box (making sure you enter "https," not just "http"), and press **Enter**. When prompted for a username and password, log on as **TestCert**. The Web enrollment home page opens (see Figure 9-16).

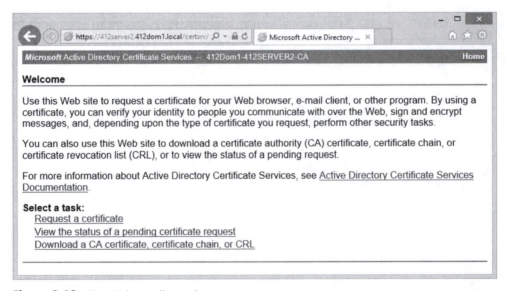

Figure 9-16   The Web enrollment home page

12. Click the **Request a certificate** link, and then click the **User Certificate** link. In the Web Access Confirmation dialog box, click **Yes**. In the message stating that no further identifying information is required, click **Submit**. In the Web Access Confirmation dialog box, click **Yes**.

13. In the Certificate Issued window, click **Install this certificate**. You see a message stating that the CA is not trusted. You could add 412Server2 to the list of trusted CAs in IE, if you want. For now, click **Install this certificate**. In the message asking whether you want to open `certnew.cer`, click **Save**. The certificate is downloaded to the default Downloads folder. (If you wanted to see the certificate, you could have clicked Open.)

14. Close Internet Explorer. Log off 412Win8, but stay logged on to 412Server2.

Using the Network Device Enrollment Service   The Network Device Enrollment Service (NDES) allows network devices, such as routers and switches, to get certificates by using Simple Certificate Enrollment Protocol (SCEP), a Cisco proprietary protocol. With this protocol, Cisco internetworking devices can request and get certificates to run IPsec, even if they don't have domain credentials. The procedure for installing and configuring NDES involves the following steps:

1. Create a user for NDES and add it to the IIS_USRS group.
2. Configure a certificate template with enroll permissions assigned to the NDES user.
3. Install the NDES role service.
4. Create a public/private key pair, using the network device's OS to enroll.
5. Forward the key pair to the registration authority on the server hosting NDES.
6. Submit a certificate request from the device to the NDES server.

 For more information on using NDES, see *http://technet.microsoft.com/en-us/library/cc753784.aspx.*

Using Smart Card Enrollment   Smart card enrollment is not so much an enrollment method as a specialized type of certificate template. It takes place through Web enrollment at a smart card station. After a user supplies credentials to request the smart card certificate and presents his or her card, the certificate information is embedded in the card.

Smart cards are used to enhance security. Users can log on to a network by presenting the card to a station with a card reader and entering their PINs, much like using an ATM card. A user designated as an enrollment agent can enroll smart card certificates on behalf of users to simplify the process. However, enrollment agents can enroll on behalf of any user, including administrators, which could pose a security risk. After a smart card is created for a user, the card can be used to log on as that user. Enrollment agents must be issued an Enrollment Agent certificate to perform this task, but considering the power an enrollment agent has, these people must be highly trusted in the organization.

To mitigate security concerns, Windows Server 2012/R2 offers restricted enrollment agents. With this feature, administrators can configure smart card certificate templates to specify which users or groups an enrollment agent can enroll in the certificate. To do this, use the "Restrict enrollment agents" option in the Enrollment Agents tab of the CA server's Properties dialog box. By default, enrollment agents are not restricted.

Configuring the Online Responder

An **online responder (OR)** enables clients to check a certificate's revocation status without having to download the CRL. To use an OR, you install the Online Responder role service when you install the CA role or later. You can install this role service on the same server as the CA role or a different server, and it requires the Web Server role service. After the OR role service is installed, it must be configured with these steps:

1. Configure an OCSP Response Signing certificate template, which is used to sign the response the OR provides to certificate revocation queries. (OCSP stands for Online Certificate Status Protocol.)
2. Configure the CA to support the online responder. An Authority Information Access (AIA) extension is configured on a CA to indicate the OR's location.

9

3. Add the OCSP Response Signing Certificate template to the CA, and enroll the OR with this certificate.

4. Configure revocation for the OR, including the settings required for the OR to reply to certificate status requests.

Activity 9-6: Configuring an OCSP Response Signing Certificate Template

Time Required: 20 minutes
Objective: Configure an OCSP Response Signing Certificate template.

Required Tools and Equipment: 412Server1 and 412Server2
Description: Now that you have configured your CA to issue certificates via autoenrollment and Web enrollment, you want to configure an online responder to field certificate status requests instead of requiring clients to download the CRL. You have already installed the Online Responder role service. Now you need to configure it.

1. Log on to 412Server2 as **Administrator**, if necessary. Make sure 412Server1 is running.

2. In Server Manager, click the notifications flag, and click the **Configure Active Directory Certificate Services on the destination server** link. The AD CS Configuration Wizard starts. In the Credentials window, click **Next**.

3. In the Role Services window, click **Online Responder**, and then click **Next**. In the Confirmation window, click **Configure**. Click **Close**.

4. Open the Certification Authority console, if necessary. Click to expand the server node. Right-click **Certificate Templates** and click **Manage**. In the right pane of the Certificate Templates console, right-click the **OCSP Response Signing** template and click **Duplicate Template**.

5. In the Properties of New Template dialog box, click the **General** tab, type **OCSP-2012** in the Template display name text box, and then click the **Publish certificate in Active Directory** check box.

6. Click the **Security** tab, and then click the **Add** button. In the Select Users, Computers, Service Accounts, or Groups dialog box, click **Object Types**. Click the **Computers** check box, and then click **OK**. Type **412Server2** and click **Check Names**. Click **OK**.

7. Click the **Enroll** and **Autoenroll** permissions in the Allow column, and then click **OK**. Close the Certificate Templates console.

8. The next step is to add the template to the CA. In the Certification Authority console, right-click **Certificate Templates**, point to **New**, and click **Certificate Template to Issue**.

9. In the Enable Certificate Templates list box, click **OCSP-2012**, and then click **OK**.

10. Next, you must inform the CA of the online responder's location. Right-click the CA server node and click **Properties**. Click the **Extensions** tab. Click the **Select extension** list arrow (see Figure 9-17), and then click **Authority Information Access (AIA)**.

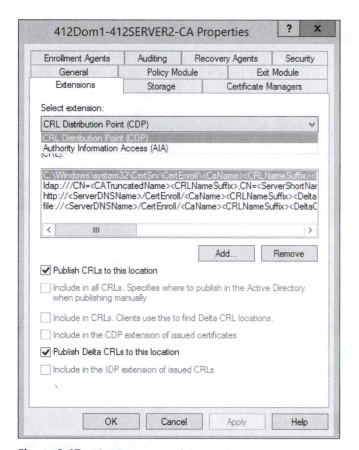

Figure 9-17   The Extensions tab

11. In the "Specify locations from which users can obtain the certificate for this CA" list box, click the entry starting with **http**. Click the **Include in the online certificate status protocol (OCSP) extension** check box, and then click **OK**.

12. When you're prompted to restart Active Directory Certificate Services, click **Yes**.

13. Now the OR server (412Server2, in this case) must enroll in the signing certificate you configured earlier in this activity. You can do this by restarting the server or requesting it manually. The next activity goes through the steps to request the certificate manually so that the server doesn't have to be restarted. Stay logged on for the next activity.

Activity 9-7: Requesting the OCSP Response Signing Certificate

Time Required: 10 minutes
Objective: Request the OCSP Response Signing certificate.

Required Tools and Equipment: 412Server1 and 412Server2
Description: To avoid restarting the OR server, you request the OCSP Response Signing certificate in the Certificates snap-in.

1. Log on to 412Server2 as **Administrator**, if necessary. Make sure 412Server1 is running.

2. Right-click **Start**, click **Run**, type **MMC** in the Open text box, and press **Enter**. Click **File, Add/Remove Snap-in** from the MMC menu.

3. Click **Certificates**, and then click the **Add** button. In the Certificates snap-in dialog box, click the **Computer account** option button, and then click **Next**. In the Select Computer dialog box, leave the default selection **Local computer**, click **Finish**, and then click **OK**.

4. In the left pane, click to expand the **Certificates** node and the **Personal** folder, and then click **Certificates**. Notice that two certificates are issued to this computer.

5. Right-click the **Certificates** folder, point to **All Tasks**, and click **Request New Certificate** to start the Certificate Enrollment Wizard. Click **Next** twice.

6. In the Request Certificates window, click the **OCSP-2012** check box, click the **Enroll** button, and then click **Finish**.

7. Click the **Certificates** folder again. You should see the new OCSP-2012 certificate in the list.

8. The last step is configuring the certificate. Right-click the **OCSP Signing** certificate, point to **All Tasks**, and click **Manage Private Keys**.

9. In the Security tab, click **Add**. In the "Enter the object names to select" text box, type **Network Service**, click **Check Names**, and then click **OK**. Click **OK**, and then close the MMC. Click **No** when prompted to save the console.

10. Stay logged on to 412Server2 for the next activity.

Creating a Revocation Configuration

A revocation configuration tells the CA what methods are available for clients to access CRLs. To create one, you use the Active Directory Certificate Services snap-in, under the Roles node in Server Manager. The steps are described in the following activity.

Activity 9-8: Creating a Revocation Configuration for the OR

Time Required: 10 minutes
Objective: Create a revocation configuration.

Required Tools and Equipment: 412Server1 and 412Server2
Description: You're almost finished configuring the online responder. The last task is creating the revocation configuration so that the CA can direct clients where and how to get their CRL.

1. Log on to 412Server2 as **Administrator**, if necessary. Make sure 412Server1 is running.

2. In Server Manager, click **Tools, Online Responder Management** from the menu. Right-click **Revocation Configuration** and click **Add Revocation Configuration**. In the Add Revocation Configuration Wizard's Getting started window, click **Next**.

3. In the Name the Revocation Configuration window, type **OR412Server2** in the Name text box. The name should describe the online responder function and include the server name. Click **Next**.

4. In the Select CA Certificate Location window, leave the default selection **Select a certificate for an Existing enterprise CA**, and then click **Next**.

5. In the Choose CA Certificate window, click **Browse** next to the "Browse CA certificates published in Active Directory" text box. The Select Certification Authority message box opens. Because there's only one choice, click **OK**. The Online Responder Signing certificate is loaded automatically. Click **Next**.

6. In the Select Signing Certificate window (see Figure 9-18), accept the defaults, and then click **Next**.

Figure 9-18   The Select Signing Certificate window

7. In the Revocation Provider window, click the **Provider** button, and then click **Add**. Type **http://412Server2.412Dom1.local/CertEnroll/412Dom1-412SERVER2-CA.crl**, and click **OK**.

8. Under the Delta CRLs text box, click **Add**. In the Add/Edit URL text box, type **http://412Server2.412Dom1.local/CertEnroll/412Dom1-412SERVER2-CA.crl**, and then click **OK** twice. In the wizard's final window, click **Finish**.

9. Stay logged on for the next activity.

To configure the CRL distribution schedule, click the Revoked Certificates folder in the Certification Authority console and click Properties to open the Revoked Certificates Properties dialog box (see Figure 9-19). The default CRL publication interval is 1 week, and the default publication interval for delta CRLs is 1 day. You can change the publication interval for the CRL from as little as 1 hour to as many as 999 years and the delta CRL from 30 minutes to 999 years. In addition, you can right-click the Revoked Certificates folder, point to All Tasks, and click Publish to publish the CRL immediately.

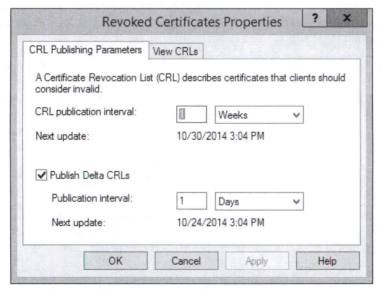

Figure 9-19   Configuring the CRL publishing schedule

One way to test the OR's configuration is to issue and then revoke some certificates. You can revoke certificates in the Certification Authority console by clicking Issued Certificates, right-clicking a certificate, pointing to All Tasks, and clicking Revoke Certificate. Then open a Web browser and go to *http://412Server2.412Dom1.local/CertEnroll/412Dom1-412SERVER2-CA.crl*. After you download this CRL file, open it. The Revocation List tab lists serial numbers and revocation dates for revoked certificates (see Figure 9-20).

Figure 9-20   The Certificate Revocation List dialog box

Maintaining and Managing a PKI

CA servers, issued certificates, and associated private keys are critical components of a network that depends on a public key infrastructure, so these components must be maintained and protected against disasters. In addition, key CA administrative roles must be assigned to responsible, trusted users to carry out the numerous tasks in maintaining a PKI environment.

Starting with Windows Server 2003, Microsoft introduced CA role-based administration, which limits the PKI tasks a domain administrator account can perform. By default, administrators can perform all tasks on a CA server. However, after roles have been assigned, administrators can perform only tasks related to their assigned roles. Whether you use role-based administration or not, four key roles must be filled to administer a CA and its components:

- *CA Administrator*—Configures and maintains CA servers. This role can assign all other CA roles and renew the CA certificate. To assign this role, give the selected user the Manage CA permission in the Security tab of the CA server's Properties dialog box.

- *Certificate Manager*—Approves requests for certificate enrollment and revocation. To assign this role, give the selected user the Issue and Manage Certificates permission in the Security tab of the CA server's Properties dialog box.

- *Backup Operator*—Not so much a CA role as an OS right. Members of the local Backup Operators group or a user who has been assigned the "Back up files and directories" and "Restore files and directories" rights can perform this role.

- *Auditor*—Manages auditing logs. Assigning the "Manage auditing and security log" right confers this role on a user.

For more on CA role-based administration, see *http://technet.microsoft.com/en-us/library/cc739182.aspx*.

CA Backup and Restore

Regular backup of all servers in a network is mandatory. When a full backup or system state backup is performed on a CA server, the certificate store is backed up along with other data. You might also want to back up the certificate database on each CA separately. The Certification Authority console includes a simple wizard-based backup utility you can use to perform backups with the following options:

- *Private key and CA certificate*—Backs up only the local CA's certificate and private key.

- *Certificate database and certificate database log*—Backs up the certificates issued by this CA. If your certificate database is large, you can choose to perform incremental backups, which back up only the changes to the database since the last full or incremental backup.

You can also use the `certutil` command-line program to back up the CA, and you can automate the process by using the command in a batch file or script and use Windows Task Scheduler to do periodic backups of the CA database.

Like backups, CA restores can be done with the Active Directory Certificate Services snap-in or the `certutil` command. Before you can restore the CA database, however, the CA service must be stopped. When you start the CA Restore Wizard, you're prompted to stop the service.

Activity 9-9: Backing Up the CA Server

Time Required: 10 minutes
Objective: Back up the CA server.

Required Tools and Equipment: 412Server1 and 412Server2
Description: Your CA server has been up and running and issuing certificates. You realize the importance of data the CA manages, so you do a backup of the CA certificate, private key, and certificate database.

1. Log on to 412Server2 as **Administrator**, if necessary. Make sure 412Server1 is running.

2. First, you need to create a folder for storing the backup. Normally, this folder is on another server or removable media. For this activity, create a folder named **CEBackup** in the root of the C drive.

3. Open the Certification Authority console, if necessary. Right-click the CA server node, point to **All Tasks**, and click **Back up CA** to start the Certification Authority Backup Wizard. Click **Next** in the welcome window.

4. In the Items to Back Up window, click **Private key and CA certificate** and **Certificate database and certificate database log**.

5. Click the **Browse** button next to the "Back up to this location" text box. In the Browse for Folder dialog box, navigate to and click the **CABackup** folder you just created, and click **OK**. Click **Next**.

6. In the Password and Confirm password text boxes, type **Password01**, and then click **Next**. In the Completing the Certification Authority Backup Wizard window, click **Finish**. The backup begins.

7. When the backup is finished, close any open windows, and stay logged on for the next activity.

Key and Certificate Archival and Recovery

If a user's private key is lost or damaged, he or she might lose access to systems or documents. If the key has been used for authentication to a system, a new certificate and key can be issued. However, if the key was used for applications such as EFS, the user loses access to encrypted documents. If a data recovery agent has been assigned to the user's documents, they can be recovered, but data recovery agents should be used only when there's no hope of the document owner regaining access to the files. By using **key archival**, private keys can be locked away and then restored if the user's private key is lost. Private keys can be lost if a user's profile is lost or corrupted or a smart card holding the private key is lost or damaged.

There are two methods for archiving private keys. Manual archival requires users to export their keys to a file by using the Certificates snap-in. The file is password-protected, and the password must be entered to import the key. The certificate the private key is related to must allow the private key to be exported. The default setting for private key export depends on the type of certificate template. For example, the default setting on an EFS or a User certificate template is to allow exportation. The default setting on a Computer or an IPsec template is to not allow exporting the private key.

The procedure for exporting the private key for a certificate is straightforward:

1. Open the Certificates snap-in in an MMC.

2. Locate the certificate for the key you want to export. Right-click the certificate, point to All Tasks, and click Export.

3. The Certificate Export Wizard walks you through the process.

The Certificate Export Wizard exports the certificate and can export the private key if allowed. You're prompted to select the format for the certificate export (see Figure 9-21). However, the only format supported for exporting the private key along with the certificate is

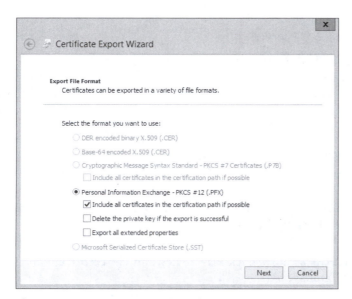

Figure 9-21 Selecting an export format for a certificate

Personal Information Exchange. If only the certificate is exported, other formats are enabled. You might want to export the certificate without the private key if the certificate is to be used on another computer or OS or for later recovery if the certificate is lost. To import a certificate and/or the private key, in the Certificates snap-in, simply right-click the folder where you want to import the key, point to All Tasks, and click Import. You're asked to supply the password used when the certificate was exported.

Manual key archival is fine for a network with few users and keys to manage. However, Windows Server 2012/R2 offers automatic key archival when manual key archival isn't adequate. Automatic key archival uses a key recovery agent (KRA), which is a designated user with the right to recover archived keys. A KRA has a lot of power, so the user should be chosen carefully. The designated user must enroll for a Key Recovery Certificate after the Key Recovery Agent template has been configured to allow the designated user to enroll. The Key Recovery Agent certificate is then added to the Recovery Agents tab of the CA server's Properties dialog box (see Figure 9-22).

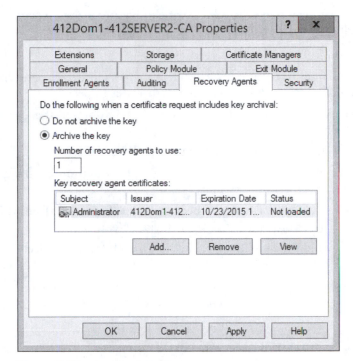

Figure 9-22   Configuring a key recovery agent

After a KRA is assigned, the key for each certificate issued from a certificate template with key export enabled is archived automatically. Multiple KRAs can be assigned to a certificate by entering a value in the "Number of recovery agents to use" text box. This number should usually be the same as the number of certificates you add to the "Key recovery agent certificates" list box that allow all installed KRAs to recover keys. The number of recovery agents can't be more than the number of certificates installed. If you specify a number lower than the number of certificates installed, the certificates are selected round-robin for each key archival procedure. In this case, you have to determine which recovery agents can recover an archived key. For example, if two recovery agents are specified and four KRA certificates are installed, two certificates are chosen for each key archival process. Either of the two KRAs can decrypt the key for recovery.

The recovery of a key that has been archived automatically typically follows these steps:

1. The user who has lost his or her private key contacts the Certificate Manager (role holder) to request key recovery.

2. The Certificate Manager locates the key in the CA database.

3. The Certificate Manager inspects the encrypted key's properties to determine which KRAs can recover the key. The Certificate Manager can copy the key from the CA database but can't decrypt the key unless he or she is also a designated KRA.

4. The key is sent to a KRA for decryption.

5. The KRA decrypts the key and sends it to the user in a password-protected file.

6. The user imports the key, using the password supplied by the KRA.

Activity 9-10: Archiving a Key Manually

Time Required: 15 minutes
Objective: Archive a private key.

Required Tools and Equipment: 412Win8
Description: You have just been issued an EFS certificate and realize you should archive your private key in case it's lost or corrupted.

1. Log on to the domain from 412Win8 as **TestCert**.

2. Add the Certificates snap-in to an MMC. In the left pane, click to expand the **Certificates** node and the **Personal** folder, and then click the **Certificates** folder.

3. Right-click the certificate, point to **All Tasks**, and click **Export**. In the Certificate Export Wizard's welcome window, click **Next**.

4. Click the **Yes, export the private key** option button, and then click **Next**.

5. In the Export File Format window, leave the **Personal Information Exchange - PKCS #12 (.PFX)** option button selected, and then click **Next**.

6. In the Security window, click the **Password** check box, type **Password01** in the Password text box and the Confirm password text box, and then click **Next**.

7. In the File to Export window, click **Browse**, and note which folder is selected as the destination folder. Type **EFSCert** in the File name text box, and click **Save**. Click **Next**.

8. In the Completing the Certificate Export Wizard window, click **Finish**. Click **OK** in the success message. Leave the Certificates snap-in open for the next activity.

Activity 9-11: Recovering a Lost Key

Time Required: 15 minutes
Objective: Recover a lost key.

Required Tools and Equipment: 412Win8
Description: Your private key was accidentally deleted, and you need to recover it from an archived backup.

1. First, you delete your existing certificate and key. In the left pane of the Certificates snap-in, click the **Certificates** folder, if necessary. Right-click the **EFS-2012** certificate and click **Delete**.

2. In the message box explaining that you can't decrypt data encrypted with this certificate, click **Yes**.

3. Right-click the **Certificates** folder, point to **All Tasks**, and click **Import**. (Note that you can request a new certificate, but a new certificate can't decrypt data encrypted with the deleted certificate.)

4. The Certificate Import Wizard starts. Click **Next**.

5. In the File to Import window, click **Browse.** In the File types list box, click **Personal Informa-tion Exchange.** Click the **EFSCert** certificate you exported in Activity 9-10, and then click **Open.** Click **Next.**

6. In the "Private key protection" window, type **Password01** in the Password text box, and then click the **Mark this key as exportable** check box. If you don't select this check box, you can't export the key again. Click **Next.**

7. In the Certificate Store window, accept the default **Personal** option, and then click **Next.**

8. In the Completing the Certificate Import Wizard window, click **Finish.** In the success mes-sage box, click **OK.** You should see your EFS-2012 certificate displayed in the Certificates folder.

9. Log off or shut down all computers.

Using Windows PowerShell to Manage AD CS

Table 9-3 lists some PowerShell cmdlets for managing AD CS. To see the full list of cmdlets for AD CS administration, type `Get-Command -Module AdcsAdministration`. To see the full list of cmdlets for AD CS deployment, type `Get-Command -Module AdcsDeployment`.

Table 9-3   PowerShell cmdlets for AD CS

Cmdlet	Description
`Add-CACrlDistributionPoint`	Adds a CRL distribution point path indicating where the CA publishes certification revocations
`Add-CATemplate`	Adds a certificate template to the CA
`Backup-CARoleService`	Backs up the CA database and all private key data
`Get-CACrlDistributionPoint`	Gets all the locations set on the CRL
`Get-CATemplate`	Gets the list of templates the CA can use to issue certificates
`Remove-CACrlDistributionPoint`	Removes the CRL distribution point
`Remove-CATemplate`	Removes the templates the CA can use to issue certificates
`Restore-CARoleService`	Restores the CA database and all private key data
`Install-AdcsCertificationAuthority`	Configures the Certification Authority role service
`Install-AdcsNetworkDeviceEnrollmentService`	Configures the Network Device Enrollment Service
`Install-AdcsOnlineResponder`	Configures the Online Responder role service
`Install-AdcsWebEnrollment`	Configures the Certification Authority Web Enrollment role service

© 2016 Cengage Learning®

Chapter Summary

- Active Directory Certificate Services (AD CS) provides services for creating a PKI in a Windows Server 2012/R2 environment. A PKI enables administrators to issue and manage certificates, which can add a level of security to a network.

- A PKI binds the identity of a user or device to a cryptographic key. The main services a PKI provides are confidentiality, integrity, nonrepudiation, and authentication.

- Some key terms for describing a PKI and AD CS include private and public keys, digital signature, certification authority, certificate revocation list, online responder, and certificate enrollment.

- An enterprise CA integrates with Active Directory; a stand-alone CA does not. Windows Server 2012/R2 Enterprise Edition must be installed to install an enterprise CA. For non-Windows devices or users, you need to install a stand-alone CA.

- A CA can be online or offline. An offline CA is more secure and usually used in a CA hierarchy with one or more online issuing CAs. An issuing CA issues a certificate to users and devices. A CA hierarchy is usually two-level or three-level. The first level is the root CA, and each level created is subordinate to the level above it.

- The AD CS role shouldn't be installed on a domain controller. An enterprise CA must be installed on a domain member server, but a stand-alone CA can be installed on a member server or a stand-alone server.

- Configuring a CA involves configuring certificate templates, enrollment options, and an online responder and creating a revocation configuration. There are four template versions, with the Version 1 templates provided for backward-compatibility, and the Version 4 templates used only with Windows Server 2012/R2.

- Certificate enrollment occurs when a user or device requests a certificate, and the certificate is granted. Enrollment can occur with autoenrollment, the Certificates MMC, Web enrollment, NDES, and smart cards.

- An online responder allows clients to check a certificate's revocation status without having to download the CRL periodically. The Online Responder role service requires installing the Web Server role service, too.

- Role-based administration limits the PKI tasks a domain administrator account can perform. Four key roles must be filled to administer a CA and its components: CA Administrator, Certificate Manager, Backup Operator, and Auditor.

- When a full backup or system state backup is performed on a CA server, the certificate store is backed up along with other data. You use the Active Directory Certificate Services snap-in to back up the certificate database and database log.

- When users' private keys are lost or damaged, they could lose access to systems or documents. Keys can be archived manually with the Certificates snap-in or automatically on enterprise CAs by assigning users as key recovery agents.

Key Terms

certificate practice statement (CPS)   A document describing how a CA issues certificates containing the CA identity, security practices used to maintain CA integrity, types of certificates issued, the renewal policy, and so forth.

certificate revocation list (CRL)   A list of certificates that the CA administrator has invalidated before their expiration dates.

certificate templates   A shell or model of a certificate used to create new certificates; it defines characteristics of the certificate, such as the intended use and expiration date.

CRL distribution point (CDP)   An attribute of a certificate that identifies where the CRL for a CA can be retrieved; can include URLs for HTTP, FILE, FTP, and LDAP locations. *See also* certificate revocation list (CRL).

enterprise CA   A server running Windows Server 2012/R2 with the AD CS role installed; integrates with Active Directory.

hash algorithm   A mathematical function that takes a string of data as input and produces a fixed-size value as output. Hash values are used to verify that the original data hasn't been changed and to sign CA certificates and certificates issued by the CA.

intermediate CAs   A CA in a multilevel CA hierarchy that issue certificates to issuing CAs, which respond to user and device certificate requests; sometimes called a "policy CA."

issuing CAs   A CA that interacts with clients to field certificate requests and maintain the CRL. *See also* certificate revocation list (CRL).

key archival   A method of backing up private keys and restoring them if users' private keys are lost.

Network Device Enrollment Service (NDES)   A service that allows network devices, such as routers and switches, to get certificates by using Simple Certificate Enrollment Protocol (SCEP), a Cisco proprietary protocol.

online responder (OR)   A role service that enables clients to check a certificate's revocation status without having to download the CRL. *See also* certificate revocation list (CRL).

public key infrastructure (PKI)   A security system that binds a user's or device's identity to a cryptographic key that secures data transfers with encryption and ensures data authenticity with digital certificates.

registration authority   A server configured with the Web Enrollment role service; also called a "CA Web proxy."

restricted enrollment agent   An enrollment agent that's limited to enrolling only specific users or security groups; available only with an enterprise CA.

root CA   The first CA installed in a network. Clients are configured to trust the root CA's certificate, and then implicitly trust the certificate of any CA that's subordinate to the root.

stand-alone CA   A server running Windows Server 2012/R2 with the AD CS role installed; not integrated with Active Directory.

Review Questions

1. Which of the following is a service provided by a PKI? (Choose all that apply.)
   a. Confidentiality
   b. Nonrepudiation
   c. Authorization
   d. Antivirus

2. Which of the following is used in both ends of the cryptography process (encryption and decryption) and must be known by both parties?
   a. Public key
   b. Private key
   c. Secret key
   d. Digital signature

3. A PKI is based on symmetric cryptography. True or False?

4. If you want the most security, which of the following should you use?
   a. Symmetric cryptography only
   b. Asymmetric cryptography only
   c. A combination of symmetric and asymmetric cryptography
   d. Secret key cryptography

5. Camille and Sophie want to engage in secure communication. Both hold a public/private key pair. Camille wants to send an encrypted message to Sophie. Which of the following happens first?
   a. Camille encrypts the message with her public key.
   b. Camille sends Sophie her private key.
   c. Sophie sends Camille her public key.
   d. Camille encrypts the message with her private key.

6. You have installed your root CA and will be taking it offline. The root CA must be which type of CA?
   a. Stand-alone
   b. Enterprise
   c. Intermediate
   d. Online

7. In a three-level CA hierarchy, the middle-level servers are referred to as which type of CA?

   a. Stand-alone

   b. Enterprise

   c. Intermediate

   d. Online

8. Which of the following identifies the CA and describes the CA's certificate renewal policy?

   a. Root CA

   b. Online responder

   c. CRL

   d. CPS

9. You're installing AD CS in your network. You need a secure environment and want to require the CA administrator to enter a password each time the CA performs cryptographic operations. Which option should you enable during installation?

   a. Select the hash algorithm for signing certificates issued by this CA.

   b. Select a cryptographic service provider (CSP).

   c. Use strong private key protection features provided by the CSP.

   d. Change the key length.

10. Version 1 templates can't be modified, but they can be duplicated and then modified. True or False?

11. A certificate is issued on July 1, 2015. Its validity period is 2 years, and its renewal period is 2 months. When can the certificate first be renewed?

    a. September 1, 2015

    b. May 1, 2017

    c. September 1, 2017

    d. May 1, 2016

12. Which of the following isn't a necessary step to configure autoenrollment?

    a. Configure a KRA.

    b. Configure a certificate template.

    c. Configure a group policy.

    d. Add the template to the CA.

13. You want to prevent tampering on your internetworking devices by issuing these devices certificates to run IPsec. What should you install?

    a. Online responder

    b. NDES role service

    c. Intermediate CA

    d. CDP

14. Which of the following steps is necessary to configure an online responder? (Choose all that apply.)

    a. Configure an OCSP Response Signing certificate template.

    b. Enroll the OR with the OCSP Response Signing certificate.

    c. Configure the OR enrollment agent.

    d. Configure revocation for the OR.

15. Which role can renew the CA certificate?

    a. CA Administrator

    b. Certificate Manager

    c. Backup Operator

    d. Auditor

16. Your CA has issued several hundred certificates and private keys to several hundred users. More than once, a user's private key has been lost or corrupted, resulting in lost data. You want to make sure your users' private keys can be recovered if needed. What should you do?

17. You want to create a separate backup for the certificate store and make sure the backup occurs every Friday at 11:00 p.m. How should you do this?

    a. Use Windows Backup to schedule a CA database backup weekly on Fridays at 11:00 p.m.

    b. Hire a technician to work Friday nights and instruct her on how to use the AD CS snap-in to back up the certificate store.

    c. Use `certutil` and Windows Task Scheduler.

    d. Use the AD CS snap-in to schedule the backup.

18. To reduce the amount of traffic generated when clients download the CRL, which of the following should you use?

    a. AIA

    b. Delta CRL

    c. CDP

    d. SCEP

19. You want to begin using smart cards for user logon. The number of enrollment stations you have is limited, so you want to assign department administrators to enroll only other users in their departments in smart card certificates. How should you go about this?

    a. Issue the designated department administrators an Enrollment Agent certificate. Publish the smart card certificate template. Have the designated enrollment agents use the Certificates snap-in to enroll departmental users in the smart card certificates.

    b. Issue the designated department administrators an Enrollment Agent certificate. Configure the smart card certificate templates with the list of users each enrollment agent can enroll. Have the designated enrollment agents use Web enrollment to enroll departmental users in the smart card certificates.

    c. Issue the designated department administrators an Enrollment Agent certificate. Configure the CA server's properties to restrict enrollment agents. Publish the smart card certificate template. Have the designated enrollment agents use Web enrollment to enroll departmental users in the smart card certificates.

    d. Configure Enrollment Agent Certificate templates with the list of users agents can enroll. Issue the designated department administrators an Enrollment Agent certificate. Publish the smart card certificate template. Have the designated enrollment agents use Web enrollment to enroll departmental users in the smart card certificates.

20. Your company runs a commercial Web site that enables your business partners to purchase products and manage their accounts. You want to increase the site's security by issuing certificates to business partners to augment logon security and protect data transmissions with encryption. What should you install?

    a. An online enterprise CA

    b. An online stand-alone CA

    c. An offline root CA

    d. An intermediate CA

Case Projects

Case Project 9-1: Designing a PKI and CA Hierarchy

You're called in as a consultant to create a CA hierarchy for a company. The company has three locations: one in the United States, one in South America, and one in Europe. Each location has approximately 1000 users who need certificates. About 75% of the users in each location are domain members running Windows 7 and Windows 8.1. The others are running a non-Windows OS and aren't domain members. Some features of the PKI should include the following:

- Web enrollment
- Autoenrollment
- Smart card enrollment, in which designated users can enroll other users
- EFS
- Automatic key archival
- Network device certificates
- Real-time query for certificate revocation status

Design the CA hierarchy, and label each CA according to its function and status (stand-alone, enterprise, root, intermediate, issuing, online, offline). The design should include a drawing showing the hierarchy as well as a detailed description, including how users and clients interact with the systems you selected. In addition, list the role services that need to be installed and the certificate template types that must be configured.

chapter 10

Implementing AD FS and AD RMS

After reading this chapter and completing the exercises, you will be able to:

- Install and configure Active Directory Federation Services
- Install and configure Active Directory Rights Management Services

Active Directory Domain Services is the foundation on which a Windows Server 2012/R2 network is built. By now, you should have enough knowledge to install and set up a secure, reliable domain-based network. However, although Active Directory Domain Services (AD DS) is the core technology in a Windows Server 2012/R2 domain, some complementary technologies installed as server roles can augment AD DS features and flexibility.

This chapter discusses two server roles: Active Directory Federation Services and Active Directory Rights Management Services. These roles use or integrate with AD DS technology to give users flexible, secure access to applications and network resources.

Active Directory Federation Services

Table 10-1 lists what you need for the hands-on activities in this chapter.

Table 10-1   Activity requirements

Activity	Requirements	Notes
Activity 10-1: Preparing for AD FS Deployment	412Server1, 412Server2	
Activity 10-2: Installing the AD FS Role	412Server1, 412Server2	
Activity 10-3: Preparing for AD RMS Deployment	412Server1, 412Server2, 412Server3	
Activity 10-4: Installing the AD RMS Role	412Server1, 412Server3	
Activity 10-5: Creating a Rights Policy Template	412Server1, 412Server3	
Activity 10-6: Exploring the Active Directory Management Services Console	412Server1, 412Server3	

© 2016 Cengage Learning®

The **Active Directory Federation Services (AD FS)** server role allows single sign-on access to Web-based resources, even when resources are in a different forest or a different network belonging to another organization. A typical situation is a user in Company A who needs to access resources in partner Company B with a Web browser, so Company B sets up a secondary account for the Company A user. The user is prompted for credentials when attempting resource access. If the number of users involved in this type of transaction is low, the extra work required to maintain users is minimal. The inconvenience of having to enter credentials each time the resource is accessed might not be a major burden. However, if many users must be maintained or users must communicate with many external companies, a single sign-on might be warranted. AD FS is designed for just this situation.

AD FS Overview

AD FS provides functions similar to a one-way forest trust, except in a forest trust, domain controllers in each forest must be able to communicate directly with one another without interruption of service. As a result, when forests are hosted on separate organizations' networks, firewalls on the networks must be configured to allow Active Directory communication, which raises security concerns. AD FS is designed to work over the public Internet with a Web browser interface. Its main purpose is to allow secure business-to-business transactions over the Internet; users need to log on only to their local networks. AD FS servers and AD FS–enabled Web servers then manage authentication and access to resources on partner networks without additional user logons.

Like most OS technologies, AD FS has its own terms for describing its components. The next sections discuss some terms and components used by AD FS.

Federation Trusts   A **federation trust**, like other types of trust relationships, involves a trusting party and trusted party. Because AD FS is designed to facilitate business partnerships, the term "partner" is used instead of "party." A federation trust is inherently a one-way trust, but a two-way trust could be formed simply by creating a trust in both directions.

A typical business partner relationship involves users on one company network accessing resources on another company network. For example, with a supplier of goods and a wholesale purchaser of those goods, the supplier is likely to be the trusting partner, and the purchaser is the trusted partner. Users at the purchasing (trusted) company might access order entry, inventory, and order status applications and databases at the supplier (trusting) company. In AD FS terminology, the trusted company is referred to as the **account partner**, and the trusting company is called the **resource partner**. In the trust relationship in Figure 10-1, the arrow points from the trusting (resource) partner to the trusted (account) partner. Users in the account partner organization are said to have a federated identity, which describes the agreed-on standards for sharing user identity information among two or more parties. This shared identity information is used to grant users privileges and permissions to resources across organizations.

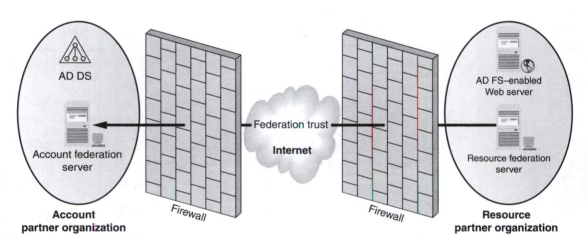

Figure 10-1   A federation trust relationship

© 2016 Cengage Learning®

10

Account Partners and Resource Partners

User accounts in the account partner can be Active Directory or Active Directory Lightweight Directory Service (AD LDS) user accounts. The resource partner organization hosts applications and other resources that are accessible to account partner users. When a user in the account partner organization wants to access these resources, a federation server in the account partner's network presents a security token representing the user's credentials to Web resources in the resource partner's network. Based on the security token, the federation server in the resource partner's network grants or denies access.

Claims-Aware Applications

In AD FS parlance, the user credentials packaged in a security token are called "claims." A **claim** is an agreed-on set of user attributes that both parties in a federation trust use to determine a user's credentials, which specify the user's permissions to resources in the partner's network. Claims typically include a user's logon name and group memberships and can include other attributes, such as department, title, and so forth. A claims-aware application is an ASP.NET application that makes user authorization decisions based on claims packaged in AD FS security tokens.

Windows NT Token Applications

Applications that aren't claims aware can still participate in AD FS. These applications rely on Windows NT–style access tokens to determine user authorization. These tokens contain traditional user and group security principal SIDs, and access control lists (ACLs) are used to determine user permissions to a resource. An NT token-based application is an IIS application that relies on standard Windows authentication methods rather than claims. This type of application might be developed by using a legacy scripting language, such as Perl or an older version of ASP that doesn't use the .NET programming interfaces.

AD FS Role Services and Components

In Windows Server 2012, the AD FS role consists of four role services that can be installed on one or more servers. The role services that are installed usually depend on whether you're installing AD FS in an account partner's or a resource partner's network:

- *Federation Service*—The function of the Federation Service role service depends on whether the network where it's installed is acting as an account partner or a resource partner. When used in an account partner network, its function is to gather user credentials into claims and package them into a security token. The security token is then passed to the federation service on the resource partner network, which receives security tokens and claims from the account partner and presents the claims to Web-based applications for authorization. A server with this role service installed is called a **federation server**.

- *Federation Service Proxy*—This role service is installed on servers in a perimeter network outside the organization's firewall. A **federation server proxy** fields authentication requests from browser clients and passes them to the federation server inside the firewall. A server configured as a federation service proxy protects the federation server from exposure to the Internet. The Federation Service and Federation Service Proxy role services can't be installed on the same server.

- *AD FS Web agents*—A Web server can host the claims-aware agent or the Windows token-based agent role service. These servers are called **AD FS–enabled Web servers**. Web agents manage security tokens sent by a federation server to determine whether the user whose credentials are described in the token can access applications hosted by the AD FS–enabled Web server. These two role services are available:

  o Claims-aware agent: An AD FS Web agent that handles security tokens by using claims.

  o Windows token-based agent: An AD FS Web agent that handles Windows NT–based tokens.

Starting with Windows Server 2012 R2, AD FS deployment has been simplified: You just install the Active Directory Federation Services role. There are no additional role services to choose. The functions of a federation service proxy and Web agents are now provided by the Web Application Proxy role service under the Remote Access role and must be installed on a separate server from the AD FS role. The server running Web Application Proxy is installed on the perimeter network when you need to provide federation services to clients on untrusted networks.

Additional components and terms in an AD FS deployment include the following:

- *Claims providers*—A **claims provider** is a server that supplies a user with claims to present to the resource partner for access to federated resources. The claims provider works with Active Directory to verify the authenticated user and then builds the claim based on user attributes. The assembled user attributes depend on the requirements of the resource partner.

- *Relying party*—The **relying party** is the resource partner that hosts the resources accessed by the account partner. It processes and validates claims issued by the claims provider and presents a token that grants access to a resource.

- *Relying party trust*—A **relying party trust** is an AD FS trust created on the AD FS server that acts as the claims provider in an AD FS deployment. This trust causes the claims provider to "trust" the relying party claims are being made for.

- *Claims provider trust*—A **claims provider trust** is a trust created on the AD FS server that acts as the relying party or resource partner. This trust causes the relying party (resource partner) to "trust" the claims provider so that claims supplied by the claims provider are considered reliable.

- *Claim rules*—**Claim rules** are conditions that determine what attributes are required in a claim and how claims are processed by the federation server. There are two types of claim rules: relying party trust claim rules and claims provider trust claim rules.

- *Attribute store*—The **attribute store** is an LDAP-compatible database that stores the values in claims. Active Directory is most commonly used as the attribute store, but other LDAP databases and Microsoft SQL Server can also be used.

AD FS 2.1 was released with Windows Server 2012 and also applies to AD FS implementations in Windows Server 2012 R2. AD FS 2.0 was available for Windows Server 2008 R2 and Windows Server 2008 as a free download. AD FS 1.1 was an installable role in Windows Server 2008/R2, and AD FS 1.0 was an installable component in Windows Server 2003. This chapter focuses on AD FS 2.1.

AD FS Design Concepts

AD FS can be deployed in several situations. Depending on the situation, you might use a combination of AD FS role services to address an organization's federated identity needs. The AD FS designs discussed in the following sections cover the federated identity needs most organizations are likely to have.

Web SSO   The simplest of the AD FS designs, the **Web SSO** provides single sign-on access to multiple Web applications for users who are external to the organization's network. This design is most often used in consumer-to-business relationships. There's no federation trust between federation servers, as with other AD FS designs, because this design has only one federation server. Usually, it consists of a federation server inside the organization's firewall and a federation proxy server (or Web Application Proxy in Windows Server 2012 R2 deployments) connected to the internal network as well as an Internet-accessible perimeter network. In addition, it contains one or more AD FS–enabled Web servers, also Internet accessible, that are connected to the organization's network. Clients requiring access to Web applications need to log on only once. A username and password must be created for each user in a directory service. Credentials are presented to the federation proxy server, which forwards them to the internal federation server, which then issues a security token after successful authentication. Figure 10-2 shows the following process for authenticating to an AD FS–enabled Web application:

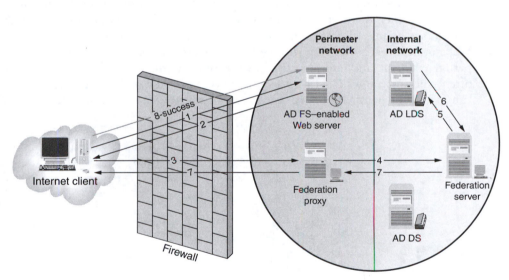

Figure 10-2   Web SSO authentication and authorization
© 2016 Cengage Learning®

The perimeter network in the figure is sometimes referred to as a "DMZ (demilitarized zone)," and there's a firewall (not shown) between the perimeter network and the internal network.

1. A user attempts to access an application on the AD FS–enabled Web server.

2. The AD FS–enabled Web server refuses access and redirects the browser to the federation proxy server's logon page.

3. The user's browser requests the logon page from the federation proxy server.

4. The user enters logon credentials, and the federation proxy server passes them to the federation server in the internal network.

5. The federation server validates the credentials with a directory service, such as AD LDS.

6. The federation server receives credential information from the directory service and creates the security token.

7. The security token is passed back to the client with the URL of the application on the AD FS–enabled Web server.

8. The client presents the security token to the Web server and accesses the application.

Federated Web SSO   The federated Web SSO design is similar to Figure 10-1, in which a trust relationship is established between the resource partner and the account partner. A federation server is running on both networks. Although not shown in the figure, federation proxy servers are often used in this design to enhance security. The Web SSO design is inherent in this design, where Internet users who aren't part of the trust can still access Web applications in the resource partner network. In this situation, the account partner users request Web services from the resource partner. The resource partner doesn't authenticate the user locally, but redirects the user back to the federation server in the account partner network. The account federation server validates the credentials and creates a security token for the client to present to the resource federation server. The federation server creates a security token for the client to present to the AD FS–enabled Web server, and the client requests the application. The federated Web SSO design supports business-to-business relationships for collaboration or commerce purposes.

Federated Web SSO with Forest Trust   The federated Web SSO with forest trust design involves a network with two Active Directory forests. One forest, in the perimeter network, is considered the resource partner. The second forest, in the internal network, is the account partner. A forest trust is established between domain controllers in both forests. In this design (see Figure 10-3), internal forest users and external users have access to AD FS–enabled Web applications in the perimeter network. External users have Active Directory accounts in the perimeter forest, and internal users have accounts in the internal forest. This design is used most often when Windows NT token applications are hosted on Web servers. The AD FS Web agent running in the perimeter network intercepts authentication requests and creates the NT security

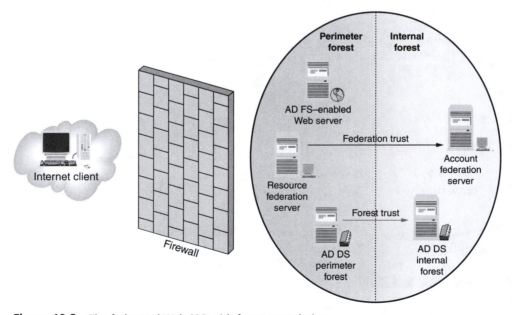

Figure 10-3   The federated Web SSO with forest trust design
© 2016 Cengage Learning®

tokens that Web applications need to make authorization decisions. The forest trust enables the Web agent to authenticate users from the internal network. External users are authenticated because the Web agent server is a member of the perimeter network forest. The federated Web SSO with forest trust design is most often used in business-to-employee relationships and allows both internal and external employees to access AD FS–enabled Web applications.

Preparing to Deploy AD FS

After you have decided on a federation design, there are a few other requirements to consider:

- AD FS 2.1 is supported by Windows Server 2012 and Windows Server 2012 R2. To use Web Application Proxy instead of Federation Proxy, use Windows Server 2012 R2 servers.

- Federation servers, federation proxy servers, and Web servers hosting AD FS Web agents must be configured with Transport Layer Security/Secure Sockets Layer (TLS/SSL), which is used by the HTTPS protocol. Firewalls must permit HTTPS traffic.

- Web browsers on client computers must have JScript and cookies enabled.

- One or more account stores, such as AD DS or AD LDS, must be running on the network. However, running AD DS on the same server as any AD FS roles isn't recommended.

- Certificates are required by federation servers, federation server proxies, Web Application Proxy servers, and AD FS–enabled Web servers. Certificates can be requested from a public certification authority (CA) or internally from an AD CS CA. Optionally, you can self-sign certificates, which works well for testing environments.

As you have seen in the diagrams of AD FS designs, installing and testing AD FS require a complex network environment and several computers. Setting up and testing AD FS with the simplest design, Web SSO, require at least four computers. Other designs could require up to eight computers, if proxies are used. Following is an overview of the steps for implementing a Web SSO design:

1. Create a service account to be used by the AD FS role.

2. Install a Web Server certificate.

3. Install the Federation Service role service on a server in the internal network.

4. Install the Federation Service Proxy role service or the Web Application Proxy role service (for Windows Server 2012 R2 deployments) on a server in the perimeter network (optional).

5. Install the Web Server role service and the AD FS Web Agent role service on the AD FS–enabled Web server.

6. Install AD DS or AD LDS to maintain the account store (the database containing user accounts). With Web SSO designs, AD LDS or a similar LDAP-compatible account store is usually used.

7. Install the claims-aware or Windows NT token-based application on the Web server.

Most of these steps involve several substeps, such as issuing certificates, configuring DNS, and so forth. Activities 10-1 and 10-2 walk you through the first steps of configuring an AD FS deployment. The Microsoft Technet Web site describes a thorough step-by-step procedure for deploying each AD FS design at *http://technet.microsoft.com/en-us/library/dn486820.aspx*.

You don't configure a full AD FS deployment in this chapter. A full AD FS deployment requires a claims-aware Web application, a Web server to host the claims-aware application, an AD FS server, a domain controller, and a client machine at minimum. However, this chapter guides you through installing the AD FS role and discusses some configuration options that should be enough for the 70-412 certification exam.

10

Activity 10-1: Preparing for AD FS Deployment

Time Required: 20 minutes
Objective: Prepare for AD FS deployment.

Required Tools and Equipment: 412Server1 and 412Server2
Description: In this activity, you create a service account and install a certificate for use with AD FS.

1. Start 412Server1, if necessary, and log on as **Administrator**. Start 412Server2.

2. On 412Server1, open a PowerShell window. Type **Add-KdsRootKey -EffectiveTime (Get-Date).AddHours(-10)** and press **Enter**. This key is used to generate Managed Service Account passwords.

3. Next, type **New-ADServiceAccount ADFSsvc -DNSHostName 412Server2. 412Dom1.local -ServicePrincipalNames http://412Server2.412Dom1. local** and press **Enter**.

4. Next, you need to install a certificate. Because you installed AD CS in Chapter 9, you issue one from the CA. On 412Server2, open Server Manager, and click **Tools, Certification Authority** from the menu.

5. Click to expand the server node, and then right-click **Certificate Templates** and click **Manage**. Scroll down, and then right-click the **Web Server** template and click **Properties**.

6. In the Web Server Properties dialog box, click the **Security** tab. Click **Authenticated Users**, click the **Enroll** check box in the Allow column, and then click **OK**. Close the Certificate Templates console and the Certification Authority console.

7. Open an MMC console and add the **Certificates** snap-in to it, being sure to click **Computer account** and **Local Computer** when prompted.

8. In the Certificates snap-in, expand the **Personal** folder, and then right-click the **Certificates** folder, point to **All Tasks**, and click **Request New Certificate**.

9. In the Certificate Enrollment window, click **Next**. In the Select Certificate Enrollment Policy window, click **Next**.

10. In the Request Certificates window, click the **Web Server** check box, and then click the **More information is required to enroll for this certificate** link (see Figure 10-4) to open the Certificate Properties dialog box.

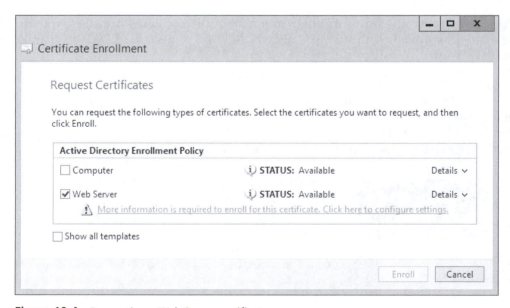

Figure 10-4 Requesting a Web Server certificate

11. Click the **Subject** tab, if necessary. Click the list arrow under Type in the Subject name section, and click **Common name**. Type **412Server2.412Dom1.local** in the Value text box, and then click the **Add** button. In the Alternative name section, click the list arrow under Type, and click **DNS**. In the Value text box, type **412Server2.412Dom1.local**, and then click the **Add** button (see Figure 10-5). In the Alternative name section, type **enterpriseregistration.412Dom1.local** in the Value text box, and then click the **Add** button. The "enterpriseregistration" alternative name is needed for device registration for Workplace Joins if you want to use this feature. Click **OK**.

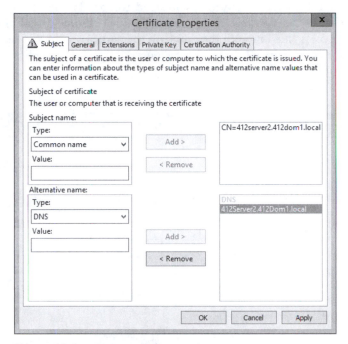

Figure 10-5   Configuring the certificate

12. Click the **Enroll** button. When the enrollment is completed, click **Finish**. In the Certificates snap-in, you see the new certificate in the Certificates folder. Close the MMC, and click **No** when prompted to save it. Close the Certification Authority console.

13. Keep both servers running and stay logged on if you're continuing to the next activity.

Activity 10-2: Installing the AD FS Role

Time Required: 20 minutes
Objective: Install the AD FS role.

Required Tools and Equipment: 412Server1 and 412Server2
Description: Install the AD FS role on 412Server2. 412Server1 must be running.

1. Start 412Server1, if necessary. Start 412Server2, and log on to the domain as **Administrator**. (Be sure to log on with **412Dom1\Administrator** so that you log on to the domain instead of the local computer.)

2. In Server Manager, click **Manage, Add Roles and Features** to start the Add Roles and Features Wizard. Click **Next** until you get to the Server Roles window.

3. In the Server Roles window, click **Active Directory Federation Services**, and then click **Next** until you get to the Confirmation window. Click **Install**, and when the installation is finished, click **Close**.

4. In Server Manager, click the notifications flag, and click the **Configure the federation service on this server** link to start the Active Directory Federation Services Configuration Wizard. In the Welcome window, read the information, accept the default option **Create the first federation server in a federation server farm**, and then click **Next**.

5. In the Connect to AD DS window, accept the default credentials, and click **Next**.

6. In the Specify Service Properties window, you need to specify the SSL certificate. Click the **SSL Certificate** list arrow, and click **412Server2.412Dom1.local**. The Federation Service Name text box is filled in with the name on the certificate. In the Federation Service Display Name text box, type **FS 412Dom1** (see Figure 10-6), and then click **Next**.

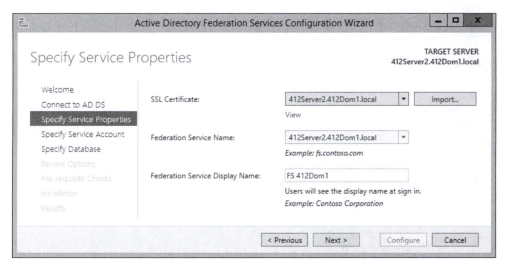

Figure 10-6   Specifying service properties

7. In the Specify Service Account window, type **ADFSsvc** (the service account you created in Activity 10-1) in the Account Name text box, and then click **Next**.

8. In the Specify Database window, accept the default **Create a database on this server using Windows Internal Database**. (If you had an SQL server available, you could use it instead.) Click **Next**.

9. In the Review Options window, review the selections, and click **Next**. (If you were going to do similar installations on additional servers, you could click the View script button to see the PowerShell script that performs the installation and use it on other servers.)

10. In the Pre-requisite Checks window, verify that all prerequisites were met, and then click **Configure**. You might see a warning about setting the SPN for the service account. You can ignore this error. When the configuration is finished, click **Close**.

11. In Server Manager, click **Tools, AD FS Management**. You use this console in the next activity.

12. Keep both servers running and stay logged on if you're continuing to the next activity.

Configuring a Relying Party Trust

Recall that the relying party is the resource partner that accepts claims from the account partner to make authentication and authorization decisions. A relying party trust sets up the trust relationship between the claims provider and the relying party (resource partner). You configure the relying party trust on the AD FS server that issues claims (usually the account partner), which in effect causes the claims provider to "trust" the relying party. To configure the relying party trust, right-click the Relying Party Trusts folder in the AD FS console and click Add Relying Party Trust to start the Add Relying Party Trust Wizard. In the Welcome window, click Start. Then provide the following information:

- *Select Data Source*—In this window, you specify how the wizard gets information about the relying party. This information is the metadata the relying party needs to create the trust, including the SSL certificate. It's usually published by the claims-aware application that users will access via federation services. Select from the following options (shown in Figure 10-7):

    o Import data about the relying party published online or on a local network: With this option, you import data from a server, usually by supplying the URL of the relying party's published application metadata.

    o Import data about the relying party from a file: Use this option if the relying party can't be contacted directly and has exported the metadata to a file. The location can be a local path or a UNC path.

    o Enter data about the relying party manually: This option requires entering a display name, choosing an AD FS configuration profile (the AD FS compatibility version), configuring a certificate, selecting authentication options, setting authorization rules, and so forth. Choose this option if the relying party application can't publish or export its federation metadata.

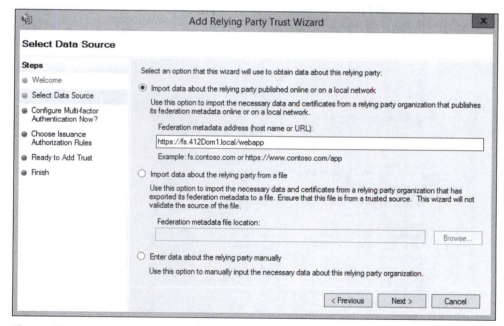

Figure 10-7   Configuring the relying party trust

- *Configure Multi-factor Authentication Now?*—Optionally, you can configure multi-factor authentication, described later in "Configuring Authentication Policies."

- *Choose Issuance Authorization Rules*—Issuance authorization rules determine which users can receive claims for the relying party. You can allow all users (default) or deny all users. If you deny all users, you must add issuance authorization rules later to allow specific users to access the relying party.

Configuring a Claims Provider Trust

You configure a claims provider trust on the AD FS server that acts as the relying party (resource partner). Doing so configures the relying party to trust the claims issued by the claims provider (account partner). To configure a claims provider trust, right-click the Claims Provider Trusts folder in the AD FS console and click Add Claims Provider Trust to start the Add Claims Provider Trust Wizard. In the Welcome window, click Start. The Select Data Source window has the same options as in the Add Relying Party Trust Wizard. That's all the information you need to enter to set up this trust.

Configuring Claims Provider Claim Rules
A claims provider claim rule determines what claims AD FS issues. Claim rules are configured on the attribute store, which by default is Active Directory. Another term for claims provider rules is "acceptance transform rules." A claim rule can pass a claim through to the relying party, or it can perform a transformation on the rule if certain attributes from the claims provider must be mapped to attributes the relying party can accept. For example, the claims provider can use the attribute "Group" to define a type of user, and the relying party can use the attribute "Role." A claim rule can transform the claim by changing the "Group" attribute to "Role" so that it's accepted by the relying party.

To configure a claim rule for Active Directory, click the Claims Provider Trusts folder in the AD FS console, and in the middle pane, right-click Active Directory and click Edit Claim Rules. In the Edit Claim Rules for Active Directory dialog box, you see a list of predefined rules. You can add new rules, edit existing rules, or remove rules (see Figure 10-8). You can also change the order in which claim rules are processed by selecting a rule and clicking the up or down arrow.

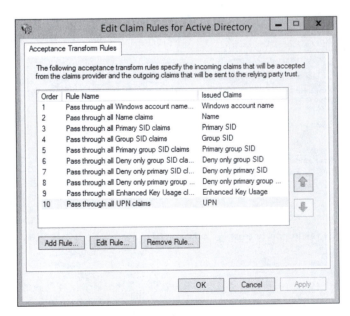

Figure 10-8   Editing claim rules

If you need to transform a claim, you click Add Rule and then click Transform an Incoming Claim. The Add Transform Claim Wizard walks you through the process, as shown in Figure 10-9.

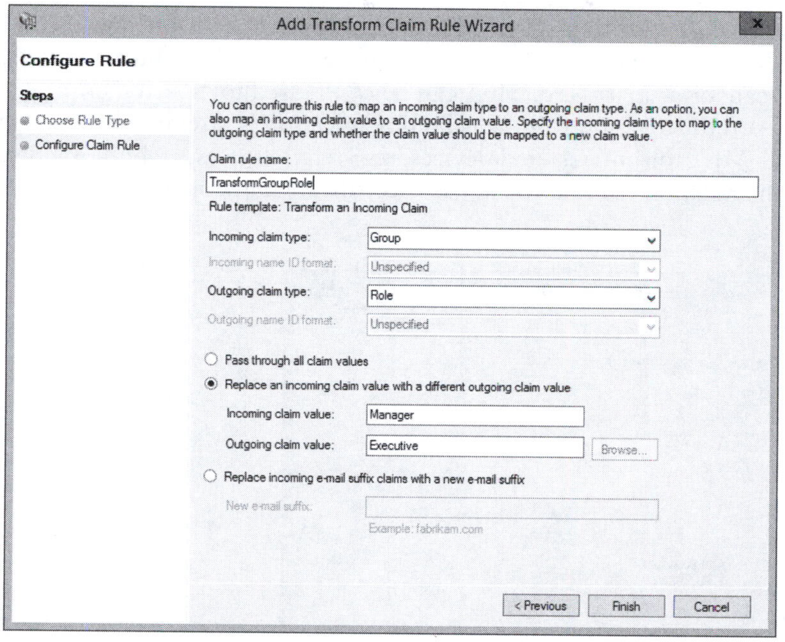

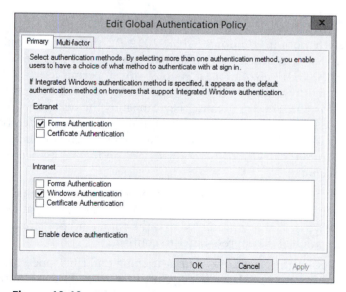

Figure 10-9   Creating a transform rule

Configuring Authentication Policies

Authentication policies enable you to determine what type of authentication is required in the AD FS system. You configure authentication policies in the AD FS console by clicking the Authentication Policies folder. There are two types of authentication policies:

- *Primary authentication*—Required for all users who access applications that use AD FS. Primary authentication can be configured globally or on a custom basis for each relying party. You configure primary authentication based on whether the user is accessing the application from the intranet or extranet (see Figure 10-10). By default, extranet access uses forms authentication (the user enters credentials on a Web form) and optionally

Figure 10-10   Primary authentication policies

certificate authentication. If both options are selected, the user can choose the authentication method at logon. Intranet access uses Windows authentication by default, and you can enable forms authentication and certificate authentication. In addition, you can enable device authentication.

- *Multi-factor authentication*—**Multi-factor authentication (MFA)** means users must authenticate with more than one method, such as using a username and password as well as a digital certificate or a smart card. MFA can be configured for specific users, groups, or devices depending on the location from which authentication is attempted (see Figure 10-11). You can enable MFA for unregistered devices, registered devices, or both. By default, the only other authentication method to choose is certificate authentication.

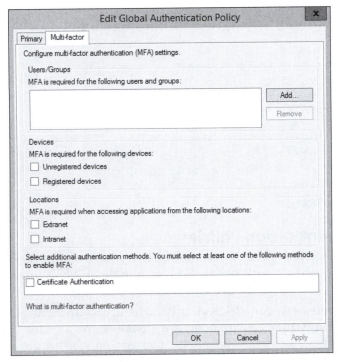

Figure 10-11   Multi-factor authentication policies

Workplace Join

Workplace Join is a new feature in Windows Server 2012 R2 that allows nondomain-joined devices to access claims-based resources securely. You can use this feature to cope with the "bring your own device (BYOD)" revolution; it enables you to permit users with smartphones and tablets to access domain resources without creating a security risk. Using Workplace Join also makes things easier for BYOD users because they can enjoy the benefits of SSO.

The mobile device used to perform a Workplace Join must trust the SSL certificate installed on the AD FS server. This is usually done by installing the CA certificate on the mobile device. In addition, you must configure the device registration service on the AD FS server. To do so, use the following PowerShell cmdlets:

- `Initialize-ADDeviceRegistration`—When prompted, enter the name of the service account you created in Activity 10-1, being sure to add a dollar sign ($) at the end of the name: `412Dom1\ADFSsvc$`. When prompted that the command prepares Active Directory to host Device Registration Service, press Enter to confirm.
- `Enable-AdfsDeviceRegistration`—After the command runs, open the AD FS console, click the Authentication Policies folder, click Edit in the Primary Authentication section, and click the "Enable device authentication" check box.

Next, you need to make sure that an alias (CNAME) record named "enterpriseregistration" exists on the DNS server that points to the AD FS server. This alias name is used by devices to find the AD FS server to perform the Workplace Join.

In addition, you need to install the claims-aware application that devices will access by installing the Web Server (IIS) role and the Windows Identity Foundation feature on another member server (separate from the AD FS server). Finally, you create a relying party trust on the AD FS server. Depending on your AD FS design, you might also want to install the Web Application Proxy role service. Here are the steps for allowing third-party devices to perform Workplace Join to access domain resources from the Internet:

1. Install a certificate from a third-party CA. A third-party CA, such as VeriSign, is needed when the devices performing the Workplace Join don't have access to the domain's internal PKI.

2. Install and configure AD FS.

3. Initialize and enable the device registration service.

4. Add DNS records for the AD FS server and the device registration alias, if necessary.

5. Install and configure the Web server and a claims-aware application.

Active Directory Rights Management Service

You have learned methods for allowing some users to access information while disallowing other users. Access to digital information stored on computers can be allowed and disallowed by controlling who can authenticate to the servers storing information, assigning permissions to files and folders with NTFS permissions and dynamic access control (DAC), and using encryption methods, such as EFS. However, what users can do with data after being granted access to it hasn't been discussed.

Active Directory Rights Management Service (AD RMS) helps administrators get a handle on this critical step in securing data. Whether protecting trade secrets, customer account information, or intellectual property, many organizations struggle with this important facet of network security. With AD RMS, an administrator can create use policies that define how a document can be used after a user accesses it. Actions such as copying, saving, forwarding, and even printing documents can be restricted. For example, suppose you send an "eyes only" e-mail to another employee. With AD RMS, you can restrict the recipient from printing the message or forwarding it to someone else.

To be effective, AD RMS requires AD RMS–enabled client or server applications, such as Microsoft Office, Microsoft Exchange, and Microsoft SharePoint. Developers can also create AD RMS–enabled applications by using the AD RMS Software Development Kit (SDK), available on the Microsoft Web site.

AD RMS Key Features

AD RMS is a server role in Windows Server 2012/R2, but it requires a client access license for each AD RMS client. Some key features of the AD RMS server role include the following:

- *AD FS integration*—AD RMS can be integrated with AD FS to set up a federated trust between organizations. With AD FS, the benefits of AD RMS can be extended outside the organization's network to ensure document security in business-to-business relationships.

- *AD RMS Server self-enrollment*—An RMS server must connect to the Microsoft Enrollment Service over the Internet to acquire a certificate, which allows the RMS server to issue client licenses and certificates to access protected content. With AD RMS, the server can self-enroll in this certificate, so there's no need to contact Microsoft servers.

- *Support for mobile devices*—AD RMS, starting in Windows Server 2012, supports mobile devices and Mac computers when you install the mobile device extension.

- *Administrator role delegation*—AD RMS enables network administrators to delegate AD RMS responsibilities to different users. There are three AD RMS administrator roles:

  o AD RMS Enterprise Administrator: This role has full administrative authority over an AD RMS installation.

  o AD RMS Service Group: This group holds the AD RMS service account. The service account is added to this administrative role automatically.

  o AD RMS Auditor: This role can view RMS-related logs and reports.

  o AD RMS Template Administrator: This role can create and manage AD RMS templates.

AD RMS Components

An AD RMS environment, like an AD FS environment, consists of several components, usually set up as separate servers:

- *AD RMS server*—The AD RMS server role can be installed on one or more servers. Whether it's installed on one server or multiple servers, the installation is referred to as an **AD RMS root cluster**. Multiple servers can be used for redundancy and load balancing. Only one AD RMS root cluster can be installed in an Active Directory forest. The AD RMS server self-signs a server licensor certificate (SLC), which allows the server to issue AD RMS client licenses and certificates. When the AD RMS role is installed, some Web server roles are also installed.

 Don't confuse the term "cluster" used to describe an AD RMS deployment with a failover cluster or an NLB cluster. Neither cluster service is required to install AD RMS.

- *AD RMS database server*—AD RMS uses a database to store AD RMS configuration data and Active Directory group membership information. An SQL database installed on a separate server is recommended for production environments, but you can use the Windows internal database for test environments.

- *Active Directory domain controller*—Servers running the AD RMS server role must be domain members, and users who use or publish AD RMS–enabled content must be in Active Directory with a valid e-mail address.

- *AD RMS-enabled client computer*—AD RMS client software must be installed on computers using AD RMS content. Windows Vista and Windows Server 2008 and later computers include the necessary software, and older clients can download it from the Microsoft Web site.

The AD RMS process consists of two distinct actions: publication of AD RMS–protected documents and access of these documents by an AD RMS client. Publication requires the user authoring the document to acquire a rights account certificate (RAC) and a client licensor certificate (CLC). With these certificates, the user can publish AD RMS–protected content, which involves the following steps.

1. Create a document with an AD RMS–enabled application and specify rights for the document. A publishing document with use policies is created.

2. The document is encrypted by the AD RMS application, and the publishing certificate is bound to the document. The AD RMS server cluster is the only entity that can issue licenses to decrypt the file.

3. The document author can then distribute the application for users to access it.

   A user accesses an AD RMS–protected document with the following steps:

1. A user attempts to access the document by using an AD RMS–enabled application.

2. The AD RMS client reads the publishing license.

3. The AD RMS server specified in the publishing license is contacted to request a use license.

4. After verifying that the user is authorized to access the document, the AD RMS server issues a use license to the client.

5. The document is decrypted, and the user can use the document according to the granted rights.

AD RMS Deployment

Before installing the AD RMS role, you must address the following requirements:

- Prepare a domain member server for the AD RMS role; its users should be people who will be using AD RMS–protected content.

- Create a service account, which must be a regular domain account because it interacts with other services and computers. The account should have a strong password and shouldn't be a member of any groups beside Domain Users; no additional rights should be granted to this account. The AD RMS configuration wizard assigns the account the necessary rights.

- Make sure the user account for installing AD RMS has the right to create databases on the SQL server, if you use an external database.

- If an external database is used, install the database server before installing AD RMS.

- Create a DNS CNAME record for the AD RMS cluster's URL; this record is used to access the AD RMS service.

When you're ready to install AD RMS, install the role and the required role services in Server Manager with the Add Roles and Features Wizard. Activity 10-4 walks you through this process, but many of the selections are described in the following steps:

1. In the Server Roles window, click Active Directory Rights Management Services. In the Role Services window, you have options to install the following role services:

   o Active Directory Rights Management Server: The main role service required to protect documents from unauthorized use. This role service is required and selected by default on the first AD RMS server.

   o Identity Federation Support: Select this option if you're integrating AD RMS with AD FS to extend document protection outside the organization's network to federated business partners.

2. You're prompted to install the Web Server Role (IIS) and several of its role services. Accept the default choices.

3. After the role is installed, click the notifications flag in Server Manager, and then click the "Perform additional configuration" link to start the AD RMS configuration wizard. In the AD RMS window, read the information, and click Next.

4. In the AD RMS Cluster window, you have the option to create an AD RMS root cluster or join an existing AD RMS cluster. For the first AD RMS server, select the default option "Create a new AD RMS root cluster." A root cluster supports certification and licensing. After a root cluster is set up, you can install additional licensing-only clusters, if needed. Click Next.

5. In the Configuration Database window, specify where the required database will be hosted:

   o Specify a database server and a database instance: If you select this option, you must enter the name of an SQL server and a database instance.

   o Use Windows Internal Database on this server: The Windows internal database can be used for test environments or for single-server cluster configurations. If more than one server will participate in the cluster, this option can't be selected.

6. After selecting the database configuration, click Next. In the Service Account window, click Specify, enter the username and password for the account you created to serve as the AD RMS service account, and click Next.

7. In the Cryptographic Mode window, you have the following options:

   o Cryptographic Mode 2: This mode provides RSA encryption using 2048-bit keys for signature and encryption and SHA-256 hashes for signature. This mode is recommended because it's more secure than Mode 1. Mode 2 is supported in Windows Server 2008 R2 with Service Pack 1 and later. Mode 2 provides regulatory compliance with the security standards set by the National Institute of Standards and Technology (NIST) in 2011.

   o Cryptographic Mode 1: Provides RSA 1024-bit keys and SHA-1 hashes. Use this mode for backward-compatibility with earlier versions of AD RMS that don't support Mode 2.

8. In the Cluster Key Storage window, you decide how the AD RMS cluster key should be stored:

   o Use AD RMS centrally managed key storage: This option requires specifying a password to protect an encrypted key, which is shared by all servers in the AD RMS cluster automatically.

   o Use CSP key storage: This option requires selecting a cryptographic service provider to store the cluster key. If you select this option, the cluster key must be distributed to other servers manually.

9. After selecting a key storage option, click Next. In the Cluster Key Password window, enter the cluster key password or select a CSP, depending on your selection on the previous window, and click Next.

10. The Cluster Web Site window prompts you to select an IIS Web site to create the virtual directory for hosting AD RMS. If you set up a virtual directory before starting the AD RMS installation, you select it here; otherwise, the Default Web Site directory is used.

11. In the Cluster Address window (see Figure 10-12), enter the address of the AD RMS Web site clients use to access the AD RMS service, which is usually hosted on the AD RMS server. You're prompted to choose an SSL-encrypted or unencrypted connection type. If

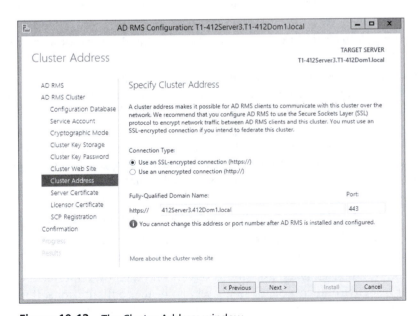

Figure 10-12   The Cluster Address window

you choose an unencrypted connection (via HTTP instead of HTTPS), you're warned that identity federation support can't be added, and you can't change the URL or port number after AD RMS configuration is finished. If you choose an SSL-encrypted connection, you're prompted to specify the server certificate in the next window.

12. In the Server Certificate window (which isn't shown if you selected an unencrypted connection in Step 11), specify the certificate for SSL encryption or create a self-signed certificate. A self-signed certificate can be used for test deployments, but you should choose a certificate from a CA for production deployments. Click Next.

13. In the Licensor Certificate window, enter a descriptive name for the certificate used to establish the cluster's identity to clients. For example, you could use 412Dom1ADRMS. You should create a backup of this certificate after the AD RMS configuration is finished because without this certificate, clients can't connect to the AD RMS server. Click Next.

14. In the SCP Registration window, you can register the **service connection point (SCP)** now or later. You must be logged on to the domain as a member of Enterprise Admins to register the SCP. The SCP provides clients with URLs for the AD RMS cluster, which must be registered for clients to access the cluster. Click Next, and then click Install in the Confirmation window. The AD RMS portion of the installation is finished. Next, you install the additional IIS role services and confirm the installation.

As you can see, setting up AD RMS takes considerable planning and several preinstallation tasks. The complexity of this server role and AD FS reflects businesses' growing need to give users and partners secure, flexible access to network resources.

The server roles discussed in this chapter are often installed as the only role on a Windows Server 2012/R2 server, so they lend themselves particularly well to virtualization. If you're using AD FS or AD RMS, consider installing these roles as virtual machines in Hyper-V.

10

Activity 10-3: Preparing for AD RMS Deployment

Time Required: 20 minutes
Objective: Prepare for AD RMS deployment.

Required Tools and Equipment: 412Server1, 412Server2, and 412Server3
Description: In this activity, you create an account for use as the AD RMS service account and install a certificate for use with AD FS.

1. Start 412Server1, if necessary, and log on as **Administrator**. Start 412Server2 and 412Server3.

2. On 412Server1, create a user in the Users container with the logon name **ADRMSsvc** and password **Password01**. Set the password to never expire, and make sure the user doesn't have to change the password at the next logon.

3. Next, you need to install a certificate. Because you installed AD CS in Chapter 9, you issue one from the CA. You prepared the Web Server certificate template for enrollment in Activity 10-1, so you don't need to do it again. On 412Server3, open an MMC console and add the **Certificates** snap-in to it, clicking **Computer account** and **Local Computer** when prompted.

4. In the Certificates snap-in, right-click the **Personal** folder, point to **All Tasks**, and click **Request New Certificate**.

5. In the Certificates Enrollment window, click **Next**. In the Select Certificate Enrollment Policy window, click **Next**.

6. In the Request Certificates window, click the **Web Server** check box, and click the **More information is required to enroll for this certificate** link to open the Certificate Properties dialog box.

7. Click the **Subject** tab, if necessary. In the Subject name section, click the list arrow under Type, and click **Common name**. Type **412Server3.412Dom1.local** in the Value text box, click the **Add** button, and then click **OK**.

8. Click the **Enroll** button. When the enrollment is completed, click **Finish**. In the Certificates snap-in, you see the new certificate in the Certificates folder. Close the MMC, clicking **No** when prompted to save it.

9. Shut down 412Server2. Keep the other two servers running and stay logged on if you're continuing to the next activity.

Activity 10-4: Installing the AD RMS Role

Time Required: 20 minutes
Objective: Install the AD RMS role.

Required Tools and Equipment: 412Server1 and 412Server3
Description: In this activity, you install the AD RMS role on 412Server3. 412Server1 must be running.

1. Start 412Server1, if necessary. Start 412Server3, and log on to the domain as **Administrator**. (Make sure to log on with **412Dom1\Administrator** so that you log on to the domain instead of the local computer.)

2. In Server Manager, click **Manage, Add Roles and Features** to start the Add Roles and Features Wizard. Click **Next** until you get to the Server Roles window.

3. In the Server Roles window, click **Active Directory Rights Management Services**, and then click **Add Features**. Click **Next** twice. In the AD RMS window, read the description and the "Things to note" section, and then click **Next**.

4. In the Role Services window, accept the default selection **Active Directory Rights Management Server**, and click **Next**. In the Web Server Role (IIS) window, click **Next**.

5. In the Role Services window, accept the default selections, and click **Next**. In the Confirmation window, click **Install**. When the installation is finished, click **Close**.

6. In Server Manager, click the notifications flag, and click the **Perform additional configuration** link to start the AD RMS Configuration Wizard. In the AD RMS window, read the information, and then click **Next**.

7. In the AD RMS Cluster window, accept the default option **Create a new AD RMS root cluster**, and click **Next**.

8. In the Configuration Database window, click the **Use Windows Internal Database on this server** option button, and then click **Next**.

9. In the Service Account window, click **Specify**. In the Windows Security dialog box, type **ADRMSsvc** in the User name text box and **Password01** in the Password text box. Click **OK**, and then click **Next**.

10. In the Cryptographic Mode window, accept the default option **Cryptographic Mode 2**, and click **Next**.

11. In the Cluster Key Storage window, accept the default option **Use AD RMS centrally managed key storage**, and click **Next**.

12. In the Cluster Key Password window, type **Password01** in the Password and Confirm Password text boxes, and then click **Next**.

13. In the Cluster Web Site window, click **Next**. In the Cluster Address window, accept the default option **Use an SSL-encrypted connection**, type **412Server3.412Dom1.local** in the Fully-Qualified Domain Name text box, and then click **Next**.

14. In the Server Certificate window, accept the default option **Choose an existing certificate for SSL encryption**, click the certificate you installed in Activity 10-3, and then click **Next**.

15. In the Licensor Certificate window, type **412Dom1ADRMS** in the Name text box, and then click **Next**.

16. In the SCP Registration window, accept the default option **Register the SCP now**, and click **Next**.

17. In the Confirmation window, click **Install**. When the installation is finished, click **Close**.

18. Log off 412Server3, and log back on as **Administrator** to update the security token so that you can access the AD RMS console. Verify that you can access the AD RMS console by clicking **Tools, Active Directory Rights Management Services** from the Server Manager menu.

19. Keep both servers running and stay logged on if you're continuing to the next activity.

AD RMS Certificate Types

AD RMS uses four types of certificates to identify servers used in the AD RMS cluster, identify client computers that access AD RMS–enabled applications, and verify the identity of users and computers accessing AD RMS content. Following is a description of each certificate type:

- *Server licensor certificate*—The **server licensor certificate (SLC)** contains the public key of the AD RMS server and identifies the AD RMS cluster. The private key of this self-signed certificate is used to sign other certificates used in AD RMS. The certificate has a 250-year validity period so that it can protect archived rights management data for a long time.

- *Rights account certificate*—The **rights account certificate (RAC)** identifies users of AD RMS content. Users are issued an RAC when they first attempt to open a protected document. A standard RAC has a validity period of 365 days. A temporary RAC, issued to users who access content from a device that isn't trusted, has a validity period of 15 minutes.

- *Client licensor certificate*—The **client licensor certificate (CLC)** is issued to clients when they're connected to the AD RMS network and grants them the right to publish protected content. It contains the client licensor's public and private keys. The private key is encrypted by the user's public key. It also contains the public and private keys of the cluster that issued the CLC.

- *Machine certificates*—A **machine certificate** is created on a client computer when it first uses an AD RMS application. The certificate is issued by the root cluster and contains the computer's public key. The private key for the certificate is stored in a "lockbox" on the computer that's associated with the currently logged-on user.

AD RMS License Types

There are two types of AD RMS licenses. A license is actually a specific type of certificate used to determine the rights a user has to publish or access protected documents:

- *Publishing license*—A **publishing license** is tied to a rights-protected document and is created when a client publishes the document. It contains a list of users, identified by e-mail address, and specifies what the users can do with the document. For example, a publishing license might specify that a user can view and edit a document but not copy it.

- *Use license*—A **use license** is issued to certain users when they authenticate to an AD RMS server and request access to a rights-protected document. This license contains the key to decrypt the document.

Configuring the AD RMS Service Connection Point

The AD RMS service connection point (SCP) is defined during installation of the AD RMS root cluster and allows domain members to discover the AD RMS cluster automatically. You can perform the following SCP management tasks in the SCP tab of the Properties dialog box of the AD RMS server (see Figure 10-13):

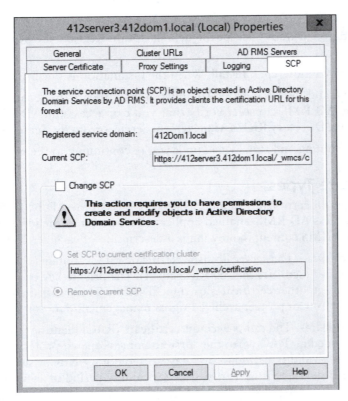

Figure 10-13   Configuring the SCP

- *Register the SCP*—You need to register the SCP if you didn't during the initial AD RMS configuration. The SCP must be registered before clients can discover and access the AD RMS cluster.

- *Change the SCP*—You might need to change the SCP if the URL of the AD RMS server has changed.

- *Remove the SCP*—You might need to remove the SCP if you're planning to uninstall AD RMS and reinstall it on the same server. You can't reinstall AD RMS if an existing SCP is found during the installation, and uninstalling AD RMS doesn't remove the SCP.

If you uninstall AD RMS before removing the SCP and need to install it again, you can remove the SCP by using the `ADscpRegister.exe` command-line tool, which is available only in the RMS Administration Toolkit from the Microsoft Download Center.

The SCP is stored in Active Directory, and only domain member clients have access to it. If you want a nondomain member client to access the AD RMS cluster, you must modify the Registry on the client computer. Create a key named Activation in the HKEY_Local_Machine\Software\Microsoft\MSDRM\ServiceLocation key on the client and enter the value of the SCP. You can view the SCP's current value in the SCP tab shown previously in Figure 10-13. For example, for the AD RMS cluster in Activity 10-4, the value is http://412Server3.412Dom1.local/_wmcs/certification.

Working with Rights Policy Templates

A **rights policy template** enables you to configure policies for determining who can access a rights-protected document and what actions can be taken with the document. When a document is published, a template can be applied to the document that specifies the rights the recipients have to the document. File Server Resource Manager (FSRM) can be used to scan documents and apply rights policy templates automatically based on resource properties or the contents of the document.

To create rights policy templates, open the Active Directory Rights Management Services console, scroll down the middle pane, and click the "Manage rights policy templates" link in the Tasks section. In the Distributed Rights Policy Templates window, click "Create distributed rights policy template," and then specify the following information:

- *Add Template Identification Information*—Give a descriptive name to the template and a description that specifies what rights are assigned.

- *Add User Rights*—Add users and groups (see Figure 10-14). You can select users or groups from Active Directory, but the account you select must have an e-mail address assigned in its properties. Alternatively, you can specify ANYONE to include all users in the organization. You can assign rights from a predefined list or create custom rights. Most of the predefined rights are self-explanatory, but a few warrant explanation:

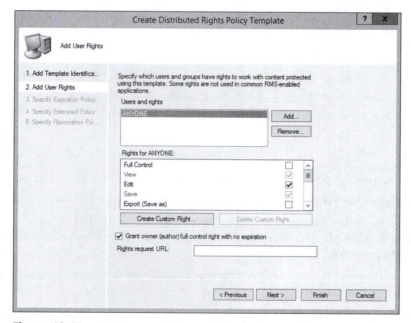

Figure 10-14   Adding user rights to a rights policy template

- o Export: Allows a user to use the Save As option when saving a document.

- o Forward, Reply, Reply All: These rights are used with protected messages created with Microsoft Exchange.

- o Extract: Lets a user copy content from a document.

- *Specify Expiration Policy*—Determine whether the published document availability expires. You can specify expiration parameters for content availability and for the use license. If the use license expires, the document is no longer available to users, and users must get another license to access the content (see Figure 10-15).

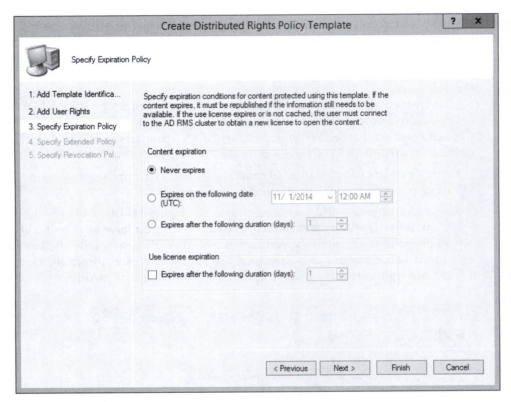

Figure 10-15   Specifying an expiration policy

- *Specify Extended Policy*—Configure additional content protection options:
  - Enable users to view protected content by using a browser add-on.
  - Require a new use license every time content is consumed (disable client-side caching): If users shouldn't be able to open protected content when they're disconnected from the network, you should enable this option.
  - Application-specific options: You can specify additional policies with values that are specific to the application.
- *Specify Revocation Policy*—You use these settings to specify that content can be revoked, which disallows access to content based on the content ID, user, or application. If you enable revocation, specify the URL of the revocation list.

Configuring Exclusion Policies

Exclusion policies enable an administrator to prevent specific users, AD RMS client versions, or applications from interacting with AD RMS content. Exclusions are configured in the Active Directory Rights Management Services console by clicking the Exclusion Policies node in the left pane (see Figure 10-16). Exclusion policies can be configured as follows:

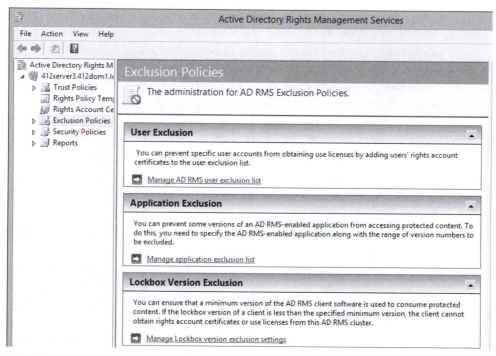

Figure 10-16   Configuring user exclusion policies

- *User Exclusion*—Prevents user accounts (based on their e-mail addresses) from acquiring use licenses for protected content. When you add a user, you must enable use exclusion before you can add the account to the exclusion list, which you do by clicking the "Manage AD RMS user exclusion list" link and then clicking Enable User Exclusion in the Tasks pane. You add domain users by specifying their Active Directory user account names. Specify nondomain users by entering their public key strings.

- *Application Exclusion*—Enable application exclusion, and then add an application to the exclusion list by entering the application's filename and its minimum and maximum version level.

- *Lockbox Version Exclusion*—This exclusion policy allows you to specify the minimum AD RMS client version that can acquire use licenses from AD RMS. If the AD RMS client version is less than the specified minimum, the client can't acquire use licenses.

Activity 10-5: Creating a Rights Policy Template

Time Required: 10 minutes
Objective: Create a rights policy template.

Required Tools and Equipment: 412Server1 and 412Server3
Description: In this activity, you create a rights policy template in preparation for publishing rights-protected content. This template gives anyone view, edit, and save rights to published content.

1. Start 412Server1, if necessary. Start 412Server3, and log on to the domain as **Administrator**, if necessary.

2. Open Server Manager, if necessary, and click **Tools, Active Directory Rights Management Services** from the menu.

3. In the left pane, click to expand the AD RMS server node, and then click **Rights Policy Templates**.

4. In the middle pane, click the **Create distributed rights policy template** link to start the Create Distributed Rights Policy Template Wizard.

5. In the Add Template Identification Information window, click **Add**. In the Add New Template Identification Information dialog box, type **TestTemplate** in the Name text box and **Test Rights Policy Template** in the Description text box. Click **Add**, and then click **Next**.

6. In the Add User Rights window, click the **Add** button. In the Add User or Group dialog box, click the **Anyone** option button, and then click **OK**.

7. Scroll through the Rights for ANYONE list box to see the predefined rights you can assign. Click the **View, Edit,** and **Save** check boxes, and then click **Next**.

8. In the Specify Expiration Policy window, click the **Expires on the following date** option button in the "Content expiration" section, and then click a date and time in the corresponding list boxes.

9. In the "Use license expiration" section, click the **Expires after the following duration (days)** check box, type **10** in the text box, and then click **Next**.

10. In the Specify Extended Policy window, click the **Require a new use license every time content is consumed (disable client-side caching)** check box. Enabling this option means users must have a network connection to the AD RMS cluster each time a protected document is opened. Click **Next**.

11. In the Specify Revocation Policy window, read the description of this policy option, and then click **Finish**. In the middle pane of the Active Directory Rights Management Services console, you see the new template. Leave this console open.

12. Keep both servers running and stay logged on if you're continuing to the next activity.

Working with Trust Policies

You might want to grant users from a different organization or forest the ability to acquire use licenses to protected content in your forest. For example, an organization is composed of two or more forests, and you want users from one forest to have access to rights-protected documents in another forest. If you have already established a federated trust through AD FS, you might want to share AD RMS content between the trusted organizations. There are three types of trust policies you can configure with AD RMS (see Figure 10-17), described in the following sections.

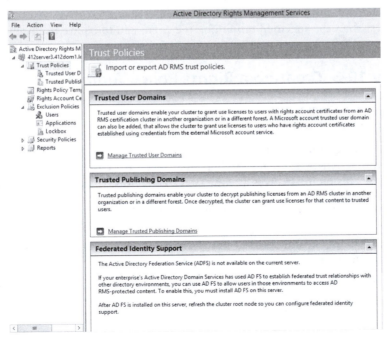

Figure 10-17   Trust policies

Trusted User Domains A trusted user domain (TUD) establishes a trust between AD RMS clusters in separate forests so that users in the trusted forest can access AD RMS content in the trusting forest. A TUD enables the trusting AD RMS cluster to accept rights account certificates from the trusted cluster and grants use licenses to its users. A TUD is a one-way trust, meaning if you have two forests, you need to establish two trusts for users in both forests to access AD RMS content in both forests. Each time a user accesses content protected by the remote AD RMS cluster, the user receives the use license from the remote cluster, so connectivity between clusters must exist.

Although a TUD doesn't require an Active Directory forest trust between forests, this trust makes it easier to work with groups of users from the partner organization because group membership data is available between trusted forests. The process of establishing a TUD has two steps:

1. *Export the trusted user domain file on the trusted AD RMS cluster*—The TUD file contains the server licensor certificate (SLC) but doesn't contain the private key. In the Active Directory Rights Management Services console, click Trust Policies in the left pane, and then click the Manage Trusted User Domains link in the Trusted User Domains section in the middle pane. Then click Export Trusted User Domain in the Actions pane.

2. *Import the trusted user domain file on the trusting AD RMS cluster*—First, copy the exported TUD file to a location accessible to a server in the trusting AD RMS cluster. In the Active Directory Rights Management Services console, click Trust Policies in the left pane, and then click the Manage Trusted User Domains link in the Trusted User Domains section in the middle pane. Then click Import Trusted User Domain in the Actions pane. Browse to the location of the exported TUD file, and enter a descriptive name for the certificate.

After a trust is established, the following process occurs when a user from the trusting partner publishes protected content, and a user from the trusted partner attempts to access the content:

1. A user from the trusting partner publishes protected content, which is sent to the user from the trusted partner.

2. The user from the trusted partner acquires an RAC from his or her local AD RMS server.

3. The RAC is sent to the trusting partner's AD RMS cluster to request a use license.

4. The RAC is validated by the trusting partner, and a use license is issued to the user.

Trusted Publishing Domains A trusted publishing domain (TPD) allows an AD RMS cluster to issue use licenses for content published by another AD RMS cluster. With a TPD, the private key and rights policy templates are exported from the trusted domain, so after the trust is established and content is published, there's no need for the trusted cluster to have connectivity with the trusting cluster. However, because the private key of the trusting cluster is exported along with the SLC, a high degree of trust between organizations must exist. Not all organizations allow their private keys to be shared with other organizations. TPDs make working with groups of users much easier because all authentication takes place at the trusted cluster, but because of the security risks of sharing private keys, they're usually used only when the two forests are in the same organization. The steps for establishing a TPD are similar to those for establishing a TUD, except you start with the trusting domain:

1. *Export the trusted publishing domain file on the trusting AD RMS cluster*—The TPD file contains the SLC, private key, and rights policy templates. In the Active Directory Rights Management Services console, click Trust Policies in the left pane, and then click the Manage Trusted Publishing Domains link in the Trusted Publishing Domains section in the middle pane. Then click Export Trusted Publishing Domain in the Actions pane. You must enter a password used to encrypt the TPD file. This password is used when the TPD file is imported on the trusted cluster.

2. *Import the trusted publishing domain file on the trusted AD RMS cluster*—Copy the exported TPD file to a location accessible to a server in the trusted AD RMS cluster. In the Active Directory Rights Management Services console, click Trust Policies in the left pane, and click the Manage Trusted Publishing Domains link in the Trusted Publishing Domains section in the middle pane. Then click Import Trusted Publishing Domain in the Actions pane. Browse to the location of the exported TPD file, enter the password entered in Step 1, and enter a descriptive name for the certificate.

After a trust is established, the following process takes place when a user from the trusting partner publishes protected content, and a user from the trusted partner attempts to access the content:

1. A user from the trusting partner publishes protected content, which is sent to the user from the trusted partner.

2. The user from the trusted partner attempts to open the protected content and requests a use license from its AD RMS cluster.

3. The AD RMS server uses the private key imported from the trusting partner to create the use license and issues it to the user.

Federated Identity Support   If AD FS is installed on your AD RMS servers, you can use the trusts established with AD FS to share rights-protected content without having to create additional AD RMS trusts. The following process occurs when a user in an AD RMS cluster publishes protected content for a user in a partner organization where an AD FS trust has been established:

1. A user from the publishing AD RMS cluster publishes protected content, which is sent to the user in the partner organization.

2. The user from the partner organization attempts to open the protected content.

3. An AD RMS server in the publishing cluster is contacted.

4. The request to the AD RMS server is redirected to a federation server in the publishing organization.

5. The federation server requests identity confirmation from a federation server in the partner organization.

6. The user contacts his or her home federation server, and the client is authenticated by Active Directory.

7. The federation server confirms the user's identity, and the user contacts the AD RMS server in the publishing organization with proof of identity.

8. The AD RMS server in the publishing organization issues a use certificate to the user.

Backing Up and Restoring AD RMS

Configuring AD RMS can be a complex undertaking, so backing up the configuration is paramount. The backup of AD RMS involves the following procedures:

- *Back up the AD RMS databases*—There are three databases: the configuration database, the directory services database, and the logging database. The configuration database is the most important, as it contains the data needed to manage account certification and licensing. The directory services database contains cached content from Active Directory, including users, group memberships, and security IDs (SIDs). The logging database contains log files about issued licenses and client activity. If you're using SQL Server to host these databases, use the SQL Server Backup tool. If you're using the Windows internal database, you must use SQL Server Management Studio Express.

- *Export the trusted publishing domain file*—The steps for this procedure were described earlier in "Working with Trust Policies."

- *Store the cluster key password in a safe place*—If you don't know the password, you can change it first in the AD RMS console by clicking Security Policies, Cluster Key Password in the left pane, and then clicking the "Change cluster key password" link in the middle pane. If you do change the password, you must do so on all AD RMS servers in the cluster.

To restore an AD RMS configuration after a server failure, restore the databases and redeploy the AD RMS role. During installation, choose the option to join an existing AD RMS cluster. When you select this option, you must supply the location of the AD RMS configuration database and the cluster key password. After the installation is finished, import the trusted publishing domain file you exported during the backup process.

Activity 10-6: Exploring the Active Directory Rights Management Services Console

Time Required: 10 minutes
Objective: Explore the Active Directory Rights Management Services console.

Required Tools and Equipment: 412Server1 and 412Server3
Description: In this activity, you review some of the options in the Active Directory Rights Management Services console.

1. Log on to 412Server3 as **Administrator**, if necessary. Make sure 412Server1 is running.

2. Open Server Manager, and click **Tools, Active Directory Rights Management Services**, if necessary.

3. In the left pane, click **Trust Policies**. Click the **Manage Trusted User Domains** link in the Trusted User Domains section of the middle pane. Read the information about trusted user domains.

4. Click **Export Trusted User Domain** in the Actions pane. Type **TUD412Dom1** in the File Name text box, and click **Save**. Notice that the file is saved in the Documents folder of the current user by default.

5. Click **Import Trusted User Domain** in the Actions pane. Read the information about importing a trusted user domain, and then click **Cancel**.

6. In the left pane of the Active Directory Rights Management Services console, click **Trusted Publishing Domains**. Notice that the 412Dom1ADRMS domain is trusted by default. Click **Export Trusted Publishing Domain** in the Actions pane. (This step is part of the AD RMS backup procedure.)

7. Click the **Save As** button. Type **TPD412Dom1** in the File name text box, and click **Save**.

8. In the Password and Confirm Password text boxes, type **Password01**, and then click **Finish**.

9. In the Actions pane, click **Import Trusted Publishing Domain**. Read the information about importing a TPD, and then click **Cancel**.

10. In the left pane, click **Exclusion Policies**. Click the **Manage AD RMS user exclusion list** link in the User Exclusion section in the middle pane.

11. In the Actions pane, click **Enable User Exclusion** and then click **Exclude RAC**. Read the information about excluding a user, and then click **Cancel**. Repeat this procedure for applications and lockbox exclusions.

12. In the left pane, click **Security Policies**. In the middle pane, click **Reset password**. This is where you can reset the cluster key password if you don't have the current password. You need the cluster key password to restore AD RMS. Close the Active Directory Rights Management Services console.

13. Shut down all running servers.

Chapter Summary

- AD FS allows single sign-on access to Web-based resources between business partners and in other situations when a single sign-on to diverse Web-based resources is needed. Most business-to-business AD FS environments involve a federation trust between an account partner and a resource partner.

- An AD FS installation in Windows Server 2012 involves four role services: Federation Service, Federation Service Proxy, and two AD FS Web agents (claims-aware and Windows token-based). In Windows Server 2012 R2, it involves only the AD FS role and optionally the Web Application Proxy role service.

- AD FS deployment include the following components: claims providers, relying party, relying party trust, claims provider trust, claim rules, and the attribute store.

- AD FS designs include Web SSO, federated Web SSO, and federated Web SSO with forest trust. AD FS 2.1 is the current version of AD FS and is supported by Windows Server 2012 and later.

- The relying party is the resource partner that accepts claims from the account partner to make authentication and authorization decisions. A relying party trust sets up the trust relationship between the claims provider and the relying party (resource partner).

- You configure a claims provider trust on the AD FS server that acts as the relying party (resource partner). This trust configures the relying party to trust the claims issued by the claims provider (account partner).

- The Workplace Join feature is new in Windows Server 2012 R2 and allows nondomain joined devices to access claims-based resources securely. This feature can be used to cope with the "bring your own device (BYOD)" revolution.

- AD RMS extends document security beyond file system permissions. It can restrict not only who can access a document, but also what users can do with a document after accessing it. The AD RMS role requires an AD RMS–enabled application to work.

- AD RMS consists of two distinct actions: publication of AD RMS–protected documents and access of these documents by AD RMS–enabled clients. An AD RMS deployment involves an AD RMS server, an AD RMS database server, an AD DS domain controller, and an AD RMS–enabled client computer.

- AD RMS uses four types of certificates to identify servers used in the AD RMS cluster, identify client computers that access AD RMS–enabled applications, and verify the identity of users and computers accessing AD RMS content.

- There are two types of AD RMS licenses. A license is a specific type of certificate for determining the rights a user has to publish or access protected documents.

- The AD RMS service connection point (SCP) is defined during installation of the AD RMS root cluster and allows domain members to discover the AD RMS cluster automatically.

- Rights policy templates enable you to configure rights policies that are applied to rights-protected documents. When a document is published, a template can be applied to the document that specifies the rights recipients have to the document.

- Exclusion policies enable an administrator to prevent specific users, AD RMS client versions, or applications from interacting with AD RMS content.

- There are three types of trust policies you can configure with AD RMS: trusted user domains, trusted publishing domains, and established trusts from an AD FS configuration.

- Backing up AD RMS involves backing up the AD RMS databases, exporting the TPD file, and storing the cluster key password in a safe place.

Key Terms

account partner   In a federation trust, it's the trusted company whose users will be accessing resources of the trusting company (resource partner). *See also* resource partner.

Active Directory Federation Services (AD FS)   A Windows server role that allows single sign-on access to Web-based resources across different forests or organizations.

Active Directory Rights Management Service (AD RMS)   A Windows server role that enables administrators to create use policies for defining how a document can be used after a user accesses it.

AD FS–enabled Web servers   Web servers that host an AD FS Web agent. *See also* Active Directory Federation Services (AD FS).

AD RMS root cluster   One or more servers configured with the AD RMS server role. Multiple servers can be used for redundancy and load balancing. *See also* Active Directory Rights Management Service (AD RMS).

attribute store   An LDAP-compatible database that stores the values used in claims. *See also* claim.

claim   An agreed-on set of user attributes that both parties in a federation trust use to determine a user's credentials. *See also* federation trust.

claim rules   Conditions that determine what attributes are required in a claim and how claims are processed by the federation server. *See also* federation server.

claims provider   A server that provides a user with claims to present to the resource partner for access to federated resources. *See also* claim *and* resource partner.

claims provider trust   A trust created on the AD FS server that act as the relying party or resource partner. *See also* relying party *and* resource partner.

client licensor certificate (CLC)   A certificate used in AD RMS that's issued to clients when they're connected to the AD RMS network; it grants them the right to publish protected content.

federated Web SSO   An AD FS design in which a trust relationship is established between the resource partner and the account partner. *See also* account partner *and* resource partner.

federated Web SSO with forest trust   An AD FS design that involves a trust between two Active Directory forests. One forest, in the perimeter network, is considered the resource partner. The second forest, in the internal network, is the account partner. *See also* account partner *and* resource partner.

federation server   A server configured to run the Federation Service role service. When used in an account partner network, its function is to gather user credentials into claims and package them into a security token. When used on the resource partner network, it receives security tokens and claims from the account partner and presents the claims to Web-based applications for authorization.

federation server proxy   Installed on servers in a perimeter network outside the organization's firewall, this service fields authentication requests from browser clients and passes them to the federation server inside the firewall.

federation trust   A trust between two networks using AD FS; one side of the trust is considered the account partner, and the other side is called the resource partner. *See also* account partner *and* resource partner.

machine certificate   A certificate used in AD RMS that's created on a client computer the first time it uses an AD RMS application.

multi-factor authentication (MFA)   An authentication process whereby users must authenticate with more than one method, such as with a username and password as well as a digital certificate or smart card.

publishing license   A type of certificate used in AD RMS that's tied to a rights-protected document and is created when a client publishes the document.

relying party   The resource partner that hosts the resources accessed by the account partner. *See also* account partner *and* resource partner.

relying party trust   An AD FS trust created on the AD FS server that acts as the claims provider in an AD FS deployment.

resource partner   In a federation trust, it's the trusting company whose resources are accessed by the trusted company (account partner). *See also* account partner.

rights account certificate (RAC)   A certificate used in AD RMS for identifying users of AD RMS content.

rights policy template   A component of AD RMS that enables you to configure policies for determining who can access a rights-protected document and what actions can be taken with the document.

server licensor certificate (SLC)   A certificate used in AD RMS that contains the AD RMS server's public key and identifies the AD RMS cluster.

service connection point (SCP)   An AD RMS component that provides clients with URLs for the AD RMS cluster, which must be registered for clients to access the cluster.

trusted publishing domain (TPD)   A trust between AD RMS clusters in separate forests that allows an AD RMS cluster to issue use licenses for content published by another AD RMS cluster.

trusted user domain (TUD)   A trust between AD RMS clusters in separate forests that allows users in the trusted forest to access AD RMS content in the trusting forest.

use license   A type of certificate used in AD RMS that's issued to particular users when they authenticate to an AD RMS server and request access to a rights-protected document.

Web SSO   An AD FS design that provides single sign-on access to multiple Web applications for users who are external to an organization's network.

Workplace Join   A new feature in Windows Server 2012 R2 that allows nondomain joined devices to access claims-based resources securely.

Review Questions

1. In a federation trust, the company whose users are accessing resources is referred to as which of the following?

   a. Account partner

   b. Claims provider

   c. Resource partner

   d. Federated server

2. What's the term for an agreed-on set of user attributes that both parties in a federation trust use to determine a user's credentials?

   a. Token

   b. Policy

   c. Claim

   d. Exclusion

3. You're installing AD FS to facilitate transactions with a business partner. You want to keep the federation server secure behind a firewall and don't want direct communication between your partner's computer and the federation server. What should you use?

    a. Federation service proxy

    b. AD FS Web agents

    c. Online responders

    d. Federated Web SSO with forest trust

4. You have several Web applications that you want trusted Internet clients to be able to access with a single sign-on. The Internet clients aren't from a single company; they can be from anywhere on the Internet. Which AD DS design should you use?

    a. Web SSO

    b. Federated Web SSO

    c. Federated Web SSO with forest trust

    d. AD FS claims-aware Web agents

5. Which of the following role services do you use with AD FS deployed on a Windows Server 2012 R2 server if you need a proxy on the perimeter network?

    a. Web Agents

    b. AD Certificate Services

    c. DirectAccess

    d. Web Application Proxy

6. Which of the following isn't part of a typical AD FS deployment?

    a. Web browsers

    b. Certificates

    c. An account store

    d. DHCP

7. Which of the following should be installed to prevent employees from printing security-sensitive e-mails?

    a. AD LDS

    b. AD FS

    c. AD RMS

    d. AD DS

8. What should you configure in AD FS when you want the claims provider to trust the relying party from which claims are made?

    a. Claims provider trust

    b. Relying party trust

    c. Trusted user domains

    d. Trusted publishing domains

9. Which of the following is the storage location for the values used in claims?

    a. Claim directory

    b. Federation proxy

    c. Federation server

    d. Attribute store

10. What's the first step when configuring a relying party trust?

    a. Configure multi-factor authentication

    b. Choose issuance authorization rules

    c. Select the data source

    d. Configure a TPD

11. What should you configure if certain attributes from the claims provider must be mapped to attributes the relying party can accept?

    a. Acceptance transform rule

    b. Claims provider trust

    c. Authentication policies

    d. AD device registration

12. You and another company are engaging in a joint operation to develop a new product. Both companies must access certain Web-based applications in this collaborative effort. Communication between the companies must remain secure, and use of exchanged documents and e-mails must be tightly controlled. What should you use?

    a. AD CS and AD LDS

    b. AD RMS and AD DS

    c. AD FS and AD RMS

    d. AD LDS and AD RMS

13. Which of the following isn't part of a typical AD RMS installation in a production environment?

    a. AD RMS database server

    b. AD DS

    c. Client certificates

    d. Microsoft Enrollment Service

14. You need to delegate AD RMS responsibilities to a junior administrator. You don't want to give the administrator more permissions than required to allow her to view RMS-related logs and reports. What should you do?

    a. Add the user to the Server Operators group on the AD RMS server.

    b. Delegate the AD RMS Template Administrator role.

    c. Delegate the AD RMS Auditor role.

    d. Add the user to the AD RMS Service group on the AD RMS server.

15. Which of the following is true about an AD RMS deployment?

    a. The database must be hosted by an external SQL server.

    b. The AD RMS role must be installed on a domain controller.

    c. The service account must be a regular domain user.

    d. The AD RMS role must be installed on a stand-alone server.

16. Which of the following is true about AD RMS installation and configuration?

    a. The SCP must be registered by a member of Domain Admins.

    b. You must use an unencrypted connection to support identity federation.

    c. A self-signed certificate can be used for the server certificate.

    d. The cluster key password can't be changed by the administrator.

17. Which of the following contains the public key of the AD RMS server?

    a. Server licensor certificate

    b. Rights account certificate

    c. Publishing license

    d. Use license

18. Which of the following is created when a client publishes a rights-protected document?

    a. Server licensor certificate

    b. Rights account certificate

    c. Publishing license

    d. Use license

19. Which of the following should you configure if you want to exclude certain application versions from accessing a rights-protected document?

    a. Exclusion policy

    b. Revocation policy

    c. Rights policy template

    d. Trusted publishing domain

Case Projects

Case Project 10-1: Illustrating a Federated Web SSO Design

This project can be done in groups. Designs should be presented to the class with discussion of their implementation details.

You have been asked to consult with a publishing company to come up with an AD FS design. The publishing company, WebBooks, wants its largest business partners, several booksellers, to be able to access purchasing and inventory Web applications running on the WebBooks Web servers.

WebBooks has a Windows Server 2012 R2 network with Active Directory. It has a Web server that's publicly accessible through the perimeter network (DMZ) and plans to add a Web server to host the purchasing and inventory Web applications. The applications are directory enabled.

Develop an AD FS design, with an accompanying diagram, that WebBooks can use to achieve its goal of giving business partners single sign-on access to its Web-based applications. For simplicity, include only one partner bookseller. You should include the following items in your design:

- A diagram, with the account partner and resource partner labeled, showing servers and server roles to run at both WebBooks and the bookseller location

- An explanation of the role each server plays in the process

- A description of how authentication and authorization to Web applications take place

Case Project 10-2: Devising an AD DS Design with AD FS and AD RMS

This project can be done in groups. Designs should be presented to the class, with discussion of implementation details.

Create a fictitious multilocation company that uses Windows Server 2012 R2 Active Directory as its primary directory service. Describe the company's business and explain why it will benefit from using the following roles and how they will be used:

- AD DS, including RODCs
- AD FS
- AD RMS
- DNS

Keep in mind that the main goal of this project is to create a company in which these roles should be used. Create a diagram showing where servers will be located and which roles will be installed on the servers, and include information about sites. Write documentation explaining why each role service is needed, and include information such as which servers will be global catalog servers and which servers will perform FSMO roles.

Present your project to the class, along with a detailed diagram showing sites, servers, role services, and so forth.

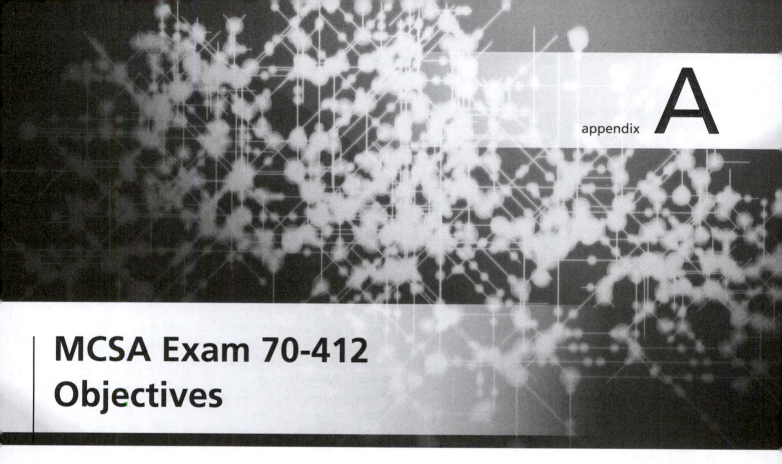

MCSA Exam 70-412 Objectives

Table A-1 maps the Configuring Advanced Windows Server 2012 Services (70-412) exam objectives to the corresponding chapter and section where the objectives are covered in this book. Major sections are listed after the chapter number, and applicable subsections are shown in parentheses. After each objective, the percentage of the exam that includes the objective is shown in parentheses.

Table A-1   Objectives-to-chapter mapping

Objective	Chapter and section
Configure and manage high availability (16%)	
Configure network load balancing (NLB)	Chapter 6: Configuring Network Load Balancing
Configure failover clustering	Chapter 6: Failover Clusters
Manage failover clustering roles	Chapter 7: Advanced Failover Clusters
	Chapter 7: Configuring Highly Available Virtual Machines
Manage VM movement	Chapter 7: Configuring Virtual Machine Movement
Configure file and storage solutions (18%)	
Configure advanced file services	Chapter 4: Configuring Advanced File Services
Implement Dynamic Access Control (DAC)	Chapter 5: Configuring Dynamic Access Control
Configure and optimize storage	Chapter 4: Configuring Advanced File Storage
Implement business continuity and disaster recovery (15%)	
Configure and manage backups	Chapter 8: Backing Up Windows Servers
	Chapter 8: Configuring Online Backups
Recover servers	Chapter 8: Windows Server Recovery
Configure site-level fault tolerance	Chapter 8: Site-Level Disaster Recovery
	Chapter 8: Configuring Multisite Clustering

Objective	Chapter and section
Configure network services (17%)	
Implement an advanced Dynamic Host Configuration Protocol (DHCP) solution	Chapter 3: DHCP Overview
	Chapter 3: Configuring Superscopes and Multicast Scopes
	Chapter 3: Implementing DHCPv6
	Chapter 3: DHCP High Availability
	Chapter 3: Configuring DHCP for DNS Registration
Implement an advanced DNS solution	Chapter 3: Domain Name System Overview
	Chapter 3: Configuring DNS Security
	Chapter 3: Configuring Advanced DNS Options
Deploy and manage IP Address Management (IPAM)	Chapter 5: Configuring IP Address Management
Configure the Active Directory infrastructure (15%)	
Configure a forest or a domain	Chapter 1: Configuring Multidomain Environments
	Chapter 1: Configuring Multiforest Environments
	Chapter 1: Upgrading Domains and Forests
Configure trusts	Chapter 1: Active Directory Trusts
	Chapter 1: Configuring Active Directory Trusts
Configure sites	Chapter 2: Configuring Sites
Manage Active Directory and SYSVOL replication	Chapter 2: Active Directory Replication
Configure identity and access solutions (19%)	
Implement Active Directory Federation Services (AD FS)	Chapter 10: Active Directory Federation Services
Install and configure Active Directory Certificate Services	Chapter 9: Introducing Active Directory Certificate Services (AD CS)
	Chapter 9: Deploying the Active Directory Certificate Services Role
	Chapter 9: Configuring a Certification Authority
Manage certificates	Chapter 9: Configuring a Certification Authority (Configuring Certificate Templates)
	Chapter 9: Maintaining and Managing a PKI
Install and configure Active Directory Rights Management Services	Chapter 10: Active Directory Rights Management Services (AD RMS)

Glossary

access-denied assistance A feature in Windows Server 2012/R2 that gives file users, file owners, and administrators methods to remediate access-denied messages when users requesting shared files should be allowed access.

account partner In a federation trust, it's the trusted company whose users will be accessing resources of the trusting company (resource partner). *See also* resource partner.

Active Directory–detached cluster A new cluster configuration option that allows deploying a failover cluster without needing Active Directory for network name management.

Active Directory Federation Services (AD FS) A Windows server role that allows single sign-on access to Web-based resources across different forests or organizations.

Active Directory Rights Management Service (AD RMS) A Windows server role that enables administrators to create use policies for defining how a document can be used after a user accesses it.

active node A cluster member that's responding to client requests for a network application or service; also referred to as an "active server."

AD FS–enabled Web servers Web servers that host an AD FS Web agent. *See also* Active Directory Federation Services (AD FS).

AD RMS root cluster One or more servers configured with the AD RMS server role. Multiple servers can be used for redundancy and load balancing. *See also* Active Directory Rights Management Service (AD RMS).

attribute store An LDAP-compatible database that stores the values used in claims. *See also* claim.

authoritative restore A type of Active Directory restore operation in which the restored DC replicates to all other DCs in the domain, and any changes made to Active Directory objects since the backup occurred are lost.

automatic site coverage A feature in which each domain controller advertises itself by registering SRV records in DNS in sites that don't have a DC if the advertising DC has the lowest cost connection to the site.

bare metal recovery A backup option that includes the system state, the system reserved volume, and the volume where Windows is stored.

block-level storage Storage seen by the storage client as a local drive.

boot configuration data (BCD) store A binary file containing settings that determine how a Windows system boots.

BranchCache A file-sharing technology that allows computers at a branch office to cache files retrieved from a central server across a WAN link.

bridgehead server A domain controller in a site that has been assigned to handle replication of one or more directory partitions in that site.

central access policies A component of DAC consisting of one or more central access rules; used to target resources on servers and set DAC permissions with group policies. *See also* Dynamic Access Control (DAC).

central access rules A DAC component for setting permissions on targeted resources; deployed through central access policies. *See also* Dynamic Access Control (DAC).

centralized topology An IPAM deployment option that has a single IPAM server for the entire enterprise. *See also* IP Address Management (IPAM).

certificate practice statement (CPS) A document describing how a CA issues certificates containing the CA identity, security practices used to maintain CA integrity, types of certificates issued, the renewal policy, and so forth.

certificate revocation list (CRL) A list of certificates that the CA administrator has invalidated before their expiration dates.

certificate templates A shell or model of a certificate used to create new certificates; it defines characteristics of the certificate, such as the intended use and expiration date.

child domains Domains that have the same second-level and top-level domain names as the parent domain in the same tree and forest.

claim An agreed-on set of user attributes that both parties in a federation trust use to determine a user's credentials. *See also* federation trust.

claim rules Conditions that determine what attributes are required in a claim and how claims are processed by the federation server. *See also* federation server.

claims provider A server that provides a user with claims to present to the resource partner for access to federated resources. *See also* claim *and* resource partner.

claims provider trust A trust created on the AD FS server that act as the relying party or resource partner. *See also* relying party *and* resource partner.

classification property A file attribute containing a value that's used to categorize the data in a file or an aspect of the file, such as its location or creation time.

client access point A name and IP address by which clients can access a clustered service in a failover cluster. *See also* failover cluster.

client affinity value An option specified in multiple host filtering modes that determines whether the same or a different host handles successive requests from the same client.

client licensor certificate (CLC) A certificate used in AD RMS that's issued to clients when they're connected to the AD RMS network; it grants them the right to publish protected content.

Cluster-Aware Updating (CAU) A new failover cluster feature in Windows Server 2012 that automates software updates on cluster servers while maintaining cluster service availability. *See also* failover cluster.

cluster heartbeat Communication between cluster nodes that provides the status of each cluster member to the cluster quorum. The cluster heartbeat, or lack of it, informs the cluster when a server is no longer communicating.

cluster operation mode A cluster parameter that specifies the type of network addressing used to access the cluster: unicast, multicast, or IGMP multicast.

cluster server A Windows Server 2012/R2 server that participates in a failover cluster; also referred to as a "cluster node" or "cluster member." *See also* failover cluster.

cluster shared volume A storage option in a failover cluster in which all cluster nodes have access to the shared storage for read and write access. *See also* failover cluster.

clustered application An application or service installed on two or more servers participating in a failover cluster; Also called a "clustered service." *See also* failover cluster.

connection object An Active Directory object created in Active Directory Sites and Services that defines the connection parameters between two replication partners.

content information A message transferred from a BranchCache server to a client that indicates to the client where the file can be retrieved from the cache in the branch office. *See also* BranchCache.

core cluster resources Resources in a failover cluster that include the quorum resource, which is usually the witness disk or witness share; the IP address resource that provides the cluster IP address; and the network name resource that provides the cluster name.

CRL distribution point (CDP) An attribute of a certificate that identifies where the CRL for a CA can be retrieved; can include URLs for HTTP, FILE, FTP, and LDAP locations. *See also* certificate revocation list (CRL).

Delegation Signer (DS) A DNSSEC record that holds the name of a delegated zone and is used to verify delegated child zones. *See also* Domain Name System Security Extension (DNSSEC).

DHCP failover A new feature in Windows Server 2012 that allows two DHCP servers to share the pool of addresses in a scope, giving both servers access to all addresses in the pool.

DHCP name protection A feature in DHCP that prevents name squatting by non-Windows computers by using a DHCP resource record called Dynamic Host Configuration Identifier (DHCID). *See also* name squatting.

DHCP Unique Identifier (DUID) A hexadecimal number, usually derived from the MAC address of the network interface used by DHCPv6 to identify clients for address leases and to create reservations.

differential backup A backup method in which only the blocks that have changed are transferred to the destination if there is an existing backup.

distributed cache mode A BranchCache mode of operation in which cached data is distributed among client computers in the branch office. *See also* BranchCache.

distributed topology An IPAM deployment option that places an IPAM server at every site in a network. *See also* IP Address Management (IPAM).

DNS cache locking A DNS security feature that allows you to control whether data in the DNS cache can be overwritten.

DNS cache poisoning An attack on DNS servers in which false data is introduced into the DNS server cache, causing the server to return incorrect IP addresses.

DNSKEY The public key for the zone that DNS resolvers use to verify the digital signature contained in Resource Record Signature (RRSIG) records.

DNS socket pool A pool of port numbers used by a DNS server for DNS queries to protect against DNS cache poisoning. *See also* DNS cache poisoning.

domain The core structural unit of Active Directory; contains OUs and represents administrative, security, and policy boundaries.

domain functional levels Properties of domains that determine which features of Active Directory have domain-wide implications and which server OSs are supported on domain controllers.

Domain Name System Security Extension (DNSSEC) A suite of features and protocols for validating DNS server responses.

drain on shutdown A new feature in Windows Server 2012 R2 that drains roles automatically and live-migrates VMs to another cluster node before the Hyper-V server shuts down.

Dynamic Access Control (DAC) A feature in Windows Server 2012/R2 that gives administrators another method for securing access to files that's more powerful than file and folder permissions based on group memberships.

Dynamic Host Configuration Protocol (DHCP) A component of the TCP/IP protocol suite used to assign an IP address to a host automatically from a defined pool of addresses.

dynamic quorum A feature that assigns a cluster node vote dynamically depending on whether the node is an active member of the cluster. If a node is no longer active in the cluster, its vote is removed.

dynamic witness A quorum feature in Windows Server 2012 R2 in which the cluster determines whether to give the witness a quorum vote, based on whether there's an odd or even number of cluster nodes.

enterprise CA A server running Windows Server 2012/R2 with the AD CS role installed; integrates with Active Directory.

external trust A one-way or two-way nontransitive trust between two domains that aren't in the same forest.

failback options Settings that specify a cluster should revert to the most preferred owner when the server is available again. The failback can occur immediately or between certain hours of the day.

failover cluster Two or more servers appearing as a single server to clients. One server is considered the active server, and other servers are passive. The active server handles all client requests for the clustered application, and the passive servers wait in standby mode until the active server fails.

failover options Settings that specify how many times a service attempts to restart or fail over to another server in the specified period.

feature file store A network share containing the files required to install roles, role services, and features on Windows Server 2012/R2 servers.

Features on Demand A feature in Windows Server 2012/R2 that enables you to remove unneeded installation files and free up the disk space they normally consume.

federated Web SSO An AD FS design in which a trust relationship is established between the resource partner and the account partner. *See also* account partner *and* resource partner.

federated Web SSO with forest trust An AD FS design that involves a trust between two Active Directory forests. One forest, in the perimeter network, is considered the resource partner. The second forest, in the internal network, is the account partner. *See also* account partner *and* resource partner.

federation server A server configured to run the Federation Service role service. When used in an account partner network, its function is to gather user credentials into claims and package them into a security token. When used on the resource partner network, it receives security tokens and claims from the account partner and presents the claims to Web-based applications for authorization.

federation server proxy Installed on servers in a perimeter network outside the organization's firewall, this service fields authentication requests from browser clients and passes them to the federation server inside the firewall.

federation trust A trust between two networks using AD FS; one side of the trust is considered the account partner, and the other side is called the resource partner. *See also* account partner *and* resource partner.

File Classification Infrastructure (FCI) A feature of File Server Resource Manager that allows classifying files by assigning new properties to them. The properties can then be used to create rules for searching or perform tasks on files meeting the criteria of the assigned properties.

file-level storage Storage that the client has access to only as files and folders.

filtered attribute set A feature of RODCs that specifies domain objects that aren't replicated to RODCs.

filtering mode An option in a port rule that specifies whether multiple hosts or a single host respond to traffic identified by the port rule. Multiple host is the default mode and allows scalability. Single host mode specifies that the server with the highest priority value handles traffic.

Flexible Single Master Operation (FSMO) roles Specialized domain controller tasks that handle operations that can affect the entire domain or forest. Only one domain controller can be assigned a particular FSMO.

forest A collection of one or more Active Directory trees. It can consist of a single tree with a single domain, or it can contain several trees, each with a hierarchy of parent and child domains.

forest functional level A property of a forest that determines which features of Active Directory have forest-wide implications and which server OSs are supported on domain controllers.

forest root domain The first domain created in a new forest.

forest trust A trust that provides a one-way or two-way transitive trust between forests, which enables security principals in one forest to access resources in any domain in another forest.

forest-wide authentication A property of a forest trust for granting users in a trusted forest access to the trusting forest.

global catalog A partial replica of all objects in the forest. It contains the most commonly accessed object attributes and universal group membership information.

global catalog (GC) server A server that holds the global catalog; it facilitates forest-wide Active Directory searches and logons across domains and stores universal group membership information. *See also* global catalog.

GlobalNames zone (GNZ) A DNS feature that gives IT administrators a way to add single-label names to DNS, thereby allowing client computers to resolve these names without including a DNS suffix in the query.

global object access auditing policy A group policy setting that affects the auditing status of an entire file system or Registry on computers in the scope of the GPO where the policy is defined.

Group Policy provisioning A method of provisioning IPAM that uses the Group Policy tool to perform tasks such as creating security groups, setting firewall rules, and creating shares for each IPAM-managed server. *See also* IP Address Management (IPAM).

guest clustering A clustering feature that requires two or more VMs with a guest OS installed and configured for failover clustering; the failover clustering occurs in the VM's guest OS.

handling priority An NLB parameter used in single host mode that determines which host handles all traffic meeting the port rules' criteria. *See also* filtering mode *and* network load balancing (NLB).

hash algorithm A mathematical function that takes a string of data as input and produces a fixed-size value as output. Hash values are used to verify that the original data hasn't been changed and to sign CA certificates and certificates issued by the CA.

heartbeat A signal sent between cluster nodes informing them that a node is up and running.

high availability A network or computer configuration in which data and applications are almost always available, even after a system failure.

highly available virtual machine A failover cluster configuration in which two or more servers with the Hyper-V role are configured in a failover cluster, and the VMs are stored on shared storage. Also called a "clustered virtual machine."

hosted cache mode A BranchCache mode of operation in which cached data is stored on one or more file servers in the branch office. *See also* BranchCache.

hot backup site A location that duplicates much of the main site's IT infrastructure and can be switched to if a disaster occurs at the main site.

hot standby mode A DHCP failover mode in which one server is assigned as the active server to provide DHCP services to clients, and the other server is placed in standby mode. *See also* DHCP failover.

hybrid topology An IPAM deployment option that has a single IPAM server collecting information from all managed servers in the enterprise and IPAM servers at key branch locations. *See also* IP Address Management (IPAM).

Hyper-V Replica A new feature in Windows Server 2012 that periodically replicates changes in a VM to a mirror VM hosted on another Hyper-V server.

intermediate CAs A CA in a multilevel CA hierarchy that issue certificates to issuing CAs, which respond to user and device certificate requests; sometimes called a "policy CA."

Internet Storage Name Service (iSNS) An IP-based protocol used to communicate between iSNS clients and servers for the purpose of allowing iSCSI devices to discover and monitor one another.

Inter-Site Topology Generator (ISTG) A designated domain controller in each site that's responsible for assigning bridgehead servers to handle replication for each partition.

intersite replication Active Directory replication that occurs between two or more sites.

intrasite replication Active Directory replication between domain controllers in the same site.

IP address block The largest unit for referring to an IP address space; consists of a contiguous range of IP addresses with a corresponding subnet mask.

IP Address Management (IPAM) A new feature in Windows Server 2012 that enables an administrator to manage the IP address space with monitoring, auditing, and reporting functions to help manage DHCP and DNS.

IP address range A pool of continuous addresses in an IP address block; usually corresponds to a DHCP scope.

IP address range group One or more IP address ranges that are logically grouped by some criteria.

IPAM client A Windows computer with the IPAM management console installed; typically used for remote management. *See also* IP Address Management (IPAM).

IPAM server A Windows Server 2012/R2 member server with the IPAM Server feature installed. *See also* IP Address Management (IPAM).

iSCSI initiator An iSCSI client that sends iSCSI commands to an iSCSI target. *See also* iSCSI target.

iSCSI logical unit number (LUN) A reference ID to a logical drive the iSCSI initiator uses when accessing storage on the iSCSI target server.

iSCSI qualified name (IQN) An identifier for iSCSI targets and initiators used to identify the iSCSI device in an iSCSI connection.

iSCSI target A logical storage space made available to iSCSI clients by a server running the iSCSI Target Server role service.

issuing CAs A CA that interacts with clients to field certificate requests and maintain the CRL. *See also* certificate revocation list (CRL).

iterative query A DNS query in which the server responds with the best information it currently has in its local database to satisfy the query.

key archival A method of backing up private keys and restoring them if users' private keys are lost.

key-signing key (KSK) A DNSSEC key that has a private and public key associated with it. The private key is used to sign all DNSKEY records, and the public key is used as a trust anchor for validating DNS responses. *See also* Domain Name System Security Extension (DNSSEC).

Knowledge Consistency Checker (KCC) A process that runs on every domain controller to determine the replication topology.

live migration An application or service installed on two or more servers participating in a failover cluster; also called a "clustered service."

load balancing mode The default DHCP failover mode in which both DHCP servers participate in address leasing at the same time from a shared pool of addresses. *See also* DHCP failover.

load weight An NLB parameter that allows configuring how much network traffic, as a percentage, each node should handle. *See also* network load balancing (NLB).

machine certificate A certificate used in AD RMS that's created on a client computer the first time it uses an AD RMS application.

managed server An IPAM component that's a Windows server running one or more of these Microsoft services: DHCP, DNS, Active Directory, and NPS. *See also* IP Address Management (IPAM).

manual provisioning A method of provisioning IPAM that requires configuring each IPAM server task and managed server manually. *See also* IP Address Management (IPAM).

Microsoft Azure Backup An online backup solution that stores backups in the cloud; they can be accessed from anywhere you have an Internet connection.

multicast scope A type of DHCP scope that allows assigning multicast addresses dynamically to multicast servers and clients by using Multicast Address Dynamic Client Allocation Protocol (MADCAP).

multi-factor authentication (MFA) An authentication process whereby users must authenticate with more than one method, such as with a username and password as well as a digital certificate or smart card.

multimaster replication The process of replicating Active Directory objects; changes to the database can occur on any domain controller and are propagated to all other domain controllers.

name squatting A DNS problem that occurs when a non-Windows computer registers its name with a DNS server, but the name has already been registered by a Windows computer.

netmask ordering A DNS feature that causes the DNS server to order the list of addresses so that the ones with a closer address match to the client making the query are returned at the top of the list.

Network Device Enrollment Service (NDES) A service that allows network devices, such as routers and

switches, to get certificates by using Simple Certificate Enrollment Protocol (SCEP), a Cisco proprietary protocol.

Network File System (NFS) A file-sharing protocol that allows users to access files and folders on other computers across a network; it's the native file-sharing protocol of Linux and UNIX systems.

network load balancing (NLB) A Windows Server feature that uses server clusters to provide scalability and fault tolerance. *See also* server cluster.

Next Secure (NSEC) A DNSSEC record that is returned when the requested resource record does not exist. *See also* Domain Name System Security Extension (DNSSEC).

Next Secure 3 (NSEC3) An alternative to NSEC records. They can prevent zone-walking, which is a technique of repeating NSEC queries to get all the names in a zone. *See also* Next Secure (NSEC).

Next Secure 3 (NSEC3) Parameter DNSSEC records used to determine which NSEC3 records should be included in responses to queries for nonexistent records. *See also* Next Secure 3 (NSEC3).

NFS data store An NFS share on a Windows failover cluster that provides a highly available storage solution for applications using NFS. *See also* Network File System (NFS).

nonauthoritative restore A type of Active Directory restore operation in which changes made to Active Directory objects on other DCs since the backup are kept and replicated to the server being restored.

one-time backup A backup type that creates a backup to a local volume or a share; the backup begins immediately.

one-way trust A trust relationship in which one domain trusts another, but the reverse is not true.

online responder (OR) A role service that enables clients to check a certificate's revocation status without having to download the CRL. *See also* certificate revocation list (CRL).

organizational unit (OU) An Active Directory container used to organize a network's users and resources into logical administrative units.

partitioned A cluster status that can occur if communication fails between cluster servers, resulting in two or more subclusters, each with the objective of handling the clustered service. *See also* cluster server.

passive node A cluster member that's not currently responding to client requests for a clustered application but is in standby in case the active node fails; also called a "passive server."

physical to virtual (P2V) migration A migration that converts a physical computer to a virtual machine.

port rule A setting that specifies which type of TCP or UDP traffic an NLB cluster should respond to and how the traffic is distributed among cluster members. *See also* network load balancing (NLB).

preference A value used to indicate priority when there are multiple DHCPv6 servers.

preferred owner The server selected as the active server for a service or an application.

prefix The part of the IPv6 address that's the network identifier.

public key infrastructure (PKI) A security system that binds a user's or device's identity to a cryptographic key that secures data transfers with encryption and ensures data authenticity with digital certificates.

publishing license A type of certificate used in AD RMS that's tied to a rights-protected document and is created when a client publishes the document.

quick migration A migration option available only between Hyper-V servers in a failover cluster; usually results in a minute or more of downtime, depending on how much memory the VM uses.

quorum A database containing cluster configuration information about the status of each node (active or passive) for clustered applications. It's also used to determine, in a server or communication failure, whether the cluster is to remain online and which servers should continue to participate in the cluster.

realm trust A trust used to integrate users of other OSs into a Windows Server 2012/R2 domain or forest; requires the OS to be running Kerberos V5 authentication.

recovery point A checkpoint that can be generated automatically so that you can revert to an earlier server state in case there's an unplanned failover and a VM is in an unworkable state.

recursive query A DNS query in which the server is instructed to process the query until it responds with an address that satisfies the query or with an "I don't know" message.

referral The process of sending a request for information about an object to DCs in other domains until the information is found.

registration authority A server configured with the Web Enrollment role service; also called a "CA Web proxy."

relying party The resource partner that hosts the resources accessed by the account partner. *See also* account partner *and* resource partner.

relying party trust An AD FS trust created on the AD FS server that acts as the claims provider in an AD FS deployment.

replica server In the Hyper-V Replica feature, the Hyper-V server where replication is enabled.

resource partner In a federation trust, it's the trusting company whose resources are accessed by the trusted company (account partner). *See also* account partner.

resource property An attribute that can be applied to a resource, such as a file or folder, and is used to classify resources.

resource property list A DAC component of containing a list of resource properties that are downloaded by servers.

Resource Record Signature (RRSIG) A key containing the signature for a single resource record, such as an A or MX record.

restricted enrollment agent An enrollment agent that's limited to enrolling only specific users or security groups; available only with an enterprise CA.

retention range A setting in Microsoft Azure Backup that specifies how long a backup should be kept.

rights account certificate (RAC) A certificate used in AD RMS for identifying users of AD RMS content.

rights policy template A component of AD RMS that enables you to configure policies for determining who can access a rights-protected document and what actions can be taken with the document.

rolling upgrade An NLB cluster upgrade method that involves taking each cluster node offline, upgrading the host, and then bringing it back online. *See also* network load balancing (NLB).

root CA The first CA installed in a network. Clients are configured to trust the root CA's certificate, and then implicitly trust the certificate of any CA that's subordinate to the root.

scale-out file server A highly available share option that provides the reliability of failover clusters and the load distribution of an NLB because client connections are distributed among all nodes in the cluster.

scheduled backup A backup type that allows specifying how often a backup occurs and dedicating a disk to backups.

scope A pool of IP addresses and other IP configuration parameters that a DHCP server uses to lease addresses to DHCP clients.

Secure Boot A feature that prevents a computer from booting from untrusted software.

selective authentication A property of a forest trust that enables administrators to specify users who can be granted access to selected resources in the trusting forest.

server cluster A group of two or more servers configured to respond to a single virtual IP address.

server licensor certificate (SLC) A certificate used in AD RMS that contains the AD RMS server's public key and identifies the AD RMS cluster.

service connection point (SCP) An AD RMS component that provides clients with URLs for the AD RMS cluster, which must be registered for clients to access the cluster.

shared-nothing live migration A live migration done between Hyper-V servers that have no common storage.

shared virtual hard disk A virtual hard disk configured on a VM in a guest cluster that's used for shared storage among VMs in the guest cluster instead of traditional SAN storage.

shortcut trust A manually configured trust between domains in the same forest for the purpose of bypassing the normal referral process. *See also* referral.

SID filtering An option that causes a trusting domain to ignore any SIDs that aren't from the trusted domain.

site A physical location in which domain controllers communicate and replicate information.

site-level disaster recovery A process with procedures and technologies an organization uses to get its network and servers running quickly after a disaster.

site link An Active Directory object that represents the path between sites and determines the replication schedule and frequency between sites.

site link bridge An Active Directory object that represents site links using a common transport protocol.

site link bridging A default property of a site link that makes it transitive. To control the transitive nature of site links, you can create site link bridges manually.

split scope A fault-tolerant DHCP configuration in which two DHCP servers share the same scope information, allowing both servers to offer DHCP services to clients.

split vote A quorum situation in which no quorum can be reached.

stand-alone CA A server running Windows Server 2012/R2 with the AD CS role installed; not integrated with Active Directory.

standby mode A cluster node that isn't active.

stateful autoconfiguration A method of IPv6 autoconfiguration in which the node uses an autoconfiguration protocol, such as DHCPv6, to obtain its IPv6 address and other configuration information.

stateless autoconfiguration A method of IPv6 autoconfiguration in which the node listens for router advertisement messages from a local router.

storage area network (SAN) A storage system that uses high-speed networking technologies to give servers fast access to large amounts of shared disk storage.

storage migration A VM migration process used to move a VM's storage from one volume to another without moving the VM to another Hyper-V server.

superscope A special type of scope consisting of one or more member scopes that allows a DHCP server to service multiple IPv4 subnets on a single physical network.

system access control list (SACL) An attribute of a file system object that defines whether and how a file system object is to be audited.

system state backup A backup option that backs up boot files, Windows system files, and the Registry. On a DC, the system state includes the Active Directory database and the SYSVOL folder.

thin provisioning The use of dynamically expanding virtual disks so that they occupy only the amount of space on the physical disk that's currently in use on the virtual disk.

tie breaker for 50% node split A situation in which a cluster is partitioned into equal numbers of nodes, and the dynamic quorum feature is used to change node votes to break the tie. *See also* dynamic quorum.

tiered storage A feature of Storage Spaces that combines the speed of solid state drives with the low cost and high capacity of hard disk drives.

transitive trust A trust relationship based on the transitive rule of mathematics; therefore, if Domain A trusts Domain B and Domain B trusts Domain C, then Domain A trusts Domain C.

tree A group of domains sharing a common naming structure.

trim A feature that allows a thinly provisioned disk to shrink automatically when data has been deleted from the disk. *See also* thin provisioning.

trust anchor In public key cryptography, it's usually the DNSKEY record for a zone.

trust relationship An arrangement that defines whether and how security principals from one domain can access network resources in another domain.

trusted publishing domain (TPD) A trust between AD RMS clusters in separate forests that allows an AD RMS cluster to issue use licenses for content published by another AD RMS cluster.

trusted user domain (TUD) A trust between AD RMS clusters in separate forests that allows users in the trusted forest to access AD RMS content in the trusting forest.

two-way trust A trust in which both domains in the relationship trust each other, so users from both domains can access resources in the other domain.

unidirectional replication The type of replication used by RODCs, in which writeable DCs replicate to RODCs, but RODCs don't replicate to other DCs.

unmapped address space An IP address or address range that hasn't been assigned to an IP address block.

UPN suffix The part of the user principal name (UPN) that comes after the @.

urgent replication An event triggering immediate notification that a change has occurred instead of waiting for the normal 15-second interval before replication partners are notified.

use license A type of certificate used in AD RMS that's issued to particular users when they authenticate to an AD RMS server and request access to a rights-protected document.

virtual IP address The IP address by which networking services provided by an NLB cluster are accessed by network clients. A DNS host record should exist for the cluster name mapped to this address. *See also* network load balancing (NLB).

virtual machine monitoring A new feature in Windows Server 2012 that allows monitoring resources, applications, and services running on highly available VMs. *See also* highly available virtual machine.

virtual machine network health detection A failover cluster feature that automatically live migrates a virtual machine to another node if its network connection fails.

virtual to virtual (V2V) migration A migration that converts a virtual machine from one vendor's format to another vendor's format.

Web SSO An AD FS design that provides single sign-on access to multiple Web applications for users who are external to an organization's network.

witness disk Shared storage used to store cluster configuration data and help determine the cluster quorum.

Workplace Join A new feature in Windows Server 2012 R2 that allows nondomain joined devices to access claims-based resources securely.

zone level statistics A new feature in Windows Server 2012 R2 that provides detailed statistics for each zone to show how a DNS server is used.

zone signing A DNSSEC feature that uses digital signatures contained in DNSSEC-related resource records to verify DNS responses. *See also* Domain Name System Security Extension (DNSSEC).

zone-signing key (ZSK) A public and private key combination stored in a certificate used to sign the zone.

Index